fundamentally aware of worthy of rework
of gods god/s politics, some consideration of &
further superstition engagement with lit

author absent from narrative

Wujek, 16 Dec. mine massacre

Revolution and Counterrevolution in Poland, 1980–1989

Rochester Studies in East and Central Europe

Series Editor: Timothy Snyder, Yale University

Additional Titles of Interest

Ideology, Politics and Diplomacy in East Central Europe
Edited by M. B. B. Biskupski

*Between East and West:
Polish and Russian Nineteenth-Century Travel to the Orient*
Izabela Kalinowska

The Polish Singers Alliance of America 1888–1998: Choral Patriotism
Stanislaus A. Blejwas

*A Clean Sweep?
The Politics of Ethnic Cleansing in Western Poland, 1945–1960*
T. David Curp

*Nazi Policy on the Eastern Front, 1941:
Total War, Genocide, and Radicalization*
Edited by Alex J. Kay, Jeff Rutherford, and David Stahel

Critical Thinking in Slovakia after Socialism
Jonathan Larson

Smolensk under the Nazis: Everyday Life in Occupied Russia
Laurie R. Cohen

Polish Cinema in a Transnational Context
Edited by Ewa Mazierska and Michael Goddard

Literary Translation and the Idea of a Minor Romania
Sean Cotter

*Coming of Age under Martial Law:
The Initiation Novels of Poland's Last Communist Generation*
Svetlana Vassileva-Karagyozova

A complete list of titles in the Rochester Studies in East and Central Europe series may be found on our website, www.urpress.com.

Revolution and Counterrevolution in Poland, 1980–1989

Solidarity, Martial Law, and the End of Communism in Europe

Andrzej Paczkowski
Translated by Christina Manetti

University of Rochester Press

This translation was funded by the Foundation for Polish Science.

A shorter version of this book was published in Polish as
Wojna polsko-jaruzelska: stan wojenny w Polsce 13 XII 1981–22 VII 1983
(Warsaw, Prószyński i S-ka, 2006 and 2007). Copyright © by Andrzej Paczkowski, 2006, 2007.

Translation copyright © 2015 by Christina Manetti

All rights reserved. Except as permitted under current legislation, no
part of this work may be photocopied, stored in a retrieval system,
published, performed in public, adapted, broadcast, transmitted,
recorded, or reproduced in any form or by any means, without the
prior permission of the copyright owner.

First published 2015

University of Rochester Press
668 Mt. Hope Avenue, Rochester, NY 14620, USA
www.urpress.com
and Boydell & Brewer Limited
PO Box 9, Woodbridge, Suffolk IP12 3DF, UK
www.boydellandbrewer.com

Copublished by the Institute of Political Studies of the Polish Academy of Sciences,
ul. Polna 18/20, 00-625 Warsaw, Poland.

ISBN-13: 978-1-58046-536-6
ISSN: 1528-4808

Library of Congress Cataloging-in-Publication Data

Names: Paczkowski, Andrzej, 1938–
Title: Revolution and counterrevolution in Poland, 1980–1989 : Solidarity, martial law, and the end of communism in Europe / Andrzej Paczkowski ; translated by Christina Manetti.
Other titles: Wojna polsko-jaruzelska. English
Description: Rochester, NY : University of Rochester Press, 2015. | Series: Rochester studies in East and Central Europe, ISSN 1528-4808 ; v. 14 | "A shorter version of this book was published in Polish as Wojna polsko-jaruzelska : stan wojenny w Polsce, 13 XII 1981-22 VII 1983 (Warsaw : Prószyński i S-ka, 2006 and 2007)"—Title page verso. | Includes bibliographical references and index.
Identifiers: LCCN 2015029788 | ISBN 9781580465366 (hardcover : acid-free paper)
Subjects: LCSH: Poland—Politics and government—1980–1989. Revolutions—Poland—History—20th century. | NSZZ "Solidarność" (Labor organization)—History. | Government, Resistance to—Poland—History—20th century. | Anti-communist movements—Poland—History—20th century. | Martial law—Poland—History—20th century. | Social change—Poland—History—20th century. | Democracy—Poland—History—20th century.
Classification: LCC DK4442 .P33313 2015 | DDC 943.805/6—dc23 LC record available at http://lccn.loc.gov/2015029788

A catalogue record for this title is available from the British Library.

This publication is printed on acid-free paper.
Printed and bound by CPI Group (UK) Ltd, Croydon, CR0 4YY

Contents

	Preface	vii
	Abbreviations	xv

Part 1: The Beginning

1	Poland—"The Weakest Link"	3
2	The Solidarity Revolution: Act One, 1980–81	11
3	"Defend Socialism as If It Were Poland's Independence"	21

Part 2: The Attack

4	The Last Days Before	35
5	"Night of the General" and Day One	54
6	Breakthrough	72
7	Reprisals and the Public Mood	97
8	The World Looks On	121
9	Battle Over	133

Part 3: Counterattack

10	Operation "Renaissance" and Lech Wałęsa	139
11	Underground	155
12	Civil Resistance	173
13	"The Anesthetic Has Worn Off"	186
14	The End of the Campaign and Wałęsa's Release	203

Part 4: Toward Positional Warfare

15	The Church between Eternity and Solidarity	223
16	Independent Society	237
17	The Party Returns to the Ring	258
18	The End of Martial Law	270

Part 5: Endgame

19	Solidarity's Revolution: The Finale, 1988–89	283
20	Escape from the Soviet Bloc and the Fall of the Empire	300
	Conclusion: The Decade of Struggle and Its Legacy	314
	Notes	323
	Selected Bibliography	351
	Index	363

Preface

On March 2, 1950, the National Security Council organized a debate on the United States' strategy in the face of the Soviet threat. One of the participants was Professor James Bryant Conant, a chemist who had been president of Harvard University since 1933. He belonged to an elite group of scientists involved with the United States' most important military undertakings during the Second World War (including the Manhattan Project). He was also close to the world of politics: he had been the chair of the National Defense Research Committee since 1941, and was High Commissioner for Germany during the years 1953–55, and then ambassador to that country until 1957. During that debate, Professor Conant said that if it did not come to war, then "the competition between our dynamic free society and their [Soviet] static slave society should be all in our favor."[1] He also predicted that the Soviet Union might Balkanize itself by 1980.

The state Moloch created by Lenin and Stalin really did collapse, both formally and definitively, as a result of "Balkanization" in December 1991. It had split into national states, just like the Ottoman Empire in the Balkans during the nineteenth and early twentieth centuries. Professor Conant's prediction was off by just ten years. Nevertheless, the year he mentioned, 1980, was not a normal year for the Soviets, nor for the entire system of their satellite states, created by Stalin in East Central Europe during the years 1944–47. In 1980, the United States led a boycott of the Moscow Olympics in response to the Soviet invasion of Afghanistan. In the end, however, this was not particularly galling, since the Kremlin could retaliate by boycotting the Los Angeles Olympics four years later. The outcome of the US presidential election was incomparably more important than America's posturing over the Olympics. The Republican candidate, Ronald Reagan, won, having announced a tough stance toward the Kremlin. After some presidents' perceived dovishness, now a hawk was in the White House. Just as important as Reagan's victory were events in Poland, the largest Soviet satellite in Europe. Since July 1, a wave of strikes had swept through the country, culminating in a general strike. This was just a couple of weeks before the Soviet leader, Leonid Brezhnev, announced the start of the Olympic Games at the opening ceremonies, and a few months before the American elections. This unprecedented series of events, which occurred without excesses, rioting, or casualties, culminated on August 30–31 with the signing of agreements between the communist leadership, headed by Edward Gierek, and the two largest strike committees (in Gdańsk and Szczecin). Among other things, these agreements stipulated that the government would grant permission for the creation of a trade union independent of the state and the communist party, which had a monopoly on power. The trade union called itself "Solidarity."

The star Polish athlete at the Moscow Olympics, Władysław Kozakiewicz, won a gold medal in the pole vault—despite the fact that the Soviet audience had tried to distract him by whistling and screaming during his run up to the jump. After winning, Kozakiewicz made a rather impolite gesture to the audience: he bent his arm at the elbow and clenched a fist, telling spectators, basically, "Up yours!" "Kozakiewicz's gesture," as it was later called in Poland, was not meant to express scorn for the audience. It was simply an expression of satisfaction, as David must have felt when he vanquished Goliath. All things considered, Solidarity itself was a bit like that gesture—one that millions of Poles, mostly workers, were showing to the ruling communist party. Because its official name was the Polish United Workers' Party (Polska Zjednoczona Partia Robotnicza, PZPR), some maliciously said that it was not Polish (because it was dependent on Moscow) or united (because there were cliques vying within it) or working class (because most of its members were bureaucrats).

The crux of the matter, of course, is not in gestures, names, or symbols, no matter how significant they might have been. The creation of Solidarity was a powerful breach in a system whose foundation was one-party rule and the support of a Soviet superpower. Solidarity's impact was particularly great because it was an autonomous organization that had, within a matter of weeks, managed to attract about nine million members from various ages, professions, and beliefs— from the intellectual elite to agricultural workers who could barely read and write. Although the worst years of the Stalinist terror had already passed, when the communist system was being formed, the country still found itself in the grasp of an ideologically driven dictatorship with a totalitarian pedigree and ambitions to control everything and everyone—deciding everything from the number of apartment buildings that should be built to the price of a box of matches.

Solidarity started the process of dismantling communism and saw it through to the end: in 1989, the system that had been enigmatically called "real socialism" collapsed, and other nations in that part of Europe followed the Poles' lead. Without the processes that had begun during the summer of 1980, the predictions of that Harvard professor most probably could not have been fulfilled.

The phenomenon of Solidarity aroused great interest around the world. In the Soviet Union and other communist states, there was concern that the Polish events would be "contagious" and have a destabilizing effect. In the West, there was an opposite reaction: what was happening in Poland and what Solidarity represented was seen as an attempt by working people (both physical and intellectual laborers) to acquire subjectivity, as a fight for the dignity of subordinates vis-à-vis their superiors, as the opportunity for a profound, positive change in the communist system, and for its democratization. At the same time, Solidarity was seen as a factor that was weakening the entire Soviet camp, which could tip the scales in favor of the Free World, hastening its victory in the Cold War. To some extent, the West reacted emotionally to Solidarity—Westerners were captivated, for example, by the exotic scenes of the strike at the Gdańsk Shipyard, which received extensive media coverage. It was, after all, an occupation strike, which in itself was a rarity, since workers do not usually report to work during labor strikes. Intellectuals played a direct role in the strike as advisors, which was unusual in the West. People admired the fact that the strike leadership was absolutely democratic. The Strike Committee meetings, almost permanently in session, and talks with the government delegation were broadcast over speakers throughout the shipyard. People were fascinated with the thirty-seven-year-old electrician Lech Wałęsa, who emerged overnight as a charismatic leader. For outside observers, it was a bit of a shock to see the extent to which religious elements permeated the strike: Mass celebrated at the shipyard, thousands of kneeling workers, hundreds of people taking Communion, crosses, portraits of the Pope and pictures of the Virgin Mary on fences and gates. What also struck observers was the contrast between this imagery and the name of the place where all this was happening—the Lenin Shipyard. Ironically, there was even a plaster bust of Lenin in the hall where the Strike Committee was meeting.

While Polish government propaganda and that of other communist countries was condemning Solidarity as a counter-revolutionary movement, most public opinion outside the communist world saw it in a different light. Books on the subject had titles such as *The Polish Revolution: Solidarity* or *Poland: Genesis of a Revolution*.[2] Solidarity was regarded as a revolution that would bring about a profound change in Poland's political system. At the time, its effect on the balance of power in Europe was of secondary significance. The international aspect of the movement became clear only after a nearly decade-long chain of events came to an end in 1989. This movement was sparked by a strike in defense of two people who had been fired for their activities in the underground opposition, and was a protest against the degradation of living conditions and the lack of civil freedoms in Poland. Two phases during this series of events have attracted the most interest among both specialists and the general public alike: the first, from 1980 to 1981, covered the strikes that led to the formation of Solidarity, and its sixteen months of legal existence; the second, from 1988 to 1989, encompassed negotiations with the government and the fall of the communist system in Poland. Academic publishers in the United States, Great Britain, France, and Germany, as well as in

Poland, published dozens (and perhaps hundreds) of books on the subject and thousands of articles by sociologists, economists, political scientists, anthropologists, social psychologists, and specialists in international relations. The first wave of these publications appeared during the years 1982–85, and dealt with the origins of the Polish revolutionary movement. The second wave came after 1989, and primarily addressed the causes of the communist system's collapse. Thus, authors did not usually limit themselves to the situation in Poland, but rather dealt with the phenomenon's broader geographical aspects. After Mikhail Gorbachev came to power in the Soviet Union in 1985 and introduced *perestroika*, developments in Poland and other East Central European communist countries were usually analyzed from the perspective of change in the Soviet Union. As the archives gradually began to open after 1989, historians began writing about the "Polish revolution" and even today it is primarily historical research that is conducted.

In writing this book, my intention was not to describe and analyze the entire Polish "revolutionary era," from the first strikes in July 1980 to the moment a Solidarity activist, Tadeusz Mazowiecki, became prime minister in late summer of 1989. Instead, the main subject of my research was just a small portion of that decade, one that lasted just over a year and a half—but which was of fundamental importance for describing and understanding the era as a whole. This was the period of martial law, which was imposed on December 13, 1981, and was lifted on July 22, 1983. An unexpected, brutal, and overwhelming attack was launched on the night of December 12–13, 1981. It was carried out by tens of thousands of soldiers, and over one hundred thousand armed functionaries of the security apparatus and militia.[3] This action put a stop to the Polish revolution and changed its character, to a certain extent. That attack and the reprisals that followed reduced the millions-strong workers' movement that had emerged spontaneously over the preceding months to a much smaller, but very determined, clandestine organization. Its political agenda took priority and overshadowed its earlier moral, communal, and utopian concerns. As an underground movement, Solidarity gradually lost its illusions about the possibility of transforming a centralized and state-controlled economy into one based on self-government and communal ownership. This change of perspective opened the way to acceptance of the free market and private ownership, which also proved to be the "road to Europe." Martial law derailed the rush to individual and national freedom that was already under way. It did not, however, manage to eliminate the tens of thousands of people who were Solidarity's main motivating force—they continued fighting, this time underground. Their hopes for a new, better Poland may have been suspended, but they had not been completely destroyed.

This book, however, is not devoted to Solidarity's ideological transformation. Rather, I would like to describe the mechanisms of martial law, and the reaction when General Wojciech Jaruzelski declared it early on the morning of

December 13, 1981. I am interested both in the decisions made on the highest levels of government and also in how they were implemented "in the field," as well as how Solidarity members responded when tanks appeared in the streets and thousands of the group's most active members were arrested. I am trying to answer the question of what martial law actually was, since its imposition was unprecedented in Polish history. Under martial law, the Military Council of National Salvation (Wojskowa Rada Ocalenia Narodowego) was created—a new, completely extra-constitutional governmental organ under the direction of the prime minister and leader of the ruling party. It was commonly known by its acronym, WRON. Heading it was Jaruzelski, the same person who was also prime minister and the party's first secretary. Can the creation of WRON, then, be called a military coup, or was it just part of a huge propaganda campaign? Whom and what was martial law supposed to protect? I will also attempt to describe in more detail main figures of the drama, General Wojciech Jaruzelski and Lech Wałęsa, as well as their closest associates.

The international context of martial law is of lesser concern to me here, since the dynamics of the events in Poland itself were of primary importance at the time. Nevertheless, some readers may not be familiar with the situation in Poland during the last years of the "short twentieth century," to use Eric Hobsbawm's description (as he called the years 1914–91 in his book *The Age of Extremes*). For them, I present in a concise manner both the events leading up to that grim day of December 13, 1981 (chapters 1–3), and those during the last years of communist rule (chapters 19–20). For anyone who wishes to learn more about the broader historical context of the period covered in this book, I can immodestly recommend my own monograph.[4] Of course, since its appearance, research has shed much more light on the period of martial law, which I take into consideration extensively here.

In writing this book, I have concentrated my research on the relatively large body of material available in Polish. These sources are largely comprised of documentary works, as far as martial law is concerned, and for the most part focus on one city, region, factory, or event. I utilized previously published biographical works, numerous memoirs, and diaries (including some by individuals in the top echelons of power), as well as hundreds of accounts that have been collected as part of oral history projects. In addition, of course, I also used materials from the official press and those published illegally. Hundreds of documents from various sources have already been published, or are available on the Internet. It is my hope that I have managed to find most of them. One source of inspiration (but also information) has been the conferences in which many of the important and sometimes even leading figures of those events have taken part. An especially important one titled "Poland 1980–1982: Internal Crisis, International Dimensions"[5] took place in Jachranka near Warsaw in 1997. Participants included Marshal

Viktor Kulikov, General Wojciech Jaruzelski, General William Odom, Professor Zbigniew Brzeziński, and Professor Richard Pipes. I also used many works published abroad, primarily from the United States, Great Britain, and France,[6] especially those dealing with Western policy toward Poland.[7] Of these, the monograph of Gregory Domber is—for the moment—the most important.[8] To my knowledge, however, no foreign monographs about martial law based on Polish archival sources exist, and studies of the decade that followed are also very rare.[9] Western scholars have concentrated on specific aspects of the larger period, particularly the years 1980–81,[10] as have the Poles, but martial law itself has been the focus only sporadically. In fact, only George Sanford's very interesting study considers the same time period as this work. Since Sanford was writing in the 1980s, however, he did not have access to confidential and secret documents, whether Polish, Soviet, or American.[11]

I carried out my own archival research systematically for over a decade. During the years 1992–96, I served as an expert for a parliamentary commission that was researching the legality of the imposition of martial law.[12] I worked primarily in Polish archives, which hold thousands of volumes containing documents from the communist party (mainly in the Archiwum Akt Nowych [Archive of Modern Records] in Warsaw), military (mainly in the Centralne Archiwum Wojskowe [Central Military Archives] in Rembertów), and security apparatus (at the Instytut Pamięci Narodowej [Institute of National Remembrance] in Warsaw). I worked in the Russian archives less often, because gaining access to documents from my particular period of interest was difficult. Some of the Soviet documents have already been published, however. As far as American documents are concerned, I have only studied those that have been published in print or on the Internet. Research in the archives was laborious, since I literally had to dig through tens of thousands of pages and look at hundreds of microfilms. I am not complaining, however—this happens to be the type of work I enjoy.

※ ※ ※

Without the events that occurred in the Soviet Union as a result of Gorbachev-era reforms, both economic (*perestroika*) and political (*glasnost'*), the communist system in Poland probably would not have fallen when it did, nor in the way in which it did. Perhaps we would have seen a long-term "rotting" of the system, or a violent upheaval of rebellious masses. Or, perhaps, we would have seen the opposite: without the birth of Solidarity (which revealed to the world the profound dysfunctionality of communism as a state system), and without martial law (which was an unsuccessful attempt to conceal the system's shortcomings once again and to quash social opposition), the Soviet leaders, even unconventional ones like Mikhail Gorbachev, would not have been forced to undertake changes that were in essence much more profound than the usual political facelifts, like the one initiated by Nikita Khrushchev. It was not enough to talk about "errors and distortions," or to postulate about the "moral and political unity of the people." The creation of Solidarity and its dogged fight in the dramatically unfavorable conditions of martial law forced them to respond to this challenge in a way that was more serious than mere verbal declarations. Lech Wałęsa's union was thus a contributing factor to the end of the Cold War, as well as East Central Europe's entry into the democratic realm—a good reason to learn more about this episode in Poland's relatively recent past.

I would like to thank the following institutions for supporting the publication of this book: the Foundation for Polish Science (Fundacja na rzecz Nauki Polskiej), which funded the cost of the translation; and my own Institute of Political Science in Warsaw for its goodwill, even beyond the official call of duty. I would especially like to thank Basia Kalabinski, for her thorough reading of the text, thoughtful comments, and diligent preparation of the index; and Christina Manetti, the translator, who coped admirably with my style, even though it can sometimes be rather Baroque, and eased my life by independently solving problems she encountered along the way. I also thank the anonymous reviewers, whose comments allowed me to correct some of the text's shortcomings, although I was not fully able to implement all of their propositions. I also would like to thank Sonia Kane and the staff of the University of Rochester Press, as well as those at Boydell & Brewer, for their solid and quick work, as well as for their forbearance with my less-than-perfect grasp of English. Last but not least, I would like to express my gratitude to Tim Snyder for his interest in my book proposal, and for helping this project get off to the right start.

Abbreviations

AIPN	Archiwum Instytutu Pamięci Narodowej (Institute of National Remembrance)
AK	Armia Krajowa (Home Army)
AWS	Akcja Wyborcza Solidarność (Solidarity Electoral Action)
CBOS	Centrum Badania Opinii Społecznej (Public Opinion Research Center)
GDR	German Democratic Republic
KKP	Krajowa Komisja Porozumiewawcza (National Coordinating Commission of Solidarity)
KOK	Komitet Obrony Kraju (Committee of National Defense)
KOR	Komitet Obrony Robotników (Workers' Defense Committee)
KOS	Koła Obrony Solidarności (Solidarity Defense Circles)
KPN	Konfederacja Polski Niepodległej (Confederation of Independent Poland)
MKO	Międzyregionalna Komisja Obrony Solidarności (Inter-Regional Defense Committee of Solidarity)
MKS	Międzyzakładowy Komitet Strajkowy (Inter-Enterprise Strike Committee)
MKZ	międzyzakładowe komitety założycielskie (inter-enterprise founding committees)
MO	Milicja Obywatelska (Citizens' Militia)
MON	Ministerstwo Obrony Narodowej (Ministry of National Defense)
MRKS	Międzyzakładowy Robotniczy Komitet Solidarności (Inter-Enterprise Workers' Committee of Solidarity)
MSW	Ministerstwo Spraw Wewnętrznych (Ministry of Internal Affairs)

NSZZ	Niezależny Samorządny Związek Zawodowy "Solidarność" (Independent Self-Governing Trade Union "Solidarity")
OBOP	Ośrodek Badania Opinii Publicznej (Center for Public Opinion Research)
OKO	Ogólnopolski Komitet Oporu NSZZ "Solidarność" (National NSZZ Solidarity Resistance Committee [pseudonym "Mieszko"])
ORMO	Ochotnicza Rezerwa Milicji Obywatelskiej (Volunteer Reserves of the Citizens' Militia)
PRL	Polska Rzeczpospolita Ludowa (Polish People's Republic)
PRON	Patriotyczny Ruch Odrodzenia Narodowego (Patriotic Movement of National Rebirth)
PZPR	Polska Zjednoczona Partia Robotnicza (Polish United Workers' Party)
RFE	Radio Free Europe
RFI	Radio France Internationale
RMP	Ruch Młodej Polski (Young Poland Movement)
ROMO	Rezerwowe Oddziały Milicji Obywatelskiej (Reserve Detachments of Citizens' Militia)
SB	Służba Bezpieczeństwa
SDP	Stowarzyszenie Dziennikarzy Polskich (Polish Journalists' Association)
SPD	Social-Democratic Party (West Germany)
TKK	Tymczasowa Komisja Koordynacyjna (Temporary Coordinating Commission)
WRON	Wojskowa Rada Ocalenia Narodowego (Military Council of National Salvation)
WZZ	Wolne Związki Zawodowe (Free Trade Unions)
ZASP	Związek Artystów Scen Polskich (Union of Polish Stage Artists)
ZLP	Związek Literatów Polskich (Polish Writers' Union)
ZOMO	Zmotoryzowane Oddziały Milicji Obywatelskiej (Motorized Detachments of the Citizens' Militia)

Part 1

The Beginning

CHAPTER ONE

POLAND—"THE WEAKEST LINK"

In June 1977, a group of analysts from various US government agencies[1] produced a memorandum more than twenty pages long entitled "Prospects for Eastern Europe." For our purposes, the following statements in the memorandum were of paramount importance: "unrest is likely to grow in Eastern Europe over the next three years.... Poland will be the most volatile, and a blow-up there, which might bring down Gierek and even conceivably compel the Soviets to restore order, cannot be ruled out."[2] The authors of the memorandum suggested that "if order should break down, both Warsaw and Moscow will want to see it restored by Polish forces, [and] only if these fail will the Soviets intervene."[3] Regardless of what one thinks of the competence of the American intelligence community at that time, one must admit that this prediction, formulated with extreme restraint, has to a large extent been vindicated—a rare event, since intelligence services err just as often as meteorologists do.

The conviction that Poland, of the eight[4] East Central European communist states, was most likely to experience violent protests was also held among members of the region's nascent democratic opposition, and even within Poland's own ruling elite. Members of both groups were aware of a growing social discontent that stemmed from the worsening economic situation. The kinds of violent protests seen in Poland took place in other communist states either not at all or on a much smaller scale. Unrest in Poland was usually sparked by economic grievances and came to resemble political rebellions against the ruling cliques. While other countries also experienced these kinds of revolts—for example, Czechoslovakia and East Germany in 1953, and even the Soviet Union itself during the Novocherkassk riots in 1962—these were just isolated events. In Poland, meanwhile, strikes and demonstrations took place in June 1956 in Poznań, in August 1957 in Łódź, in December 1970 on the coast (the largest were in Gdańsk, Gdynia, and Szczecin), and in June 1976 in several other cities, including Radom. In two cases (in 1956 and 1970), strikes were violently broken up by means of military force, including armed units, resulting in the deaths of dozens of protesters. In Poznań alone, approximately seventy people died. The mass protests in March 1968 by students and young people that occurred in virtually all the larger cities were also exceptional and unique to Poland.[5] These protests were purely political in nature, as were the youth street demonstrations in October 1957 after authorities closed the popular weekly *Po Prostu*.[6] In the 1960s, clashes occurred several times in response to the government's anti-Church (or anti-religious) measures, and some of them—such as those in Nowa Huta near Kraków in 1960—lasted several days.

One can therefore say that a certain segment of Polish society, particularly workers and students, was "overly excitable," and would quickly and frequently opt for dramatic forms of protest. To a large extent, this was a result of how the communist system functioned. Since no freedoms of speech or association existed, there were no institutional channels for negotiation. For the government, the main instrument for managing a crisis was force (the police and army), along with intense and brutal propaganda campaigns conducted in state-controlled media. Although the system was identical in the other communist states, only in Poland were there such frequent disturbances and strikes. The Polish tradition of resistance and insurrection was deeply rooted in Polish national culture, linked to nineteenth-century Romanticism and the memory of the uprisings against Russian rule in 1794, 1830, and 1863. Even under communism, children learned about these events in schools. Moreover, not everyone accepted the legitimacy of this regime, installed after the Second World War under the aegis and control of the Soviet Union. For a great many Poles, the Soviet Union was an enemy. The memory of the Polish-Soviet War of 1920 was still fresh, as well as that of the Soviet invasion in September 1939 (along with the German one), and the massacre of Polish officers in Katyń. The Poles also recalled how the Red Army's offensive was halted in August 1944, when the anti-German Warsaw Uprising broke out, leaving the Polish capital to its fate at the hands of the Wehrmacht. Moreover, the Soviet Union was considered the heir of Tsarist Russia, against which the Poles had waged futile insurrections that were bloodily suppressed.

The protests of 1956–76 were spontaneous and generally short-lived. As a result, there was not enough time to create stable centers of leadership, or for a charismatic leader to emerge. Nevertheless, some of these revolts were effective. In December 1970, strikes led to changes at the highest levels of the Polish government. (Władysław Gomułka left in disgrace after fourteen years in power and was replaced by Edward Gierek.) They also prompted the government to rescind its price hike, as would be the case later in June 1976 as well. Strikes and street demonstrations were two defining characteristics of the Polish political scene.[7]

The fact that the Catholic Church remained independent of state control and enjoyed great authority in Poland also distinguished Poland from other countries in the Soviet bloc. After the Second World War, Poland became a country that was in effect monoethnic, with a single religion (Roman Catholicism), which hampered the communists' war on religion to a significant extent. The Soviet model combated religion everywhere that communists took power, from Korea to East Germany. In the case of Poland, the war with the Church, which peaked during the years 1953–55, ended in a defeat for the atheistic and anticlerical state. After the political situation stabilized in 1956, even the communist leaders who, like

Władysław Gomułka, were deeply convinced of the need to marginalize and subjugate the Church, would appeal to the Catholic hierarchy for support, requesting that it not encourage the faithful to revolt. This tactic afforded Polish leaders more room to maneuver, while their counterparts in other communist countries could not appeal to any church because all churches, having been deprived of their autonomy, had much less authority. At the same time, however, this made Polish leadership dependent on the Church. From 1948 to 1981, Cardinal Stefan Wyszyński was the head of the Polish Church, a position known as the primate. Wyszyński was outstanding as both politician and priest. He opposed taking overly aggressive steps against the government, but was at the same time an untiring advocate of a Catholicism that was very much centered on the cult of Mary, marked by large-scale, open-air religious services in urban spaces. The enormity of these services is perhaps best illustrated by the clash between the Church's celebration of a millennium of Polish Christianity and the state's own secular festivities for the millennium of Polish statehood, both celebrated in 1966.

While the Catholic Church did not have immediate political ambitions, it did provide a cultural and philosophical alternative to official Marxist ideology. It boasted an efficient and extensive organization, which in 1977 numbered approximately 15,000 clergymen and 4,500 monks, as well as over 27,000 nuns, 5,000 seminarians, and almost 4,000 theology students. There was an elite, intellectually vibrant lay movement organized through the Clubs of the Catholic Intelligentsia (Kluby Inteligencji Katolickiej), which published several periodicals, including the popular weekly *Tygodnik Powszechny*. Since 1957, this group of lay Catholics also had representatives in parliament. There were pro-government Catholic organizations, too, whose loyalty toward the communist state was not always certain. The Church had a solid base in its ministry to the university community, which had many thousands of members, and also in its youth groups, called "Oasis." The Church's real strength, however, was of course the huge numbers of believers who came from all social classes and age groups. Even most party members considered themselves Catholic.

No one except Juliusz Słowacki, a mid-nineteenth century Polish Romantic poet, foresaw what would happen on October 16, 1978: the conclave of cardinals elected the Archbishop of Kraków, Karol Wojtyła, as pope. He became John Paul II. Edward Gierek, first secretary at the time, is said to have cried "O rany boskie!" (the equivalent of "for God's sake!") upon hearing the news.[8] While official records do not confirm this exclamation, even as an anecdote it does convey both the embarrassment and linguistic register of Poland's believers in Karl Marx, who tried to put a good face on the situation. In a telegram sent the next day to the Vatican, the Party leadership stressed that the election of Karol Wojtyła was a triumph "for the Polish people . . . who are building . . . the greatness and success of their socialist fatherland."[9] The implicit suggestion was that the new pope actually owed his new position to the fact that he was from socialist Poland. Although it may sound ridiculous, the matter did appear very serious. The Soviet minister of foreign affairs, Andrei Gromyko, went to the Vatican in January 1979. Recounting his visit to Gierek, he told him that the pope was "an ideological and political enemy" who "could cause many problems."[10]

And that is exactly what happened, as shown by the pope's visit to Poland on June 2–9, 1979, often described as his "Pilgrimage to the Fatherland." Millions of Poles turned out to see the pope, and an opinion poll reported that 87 percent of those surveyed declared they were "very interested" in the visit.[11] The Church's solid organization of the event was impressive, and it was reassuring to see what huge crowds were gathering for an event not sponsored by the communist regime. People remembered the ideas in the pope's homilies—truth, the dignity of man and his labor, the rights of the individual and collective—things that were never mentioned in Poland's official language. People also remembered the pope's exhortation: "Do not be afraid!" There can be no doubt that the new Polish pope and his tour of Poland seriously delegitimized the regime.

Something else that was specifically Polish was the country's particular form of democratic opposition, which emerged in 1976–77. This phenomenon was not exclusively Polish, however, because dissident groups had already existed in the Soviet Union since the mid-1960s. The Polish democratic opposition was comprised of groups representing a variety of ideological orientations, from post-Marxists and social democrats to Christian democrats and nationalists. Some of the most dynamic were those who had participated in the student revolt of 1968, known as the "March generation." The opposition developed over a number of years, and one of the most important experiences for those involved were the collective protest letters that were signed in late 1975 and early 1976 against proposed changes to the constitution. In mid-1976, the Polish opposition started to distinguish itself from those in other communist countries, not only because of its dynamics but also because it had managed to reach beyond strictly intellectual circles, something that opposition movements elsewhere had largely failed to do. The opposition's reaction to the reprisals against those who participated in the strikes and unrest in June 1976 was a critical moment.[12] It spurred Polish dissidents to organize themselves with the aim of offering assistance—financial and legal—to the victims of those reprisals and their families, and it finally allowed them to breach the confines of the "intelligentsia ghetto." That September, the Workers' Defense Committee (Komitet Obrony Robotników, KOR) was founded.[13] Later, other organizations came into being, such as the Student Solidarity Committee (Studencki Komitet Solidarności), the Movement for the Defense of Human and Civil Rights (Ruch Obrony Praw Człowieka i Obywatela), the Young Poland Movement (Ruch Młodej Polski, RMP), and the Confederation of Independent Poland (Konfederacja Polski Niepodległej, KPN). In its program, KPN stated that Poland's full sovereignty should be restored, and even called itself a political party. KOR's activities were the most varied; this group was also the main source of information about events in Poland for the foreign media and the West. Jacek Kuroń was KOR's best known member, not just because he was extremely active, but also because he was exceptionally creative. During the years 1964–71 he served two three-year sentences as a political prisoner.

There were no more than 2,000–3,000 people involved in the opposition, in all the organizations throughout Poland. It was nevertheless very lively and determined, and several dozen of its members could even be called "professional oppositionists." The opposition organized aid for those who had suffered as the result of government reprisals, and planned celebrations for traditional Polish holidays (commemorating the Constitution of 1791 on May 3 and Poland's independence on November 11) that were not recognized by the communist state. Sometimes several thousand people would take part in these events. Oppositionists also collected signatures for various protest letters, held hunger strikes, and organized lectures for students on subjects that had been officially banned. Above all, however, they initiated a "second circulation" of illegally published books and periodicals that were critical of the government's current activities and informed readers about the reprisals. They also presented historical facts that had been either covered up or falsified—something known as filling in the "white patches." There were discussions about possible changes to the government system and methods of exerting pressure on the governing powers in the party and state. In addition to news sheets, there were also several literary and political periodicals. These actions all took place on a scale unknown in other countries: in 1978, the political police (Służba Bezpieczeństwa, SB) confiscated approximately 300,000 pages of various printed materials, and by July of 1980 they had collected close to 600,000.[14] During the years 1976–80, the SB uncovered 35 secret "high-class" duplicating centers, and confiscated over 3,000 reams of duplicating paper and over 110 kilograms of printing ink. More than the SB's growing efficacy, this data illustrates how much underground publishing had grown.

In terms of later developments, the opposition's good contacts in the Church, which were sometimes even very close, were crucial. Priests sometimes helped create opposition organizations (one of KOR's founders was the priest Jan Zieja), and most of the anniversary commemorations began with a Mass. Hunger strikes were organized in churches, and many members of the Clubs of the Catholic Intelligentsia and the ministries to the university community participated in the opposition's activities. Many opposition activists met with Church hierarchs. Cardinal Wojtyła, Archbishop of Kraków and the future pope, was one of the bishops most favorably disposed to the opposition, but Primate Wyszyński also helped. It was not only groups from the political center or right who had contacts in the Church, however. A rapprochement was taking place between the

Church and the leftist, anti-totalitarian, anti-communist intelligentsia. The book *Rodowody niepokornych* (Pedigrees of the Defiant, 1971), written by Bohdan Cywiński, a Catholic intellectual, is an example of the efforts being made in this area. One of the leading leftist oppositionists, Adam Michnik, also wrote a book in this vein—*Kościół, lewica, dialog* (1977, published in English as *The Church and the Left*). Although most of the clergy did not participate in this dialogue, it was nevertheless apparent that the Church served as a protective shield for opponents of the regime.

Perhaps more important than gaining the Church's favor was to break down the barrier that divided the intellectuals and university students from the workers. A year after it was founded, KOR began publishing a biweekly, *Robotnik* (The Worker), whose title alluded to a tradition going back to the nineteenth century, when the Polish Socialist Party published an illegal periodical with that same title in the Russian partition. The publication's first editor was Józef Piłsudski, who had been one of the founders of independent Poland in 1918. In April 1978, the group associated with KOR and RMP formed the illegal Free Trade Unions (Wolne Związki Zawodowe, WZZ) in Gdańsk and began to engage systematically with the workers. WZZ activists distributed periodicals and other underground publications and trained people in the defense of ad hoc interests; for example, they educated workers about labor safety regulations and workers' rights. They also sometimes sponsored lectures on Polish history or economics. WZZ members took part in commemorative and other events organized by the opposition, and also staged their own in honor of the anniversary of the December 1970 massacre.

During an event in 1979, a still unknown electrician named Lech Wałęsa, who was involved in WZZ, addressed a crowd of about two thousand people in front of the Gdańsk Shipyard, where the massacre's first victims had fallen. He predicted that a memorial commemorating the victims would be erected on that spot within a year—which is exactly what happened. Similar groups, but smaller and less active, were based on *Robotnik*'s network of correspondents. In 1979, *Robotnik* published a document titled "Charter of Workers' Rights," which mentioned the right to strike and the need to create trade unions independent of the government. The document was signed by over a hundred people from twenty-six cities. Fifty thousand copies of the "Charter" were printed and then distributed in dozens of factories. The opposition in other communist countries had never succeeded in carrying out anything like this on a similar scale. In 1978–79, the first farmers' associations were created; they followed the WZZ model, publishing illegal periodicals such as *Placówka* (The Outpost). To some extent, the rivalry between KOR and other opposition groups played a role in raising the political consciousness of both workers and farmers.

The growth of the democratic opposition was spurred by political and economic developments in the international arena. The period of détente in the

1970s reached its height in August 1975, when thirty-five states, including the United States and the USSR, signed the Final Act of the Conference on Security and Cooperation in Europe (CSCE) in Helsinki. While this document sanctioned the existing borders, which was vital for Poland and the entire Soviet bloc, it contained a "trap," as one of the leading experts on Central Europe, François Fejtő, has called it.[15] One of its sections, known as the "third basket," dealt with human rights, including the freedoms of association, movement, and speech. This portion of the agreement gave the West the opportunity to air its views and to protest human rights violations, something for which the communist dictatorships of the Soviet bloc were notorious. After Jimmy Carter took office in January 1977, Washington made the defense of human rights a foreign policy priority, based on the Helsinki Accords.[16] The United States' European allies had to take this into account. Opposition activists in communist countries could now invoke the accords that their own governments had signed and demand that they be respected. To a certain extent, this limited the ability of those in power to launch reprisals.

The Polish ruling elite was especially susceptible to this kind of pressure, since the economic policies of Gierek's government (intended to modernize Poland's production potential and raise the standard of living) had been dependent, since 1971, on credits that Western banks and governments had gladly granted. Soon, however, these policies broke down when the loan repayments began to consume an ever-greater portion of the revenue from exports, making it necessary to secure further loans, which were granted with increasingly unfavorable terms. In 1975, Poland's debt totaled $8 billion, while approximately one-third of the country's export revenues were used to service its debt. In 1980, the debt rose to almost $25 billion, and the payments were more than Poland's total exports to the West.[17] As a result, the Polish economy became dependent on its creditors. It should not be surprising that, for Gierek, it was important for Poland to enjoy a reputation as a stable and liberal country. As a result, he believed that drastic measures should be avoided when combating the opposition, and above all that there should be no public trials ending in severe sentences. "Our country," said one of the high-ranking SB functionaries at a meeting with party activists, "is treated like one that ... has no political prisoners ... and this is paying off for us."[18] While it is true that there were plenty of people (particularly in the security apparatus) who advocated more radical methods, the political decision-makers nevertheless stood in their way. Of course, opposition activists were quite frequently subjected to various types of harassment — for example, 48-hour detentions, temporary arrests, searches, confiscations, and being fired from their jobs or banned from foreign travel, even to "fraternal" countries. Sometimes they were beaten—even fatally. Nevertheless, in comparison to what was happening to dissidents in Czechoslovakia and the Soviet Union, their situation was easier. As Bogusław

Stachura, the deputy minister of internal affairs, noted, "We treat them very 'tenderly.'"[19] Not only was the opposition in Poland more numerous and active than in other communist states, but it also had greater freedom to act.

The Kremlin's leaders often criticized their Polish comrades for having allowed the only large sector of private agriculture in the Soviet bloc to remain (it included 70 percent of the total land under cultivation). They also criticized Polish officials for their relatively tolerant attitude toward intellectuals, who had been expressing their opposition to the government with some frequency since 1957.[20] Vladimir Lenin once said that Tsarist Russia was the "weakest link in the chain of imperialistic states." By this logic, it can be argued that Poland, with its many idiosyncrasies, was the weakest link in the chain of communist states.[21]

Chapter Two

The Solidarity Revolution

Act One, 1980–81

Under pressure from turbulent protests, the Polish communist regime withdrew the price hike on foodstuffs that it had planned for June 25, 1976, resulting in a long period of destabilization for the system. Freezing prices for another year deepened the market imbalance since production could not keep pace with the population's income, and there were limits to Poland's ability to earmark loans for the import of consumer goods. Chaos began creeping into the centrally planned industrial sector. The government cut back on investments arbitrarily, and it proved increasingly difficult to maintain cooperation between producers. The energy balance was fragile and inflationary pressures emerged, while the lines outside shops grew longer and the black market spread. The catastrophic winter of 1978–79 that paralyzed the country for a couple of months played a role, too—over half of Poles said that the magnitude of the calamity was due to "organizational paralysis."[1] In other words, the government was responsible. By early 1980, only 29 percent of those surveyed believed that the condition of the economy was "good," in comparison to almost 60 percent four years earlier.[2] These negative feelings were exacerbated by disappointment, since the first years of the Gierek era had generally been assessed very favorably, primarily because the standard of living had been improving rapidly. Gierek himself was perceived as the opposite of Gomułka: he was tall, broad-shouldered, elegantly dressed, and traveled the country. He was direct in his contact with people, whom he did not shun. Gierek was no stranger to life abroad (before 1946 he had lived for more than a decade in France and Belgium), and he liked to have official, top-level meetings with Western politicians. These traits now began to irritate people, making Gierek seem artificial and pompous.

By granting concessions under the pressure of public opinion, the ruling clique showed itself to be weak, and this kind of "loss of face" is more difficult for those in power to handle in a dictatorial state than in a democracy. Moreover, the course of events in June 1976 confirmed workers' belief that strikes could prove an effective instrument in the fight to resolve their most pressing issues. The opposition was organizing itself, and its members were pointing out the errors, waste, and abuses in Gierek's ruling circle, about which rumors were flying. Western radio stations broadcasting in Polish, especially Radio Free Europe (RFE), played an important role in publicizing these kinds of issues.[3] In the autumn of 1978, the Polish pope emerged as a new national authority, far above those holding the reins of state power. Nevertheless, this does not mean that anti-government behavior appeared on a large scale. In the parliamentary elections of March 1980, society's voting behavior did not deviate from long-standing norms: over 98 percent of those eligible to vote took part, and approximately 99 percent of the votes went to the single list of candidates dictated by the communist party.[4] Discontent and criticism remained "dormant," manifested more often as complaints and joke-telling at home, among friends, or in the ubiquitous lines, than through participation in public events organized by the opposition. Just below the surface, however, the processes needed for this discontent to be transformed into publicly expressed dissent were simmering.

Gierek's team decided to "thaw" meat prices after the elections seemed to confirm that they had the situation under control. The new prices (at least dozens of percentage points higher) were introduced on July 1, 1980. The reaction was swift. That same morning, several factories around the country stopped production, with workers at spontaneous public meetings demanding salary increases or a return to previous prices. In the evening, a meeting of those responsible for the economy took place at the party's Central Committee. It was decided that wherever there was a strike, the workers' demands for pay hikes should be at least partially met. The first test—at the Ursus tractor factory near Warsaw—was successful: one of the government ministers came to the negotiations, and workers returned to work in exchange for the promised pay raise.[5]

This is how the first phase of this "summer of strikes" began; it was to last over six weeks. Until mid-August, strikes of varying sizes took place in over two hundred enterprises in approximately fifty locations. The course of events was generally similar to that at Ursus, although government ministers rarely came to see the striking workers. News about the protests spread quite quickly. Even though most factories did not go on strike, this did not necessarily mean that they had no discontented workers—it was simply that no one had taken the initiative to organize them. There were cases in which several factories in one place decided to strike at the same time. On July 16–19, a widespread strike took place in Lublin, with workers from approximately eighty enterprises taking part. An entire railway junction was blocked, which happened to be the one serving trains transporting supplies for Soviet troops stationed in Germany. A single government minister was no longer enough to stop this protest, however; a government delegation headed by a deputy prime minister was dispatched to resolve the matter.

In addition to demands related to pay hikes, there were others related to working conditions and the management's arrogant treatment of employees. There were also demands related to more than just one enterprise, such as the call to equalize the child benefits paid to civilians and those in the military or police force. There were calls for lowering the retirement age, abolishing Saturday as a workday, and holding democratic elections in existing trade unions. No mainstays of the system were questioned, however, whether economic (central planning) or political (monopoly of the communist party). The opposition immediately began to revive: on July 2, KOR issued a short statement in support of workers' demands for raises, and on July 11, another, more extensive document was published that contained a number of demands beyond those voiced during the strikes. For example, they demanded a "radical change of the entire economic system," a legal guarantee of the "private ownership of land," a legal right to create independent trade unions, the right to strike, abolishment of preventative censorship, a guarantee of freedom of the press, a halt to reprisals against the opposition, and the release of political prisoners.[6] Because people from the opposition rarely had access to the factories on strike, the main sources of information were the Polish language broadcasts by foreign radio stations and word of mouth (including by telephone). Even with the many temporary work stoppages and expressions of discontent, there were no excesses, which caused the party leadership to decrease its vigilance. During a meeting that took place on July 24, Gierek said that "here and there various kinds of pimples [*sic*] might pop up," but that "those minor conflicts would burn out."[7] Soon after, he left for a three-week holiday on the Black Sea at Leonid Brezhnev's invitation.

Although Gierek erred in his prognosis, the fact he left the country was not necessarily a mistake, since his presence probably would not have influenced events anyway. From the government's perspective, things took a turn for the worse. On August 14, Stanisław Kania, heading the Politburo in Gierek's absence, announced that a strike had begun at the Gdańsk Shipyard (where "people from KOR had the upper hand") and that some fellow named Wałęsa, who was "linked to Kuroń's group," was heading the strike.[8] It was true: for the first time, people from the opposition chose where and when the strike would take place, and prepared their list of demands. They were not revolutionary: pay increases, reinstatement of those who had been dismissed from their jobs at the shipyard for their involvement in the illegal WZZ, an improvement in the supply of basic goods, and the erection of a monument commemorating the victims of the December 1970 massacre. When the directors accepted these demands, however, it was announced that the strike would continue anyway because other enterprises had joined it. On August 16, the Inter-Enterprise Strike Committee (Międzyzakładowy Komitet Strajkowy, MKS) was created, led by Wałęsa. Within days, it came to represent over one hundred enterprises. Several WZZ activists were also involved. MKS announced a list of twenty-one demands, of which the first was most important: the introduction of a legal right to create independent trade unions. In addition to economic and social demands, some were also related to civic freedoms that had already been included in KOR's declaration. A second, political phase of the strike movement had begun, in which demands related to civic freedoms overshadowed those for emergency pay.

On August 18, the shipyard workers from Szczecin followed Gdańsk's lead: they founded an MKS, too, which presented its own list of thirty-six demands, similar to those in Gdańsk. Given the memory of the December 1970 massacre, it was probably not a coincidence that strikes became most politicized in those two cities, and that the creation of independent trade unions topped their lists of demands. During this time, as many as a dozen or more strikes were taking place every day elsewhere in Poland. These followed the "July model," and were generally limited to just one enterprise, without any formal organization by strike committees. New elements began to appear, thanks to Radio Free Europe and the BBC's coverage, and to an ever-larger number of flyers that were being distributed in large industrial centers, urging people to strike and informing them about what was happening on the coast. For example, on August 20, in Świdnica, in Lower Silesia, a strike began with the slogan "Solidarity with the Gdańsk MKS." Farmers' opposition groups conveyed their support for the workers on strike in Gdańsk. A group of opposition intellectuals from Warsaw went to the shipyard, where MKS appointed them as advisors. More than a dozen KOR and RMP activists were there as well, who edited a daily bulletin titled Solidarność (Solidarity). An important aspect of the Gdańsk strike was the presence of symbols and religious artifacts—portraits of John Paul II and pictures of the Black Madonna of Częstochowa. In a sense, these images served as protective shields as they decorated the shipyard gates. Open-air Masses were held at the shipyard, and were also attended by the workers' families, friends, and passersby, who all stood at the gate. This all reinforced the impression that the strikes were being transformed into a national and community social movement with deep religious and moral underpinnings.

One reason the protests spread was that the government sent groups of negotiators to Szczecin and Gdańsk, headed by deputy prime ministers Kazimierz Barcikowski and Mieczysław Jagielski, who had managed to end the strike in Lublin. Because people saw the presence of these men as a sign that the government intended to continue its tactic of making concessions, which it had employed up to this point, people's fear that force would be used diminished. This fear was not entirely unfounded, however, since plenty of support for crushing the strikes existed in the highest echelons of power. The Ministry of Internal Affairs (Ministerstwo Spraw Wewnętrznych, MSW) created a team called "Operation Summer-80" (*Operacja "Lato-80"*) that was preparing to carry out a blockade of the shipyard, militarize the ports, kidnap members of the Gdańsk MKS officers with a commando detachment, and arrest opposition leaders.[9] Most of the Politburo members, however, including the most important—Gierek, Kania, and Jaruzelski, who was also minister of defense—believed that, because of the scope of the protests, an improvised attack on the striking enterprises would be impossible, and that there was no time for longer preparations. They were not even influenced by pressure from Moscow: Brezhnev urged Gierek to take decisive action in personal letters, and the Soviet ambassador expressed a similar sentiment in his statements. Thus, the Polish leadership limited itself to propaganda suggesting that the strike would have negative consequences for the economy, alluding to the threat of a Soviet intervention. Party leaders appeared on television; Gierek alone was on television twice in the course of just one week. They also made certain personnel changes (including the dismissal of Prime Minister Edward Babiuch) that were designed to cast blame for the crisis. Gierek personally persuaded Primate Wyszyński to urge people to end the strikes during a sermon planned for a Church holiday on August 26.

By that point, however, it was probably already too late: since Monday, August 25, the strikes had been spreading like wildfire, with increasing numbers of new MKS branches being established, which meant that there were at least a dozen factories on strike in each of a number of other industrial centers. In most cases workers expressed solidarity with their counterparts who were striking on the coast, and the same twenty-one demands were often declared. On August 28, the coal mines went on strike. Not only were these mines a source of precious hard currency and the Polish economy's pride and joy, but they also represented the main political support for Gierek, who had himself been a miner for many years. According to a Ministry of Internal Affairs communiqué, on August 29 at 10 a.m., strikes were under way at 653 enterprises, with over 640,000 people participating.[10] The country was on the brink of a general strike.

That day, at a Politburo meeting, Gierek admitted that it was "necessary to choose the lesser evil, and then try to get ourselves out of this."[11] That "lesser evil" was to accept the first demand—i.e., to agree to the creation of independent trade unions. The party leadership realized the danger ("we might lose the chance to exercise power . . . we will have our hands tied") but also felt a sense of helplessness ("strength is something we lack,"[12] said Kania). Moscow silently accepted this solution. As a result, the government commission and the MKS in Szczecin signed an agreement on August 30, and the next day in Gdańsk.[13] The members of the opposition who had been arrested were released. The good judgment shown by both sides was impressive: the workers did not go out into the streets, and those in power did not attempt to use force, probably because both sides remembered the tragic lesson of December 1970.

In some parts of Poland, primarily in Upper Silesia, the strikes lasted until September 5, but they, too, ended with the signing of more agreements, which, among other things, confirmed the agreements in Szczecin and Gdańsk. Without waiting for legal solutions, the strike committees began to transform into "interenterprise founding committees" (międzyzakładowe komitety założycielskie,

MKZ). New leaders emerged, like Zbigniew Bujak in Warsaw, Andrzej Słowik in Łódź, Władysław Frasyniuk in Wrocław, Mieczysław Gil in Nowa Huta, and Jan Rulewski in Bydgoszcz. They were usually young workers, engineers, or low-level bureaucrats, and were people who were the most vocal and organizationally talented. For the most part, they had nothing to do with opposition groups, and until the strikes they generally had been no different from their colleagues. People from all over the country went on pilgrimages to Gdańsk for consultations and to express solidarity with the shipyard workers. The city began to be treated as if it were the "real" Polish capital. Nevertheless, a certain amount of chaos persisted because of the vagueness surrounding just how the new trade unions would be organized. The chaos lasted until September 17, when representatives of almost forty MKZ met in Gdańsk.

After long debates, participants decided to create a single organization that they called the Independent Self-Governing Trade Union "Solidarity" (Niezależny Samorządny Związek Zawodowy "Solidarność," NSZZ). The National Coordinating Commission (Krajowa Komisja Porozumiewawcza, KKP) was also established, comprised of representatives from each region. They agreed that a statute would be drawn up, and appointed as union chairman Lech Wałęsa, that charismatic leader of the Gdańsk Shipyard strike. No one was surprised by the tautology in the union's name, since the difference between "independent" and "self-governing" was not obvious. The idea of "solidarity," however, turned out to be the right choice in terms of propaganda, while it also conveyed well the general feeling of striving toward a sense of community. It also emphasized the subjectivity of a society treated as a whole, independent of the government (and the state)—and even as its antithesis.

The union's structure was organized geographically, not by professions or sectors, as is usually the case in trade union movements. In effect, almost all the opposition groups merged with Solidarity. Many of their activists became advisors for KKP or regional committees, and also worked for the union organizations that were taking shape. While it is true that only a few people were actually part of the union leadership, both on the national and regional levels, advisors like Jacek Kuroń, Adam Michnik, Tadeusz Mazowiecki, Henryk Wujec, Andrzej Stelmachowski, Jan Olszewski, and Andrzej Czuma played very important roles. In Gdańsk, of course, it was WZZ activists who were most prominent at Wałęsa's side. These included Anna Walentynowicz, Bogdan Borusewicz, and Andrzej Gwiazda.

Solidarity cells began springing up all over the country, not only in the fields of production or transport, but also in government offices, trade institutions, schools, universities and academic institutions, theaters and editorial offices, and even in courts and ministries. In a short time, approximately nine million people had signed up for the union—men and women, young and old, with a wide range of views, people who belonged to all social and professional groups and came from all walks of life, from professors at renowned universities to barely literate agricultural workers. About a million members of the communist party joined Solidarity, too, against which its leadership did not immediately protest. The communists even quietly counted on their membership in the group becoming one of the means by which they could gain control of this new, strange, and dangerous entity that was taking shape. Joining Solidarity was not the same as registering oneself in a trade union, which was quasi-mandatory under communism. It was a completely new experience because it meant becoming a member of a huge social movement, which took the form (perhaps only a guise) of a trade union only because of events during the "summer of strikes," and the fact that the system's authoritarian character meant this was the only viable option acceptable to those in power.

Society did not become less active after the strikes ended. On the contrary, just organizing the Solidarity cells and appointing their interim authorities meant that thousands of meetings took place, at which people who had been silent until now, or who had mindlessly applauded official speakers, finally spoke up. The vast space of public debate opened up, without any limitations, and with complete freedom in terms of who should speak, and about what. Those attending the meetings often became truly obsessed with transparency, for example, with regard to regulations governing the meetings and the selection of candidates for office in the union. People suspected manipulation and clandestine communist party or SB activity everywhere. At the same time, they strove to reach some general consensus in these debates, because "solidarity" was considered to be a synonym for "unity" and "equality." This explosion was not limited to the creation of Solidarity, but meant an almost universal impulse to create new organizations or to free existing ones from party control—something the party and state authorities found disturbing. Two competing farmers' organizations were launched in the first week of September alone—Peasants' Solidarity and Rural Solidarity. After many months of negotiations and squabbling, they united to form the Independent Self-Governing Trade Union of Individual Farmers Solidarity (NSZZ Rolników Indywidualnych "Solidarność," NSZZ RI). In the spring of 1981, the new organization numbered over half a million members. From early September, postsecondary students also began to organize themselves, and representatives of approximately sixty newly created postsecondary organizations convened in Warsaw after the new academic year began on October 1. They decided to create the Independent Students' Union (Niezależne Zrzeszenie Studentów), appointed its board, and agreed on its statute. Six months later it had about eighty thousand members, representing approximately 25 percent of all postsecondary students. In December 1980, the Individual Craftsmen's Solidarity (NSZZ Indywidualnego Rzemiosła "Solidarność") was founded. Despite its only marginal importance (having only four thousand members), its existence clearly demonstrated the desire of many groups to have their own truly "independent and self-governing" organizations. In that same period, the Solidarity union for disabled people and pensioners was also launched (NSZZ "Solidarność" Inwalidów, Rencistów i Emerytów), as well as one for taxi drivers (NSZZ "Solidarność" Kierowców Transportu Prywatnego). In mid-September, a committee was established that would act as an umbrella organization for artistic and academic associations (the Artistic and Academic Associations' Consultative Committee, Komitet Porozumiewawczy Stowarzyszeń Twórczych i Naukowych), working closely with Solidarity. It became the spokesman for professional organizations such as the Polish Sociological Association, Polish Philosophical Association, and Polish Filmmakers' Union. The intellectual organizations that were part of the "ideological front"—very important to the party—were experiencing their own kind of revolt. These included the Polish Journalists' Association (Stowarzyszenie Dziennikarzy Polskich, SDP) and the Polish Writers' Union (Związek Literatów Polskich, ZLP). In the autumn of 1980, people associated with the opposition, or close to it, assumed leadership of these organizations and transformed both of them into close allies of Solidarity.

Social ferment spread like wildfire and engulfed virtually everyone: scouts and high school students, activists and members of the communist party. Party members began pushing for a special congress to be convened, and democratic elections at all levels. Women's and youth organizations that had been party appendages were swept up in it, too, as were activists in the pro-government trade unions, which were searching intensely for a new incarnation, to avoid being devoured by Solidarity. After years of having quietly accepted the system, Poles "let loose": almost everyone was talking, making speeches, writing, and arguing, and virtually any topic was game. Solidarity was, of course, the biggest breach in the communists' monopolistic system, but hundreds of smaller gaps and cracks appeared, too. Underground publishing expanded tremendously, since many of the new, various Solidarity organizations began producing their own news sheets, brochures, and books.[14] These publications were transmitting information that was not subject to government censorship, including texts on previously taboo subjects in contemporary Polish history, as well as analyses of the economic situation.

Although the democratic opposition's intellectual output was considerable, it nevertheless had no plan ready for governing the country. In its early phase, the opposition presented itself as an egalitarian movement whose aim was to seek redress, "limited to the workers' defense . . . [and] safeguarding that agreements signed by the government are realized," as well as "demanding that the authorities respect the freedoms of speech and association."[15] It was simply acting as a trade union that was "making demands," while the addressee of those demands was supposed to insure they were met. Because people were joining the union en masse, however, with people from all across society getting involved, Solidarity was somehow gradually forced to shift its emphasis from only voicing grievances to proposing more or less specific changes. The attitude of the "addressee"—the communist leadership—also contributed to this development: it had adopted its own brand of passive resistance, such as dragging its feet in realizing the points outlined in the agreements.

Solidarity's program was first sketched out in February 1981.[16] Although it did state that "we do not intend to replace the government in [carrying out its] tasks," blame was being put on the government—or to be more precise, the communist system. "The disappearance of democratic institutions is at the root of this crisis," the authors wrote, "and the deep division between society and the government that is associated with this." Moreover, they stated that economic reforms would not suffice "unless a thorough reform of the system by which power is exercised is not carried out simultaneously." Liberating enterprises from government control and eliminating central planning were recognized as fundamental to any economic reform. In the political sphere, the main issue was modification of the electoral law for parliament and local government so that it would guarantee the ability "to submit [the names of] candidates by organizations and civic groups." This text, which became the subject of a long discussion, thus did not directly attack two fundamental canons of the system: the role of the communist party as the main organizer of political life, and Poland's position as a Soviet satellite. This moderate approach has been described as "self-limiting," and the entire situation has been called a "self-limiting revolution."[17] Although this sounds like an oxymoron (a revolution is, after all, the opposite of limiting oneself), it did convey the current state of affairs quite well: there existed both a fear of going too far, which could end with a Soviet intervention, as well as a lack of a universally comprehensible language capable of expressing these new political projects.

With time, Solidarity's transformation from a supervisor into a catalyst of change became increasingly apparent. It was a reaction to repeated conflicts with the government, and was above all due to the communist party's unwillingness to undertake reforms. For example, union representatives were the main authors of the amendment to the censorship law, as well as legislation on enterprises and employees' self-government, both of which were passed by the parliament. In May 1981, in another bill, the idea of a "social enterprise" was introduced, founded on the idea that the crew of the factory would be in charge of it. Another one was on the establishment of a Chamber of Local Government as a second house of parliament. A little later, a bill on local government itself was prepared for presentation to parliament.[18]

The union's platform, passed on October 7, 1981, at the First National Solidarity Congress, was titled "The Self-Governing Republic" (*Rzeczpospolita Samorządna*),[19] and encompassed not only economic and political reforms, but also changes in education (including the question of truthful history teaching in school), amendments to the criminal code, autonomy for universities, the need to liberate the justice system from party control, the freedom to conduct scholarly research, access to radio and television for social organizations, and autonomy for local self-government. The union platform stated plainly that "the idea of freedom and uncurtailed independence is dear to us," and that "national identity must be fully respected."[20] The program also stated that only through free elections would parliament regain a "generally recognized representative character."[21] They declared that an awareness that bloodshed was possible "requires us to realize our ideals gradually" and "to observe the balance of power that arose in Europe after the Second World War."[22] The revolution was thus still "self-limiting," a gradual one based on "an honest and loyal dialogue with the government."[23] The entire "self-governing Republic" was a utopia of sorts—a variation of the "third way" between ideocratic authoritarianism as implemented by the communist party (ruling with a monopoly of power and all-embracing etatism) and the democratic world (based on the free market and private ownership). Regardless, however, of whether this kind of project could actually be carried out, it was nevertheless a clear alternative to the communist system.

In official documents, Solidarity invariably declared it was ready to negotiate and conclude a "new social contract." Some of Solidarity's members, however, especially activists at various levels and the group's advisors, who were intellectuals, were convinced that the union was fulfilling a mission, that it was morally in the right, "represent[ing] the embryo of new life within a state that has totalitarian ambitions."[24] They believed it not only represented the captive Polish society to the government, but also in fact *was* society, representing "good," while the government embodied "evil." Through various projects, Solidarity was assuming the burden of rebuilding Poland. The trade union wanted to push forward the communist party, which had proved incapable of doing so itself.

Chapter Three

"Defend Socialism as If It Were Poland's Independence"

In choosing the "lesser evil," those in power had created an exceedingly difficult situation for themselves. Clearly, a new, independent organization would be a "foreign body" whose existence would be irreconcilable with the system's fundamental principles. Above all, it would challenge the omnipotence of the communist party, which, in Poland's case, had already been forced to accept the autonomy of the Catholic Church. The government's strategy regarding Solidarity and the other organizations that were forming under the union's protective umbrella did not leave much room to maneuver. If the system was not going to disintegrate, the union needed to be absorbed by the existing structures and subjugate itself to the "leading power," as the communist party declared in the state constitution. Various tactics could be employed to achieve this: the movement's development could be hampered, its collapse could be brought about from within, or it could be discredited. A frontal attack could also be launched by using force, and above all by isolating (read: arresting) the most active members of the union and opposition. These measures—weaken and attack—were essentially complementary, since achieving the first aim would make it easier to employ the second. Taken together, they offered a chance to make Solidarity "fit" into the system in terms of its form and personnel. Or, they would make it possible to eliminate Solidarity entirely. Since the government abandoned the use of force in July and August, however, they could not resort to it now, after they had just signed the agreements, which the overwhelming majority of both Poles and foreign observers had applauded enthusiastically.

The communist party leadership also had internal issues it needed to address. To this end, Edward Gierek was removed as first secretary on September 5, a continuation of personnel changes that had begun two weeks earlier. Gierek's successor, Stanisław Kania, was an experienced, albeit colorless, *apparatchik*, who for many years had been responsible for party control over the security apparatus and policy toward the opposition. Soon, further changes were made in the party and government apparatus which were intended to show that the party was removing those responsible for the economic disaster. These changes did not result in complete unanimity within the ruling clique, however. As often happens in crisis situations, a division arose between the "moderates" and the "hardliners." The moderates (including such individuals as Stanisław Kania, Kazimierz Barcikowski, and Wojciech Jaruzelski) advocated gradually weakening Solidarity and bleeding it of its members. The hardliners, by contrast, believed Solidarity should simply be liquidated as swiftly as possible. In the party apparatus, army, and Ministry of Internal Affairs, these hardliners (called the "party concrete," *beton partyjny*) were especially numerous. They were also strongly represented in the party's highest echelons, and included, for example, new members of Politburo Stefan Olszowski, Andrzej Żabiński, Tadeusz Grabski, and Stanisław Kociołek, and minister of internal affairs Mirosław Milewski. Although advocates of reform had certainly also appeared in the party, supporting change that would allow a permanent place in the system for Solidarity, they did not find support in the highest circles of power.

At first, Moscow's stance was similar to that of the moderates. The Kremlin's instructions for the Polish leadership issued on September 3 mentioned the necessity of "preparing a counterattack" and "a return to the lost positions in the working class." The Kremlin recommended, however, that Polish leaders "show flexibility" in their activities, and only use "balanced administrative measures if they are needed," while they were to focus on propaganda and "increased militancy in party organizations" in the factories.[1] The only innovative recommendation suggested was that "those in leadership positions [in the army]" should be attracted "to work in the party and economic sector." Such propositions implied that the Soviets saw regaining complete control over the situation more as a process, rather than as a sudden one-off operation.

Kania's team had internal divisions, and used tactics that were intended to impede the expansion of Solidarity, by delaying decisions, for example. These activities were undertaken not only at the local level, but also at municipal, regional, and even national levels. On the local level, for example, factory directors refused to provide union cells with any office space or telephones. The authorities' intentions became glaringly obvious when it came to Solidarity's registration. The group submitted its registration application (along with its statute) to the Voivodship Court in Warsaw on September 24. Time passed, but the court did not act on the matter, although the application had seemed to be a mere formality. In response, Solidarity carried out a one-hour warning strike throughout the country on October 3. After a month, the court finally approved Solidarity's registration. It changed the union's statue, however, eliminating from it the right to strike, and adding a mention of the "leading role of the party" found in the constitution. Solidarity appealed to the Supreme Court and announced that if the decision regarding these amendments was not changed, it would call for a general strike. After feverish negotiations, with this threat looming over it, the Supreme Court repealed the amendments. On November 10, the union was registered, with the agreed-upon wording. Thus, arranging this one matter took almost two and a half months, counting from the end of the strike at the Gdańsk Shipyard. The government resisted the legalization of other organizations much more aggressively. The Independent Students' Union was registered only in February 1981, five months after submitting its application and after a strike lasting many weeks. The Independent Self-Governing Trade Union of Individual Farmers Solidarity (NSZZ IR) was registered in May 1981, after the occupation of several public buildings and some extremely dangerous disturbances (about which more will be said later in this chapter). Tradesmen had to wait until June 1981 for the registration of their Solidarity branch.

These delay tactics became a mainstay of the government's strategies, in all kinds of situations, of varying degrees of importance. Solidarity even had to resort to strikes—or threats of strikes—to force the implementation of some of the points in the Gdańsk Agreement. These points included the introduction of Saturdays as a day free from work, and the publication of an official union newspaper (the first issue of *Tygodnik Solidarność* (Solidarity Weekly) appeared only in early April 1981). The situation was similar on the regional level, where there were numerous conflicts with the local administration. One such conflict occurred over granting hospitals the use of buildings originally slated for party or militia use. Also controversial was the removal of officials tainted by corruption. Negotiations regarding amendments to the laws on censorship and local government, for example, dragged on for months. There was a constant battle, complete with protest marches, over demands to improve food supplies or guarantee deliveries of rationed items (such as meat, butter, and baby formula). Eventually, these demands were successfully forced through. Not only was this kind of sluggishness part of the government's tactics, it was above all a sign that the party elites were not prepared—politically or intellectually—for change and reforms. As Solidarity strove to expand into areas that would be "independent and self-governing," it was guided by a precisely defined, and perhaps utopian, vision of general political changes. The communist party, by contrast, concentrated primarily on maintaining its monopoly of power and the political status quo.

The government's resistance to change prompted unionists to escalate their protests. Strikes were their preferred tool, and often broke out on the local level for mundane reasons. Despite Wałęsa's undeniable charisma and the union leadership's authority, many of these actions took place against their will, despite repeated appeals for calm. "Solidarity society," or at least a large segment of its elite (particularly regional activists and those from the factory committees), felt deeply frustrated, particularly during the autumn of 1981, and the union's national leadership had trouble controlling them. The party and its subordinate state services were unsuccessful in crushing Solidarity by eliciting centrifugal activities, eliminating union radicals, and arranging a split, since the unifying forces—a common enemy and hope that fundamental changes would be carried out in Poland—were stronger than their differences.

argues gov't delaying tactics 1981 helped undermine support for Solidarity.

Nevertheless, in the second half of 1981, the tactic of delaying reforms and the government's negative reaction to the union's projects, combined with worsening everyday problems, plainly had an impact on Poles' attitudes. According to research carried out in late November and early December 1981, the percentage of people who supported Solidarity dropped in one year from 89 percent to 71 percent. The number of people who believed that the government alone was responsible for the economic and political crisis fell from 61 percent to 39 percent, while those who blamed both sides (the government and Solidarity) for the conflict grew from 27 percent to 40 percent.[2] Even some union members were already having doubts about their own organization: about 8 percent of those surveyed declared that they did not support Solidarity.[3] While having over 70 percent support is more than satisfactory, in this case, the downward trend was critical. Society was already tired of the day-to-day difficulties and prolonged emotional seesaw.

Obvious to everyone were the government's tactics of avoiding reforms and postponing decisions. Nevertheless, the ruling camp was also involved in other, less visible activities, such as those of the security apparatus and its informers, who attempted, mostly unsuccessfully, to insure that decisions made by various Solidarity branches would be in line with the government's interests. Most important, however, were the government's preparations to attack the union. Even during the summer strikes, the Polish Politburo members considered imposing martial law, since the country's constitution did not sanction the declaration of a state of emergency in response to unrest or natural disasters. The idea was dropped, however, and the "lesser evil" was chosen instead. The matter was taken up again in connection with the conflict over Solidarity's registration and the union's right to announce a general strike. On October 22, 1980, the Politburo appointed a group to prepare the principles by which the state would function during such a strike. That same day, a meeting took place in the General Staff, resulting in an order to prepare the document "Propositions on the Matter of the Procedures by Which Martial Law Would Be Imposed for the Security of the State and a Definition of the Effects of Implementing Martial Law."[4]

It was not just current events in Poland that prompted these decisions, although they had brought pressure on the regime to act; they were also made because Poland's western and southern neighbors (East Germany and Czechoslovakia) had begun to show signs that they were concerned about the situation in Poland, too. As early as September 30, Erich Honecker, the East German communist leader, asked his comrades in Moscow to create a "consultative mechanism" regarding Polish matters.[5] In analyses for internal use, German Democratic Republic (GDR) politicians referred directly to the situation in Czechoslovakia in 1968, where the "consultative mechanism" ended with an armed intervention. Admittedly, reactions at the Kremlin were at first significantly less emotional than those in

Berlin. The fact that Solidarity was now registered, however, and that its membership was burgeoning, changed the stance of the Soviet leadership. Not only did the Soviets agree that their Polish counterparts should immediately take action against Solidarity, but, more importantly, they also determined that the presence of Warsaw Pact armies in Poland should support these activities, since Polish law enforcement functionaries were not yet ready.

On November 12, there was a meeting of the Committee of National Defense (Komitet Obrony Kraju, KOK), the highest party and governmental body dealing with defense and military matters. At this meeting, leaders admitted that preparations for martial law were not yet far enough advanced. They blamed their unpreparedness, above all, on a lack of coordination between the military, Ministry of Internal Affairs, and other ministries that would be involved in martial law (such as the Ministry of Justice, which had under its jurisdiction the prisons, courts, and public prosecutor's office). Some of the speakers pointed out that, in order to act, "more favorable political and social conditions" were required,[6] which meant a more heated phase of the conflict and a polarization of public opinion.

These conditions appeared soon, when, on November 21, an incident occurred in conjunction with the arrest of Jan Narożniak, an employee of the Warsaw region Solidarity branch who had acquired and publicized the secret instructions of the Public Prosecutor's Office regarding the prosecution of "illegal anti-socialist activities." Several large Warsaw factories went on strike in defense of Narożniak, demanding not only his release, but also the formation of a parliamentary commission to investigate the activities of the public prosecutor's office and security apparatus. Kania's team treated this strike like a declaration of war, and the Ministry of Internal Affairs forces were put on alert; in Berlin and Moscow there were similar thoughts. Although the conflict was amicably avoided, the Soviets decided that a meeting of the Warsaw Pact leadership would take place. On December 8, Soyuz-80 maneuvers were planned in Poland, with the participation of more than a dozen Soviet, Czechoslovak, East German, and Polish divisions. These exercises were supposed to act as a cover for the operation against Solidarity, during which several thousand activists (the lists had already been prepared) were to be arrested.

Washington—and the Vatican, too—were feverishly trying to intervene, calling on Brezhnev to abandon these activities. The Western media, primarily based on White House and State Department leaks, warned that there were concentrations of Soviet troops on Poland's borders. During the dramatic meetings which took place on December 5 in Moscow, however, Kania managed to convince his colleagues (especially Brezhnev), during a speech that lasted over an hour, that the maneuvers should be called off. And that is what happened, but the Soviet leader told Kania, "Well, okay. We won't enter [now], but if the situation gets more complicated—we will."[7] At least this is Kania's recollection.

Preparations were in full swing for the imposition of martial law, about which the public knew absolutely nothing. Poles had been perplexed by the successive conflicts between the government and Solidarity. The lack of strong leadership on the part of the government was apparent. Neither Kania nor, to an even lesser extent, Prime Minister Józef Pińkowski, in office since August, was able to provide it. The remedy was found by following a suggestion from the Soviets a few months before: on February 11, 1981, the minister of national defense, General Wojciech Jaruzelski, assumed the post of prime minister. Because of his profession and position, he was already known as "tough." Moreover, the Polish army traditionally enjoyed considerable authority, regardless of regime. At this point, it was especially important because the communist party had suffered a loss in its prestige. Even Solidarity reacted positively and suspended their plans for a press boycott, which was to be a protest against the union's lack of access to mass media. Jaruzelski brought Mieczysław F. Rakowski into the government as deputy prime minister. Rakowski had been the editor of the well-regarded weekly *Polityka*, known for its reformist sympathies, which was undoubtedly intended to "soften" the image of a cabinet headed by a military man.

Jaruzelski's new position did not hamper the secret preparations. Quite the contrary: some days after his nomination, there was a simulation, enabling him to determine any gaps that still existed in the preparations for martial law. On March 15, after the results had been analyzed, the Ministry of National Defense (Ministerstwo Obrony Narodowej, MON) and the Ministry of Internal Affairs presented the prime minister with their proposals. They said that both ministries were "in principle capable of implementing martial law,"[8] and that the only thing lacking was suitable preparation in terms of propaganda. It was proposed that they begin the operation on a Saturday night, and treat it as something meant to forestall a general strike. As soon as the party leadership made a political decision, both ministries would need five to seven days to develop the operation, which was to be launched as a complete surprise. Three possible versions of the course of events were foreseen: a "mild" one, in which few protests would occur; an "active" one, in which there would be mass strikes, but only on factory premises; and an "aggressive" one, in which workers on strike would take to the streets and attack public buildings. In an "aggressive" scenario, the memorandum to the prime minister stated, "the aid of the Warsaw Pact armies is not out of the question."[9]

In late January, the Kremlin had already decided to carry out maneuvers that it had suspended in December. It is very likely that both the simulation (*gra sztabowa*, or "game," as these kinds of command post exercises were called in Polish) and the memorandum of March 15, and perhaps even the appointment of a military man to the post of prime minister, were all related to this decision. The maneuvers were given the cryptonym "Soyuz-81": we must "let them know our forces are ready," said Marshal Dmitrii Ustinov at a Soviet Politburo meeting.[10] The exercises, at which approximately 30,000 soldiers from four armies would take part, began on March 17 and were supposed to last, as officially announced, until March 25. The entire operation was to involve over 120,000 Soviet troops stationed at the Polish borders. In the East German and Czechoslovak armies, the state of heightened combat readiness instituted in December 1980 was still in effect.

Meanwhile, the day before the maneuvers were to begin, a group of activists from the Independent Self-Governing Trade Union of Individual Farmers Solidarity (NSZZ IR) began occupying a building in Bydgoszcz, a large city in northern Poland, demanding that their union be registered. On March 19, a special militia unit forcibly removed regional Solidarity leaders, who had gone to a meeting of the local voivodship council to support the farmers' demands. Three Solidarity representatives were brutally beaten. That night, Solidarity headquarters deemed this an attack on the union and announced a state of "strike preparedness." From one day to the next, an explosive atmosphere swept the country. Solidarity held a four-hour, nationwide warning strike on March 27, demanding that those responsible for the beatings be punished and that the farmers' union be registered. An open-ended general strike was announced for March 31. Emotions in the country were running high: Solidarity's regional offices had moved to large factories, photos of the beaten trade unionists were posted everywhere, and hundreds of communist party cells appealed to Kania to fulfill Solidarity's demands. Feverish meetings were taking place, both of the union's leadership and the central government. Prime Minister Jaruzelski met with Primate Wyszyński, who also spoke with a Solidarity delegation. On March 24, the government issued an official communiqué that spoke of an indefinite extension of the "Soyuz-81" maneuvers. In Warsaw, the deputy head of the KGB, Vladimir Kryuchkov, appeared alongside Marshal Viktor Kulikov, commander of the Warsaw Pact forces. On March 27, Brezhnev telephoned Kania, told him the situation "had entered a critical phase," and recommended that martial law be imposed the day before the general strike was planned.[11] That day, Kania (as party first secretary) and Jaruzelski (as prime minister) approved a lengthy document titled "The Main Idea Behind the Implementation of Martial Law in the Polish People's Republic For Reasons of State Security," which contained the operation's basic guiding principles.[12] All forces of the Ministry of Internal Affairs were put on highest alert. Military maneuvers were underway on training grounds, and were shown every day on the television news.

On March 31, however, an agreement was reached after dramatic, emotional talks that had been taking place for a week, led by Deputy Prime Minister Rakowski and Lech Wałęsa. Both sides retreated: Solidarity called off the general strike, and the party leadership promised it would investigate the "Bydgoszcz incident" and register the farmers' union. The night of April 3–4, Kania and Jaruzelski held top secret talks with Marshal Ustinov and the KGB chief, Politburo member Iurii Andropov, in the border town of Brześć. The Soviets agreed that only Polish forces would participate in the operation, without Soviet troops. On April 7, the "Soyuz-81" maneuvers ended. From that time, Moscow's leaders left matters in the hands of their Polish comrades, and all they could do was urge them finally to act, and frighten Poles with the prospect of Soviet tanks.

Pressure on the Polish leadership was sometimes quite unceremonious, such as in early June when, at Honecker's initiative, an internal coup was attempted, in which party hardliners were to replace the Kania-Jaruzelski tandem. Both leaders emerged unscathed, and the hardliners lost Moscow's confidence. A special communist party congress in July ended in a defeat for the reformers and a weakened position for the hardliners, which to some extent stabilized the situation within the party itself. It was not any better able to mobilize, however, and its membership continued to fall. It became clear that the army would be the last resort. The oft-repeated slogan "We will defend socialism like independence" actually meant just this—that the army, not the party, was required in the fight for independence.

Preparations for the implementation of martial law were underway, as was the shift of military men to civilian positions: generals took over the ministries of internal affairs (Czesław Kiszczak, who up until now had been the head of counter-intelligence and of military police), administration, and mining and energy. "Men in uniform" appeared in the roles of voivods, deputy voivods, and mayors of large cities. Jerzy Urban was appointed as government spokesman, a post that continued to be extremely important because of the role of propaganda in martial law and its preparation. This talented, cynical journalist was a friend of Deputy Prime Minister Rakowski.

Moscow continued to monitor the situation: every once in a while, it would send people from the highest political echelons to Poland, such as Andrei Gromyko, for example; Marshal Kulikov was an almost daily visitor in Warsaw. Brezhnev called Kania many times, and had a long talk with him and Jaruzelski in the Crimea in August. Honecker persisted in his support of the hardliners who were eager for confrontation. The KGB resident in Warsaw, General Vitalii Pavlov, was in contact with them almost every day. The atmosphere was thus still tense, and Solidarity was adding fuel to the fire. The "Message to the Working People of Eastern Europe," approved on September 8 at Solidarity's First National Congress, played a special role. In it, Solidarity expressed the hope that "soon your representatives will be able to meet with ours in order to share our union experiences."[13] This statement, of course, overcame a certain "psychological barrier" (i.e., fear of the Soviet superpower) and represented a "Messianism far removed from a politics of realism," as many activists and advisors saw it.[14] Brezhnev saw the document as an "impudent prank"[15] and called Kania, asking insistently when martial law would finally be introduced.[16]

In the coming days, open letters, radical in tone, were sent to Warsaw from Moscow, Berlin, Prague, Budapest, and Sofia. On September 13, a meeting of the Committee of National Defense took place, to which Kania had been invited, although he was not officially a member of this body. The committee stated that martial law was ready from a technical standpoint, but that, as Jaruzelski said, a situation should be created in which no one could interpret the launching of the operation as a government provocation, but as something necessary. Moreover, Jaruzelski stressed that there still existed a "relatively lower stage of readiness in the economy and state administration."[17] Kania voiced similar reservations, and despite pressure from the Ministry of Internal Affairs, the body did not request that the Politburo make a decision.

Most importantly, the propaganda campaign had to be intensified, and a specific reason (or rather, pretext) had to be found that would justify the imposition of martial law in the public's eyes. There was also a problem within the leadership: Kania was not eager to employ such a drastic measure. Moreover, because of possible complications, power needed to be concentrated in the hands of one individual. The man who had been first secretary up to this point was certainly not suited to the task. Since the Kremlin doubted the hardliners' competence, none of them was a suitable candidate for the administration of martial law. Naturally, it was thought best to entrust a military man with this function. The choice was thus extremely limited: no realistic alternative to General Jaruzelski existed. The Soviets thus decided that Jaruzelski would replace Kania, who was wavering. As a result of suggestions and tactful pressure from Moscow, on the morning of October 18, the Central Committee dismissed Kania (with a small majority, 104 to 79 votes) and appointed Jaruzelski (with only 4 votes against him). The newly elected first secretary did not resign from any of his functions, so he continued to be simultaneously prime minister, chairman of KOK, and minister of defense, as well as an MP and member of numerous political bodies and boards of social organizations, such as the veterans' union. This was a unique situation for European communist states, since a current military officer had never held the position of head of state, nor had one ever occupied such a large proportion of the highest posts. In just under two months, he would assume one more.

Psychologically, the party elite found itself at a point of no return, although the decision-making mechanism could still have been stopped. In any case, other preparations were in full swing, but at the same time they were carried out discreetly, and the authorities remembered that propaganda should exaggerate the atmosphere of gloom. The official media thus presented the coming winter almost apocalyptically, announcing that electricity and heating would be turned off in cities; that factories, hospitals, and schools would be closed; and even that there would be shortages of bread and potatoes. Solidarity—being, as it was, a destructive and irresponsible power—was blamed for the chaos and anarchy. Numerous local strike actions facilitated this kind of argumentation. In one place agricultural workers were on strike; elsewhere there were teachers, yet somewhere else miners, and throughout Poland students were striking. Even the inmates in one of the prisons rose up, with two fatalities occurring during the quelling of the revolt. Various Solidarity branches came up with radical projects, such as removing communist party cells from factories.

The authorities' efforts to maintain public calm and revive the economy, as well as their concern for the common man, countered "Solidarity anarchy." Beginning on October 27, hundreds of Operational Military Groups appeared, first in villages and small towns, then in large enterprises and provincial seats. Their official task was to assist in solving local problems of daily life. Their more important aim, however, was reconnaissance, to facilitate the military commissars' activities after the imposition of martial law. The government's proposals regarding the creation of a Council of National Understanding (Rada Porozumienia Narodowego) were widely publicized. Solidarity, however, was very skeptical about these proposals, and saw them as an attempt to adorn the regime's "old façade with a Solidarity badge," which "could only deprive the union of its independence and credibility."[18]

Once preparations were complete, Jaruzelski's team launched its "offensive operations." The first of these was a Central Committee decision made on November 28 regarding a bill "on the extraordinary means of action in the interest of protecting the citizens and the state" that was to be presented to parliament. On this basis, the government could, for example, suspend the rights to strike and association, and introduce a curfew, as well as limit postal services and border crossings.[19] This legislation would thus be more about a "state of emergency" than "extraordinary means." Although the bill was not published, its very title was enough to prompt Solidarity's outrage. In fact, the bill was actually, to a large degree, a smokescreen to cover the imposition of martial law since, after all, it was supposed to be launched as a complete surprise, in the absence of any parliamentary procedures.

Considerably more spectacular was another activity: on December 2, a special Ministry of Internal Affairs unit, by helicopter landing, took control, without much resistance, of a building belonging to the Firefighting Officers' School, which striking students had occupied. This took place in greater downtown Warsaw, in view of hundreds of people and in the presence of regional Solidarity leaders, who were aiding those on strike. During the commando attack, the Solidarity office lost its phone connection. Both of these events suggested that the moment of confrontation was looming near. The union's reaction was easy to predict: on December 3, a meeting of the Presidium of Solidarity's National Commission and the chairmen of all its regional boards took place in Radom. The bill and the events at the firefighters' school were both deemed attacks on

Solidarity. The atmosphere at the meetings was emotional and determined. There were many harsh words and radical proposals (for example, appointing a government of experts). Even Wałęsa, who was usually moderate, spoke of getting rough with the government (*targanie się [z władzą] po szczękach*). Karol Modzelewski, who had been a dissident since the 1960s and had served two jail terms as a political prisoner, mocked the "Internationale" (the hymn of the communist movement), saying that "this is *their* last struggle," instead of "this is *the* last struggle."[20] It was agreed that if the parliament passed the legislation, a twenty-four hour general strike would take place, and if the government wanted to implement the legislation, an indefinite strike would begin. Two days later, at Rakowski's suggestion, Jaruzelski decided that suitably selected excerpts from the Radom meetings, obtained from a secret informer, would be broadcast by radio, and presented as key evidence of Solidarity's intention to overthrow the system.[21] It was to serve as the pretext for imposing martial law. The morning of December 5, the Politburo met and listened to information from the head of the Ministry of Internal Affairs about the situation in the country. A tough and determined tone dominated the long discussion: Jaruzelski implied they had no choice but to act (*przed nami nie ma już nic*), and at the same time noted bitterly that "it is a horrible, monstrous shame for the party that after thirty-six years in power, it has to be defended by the police."[22] In conclusion, the general said that "the decision will be made at the optimal time, within a political framework."[23]

After sixteen months, the "Solidarity carnival," as it was known (whether ironically or half-jokingly), thus drew to a close. It was not so much a carnival in the sense of amusement, but rather more a time when the sanctioned rules of social life were suspended, when people challenged the existing political hierarchy, and even the least realistic ideas could be floated, including those related to society. Although the institutions that had been keeping a tight physical and psychological hold on society did not collapse, they did find themselves sidelined during that carnival, if nothing else at least because the crowd had stopped obeying them. A feeling of individual and collective freedom dominated, and also a hope that the world would change, and that freedom was there to stay. When we talk about this carnival, however, we assume from the start that it was somehow "extracted" from normal time, and that it would have a beginning and an end. This particular carnival began on August 31, 1980, and by December 13, 1981, the time had come for it to close.

Part 2

The Attack

Chapter Four

The Last Days Before

On December 5, the Polish Politburo granted permission for the imposition of martial law and gave Jaruzelski a free hand to select the exact date. For reasons of secrecy if nothing else, the Politburo was unable to decide the date or hour that the operation—which had been assigned the cryptonyms "G," "W," or "X"—would begin.[1] According to the plans that had already been approved, the army required at least forty-eight hours after the political decision had been made to launch its operations in full force. Those same plans also stated that, optimally, the operation would begin on a Saturday night, when most workplaces were closed, making an immediate response (such as strikes and Solidarity's mobilization) practically impossible, or at least seriously hindered, until Monday. Meanwhile, since December 5 was a Saturday, the operation could not begin yet, and it would be necessary to keep its date a secret for at least a week. This would be too risky, considering the large number of people who knew about it. The preparations were still being "polished," which was not surprising, given Jaruzelski's extreme pedantry, which he also expected of all his subordinates and colleagues. It was necessary, among other things, to conduct a propaganda campaign to publicize a specific reason (or pretext) for taking such dramatic action—putting tens of thousands of soldiers and thousands of tanks and armored vehicles on city streets. A pretext—a meeting of Solidarity's leadership on December 3—did present itself, but secret police tapes made at those meetings had to be suitably prepared and publicized in the mass media for several days at least. Because Jaruzelski made the decision to start this propaganda campaign on Sunday, December 6, it could go on uninterrupted for five or six days. Which is precisely what happened.

The regional communist party offices and administration had to be mobilized as well, as did the leadership of the military and Ministry of Internal Affairs. The satellite political parties also needed to be informed of the fact that Operation "W" was drawing near, and the chairman of the Council of State had to be told about the task awaiting him. Jaruzelski was faced with a long series of meetings, consultations, and briefings. In addition, he wanted to obtain a formal assurance from Moscow that it would provide economic aid (above all in deliveries of meat, grain, and raw materials, including oil) and, if needed, military assistance. This all meant extra time was crucial. Moscow did not want to commit itself to such formal obligations, however, and so Jaruzelski also called on his Soviet comrades for direct support. Thus, via Ambassador Boris Aristov, he asked that a representative of the Soviet Committee of Economic Planning come to Poland (he came on December 8). He also asked—more importantly—that members of the top Soviet party leadership (Gromyko or Andropov) come to Warsaw.[2] Perhaps he wanted to have them nearby, so that he could saddle them with some of the responsibility. Or perhaps their presence would make it easier to prepare a decision, if necessary, about the participation of Warsaw Pact armies in the operation to impose martial law (although the decision itself would have to be made in Moscow).

Not only would the order have to be issued at least a week after the Politburo met, other factors also meant the operation had to begin before mid-December. Most important of these was that the two-month extension of service for 46,000 soldiers from an "old year" (drafted in autumn 1979) was drawing to a close. It could be extended again after December 20 only if the country was at war, or if the Sejm approved. The new recruits were considered to have been "infected" by Solidarity, and were so distrusted that the autumn draft was in fact postponed, and only about 17,000 people were inducted, about one-third of that year's total. In these conditions, discharging trained soldiers into civilian life would have meant a temporary reduction in the numbers serving in the military, something the designers of martial law could not afford.

General Jaruzelski also considered the Kremlin's invitation to go to Moscow. The visit was scheduled to take place on December 14–15. In Warsaw, Ambassador Aristov conveyed Brezhnev's extensive "verbal dispatch." It contained the following passage: "Essentially, it is not about whether or not the confrontation will happen, but rather who will begin it, what means will be used to carry it out and on whose side the initiative will remain."[3] One can easily imagine how unpleasant the tone and content of conversations with the "Bear from the Kremlin," as the Soviet General Secretary was commonly called in Poland, would have been. So it should come as no surprise that Jaruzelski preferred to avoid putting himself through that. In the end, the imposition of martial law rendered the visit superfluous. An additional argument for beginning the operation on December 12 or 13 was that Solidarity's Mazowsze Region branch, the second largest trade union organization in the country after that in Upper Silesia, had decided to stage a demonstration in downtown Warsaw on December 17, the anniversary of the 1970 massacre on the coast.

The immediate impetus for the decision to impose martial law was the spectacular breaking of the student strike at the Firefighting Officers' School by special units of the Ministry of Internal Affairs. Though government propaganda portrayed the calls for a mass demonstration in the streets of the capital as a casus belli, as far as the authorities were concerned it really was. The Christmas holidays also limited the choice of date for the start of martial law—in Poland, these are traditionally the longest holidays and the most important, for both religious and family reasons. Interfering with them by bringing the army into cities just a few days prior (i.e., on the night of Saturday–Sunday, December 19–20) was unthinkable, even for the atheistic authorities. General Jaruzelski had little room to maneuver: "We find ourselves in the role of a boxer who is cornered," he is said to have told Rakowski.[4] He could no longer delay the decision, for internal reasons, since he faced growing pressure from much of the apparatus and party *aktiv*, as well as from the officer corps and Ministry of Internal Affairs. Other considerations were the economic chaos and deepening crisis surrounding supplies of basic goods for the population. There were also external pressures, such as that from Moscow, and also from East Berlin and Prague.

It is difficult to determine exactly when the decision was made to impose martial law the night of December 12–13. During the afternoon of December 7, on sudden orders from Brezhnev, Marshal Kulikov flew to Warsaw with his adjutants. That same day, he learned from Ambassador Aristov, who had information from General Florian Siwicki, that on December 13, at 12:30 a.m., the arrests of Solidarity's leaders would begin, and that martial law would be declared at 6 a.m., at which time Jaruzelski would also make his "appeal to the nation."[5] Siwicki confirmed this information in a personal conversation that evening. So the date was chosen no later than December 7, and had undoubtedly already been determined several days earlier, perhaps even before the Politburo's meeting.

Although everything was already prepared for the operation in terms of the military and police, Jaruzelski was still afraid it might not succeed, and he vacillated. He did not conceal this from Marshal Kulikov during a conversation of more than an hour and a half the night of December 8–9. This, at least, is how it appears from General Anoshkin's transcript of the meeting—the only source available,[6] since Jaruzelski's account in his memoirs is quite superficial.[7] Above all, Jaruzelski feared they would fail to detain all of the approximately six thousand people who were slated for arrest, as well as top-ranking Solidarity members, and that protest strikes would spill from the factories into the streets. "If this spreads throughout the country," Anoshkin recorded Jaruzelski as saying, "you will have to help us, [since] we wouldn't be able to subdue huge masses [of people] single-handedly." He was also worried by the stance of the Church, which he believed could openly support Solidarity, which would mean that "we [would be] in a difficult situation."[8] In fact, this is how one can interpret the letter sent by Primate Józef Glemp on December 6 to the marshal of the Sejm and all members of parliament. In it, he warned against passing legislation related to extraordinary powers for the government, which would "disturb the internal peace, break the agreements that are being concluded with difficulty, and provoke a dangerous social conflict."[9] The general had reason to fear because this letter was penned at the request of Wałęsa and several of his advisors, with whom Glemp had met the previous day. Supporting Solidarity was a far cry from urging society to do battle with the government, which another of the primate's letters, from December 8, shows. This letter was addressed to the union's chairman, and appealed for him to "engage in dialogue" and warned against "the rashness that constitutes confrontation."[10]

In a conversation with Kulikov, Jaruzelski at one point said that, for the time being, only a "preliminary decision" had been made, that the "situation can change," and that he did not exclude the possibility of announcing a "state of emergency" instead of declaring martial law, "under the pretext that we want to avoid bloodshed.... The nation would accept this better." And it was true—a "gradual imposition" of martial law could still have been adopted until the order for the first phase of the operation was issued and started making its way down through the hierarchy, before the arrests began, the telecommunications headquarters were occupied, and large army units started to leave their barracks. Nonetheless, Jaruzelski confirmed the date, and did not even exclude the possibility that the operation would be carried out a day earlier, on Friday night (something General Kiszczak had been advocating). In the final part of the conversation, the Soviet marshal asked, "When we report to Leonid Ilyich [Brezhnev], can we tell him about your decision to begin implementing the plan?" The answer, not completely unequivocal, was: "Of course, [but] on the condition you will help us." Kulikov, however, clearly stated, "To start with, you must make use of your own possibilities." He did not rule out the use of Warsaw Pact armies, but wanted to reserve them for "later" (i.e., if the first attack with Polish forces failed). In a *post scriptum* to the transcript of the conversation, Anoshkin noted that Jaruzelski was "extremely distracted," "upset," and "inconsistent in his thinking," and that "one can sense there are many unresolved matters." As far as the last of these is concerned, perhaps he was right, but this was mainly because Jaruzelski was deliberating, as he often did.

Late that evening, Jaruzelski was behaving differently during a meeting of the Military Council of the Ministry of National Defense, the most important military body, which included commanders of the different military districts and branches, and the heads of MON's central institutions. During the meeting, the mood became apparent; Jaruzelski noted it was now "more radical than some months ago." Some speakers stated that "younger officers are also expecting [the situation] to be resolved by force."[11] Jaruzelski realized that, with such far-reaching preparations, clear expectations, and emotions that were already running high, there was no turning back: "we were moved and determined," he wrote in his memoirs. At the end of the meeting, he continues, "I went up to them [the participants at the meeting] one by one, shook their hands firmly [and] embraced each one."[12] He parted with his officers just as one does before an attack.

Jaruzelski's vacillation worried both party hardliners and the Soviet generals and leaders. The KGB resident, Pavlov, sent a dispatch to Moscow in which he cast doubt on Jaruzelski's determination, basing himself partly on the opinions of

Mirosław Milewski, one of the first secretary's main opponents. Pavlov, Kulikov, and Aristov wrote a joint letter to Brezhnev in which they expressed their fear that the Polish prime minister could lose heart.[13] The Soviets' confusion is apparent in a protocol from a Politburo session that met on December 10 at the Kremlin. They were not yet sure whether martial law would be imposed, and were "under fire" from Jaruzelski's various appeals, which included requests for a visit from top Soviet leaders, assurances that economic and military aid would be provided, and an announcement from the Soviet press agency TASS regarding the situation in Poland, which could influence the Church's stance. The head of Gosplan, Nikolai Baibakov, invited to the meeting after just having returned from Warsaw, concluded his address on economic issues by stating that Jaruzelski "has turned into a man who is unbalanced and unsure of himself."[14] In this rather chaotic discussion, one thing was presented as a certainty: "Sending [Soviet] troops is completely out of the question." When Kulikov received information about the meeting's conclusions from Marshal Ustinov, Anoshkin wrote on the note's margin: "This is terrible news for us! For a year and a half people have been rambling on about the introduction of troops—and now that's all vanished. What kind of situation is Jaruzelski in?!"[15]

Indeed, Moscow first strove for its troops (and those of its allies) to participate directly in the crushing of Solidarity. Then it tried to influence who would head the Polish communist party, constantly pressing for decisive action. Finally, the Soviet's efforts resulted in Jaruzelski's assuming the top post in the country. Now, at the last moment, the USSR was reneging on its promise to provide military assistance. Marshal Kulikov was not only an important instrument in that pressure, but it would seem that he was also personally convinced that the Soviet army should become involved in Poland. Jaruzelski, as Anoshkin noted, was "very worried because no one from the Soviet leadership came."[16] The only one who came was the deputy head of the KGB, Vladimir Kryuchkov. While he was someone important in the Soviet ruling hierarchy, political decisions were beyond his competence. Kulikov, Pavlov, and Aristov could not make these kinds of decisions independently either—or even jointly.

Kulikov was urging the Poles to action: "you have real power," "you shouldn't delay the date," "I know what work you have carried out," and "friends will remain friends," he said. Nevertheless, he himself was concerned with logistics for his staff and the Soviet personnel in Warsaw, in case of unrest and the need for a hasty evacuation. Two airplanes were to be brought to Warsaw's Okęcie airport, where they would stand by if needed. At the airport near Brześć on the Bug River (about two hundred kilometers from Warsaw), five more airplanes were to be ready. It was planned that an entire army company would be sent to protect the Embassy, and a headquarters outside the city was to be prepared for the marshal's staff. Thus it appeared that Jaruzelski was left on his own at a crucial moment.

The machinery of martial law nevertheless had been set in motion. The first troop movements took place on Friday, December 11. On that day, an Auxiliary Front Command Post was set up outside the capital; it formally served as the headquarters for all combat units of the Polish Army, which, according to the Warsaw Pact framework, were part of the planned Maritime Front (informally called the "Polish Front").[17] Similar actions were taken in three military districts—those based in Silesia, Pomerania, and Warsaw—and were carried out by land forces. In accordance with the plans for wartime, the districts transformed themselves into armies and moved their basic staff from their previous headquarters. By noon on December 12, all the extra posts were ready. Two days earlier, a group of officers from the Main Directorate of Combat Training had been sent to units stationed far away that were designated for activity in Warsaw. Following their instructions, on the night of December 11–12, the 13th and 55th motorized regiments began to move gradually toward the capital.[18]

On December 11, the special army units that were to participate in the first phase of action were put on combat alert, as well as the entire Warsaw garrison. Already beginning in early December, since the operation at the Firefighting Officers' School, the entire Ministry of Internal Affairs was on heightened alert, which meant, among other things, that vacations were suspended and reservists were mobilized. On December 11, the SB Headquarters ordered that individuals selected for arrest be closely observed. By the afternoon of December 12, all the garrisoned units that were to participate in the operations were put on full alert, but they did not leave their permanent posts. These included military academies, internal troops, reservists' detachments, Motorized Detachments of the Citizens' Militia (Zmotoryzowane Oddziały Milicji Obywatelskiej, ZOMO), and special units.

These troop movements, albeit small, could not go unnoticed. Witnesses saw only single elements of these movements—even commanders of specific units had no idea of the operation's scope. It was to be carried out according to the "basic variant," which was called "Implementing Martial Law by Surprise."[19] Maintaining absolute discretion was thus critical to success. For several weeks, the escalation of the conflict on both sides of the barricades suggested the climax was nearing. Nevertheless, everything we know indicates that those responsible for martial law managed to keep secret not only the details of its starting date (which was easiest) and the schedule of activities preceding hour "G," but above all what kinds of events would follow. This was the result of strict respect for military and state secrets, and also the high degree of discipline in the officer corps. According to a report from the Pomeranian Military District for the General Staff, it appears that "the complete operations [planned for the district's troops] were known only to those in the narrowest command circles," and that "direct preparations to undertake special actions in the field were in principle not carried out on a scale that would allow a betrayal of what the undertaking's actual nature was."[20] The division's commanders were acquainted "only with the parts [of the documentation] that directly involved them."

In the language of military instructions and orders, which is considered to be precise, there were vague terms: "special activities" meant both the operations to assume control of communications, radio, and television, as well as the blockade of cities and the movement of armored convoys through large cities. The term "improvement of position" in the context of martial law was to be understood as the occupation of the main transportation routes needed to block cities. The degree of secrecy during the preparations was such that during one of the briefings for the leadership of the military districts, service branches, and voivodship military staffs (i.e., for a group of high-ranking officers who must have enjoyed full confidence), the participants "were not shown the planning documents that had been prepared."[21] The situation was similar in the Ministry of Internal Affairs. For example, Colonel Jerzy Gruba, the commander of the voivodship Citizens' Militia (Milicja Obywatelska, MO) in Katowice, wrote in his memoirs that he had of course been prepared to implement martial law, but he did not know the details, and had found out about the date around 4 p.m. on the afternoon of December 12. It was rather a surprise for him.[22] General Anoshkin recorded the following joke in his "Working Notebook": the date that martial law would be imposed was known to four people—the first secretary of the Central Committee, the prime minister, the minister of national defense, and the chairman of the Military Council of National Salvation (i.e., to Jaruzelski alone).

Hundreds of people knew about the specific components of martial law—these were individuals from the military, Ministry of Internal Affairs, and some civilian departments, such as the Ministries of Justice, Transport, Mining and Energy, and Communications. In the second half of 1981, several ministries signed agreements with the Ministry of Internal Affairs or the Ministry of National Defense regarding the protection of their buildings (including prisons). In some of these documents, the term "martial law" was used, but in others there were more enigmatic terms, such as "state of serious danger to state security." But no one from the civilian departments knew the exact extent of the preparations, the number of troops that were to be used, or the timetable for operations. Even among the officers of the General Staff, most knew only the portions of the plans that they had themselves been working on, or those that had been essential to their own activities. So at the Ministry of Internal Affairs, only a very narrow group of people had complete knowledge about the planned activities. Even fewer people had been informed about the setting of a date for hour "G."

The generals from Jaruzelski's closest circle certainly knew the date—Florian Siwicki, head of the General Staff, who was de facto carrying out the duties of the minister of defense; Michal Janiszewski, head of the chancellery at the Council of Ministers; and Czesław Kiszczak, minister of internal affairs. Perhaps also a few higher-ranking officers from the General Staff had been informed, as well as General Tadeusz Tuczapski, who was secretary of the KOK and deputy minister of national defense. Other than Kiszczak, probably several top figures from the Ministry of Internal Affairs also knew. It was only on December 11 that Deputy Prime Minister Mieczysław Rakowski found out—and he was one of Jaruzelski's closest political associates. Stefan Olszowski and Kazimierz Barcikowski, who were Politburo members and Central Committee secretaries, also found out at that time. Both men were supposed to belong to the top decision-making leadership after the imposition of martial law. Other officials knew nothing of the plans as well. For example, the minister for cooperation with trade unions, Stanisław Ciosek, knew neither the date nor the details of the operation. For several weeks, he had been conducting more or less secret talks with the Church and was sounding the situation within Solidarity. Jerzy Urban, the government's press spokesman, who was responsible for officially interpreting the government's actions, recalled: "I supposed that some decisive move was being prepared," and "it was easy for me to imagine that it would have to take place the next Saturday."[23] But it was only on December 12 that he found out from Rakowski that something was indeed "in the works" and that he should prepare several articles that would "be suitable for a situation in which there is some kind of vague state of emergency."[24]

Most of the members of the Politburo knew neither the details of the operation, nor the date it would begin, despite the fact that this was formally the highest decision-making group in the country (and had originally authorized Jaruzelski to take action). Stanisław Kociołek, first secretary of the Warsaw Committee of the PZPR, who was regularly invited to Politburo meetings (and often took the floor there), learned only early the afternoon of December 12 that "something would happen."[25] He was told by one of the few people who were privy to that information—Olszowski. Kociołek could have imagined what was going to happen, but he found out neither when it would happen, nor what exactly it would be. So, all Saturday evening, he waited in his office for any kind of additional information. Because no one called, he went back home at a quarter after midnight. On the way, as he recounted, he "didn't notice anything unusual, perhaps only a few more militia vehicles than normal."[26] Undoubtedly everyone except the few best informed expected that the decision would be made any moment, but it is unlikely they knew at what time hour "G" would occur. On December 12, not even the first secretaries of the voivodship communist party committees, voivods, and heads of the voivodship military commands knew this information.

Because the CIA, of course, did not know the date of "G," the American administration did not either. Colonel Ryszard Kukliński, the only serious source of information from the General Staff, had been evacuated from Poland in early November because it was highly likely that he would be unmasked. At that time, the date had not yet been set. Formally, his knowledge should have been limited, but obviously directives are one thing, and reality is another. Gathering materials for American intelligence, Kukliński had of course accumulated information that went beyond the range of tasks he had been assigned. The most important thing he said both in messages and later in person, when he was already in Washington, was that the imposition of martial law would be a "Polish operation," without the participation of Warsaw Pact troops.

On November 18–19 the General Staff carried out a review of the situation that had emerged after the "disappearance in unknown circumstances" of Colonel Kukliński, his wife, and two sons. A group of Soviet specialists who had arrived from Moscow took part.[27] The awareness that Kukliński had deserted and was a traitor did not incline those involved in the consultations to abandon the plan to introduce martial law, but it did force them to make a number of adjustments. They changed the cryptonyms and signal codes of some of the operation's components, as well as the timetable for the troops' operations. They also decided to abandon the "indirect variants," leaving two of the most important ones: "imposition of martial law utilizing the element of surprise" and "gradual implementation of martial law's components before it is announced" (i.e., "creeping" into martial law). These changes were undoubtedly unnecessary, since the CIA kept whatever it knew highly secret.

Although operations were centered on the military, preparations were to an equal extent based on plans that had been developed in the event of war and those prepared at the Ministry of the Internal Affairs in the event of a "Serious Threat" (abbreviated PZ, for *poważne zagrożenie*), which meant unrest, illegal demonstrations, or strikes. The wartime plans foresaw, for example, the defense of hundreds of important objects from diversionary groups or an enemy assault. In any case, everything was all set, or so at least it would appear from the hundreds of documents that are now in open archives, or the dozens of maps, graphs, and tables related to many different aspects of Operation "W." The individuals in charge of imposing martial law were also convinced that the operation was being planned with the utmost care. The Polish army may never have been so thoroughly and carefully prepared to carry out tasks assigned to it—not even during its participation in the invasion of Czechoslovakia in 1968, or when it helped pacify the strikes and demonstrations in June 1956 and December 1970. Probably the same can be said about the security apparatus and other services of the MSW. Those who were to be the targets of the attack—Solidarity and the opposition—were not prepared for what would happen the night of December 12–13. Since the summer of 1980, Poland had been in a permanent state of unrest, exacerbated by the deepening difficulties of daily living and worsening shortages. On multiple occasions, social tensions rose dramatically. Solidarity's frequent mobilizations and a generally heightened sense of danger rendered people indifferent to signals related to the government's plans. Solidarity activists based their ideas about the government's possible actions on the "creeping" scenario that was superficially known to them, more from hearsay than from documents, which was probably what the architects of martial law intended. It cannot be ruled out that there may have also been a controlled leak for the purpose of disinformation. The bill on extraordinary powers for the government was so well known, however, that it had already reached the Sejm, and even Primate Glemp had received a copy for review. Nowhere did these documents mention martial law.

Solidarity had extremely rare contact with some functionaries of the Security Services and Citizens' Militia, or military personnel, who were favorably inclined toward the union. Thus, they could not have aided Solidarity's members much in their efforts to procure information about government preparations. These individuals would not have had extensive information anyway, and they did not know the date selected for the imposition of martial law. Even if they had already found out, it would have been too late. Some of Solidarity's activists recall signals that came in the shape of fragmentary information or vague announcements that the government was preparing to crack down on the union. Many people, however, believed that the army could not be used to impose a state of emergency because, if it was, as Janusz Pałubicki believed, then the troops "would join the [workers'] crews"[28] after being brought out of their barracks. Some, like Jacek Kuroń, believed that the "General would take aim, and take aim again, and then take his hand off [the trigger], as was his habit.... I didn't think that they were so crazy."[29] Karol Modzelewski, on the other hand, admitted, "We all overlooked the possibility of a military coup. We didn't have the logistical imagination [to have thought of it]. We were clinging too much to political tradition."[30]

The events of March 1981 brought a certain degree of experience and reflection. Solidarity decided at that time that, during a general strike, the regional boards of Solidarity would be moved to the largest enterprises in a given city. It was also recommended that a network of couriers be set up, and that the communication lines of institutions having Solidarity enterprise committees be utilized, like the railways or energy networks. Local instructions on how to wage civil resistance were prepared, along with flyers intended for soldiers (including Soviet ones). In autumn, activists from most of the regions and some of the large enterprise organizations revisited ideas from that spring. They were led more by intuition, and by their reading of the obvious signs that the government was moving toward confrontation, than by any real, specific information about what shape the conflict would take.

Those instructions mentioned civil disobedience, passive resistance, refusal to cooperate with authorities, and an occupation strike, but in general people were warned not to provoke the authorities. Solidarity reminded its audience about the principles of strike organization, the creation of alternative enterprise committees ("the second rank"), the concealment of union documents and membership lists, and the need for supplies of food, medicines, and blankets. In some of the larger enterprises, Solidarity committees organized watches or groups of guards. They believed there should be a watch so that unwanted individuals from the outside could not manage to enter factory grounds during a strike. Members of these watch groups only had white and red armbands at their disposal; no one had firearms, or any "means of direct force," not even truncheons. They had not undergone any sort of training. The National Commission had not even discussed a draft instruction, as Andrzej Gwiazda had suggested, and no group was formed that would have dealt with it.[31] It should be recalled, however, that this motion was announced only on December 12, so even if it had been carried out, it would not have had much of an effect. The lack of interest probably stemmed from the fact that, during previous strikes, the militia had never once attacked a factory, though on a couple of occasions force had been used against groups of people in public buildings (as had been the case in March in Bydgoszcz). Thus, people probably did not imagine that the authorities would storm the factories. After events at the Firefighting Officers' School, all regional boards and many smaller workplaces introduced emergency "shifts." These, however, were "alarm shifts" and only a few people were assigned to them (primarily the union's full-time employees).

Even if people had been privy to more concrete information about the government's real intentions, Solidarity, as a democratic and internally differentiated social movement with many millions of members, would probably not have been able to prepare itself organizationally for two serious and difficult undertakings. These were also, to some extent, mutually exclusive: a general strike, which requires universal and open mobilization of its members, and going underground, if the strike failed. Although some activists argued that people should prepare for civil defense, most were imagining a situation like the one during the August 1980 strikes: it would suffice just to lock themselves in the factories and hold out for a while, which would incline the government to make concessions and compromise.

According to Władysław Frasyniuk, chairman of the Lower Silesia Region, one of the union's most popular leaders, "practical activities were of lesser importance, people were above all not prepared mentally. No one expected that the supposedly weak government would turn out to be so strong that it could thrust militiamen . . . and soldiers on us, [who were] our coworkers and neighbors."[32] Many Solidarity members spoke out in favor of the idea of fighting back without the use of force. Gandhi was mentioned, as were the teachings of the Church, whose hierarchs, including Primate Wyszyński, rightly considered hardline opponents of communism, steadfastly called for moderation. Solidarity was ill prepared for a physical clash.

To sum up—for various reasons, many of the union's members did not exhibit determination. Research carried out by union sociologists during the autumn of 1981 showed that about one-third of the members belonged to the minority who believed an agreement should be reached. As Ludwik Dorn related when he reported on the results of the study, this minority "had extremely strong hopes that there would be an understanding, dialogue, or that some kind of compromise would be concluded."[33] Dorn also pointed out that "the opinion of most of the union's members diverged . . . from that of those in Poland who were not Solidarity members." Most of Solidarity's members believed, probably under the influence of statements by its radical activists, that the government was weak, and would not be capable of taking the initiative. Thus, either it would not attempt to attack the nine-million-strong union or, if it did, it would be defeated quickly. After all, for more than a year, the government had been shying away from drastic solutions, and although it often rattled its saber, it never brandished it. The real fear was Soviet tanks. Incidentally, one wonders what Solidarity's reaction—i.e., that of its leaders and members—would have been if, on December 11, the government had publicized the drafts of its decrees and orders, as well as the lists of military and militia units slated to take part in the operation, the targets they had been assigned, the lists of people destined for internment, and enterprises that were to be militarized. Would the effect have been fear and capitulation, or anger and rebellion?

In the media, there were sporadic public statements directly referring to the possible use of troops. The daily *Gazeta Krakówska*, the communist party's only regional organ edited by party reformers, published a piece on December 10 about a lecture that had taken place several days before, in which the well-known party sociologist Jerzy J. Wiatr said that "long-term military governments" were one of four possible scenarios.[34] The newspaper, however, emphasized the most optimistic variant, as indicated by the article's title: "In Order to Achieve a National Understanding, The Party Must Give Up Its Monopoly of Power."[35] In the last issue of *Tygodnik Solidarność* published before martial law was declared (the next was published only in June 1989!), the prominent journalist Ernest Skalski wrote, in an article titled "Coup" (Zamach), that a "concept of governing [had been developed] similar to that of a military occupation in a conquered country." He based himself on information that was "leaking from the [government] apparatus by a circuitous route."[36] Another popular publicist, Krzysztof Czabański, in his commentary "Czy będzie wojna domowa?" (Will there be a civil war?), predicted that "tanks would stand at the intersections" and that "police and military patrols would be swarming in the streets."[37] There weren't any details in these texts, because the authors did not know them. Incidentally, both ended their comments optimistically, in a sense. "Those who are betting on force will in this way remove themselves from the life of the country," wrote Czabański.

This was the opposite of what had happened in late November and early December 1980, when the world media reported in a very alarmed tone that there was a concentration of Soviet troops on the Polish borders. In Poland, this information was known from foreign radio broadcasts, but a year later Radio Free Europe and BBC primarily noted that tensions were rising, and reported on the stance of Solidarity, featuring statements by its leaders. At the same time, however, there were few specifics as to what the government was actually doing. Its actions were analyzed from the same perspective as observers in Poland—which means they focused on the legislation on extraordinary powers, and thus the gradual and, to some extent, overt implementation of a state of emergency (*stan nadzwyczajny*). A few isolated signals appeared, which were impossible to verify or difficult to notice. For example, on December 11, the planned official visit of French Prime Minister Pierre Mauroy was cancelled—owing to Prime Minister Jaruzelski's pressing responsibilities. The French journalist Gabriel Meretik, author of the best description to date of the "night of the general," found out ten years later that Jaruzelski, as a result, never received the gift Mauroy intended to give him on that visit—a cavalry sword.[38] The General, however, somehow managed to get along without it.

As tensions grew, life actually continued as usual, both public life and normal, day-to-day life, despite an expectation that "something" might happen. Lines in front of shops grew as the most important holidays (also from a culinary point of view) neared. Union organizations in workplaces were involved in the acquisition and distribution of onions and potatoes, and also in preparing holiday parcels for employees' children. Snowplows cleared city streets. Before going to bed, children watched the television programs aired for them. Students all over Poland were ending a strike that had lasted several weeks. At the Warsaw cinema Moskwa, less than three hundred meters from the formidable Ministry of Internal Affairs complex, the auditorium was full at every screening: it was showing Francis Coppola's *Apocalypse Now*. On Sunday, December 13, the photographer Chris Niedenthal took a photograph there that would become one of the icons of martial law: an eye-catching billboard for the film (Apokalipsa) that clearly implied a link between the name of the cinema ("Moskwa" – Moscow) and the tank that was standing in the square in front of it, whose barrel was aimed at the street.

At the Palace of Culture and Science in Warsaw, the Congress of Polish Culture was taking place. It had been organized by the recently formed Artistic and Academic Associations' Consultative Committee, a pro-Solidarity organization completely independent of the government. There, talks were being presented by luminaries of Polish arts and sciences—including poets, professors, actors, and composers. They spoke of the condition of culture in Poland, about the government's efforts to deprive it of authenticity, about censorship and "white patches" (*białe plamy*) in contemporary history, and about the new cultural and research opportunities that increasing freedom had brought. Eugeniusz Szumiejko spoke in the name of Solidarity. Szumiejko was an astronomer by profession, and a member of the Presidium of Solidarity's National Commission. He announced that on the last day of proceedings, on Sunday, December 13, the union's chairman, Lech Wałęsa, would make a personal appearance. Despite the clearly oppositional character of the congress, officials responsible for culture did appear at its inauguration: Hieronim Kubiak, a Politburo member and Central Committee secretary, as well as Deputy Prime Minister Rakowski and Minister of Culture Józef Tejchma. None came, however, to the closing session—including Wałęsa.

On December 12, the Primatial Social Council met for the first time. The Council had recently been formed by Primate Józef Glemp, who modeled it on a similar institution that had existed until 1939. This was an advisory body, and its main task was—as Glemp wrote in the text calling the Council into existence— "to study current problems in social and political life in the light of the Church's social teachings," "to give opinions as to whether the behavior of individuals and groups is ethical," and "to indicate—in understanding with the Polish primate— the areas of service to the Nation."[39] Thus, it was not a political institution. The kinds of issues it was to consider, however, were at least in part related to the conflict currently underway in Poland. The Council was comprised of twenty-eight people from various Catholic circles, but without any representatives from pro-government organizations, such as the PAX Association, and without any of the Solidarity advisors who had ties to the Church. Some of the Council's members were well known in public life, such as Stanisław Stomma (appointed as chairman), Jerzy Turowicz, and Andrzej Micewski, who had extensive political and journalistic experience. Others represented the world of academia, and there were also specialists in law, international relations, and social policy. Still others represented local groups of the Catholic intelligentsia. The meeting, inaugurated by the primate himself, was not long and ended before evening.

The most important proceedings, however, did not take place in the capital, but in Gdańsk, where a meeting of Solidarity's National Commission convened on Friday at 11 a.m. Unlike several previous sessions, which had taken place in a dignified room at the Old Town Hall, they met this time at the "cradle of Solidarity"—in the same building at the Gdańsk Shipyard where the endless meetings of the MKS had occurred for two weeks in August 1980, and where the agreement was later signed that drew the "hot summer of 1980" to a close. Thus, a union branch headquarters was located at an enterprise, as had been the recommended tactic during strikes. The meeting was essentially a continuation of those that had taken place in Radom on December 3. The resolutions passed in Radom were officially approved—those same resolutions that had provoked such a violent attack by the government-run media. The discussions, however, went much further. Some of the speakers—including Lech Wałęsa and most of the advisors, regardless of their political background—spoke in favor of moderation and warned against excessive radicalism. Others, however, put forth exceedingly bold propositions: free elections not only to the provincial councils, but also to the Sejm ("let's be honest—we dream of having parliamentary privileges,"[40] said Frasyniuk). They also posited that, in addition to a National Economic and Social Council (they even chose its twenty-four members), there should even be a provisional coalition government (Jacek Kuroń distributed his article titled "National Government"[41]), and that a countrywide referendum should be held as a vote of confidence in the current government. Moreover, a Poland-wide "active" strike should be held, which meant that products produced during the strike would be distributed directly through the enterprise (and in effect through the strike committee). "Putting forth these demands," Karol Modzelewski admonished his colleagues, "is tantamount to a declaration of war, and, I would add—war without quotation marks."[42] The atmosphere, recalled Zbigniew Bujak, was "kind of weird, heavy. The disputes backstage were different as well. Usually we argued over every sentence, over [every] resolution, and this time the discussions were about fundamental questions."[43] Lech Wałęsa was taciturn. According to Bujak, he "looked with pity on the whole situation." The union's chairman even gave some speakers a dressing down for their excessive radicalism.

In the evening, those present at the meeting began receiving news that elite units from the militia's cadet schools in Szczytno and Słupsk had started to move toward Gdańsk. The voivodship authorities, when asked about it, answered that it was part of Operation "Ring" (Pierścień), aimed at speculators and thieves. In reality, the entire "Ring" operation was simply a cover for the concentration of militia forces in preparation for martial law. But even those who didn't believe the militia's explanations believed it was a show of force, and not an attack. Later, more information started coming in from the rest of Poland and Gdańsk: troop movements had been spotted somewhere else, and elsewhere telex and telephone communications had been blocked. Around midnight, it turned out that telecommunications connections had been cut in the shipyard as well.

To some extent, the date of the National Commission's meeting affected the decision regarding the timing of hour "G"—not, however, because the authorities expected the activists gathered there would experience some sudden epiphany that would have made them reject their hardline stance, adopted in Radom. It was that the core members of the organization that was slated for destruction were all gathered in one place. These were Solidarity's "200 *molodchikov*" (in the sense of "lackeys"), as General Viktor Anoshkin called them in his notes.[44] It was a unique opportunity to apprehend Solidarity's entire elite at once. This opportunity, however, could also make problems worse: it was hard to imagine that a tight ring of ZOMO men could surround the building where the meeting room was, and that special units would sweep into the building and start scuffling with hundreds of people. This type of action would have surely ended with the use of "means of direct force," and perhaps with fatalities. No propaganda campaign could have managed to blur or deform the significance of such a drastic act of violence against a large group of individuals who enjoyed society's trust and had been voted into office through democratic elections. Or the proceedings could have lasted longer than planned, and those gathered there would have received word of the scale of the arrests, and the takeover of the union's regional headquarters, as well as its telecommunications and radio and television buildings. This information probably would have inclined them to stay in the building and begin the occupation strike immediately, led by Wałęsa and all the top union leaders, which would have been a serious complication. Fortunately for the generals, the last part of the meeting was quick and, shortly after midnight, the participants began leaving the shipyard.

While Solidarity's leadership had been feverishly debating, from the morning of December 12, the government's actions, the union's possible reaction, and plans to rebuild the country, the inevitable moment was coming when an order would have to be issued. Around 9 a.m., four generals—Jaruzelski, Siwicki, Kiszczak, and Janiszewski—met in Prime Minister Jaruzelski's office. As Kiszczak recalls, they agreed, after deciding that everything was "all set,"[45] that if they were to adhere to predetermined date, they should issue the order to begin the operation no later than 2 p.m., so the cascade of orders sent from Warsaw would make it to the executive cells in time. Then they parted ways. Kiszczak met with the head of the KGB mission in Poland, General Vitalii Pavlov, whom he informed about the schedule of planned action. Perhaps the experienced Chekist still did not completely trust Jaruzelski's team, since in his dispatch to Moscow he said that if the general had a mental breakdown, Olszowski could assume party leadership.[46] The Kremlin had already considered Olszowski as a possible alternative on previous occasions as well—first to Stanisław Kania, and then to Jaruzelski. In a diary entry from December 12, Rakowski wrote about "difficulties on the Soviet line,"[47] but in the morning Jaruzelski talked twice by phone with Moscow—along "party lines" with Mikhail Suslov, and along "military lines" with Marshal Dmitrii Ustinov,[48] which probably removed these unspecified problems. Both Suslov and Ustinov were older men, nearing the ends of their lives—Suslov, considered to be the party's main ideologist, died six weeks later, and Ustinov, minister of national defense, died three years later. From Jaruzelski's memoirs, we know that he received confirmation of Moscow's stance from these conversations—decisive support for decisive action. He does not write, however, about whether he asked for military assistance if the operation failed. I believe that even if he did, neither the question nor the answer had to have been formulated openly. Jaruzelski and his interlocutors, after all, did know the official language well, and understood what formulations like "fraternal aid" or "interests of the socialist community" meant.

The institution that was to rule the country during martial law was named only on December 12. In "The Main Idea Behind the Implementation of Martial Law in the Polish People's Republic for Reasons of State Security" of March 27, 1981 (mentioned in chapter 3), which was the "Bible" of the preparations that preceded martial law, it was assumed that "at the moment martial law is imposed, the basic functions of government and leadership in the country would be transferred to the Committee of National Defense."[49] This assumption was logical, given KOK's formal and actual position in the state structure, and because it included individuals from both the military and government (the prime minister was officially its chairman) and the Politburo of the PZPR. I was able to determine neither why nor when Jaruzelski abandoned this idea and decided instead to create a completely extra-legal institution, comprised exclusively of military men. When I asked him about it, he could not remember. According to one version, General Janiszewski thought up the name; according to another, it was General Kiszczak's idea.[50] In any case, this change of plan certainly happened no later than December 7, because Mieczysław Rakowski noted in his diary on that day that the Military-Revolutionary Council was to assume control of the country.[51] In a conversation with Kulikov on December 9, Jaruzelski spoke about the Military-Revolutionary Committee. Siwicki, however, when he talked with Kulikov on December 11, mentioned the name "Military-Revolutionary Council of Salvation for the Homeland."[52] It was only in the middle of the night on December 12–13 that Kulikov found out it would be called the "Military Council of National Salvation" (Wojskowa Rada Ocalenia Narodowego, WRON).[53] Thus, the word "revolution" vanished almost at the last minute, probably because it was reminiscent of the system's roots and ideology, which could have had limited the number of supporters of martial law. It was deemed better to allude to patriotic sentiment and loyalty to the state, embodied by the army, which was the only state institution that had maintained a relatively high level of prestige: "We chose the slogan 'Defense of the Fatherland' so as not to emphasize the party, which is not popular," declared Jaruzelski in a conversation with Kulikov.[54] Nevertheless, in his speech proclaiming the imposition of martial law, General Jaruzelski made use of ample ideological rhetoric: "the Polish socialist State," "socialist ideals," "the socialist community of nations," "socialist democracy," "there is no turning back from socialism," and "the only road . . . is socialism."[55] We can assume that, just like "state," communist propaganda naturally made people link the word "nation" with the adjective "socialist," too.

WRON was comprised of twenty officers (one more was coopted later), including four who were "civilian" ministers in the government, and three deputy ministers of national defense. Commanders from all branches of the military (ground forces, navy, and air forces) and military districts were also included, which means that essentially all of Poland's top military leaders were members of

WRON. Lieutenant Colonel Mirosław Hermaszewski, the first and only Polish astronaut, was also somehow added to WRON, as was reserve colonel Roman Leś, chairman of the board of the Union of Former Professional Soldiers. According to its own "Proclamation," announced on December 13, the Council was appointed on the night of December 12–13. It did not say, however, who appointed it. The "Resolution" regarding the Council's creation, which survives in archives and was not published at the time, is dated December 12 and says that WRON was created as the result of a decision of a "group of officers from the People's Army of Poland," which met under the leadership of General Jaruzelski "at the initiative of the Military Council of the Ministry of National Defense."[56] During a speech broadcast on the radio at 6 a.m. on December 13, Jaruzelski said that the Council had been established "today,"[57] which would have meant it had happened sometime during the preceding six hours. According to General Anoshkin's notes, however, the Council's first meeting took place on December 13.[58] It is difficult to know what to make of these contradictory pieces of information. In all likelihood, they are all inaccurate, since no meeting of the "officers' groups" took place on either December 12 or even 13 with the members mentioned, and the first meeting of WRON at which a protocol was taken took place on December 14.[59] In any case, General Tuczapski, as deputy minister and secretary of KOK, was one of the most important figures during the preparations leading up to martial law. He learned only on December 13, during a phone conversation with General Siwicki, that he was to be a member of the Council.[60] Colonel Hermaszewski, by contrast, happened to be in Moscow, when he received word from the embassy on December 12 that he should go to Warsaw, without knowing the reason. He arrived at home the evening of December 13, via the staff headquarters of the Soviet Forces' Northern Group, which was stationed in Legnica, near Wrocław. It was only then, as he watched television, that he learned that something called WRON existed and that he was a member. The first meeting took place "the next day," i.e., December 14. "There was no discussion," Hermaszewski stressed in an interview.[61] All of these details are, however, not very significant.

The most important question regards WRON's legality, both in terms of when and how it was formed. It usurped power, as far as we can see from the surviving protocols, reports, and all of the Council's documentation, and of course from the press reports about its work and decisions. WRON issued instructions to the state administration and orders to the armed forces without any legal basis for doing so. WRON is not mentioned in any document serving as a formal basis for the imposition and execution of martial law. As if that were not enough, WRON did not seek official legalization in the shape of a decree or legislation through the Council of State or Sejm, even after the fact. The fact that it was an institution functioning outside the law—or rather, above it—should thus not be a matter of dispute.

As was agreed on the morning of December 12, General Jaruzelski first informed General Kiszczak and then General Siwicki by phone, around 2 p.m., that the date of hour "G" would remain unchanged. While a lively discussion was underway at the Gdańsk Shipyard about a referendum asking whether or not the electorate had confidence in the government, and about the electoral law regarding elections to local government, telegrams began to be dispatched from the Ministry of Internal Affairs. They began with the words "I am announcing the code word 'Synchronization.' I am informing you, and ordering that [it be] carried out." Here followed a list of ten cryptonyms that were from a table of signals that referred to specific actions to be taken.

Information included under the cryptonym "Comet" (Kometa) was crucial for setting the general tempo of events. Shortly after receiving the dispatch, SB functionaries began gathering in voivodship headquarters. All barracked units were also included in this state of alert, some of whom left their garrisons in haste. A couple of hours after the minister of internal affairs issued the orders, orders also began flowing from the head of the General Staff. The headquarters of the military districts, armed forces, and central institutions of MON began to receive them at about 6:30 p.m. At 9 p.m., the commanders of the two aforementioned regiments received "Combat Order no. 01," which instructed them to begin redeployment on the outskirts of Warsaw at 3 a.m.

The operation had begun, and probably even Jaruzelski would have had a hard time stopping it. In fact, there is no evidence to suggest that he might have considered that possibility.

Chapter Five

"Night of the General" and Day One

"The evening is peaceful, as usual on Saturdays. All the women are wearing slippers (in winter they leave their shoes in the cloakroom). Two are knitting and a third has just gone to the bathroom. Suddenly, Maria hears a hollow banging and has the impression that the noises are coming from somewhere in the building, beyond the metal doors leading to the hallway. . . . The strange vibrations seem to penetrate the building's metal structure. On the control panel, lights start turning on chaotically. Maria grabs the telephone receiver and connects to the technical center: 'What's going on there?' No one answers. . . . The noise grows stronger, so she decides to go and check herself. She had just taken a couple of steps when the double doors are opened with a strong shove. Four or five soldiers burst into the big room. . . . One shouts: 'Chairs to the wall! Don't move!' The second threatens Maria with a bayonet. . . . Maria sees him go closer to the glass, beyond which are the levers and buttons . . . and start to turn them all off chaotically. 'They've gone mad,' thinks Maria. 'They're going to blow up the whole installation.' She looked instinctively at the big electric clock that had just stopped. The hands, now still, point to 11.20 p.m."[1]

This anonymous but very credible account was recorded by Gabriel Meretik. Maria worked in the telegram section of Warsaw's national and international telecommunications center. That's more or less how the Operation "Azalea" looked at 451 sites throughout the country (60 of them were in Warsaw). The rumors about equipment being wrecked or cables cut are not confirmed in the sources, but it is difficult to exclude the possibility that such events did in fact occur. In any case, just before midnight, the "civilian" telecommunications network fell silent for good. This blockade also included the telephone lines to the foreign diplomatic and consular posts. Approximately 5,000 people carried out the operation: 700 SB functionaries, over 3,000 soldiers from the MSW military units (including the Border Defense Troops), and about 1,200 soldiers from the army.[2] Some of the sites that were occupied were then defended by the army, and some by Ministry of Internal Affairs services.

One part of this operation was to take control of the radio and television stations, including the transmission equipment that was often located in remote areas. This action was carried out at the same time, although in several cases atmospheric conditions caused delays. There were no problems carrying it out: the main radio and television centers were practically empty at this time of day;

there were only a few journalists and technical staff on duty. Moreover, there were not very many targets, just about 120, but the only really large ones were those in Warsaw. Nevertheless, almost 4,000 individuals took part in this action, including 340 SB functionaries and 550 special forces troops. When the preparations were being made to occupy the radio and television, a substitute center was also set up, which temporarily took over the broadcast at Polish Radio 1 (the other programs were suspended), and individuals—both journalists and technicians—were identified who were supposed to carry out this task. Similar centers were also created in the voivodships that had regional radio and television stations. Polish Television's Program II, which was just broadcasting its popular Studio 2 program, was interrupted around 11:40 p.m., and the journalists who happened to be on the air announced that the interruption was occurring for "technical reasons." The TV headquarters on Woronicz Street was occupied by the soldiers of the 10th Battalion of the 6th Airborne Division (special forces). Units from that same division also occupied the broadcasting equipment at the Palace of Culture and Science and, several hours later, Warsaw's Okęcie airport, where a "landing operation" had taken place.

Jacek Cieszewski, a journalist from Katowice, recorded this account by Adam Skwira in the early 1980s. Skwira, a timberer from the Wujek mine, was recounting to him the arrest of Jan Ludwiczak, the chairman of the Solidarity factory committee at that mine:

> My wife woke me up at one in the morning. Actually the loud noises woke up the entire neighborhood. . . . Everyone stood at their windows and watched what was happening. Around the building where Ludwiczak lived there were several of the militia's minivans and loiterers and the building was surrounded by militiamen in storm uniforms, [who had] special truncheons, long ones. After a little while, I saw them dragging Ludwiczak out of the building, pushing him into the vehicle, and even though of course people were shouting, they left right away. We stood there, confused. After a while, I went to Ludwiczak's apartment. . . . I found that the door had been smashed in by axes. His wife and children were scared, they didn't know what was happening. There were streams of blood running down the wall alongside the door.[3]

Skwira's experience is a good example of the government's actions during Operation "Fir" (Jodła). The aim of this program was to intern Solidarity activists, some intellectuals, and also, as they said in SB jargon, "the *aktiv* of the enemy counterrevolutionary groups." Many of the arrests were dramatic: doors broken down with crowbars, handcuffs, children crying, people forced out into the bitter cold in their pajamas. Sometimes both parents in a family were interned and the children were supposed to be taken to the militia's children's section. Only a few managed to escape. People who were not even in the country—some of whom had been abroad for many months—were also included on the first lists of internees that were issued a couple of days later. Even the list that the MSW compiled of members of the National Commission, labeled "secret" and intended for internal use, included the names of people who had avoided internment and were in hiding, some of whom even participated in the strikes. Although there were undoubtedly mistakes, generally there is no reason to question the numbers in the MSW report that described the situation at 7 a.m. According to that document, 2,874 people were interned over the course of just one night.[4] Because there were 4,318 people on the lists, this meant that 67 percent of the plan was carried out. This performance, one can say, was not so bad, although in some towns there were delays and the groups carrying out the operation appeared only toward morning, when many people already knew that mass round-ups had begun, and groups of neighbors impeded the arrests, or even rendered them impossible.

The detentions—or more simply put: arrests—were carried out for the most part by armed groups of a few people, composed of a few SB functionaries and militiamen, equipped with tools to break down doors, handcuffs, and other means of "direct force," including chemical ones. In some cases, like during Ludwiczak's arrest, several to a dozen or so ZOMO men backed up these groups by surrounding the building. Some of the groups were supposed to arrest more than one person, and since each had to be detained individually and taken to the police station, several trips had to be made. No searches were carried out during the arrests, when everything took place in a terrible rush. More than just a result of the "tight schedule," this was also done intentionally for psychological effect. More than ten thousand SB and militia functionaries probably took part; the army did not.

Not all members of the National Commission gathered at the Gdańsk Shipyard were captured. Those who were not planning to stay in a hotel went to the train station and left by night trains, or set off for home by car. By some chance, not all fell into the SB's hands and hid where they could. After 1 a.m., when most had reached their rooms, ZOMO surrounded the hotels. A cordon even stood on the snow-covered beach in front of the famous "Grand Hotel" in Sopot. The trap was closed. SB functionaries, assisted by militiamen, flushed room after room, using the lists that they had made based on the hotel registration records. SB men were also on the scene, having come to see their "clients," such as colonel Jan Lesiak, who had for years been working on Kuroń's case, or colonel Władysław Kuca, in charge of the most important secret informer in the National Commission—Eligiusz Naszkowski. Police vans took those who were arrested to the ZOMO barracks on Kartuska Street.

Years later, Jacek Kuroń, who was known for not liking martyrological recollections of the past, did not hide the emotions he felt at the time: "They took me to some free-standing building on the city's periphery. They told me to get out and took me down some stairs into the cellar . . . whose floor was scattered with sand, and the wall towards which I was walking had been shot with bullets. . . . Militiamen in military uniform were standing at two of the other walls, with machine pistols slung across their shoulders. . . . Aha, that's it. Already? What a shame."[5] It ended, however, with him taking off his sheepskin coat and lying down on the floor, with a "bag full of papers" under his head, and falling asleep. In Gdańsk that night, about thirty members of the National Commission and several advisors were arrested.

Wałęsa was given special treatment. Around 2 a.m., not only did SB functionaries appear in his apartment, but so did the Gdańsk voivod, Jerzy Kołodziejski, along with the first secretary of the communist party's Voivodship Committee, Tadeusz Fiszbach. Wałęsa had already heard about the large scale of the arrests and that communications had been completely blocked. The officials informed Solidarity's chairman that martial law had been declared, and explained that he should go immediately to Warsaw for talks with government representatives. When Wałęsa refused, his guests went to contact their superiors by government telephone (residential phones and public booths were not working), and an SB team stayed in front of the apartment, ready to break inside. After a while, both messengers returned and reported that Deputy Prime Minister Rakowski had firmly insisted that he go to Warsaw. This time Wałęsa agreed and he left from the military airport about 6 a.m., when it was still dark. Wałęsa's arrest and removal to a government villa near Warsaw was part of Operation "Fir," but plans for him were a little different from those for the rest of Solidarity's leaders.

Operation "Fir" was not limited to the detaining of specific people in their apartments, in their places of permanent residence (such as dormitories), or hotels. Around 1:15 a.m., a group of several hundred ZOMO surrounded the National Commission's headquarters and Gdańsk Regional Board. After cutting electricity and forcing the grating open, they entered. The Solidarity employees on duty there who were arrested were taken to the suburb of Pruszcz Gdański and, after cursory interrogations, to the prison in Strzebielinek, near the coast, where internees from the Tri-City (Gdańsk, Gdynia, and Sopot) were gathered. If any of those detained were not on the lists of people to be interned, authorities conducted a "prophylactic talk" with them and proposed that they sign a declaration of loyalty on a form that had been prepared and printed in advance. Those who refused to sign were interned. The operation cryptonym "Maple" (Klon) was used for these talks, but this operation was supposed to start on a broader scale only after the declaration of martial law. Authorites also removed documents and printed materials from the Gdańsk Solidarity offices in pre-prepared sacks. They even took the printing equipment.

Operation "Fir" was carried out in a similar fashion in other regional offices, although of course the number of ZOMO depended on how many people were expected to be in the offices, and how large the actual premises were. In smaller regional offices, generally a few people were on duty; in larger ones, between ten and twenty. Other people were also present, sometimes there just by chance. In Gdańsk, the operation began late in order not to startle the members of the National Commission, whose meeting was still going on after midnight. In most cities, however, ZOMO had already surrounded the buildings before midnight. The reactions of the people in the offices varied, but in general they were passive. It was probably only in Katowice that the approximately thirty people present at the headquarters resisted—by using fire extinguishers and blocking doors. When militiamen breached the doors and threw tear gas inside, however, the unionists surrendered.[6] Furniture was often destroyed, as well as telephone switchboards, even though they were not working anyway. Typewriters were wrecked and papers scattered about. In Wrocław, ZOMO "broke up the press with crow-bars, and then ... simply smashed everything: cabinets, desks, telephones, radios, tape recorders." "In the heat of battle," said Frasyniuk, "they went on the third floor, where they also smashed the equipment belonging to the pro-government trade unions."[7]

In some regions, the operation took place in two stages. The main task of the first, which took place around midnight, was the internment of the people who were present in the offices—some of whom were on the lists and thus would have been arrested at home anyway—and the immobilization of the printing equipment. The second stage, usually several (but sometimes even ten) hours later, was primarily intended to take documents and destroy the rest of the equipment. During the week, about four hundred sacks of documents from twenty-four voivodships were taken to the Ministry of Internal Affairs in Warsaw. In time, the number of sacks doubled, and an ad hoc group of several dozen SB functionaries and employees of the communist party's Central Committee dealt with their contents.[8] After this second stage, the union offices were closed, sometimes sealed, and guards posted. Between the stages, however, there was generally a small interval of time to rescue something. In some cases people succeeded. Because a minimum of several dozen Solidarity offices were raided all over the country, it can be estimated that probably at least 3,000–4,000 SB, militiamen, and ZOMO took part.

In Warsaw at 1 a.m., as increasing numbers of militia cars were on the streets transporting internees, and the halls and arrest cells of some police stations were burgeoning with the "counterrevolutionaries" who had been brought there, a meeting of the Council of State began inside Belvedere palace. In addition to the council's chairman, Professor Henryk Jabłoński, who lived there, and several people from the office, who were already at the scene, most of the other members of what was formally communist Poland's highest state institution were brought by military vehicles, knowing nothing about the day's agenda, nor about the subject of the deliberations. The invitation that the escort showed them was extremely terse: they were informed that a special meeting of the council would be held at 1 a.m. Kazimierz Barcikowski, who had come straight from the Central Committee building, was the only one who knew very well why the meeting was being called. Similarly, Jabłoński only found out early the afternoon of December 12 that he would have to call the meeting; at that time he was given documents to review and approve. Henryk Boratyński, head of the State Council chancellery, was privy to the preparations—but also practically at the last moment. The meeting's protocol states that four members and the council's secretary were not present "because of a lack of communication," and one (Jerzy Ziętek) because he was bedridden.[9]

In the meeting room, besides the council's members and employees, there was a small group of high-ranking officers—including the deputy minister of national defense, General Tuczapski; the chief military prosecutor, General Józef Szewczyk; the chair of the Military Chamber of Supreme Court, General Kazimierz Lipiński; Colonel Tadeusz Malicki from the National Defense Committee headquarters, who had been dealing with the legal aspects of martial law since the summer of 1980; and the deputy minister of justice, Tadeusz Skóra. Neither the prime minister nor even one of the six deputy prime ministers attended, nor did any of the ministers from the ministries of internal affairs and defense. One of the council's members, Ryszard Reiff, the head of the Catholic association PAX, approved by the communist party, recalled that the "mood was heavy, even though almost everyone tried to mask the anxiety that was rankling them with a poorly feigned light-heartedness."[10]

Those assembled were sitting around a large, oval table, on which were lying files with drafts of documents. After he had delivered his exposé, General Tuczapski asked the council to approve the documents. Szewczyk and Skóra presented additional explanations. Barcikowski recalls that Tuczapski used the name "WRON" and "informed that the military had assumed the initiative" since "the politicians had turned out to be incapable of taking control of the crisis."[11] This was a hapless statement, since military men had already been occupying many of the most important positions in the state (including the post of prime minister and the ministers of internal affairs, administration, and mining) for many months, and there were also high-ranking officers among the members of the Central Committee of the Polish United Workers' Party. But that is of little consequence. General Tuczapski spoke "energetically, decisively, and sharply," as Reiff recalled. Nevertheless, Reiff had the courage to protest and provide broad justification for doing so. For most of those gathered, his actions did not come as a surprise, since PAX's chairman sympathized with Solidarity and thought about playing a significant role if it came to an agreement between the party, union, and Church. The well-known sociology professor Jan Szczepański put a bit of distance between himself and the task presented to the council by General Jaruzelski by complaining that there had been no chance to become acquainted with the projects being proposed. But that was exactly what the architects of martial law had intended when they decided to take the nation by surprise. A few other speakers, including Barcikowski, took the floor, but the meeting's protocol is extremely brief. It was actually a polemical dialogue between Reiff and Tuczapski, who was supported by other speakers. Only "several individuals," writes Reiff, "remained silent until the end, without concealing their despondency and sadness."

After about an hour-long debate, the four decrees and the resolution "On the Implementation of Martial Law" were passed. All the documents were dated December 12, and thus were antedated, since the nighttime meeting had begun when it was already December 13. Moreover, according to the last article of each of the decrees, they came into force "on the day of their passage," and not, as usual, "on the day of their publication." It was also necessary to wait for these decrees to be publicized since, for unknown reasons, the appropriate issue of *Dziennik Ustaw* (Journal of Laws) had not been printed ahead of time (though, after all, probably no one seriously thought that any corrections to the prepared drafts would be introduced during the Council of State meeting). The documents were passed—as it was noted in the protocol—"with R. Reiff taking a separate position . . . and J. Szczepański stating that . . . he does not declare himself to be in favor of them, but that he also does not voice an objection." Barcikowski returned to the Central Committee building, and the others probably to their beds. On the protocol, a note says that the members "who did not manage to come . . . approved the decision."

On the evening of December 13, at the Church's request, small corrections were made to the documents that had already been accepted. These changes, of course, were not presented to the Council of State, and the document in its entirety was sent to be printed only the afternoon of December 16. The first copies of *Dziennik Ustaw* (Issue 29/1981) appeared early the next morning. Later, constitutionalists carried on a prolonged debate about the legal power of the decisions of the Council of State, since, according to the constitution at the time, that organ lacked the authority to ratify decrees when the Sejm was in session. Meanwhile, such a session was in fact underway, and the next sitting was slated for December 15 and 16 (it ultimately took place more than a month late). Lawyers from KOK had mentioned the problems that could arise from such a solution ever since talk began about the conditions needed to implement martial law as a "surprise." No one in decision-making circles took heed of these warnings, however. The important thing was efficacy, and not the law.

General Jaruzelski, when he was already the chairman of WRON, spent the night in the quite deserted Office of the Council of Ministers, which was two hundred meters away from Belvedere (and three hundred meters from the Soviet Embassy). His accommodations were rather spartan, but I was unable to collect trustworthy opinions about the quality of the cuisine there. In that same building, Rakowski was also sitting in his office. After midnight, he brought in minister Jerzy Urban, undoubtedly to bolster his own courage. In the little room next to the office, Wiesław Górnicki was napping, dressed in his military uniform with its major's epaulettes. A well-known journalist, Górnicki had been Jaruzelski's ghostwriter for a couple of months. He had just finished his excruciating work on the latest version of the general's speech, which Jaruzelski was now personally polishing.

"What was going on?" a journalist asked Urban years later. "Nothing, actually," he answered. "We sat and waited. . . . It was very tense. . . . Empty talk, to kill time. . . . Mietek [Rakowski] called Jaruzelski several times."[12] A conversation with Fiszbach—who had been ordered to send Wałęsa to Warsaw—livened things up to a certain extent. Then the authorities called in Stanisław Ciosek, who as minister for contact with the trade unions was needed in order to begin talks with Wałęsa, and Józef Tejchma, who as minister of culture and art had some activity scheduled with the Congress of Polish Culture, which was supposed to resume deliberations in the morning. As the result of Tejchma's intervention, participants who showed up in the morning found a handwritten note on the door of the Teatr Dramatyczny, where the congress was taking place, with the following information: "By the decision of the Mayor of the City of Warsaw, the Congress of Culture has been dissolved." Militiamen were visible in the theater's lounge.

At 3:30 a.m., when members of the National Commission who had been caught were already in detention, General Jaruzelski went to the barracks of the air force liaison group, where substitute radio and television studios had been installed. First he recorded a statement for radio, which was expected to be broadcast at hour "G." Then he recorded the same speech in the television studio (to be broadcast at 12:00), after which he returned to the Office of the Council of Ministers. Shortly thereafter, Barcikowski went to the residence of the primate, Archbishop Józef Glemp, to inform him that martial law had been imposed. Barcikowski was accompanied by Jerzy Kuberski, head of the Office for Religious Affairs, and by General Marian Ryba, in full dress uniform, who was the deputy head of the Chancellery of the Council of Ministers. It was not just (or at least not so much) out of courtesy that they informed the head of the Church in Poland so soon. "I realized full well," said Barcikowski, "that it was the Church that had the button by which Poland could be detonated that day."[13] The primate listened "attentively and with concern" to Barcikowski's declaration, a response to which General Jaruzelski reacted with "clear relief" when he was informed about the course of the meeting. Perhaps WRON's chairman really did calm down after hearing this information, although it seems unlikely that he would have expected the primate to call on the nation to fight, and on the young people to man the barricades.

As Barcikowski, Kuberski, and Ryba were entering the primatial palace on Miodowa Street, messengers from the voivodship MO headquarters were notifying and distributing instruction packets to the first secretaries of the PZPR voivodship committees, voivods, heads of the voivodship military headquarters, and the voivodship KOK commissars. They were all instructed to turn on the radio at 6 a.m. and listen to the speech by WRON's chairman, in which he was supposed to provide them with general guidelines and sketch out a political and propaganda line for further action. It is striking that such highly trusted individuals who were in such responsible positions, or had just been appointed to them, found themselves practically among the last of those to learn of the plans. Many of them surely were waiting vigilantly, expectantly, at their workplaces—or perhaps they were even on duty—and so naturally at midnight they already knew what was happening.

Beginning the evening of December 12, the Ministry of National Defense leadership issued more orders. In the "Dziennik działań bojowych" (Diary of operational activities) entries by the Silesian Military District[14] for that date, we read, for example:

8:10 p.m.—develop emergency system of radio relay communications; 11:25 p.m.—begin regrouping forces at 3:00 a.m. in order to assume army protection of designated special sites, including designated airports; 11:30 p.m.—issue the envelope marked with the sign "Krakus" [orders regarding the tasks of specific divisions] and allow it to be opened at 5:00 a.m.; 11:40 p.m.—from 3:00 a.m. impose the State of Operational Readiness of Military Threat for the Central Institutions of MON, Military Districts [Okręgi Wojskowe, OW], Types of Military Forces [Rodzaje Sił Zbrojnych, RSZ] and subordinate troops.

And here are selected entries from December 13:

1:10 a.m.—Code "Azalea" carried out in full. All soldiers are at the sites; 1:10 a.m.—at 5:00 a.m., launch a blockade of the areas specified [in the orders] in towns, and of the seats of OW and RSZ commands, as well as their patrol; 1:15 a.m.—launch a complete group for the accelerated collection of special production beginning at 6:00 a.m.; 1:20 a.m.—bring maneuver (intervention) battalions and special sub-detachments to complete combat readiness in their places of permanent deployment until 6:00 a.m.; 1:45 a.m.—begin at 6:00 a.m. full implementation of the tasks contained in the code panel "High Water" [*Wysoka Woda*; this was a code panel prepared for operations taking place under martial law]; 4:30 a.m.—from 6:00 a.m. start regrouping the allocated tactical unions to the starting target areas according to the plan to improve the operational position of the troops ("Elaborat" envelope); 6:00 a.m.—at 6:00 a.m. open the packet marked with the password "Druggist" [*Drogista*; militarization and mobilization of the reservists] and carry out activities prescribed.

The entries in the operational logs of the other military districts, the armed forces command (air force and navy), garrisons, and central institutions of the

Ministry of National Defense look very similar or identical. It was still dark when the army began implementing martial law. Units from eleven different divisions (including two airborne) left their places of permanent deployment, and were moved by means of 1,636 tanks (over half the total owned by the Polish military), 2,043 armored personnel carriers, and about 13,000 other vehicles.[15] In other words, heavily-armed troops were sent into action.

The turbulent night was coming to an end. Thousands of people, however, were not sleeping: Jaruzelski and Wałęsa, SB functionaries and the trade unionists they had arrested, the officers on duty in the various headquarters, and people from Solidarity who were witnesses to the internments and attacks on the union's headquarters and were now looking for hiding places for themselves. Thousands of others had been awakened during the night: soldiers by the alert, local notables when the special courier rang the doorbell, and apartment dwellers by the pounding of SB officers on the doors of their unionist neighbors.

The first day of martial law was beginning. Tanks were heading for intersections, and militia and soldiers' patrols were swarming in the streets. Just like during a war.

At 6 a.m. sharp, the national anthem was played on the radio, followed by an announcer's voice: "Here is Polish Radio Warsaw. Today is Sunday, December 13. An exceptional day in the history of our state and our nation is beginning. In a moment, Army General Wojciech Jaruzelski will speak before the microphones of Polish Radio." General Jaruzelski began his nearly twenty-two-minute-long speech with the words "Citizens of the Polish People's Republic! I am addressing you today as a soldier and the head of the Polish government. I am addressing you in matters of the greatest importance. Our homeland is at the edge of an abyss."[16]

Although the country had de facto already been living under martial law for several hours, at first only a narrow circle of people knew what this meant. The Council of State's fundamental decrees were published officially in the *Dziennik Ustaw* only on December 17, as were orders from the Council of Ministers, which referred to decrees that were not yet legally in force. They concluded with the proviso "goes into effect the day of their announcement, with legal force from the day martial law was introduced." This meant the orders were retroactive, and by several days at that. But who reads *Dziennik Ustaw*, after all? Most Poles—and anyone else interested—found out about the measures contained in those documents and what they entailed gradually over the course of December 13. Since the morning, the radio had been broadcasting nothing but General Jaruzelski's speech every hour. At 10 a.m., this was complemented by the "Proclamation of the Military Council of National Salvation."

It was only after 12 p.m. that announcers, beginning with the Council of State's proclamation, read the successive decrees and orders. Similarly, two announcers dressed in military uniforms appeared on television. They lacked insignia but did have "Model Soldier" decorations. In monotonous voices, they read articles and paragraphs that were impossible to remember. Then orders issued by authorities on various levels were announced. Nevertheless, it was still after 4 p.m. that an announcement was made about the KOK order regarding the militarization of portions of the state administration and several sectors of the economy and infrastructure. According to the announcements, evading work in these units was punishable even by death! In the afternoon, it was also announced that, until further notice, a curfew would be in force from 10 p.m. until 6 a.m., and that from Monday, all schools and postsecondary schools would begin their Christmas holidays. To be on the safe side, however, the date those holidays would end was not given. The radio and television that day also broadcast various kinds of practical information, such as advice that, in case of an interruption in telephone service, people should contact the hospital, ambulance, or fire brigade in an emergency, with the help of the militia or military patrols. In the afternoon, a special, one-page issue of *Trybuna Ludu* (a central organ of the Polish communist party) was distributed, but only in some towns.

The decrees theoretically referred to a situation that could arise if imperialists insidiously attacked Poland and other "Peace-Loving Countries," but some of the instructions they contained sounded downright ludicrous, such as the announcement, made while Poland was in the midst of a deep freeze, that "engaging in tourism, sailing, and rowing on internal and territorial marine waters has been banned." Poles were also informed that "in instances justified by the need to accommodate individuals deprived of housing as the result of military operations," they could be forcibly housed with those lucky people whose houses had not been demolished. One might think that Wałęsa had cannons and bombers under his command. The most important documents were the decrees of the Council of State ("On Martial Law,"[17] "On Specific Procedures in Cases Involving Crimes and Offenses while Martial Law Is in Effect" [i.e., about summary justice], "On the Transfer to Military Courts of Cases Involving Certain Crimes," and "About the Change in the Structures of Military Courts and the Prosecutor's Military Organizational Units"), the decrees of the Council of Ministers ("On Rules of Procedure in Cases Regarding the Internment of Polish Citizens," "On the Carrying Out of Regulations of the Decree on Martial Law in the Field of Communications," "On Carrying Out the Decree on Martial Law in the Field of the Collection of Funds, Financial Transactions, Financial Services, and the Granting of Credit"), the decree of the Ministry of Internal Affairs ("On the Matter of Permission to Change One's Place of Residence during Martial Law"), and the decree of the Minister of Justice ("On the Creation of Isolation Centers"). The Council of State decree was specific: "On the Forgiving and Pardoning of Certain Crimes and Offenses"—i.e., about a general amnesty for activities before the imposition of martial law. KOK's resolutions, dated December 12 (although the Committee did not meet that day), were of fundamental importance: they detailed the creation of voivodship defense committees (Wojewódzkie Komitety Obrony), commissioner plenipotentiaries, and militarization.

Decrees of lesser importance from ministers and voivods supplemented this entire legislative packet. The additional decrees established bans on strikes and assemblies, suspended the activities of all trade unions and over one hundred social organizations (including artistic associations and the Independent Students' Union), suspended the vast majority of press publications, and allowed broadcasting only on one channel for television and radio. There was also a ban on leaving the voivodship in which one was registered as a permanent resident without permission from voivodship authorities, and limits on the amounts that could be withdrawn from personal bank accounts. In addition, a decree required that weapons (this essentially related to hunting weapons) and radio transmitting equipment, or equipment that both transmits and receives (i.e., amateur walkie-talkies), be deposited at militia stations. Correspondence and telephone conversations were to be monitored, and border traffic halted. A ban was instituted on the sale of gasoline and other vehicle fuels to private individuals, and Saturday was reinstated as a workday. On orders from the KOK, militarization was to include, for example, over 90 percent of those employees in the Ministry of Transportation, 75 percent in the Ministry of Communications, 90 percent in the Ministry of Mining and Energy, and 93 percent in the Office of Marine Economy. Over two million people were subject to militarization, which was approximately 15 percent of the total number of people employed.[18] The commissioners assigned to the voivodships and ministries had at their disposal small staffs with five to ten people (officers and soldiers). Those who were entrusted with care of the *gminas* (these are municipalities, or communes, i.e., local administrative units) and industrial plants, for the most part, had been the commanding officers in the field operations groups that had been active in those places during October and November; thus they were very familiar with the territory assigned to them. In the Council of State's decrees, some regulations were not implemented, but could have made a strong impression when broadcast in the media. One of these was the regulation that individuals from sixteen to sixty years old were obliged to render unpaid work for defense efforts. Another required farmers to supply the state with agricultural products, and also threatened that both their land and their equipment would temporarily be given to others if not properly used.

It is clear that how those regulations would be implemented—i.e., whether or not martial law could be instituted in Poland—was decided by the balance of power between those who were to carry them out and those who were subject to them, and by how determined each side was. "In each [workplace], Solidarity members were left to assess the situation themselves, and put to a test of courage when confronted with the militia and army detachments that surrounded them, and doomed to wrestle with the thought that they might be the only ones protesting," Andrzej Friszke wrote.[19] And although this description is reasonable, the situation did vary in different towns and regions. Most importantly, it was not at all clear on the morning of December 13 whether the government had definitively won. That afternoon, during a meeting of the Politburo, General Kiszczak said that "as time passes, the situation may become more difficult."[20] During the afternoon teleconference with the first secretaries of the voivodship PZPR committees, Barcikowski warned that strikes "may spread,"[21] and on December 14—during a similar teleconference—General Tuczapski admitted that "the next two days" would be decisive.[22] It seems that December 13 represented a kind of transition period, in which the attacking side had admittedly gained the bridgehead, even though it was not clear whether it would be able to hold it. This transitional state occurred mainly because it was, after all, Sunday, and only enterprises (or portions of them) that operated around the clock were functioning; offices and institutions were closed, as were schools and postsecondary schools, and the majority of military forces were still on the way to their assault positions.

In MSW reports[23] from the early morning hours of December 13, one finds information about the first reactions to the imposition of martial law: in Jelenia Góra, three strikes took place (including at the railway junction); in Wrocław, twenty people who "stormed" a building were arrested (it was the building that housed the headquarters of the Lower Silesian Regional Board, which ZOMO had surrounded). In Warsaw, flyers were distributed with an appeal for a general strike on Monday; in several locations, crowds rendered arrests impossible; three MO functionaries (in Kraków and Sieradz) refused to carry out orders. At the helicopter factory in Świdnik, the same one where the first organized strike took place in July 1980, employees began to gather in the night on hearing news of the arrests. "Around 5 a.m.," recalls Henryk Gontarz, "a messenger [from the factory] asked the parish priest to announce at morning Mass that all men were requested to report to the factory. For about ten minutes, all the alarm sirens were also turned on."[24] At 8 a.m. the first public meeting took place, a strike committee was formed, and the factory's public address system began functioning. During the day, workers and union activists who had come from Lublin gathered. They formed a Regional Strike Committee since, as it turned out, the workplaces were still empty in the regional capital. At the Wujek mine, the night shift workers came to the surface at 6 a.m. All the miners, along with their colleagues who had come from their nearby homes at their own initiative, met in the changing room,[25] where the parish priest who had been invited said Mass and, as Adam Skwira recalled, "gave a beautiful, calming sermon."[26] After the service, everyone went home. When the night shift at the Ziemowit mine had finished, people gathered, Mass was held, and everyone "listened to the radio, walked around, sat a little longer, but at about eleven dispersed," since they had "[come] to the conclusion that there was no sense in holding a strike on a Sunday."[27]

In Jastrzębie, however, a strike was announced that evening at four mines, although there were several hundred people working on around-the-clock shifts there. Over eight hundred miners from the Staszic mine in Giszowiec also went on strike. Frasyniuk, a Wrocław native, arrived in his hometown before dawn, straight from Gdańsk, and reported that "crowds showed up" at the gates of the municipal bus depot there, flags and banners were "hanging everywhere," people were heading to the strikes at their workplaces, and there was activity on the streets, despite the many patrols.[28] A Regional Strike Committee was formed, and when ZOMO entered the depot in the evening, those present moved to other enterprises. The chairman of the Łódź Regional Solidarity Board, Andrzej Słowik, also went from Gdańsk to his hometown, Łódź. Here, however, the center of protest was not in one of the enterprises, but at the regional headquarters, which ZOMO had abandoned after plundering it during the night. Since morning, people had been gathering in front of the building, which was festooned with national flags that were bound with strips of black cloth, signifying mourning. An Inter-Enterprise Strike Committee was formed and someone was shouting through a megaphone, telling people to participate in a general strike starting on Monday. Shortly after noon, a ZOMO company appeared and, along with SB functionaries, stormed the building and arrested everyone present. Those gathered on the street were dispersed. In Warsaw, the hundreds of people who were gathered in front of the Mazowsze Regional Board's headquarters were dispersed several times, until finally the MO blocked the street where the headquarters was located. In Kraków that morning, after news of the arrests overnight, the employees of three municipal transportation depots went on strike and formed strike committees. A group of students from the Mining and Metallurgical Academy, which was just ending a strike that had been going on for many weeks, moved to the Lenin Steelworks to take refuge there. At the foundry, the night shift remained on the premises and launched a strike. The strike committee began their own checks of pedestrian traffic, posted their own guards, and began using the public address system. Mass was celebrated by Father Józef Gorzelany, and the first flyers were printed.

In many cities the streets were unusually busy for a Sunday—which was especially remarkable because it was bitterly cold. People were not only gathering near Solidarity headquarters, but—much more frequently—in front of churches before and after Mass. The SB noted that priests in general appealed for calm and admonished against wrecklessness, and urged people to pray for social peace. Sometimes there were patriotic accents, prayers for the homeland, and expressions of concern about the fate of the people who had been arrested. There were people crying. In several places, ceremonies were held to bless the banners of the local Solidarity branches, something which had been announced beforehand. I have not, however, found any information suggesting that such religious services prompted street demonstrations. Undoubtedly some people went to the town centers in order to find out more about the scale of the arrests and the names of those arrested. Lists of these people were posted on parish bulletin boards at some churches; additional names were added by hand.

On the basis of eyewitness accounts, MSW reports, and previously published fragmentary studies, one can conclude that various strike organizations were established over the course of December 13 in dozens of workplaces. At least ten regional strike committees were created, people gathered in front of local union headquarters, and the first flyers appeared. Situations like the one at the Adamów mine were rare. There, the mine's Solidarity factory commission voted by a majority not to strike. The National Commission members who had escaped the Gdańsk roundup and were not caught on the way (like Leszek Waliszewski, head of the Silesian-Dąbrowa region, the largest in the country, who was caught at a train station) took action, along with many of the regional activists, although some acknowledged that opposition was impossible. "I did not call for a general strike," recalled Patrycjusz Kosmowski, chairman of the Podbeskidzie Regional Board, one of the union's best-known radicals. "I was afraid blood would be spilled. . . . I knew that [we] should go into hiding, [and] rebuild the organization."[29] Two leaders of the Mazowsze Region were in hiding, Zbigniew Bujak and Zbigniew Janas. Two well-known activists, Bogdan Lis and Bogdan Borusewicz, heroes of the August 1980 strike, also went into hiding immediately.

Five members of the Presidium of the National Commission who had escaped arrest in Gdańsk (Mirosław Krupiński, Andrzej Konarski, Eugeniusz Szumiejko, Jan Waszkiewicz, and Aleksander Przygodziński) met the next morning at the shipyard. Because almost no one was there, however, they moved to the Gdańsk Port, where there were several hundred workers present. There, they formed the National Strike Committee (Krajowy Komitet Strajkowy) and issued "Bulletin No. 1," signed at 1:20 p.m. In it, they announced a general strike of unlimited duration to begin on December 14, citing the resolution of the previous day. They demanded that "all those arrested be released" and that "martial law be revoked." Strikers were urged to "maintain discipline" and "avoid needless clashes" with militiamen and soldiers. "Our weapon," they wrote, "is calm, dignity, and ideal organization." After the two aforementioned demands were met, the text announced: "We may undertake talks with the aim of finding a basis for agreement."[30] Eventually, shipyard workers began arriving, and a couple thousand people gathered in front of the famous Gate No. 2, just next to the memorial for the shipyard workers who were killed in December 1970. The vast majority, however, went home in the evening, before the curfew.

In almost all of the many appeals and communiqués that were issued in various cities on December 13, it is noteworthy that not only were the demands identical (release of those arrested and revocation of martial law), but also the tone: they featured calls for a strike and an expectation that there would be a compromise, but also exhortations to maintain calm and discipline. That day, radical formulations, so frequent in later flyers and underground publications, appeared only sporadically. One could say that the strikes and protests were only half-hearted. People had not prepared sufficiently in terms of organization for this particular turn of events, which undoubtedly played a very important role. In addition, the urge for moderation was, to a large extent, due to the fact that many of the leaders had been removed: according to an MSW report at 10 p.m., approximately 3,400 people had already been arrested,[31] including nearly 550 from the Katowice voivodship alone. Most members of the National Commission had been taken out of action, and at least half of the regional chairmen. What hampered organization of the protests most, however, was the arrest of activists from the regional organizations and enterprise commissions, as well as full-time union employees. The arrest lists were, of course, primarily comprised of those who were the most active and radical. The fact that the telephone network had been cut posed a more serious obstacle to organizing resistance than the ZOMO attacks on the union's offices, street patrols, and blockades on major roads leading in and out of the cities. Lack of a telephone network rendered communication and coordination extremely difficult. Since no strikes were planned for entire large enterprises that day, because they were slated to start on December 14, it was difficult to foresee what the situation would be like the next day. General Jaruzelski was clearly very anxious about what would happen on Monday. During a meeting of the Politburo, he stressed several times that "shock" and "psychosis . . . terror, and gravity must be maintained."[32] Clearly, shock and fear were widespread, but these feelings were probably not yet paralyzing.

It is difficult to define exactly what influence the Catholic hierarchy and priests had on the course of events that day. As mentioned above, the institutional Church, as such, took a moderate stance. Without a doubt, it sympathized with the social movement that had emerged, but priests as a rule did not become involved in union activities other than in spiritual matters, and Primate Wyszyński, as well as his successor, announced what amounted virtually to warnings about Solidarity, though admittedly only rarely in public. Above all, Church officials feared that making demands that were too far-reaching might prompt the government to react drastically, or provoke an intervention from Moscow. Like Primate Wyszyński during the Bydgoszcz crisis in March 1981, Primate Glemp also attempted to mediate: on December 6, he sent a letter to the Sejm warning against passing the bill "On Extraordinary Powers," but during the meetings with Solidarity representatives (headed by Wałęsa), which took place on December 5, 7, and 9, he warned his guests against an escalation of demands, and even stated that the union's activists had "overstepped the authority afforded them by the world of labor."[33]

After government officials saw the primate, Bishop Bronisław Dąbrowski and Father Alojzy Orszulik, who were permanent participants in the working talks with the government, went to the Office for Religious Affairs. There, they lodged their official protest against the arrests, and requested that they be allowed to meet with Wałęsa. After a while, Barcikowski arrived, with whom both priests met two more times during the course of that Sunday. The main subject of the talks was the problem of those who were interned, particularly intellectuals and people from the cultural sphere who were linked to the Church. Conferring at that time in the Episcopate's headquarters were some of the members of the Primate's Social Council who were present in Warsaw, Solidarity advisors who had not been interned, and some members of Warsaw's Club of the Catholic Intelligentsia (whose activities, like those of the others, had also been suspended).

The imposition of martial law had not forced the primate to change his agenda that day. At 9 a.m., at the monastery at Jasna Góra, he took part in a Mass for university students which was linked with the student strike that was just ending after many weeks. There for the first time, he also referred publicly to martial law in his sermon, which—as noted in an SB report—maintained "a calm tone."[34] It really did not contain any signs of hostility toward the government, and the primate stressed several times that the situation required wisdom and calm, "so there would be no bloodshed."[35] The sermon's content was not publicized, unlike the homily that Primate Glemp delivered that evening in Warsaw, at the sanctuary of Our Lady of Grace. At the initiative of those who had implemented martial law, excerpts of this message were broadcast immediately on the radio. The tone of this sermon was much more emotional than during the primate's morning address, but by no means in the sense that Primate Glemp was urging people to take action. On the contrary, he stated that "the Church has received with sorrow the news that the dialogue which has been developing with such difficulty has broken off, and that [the authorities] have opted to make use of force." Primate Glemp also appealed for the release of those "unjustly arrested," and for "calm and for fratricidal conflict to be prevented." The primate clearly realized that his words could be met with negative reactions, which is why he stressed emphatically that he would "appeal for good judgment even at the risk of being insulted." He exhorted dramatically: "Do not undertake a battle that sets Poles against Poles. Do not risk your lives, brother workers and employees of large enterprises." He ended with the words: "Help us, Best Mother, so that no child of the Polish Nation perishes. Amen."[36]

Talks between government and Church representatives were highly diplomatic. Regardless of whether Jaruzelski suspected that the Church could summon people to resist, or whether he counted on its neutrality, he believed that its hierarchs should be approached coolly but politely. None of the documents or accounts of December 13, however, mention that the government attempted to hold any kind of talks—if only preliminary ones—with Solidarity people. Only a few days later did talks take place between Rakowski and the union's well-known lawyers and advisors—with Jan Olszewski on December 19, and Władysław Siła-Nowicki on December 22. There was one notable exception: Ciosek met with Wałęsa the morning of December 13, and in the evening Deputy Prime Minister Rakowski wanted to talk with Wałęsa. Because of a misunderstanding, that second conversation did not take place. Ciosek, as Danuta Wałęsa describes based on her husband's account, proposed a "speech on television, to calm people."[37]

According to the information Ciosek presented that same day at the Politburo meeting, Wałęsa did not express himself very clearly (as was sometimes the case) and it was not certain whether he was having difficulty formulating a clear opinion, or whether he was "not telling the whole truth" in order to win time and mislead his enemy. According to Ciosek, Wałęsa said that Solidarity had gone too far, and that the union should be headed by a new person, whom he himself would propose. He allegedly also said that the interned should be freed after signing a loyalty oath. According to Ciosek, Wałęsa also said that General Jaruzelski's speech had made a strong impression on him. At the same time, however, he refused any kind of public appearance and demanded a meeting with the members of the Presidium of the National Commission and his advisors. Trying to convince Wałęsa to make a public appearance was by no means Ciosek's own idea—he had his superiors' approval. During the aforementioned meeting of the Politburo, General Kiszczak admitted outright that it was "necessary," adding that it would be useful also to have appearances by others from Solidarity. This never came to pass, however, which created a problem, since those behind the idea probably genuinely believed they would succeed in convincing Wałęsa. In any case, if he appeared on television or even just spoke on the radio, it could have a demoralizing effect on the workers and become great political capital for Jaruzelski's team. Solidarity's leader realized this fully well, and saw no reason why he should make their lives easier. As a result, he did not appear on television, nor did he speak on the radio. "He's scum," noted General Anoshkin.[38]

Over the course of that day and evening, designated armored units—in accordance with Operation "Red Rowan"—"improved their positions" and arrived at their assault positions, one after another. The days of truth were drawing near.

Chapter Six

Breakthrough

On Monday, the fourteenth of December, a group of nine people met for the first time, who, as Mieczysław Rakowski wrote in his journal, were to "constantly monitor how the situation was developing" over the coming weeks.[1] That morning, they met in a small conference room off the prime minister's office in the historical Council of Ministers building, across the street from Warsaw's most beautiful park and the Frédéric Chopin monument. Kazimierz Barcikowski believes that, for Jaruzelski, who "clearly dominated" the others present at the meeting, "we [simply] were a select adjutant staff, which would participate in analyzing the situation and preparing decisions, which he would accept or reject."[2] Other than operational decisions, the group considered various matters of a more general nature, even strategic ones. In addition to Jaruzelski, this group included two deputy prime ministers (Rakowski and Janusz Obodowski, an economist and chairman of the government's Operational Anti-Crisis Center), three Central Committee secretaries (Barcikowski, responsible for the Sejm and contact with the Church; Milewski, responsible for security matters and justice; and Olszowski, responsible for propaganda), two heads from the ministries of defense and the interior (Siwicki and Kiszczak), and the head of the Office of the Council of Ministers (Janiszewski, Jaruzelski's jack of all trades, who had previously headed his Ministry of National Defense office).

In this group, five people were members or deputy members of the Politburo, and only two (Janiszewski and Obodowski) were not members of the Central Committee, and thus outside the party's formal top leadership, although they did belong to the narrow governing elite. Of those who were in charge of politically significant departments, only the foreign minister, Józef Czyrek, was absent. As a member of the Politburo and secretary of the Central Committee, Czyrek belonged to the highest decision-making circles. His absence may be explained by the fact that the group was primarily dealing with exclusively internal matters. Most of those in this group had extensive (at least twenty years') political experience. Four of them were military men (all were in WRON), and one (Milewski) had spent his entire career in the security apparatus. All came from approximately the same generation: the oldest, Jaruzelski, was 58; the youngest, Olszowski, was 50. They were thus the optimal age for holding executive positions: experienced enough, but still in their prime. Although they were close in age, they nevertheless came from different backgrounds: Jaruzelski and Siwicki had fought on the front,

Kiszczak and Rakowski had been young laborers in the German service during the war, and Olszowski and Barcikowski began working professionally only in the 1950s, in the communist youth organization apparatus.

This group was called the "directorate." According to Rakowski, this description had its origins "somewhere behind the scenes" and was not used externally. It is not clear whether the person who coined the term was consciously alluding to the era of the French Revolution when, after the overthrow of Robespierre's dictatorship, the Republic's Constitution of 1795 called the the highest executive power a "directorate." The government of the Paris Directorate lasted four years, and was ended by Napoleon Bonaparte's coup d'état, known as the Coup of *18 Brumaire*. Even today, this takeover remains a classic model of a military coup, and it even aroused the interest of Karl Marx. Perhaps the person who applied this name to the situation in Poland did not know French history very well, and thought the Polish "directorate" had been created as a result of the military coup d'état. Then the analogy with martial law would have been more apt. In any case, the original Directorate, as is usual for institutions of executive power during revolutions, was dictatorial in nature.

Unlike the French Directorate, the Polish one was not a constitutional organ. As a completely secret institution that had no basis in the law, it also did not bear responsibility for its own decisions, which were announced by other institutions—those of the party or state, or by WRON. From a logistical point of view, the creation of this kind of group was nothing out of the ordinary. In crisis situations, ad hoc groups often arise—small ones, meeting frequently and without unnecessary procedures, without protocols or decisions with signatures to validate them. It is, however, worth noting that when the country entered a phase of severe political crisis in mid-August 1980, the Politburo assumed all responsibility. Meeting almost every day for two weeks, it formally created the "Kania commission," which included representatives from the military and MSW. Before each Politburo meeting, it would collect and analyze information and prepare resolutions and proposals.

Thus the question arises: Where did the center of power lie after December 13, 1981? I will not try to solve this riddle here, but one should be aware that alongside the "directorate," which made operative decisions as well as more long-term ones, the Politburo and Secretariat of the Central Committee also continued to function. These were rightly considered—at least up until that point—to be the state's highest governing bodies in practice. The Politburo held meetings on December 13 and 22, and would later meet twice a month. The Central Committee's Secretariat, which was just below the Politburo in the party hierarchy, was generally concerned with the party's internal affairs, and it met only once (on December 19) during the period immediately after the imposition of martial law. The newly created Military Council for National Salvation also existed, which issued instructions and orders not only to the army, but also to the government and state administration. After December 13, it was regarded, both at home and abroad, as Poland's most important institution. Its meetings, however, did not take place very often (December 14 and 23, and later once a month), making it less a working body than a representational one—or even a façade. The Council of Ministers was also functioning, including the Government Presidium, which clearly belonged to the central elements of power, and many decisions—primarily in economic and administrative matters, for example—were discussed and made right there. The Council of Ministers usually met once a week (as did the Politburo). It also convened on the evening of December 13, when the session led by Jaruzelski lasted several hours. He did not suspend the Committee for National Defense, composed of people in the government, Politburo, WRON, and the "directorate." As a result, that same group of people met in different places and in slightly different roles. A real proliferation of ruling bodies took place, and anyone attempting to delineate their jurisdictions encounters serious difficulties.

One thing is nevertheless certain: each of these groups was headed by Wojciech Jaruzelski, who was also still the minister of defense. WRON's chairman had for some time been complaining of health problems, and sometimes vacillated, as those who worked with him more closely have unanimously testified. He was also characterized by cautious decision-making. Everything would indicate, however, that he was completely in control of both himself and the situation. Although he was probably not a person who exhibited dictatorial traits, the fact that he had spent his entire adult career in uniform and had found himself in leadership positions early on meant that he was accustomed to giving orders and demanded that they be carried out scrupulously. He also placed great emphasis on discipline and a particular brand of military bureaucracy: he required that detailed plans be drawn up in writing, as well as reports. Jaruzelski has said many times that he does not feel himself to be a politician and does not want to be one, but his road to the military's highest positions did actually begin in the Main Political Directorate of the Polish Army, which dealt with propaganda and indoctrination.

Jaruzelski's biography does deviate in one significant way from that of most officers in the "people's" (as it was called) Polish Army. Most of his colleagues came from peasant or working-class families, while he was from the landed gentry, steeped in both patriotic and noble traditions. Before the war, he attended an elite high school for boys run by the Marian order in Warsaw. After the war broke out, his family took refuge in Lithuania. In 1941, the entire family was deported to Siberia, where Jaruzelski's father died, and he worked as a logger. The young Jaruzelski did not join the Polish army that was formed in 1941–42, after the Polish-Soviet treaty; this army (headed by General Anders) was evacuated to the Middle East and later fought in Italy together with Western Allies. Instead, Jaruzelski became a soldier in 1943, when the Polish communists began forming an army under their own ideological command and political control. Jaruzelski fought on the front. After graduating from cadet school, he saw combat in the infantry and in reconnoitering detachments. He took part in heavy fighting at Kołobrzeg and went as far as the Elbe, where he had a brief chance to meet American soldiers. For many, many years this was his only direct contact with the West. At the end of the war, he held the rank of first lieutenant. He then remained in the army and systematically advanced in it from a "line" officer, who took part in the fighting with independence-oriented and anti-communist partisans in the years 1945–47, to that of a staff officer, involved mainly in training other officers. He was promoted to the rank of one star general quite unexpectedly in 1956, and was the youngest man to do so in Poland. This was the beginning of a brilliant and almost lightning-fast career: four years after achieving the rank of general, he became the head of the Main Political Directorate and, five years later, the head of the General Staff, and thus the second-highest ranking person in the military. In 1968 he was already minister of defense.

The cliquish struggle at the highest levels of the military and the anti-Semitic campaign, which was particularly intense in the military, were conducive to this last nomination. Jaruzelski was linked with the "partisans"—i.e., those who favored incorporating nationalist elements into communism. He was, however, not the leader of this faction. Because of the military positions he had held since 1960, he had many close contacts with Soviet generals, facilitated by his good knowledge of Russian. In 1961 he became a representative to the Polish parliament, the Sejm; in 1964 he became a member of the Central Committee of the Polish United Workers' Party; and in December 1970, after the army suppressed workers' strikes and protests in Gdańsk and Szczecin, he became a member of the Politburo. From that time, he participated in the work of the highest party bodies, and thus part of the narrowest circle of communist elites. Without ever ceasing to be a soldier, he became a politician simply in the course of events, which is why he—more than anyone else—was suited to directing what began at hour "G."

In the history of the People's Poland, never had so many important positions been concentrated in the hands of just one person. One could even wager that General Jaruzelski actually wielded more power than Bolesław Bierut had during the Stalinist period, or Władysław Gomułka after 1956. Of course, a direct comparison is not completely founded, since the times and conditions of exercising power—and the degree of dependence on Moscow—were different. The decision-making centers, usually formally and functionally scattered among several institutions, were in essence completely subordinate to the person—and personality—of Jaruzelski, who, from the moment martial law was imposed, simply overpowered his comrades from all the various bodies in which he was involved. Probably only at the Politburo did livelier and more open debates still take place. The division of opinions there roughly corresponded to the split that had already existed for a long time between those who supported the more and less radical solutions. Now, of course, it was no longer a matter of whether or not to implement martial law, but rather how to carry it out: about the extent of reprisals, the stance to be taken toward Solidarity, the model of the party itself, and its attitude toward the Church. But the general always had the last word in this forum, too, which assured that its administration would be competent and uniform. In other groups, Jaruzelski was simply the one who gave orders, which does not mean that he did not listen to others' opinions.

The first meeting of the "directorate" began with information about events in Poland, presented by General Kiszczak. He suggested that the strikes were starting, slowly but surely. It was difficult to gauge the actual scale of protests on the basis of reports arriving at MSW headquarters that morning, due in part to imprecise information from the field and a certain degree of flux in the situation. Actually, in this case, "chaos" would be a more suitable term than "flux." Above all, technical reasons were the cause: communications on a national and local scale had been cut, the militia had assumed control of all regional Solidarity headquarters, and many of its most active members had been isolated. According to MSW data, by the morning of December 14, a total of 739 regional board members were interned, among others, who were primarily connected with specific large enterprises, as well as 1,081 members of enterprise commissions.[3] Communication between cities or regions was practically impossible, although on December 14, for example, a courier from Gdańsk did manage to reach Świdnik with news about the National Strike Committee. In crisis situations, foreign radio broadcasts were a good source of news—as well as the only trustworthy one. It was only by December 15–16, however, that these broadcasts had more extensive and reliable information at their disposal. The attitude of factory managers and technical staff was a serious obstacle to staging strikes. The protests proceeded unimpeded only in a few cases, where participants were allowed to use the public address systems and intercoms. The plants in Świdnik, for example, were such an exception. Their director, Jan Czogała, paid for his benevolence toward striking workers by being fired for disciplinary reasons, and then interned.

In spring and autumn, Solidarity had based its strike instructions on the assumption that law enforcement functionaries would have a static presence near or around the largest enterprises, and would only employ "passive resistance."[4] Of course, on the night of December 12–13 it turned out that the militia would be not only active, but also aggressive. The armored and motorized military vehicles that moved uncamouflaged throughout the country on December 13 meant that the operation encompassed the entire army, not just its special units. On the night of December 13–14, military convoys launched what were called "demonstrative" activities. As noted in the "Dziennik bojowy" (Diary of Operational Activities) of the Silesian Military District, from

12:01 a.m. a motorized company, led by the militia, traveled along the Rybnik–Wodzisław–Jastrzębie route, and in the early morning a similar convoy "conducted demonstrative activities in the streets of Wrocław." On December 14 these kinds of movements took place in all of Poland's larger cities and industrial centers, and continued the following days. They were halted only over the Christmas holidays, but were renewed, on a smaller scale, on January 13, 1982. Convoys of military vehicles, including tanks, complemented martial law's regulations, including its militarization order. This degree of military presence undoubtedly reinforced the shock of the "Night of the General."

Beginning the morning of December 14, workers began arriving at their places of employment. Not all came to strike, however. Arkadiusz Dybowski, a miner from the Andaluzja mine, recalls that, when he arrived at the gate, members of the Enterprise Commission were already there, but were passive. He thus began calling out to the crowd of his coworkers, who were hurrying to work, "Where are you going? Think, people, what you are losing. Defend this union! ... I'm edgy and quick-tempered [so] I say: you idiots, losers!" In front of the gate stood two Nysa militia vans, and even though no one emerged from them, the miners from the first shift, which is the biggest one, "had their heads down, as if they were deaf mutes. And they went to work."[5] The strike was finally organized only late in the evening, with the miners from the night shift, the repair and preparation crews, and virtually no Enterprise Commission members. As Dybowski recalls, a big help in swaying people to resist was the "Appeal to Our Brothers the Miners," signed by the Inter-Enterprise Strike Committee in Bytom.[6] At the Ziemowit mine, there was a "sense of danger," recalls one of the miners; "I knew that at that moment nothing could be done," and "we felt that although something should be done, we didn't know what."[7] As a result, the strike announcement was postponed for a day.

There were similar situations in many workplaces, even in large ones, where the mere presence of thousands of people increased the sense of safety. Numerous public meetings and deliberations took place, and people debated feverishly about what should be done, and how, but often without much effect. The management of the enterprises often played a large role in discouraging people from protesting, and an even larger one was played by the military commissioners. These men were generally known to the crews, since they had usually been the commanding officers of the operational groups active in the field not long before, and they more or less already knew the enterprises, as well as the staff and workers who were most active. In many descriptions of what was happening on December 14 and 15, it is those officers whom people recall. In the company of managers or deputy managers, they would appear at the public meetings, where it was difficult to prevent them from taking the floor. But at the Ziemowit mine, for example, a commissioner was forced to deposit his holster and pistol in the director's office.[8]

Sometimes the local prosecutor would come in order to make it seem that the regulations of martial law were being upheld. Naturally, the SB functionaries acted with discretion. Where the management was determined and efficient enough, access to the factory broadcasting station was blocked for those on strike, or organizing a strike. Access to a microphone was often the key to gaining support for strikes. Already on December 13, at least in several cases, Polish Radio 1 programming, on orders from its directors, disheartened the workers who had gathered, and succeeded in subduing pro-strike agitation. In smaller enterprises, there were not many chances to organize protests, not only owing to the employees' frame of mind, but also—and perhaps above all—the fact that just a small group of militiamen was enough to break a strike. Beginning the afternoon of December 13, the Ministry of Internal Affairs began using the following tactic on a broader scale: it sent larger ZOMO units (companies) even to large enterprises that were on strike. Although these functionaries tried to block access to the gates and disperse people standing in front of the enterprise, they attempted to enter only relatively rarely. There were cases, however, such as at the Lenin Steelworks near Kraków, in which even commando units attempted to breach the enterprise.

The strikes either did not take any organized form, or fizzled out within a day or a few hours. A variety of factors contributed: persuasion, promises (for example, that the strikers would not be subject to reprisals), fear tactics, threats (which were frequent against workers from enterprises that had been subject to militarization), the general atmosphere of uncertainty, and threats of force, or actual force. In the Organika-Boruta plants in Zgierz, a strike began in the morning, but after 4 p.m. the vast majority of the workers left the premises; at Zamet in Białystok, a referendum was held under pressure from the commissioner, in which half of those participating condemned the strike. As a result, the Strike Committee that had already formed gave the workers a free hand, and the protest collapsed when the management succeeded in preventing the second shift from coming onto factory premises. As the result of a referendum, the strike at the Unitra-Polkolor factory in Piaseczno ended on the second day; after a day-long strike and stormy deliberations at the Konin Aluminum Works, it was decided that the protest should end; at the State Aviation Works in Mielec, by evening fewer than two hundred remained of the several thousand people who had been on strike since morning. The strike resumed the next day, but it came to a halt after just a couple of hours. Many of the strikes were relatively short; for example, an hour in the Polam Factory in Pabianice, and the same in the W-4 Department of the Hipolit Cegielski Factory in Poznań. At the Stalowa Wola Steelworks, "after two hours of being threatened by the military commissioner with reprisals," write Dariusz Iwanczenko and Jan Pisuliński, the strike "was called off."[9] In general, strikes in research institutes were short lived. There were virtually no attempts to strike in state offices and institutions. Strikes at colleges and universities were more extensive, owing to the fact that the participants were both students and, to some extent, faculty. Because classes had already been suspended, however, these strikes were not universal. Since instruction had been suspended in schools, no strikes took place at the elementary and secondary levels.

As far as I know, no one has yet made a detailed assessment of the protests that began on December 14 or had been going on since the previous day. It seems certain, however, that most workplaces did not have strikes, and virtually no governmental offices did, which of course does not mean that their employees backed martial law. It is also noteworthy that, except in only a very few cases (including Kraków and Wrocław), institutions and enterprises serving the public interest did not go on strike. These included transportation and municipal services, healthcare, and the railroads, which had been thoroughly militarized. In most of the enterprises, the strikes that did take place were chaotic. Both their organizers and participants suffered from a lack of determination. In places where strikes collapsed immediately on December 14 or did not start that day, there was not much chance for any protests to begin in the days that followed. On December 14 about two hundred workplaces were on strike in Poland, but this includes only those where a strike was officially proclaimed; thus, the number is slightly lower than it might be otherwise. Moreover, some factories went on strike only on December 15. In practice, people were not working anyway, even where no strike had been announced. In any case, productivity must have been unusually low. This, however, did not bother administrators of martial law; most important was that the protests not take on an organized character.

Serious protests did, however, take place in many large enterprises (in addition to the strikes that were short or quickly abandoned), and at public meetings and employees' assemblies, where people only protested against the imposition of martial law but did not proclaim any work stoppages. From noon on December 14, all military units were already at their initial positions, including the 16th Armored Division, which had taken a whopping thirty-five hours to move from its permanent station in Elbląg to the outskirts of Warsaw. It was at this point that the Ministry of Internal Affairs began asking the army's General Staff to send specific military units to help crush the strikes, an action most often referred to as "unblocking" the factories. The army undoubtedly played a decisive role in these operations, although in most cases it had only an auxiliary function and really only appeared when a strike was taking place at a large enterprise that covered an extensive area. The military leaders for the most part fulfilled the MSW's requests for assistance. At times, however, the General Staff had to reply that there were no free forces in a given region, such as when support was requested for the militia's operations at the steel mill in Ostrowiec Świętokrzyski.[10]

Unlike in war, when prisoners are usually taken after battles are won, now thousands of people had been taken prisoner at the very beginning of the conflict, which to a large extent determined its course. The internment of the most active union members at various levels contributed to the disorganization of the strikes, and especially to the lack of coordination among enterprises. Inter-enterprise strike organizations did develop, however, in several important regional capitals. As a rule, they generally sought refuge at one of the enterprises where a strike was taking place. The joint strike committees—which existed under various names, such as "regional" or "inter-enterprise"—began their activities on December 13 and 14 in Wrocław, Szczecin, Bytom (in Upper Silesia), Lublin (in nearby Świdnik), Łódź, Bielsko-Biała, Kraków (at the Lenin Steelworks), and Poznań. Surprisingly, no regional strike organization formed in Warsaw. The chairman of the Regional Board, Zbigniew Bujak, who enjoyed a great deal of authority, was in hiding outside Warsaw during the first days, when the strikes were taking place. This was undoubtedly a decisive factor. In Gdańsk, the aforementioned National Strike Committee was formed, and the shipyard had regional and other enterprise committees as well. Taking into account the situation after the arrests when communications had been blocked, it seems that at least some of the strikes were actually quite well organized—like in the Lenin Steelworks, in some of the mines, in Świdnik, and at the Katowice Steelworks. This was the case regardless of whether new, local leaders who had emerged spontaneously were responsible, or union activists who had been involved previously. Some of the committees published flyers and appeals, and in Świdnik they managed to publish the first issue of the strike *Biuletyn* (Bulletin). The Gdańsk Shipyard even had too many leaders; the three committees operating there simultaneously impeded each other's work. "It is extremely strange that the strike is still on," recalls Marian Terlecki, "because no one is organizing it. Most things are happening on their own."[11] As far as the shipyard was concerned, there was actually nothing strange about this; while situations did vary, plenty of people at the Gdańsk Shipyard had strike experience.

Roman Catholic Masses were a very important element of the strikes, and were probably celebrated everywhere, even if a strike lasted less than one day. Most often, priests were invited to come, but sometimes they also came at their own initiative. In addition to their pastoral roles, in the narrowest sense—such as celebrating Mass and hearing confessions—generally they also provided something akin to psychological counseling, striving to have a calming effect. They never encouraged anyone to be aggressive toward the government representatives or ZOMO functionaries who were blocking the enterprises. The example of Father Henryk Bolczyk is a special one, but probably an important one. He arrived at the Wujek mine, and as Adam Skwira has said, "the very presence of a priest had a calming effect on the people." When Father Bolczyk realized, however, that the strikers' determined mood was limiting his ability to influence them, he admitted that he should not remain with the miners any longer. "We saw him out and thanked him for coming."[12] Skwira believes that if the priest had stayed until the attack (he left the mine the evening before), the miners would not have actively resisted, and thus the resulting fatalities would have been avoided. Of course it is impossible to say this for certain. The priests did nevertheless have a calming influence on the striking workers, and also helped keep their spirits up, which in a sense strengthened their resolve. The priests who spent these first days among the striking workers probably did not know the contents of the communiqué issued on December 15 by the Main Council of the Polish Episcopate. Jaruzelski did agree to inform the bishops via military communication about the council's meeting, but the authorities prevailed upon the primate to ensure that the document would not be read aloud in the churches. In the communiqué, the bishops said that their pain was "that of the Nation terrorized by military force," a clear expression of their unequivocal assessment regarding the imposition of martial law. At the same time, however, they admitted uneasily that "a wave of emotions, bitterness, outrage, extreme hatred, and determination is growing." They issued "a fervent appeal [for Poles] to preserve the peace and to control [their] passions and anger," and to pray "for the unity of the Nation and peace in the Fatherland."[13] Even if one assumes that the bishops' words were directed at both sides in the conflict—which seems rather obvious—the striking workers were their most important audience, in particular those who had been swept away in the "wave of emotion." Despite the authorities' ban, the communiqué was read out loud in many churches (a decision of individual bishops), but only on Sunday, December 20. Thus, while Father Bolczyk could not have been familiar with it, he nevertheless acted as if he had studied it carefully.

One wonders whether the situation would have been fundamentally different if the National Strike Committee had been headed by people who truly enjoyed a large degree of authority, and above all if Lech Wałęsa had been present at the Gdańsk Shipyard instead of in isolation. While there is, of course, no reliable answer to this question, the chances of changing the course of events were rather slim, primarily because of communication problems. One can, however, assume that news that a charismatic leader was once again leading the strike would, in and of itself, have served as a mobilizing force, at least on the coast, and that resistance could have been stronger then, and lasted longer. There was, however, no "miracle weapon," nor was there any Wałęsa who was single-handedly resisting Minister Ciosek's questioning. The striking workers' chances to defend themselves actively were extremely limited, especially since troops and heavy combat equipment were being used to crush the protest. Relatively rarely, the workers prepared makeshift weapons to ward off the charging ZOMO functionaries, who were armed with batons. The workers used what they had at hand, including shovel or axe handles, iron rods, metal nuts, and rocks. If the situation changed, however, those same objects could serve to launch a counterattack. In a few places, strikers tried to take over—or did take over—the rooms where the explosives were kept (in the mines), or the devices that could cause explosions or fires (for example, the oxygen plant at the Katowice Steelworks). In some places they reckoned on being able to use compressed air cylinders, acetylene, or high-pressure fire extinguishers. To my knowledge, there was no case of striking workers having actual weapons. In accounts one sometimes hears about how bottles filled with gasoline were prepared ("Molotov cocktails"), but only according to one account was this classic insurgents' weapon actually used. This occurred in Warsaw, where an unidentified young person (who managed to escape) threw a bottle with an incendiary liquid at an armored vehicle that was driving down the street.[14] I also know of no case in which striking workers were equipped with gas masks (where would they have gotten them?), or had any substitutes, such as cloths soaked with appropriate chemicals, or balaclavas. The most usual method of defense was to throw back their aggressors' gas canisters or grenades, but the efficacy of this was limited, especially since the attacking ZOMO generally had masks at their disposal.

The striking workers' main defense might be called "passive"—preventing combat or militia vehicles from entering the enterprise, and hampering those who were intervening from moving about inside the enterprise. Thus the gates of vehicle entrances were soldered shut and the area behind them filled with heavy equipment: trucks, tractors, bulldozers, trailers, cranes, and concrete or steel disks, as well as piles of rocks. Wagons were put on tracks located within the enterprises. All of these actions, of course, could only be taken at big enterprises, such as steel mills, mines, shipyards, and large industrial factories in the machine or chemical industries, which encompassed dozens or hundreds of hectares. These enterprises were like little towns in and of themselves, with a large number of administrative buildings, production halls, cloakrooms, warehouses, garages, barracks, and packing rooms, with an internal network of roads and railroad tracks. In some places, people prepared to impede activities inside the buildings by blocking doors or boarding over windows, and in the Andaluzja mine people got ready for an underground defense. In terms of these kinds of passive defensive tactics, the miners were in the best position. The aggressors had a very limited scope for intervening in mines that had decided to hold underground occupation strikes. But, of course, a strike underground is probably the most dramatic form of protest; for one thing, its participants' fate is decided by those who control the basic equipment essential to the mine's operation and existence (such as electricity, air flow, drainage, and elevators, for example).

Virtually nowhere did anyone make preparations for supplies and sanitation. There were shortages of blankets (with the nighttime temperature falling to -15°C and even -20°C), medicines, first aid supplies, food, and water. Based on eyewitness accounts and people's recollections, only a few enterprises managed to supply the striking workers with these things on December 14 and 15. At the Andaluzja mine, the cafeteria was operating for a few days—and was quite well stocked. In general, however, the main source of food was whatever the workers had brought from home, packed by wives and family members, or sometimes simply bought in neighboring shops with money collected by the striking workers, their friends, and the neighbors who were helping them from outside. Striking miners from the Ziemowit and Piast mines, for example, made use of these kinds of sources, but deliveries organized in this way were in danger of being blocked at any moment, in which case the striking workers would be "defeated through hunger." The strike's only chance at success would have been if the authorities had repeated their tactics from the summer of 1980—i.e., if they had limited their aggressive activities to propaganda and did not besiege the enterprises. Or attack them.

Almost everywhere, government representatives first attempted to convince workers to call off their strikes. It was the commissioners who did this, accompanied by someone from the management. In places where these attempts failed, sooner or later operations began, and they followed more or less a single pattern: after the army formed a ring around the factory, armored vehicles moved into position, and tanks acted as battering rams to break down closed and barricaded gates and breach the obstacles on the other side. Although in some cases it was soldiers who entered the places where the striking workers were gathering, it was primarily only the ZOMO detachments and special MSW units, as well as SB functionaries, who actually entered the enterprises. Their task was to force striking workers to leave the enterprise and to arrest the most active members of the strike committees. When the striking workers put up a particularly strong resistance, the special units that existed at all voivodship militia headquarters played a key role. These numbered approximately five hundred functionaries. One unit stationed in Warsaw, which could be used anywhere in the country, had almost fifty people. Considering their level of training and weapons (including rapid-firing pistols), this elite force was significant, albeit small.

Sometimes "psychological preparation" preceded an attack on a striking enterprise: workers were instructed via high-power loudspeakers to leave the enterprise, the sound of gunshots was broadcast, and the engines of military vehicles surrounding the factory were revved at full force, even though they were in neutral, creating a deafening noise and a great deal of exhaust. Troops fired rockets, shone floodlights on buildings that were going to be under attack, and sometimes shot blanks from tanks' cannons.

Operations were usually launched at night, which heightened the sense of danger and impeded the striking workers' orientation. "Around midnight . . . judgment day began," recalled one of the employees from the Lenin Steelworks. "Howling, sirens, a terrible racket. And rockets from all sides. . . . At 1:55 a.m., tanks started moving from the rolling mill to the main gate; others were coming from the coking plant."[15] "The first shots were fired," wrote Henryk Gontarz from Świdnik. "Then loud reports from the tank cannons, bursts of machine gun fire

[and] the roar of tanks ramming fences.... There were enormous clouds of smoke and tear gas. Our eyes were burning, we were choking."[16] "Several tank cannons, probably up to ten, were firing," recounted Adam Skwira from the Wujek mine, "like on the front ... except with blanks.... That cannonade was embellished with pistol fire, too, as well as handguns and signal pistols. The psychosis this all caused began to spread."[17] There were similar scenes in many other places. Sometimes troops affected striking workers' psychology using very simple methods; for example, before the ZOMO men began their assault at the Polkowice copper mine, they turned off the lights in the rooms where there were over two thousand workers on strike. Tear gas was used often, and not only in the open, but also in enclosed spaces, which generally caused panic—justifiably.

After government forces managed to enter a complex, they began driving out the striking workers. Except in isolated instances when workers engaged in an active defense—such as at the Manifest Lipcowy and Wujek mines—the striking workers primarily employed two tactics: a combination of dispersal, hiding, and escape, or congregating in one place, which was the recommended course of action in instructions given at some locations. The first method was rarely effective, since the number of militiamen was usually so large that few managed to escape successfully from the area under threat. Those pursuing them had a better chance of beating people who were fleeing individually or in small groups. It was primarily strike committee members who were in direct danger of arrest who attempted to escape. This was just what happened at the Gdańsk Shipyard and in Wrocław, where the proximity of several enterprises allowed people to move from the one currently under attack to another. As a result, the following people were among those who managed to avoid capture: Władysław Frasyniuk, Józef Pinior, and Piotr Bednarz in Wrocław; Bogdan Borusewicz and Eugeniusz Szumiejko in Gdańsk; Mieczysław Gil (who hid for almost two weeks in the steel mill complex); and Stanisław Handzlik and Władysław Hardek at the Lenin Steelworks.

Concentrating large groups of striking workers in one place allowed them to avoid finding themselves one-on-one with ZOMO men chasing them, but in a certain sense this tactic made it possible for the aggressors to carry out their task, since sooner or later all the workers had to leave the premises. "We walked into an enormous production hall," recounted one employee of the Lenin Steelworks, "in which there was a crowd of [about a thousand people]. Young, strong people were put at the front of the hall, and behind them stood the others, close together, women in the middle.... We stood like that and sang, the hours passed, and no one came."[18] When armed men finally did appear, their commander first called on the workers to disperse. Those gathered there kneeled and began to sing religious and patriotic songs. The ZOMO functionaries pulled one person after another out of the crowd. Finally, the workers surrendered and left the hall, and were made to pass through a gauntlet of ZOMO men to vehicles that were already waiting outside. They were all taken to various police stations. Probably both tactics were employed simultaneously: some people escaped or hid in more inaccessible parts of the plant, others gathered in a hall or other large room. When there were not enough aggressors to clear striking workers from a workplace all at once, they entered several times, even over the course of a single day (for example, at Wrocław's Automatic Lathe Machine Factory), or over the next few nights (at the Gdańsk Shipyard or Katowice Steelworks, where clashes lasted for several days).

In their analyses of the situation, army staff officers used the term "first stage" for the operation that was carried out during the night of December 12–13. The "second stage" began on Monday, December 14: during this phase, it was primarily the army that was involved in the action. Warsaw was one of the places where the army actively participated in the suppression of the strikes. According to incomplete data, strikes occurred at about forty workplaces on December 14, including at several postsecondary institutions. The largest were at the Main School of Rural Economy (Szkoła Główna Gospodarstwa Wiejskiego) and at the Warsaw University of Technology (Politechnika Warszawska). The authorities must have considered it important to pacify the capital as quickly as possible, since it was actually the only place with a larger concentration of foreigners, making "a peaceful Warsaw" important in terms of their ability to influence opinion abroad. Moreover, it was about ensuring the highest leadership that the capital could function smoothly. As a result, in downtown Warsaw there were many patrols and combat vehicles at many intersections and strategic points (also near the villa where General Jaruzelski lived). On the night of December 14–15, the strikes at most of the larger Warsaw plants were broken: at Ursus, at the Świerczewski Factory of Precision Articles, at the Warsaw Steelworks, and at the Telecommunication Equipment Manufacturing Plant. The strike at FSO car factory (Fabryka Samochodów Osobowych) lasted less than a day more. There, about 2,000 workers were attacked on December 15 at 10:30 p.m. At the Warsaw Steelworks, 1,182 soldiers, 30 tanks, and 58 armored combat vehicles took part in the operation. At Ursus, there were 1,033 soldiers and 82 armored vehicles. It is worth emphasizing that, other than at FSO, there were not more than 500–1,000 workers actively participating in the strikes—i.e., those who remained on the premises of their enterprise overnight. During every operation, in addition to soldiers, hundreds of ZOMO functionaries also took part. Sometimes there were several soldiers and militiamen for every striking worker.

From a psychological point of view, just as important as pacifying Warsaw was liquidating the strikes in the "cradle of Solidarity," i.e., at the Gdańsk Shipyard, and in that entire region, where about fifty enterprises and institutions were on strike. After what was, to some extent, a test attack, carried out with relatively small forces during the night of December 13–14, the first serious blow fell a day later: on December 15 at 12:15 a.m., hundreds of ZOMO functionaries and soldiers from special units stormed the shipyard grounds and in a few hours forced almost seven thousand striking workers—who did not actively try to defend themselves—to leave the shipyard. They were not successful, however, in completely cleansing the area, which was very extensive and difficult to check. As a result, some of the striking workers—and members of all three strike committees—managed to hide. Because the shipyard grounds were not blocked, just a few hours after the aggressors left the premises, workers once again began flowing into the shipyard, although of course far fewer than the day before. The strike revived, and in the early morning hours of December 16, a second strike took place: tanks broke down the famous Gate No. 2, which was just next to the crosses commemorating the massacre of December 1970. This time, the operation was effective, but some of the strike committee members nevertheless managed to evade capture. On December 17–19 strikes were pacified at the Repair Shipyard and the Gdańsk Refinery, and striking workers were expelled from the Gdańsk Port. In contrast to other cities, in Gdańsk on December 16 and 17 there were violent street demonstrations in which approximately twenty thousand people participated each day, according to MSW figures. This number should be recognized as a minimum. During the turmoil many people were injured and one was killed. Smaller-scale street demonstrations took place on those same days in Łódź, Warsaw, Wrocław, and elsewhere.

The strike at the Lenin Steelworks was broken during a violent intervention the night of December 15–16. "When the ZOMO men stormed inside," recalled Stanisław Malara, "we were standing in the [production] hall. They positioned themselves in ranks opposite us. . . . Several ZOMO men destroyed the altar that had been erected on some carts, and stomped on the flags. The commanding officer had a detailed list of the members of the strike committee . . . [and] although he read the names out, no one responded."[19] After a couple of individuals had been pulled from the crowd, the commander of the ZOMO detachment called on those remaining to disperse, and they did. Similar situations occurred in other sections of this huge plant. The operation to "unblock" the steel mill involved 2,263 soldiers and 9 tanks. The strike in Świdnik was broken in a similar fashion. There, the army began the blockade the night of December 14–15, and the attack took place the next night. ZOMO detachments went up and down the streets within the complex and forced groups of striking workers to the gate. After several hours, even those who had been hiding in the nooks and crannies decided one by one to leave the plant. The only people who stayed—on orders from the commissioner—were those involved with the energy supplies.

The Warski Shipyard in Szczecin, where 8,000–9,000 people were on strike, was surrounded the night of December 13–14 by ZOMO, Border Defense Troops, and units of the 12th Motorized Division and the Navy (which had its landing craft on the Odra). The attack was carried out the next night: around 1 a.m. on December 15, tanks rammed the two most important entrances. Over a thousand ZOMO and armed soldiers, ready to shoot, stormed onto the square in front of the main building. Several dozen people were arrested, including all the members of the Regional Strike Committee, and workers gradually left the shipyard. Over the next few days, most appeared at work, but they engaged in an "Italian strike" (i.e., the scrupulous observance of regulations, which meant doing the bare minimum required at work). Flyers were distributed, and a barricade was even erected at one of the gates. In order to put a stop to the situation, in which at any moment there could be another mass occupation strike, on December 18, the management suspended the shipyard's activities until January 4, 1982. The night of December 15–16, the army carried out an operation at the Gryfia Repair Shipyard in Szczecin. This attack was not typical, because the shipyard is located on an island, so the assault was like an amphibious operation, carried out with the assistance of five amphibious warfare vessels, two tugboats, and two coastal defense vessels. Over four hundred ZOMO functionaries took part, and almost four hundred soldiers, who were equipped with two tanks and twenty-eight infantry combat vehicles. The entire operation, from the landing of intervention forces until the strike ended, lasted about fifteen hours.[20]

That same night, on December 15–16, "unblocking" operations were also carried out in the Copper Basin (Zagłębie Miedziowe) in Silesia. The Rudna mine was attacked only the morning of December 17, and at the Głogów Copper Mill the strike stopped on December 18. By December 16, the strikes in the Wałbrzych Basin had been pacified, as well as those in Wrocław itself, where about 30 enterprises and institutions (including post-secondary schools) had originally been on strike.

In Silesia the situation was different: there, special MO units actually used weapons, something that did not happen anywhere else. Also, because several mines held underground strikes, the protest in that area lasted the longest. Solidarity's Silesian regional organization was the largest in the country, and had the greatest number of large and very large enterprises (such as mines and steel mills), and thus also the greatest number of people who were active in enterprise commissions. As a result, this region also had the greatest number of people on the internment lists. Events at the Manifest Lipcowy and Wujek mines led people to believe that Silesia had "come to a standstill," or that, at the very least, all of the mines had. As usual, however, the reality was different: only twenty-five of sixty-six mines had been on strike. "Only?" one might ask. If these proportions had been maintained across other sectors of the economy, in the administration and academic and scientific institutions, then one could speak of a real general strike on a national scale. In short, the situation in Silesia was the most difficult for the authorities, which is why the Voivodship Defense Committee designated

Lieutenant-Colonel Marian Okrutny, deputy commanding officer of the voivodship MO, as commander of the pacification forces on the morning of December 14. The head of the Silesian Military District ordered that the pacification should start at the Katowice Steelworks. The minister of mining, however, General Czesław Piotrowski, ordered that the mines should be dealt with first. On orders from WRON, General Roman Paszkowski was appointed to the post of voivod.

Not all the miners protested by striking. "On Monday," Jerzy Sołowiej from the Gottwald mine recalled, "we went to work as usual.... We already knew that the Baildon [steelworks] was on strike, but none of us took any action. Our Commission's board dispersed, and the chairman was interned. So we kept on digging." Of twenty-five mines that had proclaimed strikes, nine were already done, under the influence of persuasion, the threat of force, and propaganda scare tactics, by December 14. From the morning of December 15, the army and ZOMO unblocked more mines (including the Staszic and Wieczorek mines). These operations took place more or less as they had elsewhere, except that they happened during the day, and ZOMO functionaries behaved especially brutally: they beat people as they were leaving the Staszic mine, which had been taken. The nearby workers' dormitories were also pacified ruthlessly. Monika Kobylańska wrote: "A tank positioned itself across from the dormitory. Water cannons drove up to the building, and began breaking the window panes with jets of water.... ZOMO burst into the stairwells.... 'Obstacle courses'[21] were set up for the miners in the buildings themselves."[22] In just one mine, 454 people were detained, of whom 156 were interned, 22 were sentenced by the misdemeanor court, and 4 were tried in court. No one counted how many people were injured.

That same day, the pacification of mines in the Rybnik Coal Area began. First came Jastrzębie, Moszczenica, and Borynia (where the strike lasted until December 18). The fourth mine on strike in this region was the Manifest Lipcowy mine.[23] This operation began around noon on December 15. After the army had hermetically sealed off the grounds, a tank broke down a barricade at the main entrance that was several meters high, which surprised the miners who were gathered on the square inside. After the tank, a ZOMO detachment penetrated the mine's grounds beyond the gate, but the miners succeeded in forcing the assailants out twice. "It did not come to hand-to-hand combat," said Czesław Kłosek, "[they just] threw various objects at each other."[24] During the third attack, a group of ten to twenty members of a "special unit" arrived at the area where people were assembled, and when the crowd once again tried to repel the assailants, shots were fired. Four miners were injured, including Kłosek, who was armed with a "thirty-centimeter-long wrench." The most he could have done was throw it at the ZOMO men who were hidden behind shields, but he didn't even have time for that. Militiamen, in contrast, were armed with Makarov pistols. Not surprisingly, the strike was over within a few hours.

The use of weapons at the Manifest Lipcowy mine had a twofold effect, as sometimes happens: while it did discourage some people from continuing to strike, it nevertheless made others even more determined to act. That is exactly the point at which miners from the Wujek mine "spontaneously began arming themselves," recalls Stanisław Płatek; "everyone looked for some kind of rod, stick, something to have ready."[25] The decision to pacify the strike at this mine was made on the evening of December 15, during a meeting of the Voivodship Defense Committee, in the presence of the MO's commander-in-chief, who had come to Katowice in light of the dangerous situation. Since Monday evening, the Wujek mine had already been partially surrounded by the army, and since Wednesday morning, all the squares adjacent to the miners' residential buildings, which were next to the mine, were occupied by armored vehicles and tanks. The commander of the 25th mechanized regiment, which had helped pacify the mine, had at his disposal two infantry battalions (i.e., six companies), two companies of tanks (a total of twenty tanks), and about sixty infantry combat vehicles. He designated the following forces to participate in the attack: eleven companies of various militia formations (including six ZOMO companies), eight companies of the Reserve Detachments of the Citizens' Militia (Rezerwowe Oddziały Milicji Obywatelskiej, ROMO) and Volunteer Reserves of the Citizens' Militia (Ochotnicza Rezerwa Milicji Obywatelskiej, ORMO), a platoon of tanks, twelve armored combat vehicles, and two army companies. The voivodship ZOMO commander, Lieutenant-Colonel Mieczysław Wilczyński, led militia detachments, with Colonel Zygmunt Pytko in command of the army.

On the morning of December 16, there were about 3,500 miners at the mine. At a public meeting, they had rejected an ultimatum forwarded by the commissar. They declared that they would resist the militia, but that if the army intervened, they would not defend themselves. Immediately before the order to launch the assault was given, an order came for women to leave the mine; it was heeded. The attack itself began about 11 a.m., when hundreds of people who had gathered in front of the gate—mainly miners' wives, mothers, and children—were dispersed. "Artillery preparations" began as well—which meant tank cannons were firing blanks. Half an hour later, two tanks broke through the walls and barricades in various places. The ZOMO followed them, shooting gas shells from flare pistols. Gas canisters were also thrown from a helicopter. Six water cannons were used during the operation, which was especially vicious in the bitter frost. An additional five fire trucks with smaller water cannons were called in as well. Although armored vehicles shielded the attacking ZOMO, the offensive broke down when they found themselves being pelted with rocks. In some places it came to hand-to-hand combat. First one of the armored vehicles was temporarily immobilized, then one of the tanks. The miners even took "prisoners of war"—an MO first lieutenant, the commander of one of the companies, and two non-commissioned officers. For a time, ZOMO functionaries were disoriented: "Commander, commander!" the officer from the army staff called out over a radio-telephone to the head of the militia units. "Let someone give that ZOMO a command! This all has to get moving, and, damn it, ZOMO are standing still, not moving an inch."[26]

About 1 p.m., the sounds of handgun fire were heard through the deafening racket: "At first," says Stanisław Płatek, "it seemed to me that they were shooting blanks, because I didn't notice anyone fall." When, however, the cloud of gas subsided for a moment, he "noticed a person lying [on the ground]," but when he ran up to him, he "felt a light jerk." A bullet had hit his shoulder. Militiamen from a special platoon were shooting; it was the same kind of platoon (or perhaps even the very same one) as the one that had taken part in the pacification of the Manifest Lipcowy mine the day before. Six people died on the spot, and several dozen miners were injured (three of them died in the hospital). According to the official report, nineteen of the twenty-two functionaries shot at least 156 bullets. After the shots had been fired, "the mine was as silent as a tomb," said Adam Skwira. "Like it usually is after a great tragedy," he added. The operations were interrupted and ambulances took away the injured, but the militia sometimes stopped them and pulled out people for whom they had been searching (including Płatek, who had been injured). A delegation of miners agreed with the director and commissioner that if ZOMO retreated from the mine's premises, the striking workers would also leave. The workers accepted this agreement and began leaving the mine around 6 p.m. As they left, they erected a cross by the boiler-room wall. The cross had been brought from the mining rescue station, where the miners had been shot. The army, armored vehicles, and ZOMO retreated several hundred meters. SB functionaries and members of the militia checked the identification of those leaving.

The Wujek mine massacre was a watershed, it can be argued, because not a single new strike broke out after this tragedy—no one rose up in protest against the crime committed against these workers. The next day, however, occupation strikes were still taking place in several enterprises, including some in Gdańsk, Warsaw, Wrocław, Kraków, the Copper Basin (Zagłębie Miedziowe), Gorzów Wielkopolski, Szczecin, and Lublin. At Katowice Steelworks the final pacification occurred on December 23. The fact that there had been fatalities among the miners was clearly a shock, particularly since the information provided to the public up to that point about the events at the Wujek mine had been interpreted for propaganda purposes. Although the number of workers participating in strikes was falling, probably a total of over a hundred thousand workers were still striking on December 17. After the tragedy at Wujek, strikes were staged at the Anna mine (until December 20) and the Ziemowit and Piast mines, where the protests took place underground. Miners from Ziemowit who later recounted their experiences said that after hearing the news about the events at

Wujek, "people became convinced that there is no leaving ... that we have to hold out as long as we can," and that "people became even more unyielding."[27] At Piast there were similar reactions: "on the one hand, it was painful, on the other—there was a will to persevere,"[28] recalled one strike leader, mine foreman Zbigniew Bogacz, the only member of the mine's management who persisted in the protest alongside his subordinates. When striking workers heard a rumor that ZOMO had descended to a depth of 650 meters below the surface, where there were about two thousand protesters gathered, "everyone rushed at those ZOMO with whatever weapons they had at hand" (fortunately, there were not actually any ZOMO). The published accounts by those from Piast and Ziemowit who participated in the strikes are not only excellent documents of everyday life in those unusually difficult conditions, but also a passionate testimony showing the strikers' determination. Any fears the miners had were overshadowed by the sense that they were doing something extremely important there, hundreds of meters underground: they were not only defending their own honor, but that of all who were resisting. Not even the priests who went to carry out their pastoral duties in the depths of the mine were able to persuade them to cease their protest. They had been sent by Bishop Henryk Bednorz of Katowice, who had been trying to convince the striking workers to come to the surface.

The Ziemowit mine laid down its arms on December 24, and the striking workers at Piast decided that they would remain over Christmas. Some of them were convinced that if they persisted, then all Poland would follow their lead after the Christmas holidays. They left the mine only on December 28, after two weeks of striking underground—no doubt a heroic deed. After leaving the mine, Bogacz was taken to the Voivodship MO Headquarters in Katowice, where he talked with functionaries for many hours—this conversation was essentially an argument about martial law. Next, he was put in a cell: "there, two ZOMO men received me, I could smell alcohol on their breath, one punched me right away. Later they told me to undress and hit me several more times with a truncheon."[29] Probably no one ordered the drunken militiamen to beat the exhausted "prisoner of war," but what they did fit perfectly into the logic of martial law: treating strength as their main argument—and asset—in the fight against Solidarity. This behavior was the effect of long training that they had received in their department.

The operation to implement martial law was an enormous undertaking, involving hundreds of thousands of people. Much of the powerful Ministry of Internal Affairs (including its Border Defense Troops) took part directly in these actions, mobilizing two hundred thousand of its own functionaries and soldiers. The main strike force, as has been mentioned here already many times, were the ZOMO detachments, but I have not been able to determine exactly how many functionaries were involved. The MSW units were reinforced by forty-six thousand reservists, two-thirds of whom were incorporated into over fifty mobile

ROMO units. Considering the mobilization date, only some of them managed to take part in the actions, and when they did, it was more in surrounding the areas where operations were taking place, and in street patrols, rather than in the enterprises themselves. Although ORMO volunteers were used in some cities, their numbers are difficult to determine. In all of Poland, they totaled more than a hundred and fifty thousand. ORMO troops, like those recruited for ROMO, usually took part in surrounding the enterprises that were being "unblocked" and in patrols. In any case, they were not used to storm factories. Functionaries involved in the implementation of martial law usually demonstrated utter loyalty, and cases of insubordination were rare, despite the fact that many of the militiamen with auxiliary functions were army reservists who had been called up ad hoc. This meant they had not been subject to systematic indoctrination, and were not associated with the MO.

Volunteers from "self-defense groups" also took part in patrols and various types of activities outside the striking enterprises. Even before martial law was declared, plans had been made for almost thirty thousand volunteers, but this number was exceeded. The units were made up primarily of retired officers, former MSW functionaries and members of the party apparatus. They fell under the authority of the regional party cells, but they were engaged in various actions according to the SB and militia's needs. They began to be formed on December 13, theoretically in every voivodship. In some they were called "Self-Defense Regiments," and they were usually headed by higher-ranking officers of the active service. The regiments were divided into "independent companies" (over ten in every voivodship), which in turn were divided into platoons and squads. Their headquarters were usually in local party buildings. Members of the groups received training in shooting and the use of tear gas grenades, but were unarmed when on duty. The "self-defense" units, in principle, did not help pacify strikes at the enterprises. Their main task was to patrol the streets and areas around enterprises, protect party buildings, and conduct propaganda events at enterprises (as time passed, this role became more important), and "collect information about individuals and groups whose intentions could result in terrorism or sabotage."

During a teleconference with the first secretaries of the voivodship committees, which took place three days after the announcement of martial law, Kazimierz Barcikowski pointed out that "self-defense groups must comprise part of the general forces" and warned that they should not be concentrated hurriedly, but that they should instead be "introduced with the appropriate armband in patrols wherever possible." Moreover, he admonished that members of these groups not make a show of the fact that "some of the party *aktiv* is armed."[30] Based on decisions made many months before December 13, probably no fewer than approximately 8,000–10,000 party members and functionaries from various levels (including members of the Central Committee)—who were not part of the self-defense groups—were supplied with pistols from MSW stock. Admittedly, I am not aware of any case in which any of these people actually used their weapons, but the very fact that a large group of party members was armed is, I believe, important in understanding what martial law was in the popular imagination. In any case, undoubtedly those tens of thousands of people belonging to the party's armed squads should be counted among the forces that took part in the implementation of martial law.

The SB, which had over twenty-two thousand functionaries at the time, occupied a special place in the preparation and implementation of martial law. About half of its members were operational officers. Those working in the following departments had a leading role: Department III, dealing with the opposition; Department V, created on November 7, 1981, for dealing with Solidarity in workplaces; and Department IV, for matters related to the Church. In December 1981, Department III had almost nine hundred functionaries, not including employees at its headquarters, and Department V had over sixteen hundred. In addition to their role during the round-up the night of December 12–13, these functionaries were visible primarily as the strikes were being broken and the most active striking workers were being caught, as well as those who had already attracted the SB's interest and were included on the proscription lists.

The operational officers and functionaries of the investigative department interrogated those who had been arrested and decided their fate (arrest, internment, or release). Informers were in part recruited through these interrogations and the conversations carried out as part of Operation "Maple" (Klon), as well as the half-interrogations, half-conversations with internees (which SB terminology called "operational dialogues"). By December 20, almost 5,200 people had been summoned for such talks as part of Operation "Maple." Of these, approximately 380 who refused to sign loyalty oaths were interned.[31] If we are to believe the data contained in the official reports, the recruitment was quite effective: by December 20, almost 1,600 people had been "gained for collaboration." Probably, however, as was usually the case in this kind of mass campaign, secret informers acquired in this manner were actually only of little operational value, if any.

As part of its preparation for "G" hour, the security apparatus also engaged in activities aimed at guaranteeing the ability to collect information through informers and to influence the expected strikes. Some of these activities were linked to Operation "Renaissance" (Renesans)—an attempt to usurp Solidarity, which will be discussed here separately. Conducting operational work was hampered because the traditional methods of contact with secret informers, such as making appointments by telephone, or meeting at contact points or in public places, were often not viable, either because communications had been blocked, or because it was difficult to find suitable meeting places. If a strike was well organized, then entering and exiting the enterprise was to a certain extent monitored. When martial law was introduced, there were about 12,200 secret informers on file with the departments mentioned above (two-thirds of whom were from Department V). I was unable to determine, however, how many of these were actually active, and how many only represented "dead souls"—i.e., officially registered, but no longer active. I am also unable to say anything about the quality of their work. Other than the obvious informational activities, such as supplying news about the course of the strikes and the names of workers who were most active in them, the SB primarily attempted to influence the course of events through its instructions to the network of agents who had infiltrated Solidarity.

In one of the reports prepared at the militia headquarters in Warsaw about this kind of activity, we read: "The main task of these people will be to calm the mood and to wait . . . passively for the 'situation to be clarified,' or for instructions from the union's higher officials. An operation explaining the futility of undertaking spectacular actions without coordinating them first with other union organizations will also be conducted." The blocking of telephones and telexes "allows the time necessary to calm the [public] mood and control the situation."[32] From this and other documents, we can clearly see that the aim was to defuse emotions, impede the strikes or persuade them to stop, sow misunderstandings in the strike committees, and weaken the determination of the striking workers. In addition to informers, some cadre officers also infiltrated the striking enterprises, but there is no information about their activities. SB functionaries were, in contrast, often overtly present—for example, during the talks among the strike committees and the management and military commissioners. Their presence was useful in planning attacks on the striking enterprises.

Over 53,000 soldiers took part in the implementation of martial law, which amounted to about one-sixth of the armed forces. Most participated directly in breaking strikes, which took place at sixty-two enterprises. Approximately 16,000 soldiers were assigned to protect buildings and railway lines, about 4,500 took part in Operation "Azalea," and approximately 2,300 served along with militiamen at traffic posts. By January 31, 1982, tanks taken from the barracks had traveled 404,200 kilometers, which means that each of them traveled an average of about 300 kilometers. Various types of armored vehicles moved a total of approximately 1,100,000 kilometers, which means that they each went, on average, 590 kilometers.[33] The direct costs of implementing martial law were enormous and reached several tens of billions of złotys, which covered the cost of fuel, destroyed equipment, chemicals used, increased salaries and benefits for the families of those on active military duty, and supplemental food and uniforms for the over 50,000 people who were mobilized to serve in the military and MSW.

Almost everyone—the organizers of martial law themselves, as well as foreign observers—was in agreement that the operation was carried out masterfully, and that it was a true *Blitzkrieg*. Nevertheless, analyses of the military operations offered plenty of criticism. They did not actually refer to the fact that many traffic accidents occurred during the movement of armored units. No fewer than ten people died as a result, including both soldiers and civilians, of whom two were children. The first fatality occurred on December 13, when a tank fell from a bridge near Żagań. Flagrant errors and shortcomings were mostly to blame. The activities of the 16th Armored Division in particular prompted many objections: the convoy was extremely stretched out and chaos crept in, in part because there were few maps, but also because there was a lack of preparation in terms of supplies. Soldiers in many units suffered from frostbite, and hundreds had no warm meals. There were also supply problems in other units, and some went into action with unnecessary equipment. One of the commanding officers took twelve rocket launchers from the barracks—heaven knows why—and another unit of 122 mm howitzers. Did they think that they were going to bombard the enterprises?

To sum up: the implementation of martial law was an extremely costly operation whose burden was all the more onerous because it was carried out in a country that was mired in a deep economic crisis. It brought enormous social costs and economic losses, military and MSW expenditures notwithstanding. Moreover, there were at least eleven fatalities just during the strike pacifications and demonstrations on December 16–17, as well as dozens of people seriously wounded and hundreds with more minor injuries, in addition to badly damaged buildings, equipment, and roads. Production in important enterprises was halted for many days. In terms of supplies, practically the entire national economy was in chaos. There were also difficulties in foreign trade, as well as a serious disruption to health services because communications were blocked, which may have resulted in even dozens of deaths simply because those in need of aid did not receive it, since no one knew their lives were in danger. The various hardships of daily life, which had already been going on for years, were now exacerbated for many days, and sometimes weeks. Shops were even less well stocked than usual; during the first few days after martial law was declared, even buying bread was a problem. Sometimes military and militia patrols, conscientiously adhering to martial law regulations, would disperse the lines that had formed in front of shops before the curfew was finished.

Protests in the form of occupation strikes ended definitively fifteen days after martial law was imposed. An MSW summary dated December 20, however, noted that "there has already been a breakthrough in the political and social situation of the country,"[34] which does seem to have been the case. This is relevant in that from December 15 the number of strikes and workers on strike diminished, and thus resistance clearly lost its initial momentum, and was also gradually changing its character. Marshal Kulikov's return to Moscow on the night of December 16–17 was a sign that events had taken a positive turn in the government's favor. He left just as he had arrived—secretly, and discreetly, by plane. Clearly, the Kremlin decided that help was no longer necessary. The various MSW dispatches, and even entries in "Operational Diaries," including those from the General Staff, had less and less information about the "unblocking" of enterprises, or about the number of internees. At the same time, there was ever more information about the publication of flyers and the underground Solidarity structures that were forming. As the last striking miners were coming to the surface, Solidarity went underground.

Chapter Seven

Reprisals and the Public Mood

"I am asking you, the functionaries of the Citizens' Militia and the Security Service—to guard the state against the enemy, and the working people against lawlessness and violence," General Jaruzelski said, announcing the imposition of martial law.[1] One can still somehow understand "guard the state against the enemy," although everything suggested that the state—as the general understood it—was not under threat by NATO armies or Bundeswehr commandos, but rather by the opposition of many of its own citizens. But from whose "lawlessness and violence" were the militiamen supposed to be guarding the "working people"? I would hesitate to call his appeal cynical, because neither General Jaruzelski, nor the author of the draft of this speech, Wiesław Górnicki, was a cynic, although they did often engage in conceptual acrobatics. I believe that this appeal stemmed from a kind of self-indoctrination and the fact that Jaruzelski saw reality through the prism of Marxist dogmas, and thus described it with strongly ideological language. Making use of the full force of state propaganda, those in power had been trying to convince public opinion for so long that Solidarity—and especially its "extremists"—was preparing to take power in the state by means of force, to overthrow the regime, and launch a bloody settling of accounts with its defenders, that they themselves had probably started to believe in their own declarations, and required their obedient propagandists to proclaim them as well. In their language, Solidarity was simply an enemy. A miner from the Wujek mine who was interned the night of December 13, Jan Ludwiczak, or his friend Adam Skwira, arrested a few days later, were identified with the enemy, not with the "working people," because they were Solidarity activists. It was against them that militia and secret police were supposed to be protecting the miners and shipyard workers.

The militia and secret police functionaries did not really need any prodding to act, as General Jaruzelski probably knew full well. After all, they had all been preparing themselves for a long time for precisely this kind of confrontation, which started with operations "Azalea" and "Fir." The leadership at the Ministry of Internal Affairs was a notorious advocate of a tough stance against enemies. In 1976–77, plans had even been made to kill or kidnap one of the democratic opposition's most active members, Adam Michnik, who happened to be abroad at that time. In May 1977, Stanisław Pyjas, who had been cooperating with KOR, was killed, and one of the witnesses in that case later died under mysterious circumstances. The governing clique, wanting to avoid fomenting additional tensions in society, reined in the secret police both when the opposition was organizing itself and during the August strikes. Above all, it wanted to be seen abroad as a liberal government, because of Poland's debt and the Polish economy's dependence on the West. From midnight on December 13, however, new tactics were in force, and orders went out that would surely be music to any Chekist's ears: beat the enemy. They finally had a free hand.

The examples provided here show what these tactics were like in practice during the "night of the general" and the pacification of the strikes. Ruthlessness, brutality, and aggression prevailed, and only occasionally could they have been the result of emotions unleashed during a direct clash. This was the case, for example, when striking workers defended themselves actively (at the Manifest Lipcowy and Wujek mines), or as thousands of demonstrators were being dispersed (such as on December 16 and 17 in Gdańsk). Nevertheless, government functionaries were also brutal when rounding people up from their homes, or beating those who had been detained at police stations, or when arbitrarily pulling someone out of a peaceful crowd. Aggression peaked when government forces were pursuing fleeing workers, or when those leaving a strike were sent through an "obstacle course." Zenon Szmidke, a miner from the Staszic mine, recalls that a militiaman "who was shouting ordered me to go outside the building and stand by the wall of the cafeteria. When I left the hall, I found myself between rows of ZOMO . . . [who were] shouting 'run,' and hitting [me] with batons wherever they could."[2] This kind of scene was played out hundreds of times.

The only people who had direct experience of this violence were its victims, or those who witnessed the militia's behavior. The public was mainly supposed to be impressed by the scale of reprisals. By the morning of December 22, approximately 5,200 people had been interned—almost 1,000 more than the foreseen limits. This was because the original concept of internment had changed somewhat. At first, it was intended to be primarily a preventative measure to keep those considered dangerous from organizing strikes and mass protests. The psychological impact of arresting intellectual or moral authorities was also crucial. This is why well-known cultural and academic figures—people who were unlikely to lead workers' strikes or throw rocks during street demonstrations—were detained as well as Solidarity members. From December 14, internment essentially became a type of arrest.

Internment was, however, more convenient, since it depended on administrative decisions made by the voivodship militia commandants, and as such was not subject to the control of the courts. Moreover, according to the order signed by Prime Minister Jaruzelski, the period of internment was undefined. The only limitation was an enigmatic note stating that "it will cease the day martial law is lifted." No one knew when this would happen, not even the main architect of martial law. Although some of the internees were released after several weeks (approximately six hundred were released even in time for Christmas), several hundred individuals remained in isolation for over a year. As the regulations began to be interpreted more broadly, striking workers were interned, too, along with demonstrators and people involved in organizing underground structures and distributing flyers. In the summer and autumn of 1982, numerous preventative internments took place before expected Solidarity-related events. Sometimes individuals were interned who had already been tried. For example, on May 12, 1982, engineer Zbigniew Bogacz and six workers accused of organizing the strike at the Piast mine were interned upon leaving the court building after the conclusion of their trial, in which they had been acquitted. Although those formulating the regulations had been more concerned about preventing people from committing illegal acts, in reality internment was also employed as a punishment for deeds that had already been committed. The authorities deliberately took advantage of the possibilities afforded by the institution of internment for the duration of martial law. By December 1982, a total of 9,736 people had been interned (of whom four hundred were interned twice).[3] For a single kind of activity, one could either be sentenced by a court (or court of misdemeanors) or interned. Sometimes it is difficult to discern any clear criteria for how people were treated.

People who were interned as part of Operation "Fir" were transported to over thirty predetermined prisons, where they were placed in designated buildings, barracks, or cells that were isolated from prisoners who were there for criminal offenses. In bureaucratic terminology, these places were called "isolation centers." Conditions were very harsh, particularly in the beginning. In some of the prisons, barracks were unheated and water trickled down the walls. Sometimes the water would freeze on the walls and floor. The internees were given shabby, dirty blankets, and efforts to provide medical care were hampered. In some prisons, however, conditions were better, even significantly so. Some of these centers were considered to be temporary, and the internees were moved to other prisons after a short stay. In all, there were fifty-two "isolation centers" that operated either the entire period that internment was used, or periodically. Some of the "moves" between centers were intended to prompt internal divisions among the internees, and to create the impression that the government was capable of being indulgent and magnanimous.

This is how one may interpret the decision to move several dozen intellectuals on Christmas Eve 1981 to the military holiday retreat Jaworze, where conditions were decidedly better than in the prisons. Despite their protests against this special treatment, they were held there until May 1982, when they were moved to a seaside holiday retreat in Darłówko, which became known as the "golden cage." From January 6, 1982, many of the female internees from all over Poland were moved to a holiday retreat at Gołdap, in the Mazurian Lakes region, near the Soviet border. During the first days of martial law, one of the largest isolation centers was a penitentiary in the Warsaw suburb of Białołęka, where almost three hundred people were imprisoned. Members of the National Commission and some union advisors were placed in a separate section ("pavilion IV"), where their conditions were, for a while, worse than those of the rest of the internees. One of the centers was in Kamienna Góra, in the same buildings that had once housed a satellite of Gross Rosen, the notorious German concentration camp. Of course, this prompted outrage among the internees and a protest by the Church. On instructions from the Ministry of Justice, internees were granted certain privileges, to varying degrees, compared to prisoners who were serving time for criminal offenses. The internees could have open cells, group walks (and longer ones), more frequent visits from their families, and more opportunities to buy food in the prison canteen.

In all the centers (even in the "golden cage"), constant tension existed between the prison staff and internees, who liked to express their views, demanded that regulations be respected, and often resorted to protests, such as hunger strikes. Thus, disputes were frequent and some of them ended in violent intervention by the guards, special guard units, or even ZOMO detachments. The monthly "anniversaries" marking the imposition of martial law would almost inevitably aggravate the situation. The internees would observe these dates, as was done in general by those at liberty, too, as days of protest. Sometimes these occasions were marred by extensive violence. For example, on February 13, in the internment center in Wierzchów Pomorski, more than a dozen people were severely beaten, and several dozen less severely so. Sometimes the issues related to living conditions, or family visits, gave rise to serious conflicts. The brutal pacification of the center in Kwidzyn in mid-August 1982 was sparked by such concerns. There, not only were the people gathered outside dispersed, but cells were "silenced" one by one. As a result, nearly eighty internees were beaten (almost half), including more than a dozen who were beaten so badly that they required hospitalization.[4] Sometimes, however, mass beatings were simply the result of the guards' own brutality and alcohol abuse. In the Iława prison, whose staff was notorious for its brutality, several dozen guards beat the residents of one cell ruthlessly on March 25, without any reason or even any pretext. The prison physician was not called for the victims, and an internee who was a doctor was not allowed to see them either.[5]

For the internees, the SB's activities at the centers—which included recruiting informers—were a serious problem. Sławomir Cenckiewicz has researched this topic in the context of the prison in Strzebielinek.[6] Out of the 491 people who passed through this center during martial law, various types of operational talks were held with 306 of them, and 29 were recruited. It is interesting that almost all were recruited during the first month. It is hard to say whether winning over 6 percent (29 out of 491) of the internees is a lot or a little, but the SB undoubtedly took great pains to infiltrate the community of internees so that it could conduct various kinds of disinformational and disintegrational activities. These included fomenting discord among the internees and influencing their opinions.

The SB conducted operational games (more or less subtly) in all of the internment centers. These included, for example, the granting of additional privileges (such as passes), intended as a reward for cooperating with the secret police. Rumors were also started about certain people being informers. Sometimes discipline was relaxed for internees with more moderate views, which served to further radicalize the radicals, thus intensifying polarization and heightening conflicts. At other times, privileges were simply used as a means of manipulation. For example, in one of the prisons, some of the internees had locked cells, and others had open ones. When there was an occasion for internees to sing patriotic or religious songs, the ones housed in open cells hesitated, not wanting to lose their privileges. In most of the centers, the SB conducted an operation under the cryptonym "Club Room." Permission was granted for meetings (such as name day celebrations) in the prison common rooms, which were tapped. Bugs were also placed in the cells and in the prison yards used for walks. Convincing people to cooperate was made easier by the fact that regulations did not define how long someone's isolation would last; thus, people were allowed to be released for "good behavior" or health reasons—things that operatives could use as arguments during recruitment. For the SB, an additional advantage to operational work in the isolation centers was that internees sooner or later left the prisons, so conflicts arising "behind bars" could be transferred to the underground, and the recruited informers could continue to collaborate.

In March 1982, the SB began trying on quite a large scale to convince Solidarity and opposition activists to emigrate, and they publicized it in the press. The aim was, above all, to rid the country of individuals who were a threat to the system, but probably also to foment conflict within enemy ranks. Permission to leave the country constituted a very serious temptation, since even just being granted a passport was the dream of millions of Poles. Moreover, many of those interned and arrested were rightly afraid they would not find work after their release from prison. Information spread quickly throughout Poland that most Western countries would grant new immigrants from Poland political asylum or permanent residency with few problems, and would even provide them with financial assistance and help in finding a job. At first, the main venues for finding willing potential émigrés were the internment centers, but efforts were extended to include the prison's usual inmates as well. A certain group of inmates incarcerated for criminal offenses was offered the chance to emigrate, perhaps based on the example of Fidel Castro's Cuba. In this case, authorities were undoubtedly attempting to rid the country of an unwanted element, as well as mar the image of émigrés abroad in general.

Chapter Seven

The first people willing to emigrate began to leave in the late spring of 1982.[7] By the end of December 1982, about 5,000 people (including internees' family members) had announced their willingness to leave. Permission was granted to 4,385 people, of whom 1,247 had been interned; 2,320 others were internees' family members. Passports were issued to 921 internees (and 1,756 of their family members), and 165 people (and 223 members of their families) were categorized as "conducting hostile political activities." Passports were also issued to 68 criminals (and 84 members of their families). Another Ministry of Internal Affairs document states that almost 500 internees and their families had left Poland by mid-December 1982, but that not everyone who was granted a passport used it immediately. The operation continued in the coming years, although on a smaller scale: from January 1 to December 31, 1983, about 2,600 new applications (including families) were registered. Among the internees who received permission to go abroad were 36 (of 107) members of the National Commission, 229 members of regional boards, and 527 members of enterprise commissions. These numbers represent a serious bloodletting. It is interesting that approximately one-fifth of those applying for permission to leave were from Silesia, but this figure is difficult to explain in light of the lack of research on the subject. Perhaps it is an indirect indication of how drastic the experience of the strikes was there, but it also perhaps suggests there was a conviction that a miner or skilled laborer would not have much trouble finding work abroad.

The conversations during which the SB offered people the chance to emigrate (or the fate of an exile, depending on how one looked at it) were seen as "operational talks," and were used as a chance to engage in disintegrational activities as well. The problem of whether to leave or not became a source of internal conflicts and dilemmas at the internment centers. It is very likely that the SB's emigration program was also used as a chance to recruit new informers for the intelligence service. The fact that so many people agreed to emigrate may attest to a lower motivation to engage in trade union (or political) activities after the imposition of martial law, when the degree of risk was higher. In the end, approximately one-fifth of all those interned left Poland; not all of them continued to support Solidarity actively from abroad.

The efforts to have people sign loyalty oaths—an extension of Operation "Maple"—also had a strong impact on the internees. As the research by Cenckiewicz cited above shows, almost a hundred people (one-fifth of internees) signed loyalty oaths at Strzebielinek. Half of them did so in the first month following the imposition of martial law. Because signing a loyalty oath was treated as something dishonorable, those who signed them tried to conceal their weakness, which of course gave the SB functionaries additional leverage, since they could then use this fact to blackmail them. Internment, an institution whose aim was above all the precautionary isolation of the most dangerous individuals, thus became entwined in a system in which an important role was played by various operational activities designed to exert pressure on people, and to humiliate and subordinate them.

The instrumentalization of law, including the regulations regarding internment, was essentially boundless. "On the freezing night of 12–13 December . . . they woke me up by pounding on my door. . . . They rushed me the whole time. I hardly managed to get dressed, and they packed me into a car and took me to the militia headquarters."[8] Those are not the reminiscences of an opposition or Solidarity activist, but of nearly seventy-year-old Edward Gierek, the former first secretary who was interned during the "night of the general," just like thousands of other people. The only difference was that the commanding officer of the group carrying out the arrest was one of the first secretary's own personal guards.

Over thirty people who held posts of varying importance in communist Poland shared a similar fate. Sometimes these were even leading figures, including former prime ministers Piotr Jaroszewicz and Edward Babiuch, and Zdzisław Grudzień, a former member of the Politburo. As we know from published accounts, they were treated the same as the intellectuals who were imprisoned. (They were interned not far from them, at a military holiday retreat on the coast.) Taking into account their position and material status, sincere (for the most part) attachment to the socialist state, and personal relationships with those administering martial law, finding themselves isolated in that way must have been a much greater shock for them than for the interned trade unionists or opposition intellectuals. The isolation of these high-ranking individuals, which was announced alongside the lists of interned "counter-revolutionaries," was a complete surprise to the public. It did, however, work well with some of the elements present in government propaganda since August 1980: the singling out of scapegoats and the inculcation of the idea that the crisis was directly caused by the mistakes, and even crimes, committed by specific people in power, not the communist system as such. Isolating these people was meant to provide additional justification for the internment of Solidarity activists and enable those currently in power to present themselves as a just government, combating evil regardless of who was responsible for it.

The decision to intern prominent communist party leaders was, no doubt, a cynical psychological trick. Since it was perhaps a little too transparent, it is difficult to assess what impact it had on public opinion. After a while, when the propaganda effect had worn off, it proved awkward and perhaps even embarrassing for General Jaruzelski's team. The Sejm obediently approved changes to the constitution (March 26, 1982) that introduced an institution called the State Tribunal (Trybunał Stanu), which could try Gierek and others, sanctioning their internment. In the end, however, it was decided not to hold a trial, probably primarily out of fear that it might be pointed out that some of martial law's architects (including, most importantly, Jaruzelski himself) had for years occupied places alongside the accused in top decision-making bodies.

The creators of martial law and the lawyers who crafted it may have been surprised to see that internment became the most widespread form of direct punitive political reprisal. It is striking that during the entire period of martial law (i.e., until July 21, 1983), 7,400 people were sentenced for crimes related to resisting martial law,[9] which was fewer than were interned. Trials were nevertheless more important than internment in terms of influencing public opinion and maintaining the psychosis of martial law. This was because trials could be put to good use for propaganda purposes: accounts of the trials could be published in the press and broadcast on the radio; selected excerpts could be shown on television or in cinema newsreels. In accordance with the legal acts passed on December 13, military courts were also authorized to try cases involving crimes committed in connection with martial law, in addition to the general courts, and the military prosecutors' competencies were expanded accordingly. The military judiciary was much more active than the civilian one: the military courts sentenced approximately 5,700 people "for crimes related to the decree on martial law," which was more than three-quarters of the total.

The emergency legislation of martial law introduced special summary procedures that were significantly faster: the public prosecutor had fifteen days to conduct the proceedings, and the court was required to hear the case within five days of receiving the indictment. Moreover, these summary procedures contained a very important regulation stating that punishments could amount to no fewer than three years' imprisonment, which made it a truly draconian act. In general, it was the relevant SB cells that would decide whether to deal with a deed judicially, or whether to use internment. In practice, they also made decisions about whether to send a matter to the general public prosecutor, or to the military one, who should only have dealt with crimes committed in militarized institutions or in connection with military activities. It was the public prosecutors, however, who decided whether or not to employ summary procedures. Because of the sudden increase in cases in the military courts, lawyers in the reserves were mobilized, as well as retired military judges and prosecutors. The authorities of martial law, as we see, had very strong legal instruments at their disposal to exact obedience, although of course these had been decreed from above and introduced in violation of principles such as *lex retro non agit* (a law does not apply retroactively).

In the short document "The Main Conclusions and Propositions Collected from Situational Reports," prepared on December 19, 1981, by the Main Political Directorate of the Polish Army, we read that "among soldiers . . . there exists a belief that the government is using reprisal methods that are too lenient," and that "the effects of the justice system's activities conducted according to summary procedures are not visible enough."[10] One can find many similar opinions in the various types of documents from the party, military, and Ministry of Internal Affairs that date to first few weeks, or even months, of martial law. Mieczysław Rakowski wrote in his diary on December 17 that Wojciech Jaruzelski "is pressing every day for sentences finally to start flowing." On December 23, he noted that it was important to Jaruzelski that "the first sentences be handed down."[11] In short, both "at the bottom" (if one is to believe the reports of the Main Political Directorate [Główny Zarząd Polityczny]) and "at the top" there were clear expectations that prosecutors and judges would act quickly and vigorously—and harshly. One could say that this grievance was justified, since fewer than a hundred cases had been sent to the courts by December 21. This was, however, just the beginning.

The quickest court was probably the Regional Court in Lubin in Lower Silesia. There, proceedings began already on December 17 in two cases regarding the violation of martial law regulations—as strikes were still underway in the region. Even before Christmas, trials began, for example, in Radom, Katowice, and Bytom. After the holidays, the numbers of trials—and sentences—increased from one day to the next. In late December and early January, some of the best publicized were the sentences for members of the Regional Board of Solidarity in Konin (December 28); the members of the strike committee from one of the enterprises in Bochnia (December 28);[12] Andrzej Słowik and Jerzy Kropiwnicki, Solidarity leaders from the Łódź Region (December 30); members of the strike committee from the Warski Shipyard in Szczecin (January 2); and journalists from the *Wolny Związkowiec* (*Free Trade Unionist*) news sheet at the Katowice Steelworks (January 5). On January 13, the court received an indictment against nine members of the strike committee at the Wujek mine, for whom the military prosecutor sought ten to fifteen years in prison.

At first, the vast majority of the indictments related to the strikes, but before long, many people were being tried for distributing flyers, news sheets or "continuing union activities." In Białystok, the author of a handwritten flyer reading "We demand the release of political prisoners" was sentenced to three years in prison. On December 17, a worker was tried for wearing a Solidarity armband to work with a piece of black cloth on it to show mourning on the anniversary of the 1970 massacre.[13] In Warsaw, a student was sentenced to two years in prison because on December 15 he read a flyer out loud on the street. The Air Force Court sentenced a worker at the Konin Aluminum Mill to three years in prison for creating two handwritten flyers. One miner was sentenced to three years in prison for an appeal that he scattered during a strike that said: "We will fight until our last drop of blood," which was deemed an incitement to commit a crime. Priests also became the victims of prosecutors' and judges' zeal: on December 20, Father Bolesław Jewulski from Połczyn-Zdrój was indicted for having delivered a sermon in which he, as the charge alleged, "publicly insulted and derided the social and political system of the Polish People's Republic and its leading [state] organs, and spread false information." Father Stefan Dzierżek, rector of the Jesuit college in Kalisz, was accused of displaying a symbolic nativity scene during Christmas, which "included information [!] threatening the interests of the Polish People's Republic." Father Franciszek Mazur, a Benedictine from Tyniec near Kraków, was sentenced to six and a half years in prison for distributing flyers—another example of how regulations were subject to this kind of drastic interpretation.

Since the trials differed significantly, it is very difficult to determine any patterns in the activities of the justice system. Maria Stanowska, author of a monograph on the Warsaw courts during martial law, writes that this situation was understandable since "as usual, it was specific people who decided about the form of political trials from this period."[14] Thus, for the same crime, very different sentences were handed down depending on the city and court. One could also receive an identical sentence for activities that had vastly different significances: the same sentence might have been handed down for affixing handmade flyers to a wall and for participating in a strike in a militarized factory. One of the most important factors influencing the severity of the sentence was what type of trial it was (whether it was summary, expedited, or normal). Sometimes, however, courts would change the type of procedure from summary to normal (about 20 percent were changed in this way), thus avoiding the mandatory minimum sentence of three years in prison. Most often, this procedure was applied after February–March 1982.

On the basis of what is only fragmentary data, one can conclude that the courts often refused to acquiesce to prosecutors' demands and instead gave lower or suspended sentences, and even pronounced defendants not guilty, or dismissed cases. All over Poland, during the entire duration of martial law, about 10 percent of the cases heard in military courts ended with sentences of not guilty, or with the cases being dismissed. Sometimes courts changed a "crime" to a "misdemeanor," which was subject to lighter sentencing (with a fine or detention). The example of Warsaw demonstrates the great variations in sentencing. At the Court for the Ochota District, almost 55 percent of defendants were pronounced not guilty, and in the section for the Praga district, about 92 percent were sentenced.[15] Some judges would always sentence all the defendants, and others would only acquit them. Even the Supreme Court did not always acquiesce to prosecutors' appeals, although it was considered quite "tough," as exemplified by its decision that the announcement of legal acts related to martial law on television would be equivalent to publishing them formally.

During the first weeks, most sentences conformed to the obligatory three-year minimum, but there were also significantly higher ones. The length of the sentence depended on the judge's personality and views, and on the degree to which pressure was being exerted by the voivodship defense committees, commissioners, or party authorities at different levels. Of the nine miners accused from the Wujek mine, four were sentenced to three to four years in prison (the rest were acquitted), but in the trial of miners from the Andaluzja mine, the highest sentence was five years; in the trial of miners from the Ziemowit mine and members of the strike committee at the Katowice Steelworks, sentences were seven years, and journalists from the publication *Wolny Związkowiec* from that same plant received sentences of from three to six and a half years in prison. The arrested leaders from the Lenin Steelworks strike were sentenced to three and a half to four years in prison, and the leaders of Solidarity in Łódź were sentenced to four and a half years each, although they had only been agitating for a strike. The Naval Court passed the highest sentences: in two trials related to the strike at the Maritime College, a total of ten people were sentenced, including Ewa Kubasiewicz, who received a sentence of ten years in prison (which was the highest sentence any Solidarity activist received), and the others were given three to nine year sentences. That same court meted out punishments of up to seven and a half years in prison for the strike at the Gdańsk Port.

In many cases, fines were imposed as additional punishments; for example, in the trial of strike leaders at the Katowice Steelworks, all the accused had to pay a fine from 15,000 to 20,000 złotys. Sometimes the accused would be deprived of their public rights, which could be particularly humiliating. There were judges who would not only hand down long sentences, but who would also justify them in a way that defied logic and cast doubt on the fairness of the proceedings. Patrycjusz Kosmowski, the chairman of the Podbeskidzie Region, who had been in hiding since December 13, was arrested after a month and sentenced to six years in prison. The judge from the Voivodship Court in Bielsko-Biała, who had no material evidence regarding the defendant's activities, wrote in his reasons for the judgment that "it is improbable that the defendant ... would suddenly decide to abandon all union activities."[16] The judge assumed that the accused had to have engaged in such activities at least for a while, and thus deserved a stringent sentence. As a general rule, charges and trials concerning strikes were based on the testimonies of militiamen and people from the management of the enterprise or guards. There was no photographic or audio documentation, to say nothing of written documents. If such documents did exist, they were not shown to the court. "The charges were about nothing," recalls a miner from the Andaluzja mine, "[there was] no witness who could have confirmed [that someone] specific was to blame ... that someone said something on the rostrum, that someone went [somewhere]. . . . Someone needed to be charged, the plan had to be carried out."[17] Thus, much depended on the judges, but to some extent also on the witnesses. The director of the Julia mine, appearing before the court as a witness, spoke out in defense of the strike committee and allegedly said, "If you really must try [people], then all the [striking workers] need to be tried."[18] The defendants were given suspended sentences, but the director was fired.

People who had been arrested were in a significantly worse situation than their interned colleagues. Above all, they had experienced investigations of varying lengths, during which there were often beatings, blackmail (for example, involving their families), and threats. Especially in Upper Silesia, a large number of people were suddenly imprisoned for investigative detention, which caused overcrowding and a significant deterioration in living conditions. After the court announced its decisions, those sentenced were scattered in various penitentiaries and efforts were made to keep them separated. Often they would be placed in cells with inmates who were serving criminal sentences. Nevertheless, political prisoners were sometimes concentrated, since Poland had a shortage of prisons. Two of the prisons in which there were more than a hundred inmates "sentenced for Solidarity" included one in Strzelce Opolskie, which had a tighter regime, and one in Hrubieszów. As we see from the accounts from inmates there—and there are many fewer accounts of this kind compared to those written by internees—the criminal inmates treated them rather well. They were not subject to the pressures of prison subculture. There were rarely cases of aggression or of currying favor with the guards to the detriment of the inmates. Violence among inmates was rare but did occur: a worker from Przemyśl, detained by a militia patrol with one copy of a flyer that he had found at a bus stop, was placed into investigative detention, where he died on April 3 after having been beaten by criminal inmates. It is not known, however, whether he was beaten because he had been charged with political crimes, or whether it was just a case of common thuggery.[19]

It is difficult to assess whether political prisoners were treated worse than those imprisoned for criminal offenses. The living conditions in Polish prisons were in general very bad, and sometimes even exceedingly bad, and the penitentiary authorities did not see any reason of course why a worker sentenced for participation in a strike or for distributing flyers should enjoy better conditions than anyone else. Political prisoners did not have the kinds of privileges that existed in internment centers. They were subject to the usual regulations regarding the serving of prison terms. They were in hostile or alien environments, which made their situations markedly worse. They could also fall victim to guards' aggression more easily. It was more difficult for them to receive charity from the Church, or even pastoral care, which both played quite an important role in helping care for internees spiritually and physically. The fact that they were under psychological pressure from what were sometimes quite long prison sentences, and were generally kept in very difficult conditions, facilitated the SB's operational activities. It has proved impossible, however, to find any credible documents that would shed light on just what the scope of these activities was. In any case, informers were also recruited among these political prisoners, and people were encouraged to emigrate, with promises of better treatment or shorter prison terms.

During martial law, provisions were also enacted regarding misdemeanors, and were among the legal instruments used to calm the atmosphere, discipline society, and punish enemies. Misdemeanor courts dealt with such cases. The decisions of these bodies have not yet been studied, so it is difficult to say precisely what proportion of the offenses was related to charges of political activities (participating in strikes, distributing flyers, or taking part in "gatherings"), and how many were ordinary misdemeanors against the regulations of martial law, such as breaking the curfew, leaving one's place of residence without appropriate permission from relevant authorities, or not having one's identification document. The clear majority of cases dealt with in the courts of misdemeanor were of this nature. During the entire time martial law was in force, approximately 208,000 people were punished, including 30,000 for misdemeanors associated with demonstrations, public meetings, or wearing a Solidarity pin. Over 2,000 of them were punished with arrest (and the others with fines).[20] In terms of their efficacy in applying the law, the courts of misdemeanor, unlike other courts, acted swiftly: as early as December 14 and 15, a total of 372 cases were heard. In the first ten days of martial law, almost 10,000 petitions were sent to the courts of misdemeanor, and 7,400 people were punished, including almost 600 cases in which the court ordered that the punishment take the form of detention (for up to three months).

One of the first trials that was strictly political in nature took place on December 16 in Łódź, involving twenty-two people who had been detained during a demonstration in front of the Łódź Regional Solidarity Board. Of these people, three were sentenced to detention of up to three months; the rest were fined. The courts of misdemeanor began meting out punishments in political cases on a mass scale as the result of street demonstrations, particularly in May and August 1982. For example, just in Lublin on May 3–5, 1982, 276 people were detained, of whom eight were arrested, two interned, and 170 fined.

Operation "Maple," mentioned above, represented a special kind of harassment. By December 22, approximately 6,300 people had been summoned for "warning talks" (also called "preventative talks") and were given loyalty oaths to sign. There were several different types of printed forms, which had been prepared already in January 1981, as well as new ones drawn up in autumn. The shortest version said: "I, the undersigned, declare and undertake to refrain from any activities detrimental to the Polish People's Republic, and in particular to respect the existing legal order." The talks took place at militia stations with an SB functionary, who said right away that refusing to sign could result in internment. And this really was the case: by December 22, 409 people had been interned for refusing to sign the declarations. Annotations like "as much as possible" or "as always" could be deemed tantamount to a refusal. This operation was not just about threatening the person who had been summoned—showing him or her a "yellow card"—but also about humiliating him or her and severing his or her contacts with friends and acquaintances from the trade union or opposition circles. Reactions of those who had been "loyalized" in this way varied widely: from concealing the fact to making light of it. On the basis of some of the internees' accounts, one can conclude that, in isolation centers, signing the loyalty oaths was treated generally as something that tainted those who signed them. Nevertheless, I did not find any sources suggesting that those who signed them in conditions of freedom were ostracized or condemned. Probably one does not have to add that the warning talks were also used as attempts to recruit informers. Although Operation "Maple" lasted many weeks, it was most intense in the earliest phase of martial law. By the end of 1982, warning talks had been carried out with approximately 32,000 people.[21]

The implementation of martial law, along with the strikes and the various kinds of protests that ensued, meant that the authorities were inclined to employ yet more forms of reprisals and pressure. One of the most significant was that workers who went on strike would lose their jobs. At the Katowice Steelworks, about 1,400 workers were fired; a similar number lost their jobs at the Szczecin Shipyard and in some of the mines. At the ports and shipyards of Gdańsk and Gdynia, people were fired on a mass scale. Three shipyards were temporarily closed, including the Gdańsk Shipyard, until January 4. Work was periodically suspended in at least twenty enterprises throughout the country. People were not being thrown out of work exclusively in big cities and large enterprises. In the Polmo factory in Krosno, which was not one of the giants, over two hundred people were fired. Generally speaking, a dozen to several dozen people were forced to leave their jobs wherever there were strikes. Factory directors ordered that the employee ID's of striking workers be taken from them when they left the factory, and when workers came the next day, some of them were not given new ones. In several cases, people were required to write declarations condemning the strike's "ringleaders." At the Ziemowit coalmine, anyone who had been on strike underground longer than six days was required to write this kind of declaration. Undoubtedly this was meant to filter out the most determined, since those who refused to sign were fired.

Being fired as a punishment for political activities was also used against some people who had participated in the short-lived strikes on May 13, August 31, in mid-October, and in November 1982, as well as against demonstrators who were detained. For example, at the National Aerospace Factory in Świdnik, 178 workers were fired and 10 were interned after a 15-minute strike that took place on May 13, with 70 percent participation. Mieczysław Rakowski states that, based on official statistics, approximately 55,800 people were fired from December 13, 1981, to early August 1982.[22] We can assume that many of these were thrown out for political reasons, since there were no fewer than 16,000–17,000 people who had been interned and imprisoned—which also amounted to losing one's job. It was not only workers and rank and file employees who lost their jobs, of course, but also managers. According to figures from the Central Party Control Commission, in the 207 largest enterprises, whose party organizations were controlled directly by the Central Committee, about 2,800 supervisors and executives were fired just until March 1982, and a similar number were disciplined by being demoted to lower-ranking positions.

It was nevertheless not only striking workers and employees of industrial enterprises who were fired or removed from their positions. Employees from various institutions who either took part in protests or "did not pledge" to work or manage their enterprises as martial law required were also fired. Forcing people to leave Solidarity was one of the basic mechanisms of the purges that began shortly after December 13 and lasted many months, even though the union was suspended until October 8, 1982, despite the fact that formally it was still legal. In the front line were clearly those Solidarity members in sectors that were sensitive for the regime. First, those holding various types of party leadership positions were required to engage in "self-definition." This may seem surprising but, according to membership records, on December 13, 1981, forty-five members and deputy members of the Central Committee of the Polish communist party belonged to Solidarity, as well as seventeen members of the Central Party Control Commission and thirteen members of the Central Revision Commission. These figures actually convey quite well the atmosphere and the hope placed on the changes that had taken place since August 1980. Among those seventy-five people, sixty-seven declared that they would quit the union; the others refused and were punished—as a rule, by being thrown out of the party.

It is not known how many people were removed from lower levels of the party apparatus and *aktiv*, but the processes of "self-definition" and estimating one's usefulness during martial law were similar if not identical everywhere, and took a heavy toll. In Lower Silesia, twelve members of the party's Voivodship Committee in Wrocław, for example, were dismissed, as were nine first secretaries from the communal or municipal committees, and six first secretaries from enterprise committees. Some of them were expelled from the party immediately. The entire Municipal Committee in Polkowice was dissolved. The purges were carried out all over Poland on a large scale, including in voivodships where the protests after December 13 were significantly less intense and on a much smaller scale than in Lower Silesia. In the Białystok voivodship, five first secretaries from enterprise committees were dismissed, as were thirty-three secretaries from the Basal Party Organizations, and twenty-nine members from communal or municipal offices. Poland-wide, 311 secretaries from territorial offices were dismissed (at the voivodship and municipal levels, etc.), as well as 249 secretaries from enterprise committees (in large-scale enterprises), and 1,856 secretaries from basal and departmental (podstawowe and oddziałowe) party organizations. By August 1982, approximately 235,000 people had been struck off the party registers.[23]

Many lower-level activists turned in their party cards without waiting for sanctions, which was just the tip of the iceberg, since quitting the party was becoming a mass phenomenon. All over Poland, about 10 percent of party members had turned in their party cards in the first weeks after the imposition of martial law. Removing people from their party functions was facilitated by the "Instruction on Directing the Party When a Threat to State Security Has Been Announced," passed by the Central Committee Secretariat on December 10, 1981. This document was supplemented by an instruction titled "The Party's Tasks in Conditions of Martial Law," issued a month later. On its authority, the higher party levels could suspend lower ones and regulate their personnel, in accordance with the doctrine of "democratic centralism," which had been *de rigueur* in the communist movement since Lenin's time.

Next in line was the judicial system. In five of the voivodships, the first talks with prosecutors took place on December 15 and 16. Of the thirty-three prosecutors who were Solidarity members, thirteen refused to sign a declaration stating that they were relinquishing union membership. Of this smaller group, eleven resigned their posts immediately, and two were fired because they had not submitted a "pledge." All the other employees in the prosecutor's offices who refused to quit the union were also fired. The only interned public prosecutor (Stefan Śnieżko) was, of course, also fired. In the coming days, similar events took place in the other voivodship public prosecutors' offices. An operation to "verify" (screen) judges and other employees of the court system was launched more or less simultaneously. Suitable talks were held with about 7,300 people—i.e., with all the Solidarity members, of whom 840 were judges. Despite pressure, 137 judges refused to quit, but were nevertheless allowed to remain in the court system. Thus, one could say that the judiciary got off lightly, but it was clear that, at least for a while, the Solidarity members who did keep their jobs would not be able to advance in their careers. At the suggestion of the minister of justice, who himself was soon dismissed, the Council of State dismissed twenty-five judges from their posts and accepted the resignations of eleven others. The minister, acting on his own authority, also dismissed five assessors (associate judges).[24] In some courts the pressure to leave the union was brutal: in Białystok, as Tomasz Danilecki and Marcin Zwolski write, the judges were "gathered in the court building, which was surrounded by ZOMO." They were threatened with dismissal, and even internment. As a result, all those present declared that they would quit Solidarity.[25]

Journalists and technicians who worked in the media were another professional group that found itself under fire. The suspension of most newspapers and radio and television programs facilitated the screening of journalists. There was thus no need for undue haste. In the case of journalists, it was not so much about their quitting Solidarity, but above all about ascertaining what their attitude was to the imposition of martial law, the leading role of the party in mass media and foreign policy—and more specifically to the "alliance" with the Soviet Union. "Verification talks" were carried out with about 10,000 people, including technicians working in radio and television. According to a report for the party leadership submitted in June 1982, after the entire operation had already concluded, 302 people were fired from the party publishing concern RSW "Press-Book-Movement" (Prasa-Książka-Ruch). Over 180 were forced to work outside the media, and 60 editors-in-chief were fired, along with 78 deputy editors and 57 managing editors (sekretarzy redakcji). In the Committee on Radio and Television, 227 journalists were blacklisted, 300 technical employees were fired, and approximately 20 changes affected executive positions. At other publications, approximately a hundred journalists were fired, and over twenty were dismissed from their positions.[6] The Catholic press was not subject to verification. It is estimated that about 10 percent of all journalists were expelled from their jobs.

Of course there were significant regional differences. On the coast in the Tri-City, approximately one-third of full-time journalists were fired. Poland-wide, twenty-one editorial offices were dissolved, but not all decisions to liquidate publications stemmed from a loss of trust in their editors. In some cases, financial and publishing considerations were a determining factor. One of the liquidated titles was the well-known Warsaw weekly *Kultura*; eight of the nine people in its party cell had turned in their party cards. Tried and true journalists were used for the creation of new social and cultural publications, such as the weekly *Tu i Teraz*. The verification commissions, which functioned at the levels of editorial boards or radio or television stations, were comprised of trustworthy communist journalists, but also military commissars, SB functionaries, and representatives of party branches and censorship offices. For example, in Łódź, the commission was comprised of a Central Committee plenipotentiary, an officer of the Voivodship Defense Committee, a party Voivodship Committee secretary, an SB functionary who was conducting surveillance among journalists, and the director of the district censorship office.[27] In Warsaw, there was also a "central verification team" to which appeals could be directed. The screening procedure was particularly humiliating for those who—because of their personal situations or characters—were evasive or said things that did not reflect their true views, in an attempt to preserve their jobs or at least stay in their profession. The verification of journalists, as is usually the case in these kinds of situations, aimed to eliminate people who were considered a threat, and also to discipline—i.e., frighten—the entire profession. Another blow to the field of journalism was the formal dissolution, on March 20, 1982, of the Association of Polish Journalists, which had been suspended since December 13 anyway.

The wave of purges also affected the field of education, including post-secondary institutions and academia. Teachers, as a group, were treated ruthlessly: about 110 teachers were interned, many were fired, and an even larger number were demoted from their posts (including many school principals). In Lower Silesia and the Opole region alone, almost 250 people were deemed "not useful for positions of authority."[28] In addition to school directors and Solidarity activists, history and civics teachers were evaluated particularly carefully. The Politburo ordered that schools introduce a position called "deputy director for political issues." Another form of pressure on teachers and young people was a Poland-wide program of talks in schools about martial law by lecturers from the army's Main Political Directorate. According to an official report, during the first ten days after the extended Christmas holiday (i.e., after January 5), twenty thousand such talks took place, at which approximately fifty thousand teachers were said to have taken part, as well as 1.3 million pupils.[29] These figures, like many statistics prepared by the military, raise many doubts because of their tendency to inflate the numbers.

The academic community was dealt with very radically, although people were more often removed from their posts (demoted) than fired. By December 15, 1981, the Conference of Post-Secondary Rectors had already been dissolved. This body had just recently been created and enjoyed a great deal of authority in the field of post-secondary education. In the Tri-City, all rectors of post-secondary schools were dismissed and almost every faculty member was verified (3,553 individuals).[30] At Maria Curie-Skłodowska University in Lublin, five deans were dismissed (and one other was interned). The Institute of Theoretical Physics at the Silesian University ceased to exist because so many of its faculty had been fired. It was probably the most intensively verified school in the country. Its rector, August Chełchowski, and prorector, Irena Bajerowa, were interned. By the end of the 1981–82 academic year, fourteen rectors had been dismissed, as well as twenty-five prorectors and eight deans.[31] At each post-secondary school there were dozens of people who were interned, removed from executive positions, or fired. In all, these actions probably affected several thousand people.

The wave of purges was carried out on the basis of a circular issued on December 17 by General Janiszewski, as the head of the Office of the Council of Ministers. The purges affected the state administration both in the capital and in the provinces, and primarily included people who were in executive positions in industry and various other sectors of the economy, including the chairmen of the communal farmers' cooperative Rural Mutual Aid Society (Samopomoc Chłopska). Solidarity members who also had positions thanks to the *nomenklatura* system—i.e., those who required approval by the appropriate party committee (from the Central Committee at the top, all the way down to enterprise committees)—had to perform "self-definition." Their behavior during the imposition of martial law, strikes, and protests was also assessed.

In all of Poland, thousands of people were fired, above all those who had been expelled from the party or had turned in their party cards. In the Wrocław voivodship, all the councilors in self-government at different levels who were party members were verified. Six percent of them were presented with a proposition they could not refuse: to relinquish their mandate, even though they had formally won it in a popular vote.[32] According to information collected by the Warsaw Commission for Party Control, within a month after the imposition of martial law about 110 individuals from the central state administration had been expelled from the communist party. This included five deputy ministers, two departmental directors, thirteen federation (zjednoczenie) directors and deputy directors, eight directors and deputy directors of the foreign trade headquarters, fifteen enterprise directors, and thirty-two directors and deputy directors of state institutions.[33] Not all were expelled from the party—and automatically dismissed from their positions—for belonging to Solidarity or for their "inappropriate stance" during the imposition of martial law. People who were considered to be embezzlers or who used their positions to enrich themselves shared this same fate. Gierek and other prominent politicians, some of whom were accused of similar offenses, suffered internment for this reason. Eliminating them, however, was simply a "side effect" of martial law.

WRON's chairman, Jaruzelski, spoke out several times against taking revenge on Solidarity members who had become such a nuisance to the party activists, especially at enterprises. Sometimes Solidarity's activists slighted or threatened them, and in the weeks leading up to December 13, some people began to say that the party should be removed from the workplace. The fact that General Jaruzelski needed to repeat these kinds of admonitions demonstrates that this was quite a common phenomenon. Although around one-third of the party members belonged to Solidarity, many, perhaps even most, party members harbored animosity toward those whom they perceived as avowed enemies of the socialist state—power-thirsty, imperialist lackeys who were sowing chaos. This sentiment, it seems, was particularly strong in the party apparatus (and the party employed approximately twenty thousand people at that time), in the ministries of defense and the interior, and also among retired party functionaries, various departments of the Ministry of Internal Affairs, and military men.

After the imposition of martial law and the ruthless settling of accounts with Solidarity, these party members undoubtedly had a sense of *Schadenfreude*. Many did not intend to stop there, however, but rather pushed to eradicate the evil completely, by firing people or dismissing them from their posts, and through mass arrests and harsh sentences. In many workplaces, party activists smashed the Solidarity display cases, and destroyed union documents and publications. Members of party self-defense groups (or the "party guard" as they were sometimes called) appeared in factory shops and office corridors, wearing armbands with "PRL" on them (which stood for Polska Rzeczpospolita Ludowa, or the Polish People's Republic). On January 25, legislation confirming the Council of State decrees on martial law was passed, with one vote against and five abstaining. At this session, an MP from the communist club, Janusz Przymanowski—a colonel and well-known writer—praised the creators of martial law in a florid speech. He said that they had proven themselves to be sharp readers of *The Iliad* and "eviscerated the [Trojan] horses before night fell."[34] At a time when there were no fewer than ten thousand people sitting in Polish prisons, and the earth over the graves of the slain miners was still fresh, albeit frozen solid, words about "eviscerated horses" sounded inappropriate and sinister. The members of parliament, however, reacted to them—as noted in the protocol—with "mirth" and "applause," which probably conveys well the intensity of what was not mere animosity, but even true hatred of the vanquished enemy, who now had to be humiliated, too. Even General Jaruzelski (who, after all, counseled people not to succumb to their emotions) commented on the need to "root out counterrevolution" in one of his speeches before the party *aktiv* at the Ministry of Internal Affairs, and called the people who made up the underground "trash" and "weeds."[35] And we know how trash and weeds should be treated: they should be removed.

An extremely intense propaganda campaign reinforced these antagonistic feelings. The authorities of martial law engaged all possible means in this effort, including the military. In the first few weeks after December 13, the Headquarters of Propaganda and Agitation of the Main Political Directorate (Główny Zarząd Polityczny) printed several dozen different kinds of anti-Solidarity posters in print runs of half a million, and about three hundred flyers with runs of 660,000. Special operational groups created as part of the political sections of the military districts, and different branches of the armed services, were equipped with portable broadcasting stations and field printing presses. The total number of flyers produced amounted to many millions. Polish Television's Program I, which had a monopoly, played a special role, particularly its news broadcast "Television Journal" (Dziennik Telewizyjny), which aired at 7:30 p.m. A central propaganda headquarters was formed just before December 13 to coordinate the activities of all the media and information services. Its directors were Stefan Olszowski, Mieczysław Rakowski, and General Tadeusz Szaciło (on behalf of the party, government, and military, respectively). The propaganda headquarters guaranteed a relatively unified message in terms of both information and propaganda. "Black propaganda" comprised a considerable portion of the campaign. In this type of propaganda, presenting the opponent in as negative a light as possible was more important than praising the government's own accomplishments. In this campaign, it was not so much the tricks used that were new, as the intensity of the invectives, and the fact that the attacks were directed against specific individuals. The journalists taking part in this smear campaign often used material given to them by the SB, collected as part of their undercover operations, and the information was often libelous and full of inaccuracies. They exploited xenophobic feelings as well, with references to the "non-Polish" backgrounds of various union activists. Sometimes they also used coincidences: for example, when people happened to have the same last name, as was the case with Janusz Onyszkiewicz, one of the best-known union activists, and Myroslav Onyshkevich, known by his wartime pseudonym "Orest," a leader of the nationalist Ukrainian partisans. Clichés familiar from the anti-Semitic campaign of 1968 resurfaced, such as references to the "sons of the VIP's from the 1950s," "Zionist roots," the "revisionist mafia," and relatives who "served in the Wehrmacht." Journalists also strove to criminalize both Solidarity's activists and the union itself. One timeworn method was to publish information about the arrest of a Solidarity activist and that of a speculator or even murderer side by side. After authorities assumed control of union offices, functionaries searched through the documents there for evidence of embezzlement, corruption, and evading regulations, as well as any traces of plans for aggressive undertakings, or stockpiling of weapons. In the end, nothing specific would be found. All of these actions were intended to justify the reprisals, while legitimizing the authorities—WRON and the communist party—as the only guarantors of order and public peace. One can even say that, after the imposition of martial law, official propaganda played a role that was actually repressive—it served not only to discredit the enemy, but also to scare the public. Forced underground, Solidarity struck back however it could, but its counter-propaganda, which often used similarly strong language and slogans, could not compete, in terms of its reach, with the powerful mass media that were completely under communist control.

Also shaping the popular mood was a series of restrictions designed to prevent public gatherings, which necessitated depriving people of sources of amusement: all sporting events were suspended (on the Baltic coast, this ban lasted all the way until mid-February), as were theatrical productions and film screenings. Museums and libraries were closed. Even lottery fans were deprived of the chance to get an adrenaline rush and experience the thrill of winning, since lottery drawings were halted on December 13. Restrictions affecting social communication influenced the atmosphere, too: Radio Two was relaunched on January 17, Radio Four in mid-February, and Radio Three only in early April 1982. Local television programs began operating again on February 8, and Program Two on February 15. Dailies appeared even before Christmas, but it was only in February that weeklies and monthlies renewed publication. In Kraków, cinemas and theaters reopened already on January 5, but in Warsaw it was ten days later. In Gdańsk, in contrast, this happened only on February 2. For many weeks, various television and radio programs showed little variation—monotonous reports showing that "life is returning to normal" dominated, and there was much about the military and war, and, in the middle of winter, materials from the summer Soldiers' Song Festival in Kołobrzeg were shown. The first few days, there was mostly classical and military music. Only children were treated better, because their favorite programs quickly returned to the air.

On January 5, telephone service was restored only "as a test" in the ten least populated voivodships. When it was restored in all cities on January 10, one heard an automatic warning ("conversation monitored") upon picking up the receiver, and a statement to the effect that the monitoring was aimed at making it impossible to use "telephone communications for activities endangering the interests of state security." Inter-city phone service was renewed throughout Poland only in late March.

Letters and parcels, both domestic and international, were censored. At first, packages and telegrams could only be sent from selected post offices. Postal censorship offices created in the Ministry of Internal Affairs and at voivodship militia headquarters carried out a huge amount of work: by the end of 1982, approximately 82.2 million letters had been inspected (15 percent of the total number), of which 930,000 were confiscated (including Solidarity flyers, postcards that had been sent from abroad demanding that those sentenced be freed, and collective protests sent by Amnesty International). About 130,000 pieces of post were slated to be used for operational purposes, or in trials; approximately 32,500 letters were examined by chemical means (in an attempt to find encrypted messages); nearly 11 million telegrams and telexes were censored; and about 3 million packages were examined (for example, about 6,000 records and 10,000 cassettes with texts and music deemed to be anti-state were confiscated).[36] The use of these radical means of blocking the exchange of information and opinions, not only in the media but also among individuals, meant that a large variety of rumors, some of them very strange indeed, were circulating in Poland, as is usually the case in such conditions. There was talk of hundreds of people killed, and of thousands being herded to stadiums and dying of exposure there. It was also said that soldiers were being shot for refusing to carry out orders, and that people were being deported "to Siberia." These rumors mixed old Polish fears (deportation to Siberia was the fate of many nineteenth-century Polish insurgents) with new models of repression rooted in distant parts of the world (camps were located in stadiums after General Pinochet's coup d'état in Chile).

During the first few weeks after martial law was introduced, extremely serious shortages, including those of basic foodstuffs, aggravated the public's sense of uncertainty and fear. Although Poles were used to constant shortages, they now faced difficult challenges in their daily lives. In general, one person was allowed to purchase only one to two items, or packages/bottles, of non-rationed goods. In Gdańsk in early January, people could buy no more than two loaves of bread, one kilogram of pasta, two liters of milk, or three boxes of matches. In Kraków, people could only buy one loaf of bread at a time during almost all of December.[37] The supply situation was so bad that occasionally there would be calls for the introduction of bread and potato rationing. In order to improve distribution and shorten lines, items "without cards" (i.e., that were not rationed) were sold directly from trucks in some cities, and stalls with foodstuffs were opened in shoe, toy, or clothing stores. But obviously these types of steps did not mean that the amount of goods increased.

The rationing system was constantly being perfected. Attempts were made to unify it by means of a circular issued on December 30 regarding the new principle of rationed sales and a new requirement that rationing cards be registered in a specific shop. In order to satisfy consumers' various needs, authorities introduced an entire complicated system of "interchangeable products" (for example, vodka for candy) and "linked sales" (*sprzedaż wiązana*).[38] In one city, if you brought fifteen empty bottles back to the store, you could get a coupon for 100 grams of coffee or 150 grams of candy, but more than forty-five bottles could not be returned at a time, probably in order to discourage speculation. In general, however, the coffee was vile anyway, and candies were of extremely low quality. In many places, especially in smaller towns, the rationing card system was on the verge of collapse, since the small shipments did not afford any stability. Now there were lines for everything—except maybe for newspapers.

The "black market" in such situations usually serves as a "safety valve," but after December 13 the regulations of martial law hampered its operations further. At that time, the courts of misdemeanor passed judgments in thousands of cases that fell under the general category of "speculation": from the "unfounded accumulation of supplies" in stores to "criminal purchase of goods" and unregistered door-to-door sales (primarily of meat). By this definition, almost anything could become an object of speculation, from toilet paper to furniture and refrigerators. Gasoline and other fuels were among the most sought-after goods—of course, second only to meat and sausages. The fuel shortages affected everyone in the national economy who did not enjoy special privileges, not just ordinary car owners and speculators. People were urged to save fuel, and the Kraków Automobilklub organized "economical driving rallies" (*rajdy ekonomicznej jazdy*). (The record-holder used only 3.3 liters of gasoline to go 100 kilometers with his Fiat 600.) Gasoline was undoubtedly one of the most important items targeted for fraud-based trade, both before and after January 31, 1982, when it was officially rationed.

Because the production and sale of alcohol was regulated, the illegal distilling of alcohol flourished, and finding "private vodka" (*bimber*) supplies was not much of a problem. These kinds of sins, however, had been notoriously committed en masse ever since the economy of shortages began—i.e., almost the entire time that communist Poland had existed. There were many patrols and checkpoints; by the end of 1982, the patrols had verified a total of almost 2.9 million people's identity documents and almost 1.8 million vehicles. Somehow, during martial law, the methods of combating speculation were automatically made more stringent. And the black market prices and costs of this "small producers' corruption" also rose, since the sellers' increased risk was taken into account. Soon, the government's official campaign to combat speculation featured some of the most socially convincing slogans. Since, however, it did not have any serious impact on the actual levels of supplies or the population's buying power, it had a negative impact on the public mood, and served to reinforce popular convictions about the government's repressive nature. The authorities nevertheless were unbothered by this; the government was now more interested in eliciting fear than in cultivating their citizenry's affection.

One must be aware of the fact that, in the twentieth century, Polish society had experienced incomparably more difficult periods, and had suffered extremely heavy losses. In comparison, the number of victims resulting from the imposition of martial law was negligible. For many Poles, everything that happened after midnight on December 13, 1981, was still a shock—an event not so much unexpected as incomprehensible, which prompted clear associations with the Second World War and German occupation. In one of the publications featuring occasional poetry—a genre flourishing at that time—one of the poems was a recasting of a well-known "doggerel song" from the Second World War, which began with the words "on the first of September of that memorable year / the enemy attacked Poland from a neighboring country." Forty years later, an anonymous poet wrote:

On the thirteenth of December of that memorable year
Poland was attacked by an enemy from its own people.
Today the uniforms are Polish instead of those hated ones,
A bayonet aimed at its own bloodied Nation.

In another poem, written in that same convention, we read:

On the thirteenth of December of that memorable year,
The enemy did not have to come from a neighboring country
Because he was here on the spot, he was in Poland,
While one hand was outstretched, the other preparing to strike.[39]

This was precisely how very many Poles saw—or rather perceived—what had happened. Most of all, these awkward poems express a bitterness, arising not so much from a sense of defeat, but from the authors' realization that it was in fact fellow Poles who had been "preparing that blow."

Chapter Eight

The World Looks On

Operation "Azalea" had not succeeded in blocking all channels of communication, so the night of December 12–13, about 1:30 a.m., when the Council of State was still in session, the Warsaw correspondent of Agence France-Presse sent an urgent dispatch to Paris (via Vienna) about the worrying events in Warsaw. At 2:10 a.m., the press attaché at the United States Embassy, Steve Dubrow, and the embassy's political advisor, John Vaught, sent an encoded dispatch to Washington by satellite, which arrived at the Eastern European Desk at the Department of State and the National Security Council around 8:15 p.m. EST (on December 12). In it, they said that telephone communications had been cut, Solidarity activists in Warsaw had been arrested, the militia had occupied the trade union's Mazowsze Region headquarters, and convoys of military vehicles had been observed on the streets. And, most importantly for public opinion in the West and for American politicians, no Soviet military presence had been noted. In Washington, it was Saturday evening, and no authority figures were present who could have made any decisions: President Ronald Reagan was spending the weekend at Camp David, Secretary of Defense Caspar Weinberger was in a plane flying from London to Washington, and Secretary of State Alexander Haig was in Brussels, about to embark on a long trip to North Africa, the Near East, and South Asia.

In the situation room at the White House, a group of people gathered who could only analyze the situation. John Davis, director of the Eastern European and Yugoslav Affairs Office in the Department of State, organized the meeting. (Later, he was ambassador to Poland for many years.) Vice President George Bush attended, along with the White House chief of staff James Baker and admirals Nance and Poindexter. Among those present, the person who was best informed about Polish affairs was the well-known historian Richard Pipes, who had been born in Poland and was a Harvard professor specializing in Russian history. He was also an advisor to the National Security Council on matters concerning Eastern Europe and the Soviet Union. The news that "something" was happening in Poland was already making the rounds of the press agencies. After consultation with Haig, who had been awakened in the middle of the night at the Hyatt Hotel where he was staying, it was decided that the Department of State would issue a short communiqué. It was announced at 10:20 p.m. Washington time (4:20 a.m. Central European Time), and was extremely brief: "No Soviet troop movements have been noted."[1]

From the perspective of international relations, Soviet involvement was, of course, a key question, since the deployment of Soviet troops in Poland, whether or not other Warsaw Pact troops joined them, would have been a declaration of war, of sorts: it would have caused a dramatic escalation of the "Second Cold War," which had been underway since the Soviets invaded Afghanistan in December 1979, even though it would not have meant a military intervention by the United States or NATO. The term "Second Cold War" is sometimes used for the period of tensions that followed many years of coexistence—stormy, yet nevertheless longlasting coexistence—between the two super powers and military blocs. The United States placed economic sanctions on the Soviet Union at the time, sent aid to the Afghan guerrillas, increased military spending, withdrew from the SALT II disarmament talks, and boycotted the Olympic Games, which took place in Moscow during the summer of 1980. This period was not as "hot" as the "First" Cold War, that of 1948–55, but unlike the one-off violent escalations of the past (in 1961, when the Berlin Wall was built; in 1962, when the Cuban Crisis took place; or in 1968, when Warsaw Pact troops invaded Czechoslovakia), it began acquiring the traits of a more permanent phenomenon.

Both the American administration and the allied governments found themselves in an awkward position, for several reasons. Most importantly, although intelligence sources had been suggesting for some time "that something extraordinary is afoot," as it was described in a note to NATO's Secretary General on December 9,[2] they were all surprised when martial law was actually imposed. In fact, until General Jaruzelski gave his early morning speech, no one knew what kind of legal framework would exist for the activities launched against Solidarity. This awkward situation was exacerbated by the fact that neither NATO members nor the alliance as such was prepared for the possibility that the operation would use exclusively Polish forces, with foreign armies kept in reserve. Douglas J. MacEachin, who was for many years a CIA officer dealing with the Soviet bloc, explained the situation convincingly. He noted that Colonel Ryszard Kukliński in the Polish General Staff was indeed a very good source of information. Nevertheless, in intelligence circles, as well as in the highest spheres of government (the president and his closest associates, the National Security Council, and the Department of State, for example), the plan to implement martial law using exclusively Polish forces, which they knew about, "was judged from the beginning as not likely, and the evidence flow was examined in terms only of what was a priori considered likely."[3] This is not surprising: generals usually prepare a new war based on previous ones, which they themselves have observed, or which they have studied at military academies. The experiences of 1956 in Hungary, 1968 in Czechoslovakia, or the most recent ones in Afghanistan, suggested that Moscow would react to destabilization among its allies (vassals) by sending its army. The frequent juxtaposition of the "hard-headed" Kremlin and the "liberal" tendencies of some of the leaders in other communist countries probably contributed to the disbelief in General Jaruzelski's determination. In light of both these assumptions, the idea that General Jaruzelski could send tanks out onto city streets and to factory gates seemed so unlikely as to be impossible.[4]

As a result, the first reactions were evasive: the answer of French Foreign Minister Claude Cheysson to a journalist's question "What is the government doing?" was downright defeatist, if not cynical: "Nothing, of course, we won't do anything." "We will follow [the situation] as it unfolds," he added.[5] The communiqué issued by the French government on the evening of December 13 did not disavow the minister's statement, though it did express "enormous concern." This communiqué emphasized a hope that "dialogue would be renewed" in Poland, and that "civic and trade union freedoms" would be reinstated. At the same time, it noted that the decisions of the Polish authorities "would remain within the framework of internal sovereignty."[6] Thus, most important was relief that there had been no Soviet intervention. The German chancellor Helmut Schmidt—who happened to be on an official visit to the GDR at the time—was unusually restrained. Having been informed of events in Poland early that morning, he decided this was not reason enough to cancel a fruitful meeting with Erich Honecker—the first such high-level encounter in more than a decade. For him, of course, German-German relations were obviously the priority. The chancellor's position, which has been described as "highly cautious and reserved,"[7] impeded a united reaction in the West. Nevertheless, from early that morning there had been intensive consultations by phone among the "big four" NATO foreign ministers. At 4 p.m., Haig, Cheysson, Hans Dietrich Genscher, and Lord Peter Carrington met in Brussels at the office of the NATO Secretary General, Joseph Luns. After the meeting, no official communiqué was issued, and Haig's statement to the journalists was very enigmatic: "The Polish people should find a way on their own to overcome the current difficulties and achieve a compromise between the forces that exist there."[8] Haig probably stressed that the Poles should find a solution on their own out of fear that Warsaw Pact troops would take part in solving the crisis in Poland after all—something we know was really being considered as an option if the operation led by General Jaruzelski failed. Having discussed the matter with President Reagan—who returned to the White House on Sunday afternoon—Haig made at least one decision attesting to the gravity of the situation: he cancelled an important trip to Africa and Asia that had already been prepared in detail, and soon returned to Washington after a meeting of the NATO foreign ministers.

During the Politburo meeting of the Polish communist party, which was held at noon on December 13, foreign minister Józef Czyrek calmly reported on the reaction abroad, based on discussions with the ambassadors of some Western countries and a dispatch from Poland's embassies. He even seemed perhaps pleased that all of them had taken a "balanced stance," to use diplomatic language. According to Romuald Spasowski, the Polish ambassador to the United States, Czyrek thought only the American reaction was somewhat harsher, since Polish-US trade relations were a consideration. Minister Czyrek included a statement by the West German ambassador in Warsaw, who allegedly said that "if no blood is shed, there will be no strong reaction."[9] Czyrek reported on the informational activities that his department had been conducting since early that morning: in addition to the instructions that they had sent to all Polish ambassadors at 8:20 a.m., they sent a dispatch to many governments from both military blocs and to the Secretary General of the United Nations, informing them that the question of martial law might be put before the UN Security Council. They even sent a delegation to the International Labor Organization, whose headquarters are in Geneva. There, the delegation attempted to explain why the trade unions had been suspended. Warsaw Pact states were also included in these activities—the head of WRON had already met personally with the communist bloc ambassadors at 9 a.m.

While Western governments were cautious, public opinion swiftly made itself known: a public gathering began at 10 a.m. on Sunday at the Mickiewicz monument in Paris, comprised mainly of Poles at first. In the afternoon, in response to an appeal from union headquarters, thousands of people (according to the organizers, as many as 50,000–100,000) gathered near the Polish Embassy.[10] In Rome, as John Paul II was reciting the Angelus at noon, hundreds of Poles came to St. Peter's Square to hear him. In the afternoon, people gathered at the Polish Embassy in Cologne. The media were not as restrained as the politicians, but one could also detect a sense of relief in the Western press that Soviet troops had not appeared in Polish streets. Articles even appeared praising General Jaruzelski's decision. There was not much factual information, and what little existed was haphazard, not only because of the serious problems relaying information from Poland, but also because information was difficult to obtain, since foreign journalists had been banned from traveling outside of Warsaw. As usual, the press conferences held by Minister Jerzy Urban, the government spokesman, contained more propaganda than information. The first took place on the afternoon of December 13.

The West's attitude changed beginning on December 17, and was apparent not only in the media, but also in politicians' actions. Of fundamental importance in this respect was undoubtedly the fact that, on December 16, miners' blood was shed at Wujek, which gave an added dimension to the military operation that had been underway throughout Poland for several days.[11] More and more information was flowing to the West, both through journalists and via diplomatic or intelligence channels. It was becoming easier to grasp just what had happened—including the military's part in brutally breaking up the strikes, and the scope of the reprisals both against the trade unionists and the intellectuals and artists.

Perhaps analysts came to the conclusion that the scales were tipping in the government's favor, and so, in order to support Solidarity, protests against WRON should be stronger. This delayed reaction was a result of the fact that the constant talks among NATO member states, as well as internal ones taking place within in each, had to take some time. They could afford to do so because the Soviet troops stationed in Poland had not left their barracks, and those standing on alert beyond Poland's borders had not made any significant movements. The growing pressure of public opinion also undoubtedly influenced Western politicians: since December 14, demonstrations took place in front of Polish consulates and embassies in Toronto, Montreal, Stockholm, Bern, The Haag, Rome, and Paris (where demonstrations were practically permanent), for example, as well as in over one hundred French cities, Cologne, Frankfurt, and Boston. Trade unions were becoming increasingly active in the protests. Even some communist parties, such as those in Italy, Spain, Holland, Great Britain, and Belgium, condemned martial law.

Polish military intelligence reported on December 16 that special exercises had taken place in Sweden in anticipation of a large influx of refugees from Poland. (But how? By sea on kayaks and sailboats? In winter?) Some military units were also put on alert.[12] On the afternoon of December 15, in accordance with the guidelines prepared in March 1981, NATO headquarters announced a state of heightened alert, and the Polish anti-aircraft defense noted that there were more frequent flights by NATO reconnaissance planes over the southern Baltic. Of fundamental importance, however, were the reactions expressed in public statements issued by governments and various political institutions.

President Reagan tried to set the tone: on December 14, he spoke by telephone with John Paul II, with whom he subsequently maintained quite regular contact. On December 17, he made a speech broadcast on television. It was emotional both because of the president's own temperament, and probably also because there was hope it would send a clear signal to General Jaruzelski to withdraw. The European Parliament also made a statement condemning martial law and demanding that civil and trade union rights be restored in Poland. The Presidium of the German Social-Democratic Party (SPD) also made a statement, which was important to Jaruzelski's team because SPD was one of the ruling parties in West Germany, and its *Ostpolitik* assumed that good relations with communist countries would be maintained. In a special communiqué, the SPD demanded respect for trade union rights and the release of those who had been arrested, but made no mention of any sanctions against Poland. The next day, the West German Bundestag passed a resolution recommending that the government cease economic aid to Poland as long as the restrictions of martial law remained in force. This time, too, however, there was no mention of direct economic sanctions. France stook a somewhat firmer position, which inspired the office of the International Labor Organization to send a letter to Prime Minister Jaruzelski, demanding that trade union freedoms be reinstated. France also initiated a discussion about the situation in Poland at the Socialist International, which could have been important because several major Western European states had socialist governments. Moreover, France suspended credit to Poland, with the exception of those involving foodstuffs.

On December 19 Minister Czyrek presented the international situation at a meeting of the Secretariat of the Central Committee. He had to admit that it "had developed unfavorably for us,"[13] primarily because Washington's position was becoming increasingly firm. The Americans had de facto suspended economic relations—they had blocked credit for $100 million for the purchase of corn (which Reagan had already decided on December 13). In addition, they had taken steps to have the matter addressed at the United Nations. A new theme emerged in comments by American politicians: the suggestion that the imposition of martial law was actually something that Moscow had forced on the Poles—which meant the Soviet Union was being saddled with responsibility for events in Poland.

Within a couple of days, leading Western powers had prepared their position regarding three fundamental demands: 1) release of those who had been arrested; 2) reinstatement of civil rights (including trade union activities); and 3) renewing the talks with Solidarity and the Church that had been interrupted by the imposition of martial law. There was no agreement, however, on the matter of sanctions. The US undersecretary of state, Lawrence Eagleburger, arrived in Western Europe with a special delegation. Personally, he had a high opinion of Jaruzelski and considered him to be a "brilliant, intellectually independent officer, who has a decided preference for action."[14] He was, however, unable to reach a common position, or to come to any agreement regarding the packet proposed by Washington. In this situation, on December 23, after three days of consulting with the National Security Council, President Reagan announced a relatively broad set of sanctions, but only on behalf of the United States. These included suspension of the credit guarantees for exports to Poland that the federal US Export-Import Bank had granted, withdrawal of an agreement on fishing by Polish boats in US waters, a tighter embargo on technology exports, and closure of American air space to Polish planes. There was also a demand that allies limit the sale of high-tech equipment to Poland.

The announcement of sanctions itself was done in a dramatic fashion—it happened during a speech televised before Christmas, during which the president urged Americans to light candles in their windows during the holidays to show their support for the Polish people. That same day, Reagan demonstratively received Poland's ambassador to the United States, Romuald Spasowski, who had refused to obey his government and asked for asylum in the United States. Widely distributed footage and photographs showed Reagan putting his arm around a weeping Mrs. Spasowska. Reagan also sent a letter to Brezhnev on December

23, in which he wrote about "the pressures and threats which your government has exerted on Poland to stifle the stirrings of freedom."[15] Six days later, again without conferring with his allies, Reagan announced new sanctions against the Soviet Union, saying that Moscow "bears a heavy and direct responsibility for the repression in Poland."[16] A gala concert dedicated to Poland took place in the Paris Opera that evening, attended by the wife of French president François Mitterand, along with legendary Polish-born pianist Arthur Rubinstein and many members of the government. There were only socialists in attendance, however; no representative of the coalition communist party came.

Sanctions against Poland became the subject of a debate that the European allies managed to conclude constructively since, from their point of view, it was above all a political problem. Sanctions against Moscow, however—especially regarding the ban on exporting equipment and technology for the construction of pipelines to bring oil and natural gas to Western Europe—were of an economic nature. Clearly, neither the Germans nor the French wanted to agree to this. The most critical stance on sanctions was in Bonn, but even French prime minister Pierre Mauroy told Washington in no unclear terms that "it is simpler to pull out a little wooden sword [*sabre de bois*], since one isn't in danger oneself."[17] As a result, the foreign ministers of the European Community, who gathered on January 4, 1982, rejected a proposal for sanctions against the Soviet Union, while the sanction aimed at Poland was only limited in scope (encompassing the suspension of economic aid and sale of food surpluses at low prices). Diplomatic consultations were still underway, but Washington did not manage to obtain full or at least significant support even during the meeting of NATO foreign ministers, which took place on January 11 and was devoted to the question of what the reaction to martial law should be. Some countries gradually introduced some restrictions, such as regarding the movement of Polish airplanes or diplomats—the latter being a reaction to the restrictions introduced within Poland itself. Government credit guarantees were also frozen, for example, and talks on Poland's joining the International Monetary Fund were also suspended.[18] In the longer term, one of the most painful measures for General Jaruzelski and his group was the decision to suspend negotiations on extending Polish debts and the granting of new credit, which the consortium of Poland's creditors (the Paris Club) passed on January 14. The only NATO member that refused to impose any sanctions whatsoever on Poland was Greece, ruled by the leftist socialist Andreas Papandreou.

This obvious dualism—the decisive reactions of Washington and the very muted ones of the rest of the NATO member states—was to last for many years. Poland's ruling clique strove to take advantage of this by conducting propaganda that was at once both anti-American and pro-European. This did not change the essential issue: after the imposition of martial law, the West (actually the United States) could make attempts to conduct an active policy toward Poland, presenting

General Jaruzelski and his team with demands, with some instruments (albeit weak ones) at their disposal to do so. They provided modest and discreet (but nevertheless quite effective) financial aid for Solidarity, as well as propaganda—including, most importantly, the widely viewed television program "Let Poland Be Poland," broadcast on January 13. Political and diplomatic isolation also hurt Poland's prestige, as well as that of General Jaruzelski.

Most important, of course, were economic sanctions, although in December 1981, the Americans remembered not to overplay their hand. When Solidarity was definitively delegalized in October 1982, Poland lost its "most privileged" status in trade with the United States—something that it had enjoyed since 1960. (Of the other communist countries, only Romania and Hungary also had this status, since 1975 and 1979, respectively.) It is difficult to say anything for certain, but although these sanctions were significantly less painful than the Polish government's propaganda made them out to be, Polish exports to the West really did fall dramatically in 1982: by 84 percent to the United States, 18 percent to West Germany, 30 percent to France, and 21 percent to Great Britain.[19] More importantly for the situation in Poland, Poles noticed the sanctions, and the propaganda attempts to provoke a wave of criticism against the United States made them a subject of particular interest—but not always in the way that those behind the propaganda intended. In reviewing the documents about the debates underway in the top party leadership regarding Poland's international situation and these economic repercussions, and the analyses and proposals presented to them, we find many examples of attempts to mitigate the American reaction. The conferences for foreign journalists held by the government's press spokesman, Jerzy Urban, were one expression of General Jaruzelski's powerlessness in the face of sanctions and pressure. Although Urban did provide the Americans with plenty of caustic, often humorous remarks, his comments usually did not reflect reality.

While martial law may have surprised the West, it did not surprise Moscow, which is why no one thought to wake the "old bear"—as Leonid Brezhnev was popularly called—in the middle of the night to tell him that tanks had rolled into Polish cities. And even if he had been awake anyway because he happened to be having a sleepless night, then it was certainly not on account of Poland. Armored units of the Soviet army from the Western military districts were in combat readiness, as were those stationed in Poland, where Marshal Kulikov was personally monitoring the situation. In East Germany, Honecker had been notified of the planned date for the imposition of martial law. His minister of defense, Heinz Hoffmann, informed him that martial law would be imposed in Poland "before 15 December."[20] Because the Germans knew that the operation should begin on a Saturday night, they could have assumed that it would be the night of December 12–13. In any case, the East German military was put on heightened alert, and security along its border with Poland was reinforced. Information about the introduction of martial law might have reached Czechoslovak president Gustav Husák in a similar way—i.e., via military channels. In any case, Czechoslovak and East German army units (three divisions in all) had been ready for operations in Poland since December 6, 1980. In East Germany, the order related to this plan was rescinded only on April 5, 1982, which means it was in force for fifteen months.[21] The situation was similar in the Czechoslovak army. The "lesser allies," however, were not privy to the details of the preparations for martial law from March–April 1981, when the joint maneuvers "Soyuz-81" took place. They also did not participate in consultations in Warsaw at which military and KGB delegations from Moscow also took part. During the yearly meeting of the Warsaw Pact's ministers of defense, which took place in Moscow on December 4, 1981, only the political aspects of the situation in Poland were discussed, not the military ones. This does not mean that the ministers—especially the East German one—did not have their own sources of information in Poland. But had those sources themselves been informed in detail about when martial law would be imposed? Other communist leaders knew even less than Honecker and Husák, though of course they expected that a crisis would eventually come, and that finally the Polish government would have to take radical steps. Actually everyone, including Hungarian leader János Kádár, who had the reputation of being a "dove," and Romania's Nicolae Ceauşescu, who had already been distancing himself from many elements of Soviet policy for a long time, believed that a solution to the Polish crisis would come only if Solidarity were crushed.

As was to be expected, Brezhnev's reaction was very positive: not only did he call General Jaruzelski first thing in the morning to congratulate him, but the Soviet leadership also sent a letter to its allies/vassals stating that it had known about the planned operation. In that letter, the secretary general said that "the actions of our Polish friends are an active step in repulsing counterrevolution and in this sense are in keeping with the general line of the fraternal countries." Moreover, he asked that they be granted "moral and political support" and "additional economic assistance."[22] It is worth noting that while the Romanians did not receive this dispatch from Moscow, the Soviet leadership did send it to Cuba, Mongolia, Vietnam, and Laos. (Of course, it also went to Prague, Sofia, Budapest, and Berlin.) János Kádár reacted immediately: in a dispatch to Jaruzelski, he wished him "much success in the fight to defend the happiness of the Polish people and the universal interests of socialism, progress, and peace."[23]

On December 13 meetings of the top leadership in some of the other communist bloc countries were already taking place. In Bucharest, which did not receive a copy of Brezhnev's appeal, debates about economic aid for Poland took place on December 17, after a letter arrived from Warsaw requesting it. The Romanian leadership was clearly unwilling to contribute aid, primarily owing to Romania's own economic situation, and they decided that additional deliveries would not be donations. Ceaușescu pointed out to his colleagues that the chaos in the Polish economy after December 13 was due to the fact that Moscow had forced Poland to introduce martial law ("they were not the ones who decided,"[24] he said), but at the same time he grumbled about the introduction of free Saturdays in Poland. When he asked those gathered, "What are we going to do?" his wife, who was a member of the Politburo, replied, "In any event—they must pay." In Budapest, the thinking was less commercial; there, they decided to send aid in the amount of almost 40 million transfer rubles, and replied, "We will speak at a later date about the repayment of [its] value."[25] The approach was similar in Prague, where it was decided that most of the extra deliveries (worth more than 800 million crowns) should be treated as a loan not subject to repayment.

This approach was not the result of any particular animosity toward Poland or General Jaruzelski's team—though probably such feelings were also present—but rather because of the problematic economic condition of the countries to which the Poles had addressed their appeal for assistance. Even those who were in the best situation—such as East Germany or Czechoslovakia—were always functioning on the margins of market equilibrium, and had no surplus of the food or raw materials that the Poles wanted. At the Romanian Politburo session mentioned above, Ceaușescu carried out complicated calculations about how much meat and oil would have to be cut from Romanians' diets in order to increase deliveries of those products to Poland. Even the Soviet superpower found itself "pushed to the limit," as Brezhnev said at the Politburo session on January 14, 1982.[26] The Kremlin's restraint in response to the Poles' requests stemmed thus not from a desire to keep them on a tight leash, but from objective limitations. All communist countries did nevertheless offer "fraternal" assistance in one form or another, as well as increased deliveries, which, however, could have been noticeable on the local market only after a certain time had passed.

Just after martial law was imposed, military intelligence sent a report to the communist leadership in Poland stating that some in the United States believed that "Poland had become an experimental testing ground, in which a system of military government in Eastern European states is being tested."[27] Since suitable research has not been done on the subject, it is difficult to say whether a debate on the subject really did take place, if only in Moscow. It should nevertheless be noted that, as early as September 1980, there was talk of an increased role for military men in the country and of positions in the administration for them. These rumors proved true in February 1981, when General Jaruzelski assumed the post of prime minister, and the tendency to appoint military men to high positions grew more frequent during the early period of martial law. In the Soviet leaders' letter of December 13, 1981, to their allies (cited above), they said it was "particularly important" that "the leading role of the PZPR [Polish communist party] be confirmed." A month later, during a meeting of the Politburo, Brezhnev stated with satisfaction that "it looks as if Jaruzelski does not intend to dissolve the party, or to change its name, but rather to use martial law to cleanse it thoroughly."[28]

Ceaușescu, on the other hand, believed that a division had occurred in the Polish party, and he spoke sympathetically about the "former activists, communists," who would take care of "rebuilding the party on a healthy foundation,"[29] from which it might be inferred that he did not much trust his Polish counterpart. A few weeks later, in a conversation with Rakowski, he clearly distanced himself from the changes that had taken place in the ruling structures in Poland. Supporting the idea that the crisis should be resolved without outside intervention (about which the "Carpathian Eagle" was very sensitive), he expressed his doubts as to whether the chosen form was suitable: "the army will not replace the party . . . if martial law is not abandoned quickly, the trust of the working class will not be recovered. . . . The party cannot remain in the shadow of the army."[30] It seems that the other Soviet-bloc parties observed with a certain amount of unease how the party in Poland was "half a step" behind the army, particularly if this balance of power was to last for a longer period of time, or even become the Polish communist party's permanent contribution to the achievements of Marxism-Leninism. This may have been more the result of doctrinal reasons than ad hoc political ones. In a certain sense this is exactly what happened, since it was obvious that both the army and the security apparatus were the main pillars of the system right up until 1989.

On December 27–29, at General Jaruzelski's initiative, three members of Hungary's top leadership visited Warsaw, where they shared with the Poles their experiences of fighting "counterrevolutionary forces," and told of how their own "socialist consolidation" took place in 1956–57. In a report presented to Kádár, they did not write about their recommendations to their Polish comrades, but rather noted the divergence that existed within the Polish leadership, and the fact that the activity of the army "[was] delaying development of the political offensive" as far as the party was concerned.[31] The problem of which approach to adopt was one of the hottest topics discussed during the Politburo meetings and those of the Secretariat of the Central Committee, as well as during debates in various other party circles. On the one hand, there was the "Hungarian approach"—i.e., dissolving the party and creating a new, avant-garde one, while employing brutal police and administrative methods in order to consolidate power. On the other, there was the "Czechoslovak approach" (from 1968–69), which meant a thorough purge in the party and state administration, but without disturbing the party structures, and without using direct reprisals (arrests, trials) on a broad scale, a process known as "normalization."

Most of those who were considered "healthy elements" within the Polish communist party, who had long argued that counterrevolution should be vigorously combated, demanded after December 13 that there be severe punishments. They also urged that the Polish communist party be dissolved and that a new, truly Marxist-Leninist party be created, without "rightists" and opportunists. Since Jaruzelski was able to maneuver quite deftly, the party structures remained, and the purge—although numerically significant—was only partial. After a few weeks of martial law, both the ideological and political implications of having the army participate directly in the exercise of power, as well as the problem of transforming the party itself, were no longer in the forefront—though they did not disappear entirely. When General Jaruzelski was on an official visit to Bucharest in early June 1982, Ceaușescu made critical remarks about the army's replacement of the party and the prolongation of martial law. The Polish leader responded that it was not the generals but the party *aktiv* that was "in favor of maintaining martial law," because "the party has not yet completely recovered all its strength."[32] In any case, the Polish example was not emulated in other communist countries—at least not in European ones, probably because none of them was in such a deep crisis.

By imposing martial law, General Jaruzelski's group did achieve peace outwardly, in a sense. Those who were indignant that martial law had been imposed (the West) could not really do anything serious to Jaruzelski's group. Although they hindered WRON's activities, by no means could they remove it from power. Those who had previously been urging aggressive action (the communist bloc) were satisfied and thus stopped wielding pressure, which would have been simply superfluous in the new situation.

Chapter Nine

Battle Over

During a Politburo meeting on December 22, 1981, General Jaruzelski said, "We have won the first battle."[1] His use of military language is not surprising, considering both his profession and the situation; however, he added cautiously, "We have not won the campaign (which will take several months)." More importantly, he admitted that one should not triumph prematurely, since "it will take ten years to recover from the devastation in [people's] consciousness and lift the economy from ruins"—in other words, to win the war. It is difficult to take issue with this statement, even if some of the skirmishes of this battle had not yet been won: as the general was saying these words, miners from Ziemowit and Piast were still protesting underground, and a group of striking workers persisted at the Katowice Steelworks. Victory could, however, be proclaimed, since the enemy's main forces had been broken and its center crushed.

Nevertheless, this did not mean that the troops would return to their barracks. While it is true that most units had been withdrawn from the streets on January 7, approximately twenty-eight thousand soldiers from those assigned to "special tasks" remained in or near nine designated large cities (Bydgoszcz, Gdańsk, Katowice, Lublin, Łódź, Poznań, Szczecin, Warsaw, and Wrocław), about seven thousand were at training grounds and could reach the area of operations within thirteen to fifteen hours, and about thirty-five thousand returned to where they were permanently stationed, where they could be deployed in one and a half to two days. These units had a total of about seventy thousand soldiers. Moreover, specially designated reserves of about twenty thousand soldiers were kept "on permanent readiness for action . . . throughout Poland," about nine thousand were guarding selected sites (including weapons and ammunition plants), and about two thousand were posted along communication routes.[2] In all, over a hundred thousand soldiers were in various degrees of readiness or already deployed. The battle had been won, but the troops had not yet left the field.

The army did not limit itself to guarding, pacifying, and maintaining the psychosis of martial law. It also assumed a key position in the state administration, the economy, and the communist party: eleven military men were ministers or deputy ministers in civilian departments, thirteen were voivods or deputy voivods, and nine were secretaries of the communist party's voivodship committees. In all, 136 officers had been delegated to high positions in the party and state apparatus.[3] Military men headed both chancelleries that served the highest levels of government: the Office of the Council of Ministers (General Janiszewski) and the Central Committee of the Polish United Workers' Party (Colonel Bogusław Kołodziejczak). General Tadeusz Dziekan became director of the personnel department at the Central Committee of the party. After General Siwicki was coopted as deputy member of the Politburo in October 1981, that same distinction was accorded in February 1982 to General Kiszczak, who was the minister of internal affairs at the time, but also a professional soldier.

That situation, which was exceptional in the context of European communist states, was not temporary, since up until 1989 there had always been at least three generals in the party's top leadership body. One can thus truly speak of a partial militarization in the highest echelons of power. Military men were also delegated to key ideological positions. For example, officers were appointed as deputy school superintendents "to strengthen the Ministry of Education's regional apparatus" in all the voivodships.[4] The army dealt not only with pupils and teachers, but also took upon itself resocialization tasks: in January 1982, sixty-five "field companies" were created (i.e., what amounted to penal companies for about seven thousand people from the "dregs of society"). Reeducation was "carried out through education in conditions of discipline and military order and intensive ideological and political influence."[5] More specifically, this was achieved by sending these people to hard labor on earthworks and construction projects.

Militarization also took place through the introduction of military commissioners (*komisarze wojskowi*), who on December 13 were assigned to 30 ministries and central offices, each of the 49 voivodships, 225 cities and municipal districts, 2,070 communes (*gmina*, rural administrative units), and to 1,003 workplaces and institutions (including the Polish Academy of Sciences). Approximately 4,700 officers became commissioners and about 2,700 soldiers assisted them, which is approximately 7,500 people in total.[6] They were involved not only in monitoring, but also had a decision-making role. In the vast majority of cases, however, it was not within their competence to manage, or even monitor, the institutions or enterprises to which they had been assigned. This was probably not very significant, however, since, as people accustomed to life in a closed military structure, they were quite adept at integrating into the centralized and hierarchical economy, as well as into similarly organized central institutions and regional administration. Although they were able to restore order immediately, they certainly were not suited to initiating any kind of change. But this was not their task. The aim of their presence was simply to hold on to the conquered territory—just like after a battle.

The presence of commissioners was necessary because of the situation in the Polish communist party, and especially at the enterprise level. From July 1980, when large numbers of people began to quit the party, until mid-1982, the ranks of the Polish communist party shrank by almost a million people, which was almost a third. In June 1980, about 25 percent of those employed at the 207 largest and economically most significant enterprises (accounting for 1.3 million employees) were party members; by late August 1982, this number fell to just under 18 percent. Particularly important—and distressing to the party leadership—was the fact that the party lost about 40 percent of its working-class members at those leading enterprises. As a result, the party could not monitor workers so closely, which seriously limited its ability to mobilize them. To compensate, it instituted the "workers' guards," which were meant to strengthen the party's presence in the factories at least somewhat. The problem, however, was not limited to party cells, though those were the most important. As soon as Solidarity emerged, the party's chances of influencing the coopted mass social organizations were drastically reduced. Using Lenin's own term, these groups were known as the party's "transmission belts." Official (pro-government) trade unions had already lost their mobilizing powers in the summer of 1980. After the imposition of martial law, they needed to be suspended anyway, just as Solidarity had been. The significance of other organizations also waned, such as the Women's League (Liga Kobiet) or the Union of Socialist Polish Youth (Związek Socjalistycznej Młodzieży Polskiej), not to mention the Polish-Soviet Friendship Society (Towarzystwo Przyjaźni Polsko-Radzieckiej). After December 13, feverish efforts were made to revive the old "transmission belts" and create new ones.

In late December 1981, an initiative (directed from above) was launched to create loosely constituted "citizens' committees of national salvation." Their name itself alluded to WRON, and the slogan "national salvation" became one of the main officially promoted mottoes at this time. Actually, it was simply a propaganda ploy, since of course it was about saving the state (system) and not the nation, which was perhaps actually "healthier" than at any other time in the history of communist Poland. In addition to party members, members of the Democratic Party, United Peasant Party, mass organizations, and people outside the party were supposed to be involved in the "citizens' committees'" activities as well. The movement was in a certain sense an attempt to create on the local level an equivalent of the Front of National Unity (Front Jedności Narodu), that venerable fake, which since 1952 had been feigning the cooperation of legal parties and organizations. In late January 1982, there were already nearly two thousand committees with several tens of thousands of members, with Party members comprising 54 percent. Most of these committees were established on a territorial basis (*gmina*, municipal district, municipality, etc.). Many, however, were also founded in workplaces (the committees existed, for example, in 92 of the 207 most important enterprises mentioned above).

The number of committees grew quickly, but their role was increasingly difficult to define, since those in charge of martial law gradually made the reestablishment of the trade union movement their main focus. This did not happen, of course, without the help of the army—or, to be more precise, without the army's Main Political Directorate, which developed the citizens' committees' ideological and policy guidelines and operating principles."[7] Committee representatives were honored by being invited to a meeting of WRON, widely publicized in the media, on March 11. This kind of meeting was natural insofar as the committees, as the protocol stated, were an "extension" of WRON.[8] The army plugged various holes that had arisen in the system, replacing party organizations or complementing them with activities aimed at indoctrination, conducted right "in the field." I have already mentioned the talks given to school-age youth in January 1982 (see chapter 7), but similar events—carried out by specially prepared propaganda groups (usually one officer and two or three soldiers)—were later also carried out in workplaces and post-secondary institutions.

The post-battle landscape was thus not entirely clear. True, the enemy had been routed, and most of its leaders and most active members had been taken prisoner, but the party, which saw itself as the victor, had not emerged from the fight entirely unscathed itself. It had also lost many of its supporters, and the crisis within its own ranks deepened.

Part 3

Counterattack

Chapter Ten

Operation "Renaissance" and Lech Wałęsa

The preventative arrest of thousands of Solidarity activists and the stubborn hunt for anyone who managed to escape the round-up of the night of December 12–13 were not carried out just to isolate those who were most active, or considered to be most dangerous. It was also the aim of this operation to cleanse the territory, so that new people could replace those who had been imprisoned—SB collaborators or individuals considered sufficiently conformist to accept the changed operating conditions of the union. From this technical point of view, it was actually the SB that was carrying out these activities, but the idea for them arose directly from the communist elite's perspective on reality. Thus, it would be difficult to claim that the police had come up with it on their own. Without referring to earlier examples—although these can indeed be found in communist Poland's history—I would like to point out that executive and analytical circles within the party had already begun differentiating between striking workers and the opposition during the strikes in 1980. This trend did not change after Solidarity was founded. Almost all the government's efforts to force the union into communist state structures were grounded in a belief that it was necessary (as the propaganda often said) to sever the "healthy, working-class current" from the "dirty, anti-socialist scum," i.e., the anti-communist opposition. As time passed, that clear, dichotomous picture was destroyed because it turned out that some of those Solidarity activists who had previously shared nothing in common with the opposition were much more radical than people from KOR or the Free Trade Unions, who had been working for years to effect change, or even to overthrow the regime. Thus, the term "extremists" became more popular, both in official propaganda and during secret meetings. The term "extremists" now encompassed both the "new" radicals as well as the "old" oppositionists. The number of individuals who the government thought should be "cut off" from the mass of many millions was thus increasing.

Since August 1980, the basic aim of the party leadership was to purge the union of these "extremists." In order to do this, they attempted to influence the Church so that it would not support KOR activists ("the Kurońs and Michniks"). This was a relatively simple task, since neither Primate Wyszyński nor most of the hierarchy trusted the people in the opposition because many of them had leftist pasts and liberal views. Similarly, the bishops did not trust the "extremists," given their view that excessive radicalization endangered the social peace and engendered a threat of confrontation. The communist party, however, could not count on the

Church's clear and publicly expressed disapproval of those whom the Church itself wanted to marginalize or eliminate from Solidarity. Various propaganda activities also served to "cut them off," as did official statements (including Central Committee resolutions, Politburo communiqués, appeals, and proclamations), as well as speeches and articles by party activists that were openly directed against the "creeping counterrevolution," as they called it. Their aim was to discredit the "anti-socialist powers" in order to limit their influence.

The security apparatus was one of the main means of accomplishing this goal. It was constantly launching activities designed to bring about Solidarity's disintegration, employing its network of agents, who produced fake flyers and union newspapers. The SB also provided materials for "black propaganda" that the media engaged in, and would distribute flyers and posters (on its own or in collaboration with military propaganda) degrading the opposition. These activities did not have the expected results, however. It is true that many ideological, political, group, regional, personal, and ambition-related conflicts existed within Solidarity, and on several occasions it even seemed as if the union was on the verge of breaking up. In the end, however, it was consolidating factors that prevailed (most importantly, a common enemy), and the union remained united.

The problem of "what to do with Solidarity" did not arise in the party leadership's agenda, even when the situation grew tenser in late November and early December 1980, or in March 1981. At that time, it was touch-and-go whether the leadership would launch a frontal attack on the union, by means of Soviet troops. The authorities assumed that Solidarity should continue to exist—as long as it underwent an appropriate transformation, which meant above all the elimination of its "extremists." This problem nevertheless became one of the most important, since preparations for martial law were already advanced. On September 13, 1981, a meeting of the Committee for National Defense confirmed that the army and the Ministry for Internal Affairs were fully prepared to implement martial law. Stanisław Kania said outright that the main aim "should be to bring about changes in Solidarity [to make it] a trade union that has a socialist character."[1] Poland's Soviet friends knew about this idea, as shown in a dispatch sent by the head of the KGB mission in Warsaw, General Vitalii Pavlov, to the KGB's Moscow headquarters in early December 1981. In it, he wrote (exaggerating greatly) that there were secret SB informers "at all levels of Solidarity," and that after martial law was declared and the union's leading members were arrested, they would have a significant role to play.[2]

Specific activities aimed at assuming control of Solidarity had been carried out on the local level at least as early as September 1981. In late September, a Warsaw SB cell informed the Ministry of Internal Affairs that it had substitute teams prepared for several of Solidarity's enterprise commissions, and that it was working on the creation of similar teams in several other workplaces as well. In a later assessment, the SB admitted that, in Warsaw alone, "it [was] becoming necessary" to change the workplace commissions in forty-six enterprises and institutions. Twenty-four informers were to help achieve this, along with seventy various "operational contacts."³ Also taken into consideration were people unconnected to the SB who were nevertheless in conflict with the union's leadership. These were people who had, for example, been removed from positions in Solidarity because of their overly moderate views and unwillingness to politicize the union. Functionaries were to involve them in their activities, and "every method of [winning them over] [was] admissible," as a directive stated. The same directive also advised that efforts should be made to "scare" the candidates. Similar operations were carried out in all voivodships. In addition to changing the composition of the enterprise commissions, preparations were also made to assume control of the regional boards in a similar manner.

In chapter 6, I mentioned that it was not possible to determine whether or not any of those "replacement teams" were active during the strikes—and if so, how many. According to the SB's guidelines, their main task was to provide information about events and to have a calming effect on the protests. In the plan prepared for Białystok, for example, the SB assumed that if there was no one from the local Solidarity leadership present in one of the enterprises, two informers, chosen "because of their activities to date and their personal predispositions,"⁴ would organize a meeting and create a provisional commission, with one of them becoming its chairman. Their task was, above all, to prevent workers from leaving the premises and to warn the striking workers that any propositions of that nature would constitute a provocation. Moreover, participating in the strike would provide the informers with a legitimacy that would allow them to continue their activities in the union, and enable them to influence the union's regional leadership. The plan even outlined details such as how the SB would communicate with one of them: his wife was to be used for this purpose (she would also have to be recruited).

During the strikes, just as important as influencing specific protests was the need to elicit the quickest possible public declarations of loyalty from the best-known Solidarity activists, as well as their recognition of the fact that martial law was a *fait accompli*. Of course, the higher someone's position and the more prestige he had, the more valuable he was. Channel 1 television news—the only one that was operating—broadcast the first "loyalized" activists as early as December 16. For many days thereafter, others appeared as well. Although there were a few top stars among them who really did enjoy nationwide authority, the majority was comprised of leading activists from across Poland: the chairman of the Board of the Wielkopolska Region Zdzisław Rozwalak (who, however, said a couple of weeks later, at a specially called conference, that he had acted under pressure); the chairman of the Board of the Słupsk Region, Wojciech Zierke; the chairman of the Board of the Region in Leszno, Eugeniusz Matyjas (who was later active underground); the press spokesman of the National Commission, Marek Brunné; and an entire group from the Board of the Region in Piotrków, headed by chairman Mieczysław Lech. Participants in the August 1980 strikes also appeared on television, having been removed from center stage earlier, as did the founders of the regional offices of Solidarity, such as Stanisław Zawada from Kraków, Jerzy Piórkowski from Wrocław, and Jarosław Sienkiewicz from Jastrzębie. Only Sienkiewicz—who as early as November 1980 had been suspected of having links to the SB—attacked Solidarity activists directly in his televised statement. Others limited themselves in general to brief statements expressing their loyalty to the authorities of martial law. For some of them, these declarations were the price they paid to avoid internment.

It is difficult to say what influence these statements had on the striking workers and on Solidarity members in general. They were undoubtedly perceived as part of the propaganda campaign, in which well-known figures from outside the party establishment also participated, including writers (such as Wojciech Żukrowski), artists (such as the graphic artist Julian Pałka), scholars (such as Professor Gerard Labuda), and actors (such as Stanisław Mikulski). Lists of over a hundred possible participants in this campaign had already been compiled in September 1981.

Although it was relatively easy to find a few famous people who were ready to speak out publicly in support of WRON, it was much more difficult to convince a larger group to do so. On December 23, a meeting (publicized by the media) took place between General Jaruzelski and Deputy Prime Minister Rakowski, with several dozen representatives from academia present. This conference, however, turned out to be a failed attempt to neutralize one of the groups that wielded the strongest influence on public opinion. The media emphasized the participation of the head of the Polish Academy of Sciences, the well-known medievalist Aleksander Gieysztor. They neglected to mention, however, that rectors of the three largest institutions of higher learning in Warsaw did not attend—Henryk Samsonowicz of the University of Warsaw, Władysław Findeisen of the Warsaw University of Technology, and Maria Radomska of the Main Agricultural School. If one manages to cut through the diplomatic language of the official communiqué issued after that meeting ("in the long and honest discussion, the following [participants] took the floor"; "they conveyed to the prime minister [their] opinions"), it seems that at least some of the participants at those talks refused to give the administrators of martial law their vote of confidence. According to informal notes taken at the meeting by the physicist Professor Jerzy Pniewski, Jaruzelski was not satisfied with how the meeting went, and stated in conclusion that "nothing can make us retreat in our defense of the state."[5] Shortly after the meeting, some of the participants signed a letter demanding the repeal of martial law. The minister of science, higher education, and technology, Professor Jerzy Nawrocki, resigned from his post in protest.

Undoubtedly just as important as what was happening on television screens and in the press were activities behind the scenes that were intended to subordinate Solidarity to the government. One example was the series of meetings between Minister Ciosek and several Solidarity activists, including SB informer Eligiusz Naszkowski (mentioned in chapter 5; Ciosek was probably unaware of his link to the SB). Naszkowski was brought to the minister on December 22, straight from the internment center. According to the SB's plan, he was to be freed from internment in order to develop contacts with activists from other regions. His departure for Warsaw ultimately exposed him, however, and he could of course no longer play the role for which he had been prepared, and which he had clearly been willing to do.[6]

SB functionaries carried out "operational talks" with members of Solidarity's National Commission, with those who were interned and those still at liberty (without including, of course, those who were in hiding). By mid-January, about 60 members of the commission (out of 107) had been "questioned." Most of them had been willing to speak out critically about Solidarity's activists and wanted the union to have a "working-class nature." It is impossible to tell whether these kinds of statements were sincere, or whether fear of reprisals prompted them. It would seem reasonable to assume that at least some of those questioned simply lied, saying what was expected of them in order to secure peace and security for themselves. The SB carried out similar conversations with lower-level activists. Over the course of just under two weeks, about 1,150 people were selected for positions in the reformed Solidarity, including 180 for the regional boards. It is not known whether they had all talked with the authorities, but considering their numbers, this seems unlikely. We also do not know what sort of opinions prevailed among those who were interrogated. For example, the SB in Słupsk only asked the opinion of Solidarity members who were secret agents! Out of these 81 quite unusual respondents, as many as 83 percent said that Solidarity should not be made illegal, and 54 percent said that there should not be a trade union monopoly, which would mean that there would be many different kinds of trade unions in workplaces.[7] Although this case seems curious, it would appear to show that at least the Ministry of Internal Affairs took the problem of how to influence the union's future seriously. According to procedures in force at the MSW, Operation "Renaissance" was launched on January 19, 1982. In fact, it had already been underway for a couple of months. Often, it is difficult to find a semantic relationship between the cryptonym and the thing to which it refers, but in this case the name was obvious: the operation was supposed to help bring about the trade union's "renaissance"—under the SB's supervision.

After December 13, the question of what to do with Solidarity was one of the most frequent questions during top-level meetings, including those of the "directorate," as we see in the protocols from meetings of the Politburo and Secretariat of the Central Committee, as well as the memoirs of Kazimierz Barcikowski, or the diaries of Mieczysław F. Rakowski. Thus, the SB did not undertake activities on its own initiative, but rather took direct political orders and acted based on its knowledge of the intentions of its political superiors. Jaruzelski said during his radio and television speech on December 13 that the "healthy current" would "remove from itself the prophets of confrontation and counterrevolution by its own strength and in its own interest."[8] He undoubtedly realized that he should not be too gung-ho, and that this "current" should somehow be supported. And because it would have to be discreet, only the SB would be able to provide the needed support. On December 19, during a meeting of the Central Committee Secretariat, the first secretary charged Rakowski with the preparation of a plan for further action, cautioning that it was a "necessary evil" and only "one of the variants." He then sketched out its general outline: "the unions [should be] politically uniform, pro-socialist, but not anti-Church." And he added, stressing, "pro-Church, pro-socialist."[9] The successful joining of these two elements in a mass organization would mean the squaring of the circle had been solved. The deputy prime minister had his work cut out for him.

In any case, Jaruzelski's team—at least those closest to the first secretary in their views—first assumed that a union called "Solidarity" should continue to exist. It only had to transform itself, both in terms of personnel (as far as its leadership was concerned) and organization, as well as its platform, so that it could function within the system's framework without any serious problems. It was not clearly stated whether it was supposed to be just another "transmission belt," like many others, such as the Women's League or the Union of Socialist Polish Youth, or whether it would enjoy some greater degree of autonomy. The stance of the Church surely was of great significance in these discussions. Without expressing its opinion about legal and personnel changes, it declared itself in favor of Solidarity's continued existence—and also the cessation of reprisals and release of the interned. Some within the party's leadership of course opposed this concept. They were in favor of putting an end to Solidarity swiftly and definitively. They believed it had completely compromised itself and that there was no sense in wasting time on reconstructing and reviving it in a new form.

During a Politburo meeting on December 22, the most determined hardliners were against recreating Solidarity in any form, but there were also just as many who supported the idea of trying instead to transform Solidarity. It seems that most of the party apparatus was of an opinion similar to that of the hardliners, including the secretaries of voivodship committees. This was also the case in various party circles revived by the revolutionary spirit, including those who had helped organize the "workers' guards." If General Jaruzelski was in favor of keeping the union (after its transformation, of course), he did so more for pragmatic reasons than those of principle: "We cannot say that we are liquidating Solidarity.

This is not realistic." He said it was "necessary to combat the false view that we implemented martial law in order to liquidate Solidarity completely."[10] In reality, it was not about its complete liquidation, but about depriving the union of its identity and weakening it to the point that it would become obedient.

An analysis, neutrally titled "Prospects for the Solidarity Trade Union," prepared on December 21 at the Ministry of Internal Affairs,[11] laid out the arguments in favor of maintaining the union quite clearly: a) Solidarity drew its base from workers at large enterprises; b) it arose from a protest that was "by any measure justified"; c) maintaining the union would be proof that martial law was not aimed against Solidarity as such, but against attempts to destroy the system; d) the existence of the union would facilitate the restoration of social peace, and e) would even be "a guarantee . . . against [future] crises and dramatic social conflicts." Two days later, the deputy minister of internal affairs, Bogusław Stachura, established an operational group that was to coordinate all the Ministry's Solidarity-related activities. Józef Sasin was named its head, and it was comprised of eight higher-level functionaries from all of SB's operational departments (except intelligence). Sasin was director of Department V (dealing with religious, political, and social organizations).

Similar groups were created in each voivodship headquarters. Over the coming days, additional analyses were drawn up defining the scope and aims of the security apparatus. These studies included a proposition to activate the still-secret "initiative groups" in the union at the enterprise level, and even at the voivodship level. It was assumed that the pro-government "trade unions" should be supported, as well as the autonomous ones (those linked neither to the communist party nor to Solidarity), which had also been suspended. It was expected that these activities would lead to the elimination of "anti-regime elements" within Solidarity, changes in its organization, and a general weakening of its numbers. The aim was that Solidarity should not have more than 5.5 million members—i.e., fewer than half of those employed in the state-run economy. There were even plans for Solidarity to hold a national congress—after the restrictions of martial law were lifted, of course. The aim of this congress would be to retract the program passed at the First National Congress of Delegates in October 1981, to change the statue, and to select new leaders. The SB authorities decided that, for the time being, it would be appropriate to create informal structures in workplaces that would have the character of "social sections." They advised that "the information network's most valuable units" should not be part of this initiative, since presumably workers would not completely trust these sections. The SB foresaw, probably correctly, that the workers would see these groups as being populated to a large extent by individuals linked to the government.[12]

The intellectual effort of the SB functionaries was thus considerable, but the state of research to date does not allow us to assess to what extent it was effective in practice. We do not have a clear picture of how many of these "initiative groups" were finally created, to what extent they really had an impact, or how many people they managed to divert from underground activities (with time, this probably became the main aim of the entire operation). These activities undoubtedly caused some of Solidarity's members to distance themselves from the union—usually just to the sidelines, but occasionally to the area controlled by the SB, and thus also by the communist party. A large number of Solidarity's members then did the same, whether following the others' lead or on their own. Even if they had been popular local leaders until recently, however, the activists were not to blame for the departure of a great number of Solidarity's rank and file members, as well as other activists. It was more the result of Poland's general situation, the psychological pressure of martial law, and a sense they were in danger because they were members of an organization that had been suspended—and actually made illegal.

Efforts to avoid "errors committed in the past in relation to various mass organizations and social movements" (according to an analysis dated December 21) were to be an important element in planning Solidarity's future. Barcikowski expressed this idea more clearly during a meeting of the Joint Commission of the Government and Episcopate, which took place on January 18: "our aim is not to repeat the mistakes that were committed [in dealing with] Home Army circles."[13] He was alluding to the unprecedented reprisals (over eight thousand people were killed, and over three thousand death sentences were carried out) against an enormous mass of soldiers who had belonged to the largest armed resistance of the Second World War. The communist state launched these reprisals as early as 1944, and they continued until 1956, as did the propaganda deriding the former Home Army (Armia Krajowa, AK) fighters. The most glaring example was a famous 1945 poster with the slogan "AK—the reactionaries' bespittled dwarf." Despite the communists' intentions, the reprisals aimed against the former soldiers and attempts to degrade them only served to strengthen and mythologize the AK's heroic image. The Warsaw Uprising of 1944 became the symbol not so much of the struggle against the Germans, but more generally the struggle for independence, against the Red Army as well, which had brought the communist system to Poland "on its bayonets."

The "mistakes of the AK" came up many times in debates over Solidarity itself and also more generally, in discussions about Poland's social consciousness. During a briefing of MSW's directors in June 1982, General Kiszczak warned his subordinates, "We cannot allow a mass Solidarity complex to arise, a socially resonant myth of an organization unjustly persecuted by the government, as happened with AK in the past."[14] Many people from the party establishment and its intellectual base were aware of the role that symbols and myths play. A future member of the Politburo (1988–89), the well-known psychologist Professor Janusz Reykowski, stated outright in June 1982 that "Solidarity was a movement that embodied a certain social ideal; this ideal took on the form of a myth—the myth of rebirth."[15] And a battle against myths is difficult, if not impossible, to win. At a meeting of the Politburo on June 16, 1982, the problem of Solidarity was debated again. Jan Łabęcki, a worker from the Gdańsk Shipyard, whose days in that body were already numbered, said in essence the same as Reykowski, if not so elegantly. Solidarity, he said, "functions like a sacred cow in our reality . . . the workers identify with Solidarity to spite [the party], in normal conversation it comes out that Kuroń, or some other guy, or other guys, really did stir things up, that they don't identify with them, that they are against [them], but that Solidarity is theirs." "We aren't able to conquer Solidarity as a symbol," concluded the shipyard worker, "it will always exist and will always be against us."[16] How could one not believe in the wisdom of the working class?

General Jaruzelski and his team undoubtedly delayed making the final decision to announce Solidarity's disbanding, not only because they were afraid of heroizing it, but also because they were apprehensive about what society's response would be—strikes and demonstrations. And, having an exceedingly low reputation abroad, they did not want to come into additional conflict in the international arena. It was also difficult to disregard the position of the Church completely, since it had become, particularly since the summer of 1980, a tremendously significant factor in Polish politics. In short, there was philosophizing, and Jaruzelski was basing himself on generalities. In a long exposé, delivered in the Sejm on January 25, when the legislation sanctioning martial law was passed, he devoted just three paragraphs to the trade unions and mentioned the word "Solidarity" just once, when he talked about "Solidarity's extremist forces."[17] A reader not familiar with the situation at the time might have had problems understanding who exactly had caused the country to be "standing at a precipice," since Solidarity was scarcely mentioned at all. Martial law, in contrast, was depicted as having rescued Poland from falling into that abyss.

In that speech, Jaruzelski said that, as far as the trade unions were concerned, there "were no ready solutions at the moment," but he assured his listeners that "the coming months should bring a concrete answer in the matter."[18] Not one word was mentioned about trade unions in the Central Committee's official, synthetic resolution, which was passed on February 26—its first meeting since the declaration of martial law. The problem was raised again, however, during meetings of the "directorate" and the Politburo. These high-level bodies considered, for example, how the word "independence" (*niezależność*)—which was part of Solidarity's official name—should be understood. (They came to the conclusion that it should be a "partnership with the administration.") They also considered another element in its name, *samorządność* (self-government, autonomy), which they decided was supposed to mean autonomy with relation to the party, but with recognition of its "leading role."

Not much resulted from all these debates, although there was an awareness that the Solidarity question was of strategic significance. Jaruzelski and some of central government's leading figures clearly took pains to reduce the heated conflict that had been underway since December 13 to a clash just between the government and "extremists" (no matter how broadly this term was conceived). They strove to leave as much of society as possible outside this war, and to grant this segment of society a neutral status, if not that of government supporters (since that might be impossible). Since this part of society was not participating in the battle, it would also not be the target of the state's aggression. In June 1982, General Jaruzelski spoke to the security apparatus elite about the need to "liquidate the counterrevolution." Through a quite refined metaphor, however, he told his audience that the counterrevolution "is hiding in the human forest." He added that, "although this forest is not yet favorably inclined towards us, we may not cut down all its trees."[19]

Another time, in a conversation with Ambassador Boris Aristov, he said that "we cannot persist in martial law as if we were living in a bunker." He added: "We must conduct a dialogue with society."[20] The word "dialogue" should be understood here in the spirit of the communist dictatorship's particular vocabulary, in which all channels of social communication were under government control, and only those granted special license from the government were allowed to speak out publicly. Jaruzelski, unlike the "hardline" party radicals, strove to neutralize the "silent majority." The hardliners, or the "communist extremists," in contrast, believed that martial law was a good opportunity to return to the party's Leninist roots, to revive the party's fighting spirit, to transform it into a true avant-garde of the working masses of the cities and countryside. Thus, they urged "forests be cleared" far and wide, regardless of cost. Jaruzelski did not forget that Solidarity was a movement many millions strong, and that a conflict with it should not be pursued any more than necessary.

As early as December 16, 1981, during a teleconference with the first secretaries of the party's voivodship committees, Jaruzelski said: "We must think not only about today, not only about tomorrow, but we must also think . . . of what will happen ten years from now. . . . That is why today, in adopting these harsh, determined means, we cannot do anything that might interfere with the building of the bridge that must be created between our party and the people."[21] To simplify greatly: just like Solidarity was—according to the Jadwiga Staniszkis's famous thesis—a "self-limiting revolution," so for Jaruzelski martial law was to be a "self-limiting counterrevolution." But that same day, as the general was spinning his visions of building a bridge between the government and society, miners were shot at the Wujek mine.

To a large extent, the implementation of Jaruzelski's plans for Solidarity depended on Lech Wałęsa. On the morning of December 13, Minister Stanisław

Ciosek spoke with Wałęsa when Solidarity had not even been suspended yet. A few hours later, Ciosek reported on his conversation during a Politburo meeting. Wałęsa was, of course, a key figure in the strategy to assume control of Solidarity. No one, however, was in a position to guarantee that all would follow his lead if he were to agree publicly to concessions. Perhaps there were hopes that some people would declare him a traitor, which would bring about the union's fall that the government so desired. Wałęsa's speech lacked a direct declaration of loyalty to the authorities of martial law and was limited to a call for the strikes and protests to end. Nevertheless, it might have been at least partially effective. In any case, Wałęsa was isolated in a comfortable villa in Chyliczki, near Warsaw, though it was a far cry from extravagant elegance. He was under strict supervision in conditions similar to those of house arrest—except it wasn't his house and none of his family members were with him. He was put someplace to keep him close at hand, which facilitated attempts to convince him to make concessions and to exert various kinds of pressure on him. As he recalled, "I was handed over to SB's experts for processing."[22] In internal documentation, he was given the cryptonym "333," which said nothing.

Wałęsa was a stocky, moustachioed worker in his thirties from rural Poland, an electrician who had a trade school education and only a very modest level of general knowledge. In August 1980, this father of six children (and there were still more to come) unexpectedly became a charismatic strike leader, and then that of Solidarity. He had (and continues to have) a very strong personality, with what are frankly authoritarian tendencies, and is also an egotist with a strong sense of his own exceptionalism. During an interview in the summer of 1981, he said, "I was always alone, I am [now], and probably will be,"[23] although he was, after all, the head of a large family and the leader of an organization numbering many millions of people, surrounded by dozens of helpers, hired applauders, and enemies. Even at that time, he was consumed by a sense of mission and was sure of his own great abilities: "I have a vision," he said in the same interview, "and I am capable of putting many things in order, of bringing about the kind of Poland we would like to have. I am able to outmaneuver and win everything."[24]

As a child, he was a troublemaker; in his youth, he was energetic and resourceful, with a tendency to lead. This characteristic was apparent, for example, when he was promoted to corporal and squad commander after a year in military service: "He liked discipline, he was demanding, but understanding," recalls a former comrade-in-arms.[25] Wałęsa was very active in the events of December 1970, when as a worker at the Gdańsk Shipyard he took part in the strike and was a member of the strike committee. His arrest by the SB just after the bloody quashing of the workers' protest led to an episode that was to weigh on him later, even today. It was then that he agreed to provide information about the situation in the shipyard, and was registered as an informer with the code name "Bolek."[26]

Chapter Ten

In the fragmentary archival materials that survive, we find confirmation that he did indeed provide some information, but he was increasingly unwilling to do so, until he finally refused to cooperate and, after a few years, he was "eliminated from the network," as SB jargon called it.

Having been fired a couple of times for "mouthing off" to his superiors, in 1978 he found his way into the newly organized democratic opposition and became involved in the Free Trade Unions, which were in KOR's sphere of influence. From there, it was a straight path for Wałęsa to become strike leader, and to also lead millions of Poles who were demanding changes and striving to bring them about. Although Wałęsa had many adversaries in Solidarity, some of whom had ambitions of becoming his rival, the general view was that he was the union's real and indisputable leader. He often spoke clumsily, violating the tenets of literary Polish, but he had an excellent rapport with crowds, which were primarily comprised of first-generation workers, usually from peasant stock, with a background similar to his, who were uneducated and reacted emotionally. In many respects, he was simply one of them, which was his main strength. His great political intuition was intertwined with a common-sense, pragmatic view of the world of politics: "It's not important who is sitting opposite me, it's important to outwit him, eliminate him, and win what can be won."[27] Although he may have been lonely, he was not easy pickings for General Jaruzelski's clique.

Convincing Wałęsa to capitulate was an extremely important task, and authorities employed various instruments to this end. Since the leader of Solidarity was a deeply religious Catholic, one of these tools was the Church. Thus, it is not surprising that, as early as December 13, Wałęsa was allowed to meet with Bishop Bronisław Dąbrowski, secretary of the Conference of the Polish Episcopate and member of the Joint Commission, and with Father Alojzy Orszulik, director of the Episcopate's Press Office and the Church's secretary in the Joint Commission. Both had been having frequent talks with people in the government for some time, and were well acquainted with those in the party responsible for relations with the Church, particularly Barcikowski. Their first meeting with Solidarity's leader while in isolation took place on December 14. According to a brief note, composed by Father Orszulik for John Paul II, the conversation "was about the possibility of undertaking a dialogue between the government and presidium of the National Commission." Wałęsa allegedly said that "he was ready for talks after 17 December," but that he steadfastly requested to meet with his advisors.[28]

Both clerics encouraged Wałęsa to hold these talks, but it would depend on General Jaruzelski whether or not they would take place, under what conditions, and with what aim. Next, Solidarity's chairman spoke once again with Minister Ciosek, who came on December 18. The meeting must have been unpleasant for the government guest, since Wałęsa was irate after the tragedy at the Wujek mine and—if one can use this expression—mutinous. Two days later, when Father

Orszulik came again, Wałęsa told him that he would not "talk with the bandits who shot at my people."²⁹ Solidarity's leader really did prove obstinate about this. He was not swayed by a meeting with the papal envoy, Archbishop Luigi Poggi, nor even by a visit of several days from his wife Danuta, who was eight months pregnant. The tone of John Paul II's letter to General Jaruzelski, a copy of which archbishop Poggi gave to Wałęsa, might have actually persuaded Wałęsa to stand his ground. The pope addressed Wałęsa directly, which undoubtedly raised his spirits: "I assure you," wrote John Paul II, "that at this especially difficult moment I am with you and your family with all my heart, with all who are suffering."³⁰

During later visits, Father Orszulik persistently tried to persuade Wałęsa to hold talks with the authorities. Wałęsa, however, at first objected resolutely: he announced he would go on a hunger strike, and also that he wanted to escape. He also believed "we are close to victory," and that, within two weeks, "they will have to come to us on their knees."³¹ He drew information not only from those who were visiting him, but also from the media (including the Polish broadcasts of Radio Free Europe, which he listened to as much as he could). When he realized that the workers' will for active resistance had been extinguished, he told the priest on December 27 that he was ready for talks. His conditions, which he conveyed on January 6 in a *pro memoria* that the Episcopate presented to Barcikowski, were essentially impossible for the authorities to accept. His conditions stipulated that, during the talks, which should be conducted on neutral ground, members of the Presidium of the National Commission and certain experts (whether at liberty or interned) would participate on Solidarity's behalf. These included Tadeusz Mazowiecki and Bronisław Geremek. Wałęsa summarized the content of the future agreement thus: "[Return] the union to its statute, and the army to its barracks."³² Instead of an unequivocal answer, the "directorate" again sent Minister Ciosek for talks.

In excerpts from his notes and a report submitted to Rakowski, we see that Wałęsa, standing by his initial conditions, agreed that Solidarity should be changed (it should be "calmer," he said), should stop playing the role of a "political organization," and should eliminate radicals ("do them in politically"). Wałęsa was ready to give Jaruzelski his "word of honor that [he] would respect the rules of martial law and not conduct any conspiratorial work," but, he warned, "I won't sign any declaration like that because I'd be done for." According to Ciosek, his interlocutor "gives the impression of being relaxed and sure of himself," and he "feels he is the Union's leader."³³ In analyzing the words of Solidarity's chairman, Rakowski and his subordinate concluded that "it is not certain when what Wałęsa is saying is a clever tactic and when it is [his] true view."³⁴ They seem to have hit the nail on the head: Wałęsa, as a consummate risk-taker, was careful not to lay all his cards on the table, always to have something up his sleeve, and to bluff as boldly as possible.

Both the Church's urging to find a formula for compromise, encouraged by the government, and Minister Ciosek's "pestering" fit within the limits of normal negotiation games. Authorities also employed other tools, however, which were still not physical, although they may have been less refined. On December 17, 21, and 29—and thus almost alternating with Father Orszulik—a colonel named Władysław Iwaniec, Wałęsa's immediate commanding officer from his military service more than fifteen years earlier, visited Wałęsa. At that time, Iwaniec was a first lieutenant. This was surely an attempt to put psychological pressure on Wałęsa, since it was supposed that Wałęsa might have something to hide from his time in the army. Even if there weren't any "skeletons," then this appeal to the authority of his former superior might have some impact. The next idea was even more insidious. On January 20, Lieutenant-Colonel Czesław Wojtalik showed up unexpectedly at the luxurious Branicki palace in Otwock, near Warsaw, where Wałęsa had been transferred from Chyliczki. Wojtalik was an SB functionary from Gdańsk, who had overseen the Gdańsk Shipyard case in the 1970s, at which time he had had personal contact with "Bolek" (i.e., Wałęsa). Wojtalik's very presence was undoubtedly supposed to break Wałęsa, since it was quite clearly a form of blackmail: if you don't make concessions, we'll announce you were a secret informer. So much importance was placed on this meeting that General Kiszczak even told his Soviet colleague, General Pavlov, about it.[35] Wałęsa managed to withstand it all, even in isolation.

During the first official meeting of the Joint Commission since the imposition of martial law, Barcikowski reacted skeptically to the Church's postulates about the adoption of decisions aimed at preserving Solidarity, cessation of reprisals, and the launching of negotiations. He said, "The longer that talks last, the more unproductive they become," and accused Wałęsa of making "contradictory statements."[36] This was true, but that was exactly how Wałęsa thought politics should be conducted with the government, which he didn't trust one whit. In the end, however, pressured by Father Orszulik, he submitted a written statement in which he said, "I am ready for talks without any preliminary conditions and according to the guidelines established by the government and Episcopate representatives." In his memoirs, Wałęsa admitted that "I made so many concessions that in the end I arrived at the propositions put forth by the Church." He also said that "the story of our talks [with Father Orszulik] is actually the story of how the conditions I had set were gradually eliminated."[37] Among those in charge of martial law, however, the scale was already tipping toward the reintroduction of exclusively pro-government trade unions, without Wałęsa, any moderates, or even Solidarity members who had conciliated. In a certain sense, the moment when Solidarity's chairman was handed an internment order on January 26 symbolically summed up this entire episode. It happened the day after the prime minister presented his exposé in the Sejm. The order was dated December 12, 1981, so we can say that this episode, and maybe even this phase of martial law, lasted six weeks. For almost another four months, Wałęsa was kept "close at hand," near Warsaw, where not only Father Orszulik and other priests visited him, but also his wife, and even his children. This was a real "golden cage," but most often he was there alone with his guards. His situation was probably particularly difficult after he was moved, on May 11, to a government center in Arłamów, several hundred kilometers from Warsaw in southeast Poland, near the Soviet border.

Meanwhile, Rakowski's team was at work carrying out tasks that General Jaruzelski had ordered. On February 22, it announced the "Propositions of the Committee of the Council of Ministers on Trade Unions Regarding the Future of the Trade Union Movement."[38] This document had been discussed at a meeting of the Politburo two days earlier, when opinions were divided. Some believed that the name "Solidarity" should be kept (including Jan Łabęcki, Hieronim Kubiak, and Zbigniew Messner), while others believed that initiating a public discussion was senseless (including Jan Główczyk and Zofia Grzyb). No significant changes were introduced, however. The document was formally an invitation to discuss the matter, but it was sent to Solidarity's rank and file members, and only to those activists who—as it was written—"were not responsible for the union's mistakes."[39] As one of the Politburo members put it, in terms of its demands, the document was too "rambling," and its authors used generalities. They also used a magic, but already hackneyed, formulation that said there "can be no return to either the situation before August 1980 or before 13 December 1981."

The propositions were based on the idea that the trade union movement would be built "from below"—first in the workplaces, disregarding the already existing union organizations. The document stated definitively that the movement would be organized according to trade, rather than regionally, as it had been up to now. Of course, its authors also ruled that "individuals known for their destructive stance" would have to be banned. No specific names were mentioned, but everyone knew who was meant anyway. The bill on trade unions, after long debates and numerous consultations involving a wide variety of participants, had already made it through much of the legislative process by early December 1981, but it was not taken into consideration. (It had been accepted by Sejm committees.) A document dated February 22 had accepted the term "pluralism," but it was presented very enigmatically. It was apparent that the problem had made the communist party leadership weary; after all, for Jaruzelski, keeping the name Solidarity had been a necessary evil anyway. The first reactions from underground Solidarity were decidedly negative. People saw the document as evidence that, for the government, any trade unions would have to be subordinate to the party.

The publication of the document prepared by Rakowski can be seen as a sign that the government, in fact, had decided not to preserve Solidarity, and thus would also no longer be using the union for its own aims. As far as formally liquidating the union went, the problem was not so much making the decision itself as setting a date for it to take place. The fact that it took place only in October, after many months' delay, was certainly not because anyone in the party leadership had nurtured hopes that they would succeed in winning over Wałęsa, or reach an agreement with leading underground activists or those in prison. The decision was made then for completely pragmatic reasons: they thought that, over the course of a few months, emotions in society would not be running so high, and thus reactions to the union's liquidation would be weaker and no longer constitute a threat to the country's general stability. It was becoming increasingly clear that Solidarity was gaining strength and organizing itself underground. It was also becoming obvious that the chances of opposing it with another legal, socialist Solidarity were close to zero. The maneuver sometimes used by communists—vassalizing a foreign or enemy element and incorporating it into its own system—had failed this time. The vast majority of Solidarity's leaders at various levels had refused to participate. Although members may often have been passive, with many leaving the organization, they were not necessarily traitors willing to shore up the government's victorious camp. All of the SB's intensive work, laboriously written instructions and plans, its vast recruitment, and dozens of operational schemes had not proved very useful. Thus, the authorities made a political decision to abandon the whole plan. All that remained after Operation "Renaissance" were documents in the archives, and the hundreds of people whose wills the authorities had managed to break.

Chapter Eleven

Underground

Solidarity's transition to operations underground was a smooth one, and began as early as the night of December 12–13. Some of its activists—including very prominent ones, such as Zbigniew Bujak, Zbigniew Romaszewski, and Bogdan Lis—went into hiding that night and did not take part in the protests in factories and other workplaces, which of course by their very nature were not secret. The first larger group of activists in hiding was comprised of those who had taken part in the strikes but managed to avoid arrest after they had been broken. Many of these activists "went underground" immediately. Sometimes they did so as a group, such as in Białystok, where about ten people from the Regional Board first took refuge at the presbytery of St. Roch's. Then, dressed in cassocks, they were taken to the parish church and only from there to their individual hiding places.[1] The regional activists from Częstochowa attempted something similar, but failed. Six took refuge at the Jasna Góra sanctuary. The militia removed them brutally and unceremoniously, chasing away the pilgrims gathered there in the process and arresting many people inside the church. As the Paulists living there emphasized, not even the Gestapo did this during the occupation.[2] Priests helped many union activists. In the first months, there were people in hiding in every Solidarity region. In some regions, the largest or most active, several dozen people or more were in hiding. Some of the activists from the Independent Students' Union were also in hiding, as well as people from the pre-August opposition, and activists from the Independent Self-Governing Trade Union of Individual Farmers Solidarity (NSZZ IR). Sometimes, people whom the SB were not interested in went into hiding, too—which was understandable, considering the emotional atmosphere. Not surprisingly, people were apprehensive after seeing tanks on the streets, hearing rumors that the army had attacked striking enterprises, and learning that hundreds of people had been arrested.

Just how many people were active in the underground in a strict sense is difficult to establish. During the first months of martial law, probably hundreds of activists were in hiding. This number tended to wane, since although new people may have been joining—including people who had just been released from internment, or those who only became seriously involved in underground activities later—many more people were still being caught. There were also increasingly frequent cases of people "coming to the surface" for personal or family reasons, or because they were having difficulties staying in hiding. Sometimes their return home was negotiated with the SB, but this happened very rarely as long as martial law was in force. The most important of these cases was when a group of Gdańsk activists from the Young Poland Movement revealed themselves in June 1982. Staying underground for a long time required a well-organized and competent support system, and hiding required a great deal of time, energy, and money. Record-holders like Bujak or Kornel Morawiecki did, however, manage to hold out until 1986–87.

In the beginning, methods of hiding were improvised and amateurish. Even those active in the democratic opposition before Solidarity had not been accustomed to functioning in complete secrecy before the declaration of martial law, even though they had experience concealing their activities at least to some extent. They did, however, learn how to avoid being tapped, or how to "break loose" from the secret police if need be, most often by learning from their own mistakes. But then they would return home as usual. Yes, a more or less artfully camouflaged "Bureau B" (the "external observation" department) functionary could be waiting in front of their building—but they were not in hiding. Most of those who went underground after December 13 had certainly read books about the AK, some of which were even part of school reading, such as *Kamienie na szaniec*, the famous book by Aleksander Kamiński on the AK underground. Alternatively, they might have read about other underground movements, which were so common in Poland's nineteenth- and twentieth-century history. Although they already might have had some idea of how to go into hiding, the first guide adapted for the current situation was the brochure "Mały konspirator" (Little conspirator), written by Czesław Bielecki, which appeared only in 1983. It nevertheless caused a sensation: ten editions came out in just one year.

Neither Solidarity nor any of the other political opposition groups had cells devoted to "legalization" activities, so the union's activists—even those who had been designated for the "second lines"—had no false documents ready. Incidentally, unless someone was well-known or had "non-kosher" documents such as flyers or typewritten copies, people could confidently present their documents to be checked during the first few weeks of martial law, since the street patrols did not have any arrest warrants or wanted lists. These lists appeared later, as the prosecutor's office launched inquiries and the SB established formal operational reports. In early January, for example, the Warsaw SB was only looking for thirty-six people from Solidarity's Mazowsze Region leadership. The situation of Solidarity employees was worse, since their positions were listed under employment details in their identity papers, and martial law rules required that people carry this document with them at all times. Understandably, this fact could easily spark the interest of those checking documents, even if it was just a rank and file soldier or ZOMO functionary. Problems also started when someone would break one of the rules of martial law (such as the curfew), since those apprehended were supposed to be taken to the militia headquarters, where authorities could check whether the person was of interest to the SB. Even if the militia registered thousands of people every single day for that type of infraction, the chances that they would catch someone who was in hiding were nevertheless not very great. The fact that the telephone lines were blocked, a serious problem for both everyday and conspiratorial activities, paradoxically also aided those who were in hiding and all the "conspirators." This was because the SB could no longer use telephone tapping, that important operational tool, to acquire information about who and where these conspirators were, and what they were planning.

No false documents had been prepared for those in hiding, and neither had apartments, or places where people could meet. While there is nothing strange in this, it would have been strange indeed if a legally operating, million-strong trade union had issued false documents to its members and prepared itself logistically, even in terms of supplies, to function underground. At first, finding a place was not very difficult, although it did require some effort. Later, the situation became increasingly complicated, in part because of the demands of conspiratorial work, which meant frequently changing one's place of residence, meeting places, and spaces used for printing shops, not returning too quickly to "old addresses," and not availing oneself of the services of friends, family, and people active in illegal activities.

Hiding was significantly easier in large cities than smaller ones, where "everyone knows everyone." Very often, the secret accommodations or meeting places were at the homes of older people. Sometimes, the people offering refuge had experience dating back to the German occupation, and this new underground work was a present-day continuation for them. Because of the state control of foodstuffs (including meat, butter, and cereals), providing those in hiding with food posed a problem. The funds for those in hiding were also relatively modest. The entire underground movement required significant funds—especially for its printing activities—and the support from abroad (in the form of money or equipment) began arriving on a broader scale only in 1983–84. Not counting the chance parcels (which sometimes went to random people), money began arriving more systematically from abroad in mid-1982.

According to the Solidarity Coordination Office in Brussels, it sent about $10,000 to Poland in 1982 and approximately $62,000 during all of 1983.[3] Foreign Solidarity representatives used many of the financial resources received from Western trade unions to cover the costs of offices, salaries, publications, etc., but above all to purchase the printing equipment sent to Poland, and sometimes also electronics (parts for radio transmitters or equipment for monitoring the SB and MO radiotelephone conversations). Solidarity's own funds, from the sums withdrawn from banks before December 13, were inadequate and unrenewable, if they existed at all. The Wrocław underground had the largest funds, since 80 million złotys had been taken out of the Regional Board's bank account and deposited with Archbishop Tadeusz

Gocłowski shortly before the imposition of martial law.[4] The Mazowsze Region had 10 million złotys that it had acquired in a similar fashion. The regularly collected union dues made it to higher structures only with difficulty. Most often, they were used locally, in the enterprises; to a large extent, they were used to help the reprisal victims' families, and those fired from their jobs.

Solidarity underground would surely have failed if the underground had been comprised only of "conspirators" in the strict sense—i.e., those who were in hiding, and those who were helping them directly (for example, people providing accommodation). But most people who participated in underground activities lived and operated "on the surface"; they lived in their own homes, went to work, or pursued their educations, had rationing cards in their own names, and had normal family and social lives (which were actually blossoming during the curfew). So, the vast majority of those who were released from internment or from prisons after finishing their sentences (and who didn't leave the country) did not go "underground." Of course, some of those "surface people" (known as *jawniacy*) sometimes went underground every once in a while—for example, if they were involved in underground printing activities, or were going on longer visits to see someone in hiding (something not many people did).

Except during the first few months of martial law, when the number of people in hiding was at its height, it was largely people who were living "like everyone else" who were involved in both the secret enterprise and inter-enterprise commissions, and most of the illegal publications (including printing and distribution). Often they played very important roles for the people in hiding (as couriers, for example). Bogumiła Kowalska, who retired early because she had been fired, recalled, "Three times a week, I'd go to the underground office of the Mazowsze Regional Executive Commission, pick up mail there, which I'd take in normal bags to the staff of *Tygodnik Mazowsze*, and to Zbyszek [Bujak] and Wiktor [Kulerski]. Then I'd go back to the office with their mail, and often in the afternoon, I would [take them] to the meetings. . . . I was really tramping all over Warsaw. . . . I used to hurry to make it home before the curfew."[5] Entire families were involved in underground activities (which is natural); even children were sometimes entrusted with delivering packages in the near vicinity. In the winter of 1982, the underground asked people to go out with bags or backpacks, to make it harder for patrols to catch everyone who was transporting large quantities of flyers, newspapers, or reams of paper. Sometimes it seems that some people continue to heed this appeal even today. Church circles played a very important role in the creation and existence of "underground" Solidarity, but that was going on underground as well as above. I use the word "circles" intentionally because, based on the information we have to date, priests were the main support, particularly the parish priests and vicars, and less often the Church hierarchy, i.e., the Episcopate. (On this specifically, see chapter 15.)

During Operation "Fir" and in the days that followed, during the strikes and confusion that prevailed, activities were more or less spontaneous. These were consciously or unconsciously based on the belief that the union was now facing a prolonged period of underground existence. Thus, people rescued whatever they could from union headquarters and offices—typewriters, printing equipment, paper supplies (and of course banners!), which were then stashed in improvised hiding places. In some regions, some of the equipment had already been hidden earlier, and some publishers' underground printing equipment predated August 1980. In Białystok, where the SB and ZOMO were probably operating sluggishly, on the afternoon of December 13, one of the activists from the Confederation of Independent Poland simply drove up to the headquarters of the Regional Board in a truck and took away three duplicating machines, typewriters, stencils, and quite a lot of paper.[6] Sometimes, "communal property" was "appropriated" in order to acquire equipment and paper; in other words, it was stolen from factories and institutions. Eventually, a black market emerged for paper bought from dishonest enterprise employees (who were nevertheless "working for a good cause") and wholesale warehouses. In the beginning, typewriters were in demand, too, and there were thousands of those in private hands (others were available in institutions). Silkscreen, which had already been adapted for underground use in 1978, facilitated the printing of many copies without a suitably equipped room or any heavy and noisy machinery, which would also break frequently. Most commonly used, however, were mimeographs, which were quiet and relatively small and could fit into a couple of bags, along with the printed materials produced. Virtually every enterprise used these machines—most common were Gestetner and Roneo Vickers—so thousands of these could be found throughout Poland. From there, many "leaked" to the underground.

Even those who did not believe in the famous government propaganda slogan "Poles Can Do It" (Polak potrafi), actually did manage to "do it": an impressive number of minor improvements were made to equipment for the purposes of underground printing, utilizing substances having nothing to do with polygraphy. A real hit was ink made out of a paste called "Komfort" that was normally used to wash grease from hands, but "handymen" could make ink from almost anything. Szczepan Rudka, in his book on the underground press in Wrocław, gives this recipe for printer's ink: "It was made out of flakes of gray soap (the most commonly available), to which India ink was added. The resulting mixture was heated until it started to boil. Any impurities were skimmed off the top and discarded, after which the solution was cooled. While it was coagulating, eau de cologne was added to it, or a fifty percent solution of alcohol. Sometimes other liquids containing alcohol were used, such as methylated spirit, the medicine 'Acnosan,' or strong moonshine."[7] Obtaining the latter was not a problem. One could produce it oneself, and what wasn't used for printing could be consumed in a more natural fashion.

During the first months of martial law, virtually no printing equipment succeeded in making it into Poland from the West, especially professional-quality machines. Bigger shipments began in mid-1982. Exactly how much equipment the underground was using is something we will never know. Even in Rudka's work there is no general summary of the "duplicating power" of Wrocław's underground printers. The SB estimated that underground printers could produce about a million pieces of A4-format paper at a time. I have not been able to verify this number, nor do I know on what basis the MSW experts calculated this figure, or to which period of time they were referring. From their point of view, this estimate was not so important for defining the scope of underground printing's influence in Poland in general, as it was for determining how many flyers—to urge people to strike and announce a strike's aim, date, and time, for example—could be quickly produced underground. It is difficult to imagine a situation in which all the union's structures and groups that had access of any kind to printing equipment could be mobilized to act simultaneously in order to achieve one task. But if we accept the SB's reasoning and calculations, it would mean that the underground could disperse about two million flyers throughout Poland. Although this was a considerable amount, it was, of course, only a fraction of the government's own printing capacity.

In terms of numbers, periodicals definitely dominated underground publishing during the first year of martial law. Most often, these were little newspapers with just a couple of pages. As early as January, however, other multiple-page publications began appearing, among which the majority (about two-thirds) were brochures with ten to twenty pages. Over the course of 1982, at least 280 titles were published. At first, it was mostly "current" texts: collections of occasional poetry, analyses of the causes and course of martial law, or documentation regarding events since December 13 (such as almanacs). Some of these publications were prepared by ad hoc groups that did not become permanent publishers. Some of the publishing houses that had already existed within the opposition before 1980—such as NOW-a, Krąg, or Głos—renewed their operations relatively quickly, thanks in part to the fact that they had managed to keep some of their printing equipment and (despite internments) some of their staff. New publishing ventures were soon launched, of which the most important in 1982 was probably CDN, at least in terms of numbers of publications. CDN grew out of a group that had been publishing a small newspaper that had its base of support in the Solidarity enterprise commissions in several Warsaw factories.

Some of the larger periodicals also began publishing their own book series, such as Warsaw's *Tygodnik Wojenny* (War Weekly) and Kraków's *Obserwator Wojenny* (War Observer). With time, publishing houses like Przedświt, Wydawnictwo Społeczne KOS, and Słowo strengthened their presence as well. At first, distribution of these printed materials posed a serious problem, since the previous network had been eliminated during Solidarity's existence, and the creation of new ones required time. Władysław Chojnacki has estimated that print runs fluctuated between 400 and 2,000 copies—i.e., were relatively small. Some of the books, however, had print runs of over 5,000, and even as many as 8,000–10,000. George Orwell's *1984* had one of the largest print runs; in just one of its editions (and there were many), 17,000 copies were produced.[8] The illegal news sheets, of course, had much higher print runs, and reached even as many as 40,000–50,000 copies. Over half of all printed materials were published in Warsaw. Despite what were sometimes close contacts with union structures or political groups, publishing represented a separate and well-hidden segment of the underground.

It is difficult to determine how many people were active in Solidarity's underground activities, the emergent political groups (although their numbers started burgeoning only in 1983–84), the publishing of independent news sheets and other materials, and how many were active in the extremely varied forms of social resistance, such as in the field of culture. In 1983, Zbigniew Bujak stated that there were about 300,000 people directly involved in "union work," and he estimated the number of regular readers of the news sheets and underground printed materials and those paying union dues to be about 1.2 million.[9] Two years later, when underground activity experienced its first crisis, he estimated that about 50,000–70,000 people were participating directly, and that about 200,000 were more loosely involved.[10] A lack of sources does not permit us to verify these estimates, but the numbers Bujak gives seem in both cases to be too high. One can, however, say with confidence that during martial law, and until 1989, underground Solidarity was not only the core of resistance and social opposition, but was also a large-scale social phenomenon. As a result, "clearing it out" (as Jaruzelski said) was a difficult task, and a delicate one that would be impossible to achieve quickly without resorting to truly Stalinist methods. Anna Dodziuk, one of the editors of *Tygodnik Mazowsze*, recalls, "They would have to put us to the wall and shoot us. And if they don't put people to the wall and shoot them, then . . . people get ready to resist."[11]

General Jaruzelski's comment about the "human forest . . . which is not favorably inclined towards us" prompts the question of what society's attitude toward Solidarity actually was. This question is difficult if not impossible to answer. Public opinion polls conducted at the time, both by official institutions and by independent sociologists, are burdened by a high margin of error. Moreover, depending on who was conducting them, they show significantly different results (not unusual for sociological studies). The studies conducted on a Poland-wide sample by the state-run Center for Public Opinion Research (Ośrodek Badania Opinii Publicznej, OBOP) in June 1982 show that a clear majority (about 62 percent) of those surveyed believed the imposition of martial law was justified, and a large percentage (about 40 percent) stated that they were not troubled by the restrictions introduced on December 13.[12] Information from another OBOP survey in mid-January is striking, and suggests one should treat this type of research very cautiously. It concluded that just 8 percent of those questioned believed that "suspension of the trade unions, the lack of union press [publications] and printed materials" was a "severe restriction."

Research conducted in May and June 1982 by party sociologists among four thousand workers from large-scale industrial enterprises (i.e., in a very specific social group that was crucial for evaluating Solidarity's impact) brought different results. These are not fully comparable, owing to the fact that a different set of questions was used. According to this research, almost 80 percent of those surveyed believed that Solidarity looked after workers' interests either well or very well. Only 9 percent believed that the union was most responsible for the need to impose martial law, while one-third said it was solely the government that was responsible. In February 1982, a survey of university and secondary school students was carried out in Warsaw, commissioned by the Socialist Union of Polish Students. Young people in large cities constitute a unique social group and their views cannot be said to represent those of young people as a whole, and especially not those of the general adult population. It is striking, however, that the picture this survey gives is entirely different from OBOP's. Among the students surveyed, 69 percent believed that the decision to impose martial law was wrong. About 52 percent believed that the decision was motivated by the "desire to maintain power," and only 5 percent were convinced that it was in order to prevent civil war. In contrast, according to a report done by independent sociologists (unfortunately using research that was based on an unrepresentative sample, and only in the Warsaw metropolitan area), about 80 percent of those surveyed believed that the imposition of martial law was wrong, 53 percent that it had been caused by chaos, 64 percent that it would divide the nation, and about 77 percent were convinced that Solidarity would still exist after martial law was lifted.

Although it is probably not justified to make general conclusions based on this research, except that obviously the Poles were deeply divided, one can risk the following hypothesis regarding the social mood and attitude in the first half of 1982: Solidarity had the most supporters (and the government had the most opponents) among workers from large-scale enterprises, and big-city youth and urban residents. In the countryside, and in small towns with no industry, support for the union was significantly lower, which is to say negligible. Another hypothesis suggests that while it was the workers from some of the large enterprises (miners, steel mill workers, shipyard workers) who were most radical in the first days after martial law was declared, as reflected by the strikes, later it was the urban youth who were among the most radical opponents to martial law. In any case, even though the "human forest" may have been extensive and thick, it clearly did not include all of society.

The process of transforming legally operating union cells into underground structures recalls Chaos in Greek mythology—i.e., the state of "unorganized *Ur*-material" from which an ordered world would eventually emerge. This comparison is, of course, an exaggeration, not just because of the difference in scale: the Greeks meant the entire world, whereas, for the Poles, it involved only a particular trade union in a medium-sized country. The inadequacy of the comparison stems mainly from the fact that a certain order had already existed before December 13, albeit a broken one. Thus, perhaps we should speak of ruins rather than *Ur*-material.

On the enterprise level, it was relatively simple to go underground, although this, too, had its problems, in part because of the mass internments and arrests. We do not yet know how many of the enterprise commissions were reestablished. On the basis of various bits of fragmentary information, one can conclude that this number was surely not less than half, although regions and towns varied greatly—for example, in Wrocław in mid-March, about two-thirds of the union cells in factories were operating. Different trades also varied, but the Solidarity organization in administrative offices and very small enterprises did not stand much chance of reestablishing itself. Wherever secret commissions were formed, attempts were made in general to respect the results of the commission elections that had taken place earlier. Often, however, it was impossible to gather a representative and an active quorum, whether because of internments or arrests, or because people had withdrawn from public activities. Thus, people with no formal mandate from the electorate began to be active.

It is difficult to say whether or not in the beginning—when Chaos was being transformed into order—the SB's activities aimed at penetrating the underground were effective. There were certainly numerous instances when informers or people in "operational contact" with the secret police had been part of commissions earlier, or joined them only after December 13. There is no group data on their numbers or the degree to which they were active. Probably these individuals were entrusted with collecting and conveying information, rather than more active roles. It is possible, however, given that Operation "Renaissance" was underway, that many of them were charged with tasks that went beyond the mere collection of information. As research to date has shown, only in later years were the structures of underground Solidarity penetrated more deeply.

Many of the enterprise commissions actually went underground "in mid-flow"; some of them, especially from the large enterprises and universities, became very active immediately. At first, they concentrated on collecting dues and assisting the families of those who had been arrested or fired. Some of the commissions had so many people to take care of that they had to resort to assistance from charity drives, undertaken by the Church on a large scale. Some activities aimed at providing information and promoting the union's cause. From late December, there were increasing numbers of underground news sheets, only some of which were continuations of earlier publications. For example, in January, Solidarity commissions either launched or renewed publishing activities at the following enterprises in Wrocław: "Mera-Elwro" (electronics factory), Zakłady Naprawcze Taboru Kolejowego (railroad repair workshops), Miejskie Przedsiębiorstwo Komunikacyjne (municipal communications company), Pafawag (locomotive factory), and Fadroma (construction equipment factory). In February, publishing began at Dolmel (electric machinery factory), in March at FAT (lathe manufacturer), in April at Agromet-Pilmet (agricultural equipment factory) and Hydral (aluminum castings manufacturing). The Solidarity cells at the Wrocław post-secondary institutions also published news sheets. Moreover, from December 14, *Z dnia na dzień* (From one day to the next) was published; it was not liquidated after the strikes were broken.

On the basis of incomplete data, Władysław Chojnacki determined that 770 illegal publications were produced during 1982, of which most were enterprise or inter-enterprise Solidarity publications.[13] In fact, each self-respecting enterprise commission published a bulletin as a point of honor. Traditional community service was impossible because of the suspension not only of the trade unions, but also of the workers' self-government, which after Solidarity's creation mostly was liberated from the auspices of the communist party's cells in the workplaces. After the imposition of martial law, the government did not rush to revive the self-government out of a fear that it would create the opportunity for underground Solidarity to influence the life of the enterprise directly. For a long time, secret enterprise commissions were thus somehow left to organize mutual aid, present general demands (such as releasing those who had been arrested and re-legalizing the union), and organize protests.

In several large cities, after the wave of strikes had been broken, inter-enterprise structures were created alongside secret enterprise commissions. These did not aspire to replace the regional offices. In Warsaw in late February 1982, the Inter-Enterprise Workers' Committee was formed, and about forty enterprises concluded an agreement (initiated by Adam Borowski) in early March. It was known as the "CDN Agreement," based on the initials of a little publication it issued, *Ciąg Dalszy Nastąpi* (To be continued). In April, the two initiatives merged and adopted the name Inter-Enterprise Workers' Committee of Solidarity (Międzyzakładowy Robotniczy Komitet Solidarności, MRKS). Already in January, a group of several enterprise committees named themsleves NSZZ Solidarity Inter-Enterprise Coordinating Committee (Międzyzakładowy Komitet Koordynacyjny NSZZ Solidarność, MKK), which then associated itself with a publication titled *Wola* (Warsaw's Wola district was home to most of the enterprises that were included in MKK). There was a similar situation in Łódź, where in late December and early January the Solidarity Inter-Enterprise Coordinating

Committee (Międzyzakładowy Komitet Koordynacyjny NSZZ "Solidarność," MKK) and the Solidarity Inter-Enterprise Committee (Międzyzakładowy Komitet NSZZ "Solidarność," MK"S") were created, for example.

Throughout Poland, several dozen similar structures were probably established, including in smaller centers (such as the Solidarity Committee for Inter-Enterprise Coordination in Pruszków). They were created in the organizational vacuum that arose wherever the union's regional leadership did not reactivate quickly, or wherever there were internal conflicts, which were generally rooted in disputes predating martial law. Later, differences also arose between the inter-enterprise structures and regional leadership about their choice of tactics.

After December 13, organizations began emerging that were not associated with any enterprises or previously existing Solidarity structures. Many academic cells of the Independent Students' Union were reactivated, often under a different name, such as the Academic Resistance Group, the Academic Self-Defense Movement, and the Student Committee for the Defense of Democracy. Some Independent Self-Governing Trade Union of Individual Farmers Solidarity organizations resumed their activities as well. On December 20, groups of friends in Warsaw began establishing small conspiratorial groups at work or in their homes. The anonymous people behind this initiative announced their appeal as the founding group of the Solidarity Defense Circles (Koła Obrony Solidarności, KOS).[14] These were supposed to be small, informal groups, created by a "system of fives": one person selected five coworkers, each of whom could create a new group of five, and so on. The name KOS was universally accepted and, during January, at least several dozen of these KOSes were created in various cities. From mid-January, *Kos* (Blackbird) was published, which turned out to be one of the longest-lived underground publications, lasting until 1989. During 1982, publications titled *Kos* appeared, for example, in Gliwice, Kielce, Wrocław, and Kraków. Most of the KOSes joined the Solidarity structures quite quickly, or began to cooperate closely with them.

Underground structures also began springing up around the editorial boards of the new publications that were not directly connected with either the union or the Independent Student Association. On January 7, on the initiative of Jan Strękowski, *Tygodnik Wojenny* (War Weekly) began publication. For the entire period of its existence, until March 1985, it was one of the best-known titles of the underground press. In Warsaw alone, in addition to those publications already mentioned here, the following were also launched in January: *Wytrwałość* (Perserverance), a publication of the Solidarity Resistance Movement, *Przetrwanie* (Survival), which described itself as a publication of the members of the Solidarity trade union, *Niepodległość* (Independence) (with time, a political party grew around the group involved with this publication), and *Karta* (Charter), which still exists today as a journal of contemporary history. Entirely new groups also formed, linked neither with members nor organizations from before December 13.

One of these, with a bombastic name, was the Armed Forces of the Polish Underground, which became known for the fatal shooting of a non-commissioned officer of the Citizens' Militia on February 18, during an attempt to disarm him. The subsequent trial ended in very severe sentences. This group was founded by students from a technical school from Grodzisk Mazowiecki, near Warsaw. It alluded—perhaps consciously—to the underground youth movement during the years 1947–55. At that time, several hundred secret organizations for students and young workers existed. Some of them acquired weapons and planned to use terror. Almost all of them adopted proud-sounding names, even if the group was only comprised of a few teenagers. The security apparatus employed drastic methods to combat them. They even had to create a separate prison for minors (in Jaworze), which was only liquidated in 1955. During martial law, the scale and types of activities that the underground youth engaged in were, of course, completely different. Nevertheless, this type of resistance did reemerge after December 13. For example, among the twenty-three secret organizations discovered in the Piotrków voivodship in 1982, seven were comprised of school-aged youth.[15]

The operation carried out by the group from Grodzisk prompted discussions in the underground about what means should be employed in the current fight. Almost unanimously, it was decided that the actions of the Grodzisk group set a negative example, and should even be condemned. In general, in the first weeks after the imposition of martial law, its opponents created a colorful and varied mosaic of various kinds of organizations and groups, from those who were a continuation of previously existing Solidarity organizations, to those that were completely new, and which sometimes had nothing to do with the union at all. It was significant that many, perhaps even the majority, of the places vacated by those who were interned or arrested were occupied by people who had previously been unknown or not well known, who had not been in the "second ranks" but in the "third ranks," or even further removed. These people believed that, in the conditions of martial law, it was pointless to wait for the initiative to come "from above" and to limit oneself to lamenting the situation. Instead, one should undertake concrete steps. "Was I supposed to sit at home like Bujak?" asked Adam Borowski from the MRK"S," "Sit and think about what to do, and so on?"[16] The variety of initiatives and their spontaneity did not help in reestablishment of the Solidarity regional offices. On the contrary, they compounded the underground union's problems in establishing a central authority.

In most cases, regional organizations formed slowly, adapting their shape and personnel to the new conditions. Of course, in some instances they formed very quickly, such as in Wrocław, where the Regional Strike Committee (Regionalny Komitet Strajkowy) created on December 13 simply continued, as it had in Lublin and Rzeszów, too. Sometimes, however, there were situations in which regional authorities took their definitive shape and announced their existence only half a year after martial law was declared. In some important cities, and even very important ones, like Gdańsk, the new regional leaders announced themselves only in early May. The delay was not because many of the regional activists had been eliminated at the regional level, since the problem existed everywhere. It was also not because there were some special difficulties in communication, because those were the norm in every city. It was also not because there were too few people whose authority was sufficiently great and broadly accepted. On the contrary: in Gdańsk, well-known activists such as Bogdan Lis, Bogdan Borusewicz, and Aleksander Hall were in hiding. It was difficult to make relatively quick decisions regarding the creation of regional organizations because some of the leaders had doubts as to the form and character of the union's underground leadership. In addition, there was an expectation that the authorities of martial law—under pressure from international opinion, the Church, or civil resistance—would nevertheless decide to begin talks and "unsuspend" the union. In the end, however, until mid-1982, Solidarity's new structures did take shape in most regions. They had a variety of names, such as the Temporary Regional Board, Temporary Regional Commission, and the Regional Executive or Coordination Commission. In addition to those locations already mentioned, organizations also were established in Kraków, Toruń, Łódź, Katowice, Poznań, Bielsko-Biała, Krosno, Szczecin, Białystok, and Olsztyn.

The fact that these organizations were set up, however, did not mean that they actually influenced the activities of the trade union organizations that existed in their regions. Sometimes several structures aspiring to lead the entire region would exist for a long time. For example, in Silesia at one point, five regional structures existed. In Łódź, where there were as many as eight, it was only in 1984 that they were partially united. Moreover, some enterprise commissions from large workplaces remained independent of the regional authorities. In the inter-enterprise structures, a similar situation existed. The need to respect conspiratorial rules meant that there was usually no direct contact between the regional level and enterprise commissions. Another problem was that some of the secret regional leaders—and sometimes even most of them—were using pseudonyms, which did not inspire trust.

The main channel for communication "from the top down" was announcements in underground news sheets, or through courier systems that did not function very well. This, of course, greatly lengthened the process of making and announcing decisions. Sometimes these kinds of publications began appearing even before the new regional structure officially announced its existence. This was the case in Warsaw, for example, where *Tygodnik Mazowsze* (Mazovian Weekly) began publication on February 11, while the Regional Executive Committee (Regionalny Komitet Wykonawczy) issued its first declaration only three months later, on May 8. *Tygodnik* was run by Helena Łuczywo, who had headed a group that had been involved in the underground since 1976. They had been producing the *Biuletyn Informacyjny* (copied on typewriters) since December 16, 1981. *Tygodnik* quickly became the most important and prestigious underground publication, both because of its excellent information and commentary, and because of its good contact with the main leaders of underground Solidarity. Over time, however, all existing regional authorities had their own news publications.

The story of how Solidarity's main headquarters was founded is a good example of the ambivalence, uncertainty, and vagueness surrounding the transformation and creation of union structures.[17] Eugeniusz Szumiejko and Andrzej Konarski, members of the National Strike Committee, were the first to suggest the creation of a main headquarters. They had gotten off lightly during the pacification of the shipyard and ports in Gdańsk. One month after martial law was declared, they announced the formation of the National NSZZ Solidarity Resistance Committee (Ogólnopolski Komitet Oporu NSZZ "Solidarność," OKO), signing themselves with the group pseudonym "Mieszko"—the name of the first historical ruler of Poland in the tenth century (!). This choice was rather unfortunate and could have even seemed like a schoolboys' prank. They used the pseudonym not only for conspiratorial reasons, but also because neither was well known, and their names would have not meant anything to anyone. They hid in Gdańsk itself, with backing from a small group of local activists, but they did not have any contacts among well-known Gdańsk union leaders, nor with Solidarity leaders from other cities. In their "Communiqué No. 1" they stated that OKO did not aspire to represent the union to the government, but that that it aimed instead to coordinate underground activities, primarily through self-organization and passive resistance.[18] They made contact with Wrocław (the hometown of both men), Kraków, and Warsaw, thanks to Szumiejko's exceptionally energetic efforts just after the announcement of OKO's founding. This was, however, awkward for the union's regional leaders who were in hiding, who were presented with a fait accompli.

Nevertheless, in both Wrocław and Kraków it was decided to back "Mieszko's" initiative. In Wrocław, supporters included Władysław Frasyniuk and Kornel Morawiecki, who was even more determined. In Kraków, Władysław Hardek, the de facto underground leader in Małopolska, stood behind them. According to them, OKO's members should use their real names, which had already been the accepted practice in the pre-1980 democratic opposition in Poland. Szumiejko and Konarski planned to create four regional districts (North, South, East, and West), represented in OKO, which would direct activities in their area. This scheme was somewhat reminiscent of the ideas underpinning the military underground during the Second World War or the structures of the secret anti-communist organization Freedom and Independence (Zrzeszenie Wolność i Niezawisłość) during the years 1945–48. Szumiejko managed to make contact, albeit irregular, with Wałęsa while interned. Szumiejko was even appointed his plenipotentiary. Not everyone was enthusiastic about Szumiejko's idea, however. Some of the Warsaw leaders (such as Bujak and Kulerski) were against the idea of creating a central headquarters. Some in Gdańsk (such as Lis, Borusewicz, and Hall) also expressed their doubts. They distanced themselves from OKO in part because of their reservations regarding Konarski, who was suspected of having personal ambitions and ambiguous contacts with the SB. Deciding on strategy proved to be the fundamental problem, however, and strategy should determine organizational forms.

From a simplified view of the situation, it is clear that these differences reflected the ever-present division into moderates and radicals. In Polish history, too, this was often the case, such as before the January Uprising (1863–64), when there was a serious conflict between the "reds" (radicals) and the "whites" (moderates). After martial law was imposed, Wiktor Kulerski was the first to present the most thoroughly developed moderate viewpoint in a text titled "Innej drogi nie mamy" (We have no other way),[19] dated December 21, when several strikes in Silesia were still underway. In this document, distributed in the form of a typed manuscript, the author argued that active resistance was impossible when faced with escalating violence and the government's overwhelming advantage. He thus proposed that people should instead engage in passive resistance, and that there should be an "internal self-organization of society." Instead of occupation strikes, for example, people should slow down the rate at which they work as a form of protest—one that would not provoke reprisals. He also believed that people should create a "loose network" of "people of goodwill," self-help funds, and publishing houses. He urged that people should wear black ribbons and armbands as a sign of solidarity as long as martial law was in force. He did not mention the union's leadership, clearly assuming that a transition period was in progress, and that as long as the communist party might make concessions and negotiate Solidarity's reactivation, one should not represent statutory authorities.

Several weeks later, in a joint interview with Bujak printed in the first issue of *Tygodnik Mazowsze*, Kulerski essentially stood by his position: "not strikes, not going out into the streets, but training people in how to act together and cooperate, raising social and national consciousness, counteracting propaganda, [and] revealing the truth."[20] This concept, called the "long march" strategy, or that of "underground society," was based to a significant degree on the opposition's pre-Solidarity experience, but it also referred to some of the union's basic principles, including that of non-violent struggle. The skepticism toward establishing a central headquarters was one effect of adopting this kind of strategy, as was the negative attitude regarding the creation of a hierarchical underground organization.

Jacek Kuroń presented the opposing view most expressively and emphatically in his article "Tezy o wyjściu z sytuacji bez wyjścia" (Theses on the way out of a situation from which there is no way out), which was smuggled out of the prison in Białołęka, near Warsaw.[21] Kuroń, a well-known and respected cofounder of KOR, assumed that the cold, hard facts of occupation, terror, and economic disintegration would create conditions for spontaneous mass reactions, unchecked demonstrations, and terrorism, and thus for revolution, which would prompt a Soviet intervention. Only a suitably disciplined power, "organized around a central headquarters," would be able to prevent this scenario from becoming a reality. Through its actions, this entity would force the government to compromise, or would lead the "elimination of the occupation with a collective, organized demonstration." It would happen as the result of a "simultaneous blow to all centers of power and information."

Years later, Kuroń made negative comments about this concept, but he had already uttered the words, and his authority was irrefutable. This strategy was called the "general strike strategy," although one can see in Kuroń's text a vision closer to that of a national uprising or armed revolution ("blow to the centers of power"). Zbigniew Romaszewski took a similar stance, although he concentrated more on organizational issues. He stressed the significance of communication—and thus inter-enterprise agreements—and also the necessity of building modern means of communication, including radio transmitters. According to him, effective communication was very important, since calling and carrying out a general strike without it would be impossible. Romaszewski assumed that in Warsaw, for example, twenty to thirty large enterprises should undertake an occupation strike, while others carried out an absentee strike. Street demonstrations could "distract some of the government forces." Romaszewski was in favor of creating an "underground state" similar to that which had been active in occupied Poland during the years 1939–45.[22] These are just the outlines of the most emphatic ideas and statements; clearly, they do not represent the entire discussion that took place in underground publications, particularly the part expressed during innumerable debates not preserved in print. Compared to the official statements that were often made in Aesopian language, the openness of these texts is striking, even in those that could be interpreted as calls for a coup d'état (such as Kuroń's proposition that there should be a strike "against the centers of power").

During the time when these (and other) concepts were being discussed, Szumiejko and the four regional leaders (who were also communicating amongst themselves) were engaging in lively correspondence. This debate was, of course, impeded by the fact that its participants were all in hiding in different places and cities. Moreover, some of the "debaters" were in prison, so even the circulation of texts (letters, document drafts) took a long time. After a while, a compromise draft was agreed upon, which rejected the idea of a centralized structure (OKO plus the districts). The executive center was to be called the Temporary Coordinating Commission (Tymczasowa Komisja Koordynacyjna, TKK), which reflects its character quite well: its function was more to organize cooperation than to issue orders.

The founding of the TKK was announced on April 22, and was signed by Zbigniew Bujak, Władysław Frasyniuk, Władysław Hardek, Bogdan Lis, and Eugeniusz Szumiejko, on behalf of the four regions. Among them, only Szumiejko was an intellectual in the narrow sense of that word: he had a degree in astronomy, and was working as a computer specialist in a research institute. The others were skilled workers or technicians: Frasyniuk was a city bus driver, Hardek was a technician in a steel mill, Lis worked at a lathe, and Bujak was an electrician in Poland's largest tractor factory. They were all from approximately the same generation: the oldest (Hardek) was thirty-seven, the youngest (Bujak and Frasyniuk) were twenty-eight. All had grown up under communism. Lis had been a communist party member for several years before the autumn of 1981, and had even been a local union activist. Three of them had been in contact with the opposition before August 1980, to greater or lesser extents. Lis, as a party member, had been active since 1978 (along with Wałęsa) in the Free Trade Unions of the Coast; Bujak and Szumiejko had cooperated with KOR in Warsaw and Wrocław, respectively. Except for their previous cooperation with the opposition, their ages, levels of education, and vocations were generally all in line with those of Solidarity's leadership as a whole. Solidarity's leadership was made up primarily of relatively young people from factories and large enterprises. All of TKK's members had played important roles in the August 1980 strikes. After the strikes were over, they became part of the union's regional leadership. By the spring of 1982, they had thus already had brief but intensive political and organizational experience.

The documents made public on April 22 were moderate in tone, and the proposed action did not go very far.[23] The "Declaration on the Forms and Methods of Union Activities" made reference to the proposition regarding "underground society," with an appeal that each workplace should, for example, create a community assistance committee, discussion clubs (!), and printing shops (and that larger enterprises should produce their own publications). In the "Declaration on a National Agreement," TKK recognized that in negotiations with the government, it would follow the "Theses of the Primatial Social Council," which had been announced on April 8 and were approved by Primate Glemp. These were in line with the stance the Episcopal Conference had expressed in late February. At that time, the hierarchs said that martial law should be "ended as quickly as possible," and that Solidarity, as an organization "with broad public approval," should become one of the parties to conclude a new social contract. TKK's only precondition for talks was the release of all those interned, as well as an amnesty for those arrested and sentenced. These documents included a call for fifteen-minute strikes to be held in all workplaces on May 13, and for all traffic to stop at noon for one minute, during which time people should "sound their horns." Only the last sentence was stronger in tone: it declared that a general strike would be called "if it cannot be avoided." These words were certainly not the roar of a lion sure of his own strength. Nevertheless, the underground union had been built and—regardless of its name—equipped with a main headquarters. Solidarity and the opposition were closing ranks.

Chapter Twelve

Civil Resistance

The strikes sparked by the declaration of martial law were still underway when other forms of protest began emerging. In Polish writing on the subject, the term *opór społeczny* ("civil" resistance) is usually used to describe them. One may question whether this term is appropriate, since it is semantically close to the Second World War term *ruch oporu* ("resistance movement"), reserved for armed operations, particularly for partisan warfare and terrorist acts. The adjective *społeczny* ("social," "collective") allows us to remove or minimize this discrepancy, but we should, however, realize that this term is very broad, encompassing an enormous number of extremely varied types of activities, including the idea of "resistance movement," that is, acts involving physical conflict. The overwhelming majority, however, used peaceful means, close to what we often call "civil disobedience." The term "civic resistance" does not exclude the possibility of people acting on their own; it can actually be comprised of a series of actions undertaken by specific individuals who are not acting together. Under communism, for the most part, no organized, collective forms of opposition to the system existed. Instead, there were only isolated, individual acts of protest. Each year, for example, large quantities of anti-state graffiti appeared, as well as typed or handwritten flyers, and anonymous anti-state or anti-communist letters. Red flags would be ripped down occasionally, or party slogans defaced. The communist regime's ideological and repressive character meant that all criticisms were also regarded as anti-state behavior, even if they were in private letters or conversations. The SB observed these types of deeds, and those who expressed criticism—if discovered—were sentenced or suffered reprisals, for example, by being expelled from their place of study or fired from their jobs. Thus, the very nature of the system resulted in an extremely broad concept of "civil resistance," the limits of which were practically impossible to define.

After the declaration of martial law, individual forms of protest faded into the background, since Solidarity existed. The trade union was regarded by many, if not most, of its members as a form of opposition not only against the current ruling clique, but also against the regime as such. Nevertheless, in the first weeks after December 13, many individual acts of protest occurred in various places. In writing about the types of government reprisals aimed at forcing people to respect the regulations of martial law (see chapter 7), I mentioned that people were punished for posting handwritten flyers. There were hundreds of these cases, although in general the flyers did not summon people to participate in some kind of action (strikes or demonstrations), but rather simply expressed their authors' protest through texts or drawings related to martial law.

It is difficult to discern, based on the existing sources, whether these types of acts were purely individual in nature, or whether the authors of the flyers (or graffiti) were in some way associated with Solidarity or another organization. One can assume that people involved in making flyers or writing graffiti were usually connected with Solidarity or some other opposition group. Even if these were individual reactions, they stemmed from a sense of belonging to an organized movement. Other expressions of public opposition included the hanging of Polish flags at sites of symbolic significance for Solidarity (such as at the Wujek mine or the monument to the fallen shipyard workers in Gdańsk), or at particular moments (such as on the thirteenth of every month). At such times, flags with the union's name written in unusual ways (such as *solidaryca*) would also appear, as well as flowers and candles. After April 15, 1982, a conflict began over a cross made of flowers and candles on Warsaw's Victory Square (Plac Zwycięstwa), which lasted many weeks. The cross was erected on the spot where the pope's altar had stood during his visit in 1979, as well as the catafalque with Primate Wyszyński's coffin in 1981. At night, security would remove the flowers, and in the morning people would replace them with new ones. During the day, the militia and SB tried to discourage people from congregating by checking their identification cards and photographing anyone who assembled there.

The use of flyers, graffiti, and posters became so widespread that special groups were created to counteract this trend. They were comprised of ORMO members and "workers' guards," who generally operated at night, during the curfew, painting over or "scrub-brushing" the graffiti with water and cleaning agents. Consequently, the resulting white (or black) patches on walls became a typical sight in urban landscapes. Flyers scattered on the ground were gathered up just as scrupulously, and those posted on walls or elsewhere were torn off. Propagandists of martial law launched their own kind of "battle for the walls" relatively quickly; where protest symbols or texts appeared, they would put others similar in form but opposite in content. For example, they would draw two vertical lines through a painted letter "S," transforming Solidarity's initial into the symbol for the American dollar. They also produced many posters and flyers whose main aim was to reveal Solidarity's ties to "anti-social elements," who in turn were linked to imperialism or the "reactionary camp."

The repertoire of symbols and anti-government slogans employed at that time has not been catalogued. Here are a few of the best known: *Wrona orła nie pokona* (The crow will not defeat the eagle; *wrona* [crow] refers here to WRON), *WRON won za Don* (Send WRON beyond the Don [River]; here, *won* is the Russian word *von*, meaning "out"), *Zima wasza—wiosna nasza* (Winter is yours, spring is ours), and *Zaraz wracam—Solidarność* (I'll be right back—Solidarity). The army's prominent role, and the Polish term for martial law (*stan wojenny*, literally "state of war"), made allusions to the German occupation and Second World War inevitable. Thus, graffiti appeared equating the Polish United Workers' Party and the Nazi Party ("PZPR = NSDAP"), along with "ZOMO = Gestapo." Just like wartime acts of "little sabotage," as it was called, Poles drew gallows on walls in 1982, too, but instead of Hitler and swastikas, five-pointed stars or the abbreviations PZPR and ZOMO were hanging on them. The letter "S" often appeared as part of an anchor, which was an allusion both to the famous anchor symbol of *Polska Walcząca* (Fighting Poland) from the occupation, as well as the memorial to the fallen shipyard workers, which is in part comprised of anchors, a Christian symbol of hope.

Another possible allusion was the relatively recent military coup d'état in Chile in 1973, which was well known because of the intensive communist propaganda condemning that country's military men. Parallels were also facilitated by the fact that General Jaruzelski, like General Augusto Pinochet, would appear in his military uniform and dark glasses. Jerzy Urban, the government's press spokesman, was also the target of propaganda attacks and gibes. Solidarity and opposition circles hated him, above all, for his unabashed cynicism, but he also had physical characteristics that lent themselves readily to caricatures (his corpulence, bald head, bulging lips, and large, protruding ears). Jaruzelski was, however, the main icon of visual anti-regime propaganda. Jaruzelski's military cap and dark glasses dominated caricatures, but sometimes they also featured five-pointed stars and things like gallows, a horsewhip, a pistol, a machine gun, or handcuffs. A favorite motif in the drawings was a crow (*wrona*, an allusion to the abbreviation "WRON") in dark glasses and a general's cap. The symbol "V" (for victory) was also used—a reference to the Second World War and Churchill's famous gesture. General Jaruzelski, however, helped to popularize the symbol when he announced in one of his speeches that "no Polish word begins with that letter" (since "V" is only used in foreign words), and hence deemed its use to be anti-Polish. Solidarity propaganda did not shy away from humor or even self-irony, and its proponents instead drew a rabbit, whose alert ears made the letter "V," even though that animal is far from being a synonym for courage and fighting spirit.

The internees were one of the most productive groups in the propaganda war. Since they had little else to do, many of them wrote poems and songs, or devised slogans and symbols which quickly found their way out of the internment centers. It was precisely in this kind of isolation that people came up with the production of stamps for making impressions of slogans or drawings, and postage stamps and cards (although, of course, they did not send them via the state postal service as postcards). The largest number of these appeared for Easter 1982, when the traditional symbols of resurrection and rebirth were used. With time, this type of propaganda moved from the street and crudely made flyers to increasingly numerous news sheets. It was also used as part of fundraising campaigns (the postage stamps or postcards were treated as a symbol of having donated money to the Solidarity cause). A couple of years later, the stamps—sometimes in color, and often graphically quite sophisticated—were traded on the black market, providing their creators with a good income. Some of them had little to do with Solidarity, or the opposition, and were produced purely as a business. The themes appearing on walls, in flyers, in news sheets, and on stamps were a mix of martyrological elements, allusions to the Polish patriotic tradition, and biting, or even brutal, satire.

Occasional poetry was a popular form of protest. Underground publishers printed poetry of varying quality. Early on, it was more common for these poems to circulate as manuscripts, which were written on thin sheets of copy paper. The first copies of anthologies printed on duplicating machines appeared as early as January 1982. By the end of that year, several dozen had been published. In the winter of 1982, the first small volumes by well-known poets devoted to the drama of martial law were also printed.

> Blood blood blood on a uniform
> Blood on boots, blood on the wall [. . .]
> Blood flowing from chimneys' muzzles
> Flowing down the chests of workers' sons . . .
>
> [Krew krew krew na mundurze
> krew na butach krew na murze (. . .)
> krew wybiega z luf kominów
> krwawią piersi robotniczych synów . . .][1]

These lines, penned by Krzysztof Karasek, a leading young poet, convey the message of this type of poetry well. In the words of Anna Skoczek, it was characterized by a "traumatic tone of lyrical expression."[2]

The poem, regardless of how we assess its worth, was of course an expression of individual protest, but it was also part of "popular resistance" as a whole. Just as poetry should be treated as one of its elements, so should the songs about martial law, which began circulating quite quickly via audio cassettes. More so than poetry, the songs harked back to traditions predating martial law. The opposition bards became popular after the founding of Solidarity thanks to various demonstrations and events, such as the Independent Song Festival, which took place, still legally, in late August 1981 at Sopot's Opera Leśna. In the new conditions, well-known songs such as Jacek Kaczmarski's "Mury" (Walls) or Jan Pietrzak's "Żeby Polska była Polska" (Let Poland be Poland) became the unofficial hymns of the underground union and, more broadly, of "underground society." Probably the most telling song of the martial law period was the bitter "Ostatnia szychta na KWK Piast" (Last shift at the Piast coal mine), sung by Krzysztof Kelus to words by Jan Zazula:

... Boys, leave Piast already
It's time, boys, to leave this hole,
The women are crying, they baked you cakes,
The golden cage will take you up ...

[... Wyjeżdżajcie już chłopcy od Piasta
Pora chłopcy opuścić tę dziurę,
Baby płaczą, napiekły wam ciasta,
Złota klatka uniesie was w górę ...][3]

The songs of martial law, like the poetry, flyers, and graffiti, also made use of political satire, despite the fact that they were often marked by trauma and hatred. Allusions to well-known anti-German wartime satire were especially popular. For example, in a clever move, Radio Solidarity's call sign was the first few bars of an easy-to-remember song from that time. The melody was extremely well known because it had been passed down from generation to generation. Radio Solidarity made its inaugural broadcast in Warsaw on April 12, 1982. Radio Free Europe also played an important role in popularizing the poetry of martial law. Jacek Kaczmarski hosted a separate program devoted to poetry. Most cassettes in circulation were probably recorded from that radio station's broadcasts, though the underground later also produced its own cassettes.

During the first months of martial law, some people expressed their opposition in ways that harked back to the tradition of "national mourning" during the January Uprising of 1863–64. In some circles, people would dress in black, though they were usually from the intelligentsia rather than the working-class. During martial law, of course, there was no expensive mourning jewelry, as Polish women had worn 120 years earlier. Instead, people would pin to their blouses or lapels little black crosses with a "crucified" miniature eagle, or the letter "S" combined with an anchor. Another symbol of opposition was to pin resistors (*oporniki*) from radios onto one's clothing. (The word did not originally mean "a person who resists," only "resistor" in the electronic sense.) A jury could have people arrested for wearing these symbols, as happened to a student from Toruń, for example. Resistors became one of the most popular symbols, as shown by the fact that at least seven news sheets were titled *Opornik* (Resistor) in 1982. Some activists who were released from internment or arrest kept the beards they had grown in prison, a distinguishing mark, and the fashion for moustaches—quite common among the working class—was clearly linked with Wałęsa (who himself wore a beard for several months after his arrest, and even long hair).

Chapter Twelve

For a while, it was quite popular to pin miniature Solidarity symbols onto one's clothing. These were sometimes black letters (instead of red) on a white background, as a sign of mourning. Sometimes people who demonstrated their attitude toward martial law in this way became a target of aggression by ORMO functionaries, "workers' guards," or patrols. In January 1982, Radio Free Europe suggested people turn off the lights in their apartments and burn candles in their windows in memory of the victims of martial law—an idea that quickly caught on. Another initiative, which could only be undertaken on a small scale, was to send books by pro-regime writers who had publicly expressed their support of martial law to their authors' home addresses.

Just before the one-month "anniversary" of the imposition of martial law, the *Kos* news sheet published a twelve-point "occupation code of conduct"[4] signed by Zbigniew Bujak, Zbigniew Janas, and Wiktor Kulerski; it also appeared as a flyer. As was often the case, role models from the Second World War inspired this publication, too. The code of conduct, whose title was a motto of Józef Piłsudski's—"Być zwyciężonym i nie ulec to zwycięstwo" (To be defeated and not submit is victory)—urged people to work together to provide assistance to those in prison and their families, and to those who had been fired, as well as to copy and distribute flyers, and to aid those in hiding and those working in the underground. The code of conduct's author appealed to party members to turn in their cards, and to everyone to "use passive resistance" in the workplace—without explaining, however, what this resistance should consist of. The code of conduct did not demand that people refuse to sign loyalty oaths, but rather suggested that people should communicate with others in similar situations, and that people should make decisions "in keeping with their conscience" and according to the "principle of acting in solidarity." Its authors also called for a "social boycott" against "informers, lackeys, and zealots," and those who had "supported the junta." This boycott entailed neither greeting nor talking to such individuals: "Let them feel they are surrounded by a void." There is no way of telling what the effect of this appeal was; it did not really initiate any new models of behavior, but rather only reinforced and legitimized those already in use, thanks to the names of its signatories.

Other codes of conduct also appeared with time, such as those for academicians, journalists, and actors. Although none of these forms of protest posed a threat to the government, taken together they had a clear impact on the social atmosphere: they fostered a feeling of membership in a broader community, and allowed those who were not so courageous to express their views while not posing much of a risk. Since these activities suggested attitudes hostile to martial law, they exerted pressure, to a certain extent, on those who were responsible for it.

Activities such as the boycott organized by actors and others involved in the theater were more significant, since these were public protests involving larger groups. Moreover, they were carried out by well-known people, some of whom were even extremely popular. An informal meeting of several general directors from Warsaw theaters, which took place already on December 17 at the initiative of director Zygmunt Hubner, decided on this particular actors' boycott. As Andrzej Łapicki recalls, "It was decided that they would stage a protest by having a policy of restraint regarding participation in the mass media [outlets] that were supporting martial law most actively—i.e., radio and television."[5] At the same time, it was agreed that the theaters should continuing functioning normally. The Solidarity of Film and Stage Artists issued a statement titled "Actors' Ethics in Martial Law," which was a code of professional conduct. Participating in television programs, and not just in propaganda shows, was seen as "collaborating with the regime," and as sanctioning the brutal pacifications, reprisals, and purges.

Some of the underground news sheets, beginning in mid-January 1982, published "black lists" of collaborating actors (the total number was approximately sixty), and appeals to the public to boycott their theater appearances or to "applaud them off" the stage. On January 29, 1982, at the National Theater in Warsaw, during a performance of Stanisław Wyspiański's *Wesele*, one of the canonic works of Polish theater, the well-known actor Janusz Kłosiński was "applauded off." Earlier, he had appeared on television in support of martial law. "I saw his face," recalled Adam Hanuszkiewicz, who was directing the performance, "and I got scared. He was as pale as a corpse."[6] Nevertheless, Kłosiński returned to the stage in the next scene. Others who were "applauded off" in this way included the famous pianist Halina Czerny-Stefańska, and well-known opera soloists Andrzej Hiolski and Leonard Mróz. During a performance of a romantic play, coughing and loud clearing of throats drowned out the lines of actor Stanisław Mikulski, who had recently participated in the government propaganda campaign. "His mouth was moving, but his voice was completely lost in the noise," recalls a witness.[7] The play was about Polish independence, and Mikulski happened to be known best for his role as Hans Kloss in a TV spy series in which he played the role of a Pole in the service of the Soviets. As such, he became associated, in the popular imagination, with everything that impeded Polish independence.

The rebellious theater community did approve of some of the stages and actors who were following their lead, and productions that had an oppositional slant. Despite the censors' efforts, there were still plenty of these productions, since political allusions could always readily be found, whether in Greek tragedies or in Shakespeare. Sometimes Solidarity organizations at enterprises would collect money for actors whom the authorities had deprived of their livelihoods—by not showing TV programs in which these actors had taken part, removing plays in which they had acted from the repertoire, and even firing them from their theater jobs—in retaliation for participating in the boycott. The boycott was not the only "negative" activity that actors and theater people engaged in, however. On March 17, 1982, a performance of T. S. Eliot's *Murder in the Cathedral* was staged at Warsaw's St. John's Cathedral, in an interpretation that highlighted allusions to the current situation. It was a production by one of Poland's most famous directors, Jerzy Jarocki. It had been withdrawn from the Dramatic Theater's program along with other ten other productions in Warsaw theaters which had been suspended after December 13 as the result of a decision made at the municipal Department of Culture and Art.

Many directors and actors not only fought to stage productions that the authorities disapproved of, but also brought their art out from behind theater walls. Some of the elite responsible for martial law were displeased by this, or even irritated—like General Jaruzelski or Deputy Prime Minister Rakowski, since good relations with intellectuals and opinion-makers were important to them. The minister of culture, Józef Tejchma, even organized a special meeting with the members of the theater and film community, but it ended without any clear compromise. Other artistic circles called for boycotts as well: in April 1982, the Warsaw Artists' Solidarity appealed to artists not to participate in official shows. As a result of this appeal, the International Poster Biennale was cancelled in Warsaw, as was the International Graphics Biennale in Kraków. The party hardliners had no doubts: they saw a boycott of the boycotters as the most appropriate reaction, and the only effective one. As a result, over the course of two seasons (1981–82 and 1982–83), the directorship of twenty-three theaters changed, and censorship became markedly more active.

In Świdnik, known for the strikes there in July 1980 and those after the imposition of martial law, the television boycott gave rise to a very particular form of mass protest: people would go out into the streets and walk around during the *Dziennik Telewizyjny* (evening television news program), the main mass propaganda tool. It is not clear who came up with this idea, but people began implementing it, at underground Solidarity's urging, from February 5, 1982.[8] The residents of neighboring towns followed Świdnik's lead. Several hundred to a couple thousand people would take part in these "walks." In order to block this initiative, the authorities took decisive action: they set the curfew at 7 p.m. (which meant that the "walks" were moved to 5 p.m.). In addition, all the telephones in Świdnik were again blocked, a ban on vehicular traffic was imposed during the demonstration, the identity cards of people on "walks" were checked, and participants were threatened with being thrown out of their jobs. Some people continued their protests in more camouflaged forms, for example, by beating their carpets at a designated time. The authorities' harassment and an appeal by the parish priest, who called for them to cease their protest, convinced most to stop.

The example, however, spread throughout Poland, having been promoted by Radio Free Europe and the underground press, and for a while "television walks" were taking place in Elbląg, Bielsko-Biała, Ursus, and Sochaczew, for example. In Białystok, the "walks" were staged from May 4–20 on the town's main street (ul. Lipowa). They took place regularly, three times a week, at which three to four thousand people would participate, including mainly high school and college students.⁹ Residents of some cities (for example, Sieradz), instead of taking walks, would place their television sets in their windows during the television news to demonstrate their boycott of the program.

As time passed, however, the atmosphere became less tense than it had been during the strikes, and especially after the massacre at the Wujek mine. Nevertheless, in many Solidarity circles, there was a tendency to adopt more radical, or even terrorist-like, forms of resistance. Nowhere, however, did the union as such sanction these acts. Even the advocates of a general strike were restrained as far as the idea of using force was concerned. People continued to imagine that this kind of strike would be similar to those that had swept the country in August 1980. This time, however, emphasis would be placed on the need to prepare seriously for the defense of the enterprises. As usual, however, in situations marked by great social tensions, some people or groups believed it was necessary to go on the attack immediately.

Undoubtedly many members of the numerous youth groups dreamt of launching urban guerrilla warfare. Some of them even had access to weapons. No one, however, actually used them. But it wasn't only the young people who were inclined to resort to radical forms of protest. In the first months of 1982, several operations took place that did bear traits of terrorist attacks, except that they were directed at buildings rather than people. One notable exception was the aforementioned disarming of a non-commissioned officer of the Citizens' Militia in a Warsaw tram (see chapter 11). In February, members of the Confederation for Independent Poland in Białystok, along with a Solidarity activist, committed arson twice (against the militia station and a shop run by the military). According to documentation of the investigation, which until now has remained unverified, this group planned to blow up the building of the provincial communist party headquarters in Białystok.¹⁰ In Silesia, in Wodzisław, a group from an organization calling itself the Polish Legion blew up a plinth with the symbol of the USSR that had been erected in commemoration of the Soviet soldiers who had fallen in the area during the fighting in 1945. Explosives were also laid in the town hall in Olsztyn, in a trade school in Poznań, and in Wrocław at the monument to the fallen militiamen from 1945–48.

Particularly spectacular was when a group of young people doused the Feliks Dzierżyński monument in Warsaw with gasoline and set it on fire in February 1982.¹¹ Dzierżyński (Dzerzhinsky) was a Pole who had been a Bolshevik leader and founder of the Soviet secret police, the Cheka. Perhaps best known was a case in which explosives were found outside a gas station in Lubin, in the Copper Basin, on February 13. Bombing activities were renewed there in mid-September, clearly in reaction to the shooting of three people by the militia during a demonstration on August 31. The discovery of more explosives, and some actual detonations, made the entire voivodship militia stand up and take notice. As a result, the Third Department of the Ministry of Internal Affairs took over direct supervision of the investigations. It was only in January 1983 that "the Lubin bombers" were finally arrested. A total of thirty people were sentenced in several trials; the longest sentence was for five and a half years in prison.[12] Bombings, however, were a rare occurrence.

Catholic Masses were especially important in terms of social mobilization. They were often called "Masses for the Fatherland," and were held for the victims of martial law, as well as for those interned, arrested, and fired from their jobs. These Masses were held even as early as December 13, and many were held especially during the Christmas holidays. During these services, the priests more or less openly condemned martial law and honored the memory of the victims. Later, too, in dozens of churches all over Poland, Sunday services contained similar themes. January 13, 1982, making one month since the imposition of martial law, fell on a Tuesday. Only a few churches held special Masses that day, whether at the initiative of the parish priests (such as in Stalowa Wola), or at the request of Solidarity activists (as in Wrocław). In Warsaw's St. Stanisław Kostka church, the Solidarity branch of the Warszawa steel mill (whose chaplain was Father Jerzy Popiełuszko) requested that a Mass be said on January 13, but it actually took place only four days later. In February, the parish priest, Father Teofil Bogucki, and Father Popiełuszko decided that they should revive the custom, started in October 1981, of having one of the Masses on the last Sunday of the month dedicated to the Fatherland. Beginning in February 1982, the monthly services conducted by Father Popiełuszko or Bogucki became a permanent element of Warsaw's spiritual and patriotic life.

Starting on January 13, the Masses held on the thirteenth of each month, marking the imposition of martial law, became increasingly popular, even though they took place in only a few churches. Until May 13, attendance of these Masses (in some cities, this might have meant even several thousand people) was in general not associated with any collective protests by those leaving the churches after Mass. Kalisz was perhaps an exception: from January 13, after every Mass said for Solidarity in the Jesuit church, those attending the service would organize a short demonstration afterward and lay down flowers in the shape of crosses.[13]

In some cases, Masses for the Fatherland would be carefully prepared, not only from the pastoral point of view, but also in terms of aesthetics. Well-known actors would participate in them as readers, professional artists would prepare the decorations, and sometimes there was even special music for the occasion. Above all, however, the very fact that so many people were attending Masses that had such a clear message was important for the general atmosphere in society. These Masses were a visible expression of support for Solidarity and opposition to the authorities of martial law. They also attested to the fact that many people in the Church supported the persecuted union.

Although strikes were the most important instrument at Solidarity's disposal for several months after the December strikes had been broken, they turned out not to be useful in practice. This was because of the subsequent reprisals, as well as the drastic weakening of the union's organization and the fact that monitoring was ramped up extensively, not only on the streets, but also in the workplace. Various union entities appealed for work stoppages to take place the thirteenth of every month. Although those calling for such action clearly cared about the workers' safety (the strikes could be disguised, for example, as "breakfast breaks"), most of the crews were not enthusiastic. Underground news sheets did report that, here and there, crews had responded to the appeal. Because of the nature of this kind of strike, however, it was difficult to notice anything outside a factory where some of the workers were participating. In his work on martial law in Mazowsze, Tadeusz Ruzikowski even describes it as a "secret protest,"[14] which in itself is a contradiction in terms. Frasyniuk estimated that extending the time of the one-to-three-minute strikes (as had been the case in January) to fifteen minutes made it significantly more dangerous: "a quarter of an hour was enough for the authorities to find out who its organizers were."[15]

There were hardly any mass meetings, speeches, or even public readings of flyers. In general, factory supervisors, ORMO, "workers' guards," and military commissioners were well aware of the crew's weak points. The SB would undertake preventative measures, carrying out "warning talks" with activists who were well known to them. They threatened those who took part in the protests with being transferred to positions with lower pay, at the least, or, at the worst, with being fired, or even interned. According to SB data, which could be on the low side, in Wrocław (clearly a bastion of Solidarity) just under two thousand people took part in strikes lasting several minutes that were staged on January 13 in nine enterprises. On March 13, no more than twenty-five people participated in strikes at any enterprise.[16]

In some cities—for example, in Wrocław and Gdańsk—people reacted more strongly to the drastic price increases that went into effect on February 1. On average, the price of food went up by 250 percent, and fuel and energy by 200 percent. Carrying out this "price-income operation" (as it was officially called) on such a scale would not have been possible without the shield of martial law. Nevertheless, strikes in response to the price hikes were so weak that authorities needed to take no special steps, other than punishing the cities where the protests were taking place by extending the curfew and interning participants. While it is true that strikes were held on January 29 in seventeen enterprises in Wrocław, in none of these did more than 150 people take part, according to the SB's figures.[17] In Gdańsk there were no strikes, but the "Solidarity Day" announced for January

30 coincided with the date that price hikes were to take effect, which might have increased the number of people at the demonstration. In any case, no more than several thousand people participated in the demonstration at the Monument to the Fallen Shipyard Workers. After ZOMO attacked the demonstration, it turned into a riot: protesters pelted the voivodship communist party headquarters with Molotov cocktails, and clashes continued into the evening. Most of the demonstrators were young people, as was the case in the few other street demonstrations that occurred. Union leaders could take heart in the fact that the youngest generation of Poles was taking the lead. They were probably aware that street protests which were not associated with factory strikes would attract neither workers nor average Solidarity members. The events on Gdańsk streets suggested that a generational "changing of the guard" among protesters was afoot. As a result, methods would also need to be adjusted. During the first few weeks after the imposition of martial law, a great variety of oppositional forms emerged, although few were completely new (such as the "walks"). None of them, however—not even all of them taken together—threatened the communist party leadership, which rested on the formidable threat of force, palpable even when troops were no longer present in the streets, but instead remained in their barracks in a state of "heightened readiness." These activities were not a threat to the regime because, as usual, it was only a small portion of Solidarity's members who actively took part in these types of undertakings. Just as the three-million-strong communist party proved unable to stop the wave of strikes in August 1980 and subdue the independent union, Solidarity, too, with its nine million members, also failed to mobilize all its members and launch an adequate and vigorous response to the events of December 13.

The vast majority was simply exhausted, not only from the constant difficulties in procuring basic goods, but also from daily troubles caused by the regulations of martial law, which were devised not only to paralyze the enemy's efforts but also to discourage Poles as a whole from engaging in any kind of activities unacceptable to the authorities. In short, it was all designed to make society acknowledge that the party dictatorship was once again the only option guaranteeing stabilization. If people obeyed the orders of martial law—and did not support the enemy—then the regime would reward them by retracting some of its strict regulations. This was in accordance with "the elastic approach" advised in the general directive regarding regulations. The reward, however, could be rescinded at any time. In Poznań, for example, after a large, violent demonstration on February 13 (during which the militia fatally beat two people),[18] authorities suspended the sale of gasoline for private cars with Poznań registrations and banned cars in the city. They also suspended film screenings and theater productions.

Under the conditions of martial law, the millions of Solidarity members could naturally not react the way they would have wanted. A minority, who became something of an avant-garde, determined the way they *did* react. The lack of backing for this group from others in Solidarity, however, became a problem. Perhaps the situation would have been different if there had been some extraordinary circumstances, or if someone very charismatic had actually led one of the strikes or demonstrations—i.e., someone who was physically present, right there at the scene. There was, of course, no guarantee that someone like that would necessarily have attracted others, regardless of whether this passivity was rooted in a fear of reprisals or a feeling of helplessness and loss of hope in the possibility of real change. Frasyniuk was skeptical: "charismatic leaders won't save us . . . without any initiative from below, if able organizers don't emerge, we won't manage to do anything . . . society will keep quiet—either because people have been intimidated, or because they are fed up and disheartened."[19]

Chapter Thirteen

"The Anesthetic Has Worn Off"

During the debates over Solidarity's tactics, people were not just exchanging views. In some cities, a deepening gap arose between the union's generally moderate regional branches and more radical groups. The latter believed that a clear schedule of operations should be drawn up, culminating in a general strike; in addition, they also thought there should be demonstrations, a centralized decision-making process, specific preparations for the active defense of striking enterprises, impressive events, a more aggressive propaganda campaign, and efforts to influence the mood among the rank and file who were implementing martial law, particularly those in the military. "We should show ourselves," said Adam Borowski of MRKS in an interview published in May 1982. "We should show that we are here, that we represent a force, that we are organized. Because the government is not afraid of an inert mass."[1] People in many Solidarity circles were dismayed at the lack of decisive actions and that people were not encouraged to participate. This sentiment was apparent not only among those directly involved in the underground, but also among people who had decided to wait it out.

As the research to date and known documents show, two of the groups who were most vocal in expressing their discontent were the MRKS in Warsaw and a group in Wrocław centered on Kornel Morawiecki. (Morawiecki was known for his radicalism, which he expressed, for example, in his autumn 1981 text "Appeal to Soviet Soldiers Stationed in Poland."[2]) Radical views, like the ones espoused by these two groups, could undoubtedly be found everywhere, but it is difficult to say anything certain about their reach, or their social and geographic distribution. In any case, an analysis of the collective forms of expressing dissent, such as strikes or demonstrations, does not indicate a significant increase in the number of participants. Nevertheless, the events held on the monthly "anniversaries" of the declaration of martial law on the thirteenth of every month were better attended in March or April than in January. But even if approximately the same number of people took part in specific activities, monthly "anniversary" events were organized throughout Poland beginning in February. Thus, the total number of people engaged in this type of protest was significantly greater than it had been at first.

More dramatic events also took place, such as the "march of silence" staged by workers at the Lenin Steelworks in Nowa Huta. Flyers and posters announced it beforehand. On April 30, after the first shift ended, several thousand workers marched from the gates of the steel mill to the main square of the city. No ZOMO were present along the route of the march, probably because the march took place the day before the official "working people's holiday" (i.e., May 1).[3] Regardless of the authorities' motives, their absence encouraged those who were hesitant to participate in events of this type later on.

Probably most impressive was the Radio Solidarity broadcast in Warsaw at 9 p.m. on Easter Monday (April 12). Zofia and Zbigniew Romaszewski were behind this undertaking and, within a couple of months, it had numerous imitators in many cities across Poland. Ryszard Kołyszko constructed the transmitter, and Marek Rasiński and Janusz Klekowski made the broadcast from the roof of a tall building downtown. The eight-minute program, recorded on a cassette tape, began with a theme from a well-known satiric song from the German occupation, "Siekiera, motyka . . ." (Hatchet, hoe . . ."), with Zofia Romaszewska as the announcer. In the middle of the program, there was a pause during which the listeners were asked to turn off their lights if they could hear the broadcast. "All of Warsaw flickered," recalls one of the organizers, "in nearby buildings, people opened the windows, people ran onto their balconies, triumphant shouts could be heard. . . . I had a knot in my throat and tears in my eyes."[4] The actual content was less important than the broadcast as "a symbol that Solidarity [was] alive," as Zbigniew Romaszewski put it, and, perhaps even more importantly, that it could thumb its nose at General Jaruzelski.

Radio Solidarity was clearly an important event, but the development of an independent (or "underground") news system was an even more significant factor in terms of changing the popular mood and situation in society—though of course it was not the only one. Despite many irksome setbacks at the underground printing shops, publishing activities at the union's enterprise, inter-enterprise, and regional branches gathered steam as the situations there stabilized. The flow of information steadily improved, in specific factories and cities as well as on a national scale. Some of the news sheets, especially those in Warsaw, reached many other towns and cities in Poland. Reprinting articles and sharing information was very common. Quite quickly, *Tygodnik Mazowsze* began acting as a press agency, providing material for various other publications while intensively expanding its own network of correspondents. It was probably in contact with the editorial offices of all the regional news sheets, as well as the more important enterprise ones. The more significant regional bulletins played a similar role; most often, these were directly linked with the union's local underground branch. Previously existing political groups were becoming increasingly active, and new ones were being formed, which meant that there were ever-greater numbers of publications as well—including influential political ones—some of which were not necessarily connected with Solidarity at all.

Radio Free Europe and other foreign radio stations broadcasting in Polish played a very important role in the dissemination of information on a national scale. In addition to the BBC and Voice of America, which were well known, there was also Radio France Internationale, or RFI. Since February or March, these stations had broadcast numerous news items about various kinds of protests, and were receiving information from foreign correspondents in Poland. Despite the authorities' efforts to hamper these journalists' work, and the fact they were now under the "care" of counterintelligence, they nevertheless had quite good contacts within Solidarity and opposition circles. They were not put off by the threat of being expelled from Poland—a fate that did befall a number of Western correspondents in 1982. The Polish sections of foreign radio stations monitored Polish Radio, and RFE even kept tabs on Polish Television. They also made use of the underground press to whatever extent they could, especially since more material was making it out of Poland now that increasing numbers of people were traveling to the West. Foreign (émigré) Solidarity organizations had their own sources of information in Poland—sometimes via diplomatic posts—which they would then convey to RFE, BBC, and RFI.

The authorities of martial law accused these stations of actually instructing and issuing directives to underground organizations and opposition circles. It is true that they did convey various appeals and announcements on the air, including those related to the organization of strikes or demonstrations. According to the partially preserved data from the state-run Center for Public Opinion Research (OBOP), 53 percent of those surveyed listened to RFE in 1981; in 1982, the figure was over 49 percent. These were the highest numbers in this radio station's history.[5] The BBC, Voice of America, and RFI's Polish broadcast also had large audiences, which may have overlapped with RFE's to a large degree. Based on this information, one can estimate over half of Poles received information from non-government sources. RFE's popularity at that time was in part thanks to a program broadcast since Christmastime, "Pomost do kraju" (Bridge to Poland), which relayed information to families in Poland from relatives who were abroad when martial law was declared. In half a year, approximately a hundred thousand such announcements were broadcast.

Some people involved in those events, from both sides of the barricades, have noted the change in popular mood. Years later, Marek Ochocki, who in 1982 was the commandant of the voivodship militia in Legnica, said that "in late April [1982], the anesthetic wore off and the patient revived."[6] Similarly, Tadeusz Jedynak, who was the leader of underground Solidarity in Upper Silesia, believed that "society was numb for half a year at most."[7] There is no way for historians to say with any scholarly certainty why a change in atmosphere took place. Subsequent events, however, clearly showed it to be the case. Despite the moderate tone of its publications and appeals, TKK may have had a galvanizing influence on Solidarity members, especially since it was operating openly. Radical circles were increasingly active, supported by important events such as the launch of Radio Solidarity. Looking at it from a slightly different perspective, one might conclude that, after the initial shock of martial law, people had grown accustomed to the situation. The fact that there were fewer and fewer outright restrictions and problems facilitated this adjustment. Even though reprisals followed almost all public expressions of resistance, such as strikes and demonstrations, martial law slowly "lost its teeth" and no longer invoked fear.

In an appeal dated April 22, TKK called on people to participate in a strike on May 13 and to stop vehicular traffic for one minute at noon (see chapter 11). The protests planned in the regions and enterprises were supposed to complement those proposed by the union's headquarters. The date was chosen to coincide with the monthly "anniversaries" that were already being observed everywhere. Thus, TKK was not proposing anything new, and its appeal did not mention street demonstrations. People thought that the fight should be waged in the enterprises, which is why TKK did not allude at all to the upcoming May 1 holiday—the traditional leftist (but not just communist) workers' holiday—and to the May 3 holiday commemorating Poland's 3rd of May Constitution in 1791. It had been a national holiday for over a hundred years, and it enjoyed the status of a state holiday during the interwar period. During the communist era, however, it was banned.

Some of the underground organizations planned protests on those days. For example, MRKS urged people via Radio Solidarity during its April 30 broadcast to participate. The regional organizations, however, such as the one in Gdańsk, generally called on people to boycott May Day celebrations and to remain at home, or picnic in a park instead. Regardless of their motivations, they simply were not in sync with the public mood, which the "radicals" apparently had a much better sense of. It was no coincidence, therefore, that throughout Poland the first large-scale street demonstrations took place then. To a large extent, these demonstrations were spontaneous. In Gdańsk, the May Day "counter-parade" was nearly as large as the official state-sponsored event. Between 10,000 and 20,000 people took part, and in Warsaw the turnout was similar. In the capital, the official demonstration looked "quite sad," as Rakowski put it,[8] despite the fact that approximately 170,000 people attended. In Nowa Huta the situation was similar, too, and from a thousand to several thousand people participated in demonstrations in Rzeszów, Lublin, Szczecin, Łódź, Toruń, Bielsko-Biała, Białystok, and Elbląg. In all large and medium-sized cities and towns, there were public protests, which usually began after Mass. The militia did not intervene, but rather limited itself to cordoning off the official May Day demonstrations.

Perhaps the militia's passivity helped make the demonstrations on May 3, Constitution Day, even more widespread. This time, however, demonstrators were attacked almost everywhere, which usually meant hours-long skirmishes with ZOMO. The most widespread clashes occurred at the largest demonstrations. Many participants who had been dispersed earlier took refuge during Mass in the Basilica of St. Mary in Gdańsk, which was literally under siege. Rockets fired by the militia set the choir and organ on fire, and a copy of the famous painting *The Last Judgment* by fifteenth-century Dutch painter Hans Memling was damaged. Thirteen people suffered gunshot wounds. Thanks to the presence of mind of the parish priest, Father Stanisław Bogdanowicz, they managed to bring the fire and panic under control, but the street clashes lasted until late that night.[9]

The situation was similar in Warsaw, where there were skirmishes from 4 p.m. until midnight in and around the Old Town. Barricades were erected and the pungent odor of tear gas lingered in the narrow little streets for several days afterward. In Elbląg and Szczecin, more clashes with ZOMO took place on May 4, and in Lublin on May 5. In all, the militia probably detained several thousand people. In Szczecin itself, the number was around six hundred, in Elbląg over three hundred, in Lublin nearly three hundred, and in Toruń over two hundred. Several dozen people were arrested, and many more were interned. There were more fatalities as well: one person was killed as the demonstration in Warsaw was being dispersed,[10] another was poisoned with gas in Szczecin, and a third was fatally beaten in Kraków. Almost all descriptions of the demonstrations that swept through Poland at the time note that many of the participants were young, including some who were just school-aged. The Ministry of Internal Affairs was very concerned, and, as Rakowski wrote in his notes, demanded that both university and secondary school students should be "brought to order."[11] The usual punishments were employed; in Warsaw, for example, telephones were blocked again, and the curfew that had been lifted just a few days before was reinstated. Because of the young people's involvement in the clashes, the curfew for those less than eighteen years old was set at 8 p.m.

According to the Ministry of Internal Affairs, on May 13, the strikes that TKK had been calling for took place in 113 enterprises, but this is probably a low figure. Underground news sheets gave much higher numbers: in Warsaw alone, it was said that strikes took place in fifty-three enterprises (while, according the Ministry of Internal Affairs, the number was just twenty-seven). In Wrocław and in Lower Silesia, over thirty enterprises and institutions went on strike, and several dozen in Małopolska. In each of the following cities, ten to twenty also joined the strike: Szczecin, Łódź, and Rzeszów. This was the largest protest strike since the opposition was broken in mid-December 1981, but its mass character was primarily owed to the fact that it included most of the larger cities and industrial agglomerations.

So, while this was an extensive strike, it was also a shallow one—"shallow" not only because it lasted only a short while, but also because there were not many factories that had most of their crews interrupt work, as happened, for example, in the Lenin Steelworks, at the helicopter factory in Świdnik, and in the Cegielski Factory in Poznań, which made engines. In these plants, several sections stopped work, as did the National Rail Carriage Factory (Pafawag) in Wrocław. Even in most of the large factories, only several dozen people went on strike, or at most several hundred. In some, only ten to twenty people stopped work, or even fewer, although striking in such a small group was a heroic deed to be sure. There was, by and large, a consensus that the strike action of May 13 was quite a failure.

Demonstrations also took place on May 13 in several cities, including Gdańsk, Warsaw, Poznań, Olsztyn, and Leszno, but on a much smaller scale than those ten days earlier. The exception was Kraków, where there were clashes when a crowd of 10,000–20,000 gathered on the main square after leaving a Mass said for John Paul II (on the anniversary of the assassination attempt) at St. Mary's Basilica. ZOMO units, who were ready to intervene, attacked those present. After a couple of hours, the skirmishes were dispersed with water cannons and tear gas. The militia arrested over 160 people (half of whom were students). In Poznań, one person died after having been beaten. Even if significantly more strikes took place on May 13 than the MSW officials reckoned, still probably only about 40,000–50,000 workers participated—not very many, if one takes into account the heightened emotions after May 1 and 3.

One of the reasons for the relatively low participation in these strikes was probably the SB's increased efforts in the wake of the demonstrations in early May. SB functionaries carried out a large number of "warning talks" (there were over a hundred in the Rzeszów voivodship alone, for example), and directors and supervisors threatened their workers with repercussions if they took part in the strikes. In order to discourage people from engaging in oppositional activities in the future, harsh steps were taken immediately. In Świdnik, for example, after the strike, approximately two hundred people were fired from their jobs. The campaign to collect money for these people was eventually undertaken on a national scale; in December 1982, the Fund for Aid to the Repressed was created. At the FSM car factory in Bielsko-Biała, where just over two hundred people participated in the strike, thirty-one people were fired, five were interned, and one was arrested. In Kraków and Nowa Huta, over forty people were interned in connection with the strike and demonstration. In all of May, approximately a thousand people were interned throughout Poland, both in connection with the demonstrations and strikes, and for underground activities.

The relatively low turnouts during the strikes of May 13 might have calmed the authorities, but the events from earlier that month deeply concerned them. At one of the "directorate's" meetings, General Jaruzelski said, "We are dealing with a new standard," because "the masses have gone into the streets."[12] Most of those assembled, wrote Rakowski in his notes, "declared that what had happened should be used to intensify the reprisals," but Jaruzelski turned out to be more restrained, as usual: "He recommends that decisive action be taken, but that it must be well thought out and selective." Perhaps one such "well-thought-out" action was General Kiszczak's initiative to propose to Zbigniew Bujak that he come out of hiding, with a guarantee of safety.[13] The TKK member responded that he was, of course, a proponent of talks, but that in order for them to take place, all those interned must be released, those sentenced must be amnestied, and all those in hiding must be given guarantees of safety. If Bujak had come out of hiding, it certainly would have been a heavy blow to the underground.

In Moscow, however, and also in Polish hardliner circles, the clear preference was to have Bujak captured. The fact that many well-known Solidarity activists were successfully in hiding was treated as evidence that Jaruzelski's team was too lenient. People in the general's circle, on the other hand, were still considering whether to release Wałęsa, who was making it impossible to do so by stubbornly repeating that he could undertake talks only as a free person, and with the entire Presidium of the National Commission. There were few proponents of such a radical step in dealing with Wałęsa anyway, and Jaruzelski, even if he was cautious, rejected the possibility of negotiations with Solidarity people. He expected only that they would either surrender or be captured.

For the SB, the events of early May were a catalyst. As early as January, the SB had managed to neutralize several well-known underground activists, and to break a couple of large, union-related organizations. The SB could not, however, boast of any really spectacular success. It often made triumphant public announcements regarding how many printing presses it had uncovered, and how many copies of printed materials it had confiscated, but underground publishing continued to flourish anyway. For the government's opponents, these official numbers were evidence more of the underground's activities than of how successful Kiszczak's people were. Most of those arrested had not been apprehended thanks to operational activities, but because of their role in the strikes and demonstrations, or because they were distributing flyers.

In January 1982, the Bureau of Investigation at the Ministry of Internal Affairs began to prepare for the trial of seven leading union activists and four members of KOR. On February 1, the Chief Military Prosecutor's Office formally launched the investigation. Months passed, and thousands of pages of case documents already existed, but there still had been no political decision for these trials actually to take place. There was nothing to boast about. In addition to the general lack of success in prosecuting underground leaders, there were also discrediting blunders, such as the release of Jan Narożniak by MRKS on June 6. Narożniak, known from events in late November 1980, was shot when he was being arrested by chance. While he was in the hospital, monitored by the SB, doctors helped arrange his transport to a hiding place. The underground had other successes as well: after Warsaw's Radio Solidarity began operations, other analogous initiatives (which were nevertheless completely independent of one another) were launched in Poznań (on May 12), Gdańsk (June 8), and Kraków (June 12). Although the SB confiscated some transmitters, it did not succeed in silencing the stations, despite the fact that the Second Directorate of the General Staff—i.e., the military intelligence—had been enlisted to help in the search.

In the statistics, the operational activities of the security apparatus appeared to be quite substantial: in the first six months of 1982, almost seven thousand people were recruited to collaborate, of whom one-third had been obtained through the department dealing with Solidarity and workplaces—i.e., the most important segment of society in terms of current concerns.[14] As is usually the norm during periods of mass recruitment, however, many of these informers provided only general information and did not have access to more important conspiratorial cells. At a meeting with the leadership of the Ministry of Internal Affairs, General Kiszczak complained that there were only six informers for every SB operational functionary, a number which "does not provide us with even a mediocre understanding of our enemy. . . . We are constantly being taken by surprise, or we are helpless when confronted with things."[15]

Another report estimated that in Warsaw, for example, there was an exceptionally low level of infiltration among teachers and schoolchildren, and that the intelligentsia was also insufficiently infiltrated. There was also a shortage of agents in the largest industrial enterprises: in the FSO car factory, which had thousands of employees, there were just nineteen informers; in the Warsaw Steelworks there were thirty; and in the Ursus tractor factory there were thirty-five. With its sudden surge in responsibilities, the SB was finding it had a serious staffing shortage and asked the prime minister to allow it to hire additional employees. "Recruitment is necessary," General Kiszczak said at a meeting of the Ministry of Internal Affairs leadership, "on the same principles as during the years 1944–46, which means recruiting the kind of people who want to fight the enemy."[16] So once again, in order to become an employee of the security apparatus, the most important thing was not one's qualifications but one's ideological motivation.

The need to penetrate the underground became increasingly urgent, as was the need for success. The creation of the SB Research Office at the Ministry of Internal Affairs on June 1 was an attempt to improve the efficacy of the efforts of the security apparatus. This unit, however, was not dedicated to analysis or prognostication, as its name would suggest, but was rather a group of several dozen experienced functionaries, led by Colonel Władysław Kuca. It was supposed to lead and coordinate activities designed to combat underground

Solidarity's most important cells. The Research Office was focused primarily on long-range plans aimed at bringing about the disintegration of the organization, rather than everyday operational tasks meant to discover and liquidate specific conspiratorial cells. When Lech Wałęsa emerged as one of the main candidates for a Nobel Peace Prize, he became one of the prime targets of these activities. The Office gathered evidence that was meant to discredit the union leader as a long-time SB secret informer. It presented these documents to the Norwegian Embassy in Warsaw, as well as to several members of the Nobel jury, via intelligence channels (operation "Ambassador"). The secrecy that surrounds the process of selecting Nobel winners does not allow us to determine whether Wałęsa failed to win the prize at that time because of this information. In any case, the Research Office took credit for the fact that Alva Myrdal and Antonio García Robles won the prize for their disarmament work instead.[17] Another of the Research Office's more long-term projects was to inspire the establishment of a conspiratorial organization called the Inter-Regional Commission for the Defense of Solidarity (Międzyregionalna Komisja Obrony Solidarności, MKO), which it then controlled. Its publication, *Bez Dyktatu* (Without a dictate), was printed in the Ministry of Internal Affairs printing shop.

After the arrest of important union activists just as the underground was forming, the SB's first significant successes came only in the summer of 1982. These included the arrests of Stanisław Handzlik in Kraków (June 24) and Adam Borowski (July 12) and Zbigniew Romaszewski (August 29) in Warsaw. Handzlik was arrested thanks to the help of informers as the result of an operation lasting many months. The other two were also caught with help from informers. The SB gradually intensified its activities, and in addition to pursuing leading activists, it was primarily interested in radical organizations, which posed the greatest threat. These organizations included not only MRKS but also Fighting Solidarity (Solidarność Walcząca), which was founded in June by Morawiecki, mentioned above. This organization arose as the result of a split, and although some of the structures of the Regional Strike Committee and Fighting Solidarity overlapped, their differences deepened with time, and a conflict of sorts even emerged with the regional leadership, headed by Frasyniuk. On July 1, the SB created a special group (at first known by the code name "Scout") to uncover Morawiecki and his organization. It was comprised of officers from various sections. It was only after a year and a half, however, that the SB saw its first significant successes in the battle against Fighting Solidarity.[18]

Since there were now so many people "of interest"—as SB language called them—it was essential to decide on general aims and set priorities. This was done through orders and instructions sent from the headquarters, and also meetings of top functionaries. Representatives of the top echelons of the government, including General Jaruzelski, would sometimes also attend these meetings. The first secretary of the Central Committee would not go to give professional advice and share operational knowledge with his colleagues, of course; he was there to motivate the functionaries and explain the position of the party leadership. At the meeting that took place on June 6, he spoke about the special value of the "brotherhood of the army with the MO and SB, confirmed in battle," and about the "intense class struggle" underway, in which "US imperialism" had a special place. He admonished his audience to "win over and emphasize the forces that support us," although they were still in the minority. He stressed that "the enemy must know that . . . his knuckles will be rapped," but that authorities should make efforts not to engage in this task blindly, so as to bring about polarization in society ("while showing forbearance"). It should not be surprising that WRON's chairman habitually referred to the supreme model, Feliks Dzerzhinsky, "who was ruthless towards the enemies of the revolution, but was at the same time a symbol of concern and care for homeless children." The conclusion was simple: in this "noble and difficult joint cause of ours, although one's hand may itch, one may not go too far."[19] *Sapienti sat.*

The Research Office, however, was working on more concrete guidelines. For example, one of the texts distributed in the field was titled "Guidelines for Operational Work in the Field of Demasking, Surveilling and Liquidating Conspiratorial Groups and Organizations." It stressed the necessity of quickly and completely eliminating small groups or organizations that were forming in smaller workplaces in order to prevent them from expanding. As far as the larger and more significant centers of resistance were concerned, the opposite approach was actually recommended: engage in "active and thorough surveillance," attempt "to bring them under operational control," and then "use them for destructive and disinformational activities." Bringing a given organization under "operational control" meant obtaining enough information about it (and access to it) to destroy it from the inside, or direct its activities in a way that was advantageous to the SB. To this end, the SB even recommended creating its own "sham conspiratorial groups" whose aim would be, for example, "to absorb the existing groups and disintegrate illegal organizations."[20] An important aim was to understand the underground well enough to make a spectacular arrest or uncover an underground printing shop at some politically expedient moment, or for propaganda purposes. This may have been the motive for the arrest of Zbigniew Romaszewski just before the Solidarity street demonstrations planned for August 31. I do not believe, however, that the SB was able to overcome the limitation that is perhaps best described by the old saying "those doing the following know more than those who are being followed think, but less than their superiors want."

Within the underground movement, people had varying interpretations of the unexpected but indisputable success of the May Day and Constitution Day demonstrations, as well as the less successful strikes of May 13. The radicals believed that they should keep up the momentum: "we are betting on a constant uphill battle," wrote Kornel Morawiecki in June, "which if conducted doggedly and with determination will tip the scales of victory in our favor."[21] The leader of Fighting Solidarity (Solidarność Walcząca)—whose name alluded to the term "Fighting Poland" used during Nazi occupation—did not put any restrictions on the types of methods that could be used. He wrote that all tactics were fair play, "including terrorist activities." In the TKK, in contrast, there was a widespread belief that the wave of revived social unrest should give the government pause for thought, and make it inclined to compromise.

There were also fears that encouraging strikes further would prompt intensified reprisals in workplaces, which would eliminate the most active individuals. Their presence would be needed if the union wanted to use its most powerful weapon—still considered to be a general strike. The delicate situation created by John Paul II's planned second visit to Poland was also taken into account. Without the authorities' permission, the pilgrimage would not be able to take place, of course. The Church, always moderate, encouraging all sides to come to an understanding, stressed that emotions should not be stirred. Meanwhile, on June 8, during a meeting of the Joint Commission of the Government and Episcopate, the government side declared that "currently the conditions do not exist" for a papal visit.[22] Not without reason, the government believed that the papal visit would amount to a show of support for Solidarity. They believed it would be difficult to gauge the emotional intensity and general impact of the visit, which could lead to unpredictable situations. It was thus suggested that a suitable date for the pope's visit could be the 300th anniversary of the Battle of Vienna, in which the role of the Polish army proved decisive in the victory over the Turks, and for which grand celebrations were being planned. The anniversary, however, fell on September 12, 1983, which meant that the authorities had allowed themselves over a year to bring about a situation in which a great gathering of Poles would not pose any threat to them.

TKK anticipated that the government might use the state holiday on July 22 to open the path to negotiations in some way. In the past, the communist holiday had been used for the declaration of amnesties. This seemed especially likely since the Sejm was supposed to be in session the day before the holiday. As a result, underground Solidarity leaders appealed for demonstrations and strikes to be postponed until July 22. They also announced that if all internees were released and those imprisoned were amnestied, then "for the time being strikes and demonstrations should be suspended."[23] In closing, its authors added that rejecting this initiative would "force the union once again to resort to various means of pressure, including a general strike." A resolution titled "Five Times Yes" (*5 x tak*), announced on July 9, was in the same vein. It repeated the union's well-known demands regarding victims of reprisals and re-legalization of the union's activities. Three further points covered the principles on which a "national understanding" should be based, and what its aims should be. It even declared that Solidarity would strive to resolve all conflicts through negotiations in order to "reduce the need for strikes to a minimum."[24]

The government, however, did not intend to respond to these propositions at all. Ignoring them was seen as an effective way of reducing the prestige of the underground union, which after all was not recognized as a partner, but seen only as an enemy that should be destroyed. This is why the prime minister did not mention any plan for talks with Solidarity in his Sejm speech. Instead, he announced that about nine hundred individuals—including all the women—were being released from internment (in most cases, these were "temporary releases," which meant that at any moment the releases could be repealed). This information was accompanied by an announcement that WRON anticipated the lifting of martial law at the end of the year. All this news confirmed that reprisals would continue for quite some time. Jaruzelski announced the founding of the Patriotic Movement of National Rebirth (Patriotyczny Ruch Odrodzenia Narodowego, PRON), which was supposed to replace the Front of National Unity that had existed until then. Like it, PRON would also be a sham, with only a minor facelift. There were certainly no plans to incorporate Solidarity into that institution. From Deputy Prime Minister Rakowski's speech, it became clear that "grassroots" trade unions would be created only at the workplace level. He gave no reason to hope that Solidarity's activities would be revived in any form, not even as envisioned within the framework of Operation "Renaissance."

Not surprisingly, TKK was disappointed. On July 28, in an announcement titled "Five Times No," it stated that the Sejm session was "the latest evidence that the government refuses to cooperate with society."[25] At the same time, the TKK also published its preliminary platform guidelines, titled "Underground Society."[26] These were an expanded version of those presented in April. The new guidelines emphasized the role of self-organization on the local level and stressed that "the underground society movement" should be decentralized. The idea of a "self-governing Republic" was mentioned several times, and had its origins in the union's program, which the First National Congress of Delegates had approved in 1981. The document did not mention using a general strike as a weapon, and it addressed society as a whole, not solely Solidarity members. In a separate statement,[27] TKK called on all union cells to organize "peaceful demonstrations" on August 31, the second anniversary of the signing of the Gdańsk Agreement, and urged union members to take part. This appeal mentioned no strike.

While TKK tried to concentrate all the protests on one specific day, it was not able to keep the regional or local organizations from organizing their own events, especially in light of its own declarations about decentralization. On June 28, the exact day that TKK had appealed for a moratorium on demonstrations, the largest demonstration to date took place in Poznań, with 10,000–20,000 participants.

Demonstrators took to the streets for the anniversary of "Black Thursday," the day the army brutally intervened to crush a strike and demonstrations in 1956, taking seventy lives. On the next monthly "anniversary" of martial law (August 13), demonstrations took place in Wrocław, Gdańsk, Nowa Huta, and Warsaw. Next, a series of demonstrations took place in conjunction with anniversaries related to the 1980 strikes: August 16 in Warsaw, August 18 in Szczecin and Elbląg, August 20 in Ursus, August 26 in Wrocław, August 27 in Łódź, August 29 in Jastrzębie, and again in Szczecin on August 30.

All were pacified by ZOMO units, and were accompanied by clashes of varying duration. Dozens of people were detained, and larger numbers of people were being interned. As a result, more of the most active individuals were eliminated; at the same time, these events kept the atmosphere tense and encouraged people to mobilize. They can also be seen as a dry run, done in stages, for the nationwide protest that was planned. Some of the underground organizations (for example, the Special Groups organized in Warsaw by Teodor Klincewicz, which were cooperating with the regional leadership) prepared equipment needed for fighting or resistance: they produced caltrops for the immobilization of militia vehicles, collected bottles with flammable liquids, and planned to spill lubricants on the roads to slow ZOMO convoys. They drew up schedules and selected venues for the demonstrations in more detail than usual: for example, in Warsaw and Wrocław, four meeting points were designated in order to impede the militia's activities. Banners and flags were readied everywhere. Flyer campaigns intensified and there was much more graffiti on walls and posters than usual. In TKK circles, people wondered whether a general strike should be announced, as a natural continuation, if the protests were successful on a mass scale throughout the country. In short, a general offensive was declared against the regime responsible for martial law.

The other side was also preparing itself carefully for the battle. Several dozen military units were earmarked to provide assistance in pacification operations. All those that were working in production or helping with the harvest were recalled to their barracks. Maneuver and reserve battalions were maintained, and special subunits were supposed to be ready for action within two hours of receiving orders. Transport planes and convoys of vehicles for use by the MSW were prepared; security at radio, television, and communications buildings was increased; and one battalion of landing troops (special forces) was sent to Okęcie Airport in Warsaw. Plans were made to carry out shows of force in larger urban agglomerations, as was done in December 1981—which meant that convoys of armed vehicles were to drive through city streets. Military commissioners received orders to remain on the premises of enterprises and institutions under their command on August 31. Approximately six thousand officers were dispatched to meetings in large workplaces with the aim of carrying out propaganda and warning talks. Meetings between designated political officers and parish priests were also foreseen.

Beginning on August 19, the MSW—under the pretext of the campaign against speculation and corruption—began a series of "nationwide disciplinary operations." These actions included radically increasing the number of patrols, which would also enter the grounds of large industrial enterprises. ZOMO and ROMO units were mobilized and put on full alert, petards and gas canisters were stockpiled, and water cannons repaired, among other things. During the last week of August, the SB carried out a whole series of preventative measures. At a meeting of the Secretariat of the Central Committee, General Kiszczak stated that about 880 searches had been carried out, during which over 300 people were detained, and almost 70 were arrested. "Warning" talks also took place with approximately 650 individuals, and internments followed.[28] These figures are undoubtedly incomplete, since the MSW could not yet have had information from all over the country on the day that the meeting took place (August 30). Preparations for responding to protests were facilitated by the fact that the meeting places and routes for marches were widely known—and were even persistently publicized by the underground. The SB had some information about secret preparations, too.

For its part, the Central Committee mobilized the party *aktiv*. In some workplaces, the half-dormant "political and defensive detachments" were revived—i.e., the former "self-defense groups" (*grupy samoobrony*). The voivodship PZPR committees prepared various types of propaganda activities, primarily flyers and posters. In the Tri-City, however, delegations from the newly formed interim voivodship branch of PRON were to lay flowers at the Fallen Shipyard Workers' Memorial in Gdańsk, and at the plaque commemorating the massacre of workers in December 1970 in Gdynia—on August 30 rather than 31, just in case. Meetings were held with the directors of large enterprises, mayors, and voivods. Representatives of the voivodship defense committees and military commissioners took part as well. According to the information received by the Central Committee from the voivodship committees, street demonstrations were expected in at least twenty-five of the forty-nine voivodships, and numerous actions at workplaces.[29] The press and media were full of warnings and slogans like "We have only one Poland" (and the enemy wants to destroy it), as well as materials besmirching Solidarity and its activists.

When Minister Kiszczak appeared on television on August 25, he warned the organizers in a dramatic tone that they would not escape punishment. On August 18, during further talks with Bishop Dąbrowski, Kazimierz Barcikowski said that discussions about the date of the pope's visit could be held only "after that watershed date" (i.e., after August 31), since "the underground is preparing for a test of strength."[30] The government was clearly launching the largest mobilization of forces since December 1981, and not only Solidarity, but also the communist party leadership, saw whatever happened on August 31 as the second decisive battle (after that of December 13). During the ceremony at Jasna Góra on August 26, Primate Glemp—just like Primate Wyszyński two years earlier at that same spot—exhorted the two sides before battle: "It is not the street that should be a place of dialogue. Enough blood has already flowed in our streets."[31] He was unable to prevent the confrontation, however. It was not only the primate who believed that the risk of demonstrations should be avoided. In mid-August, two Solidarity advisors, Wiesław Chrzanowski and Jan Olszewski, a defense lawyer well known for his work on political trials since the 1960s, had already asked Wałęsa (via Father Orszulik) to appeal to Zbigniew Bujak to call off the protests. While the union leader acknowledged he was "against street demonstrations," Orszulik recalled him saying that "at the moment, he [didn't] see any other choice." "There will be casualties," he added, "and they will bear fruit, too."[32]

An official MSW communiqué reported that, on August 31, demonstrations took place in sixty-six cities, with one hundred eighteen thousand people taking part.[33] While there is no reason to question the first of these figures (it was quite easy to determine), the second is only an estimate. It is probably too low, which is usually the case when law enforcement officials evaluate the size of demonstrations they are supposed to quash, just as protest organizers exaggerate their own numbers. For example, according to the information given in Kraków underground news sheets, fifty thousand people were said to have participated at the demonstration in Nowa Huta. Taking into consideration its population, this seems an unlikely figure. Even the information published underground varies. For example, *Tygodnik Mazowsze* estimated the number of demonstrators in Warsaw to be twenty thousand, whereas *Tygodnik Wojenny* said it was only "several thousand." According to the MSW figures, as many as seventy thousand people took part in the protests in the capital.[34] Thus, perhaps one can conclude that although many more people participated in the demonstrations than was announced officially, in reality the actual number was difficult to pin down.

The demonstrations in large cities and agglomerations were most numerous—in Warsaw, Gdańsk, Wrocław, and Nowa Huta, from ten thousand to several tens of thousands participated. In the two great industrial districts—in Lower and Upper Silesia—individual demonstrations did not exceed several thousand people. They took place, however, in many towns, often neighboring ones, so in each of those regions a total of ten thousand to twenty thousand demonstrators probably participated. From a thousand to several thousand people took part in the demonstrations in Kraków, Szczecin, Częstochowa, Lublin, Koszalin, Bielsko-Biała, Konin, Bydgoszcz, Przemyśl, Elbląg, Gorzów Wielkopolski, and Łódź. From several hundred to a thousand people demonstrated in other smaller towns, such as Nowy Targ, Bochnia, Kartuzy, Garwolin, Świdnica, Kłodzko, and Bielawa. Some of the demonstrations took place in two installments: they began in the morning, but the main wave of participants took part in the afternoon, after work. Some of the demonstrations began after people left Mass—after the special services that had been requested. Others congregated in places associated with the 1980 strikes, at former Solidarity headquarters, or near other symbols of the 1970 and 1976 revolts.

Regardless of where and when the demonstrations began, they were inevitably attacked by ZOMO functionaries (and other militia formations), usually immediately, with tear gas and water cannons. Thus, the demonstrations were not "peaceful" in the sense that the attacks invariably prompted the crowds to defend themselves: people threw rocks, returned the gas canisters, built barriers (and even barricades), hurled Molotov cocktails, and set fire to militia vehicles. In some towns—for example in Konin, Częstochowa, and Gorzów—people attempted to attack the communist party's voivodship headqurters. In Nowa Huta, a crowd attacked one of the militia stations twice. The longest and most serious clashes broke out in Nowa Huta, Wrocław, and Gdańsk; in Warsaw, the fighting occurred throughout downtown, and even spread to the Praga district, on the other side of the Vistula. There were relatively few flags and banners, but considering the course of events—attacks, counterattacks, and ensuing chaos—they were more a hindrance than a help. In just a few cases did military units appear in the streets (including a company of special forces in Nowa Huta).

In Lubin, a small town in Lower Silesia, events took an unexpectedly bloody turn. There, an armed ZOMO platoon began shooting at the crowd, which was standing just a stone's throw away. "They moved their machine pistols out in front of them and shot," recalls a witness. "An incredible panic broke out, but not immediately, because no one expected that it was live ammunition. It was only after a few casualties fell to the ground that people began fleeing."[35] Militiamen kept shooting at them as they fled, chasing them by car ("they drove like cowboys," recalls a witness). At least six hundred bullets were fired. Two people died on the spot, another died in the hospital, and about ten more people sustained gunshot wounds. Lubin's residents were so outraged that, despite the risk, they staged more demonstrations over the next two days. On September 3, the day of the victims' funerals, eight hundred militiamen and three hundred soldiers were dispatched to Lubin.

The militia used firearms in Wrocław, Nowa Huta, and Gdańsk as well, but the manner in which they were used in Lubin was exceptional. Two people died from gunshot wounds in Wrocław and one in Gdańsk, and two (in Kielce and Częstochowa) died as the result of other injuries. Several hundred people were injured. There were also many militiamen injured, a dozen or so seriously. The official MSW communiqué stated that approximately 5,100 people were detained throughout Poland, of whom 70 percent were less than 30 years old. Over 3,000 people were put before courts of misdemeanor, and approximately 130 had their cases heard in court.[36] (The case of two priests from Gdynia was special; their trial ended only in November, with a three-year prison sentence.) The voivodship militia commandants issued many internment warrants. Hundreds of people were fired from their jobs.

The battle was over. The communist party and General Jaruzelski's team had held their position. This was their latest success in the campaign that had been underway since December 13.

CHAPTER FOURTEEN

THE END OF THE CAMPAIGN
AND WAŁĘSA'S RELEASE

During a Security Service meeting on September 2, General Władysław Ciastoń, head of the Security Service and deputy minister of internal affairs, cautiously assessed that the demonstrations "did not turn out to be a success for Solidarity," but their size was "larger than the optimistic version assumed [by the MSW]."[1] General Jaruzelski voiced a much more unequivocal opinion: first, on September 1 at the WRON meeting, and then a day later at a Politburo session, he said that "the Solidarity extremists had played their funeral march."[2] At that same meeting, General Kiszczak stated that Solidarity's leaders had "lost their social mandate." It is not clear whether this was because the minister of internal affairs thought the demonstrations had a low turnout, or because Solidarity had found it necessary to urge people to participate. In any case, the result was the same: it was definitively confirmed that there would be no talks. Many Church hierarchs were of the same opinion: "on 31 August Solidarity prepared its own funeral," Archbishop Dąbrowski wrote in his diary, unconsciously repeating Jaruzelski's words.[3]

The administrators of martial law decided that they were the indisputable victors, and thus they decided to strike while the iron was hot. On September 3, the public prosecutor's office filed formal charges against KOR members who had been interned up to that point, and issued warrants for their arrest: Jacek Kuroń, Adam Michnik, and Henryk Wujec, as well as Mirosław Chojecki and Jan Józef Lipski, who were both abroad. Upon hearing his colleagues had been arrested, Lipski returned to Poland—and to prison.[4] Zbigniew Romaszewski joined them. He was already awaiting trial, which would later be known as the "Radio Solidarity Trial." The prosecutor's charges were more serious this time than those that were usually heard at typical martial law trials. The charges referred to article 123 of the Criminal Code, relating to individuals involved in the organization of conspiratorial activities "whose aims were to deprive [Poland of its] independence, secede part of [Poland's] territory, overthrow the regime by force, or diminish the defensive capabilities of the PRL [Polish People's Republic]." The highest possible sentence for these offenses was death.

A few days later, the government made a more important decision: the Parliament would pass legislation about trade unions that would finally bring about Solidarity's formal delegalization. Although authorities attempted to keep this matter under wraps, it became an open secret. The public at large, and prominent Solidarity activists, learned about it from various quarters—including from people with links to the Church who often met with government representatives. The Church strove to prevent General Jaruzelski from taking that step in confidential talks as well as in official declarations. On September 16, after the 187th Conference of the Polish Episcopate had concluded, the bishops in their communiqué unequivocally stated—albeit in a very measured tone—that "the working people wish to have their own, independent representation: trade unions, including Solidarity and Independent Self-Governing Trade Union of Individual Farmers Solidarity . . . [and] students expect a suitable organization for themselves."[5] At the last minute, Primate Glemp intervened. He pointed out to the authorities that Solidarity's planned delegalization (and therefore also the inevitable demonstrations) would fall on an unfortunate date—the canonization of Father Maksymilian Kolbe on October 10, which had been planned for a long time.[6] Virtually every Polish bishop was traveling to Rome for the ceremony, and the primate had also planned to travel to the United States. He would have to call off both trips, he reasoned, because he would need to be in Poland during Solidarity's delegalization, since his absence would have been interpreted abroad (and at home) as proof of instability. These efforts, however, were in vain. The authorities of martial law were already determined to put an end to the ambiguous situation in which their main antagonist, Solidarity, still legally existed—even though, in their opinion, it had already been defeated.

After August 31, most of the union's members, and especially TKK's leaders, had lost their self-confidence. The magnitude of the protests, however significant they might have been, was smaller than expected. Most importantly, it was striking that only in a few instances (such as in Nowa Huta or the Gdańsk Shipyard) did the workers organize demonstrations as they emerged from their workplaces, or joined one that was already underway. The large number of young people among the participants was noteworthy. According to data from Ministry of Internal Affairs documents, the Wrocław demonstrations, for example, were comprised overwhelmingly of workers. Of the 645 people detained, 377 were workers (including 178 from large enterprises), 91 were white-collar workers, and 99 were students and pupils. The demonstrators were nevertheless primarily young people: 28 people were younger than 18; 337 were aged 18–25; 195 were 26–35. Most had only elementary or basic vocational school educations.[7]

If one were to generalize based on these figures, one could say that the average demonstrator was a young student or worker who had not yet been employed for long, and thus had a relatively low place in the employment hierarchy. Their participation in the protest was probably influenced by their physical mobility, lack of commitments (families), lack of fear for their status (since it was low anyway), and also their natural thirst for action, or even a need to blow off steam.

These individuals were impressive during the street skirmishes, but their significance at the factories was relatively small, and older workers clearly limited their own involvement. Thus, the place of the enterprises within the union's tactics and strategy became a problem. Eugeniusz Szumiejko posed the problem radically, saying, "It's as easy as pie: whoever has the enterprises holds the hammer in his hand; whoever doesn't will only be a symbol, moralist and myth."[8] Meanwhile, from the experience of the various "monthly anniversaries"—including the most successful of them, in May—one could infer that the popular resistance movement was more at home in the streets than it was in the factories. Whenever several thousand or even several hundred people with similar thoughts and feelings congregated, the movement was surer of itself and bolder than in the enterprises, where those who had remained faithful to Solidarity were being watched carefully by their supervisors and party activists. Above all, their numbers were small, compared to those of their indifferent, passive colleagues—i.e., those of the crew who became the "silent majority." Increasing the numbers of this group was one of the government's strategic goals.

These were serious dilemmas for TKK's members. On September 2, they met secretly in Nowa Huta, one of the union's main bastions in these struggles. Their aim was to decide whether to announce a general strike as a continuation of the street protests. From firsthand accounts, recorded at the time as well as later, we see that the discussion was stormy and even, according to Andrzej Friszke, "dramatic."[9] Władysław Frasyniuk and Władysław Hardek proposed issuing an appeal for people to demonstrate and hold strikes as a phase in preparations that would culminate in a general strike. Zbigniew Bujak, Bogdan Lis, and Eugeniusz Szumiejko, however, believed that this was a risky concept, and might not be greeted with the necessary support. If it failed, they thought, TKK as a whole would be held responsible. Bujak suggested that the committee should have an elected chairman, which would make it possible to rationalize the decision-making process and pin responsibility on a specific person.

Finally, a compromise was reached. The resulting decisions, publicized in six announcements issued on September 6, recommended "refraining from any activities not coordinated by TKK or the union's regional authorities,"[10] and set the dates for the protests: the second anniversary of Solidarity's registration (November 10) and the sixty-fourth anniversary of Poland's independence (November 11), which still lay quite far in the future. Union leadership would announce later what forms these protests would take. They also urged people to pay their respects on September 30 to the victims of the demonstrations on August 31 by observing a "minute of silence and displaying a symbol of mourning on their clothing."[11] Another document stated that, "despite the deep chasm that the government has dug between itself and the nation, an agreement is still our aim, and the only chance of emerging from this crisis."[12] Thus, the main goal was still supposed to be a compromise. The TKK confidentially agreed to hold a meeting when news of the union's delegalization had been confirmed. If, for some reason, the meeting could not take place, then union leadership would prepare three possible reactions to this legislation, according to what form the legislation took, and what its formal justifications were.

Some regional and enterprise organizations did not survive until the end of September, however. On the next "monthly anniversary" (on September 13), street demonstrations took place, the largest and most tumultuous of which were in Wrocław and Nowa Huta, which had already become the norm. Smaller-scale demonstrations took place in Łódź, Świdnica, and Bielsko-Biała, for example. In Szczecin, there were three demonstrations from September 11 to 18. According to Antoni Dudek and Tomasz Marszałkowski, the appeal for people to pay their respects to the victims turned out not to be terribly effective. In their estimation, "the wave of social unrest . . . began to subside rapidly."[13]

Underground activists still counted on being able to sustain the resistance through strikes and mass events. The government, however, was once again surprised Solidarity's leadership. Jaruzelski's team was preparing itself assiduously to pass the legislation, beginning with its decision that voting should take place in the Sejm on Friday (October 8), which naturally delayed the chance for protests in people's workplaces by a couple of days, until Monday. The Ministry of Internal Affairs was fully mobilized, and the army was also put on alert (including about sixteen thousand soldiers from mobile battalions). In addition to its own tasks—such as patrolling large cities and preparing helicopters to spread chemical substances—the army put airplanes, helicopters, and trucks at the Ministry's disposal. Władysław Frasyniuk's arrest on October 5 was a very well-aimed preventative strike. Frasyniuk, leader of one of the most important and active regions, was the first TKK member to be caught. The moment of his arrest was carefully planned. As a result, it not only had a serious psychological impact on a national scale, but it also paralyzed TKK's decision-making process to a certain degree.

The Sejm did indeed pass the legislation on October 8, with twelve votes against and ten abstentions. Among other things, the agreement established that all trade union registrations, of existing unions as well as those suspended since December 13, would lose their legal power. On October 9, TKK published a statement that it had prepared earlier, announcing that it was refusing to recognize the Sejm's decision. It called for a four-hour strike on November 10.[14] The appeal was published as written, when its authors were still operating under the assumption that the Sejm vote would take place in the second half of October, or even late October. As a result, people could not understand why that date had been chosen, since surely it did not take a whole month to get ready for that kind of strike. Apparently, it did not occur to them to postpone the announcement, or to designate an earlier date for the strike, but it is true that TKK had no chance to react quickly to events. President Reagan's decision was much more appropriate in this situation: already on October 9, despite the fact that it was a weekend, the American administration announced it would strip Poland of its most privileged nation status in trade with the United States.

The entire series of events associated with the union's delegalization demonstrated that central leadership for underground Solidarity, since it had always been something akin to a federation of regions, became dysfunctional when quick decisions were needed. Of five TKK members, only two, Lis and Szumiejko, were in the same city (Gdańsk). Since using telephones was clearly out of the question, the underground union's leading activists were dependent on messengers traveling by rail or car. This meant, for example, that someone who sent a letter from Wrocław to Gdańsk could receive an answer in eighteen to twenty-four hours at the earliest. As a result of the communication confusion, the Enterprise Commission at the Gdańsk Shipyard began its strike the morning of Monday, October 11, but Solidarity's regional leaders, and also TKK members who lived in Kraków, Wrocław, and Warsaw, learned of it only after the fact. Because organizers needed two to three days to launch operations in their territories, demonstrations in other cities began on October 13. That very same day, the strike in Solidarity's cradle collapsed—after it had been announced that the Gdańsk Shipyard would be militarized and numerous ZOMO detachments had been sent.

Workers at the Gdańsk Shipyard were the only ones who decided to hold a regular strike. Although it was limited to just one shift and only part of the crew was involved, demonstrations and violent clashes took place in the streets over two consecutive days (October 11 and 12) after the shipyard workers left the enterprise. During these demonstrations, protesters threw rocks at militia stations, the voivodship communist party building, and the Soviet consulate. Many people were injured and beaten. While it is true that the militia did not use firearms, one of the demonstrators died after having been hit in the head with a petard. Approximately 270 people were arrested, and about 200 shipyard workers were fired.[15] After the strike ended, so did the demonstrations in Gdańsk. In nearby Elbląg, about 1,500 people demonstrated on October 13. The demonstrations in Wrocław took place on a larger scale. On October 13, the militia spent all afternoon dispersing people who had gathered on Grabiszyńska Street, in the part of town where the striking enterprises were located. The main march, however, formed in the evening after a crowd left the cathedral on the monthly "anniversary" of the imposition of martial law. The skirmishes engulfed almost all of Old Town and lasted until late at night. Strikes were launched in a dozen or so enterprises in various other cities as well, but they were very brief and did not have many participants. The strike at the Cegielski Metal Works in Poznań was more extensive: on October 12, almost half its workers stopped work in some of its sections; in one of them, almost 70 percent stopped. A rally took place, and one of the Solidarity activists managed to summon people to the meeting through the public address system. In Poznań, however, the protest did not spread into the streets.[16]

The most serious demonstrations took place in Nowa Huta, where, on October 13, after the morning shift emerged from the Lenin Steelworks, a crowd of several thousand took off in the direction of downtown, shouting chants, including some in praise of President Reagan. For a couple of hours, a "battle" raged at the Lenin monument, access to which was being guarded by the militia, and the neighborhood militia station was violently attacked. One of the plainclothes SB functionaries, fleeing from the mass of demonstrators, fatally shot twenty-year-old Bogdan Włosik. This prompted another demonstration the next day, and once again there were clashes that ended late at night. Because skirmishes occurred on October 15, larger forces were deployed, including 450 cadets from the militia school in Szczytno, and the special forces troops helped blockade the neighborhood. During the three days of demonstrations, about 350 people were detained locally, and 1,500 all over Poland.

Strikes took place in several dozen enterprises, and probably no more than 20,000–30,000 people participated. Some of the strikes were not actually noticeable, since too few people took part, and the work stoppages themselves were only short-lived. In some of the cases, the steps taken by enterprise directors and supervisors were effective, such as at the Zamech factory in Elbląg, or the Polkolor factory in Piaseczno, outside of Warsaw. The strikes only became more significant and resonated with society when demonstrations accompanied them, or at least when crowds gathered at factory gates.

Despite the bravura and determination of the many thousands of people who had decided to protest and fought hard against the militia, the events of October 11–15 must be deemed a defeat. Many underground activists felt the same way, since they saw that when the government struck hard and decisively, Solidarity was not able to oppose it effectively. Nevertheless, the underground organizations, including TKK, decided that it was not yet time to lay down their arms. In a declaration dated October 20, TKK once again called for strikes and demonstrations on November 10, and also for people to participate in the celebrations of Poland's independence the next day. The strike-related protests were supposed to be extended to eight hours, and, more importantly, workers were urged to start marches upon leaving their factories. TKK leadership announced that a "week of workers' protests" would take place on December 13–17, in conjunction with the anniversaries of the imposition of martial law, the killing of miners in the Wujek mine, and the massacre on the coast in December 1970. They also declared that a general strike would be staged throughout Poland in the spring of 1983.[17] Taking into consideration the rather unimpressive scale of the protests after the union's delegalization and the obvious problems in properly coordinating activities, setting such a distant date (six months away) might suggest that the proposition was more a desperate attempt to "escape to the future" (which meant that TKK faced the very serious risk of losing its authority), than the result of a rational analysis of the existing situation and available options.

The government treated this menace seriously: "we are still sitting on a barrel of gunpowder," Rakowski wrote in his diary;[18] General Janiszewski interpreted the strike announcement as a challenge.[19] In its calculations, Jaruzelski's team was increasingly reckoning with the possibility that Jaruzelski's opponents within the communist party would use the repeated protests to argue that the group behind martial law did not have the situation under control and was unable—or unwilling—to use their successes to date to eradicate Solidarity completely. For this reason, preparations to pacify the strikes and demonstrations were similar to those before August 31. Significant numbers of troops were sent to all large cities: from a thousand in Silesia to two thousand in Warsaw and Gdańsk. Significant numbers of military vehicles (and airplanes) were readied for the transport of militia units. On November 9 the Ministry of Internal Affairs declared a state of "full alert." This time, however, they paid particular attention to propaganda efforts, as well as those intended to wield psychological pressure on the populace. The SB carried out hundreds of talks meant to frighten people, preventatively detained several hundred individuals, and interned dozens. Experienced SB operational officers were sent to the sixty-five largest enterprises which the Central Committee had selected, and to post-secondary institutions. There, they carried out "warning talks" with hundreds of people. The Ministry of Internal Affairs delegated functionaries of its Department IV, which dealt with the Church, to "preventative talks" with parish priests and vicars in urban parishes and industrial agglomerations. As early as October 21, the director of Department V of the Ministry of Internal Affairs ordered the identification of individuals in all voivodships "who were being recruited from large enterprises threatened [with strikes] and were suspected of inciting and organizing the most recent strikes and street skirmishes," but against whom there was no cause for arrest.[20] By November 10, about fifteen hundred such individuals were called up for three-month military exercises. They formed over twenty companies, which were scattered on various military exercise grounds far from any large cities. These can be seen as a kind of penal military unit.[21] In Wrocław, the SB repeated its October maneuver: on November 8, Frasyniuk's deputy, Piotr Bednarz, was arrested, along with eleven other people. The arrests were meant to be a clear signal that the underground structures there had already been penetrated to a large extent, which suggested that the SB was monitoring the underground, and that it could perhaps even influence its activities. For two evenings, November 7 and 8, state television aired extensive coverage of the meeting between Rakowski and people who had written letters to him. The general impression from these programs was supposed to suggest that the country's situation had already stabilized, and that the difficult social issues could be solved peacefully—something that the underground, which was isolated, was undermining. The meeting between Jaruzelski and Primate Glemp on November 8 was important in terms of propaganda. A communiqué issued after that meeting announced the date of John Paul II's visit (June 1983), and appealed for the public to remain calm and for there to be no work stoppages. The primate made a personal television appearance to express his opinion that the visit and public calm were closely connected; without calm, the Holy Father would not come to Poland.

On Wednesday, November 10, the strike action failed, and in Andrzej Friszke's assessment, it constituted quite simply "a spectacular failure of the underground."[22] The illegal *Tygodnik Mazowsze* deemed it a "defeat." According to figures from the Ministry of Internal Affairs, the strikes took place in just twenty-eight enterprises (of which nine were in Wrocław) and in thirteen voivodships, with several thousand people participating.[23] Perhaps the numbers were a bit higher, but in general not many people took part (in one factory, only a single worker stopped working), the strikes were short-lived (from ten minutes to two hours), and there were no gatherings—neither large mass meetings, nor any that were just for the factory crews. This does not mean, however, that Poland was dominated that day by an atmosphere of intensive, constructive work, as the official media were reporting the next day, or that everyone was enthusiastically exceeding their norms, like at the Rosa Luxemburg Factory in Warsaw, where General Jaruzelski paid a short visit. In many factories, there was a nervous atmosphere, uneasiness, and excitement, but deciding to strike still was not easy. What proved "Solidarity was alive" was more what was happening in the streets than the behavior of people in the factories or institutions, just as during the preceding months. The militia, reinforced by army troops, was of course gaining the upper hand.

After the October defeat, it was now relatively calm in Gdańsk, and the two other bastions of Solidarity, in both Wrocław and Nowa Huta, were also disappointing. While it is true that those cities saw relatively large demonstrations, their course was less violent than those in August or October. In Wrocław, the demonstrations began at several points in the city around 3 p.m. Members of the Border Defense Troops and the military police assisted the ZOMO functionaries. For a while, they managed to control the downtown area. The clashes lasted almost until midnight, primarily just downtown and on Grabiszyńska Street, which had already become notorious throughout Poland (it was called *zomostrada*, a play on the Polish word for highway – *autostrada*). The militia detained a total of nearly three hundred people. The next day was incomparably calmer, perhaps because a contingent of almost a thousand cadets from the militia academy in Szczytno appeared in the city. After a Mass for Poland's Independence Day on November 11, almost everyone who had attended went home. In Nowa Huta, when the steelworkers left after the first shift, the traditional march formed, but this time the people began to disperse relatively quickly. The more ardent demonstrators ran into a blockade, in which soldiers from the MSW military units were taking part, with bayonets atop their Kalashnikovs. It didn't look very inviting. The next day, no demonstrations took place in Nowa Huta because of the ZOMO forces that had amassed there.

This time it was in Kraków that the demonstrations took on a more violent nature, both on November 10 and 11. Primarily post-secondary and high school students took part, and the dormitory district was one of the areas where clashes took place. Over the course of two days, the militia detained a total of about 170 people. A relatively large demonstration took place on November 10 in Warsaw, where a crowd of several thousand (according to various sources, 3,500–8,000 people) gathered in the vicinity of the Supreme Court, where Solidarity had been registered in 1980. One of the demonstrators, beaten by the militia as the crowd was being dispersed, died in the hospital a few days later. On November 10, demonstrations also took place in Toruń, Częstochowa, Kołobrzeg, Lubin, Łódź, Poznań, Dzierżoniów, and elsewhere. There were fewer demonstrations on the anniversary of Poland's independence on November 11, and these were much less violent. In addition to Kraków, which has already been mentioned, they took place in Warsaw, Toruń, and Częstochowa. In Toruń, the irritated rector of Nicolaus Copernicus University suspended classes and ordered the eviction of many dormitory residents. At the University of Warsaw, the rector suspended classes at one of the departments. Masses were held in almost all the larger cities, but no large gatherings or marches took place afterward.

There was essentially only one conclusion from all the protests that took place after August 31—that underground Solidarity was losing its initiative and ability to mobilize people on a larger scale. This meant that, whether it wanted to or not, it would have to recognize that the "long march" would remain its only real strategy. Of course, no one knew whether it would be an effective one. In an announcement on November 22, TKK humbly admitted that "the course of events . . . throws into question the Union's tactics up to this time," and that it was now faced with the task of "developing new forms of resistance."[24] At the same time, in a separate document, the union called on the government to conclude an agreement "that could create an appropriate climate to bring the country out of the economic crisis."[25]

Administrators of martial law kept up the momentum and launched new political and propaganda-related activities day after day. On November 12, General Jaruzelski went to pay his respects to the parents of a young man who had been shot at Nowa Huta. On November 15, a terse communiqué about a WRON meeting stated that it had presented the Sejm Presidium with a proposal for it to call a session of parliament on December 13, which was interpreted as an announcement that martial law would be lifted that day. The PRON Initiative

Commission (Komisja Inicjatywna) also appealed to the Sejm to "approve the end of martial law as quickly as possible." In late November, over two hundred internees were freed, and "only" slightly over a thousand people remained in the internment centers (but at least another fifteen hundred people were still imprisoned). Nevertheless, there were still signs that the government did not intend to relax the rigors of martial law completely: on November 24, the Voivodship Court in Wrocław sentenced Władysław Frasyniuk to six years in prison (and suspended his civil rights for four years), and two days later sentenced a Belgian, Roger Noel, to three years in prison after he was charged with transporting parts for the construction of radio transmitters to Poland for Solidarity.

While the November crisis was underway, unexpected events elsewhere completely beyond the control of Poland's ruling clique also influenced the situation: on November 10, while the Polish communist leadership was vigilantly monitoring news about the scale of strikes and demonstrations, Leonid Brezhnev died. The Soviet ruler, who was a sworn enemy of Solidarity, demonstrated an admirable degree of pragmatism in his treatment of Poland and its rulers. Despite his fears and uncertainty, he agreed with Kania and Jaruzelski that they should rely solely on Polish forces to deal with Solidarity. He trusted Jaruzelski, whom it seems he did not particularly like, despite hardly knowing him. The death of Brezhnev—who was very often caricatured, because of his appearance, as a dangerous but stupid bear—meant there could be a power struggle at the Kremlin, in which a more moderate politician would ultimately win. It was thought that this situation would at least temporarily reduce interest in Polish issues, which would in turn weaken the position of Poland's own hardliners, for whom Moscow's support was of fundamental importance. Brezhnev's successor, Iurii Andropov, head of the KGB, was very well informed about Polish affairs. Andropov was one of Jaruzelski's backers and was a member of the Suslov commission, which had been appointed in August 1980 to deal with the Polish problem. Thus, one can say that, in some respects, for Jaruzelski, Brezhnev's death was good news.

As a result of the mounting tension during the wait to see what would transpire in the factories and streets on November 10 and 11, the authorities launched many different propaganda activities. The most important of these was a communiqué, read on November 11 during the afternoon news, announcing that Lech Wałęsa had been released from internment. The letter Wałęsa sent to Jaruzelski (dated November 8) was also read. The text was only a couple of lines long. In it, Wałęsa proposed "meeting and seriously discussing interesting subjects," and expressed his conviction that "with goodwill, we will certainly find a solution." The letter ended with an odd signature: "Corporal Lech Wałęsa."[26] Many conflicting interpretations of this signature appeared, but his half-joking tone (a corporal is writing to a general) gave Solidarity's chairman some room to maneuver, in case he might later need to distance himself from this gambit.

Isolated in Arłamów, the union's leader undoubtedly did not fully realize that the letter, which he had to write as a condition of his release, was actually an element of a long-term project that can be described as "Operation Wałęsa." Poland's topmost leaders were directly involved in these activities. At the very latest, it began when the general's close inner circle decided that Solidarity's chairman would not be arrested just like any other activist when martial law was imposed, but that he would be granted the status of "government guest." Later, that same group decided that he would enjoy special conditions during his internment. Humanitarian impulses were not a motivation for this decision, but rather long-range political calculations. Behind closed doors, contemptuous and at times even disdainful remarks were sometimes made about Solidarity's chairman: "he's an insignificant person, a rogue, sly fox, a cunning fellow who wants to deceive his partner," said Kiszczak at a Politburo meeting.[27] At the same time, however, people from the first secretary's inner circle believed that Wałęsa should not be alienated, since he could serve as a link to a particular segment of society—an asset that might well become necessary one day. Treating him too drastically, they calculated, would be detrimental to the government's image not so much among Solidarity's ardent supporters—about whom they frankly did not care very much—but more in terms of opinion abroad. They also reckoned that if the situation suddenly became more serious, perhaps Wałęsa could be convinced to pacify any overly radical activists. As a result, discussions often took place about whether or not releasing him was advisable.

After December 13, however, steps were taken to try to induce Solidarity's leaders to cooperate, or rather collaborate, with martial law's authorities. At first, this was done intensively; later, efforts were always persistent, although less intensive. In summer, Wałęsa was probably recovering mentally, while his wife and all of his children spent six weeks with him in Arłamów. After this long summer hiatus, the authorities renewed their efforts. At this time, Father Orszulik would visit him and bring him not only news but also some of the underground announcements and documents. As Wałęsa confided to Orszulik, "my guards suggest that I write to General Jaruzelski and request I be released."[28] Wałęsa, however, systematically refused to do so: "I didn't ask the general to lock me up," he told Father Orszulik, "so I'm not going to ask to get released." Despite Wałęsa and his guest's efforts to avoid speaking where they might be tapped, General Kiszczak had tapes from those conversations at his disposal. When SB Research Office specialists were preparing activities designed to discredit Wałęsa, they secretly recorded a conversation between Wałęsa and his brother Stanisław, who visited him on September 30. In that conversation, during which the brothers indulged in alcoholic beverages, their topics of conversation included family financial matters.

In late August, Father Orszulik announced to Wałęsa that "perhaps in the near future talks with government representatives [would be] proposed."[29] Orszulik based this statement on knowledge he had gleaned from the constant meetings between Episcopate and government representatives, which he sometimes attended. The "near future" lasted a little over a month; on October 4, Minister Ciosek really did travel to Arłamów. Wałęsa did not want to receive him immediately, but they eventually did talk for about two hours, during which the minister presented a bill on trade unions. (Four days later, the Sejm was supposed to vote on this bill.) He offered to release Wałęsa if he agreed to accept a state function—a place on the PRON National Council (which did not yet exist), or the parliamentary Consultative Council on Trade Unions (which was just being formed). Wałęsa rejected these propositions, and wrote a brief extemporaneous statement addressed to the chairman of the Council of State, the minister of justice, the marshal of the Sejm, and Primate Glemp. In it, he said that the proposed legislation "destroys the hopes raised by the social agreements that have been signed" and "will lead to even greater errors and distortions on the road to building socialism in our country."[30]

Wałęsa's reaction was the subject of a lively exchange of opinions, at a Politburo meeting as well as in numerous conversations (mainly by telephone) between Jaruzelski, Kiszczak, and Rakowski, who still wondered whether it would make sense to release him. The party hardliners (such as Mirosław Milewski) were staunchly against his release, and believed that the film of the "brothers' conversation" made by the SB should be broadcast on television to utterly compromise Wałęsa, a tactic that Jaruzelski's closest associates opposed. Finally, Wałęsa took the initiative and wrote his famous letter on November 8. In General Jaruzelski's circle, it was decided that the letter should be "more serious," and a suitable text was prepared that was "written in Wałęsa's style," as Rakowski remarked.[31]

On November 9, the day before the planned protests, General Kiszczak went to Arłamów with a special mission, which correspondingly increased the importance of the talks. Wałęsa rejected the text that Rakowski's team had produced, and insisted on the one that he had written himself, although he of course knew that key words were missing: a request that he be released, and an appeal for no strikes. Solidarity's leader was eager to be active again, but this was going to be possible only after his isolation ended. He was determined and self-confident. Based on SB reports from Arłamów, we know Wałęsa allegedly said in one of the conversations that "in five years, all this will crack anyway."[32] One has to admit that his estimate was not far off; just seven years later, Poland already had a government headed by Tadeusz Mazowiecki that had been initiated by Lech Wałęsa. Mazowiecki had been one of the thousands of people associated with Solidarity who were interned after December 13.

On November 10, the first strikes and demonstrations began, but were not very widespread, as it soon turned out. Wałęsa was still biding his time in Arłamów, and there was odd wrangling underway about Wałęsa among the top leaders of

The End of the Campaign and Wałęsa's Release 215

martial law. Kiszczak and Rakowski wanted an announcement to be made that day about Wałęsa's release. The head of the Ministry of Internal Affairs said that they had to have some kind of "bridge" to society, and that they could not "rely on truncheons and ZOMO" (said "policeman number one"!). He believed that delaying the decision would mean that "the effect will be lost,"[33] by which he meant the disorientation of demonstrators and striking workers. Jaruzelski, however, not wanting to take risks, recognized that they should wait until the results of the first day of the protest were known, especially since Solidarity's chairman had not signed any document directly referring to the protests. Thus the communiqué about Wałęsa's release did not actually serve to assuage the situation, since there was not much need to do so. On the contrary, it could be seen as proof of the government's power, since it could afford to free its greatest foe—although freedom in an authoritarian regime was relative.

On November 12, Deputy Prime Minister Rakowski noted in his diary, "Now the question arises—what next with Wałęsa?"[34] Since they had already answered the question "What next with Solidarity?" (and it was formally liquidated), the next one, logically, had to be about its chairman—or, as it was often written in the official press—"the former chairman of the former union." Before this topic became the subject of frequent debate, however, a detailed plan for putting Wałęsa under house arrest was drawn up on General Jaruzelski's orders. In accordance with that plan, Bishop Dąbrowski and the Vatican were given cassettes with the "brothers' conversation," in order to deprive Wałęsa of Church support, especially that of the primate and pope.[35]

The next day Wałęsa was taken to Otwock, where his statement was filmed for television. Because of his protests, it was never broadcast (but it was not destroyed), and he spoke with Colonel Kuca, head of the SB Research Office. On November 14, he had a longer meeting with a representative of the Chief Military Prosecutor's Office and the director of the Criminal Investigation Office of the Ministry of Internal Affairs.[36] They instructed him about the need to observe the regulations in force, and discussed the crimes that Wałęsa could commit, such as publicly calling for the legislation on trade unions not to be recognized. They also warned against him wearing a Solidarity pin in his lapel, because he could be fined. Sometimes the conversation almost became a political debate, in which Wałęsa tried to convince his interlocutors (simplifying his complicated arguments here) that he always strove to come to an agreement, to sense the government's intentions, and not to engage in frontal attacks. He also stressed that he was unfavorably inclined toward the radicals and some of his advisors, and particularly toward people associated with KOR. Moreover, he assured them that he was comfortable maintaining contact with government representatives, even the voivodship militia commandant and the local chief of the SB. Solidarity's chairman agreed, as he had occasionally in the past, with some of his interlocutors' opinions, but he steadfastly refused to sign the declaration presented to him, despite its neutral content: that he was acquainted with the "contents of the penal code on matters of . . ." with a list of the crimes that (it was believed) he could commit, and a warning that he would be held responsible. Late the night of November 14, Wałęsa was taken home, where not only his family was waiting, along with a large group of journalists, but also a crowd of a couple thousand people who had doggedly stood in front of his apartment building. Wałęsa addressed them many times through the window.

In a statement dated November 22, the TKK declared it was ready to "submit to Lech Wałęsa's decisions," who "for us is still the Union's chairman, elected in democratic elections."[37] The announcement continued in an unremittingly amicable tone, stating that Wałęsa's release "has opened new possibilities for a truce with the government." A stop was also put to the rumors circulating among those in government that some TKK members wanted to reveal their identities. Out of consideration for their safety, Wałęsa made no attempts to contact those in hiding personally, especially TKK members. He nevertheless had no intention of respecting what communist Poland's public prosecutor and chief examiner had tried to put into his head. Neither did he heed advice that he should really go visit a spa for a while—but not just because he did not feel ill or particularly tired. He simply threw himself into a whirlwind of activity: his apartment in the huge building that was part of Gdańsk's Zaspa housing estate became a place of constant pilgrimages. The visitors were primarily foreign journalists, but many people associated with Solidarity from all over the country also came.

Not wanting to depend entirely on intermediaries, Wałęsa, together with some of his close associates, prepared the text for a speech that he wanted to make on December 16 at a rally on the anniversary of the massacres in December 1970 and at the Wujek mine. Solidarity in Gdańsk organized that rally, despite the fact that TKK had called off the commemorations. Since Wałęsa's apartment was not only guarded by permanent militia sentries, but was also being tapped and photographed, the SB of course knew about this plan. The entire development was blockaded already the day before, and on the morning of December 16, the militia flushed out the area around the building, surrounding it with a tight cordon. Wałęsa was taken by force from his apartment and pushed into a waiting car. They drove him around the city for many hours, until the rally at the shipyard was over. The event's organizers, however, had been given a cassette recording beforehand, so the several thousand people gathered there were able to listen to Wałęsa's speech anyway.

The speech was very measured. Wałęsa did not call for violence; quite the contrary: "I ask you," he said in closing, "return peacefully to your homes, think about what [I said], and work towards those aims. Don't let there be even greater losses today. And let everyone else go back home. Let's not allow ourselves to be pushed away from our peaceful attainment of the aims we have set for ourselves."[38] Despite the conciliatory tone, even Rakowski, an ardent proponent of Wałęsa's release, was very upset when he learned of this speech: "probably the time has come," he wrote in his journal, "to broadcast the film of [Wałęsa's] conversation with his brother,"[39] although he himself believed that material was a fake that the secret police had put together. A month after his release, the "former chairman of a former union" began causing problems. This was to happen with increasing frequency. The whole story is a little reminiscent of a game of cat and mouse, except neither side considered itself to be the mouse: one thought it was a bold, dangerous tomcat, the other that it was a sly alley cat. This is just how Wałęsa saw himself. One day, he told Father Orszulik, "They think that I'm a bumpkin . . . but I'd sell them all down the river."[40]

The idea of easing martial law's restrictions had already been considered for a long time. A few people in the ruling elite had even mentioned the need for such steps shortly after December 13. The plan for the implementation of martial law assumed that specific prohibitions would be lifted, depending on how the situation developed. The immediate restrictions affecting the population as a whole began to be revoked after just a few weeks. These included the curfew, restrictions on travel, and the blocking of bank accounts. No schedule was ever presented to the public, however. It was only in his speech in July 1982, referred to above, that General Jaruzelski mentioned the end of the year as a possible timeframe. He was not speaking of any definitive end to martial law, however, but rather only about its "suspension," which was not regulated by any legislation. The initial steps were nevertheless taken, which is shown in the document "Comments and Propositions about How to Resolve the Political Crisis and End Martial Law," prepared by the Central Committee apparatus in late June and early July.[41]

Authors of the document assumed that "maintaining martial law too long would cause certain negative phenomena" both in Poland's internal situation and in terms of its international relations. To avert this, they proposed changing the current situation gradually; a strategic aim of the entire process was to be "the implementation of essential modifications to the structures of the socialist state." They presented these "modifications" rather vaguely and imprecisely, but at least one project was truly innovative: "the creation of the office of president of the Polish People's Republic, elected for a period of 5–7 years, who would hold executive, civilian, and military power in his hands."[42] There is no doubt that General Jaruzelski would be the only one fit for an office defined in this way. This proposal was not pursued immediately, but it was suggested again a few years later, and in a very different context. For the time being, martial law itself was the focus.

On November 18, during a special session of the Politburo, a crucial meeting took place regarding the suspension of martial law. This was a week after the government had proclaimed that Solidarity had definitively been defeated, and after

Wałęsa's release. The fact that people from outside the communist party leadership were in attendance—a very rare occurrence—made this meeting special. In fact, some were not even party members at all. Point 1 in the agenda was described quite enigmatically: "The Current Social and Political Situation in the Country and the Long-Range Conclusions That Can Be Drawn from It."[43] Among those invited to consider this first point was the Marshal of the Sejm, Stanisław Gucwa, of the United Peasant Party, a satellite of the Polish communist party. Others included the Presidium of the Council of Ministers and the "allied" deputy prime ministers—Roman Malinowski from the United Peasant Party, Edward Kowalczyk from the Democratic Party, and Zenon Komender from the Catholic PAX association. The chairman of the Council of State, Henryk Jabłoński, also took part in the meeting, along with the minister of justice and the prosecutor general of the Polish People's Republic. Among the guests was Michał Atlas, director of the Central Committee's Administrative Department, who (as Jaruzelski and Kiszczak knew) was a hardliner. Since at least 1980, he had been a "permanent contact" for East German diplomats and secret police (Stasi). As usual, General Janiszewski, head of the Office of the Council of Ministers, also took part.

First, General Jaruzelski gave the discussion direction by presenting three variations: martial law could be lifted, suspended, or maintained. He then said that suspension "would yield the most benefits," and that WRON supported this kind of solution. Thus, the meeting was probably more like a consultation and an airing of ideas about the process of suspending martial law, rather than about really choosing one of the suggested solutions. Among the more than a dozen people who voiced their opinions, only three supported the idea of lifting martial law quickly (Gucwa from the United Peasants' Party, and Politburo members Hieronim Kubiak and Stanisław Kałkus). The person recording the meeting's protocol failed to note some people's choices clearly. The first secretary's most important argument was probably that suspension—"if the appropriate legal acts are passed"—would make it possible to reinstate martial law at any time: "This safety catch is important, because difficult problems lie ahead of us, related among other things to a difficult food situation." "It is necessary to control the situation," he added, "because of the pope's visit." Unexpectedly, he proposed a propaganda move: "make 13 December an anniversary" and call it "Day of Salvation" or the "Holiday of Salvation." The perversity of this idea is surprising, but it reflects the logic of martial law's defenders. "Salvation," like "Rebirth," was part of the repertoire of most important and frequently used terms.

Interestingly, it was not the minister of justice who presented the proposed package of legislative changes, but rather General Siwicki, chief of the General Staff, who had not been regarded as a legal expert up to then. One can thus assume that he was simply outlining something that the General Staff or the Committee for the Protection of the Country had prepared. Siwicki said that of "fifty martial law regulations," six were to be abolished, thirty-two would be suspended, and seventeen would continue to be in force, or would be "examined." Either the person taking the protocol or the general was in error, because there was actually a total of fifty-five regulations. In any case, Siwicki proposed important changes in the field of labor relations. In militarized enterprises, employees could not quit their jobs of their own volition, and one could be fired for taking part in strikes or demonstrations. Administrative decisions made by rectors at universities would continue to be grounds for expulsion, as would the voivods' right to suspend principals, including "principals of post-secondary schools" (probably referring to rectors). General Siwicki stated that "the situation does not allow for an amnesty." The only possibility was to make use of the right of pardon, which could affect five hundred to seven hundred people who demonstrated contrition, comported themselves irreproachably, had not committed "serious deeds," and, for example, had small children. He foresaw the abolition of the internment centers and, as a result, the arrest and charging of some of the internees ("this affects 120 individuals," he remarked). He also proposed that voting in the Sejm take place on December 13, and that martial law be suspended on January 1, 1983.

In other lengthy speeches, Barcikowski and Kiszczak reported on Poland's political situation. Only some elements of these are remarkable, such as Barcikowski's reminders about the need to "build a political space" with the help of PRON and self-government, hastening the organization of new trade unions, and even preparing amendments to the constitution. Kiszczak's comments, in contrast, were interesting because of what he said about plans for internees. The minister of internal affairs believed that eighty to ninety people should be subject to criminal proceedings, including six individuals who could be prosecuted for "conspiratorial activities" (Andrzej Gwiazda, Seweryn Jaworski, Karol Modzelewski, Grzegorz Palka, Andrzej Rozpłochowski, and Jan Rulewski). To the minister's obvious dismay, no grounds were found for the arrest of another four (Marian Jurczyk, Janusz Onyszkiewicz, Andrzej Sobieraj, and Antoni Tokarczyk). When Jaruzelski interjected, "And what about Geremek?" the answer was: "No grounds." Kiszczak was nevertheless hopeful: "After examining [the matter], maybe a clause will be found for them, too." Ideas of varying caliber also arose in the discussion: the prosecutor general, Franciszek Rusek, for example, proposed declaring an amnesty that would be directed primarily at those who were still in hiding. Minister of Justice Sylwester Zawadzki raised a formal problem; he pointed out that the decree on martial law did not foresee the possibility of "suspending" it, but only "revoking" it. This discovery prompted a short but lively discussion, in which Roman Malinowski of ZSL admonished lawyers "not to create difficulties." Deputy Prime Minister Obodowski then demanded that the Council of Ministers be given authority in economic matters. In his summary, General Jaruzelski pointed out that it would be expedient to "send as many people as possible who are currently serving prison terms abroad." In comparing the law that the Sejm finally passed on December 18 titled "On the Special Legal Regulation during the Suspension of Martial Law"[44] with the protocol of the Politburo session a month earlier, it is apparent that the legal plans were determined by the party's highest body, and were only polished later. In the end, it was decided not to announce an amnesty, leaving the right of pardon as the only possible option. This of course required prisoners to write a request to the Council of State. Not many people made use of this tactic. On December 23, however, the internment centers were closed and—with the exception of seven leading union activists affected by the public prosecutor's sanctions (Seweryn Jaworski, for example, was added to those named above)—all their residents went home for Christmas. The prisons, however, were still full.

When General Jaruzelski announced at a Politburo meeting on December 22, 1981, that "several months" would be needed to win the campaign, he was being too optimistic, though admittedly he was not very far off. The campaign was definitively won on November 10, and the suspension of martial law was actually just one more element in the government's victory. Nevertheless, at that same meeting, the first secretary announced that "ten years would be needed" to win the war. And, indeed, the conflict tormenting Poland was not over yet on December 31, 1982. There was more to come.

Part 4

Toward Positional Warfare

Chapter Fifteen

The Church between Eternity and Solidarity

When martial law was imposed, the position of the Catholic Church in Polish society and public life was very strong, but also fragile. It was strong because the Poles belonged to that ever-smaller group of "religious" European nations; i.e., most Poles regularly attended Mass, and the parish priest was still a local authority. The Church in Poland had deep roots in society, both because it was traditional, and also because it was a spiritual alternative to communism. Many Poles regarded that atheistic system as alien and something imposed upon them against their will. The Church's position was also strong because for over thirty years, since 1948, Primate Stefan Wyszyński, both an outstanding priest and statesman, had stood at its head. He was eminently able to formulate the nation's essential needs and expectations in the language of faith. Finally, it was also because Cardinal Karol Wojtyła was elected pope in 1978, and thus became overnight the principal authority for the vast, and probably overwhelming, majority of Poles. His election as pope also sparked a tidal wave of national pride. These were the "positive" sides of power.

The Church also enjoyed its position thanks to the fact that the atheistic communist system had been experiencing, since the mid-1970s, yet another crisis in its short history. The clearest and also most dangerous manifestation of this crisis was the emergence of Solidarity, a mass movement whose protests were constantly expanding into new areas. While it is true that the exact position of the Church cannot be assessed empirically, one can with a large degree of certainty assert that, without the role of the Church, primate, and "Polish pope" in the Vatican, Solidarity would not have taken the shape it did. Although these three conditions alone did not suffice, they were essential. It would be difficult to imagine that there could have been any other main bases of support in Poland for a social movement of that magnitude. Clearly, the link to Christianity was certainly crucial. The communists ruling Poland, despite their varying degrees of antagonism to religion and the Church, had already invoked Primate Wyszyński several times in the past during moments of crisis in hopes that he would help calm the public mood. This was the case in October 1956, when Władysław Gomułka, the charismatic and respected communist party leader, feared he would lose control of the country's flood of emotions. Edward Gierek did the same in 1970, though the situation was not as tense, when he assumed power after Gomułka in the traumatic atmosphere following the massacre of striking workers on the coast.

The primate did not refuse to help, primarily because he believed that social peace is a value in and of itself. Because of the unprecedented losses that the Poles suffered during the Second World War and the first postwar years, he believed that any danger of bloodshed should be averted. Being a *homo politicus*, he knew that by assisting in this way he was actually expanding the Church's ability to act. Wyszyński was sorely disappointed by Gomułka, who launched a Bismarckian *Kulturkampf* as soon as he had succeeded in gaining a tighter grip on power. In the end, the primate emerged triumphant from this duel.

The "golden years" of the Gierek era passed quickly, and in August 1980, when strikes began to threaten his rule, he recalled the old saying, *jak trwoga to do Boga* (when in fear, God is dear), and asked again for help. The primate obliged, but this time it was obvious that the Church had in fact become the main guarantor of social peace. Although its sympathies were with those in society who were rebelling, it served as an arbiter on the Polish political scene. Therein lay the delicate nature of the situation. The Church wanted to support society's demands and national aspirations, expressed by Solidarity and the smaller groups gathered around it. On the one hand, the Church needed and wanted to guarantee to the ruling communists that these efforts to effect change would not get out of control, and that it would moderate any radical tendencies. Solidarity's own moderate stance, on the other hand, was supposed to insure that the government would not resort to violence, whose instruments were all in its hands.

The death of Primate Wyszyński in May 1981 and the short-lived *Treuga Dei* that followed did not fundamentally change the situation. As a result, the newly appointed Primate Józef Glemp quickly stepped into Wyszyński's shoes. Wyszyński had been known as the "Primate of the Millennium" because it was he who had clearly won in the state-Church rivalry over the Polish millennial celebrations in 1966. We do not know, and will never know, whether Wyszyński would have been able—by virtue of his spirit, character, and intellect—to delay or prevent the use of force and the imposition of martial law if he had been in office longer. It seems this would have not been very likely. What is certain, however, is that Primate Glemp's intensive efforts, which became feverish in the weeks leading up to December 13, misfired: he was not able to induce Solidarity's leaders to renounce their radical ideas and shelve the activists most hated by the government, nor to stop General Jaruzelski in his march toward martial law. What happened the night of December 12–13 was thus, in a certain sense, a defeat for the institutional Church, and also for Primate Glemp personally, for he had proved unable to stop the course of events.

This was not, however, a complete disaster. Regardless of the hypocrisy that characterized the attitude of those in power toward the Church (and religion in general), one of the elements in the political package that Jaruzelski and his closest associates had prepared for the period of martial law was that the government would treat the Church as its most important partner—and actually its only one. On January 18, 1981, during the first meeting of the Joint Commission of the Government and Episcopate under martial law, Kazimierz Barcikowski stated outright: "Today two forces will appear in public life which will be defining a solution: the party and state on the one hand, and the Church and lay Catholics on the other."[1] A declaration of war against the Church—as the government had made against Solidarity—would have been an extremely risky undertaking, at least for General Jaruzelski's team. In such a scenario, advocates of a return to Stalinist methods probably would have made quick work of them too, since any war against the Church would otherwise have been doomed to defeat. Moreover, the Polish communist party had no shortage of people who could invoke the support of Big Brother and expect the "smaller brothers" from the west and south to come to their aid. In its eternal mission, the Church acknowledged the situation forced upon the country on December 13, and strove to minimize the evil that was threatening the nation and to avoid confrontation with the government as much as possible. After December 13, Solidarity had disappeared from the triangle it had formed alongside the party and Church. Only the "axis" was left, as General Jaruzelski put it—i.e., a bipolar arrangement. In any case, for the Polish communist party, Solidarity had ceased to be a political subject, and could only exist if pushed into the role of an object.

Other than in the purely spiritual, religious, and ecclesiastical sphere, the Church was active in several other fields during martial law that are characteristic for the period. It should be made clear, however, that while the Church's structure may have been centralized and hierarchical, it was not ruled with iron discipline. As a result, people of the Church sometimes had diametrically opposed views. Some of the Church's characteristic activities during martial law included (but these were of course by no means all of them) efforts to conduct a dialogue with the government in the public forum; pastoral care and charitable aid for those directly affected by martial law, but not limited only to them; helping the faithful cope with what happened on and after December 13; and providing the space (or cover) for the activities of people from Solidarity, and joining them on the "long march."

The search for solutions was reserved for Glemp and his immediate associates and bishops, who belonged to the highest echelons of the institutional Church (the Main Council of the Polish Episcopate), and those ordinaries who were striving to find local solutions in their respective jurisdictions. John Paul II of course towered over all of these and was the highest authority. The Church's immediate reaction to the shock of martial law was to express the need to minimize existential pressures. (On Primate Glemp's statements to that effect, see chapter 5.) The pope's appeal, which was unusually short out of necessity, was similar to Glemp's.

The pope read his on December 13 on St. Peter's Square after his recitation of the Angelus. In it, he said, "Polish blood cannot be spilled, because too much of it has been spilled [already]."[2]

Glemp and John Paul II's appeals seem to have been coordinated, as suggested by the fact that during a general audience on December 16, John Paul II included a direct quotation from a homily by Glemp, delivered three days earlier in Warsaw. He admonished those in power much more overtly than the primate had, however, telling them that "the strength and authority of the government is expressed through a dialogue and not by the use of force."[3] A communiqué approved by the Main Council of the Episcopate on December 15 was decisive in tone (the primate had agreed for the document not to be circulated in churches). A memorandum with that same date was submitted to the government. After the Wujek mine massacre, Glemp's statements were almost hysterical (he used words such as "I beg" and "I beseech you"), but he was not clearly placing the blame for the bloodshed solely on the administrators of martial law. During a Mass in Gniezno the day after the massacre, he said, "The hatred that has been accumulating for a long time is beginning to mount." He directed his appeal for peace not only to the government, but also to everyone: "Do not raise a hand in hatred against each other."[4]

In a letter from John Paul II to General Jaruzelski on December 18, however, the papal appeal was completely unequivocal: the general was to "cease activities that bring about the shedding of Polish blood."[5] Appealing to the general's conscience, as well as to all of those "with whom the decision now lies," the pope remarked that spilled blood "cannot burden the consciences and stain the hands of our Compatriots." The general was to "return to the road" of peaceful dialogue. Copies of this appeal were supposed to be distributed via diplomatic channels, and the pope also sent one of them, along with a short personal letter, to Wałęsa, which must have been particularly unpleasant for Jaruzelski. Reacting to the very harsh tone of the pope's message, a government representative threatened that the special Vatican envoy to Warsaw, archbishop Luigi Poggi, would not be officially received by anyone, and that the addressee would not accept the pope's letter. After the Vatican conceded and withdrew the letter from "diplomatic channels," Jaruzelski, with his usual flexibility, nevertheless met with the archbishop and responded to John Paul II with a long letter on January 6. In it, he said, "We have nothing against Solidarity's activity as an independent, self-governing trade union, headed by responsible people who are working within their statutory framework."[6] At the same time, however, he hinted that how long martial law would last would "depend only on society." This meant, simply put, that it would depend on whether society would support Solidarity, or whether it would humble itself and once again obey the government.

While the pope did not hesitate to invoke the name "Solidarity" in his public statements, or at least use the word "solidarity" (with a small "s"), the

Episcopate, and particularly Primate Glemp, avoided using it outwardly. In confidential conversations and unpublicized letters to the government, they nevertheless steadfastly defended both the union as such and its members. For instance, they protested against the requirement that officials in the state sector and justice system sign "loyalty oaths," and demanded that internees be granted special rights when in prison. The primate and his closest associates, as well as most of the hierarchs, took the government representatives at their word when they said that Solidarity might be "unsuspended" if it underwent fundamental changes. Taking these assurances at face value was even easier for Glemp, because he also had many reservations about the activities of the union leadership during the period leading up to martial law. In fact, he was even hostile toward some of the union's leaders, and he had a particularly bad opinion about people connected with KOR and those he considered to be incorrigible leftists and political troublemakers. In this respect, his attitude was quite similar to those from the government camp. The primate's views on the matter did not have any impact, however, since neither he nor any of the hierarchs ever suggested their imprisonment was justifiable or right.

Increasingly, it seemed the idea of restoring Solidarity was slipping farther and farther off the agenda. Signs that this was the case included Wałęsa's formal internment (January 26) and the government's statement on the future of trade unions (February 22). Nevertheless, the primate and Episcopate invariably continued to pursue the matter. They also continued to demand the release of Wałęsa and the internees, a declaration of amnesty for those sentenced, a guarantee of safety for those in hiding, and assurance that people would not be fired because of their union activities. The communiqué from the 183rd Conference of the Polish Episcopate was a direct response to the government's stance of February 22. The conference took place several days later, and for the first time proposed that a "new social agreement" be reached.[7] It was to be concluded between the "ruling power" and "credible representatives of organized groups in society," including Solidarity. So as not to limit himself to slogans and generalizations, Primate Glemp sent the "Theses of the Primatial Social Council"[8] to all the bishops on April 8. This document outlined an idea that the more extensive "Propositions of the Primatial Social Council on Social and Economic Matters" would further develop one month later.[9]

The "Theses," which came about as the result of the Council's lengthy discussions, stated outright that the government's position "gives the impression that it is avoiding social dialogue about a national agreement." The only way to attain such a dialogue would be to "uphold the social contracts that were concluded in 1980," including their main point, which was the right to "create independent trade unions." The "Theses" could not appear in any legal publication (Catholic ones had not even been restored yet), so they circulated in handmade copies, appeared in the internal Episcopate bulletin, in the underground press and abroad (most often as excerpts). The government completely rejected (actually ignored) them. They nevertheless became part of the underground's program, as the April 22 announcement from the newly formed TKK demonstrated.

This did not mean, however, that all the underground groups, or even all members of the clergy, accepted the formulations found in the "Theses" and their implied conclusions. Father Franciszek Blachnicki, who was in Rome at the time, was a radical critic of the "Theses," for example. He believed that the document's authors "had adopted the ideas and opinions of official government propaganda." Moreover, he argued, they made groundless claims that some responsibility for the current situation fell on Solidarity, too, regardless of the mistakes it had made. Above all, he accused them of minimizing ethical issues and of excessive pragmatism, comparing it to the political line proclaimed by the Catholic PAX Association years before—which can even be seen as an insult. This charismatic cleric actually said that adopting the "Theses" as an official position could become a "source of a profound discrepancy between the official stance of the Church . . . and society," which had "matured over recent months and years so much that it cannot be diverted from its fight for full liberation."[10] There is no reason to doubt that many Polish clergymen were of the same mind, which did not necessarily imply, of course, that they were rising in open rebellion against the Church hierarchy.

There is too little information about the Episcopate's discussions to say whether some of the bishops shared similar doubts about the "Theses," and more generally about the moderate position expressed by the primate in that document. Nevertheless, it is remarkable that only a few bishops had contact with the underground—pursued, of course, only very cautiously. One of these was bishop Henryk Gulbinowicz, the Wrocław ordinary. Of the primate's close associates, probably only Father Orszulik had underground contacts. He mediated between underground activists and Lech Wałęsa on more than one occasion. In any case, Primate Glemp did not react to TKK's attempt to establish indirect contact. Not even the Primatial Social Council reacted to its proposition, despite the fact that Andrzej Wielowieyski was a member, and one of Solidarity's most important advisors prior to December 13. This avoidance of activists and underground organizations was likely due to caution, but it was probably not the only reason. A dislike of "extremism" undoubtedly played a certain role, and the underground in general, of course, can be seen as falling in that category.

The primate was ambivalent toward the underground union. In a homily he gave at Jasna Góra on August 26, 1982, he appealed for the release of Wałęsa and the internees, and asked that preparations be made for an amnesty. In doing so, however, he omitted what had been a non-negotiable point up to then: the restoration of Solidarity's rights to engage legally in its activities. Instead, he proposed that a date for John Paul II's visit to Poland be set. Ten days later, Bishop Ignacy Tokarczuk gave a homily during a farmers' pilgrimage to the same shrine. In his message, however, he returned to the conditions presented to WRON just after the imposition of martial law, including the "restoration of trade union activities, led by Solidarity."[11] The communiqué from the proceedings of the Plenary Conference of the Polish Episcopate was formally the most important document expressing the Church's position on current affairs. The conference took place just after the Sejm passed the legislation delegalizing trade unions, and the communiqué contained a reference (albeit a very cautious one) to Solidarity as an independent representative of the working people. Even if differences of opinion (which were verbalized) did exist within the Episcopate itself, for the public, at least, it was the primate's position that was most prominent, because he was a realist who understood that facts were most important. Realizing that the rigors of martial law—including internment—would sooner or later be abolished, he made the problem of John Paul II's visit one of the main points in his talks with government representatives. To achieve this goal, he was prepared to make many concessions.

Some of these concessions were met with criticism, certainly among the "rank and file" clergy, and perhaps also within the Church hierarchy. Objections included the primate's meeting with General Jaruzelski on November 8 (discussed in chapter 14), and his appeal to theater people to "return to their normal activities"—i.e., to stop their boycott. It was not a coincidence that Glemp announced this appeal during the "Evening of One Poem," which was taking place as part of the Week of Christian Culture, something that had already served for some years as a place for meetings of the archbishop of Warsaw with intellectuals and people in the arts. The appeal left a bitter aftertaste, in part because Glemp issued it on November 29, the anniversary of the outbreak of the November Uprising of 1830, and thus on one of the most important dates in the history of Poland's struggle for independence. The Union of Polish Stage Artists (Związek Artystów Scen Polskich, ZASP), associated with the defiant boycotters, was suspended the next day, and was disbanded by an administrative decision two days later. It seemed—probably intentionally—as if the authorities had waited for the primate's countersignature before making their move. Actually, however, the harshest form of the boycott was fizzling out, and ZASP's delegalized leadership soon decided to suspend the boycott when martial law itself was suspended. Glemp was thus acting in good faith, but many members of that group and underground activists believed that his actions were a grave mistake.

The fact that the Church, or at least its leadership, took a moderate stance and did not urge people to fight was nothing unusual. In the end, during the entire existence of communist Poland, the Church had employed, to good use, the "long march" strategy rather than sudden bursts of resistance. In this respect, John Paul II's visit was to be a "pilgrimage of national hope," as Archbishop Achilles

Silvestrini[12] told Minister Olszowski—and thus an event whose significance could not be overestimated. The government stipulated many different conditions and created a variety of obstacles. The meeting between the pope and Lech Wałęsa was one of the points of contention. Unlike those in power, John Paul II regarded this meeting with Wałęsa as something that should clearly take place. General Jaruzelski, however, first tried to dissuade the pope via diplomatic channels, and then tried to convince Glemp to exert pressure on Wałęsa so that he would decide against the meeting. In the end, Jaruzelski yielded but did not agree to the Vatican's delicately presented request to lift martial law definitively before the pope's arrival. In fact, quite the opposite occurred: the authorities stated outright that martial law would be lifted if they were satisfied with how things went during the pope's visit.[13] The government's fear of the possible reaction of the crowds, and the threat of unrest, was too great.

The state apparatus prepared for the visit assiduously. The army undertook appropriate action, had somehow routinely raised the level of alert in selected combat units, and was readying means of transportation for their colleagues from the Ministry of Internal Affairs. In General Kiszczak's ministry, there were plans to engage ninety-seven thousand militiamen, intersperse approximately seven thousand plainclothes SB functionaries among the crowds, deploy a special anti-terrorist group near places on the pope's itinerary, and assign the pope bodyguards who would prevent any person who exhibited a connection to Solidarity from getting near him.[14] Fears were so great that the top leadership—the "General's Quartet" (Jaruzelski, Kiszczak, Siwicki, and Janiszewski)—decided they should be ready to reinstate martial law just six months after its suspension. They gave these undertakings the collective cryptonym "Dawn" (Zorza), which inadvertently alluded to the expectations of society, as well as those of Solidarity members, that the pope's visit would be like dawn after the night of martial law.

During the first meeting with the pope, Rakowski noted, General Jaruzelski "was extremely nervous. For the first half of the speech, his legs were shaking so much that I couldn't even look at him."[15] The pope's visit took place June 16–23, 1983, in an atmosphere of enthusiasm and adoration. Emotions were indeed running high, but none of the frightening scenarios that Jaruzelski's team had feared actually came to pass. A demonstration of several thousand people took place in Warsaw on the day of the pope's arrival, and in Nowa Huta the militia attacked a march with more than a thousand participants that had formed after a papal Mass. The underground's leaders did not take part in meetings with John Paul II so they would not be accused of taking advantage of his visit. Millions of Poles participated in the papal Masses: according to figures from the Ministry of Internal Affairs, almost 7 million,[16] which should be regarded as a minimum estimate. The Church, in contrast, estimated the number of participants to be at least 9 million. During all the events, which took place in eight locations, dozens of flags and banners appeared, proclaiming, for example, "The Solidary Nation Greets You," "Freedom for Solidarity," and "Solidarity Is Fighting and Will Win."[17] Other than the sign of the cross, the most common symbol seen was the letter "V" so disliked by Jaruzelski: over the countless numbers of people in the crowds, a forest of hands with outspread fingers would appear every so often.

The homilies did not include very many strong, extemporaneous political accents, and the pope did not directly address issues that were thorniest for the government. Nevertheless, he often referred to the ideas of freedom and solidarity, and spoke about human and civil rights, condemning the trampling of human dignity. He also said that dialogue and coming to an agreement were the only way and referred, in this context, to 1980, recalling the "August movement." When Jaruzelski was told that there were "strong political accents alluding to events of the past two years"[18] in the pope's address during his meeting with young people at Jasna Góra on June 18, WRON's chairman was not only "worried" but also "furious." The next day, high-ranking representatives from Jaruzelski's administration formally lodged a protest against—as they described it—"inciting a rebellion against the government." They asked dramatically "whether the Church wants wrangling and religious war in Poland"[19] and threatened to modify the itinerary of the pope's visit.

This reaction clearly shows the tension that existed within the government camp. The administration was seeking a pretext that would make it impossible for the pope to meet with Wałęsa. In the end, the meeting took place after the official part of the visit had concluded. Logistical support for the Wałęsas and four of their children was provided by the Government Protection Bureau (Biuro Ochrony Rządu, BOR), which transported them over 700 kilometers by helicopter from Gdańsk to the Tatra Mountains, where the meeting took place in one of the lodges. It was very short and completely private and informal, in the lodge's modest, undecorated cafeteria. One might say that it was superficial; even Wałęsa recalls the meeting with fondness, but not with enthusiasm.[20] Nevertheless, it was a positive sign for Solidarity.

In his assessment, George Weigel, one of the leading experts on John Paul II's pontificate, has said that the pope's visit to Poland showed that "the Church would not cut a deal with the regime without Solidarity."[21] It is not clear whether this statement is completely correct, unless Weigel is referring to the pope's own intentions (about which there could of course be no doubt) and not those of the Polish bishops. Those close to Jaruzelski believed that some in Polish society had seen the pope's visit as a legitimization of martial law, and that the unplanned one-on-one conversation at the pope's own request the day before his departure was—as a party report stated—"a serious success for us."[22] Jaruzelski's team also saw John Paul II's visit to Poland as a "spectacular factor that broke through the West's diplomatic and political blockade."[23] It nevertheless seems that this description was an exaggeration, since Poland's strict (though not total) diplomatic isolation would still be in force for over a year. In any case, John Paul II came and went, and nothing spectacular happened. The people associated with Solidarity got a breath of fresh air, and the government's conviction that it was firm in the saddle was reinforced.

Another factor that linked those associated with the Church to Solidarity was the help they provided to victims of martial law, especially to those interned and arrested, and their families. Since December 17, when the Primatial Aid Committee was formally created in Warsaw, a total of thirty-six similar institutions had been founded in every diocese. Many priests were active in these committees, but it should be pointed out that, without laypeople doing all the legwork, this kind of large-scale charitable project would have been impossible. And although these laypeople had no experience in charity work, it turned out that they did an excellent job of organizing their activities. At first, they depended on ad hoc collection drives and people's generosity, which sometimes meant donations of time, a car, or—of utmost importance during fuel rationing—a canister of gasoline. They collected money and foodstuffs primarily during Mass; many donors went directly to their parish priests or religious orders, and most often to diocesan aid committees. These committees developed specialized sections, such as those dealing with legal or medical aid. At first, one of their very important functions was simply to act as a source of information, since it was necessary to determine where those detained were being held, which families needed help, and what kind. In 1982, the Warsaw committee alone (known as the "primatial" committee) provided families with assistance in the amount of approximately 12.2 million złotys, and distributed about 6,400 packages, each weighing 5–10 kilograms.[24]

From February 1982, the trickle of foreign assistance began to grow. At first, only parishes or diocesan committees received it. Aid from various Western European countries, usually organized by trade unions, had been received in Poland even before December 13, but the imposition of martial law prompted millions of people to act. In addition to the demonstrations in front of Polish Embassies and other shows of support for Solidarity, material aid also began flowing into Poland. During 1982, nearly seventy large truckloads of aid arrived just to the primatial committee in Warsaw, each one carrying many tons.[25] In the Federal Republic of Germany, in addition to the transports sent to institutional recipients, there was also a project aimed at sending packages to specific people. Albrecht Riechers estimated that, in 1982, Germans spent approximately 430 million marks for food, clothing, and medicines that were sent to Poland.[26] It was clear that these kinds of large donations could not be received by people who were directly affected, especially since medicines were also being sent, and even medical equipment. The packages began to be given to care facilities, orphanages, and state-run hospitals. Many donors and benefactors struck up direct contact with these institutions, which was necessary, for example, when medicines and medical equipment were involved. Transports were relatively quick to start using the underground for relaying information, letters, money, printing equipment, and parts for radio transmitters. Seventeen duplicating machines and seven offset machines were smuggled just from the Swedish port of Malmö from June to December 1982, not to mention matrixes and small spare parts.[27] This entire large-scale charity campaign would not have been possible, of course, without the Church, which acted as an umbrella for it, and without the space that it made available for these activities.

In looking at the various types of popular resistance after December 13, it is apparent that many of the demonstrations would begin after people left church. One could even say that this was a typical way of organizing a street protest, and also the easiest: it enabled a critical mass of sorts to develop inside the church, whose existence (i.e., a gathering of people inside a church) could not be stopped by the militia or ZOMO. These forces had to refrain from doing so, of course, only as long as the government did not openly declare war on the Church. General Jaruzelski's team, however, did not want to opt for this, despite pressure from the hardliners and Moscow's complaints that they were being too weak.

As a result, some of the churches—just like some of the enterprises—became "Solidarity fortresses." Actually, with time, there were fewer of the latter than the former. For many people, priests were just as important as (and perhaps even more important than) underground leaders. These priests included Jerzy Popiełuszko in Warsaw, Henryk Jankowski in Gdańsk, Mirosław Drzewiecki in Wrocław, Wacław Lewkowicz in Białystok, Stefan Miecznikowski in Łódź, Kazimierz Jancarz and Tadeusz Isakowicz-Zaleski in Nowa Huta, and Leon Kantorski, Czesław Sadłowski, and Stanisław Małkowski, who were known for their work with the democratic opposition before August 1980. Special Masses for the Fatherland and for Constitution and Independence Days (May 3 and November 11) were said, along with others requested by enterprise committees or simply people linked with Solidarity, for anniversaries such as the massacre on the Baltic coast (December 17, 1970), the massacre at the Wujek mine (December 16, 1981), or various local occasions. These Masses would take place in dozens of churches in all the larger cities.

The priests celebrating these Masses did not always give sermons that the government perceived as political. Often, the very fact that people had gathered at a Mass for such an occasion was sufficient to render them important political events. Numerous churches thus became foci for the expression of patriotic feelings. Not everyone gathered there had to be strict Roman Catholics. A leading specialist on the history of the Church in Poland, Father Zygmunt Zieliński, believes, in fact, that "a certain type of martial law religiosity was forming," and that prayer was becoming "one of the forms of protest."[28] Many other manifestations of spirituality can be seen as falling into this category, such as pilgrimages to Jasna Góra, which would sometimes also coincide with the anniversaries of the August 1980 events, and the workers' pilgrimages in Piekary Śląskie. Lay culture with no direct connection to religion also began moving into the churches on quite a large scale. The artists and performers involved simply had no other place to voice their protests—through their own creative means—against the realities of martial law.

As early as December 23, 1981, Bishop Dąbrowski, secretary of the Polish Episcopate, asked the minister of justice to guarantee internees the chance to worship. A positive decision was made immediately at what must have been some higher level, and Primate Glemp appointed the first chaplain for the internees on December 24. This was Father Jan Sikorski, who was sent to the Białołęka prison near Warsaw and was already saying Mass the day after his nomination. Before long, spiritual caregivers for the internees supplemented the existing network of prison chaplains, although the government was not at all pleased with this initiative. Specific bishops, ordinaries, and suffragans were granted permission (if they requested it, of course) for one-off visits to internment centers. The prison authorities, as instructed, tried to hamper the chaplains' work, but they were not able to block it entirely. At the same time, charity aid began arriving at the internment centers and prisons, too. Some of the chaplains played the role of liaisons between the prisoners and the outside world—unofficially and even illegally. They supplied them with underground news sheets, and conveyed to them opinions and information on various current topics. They would also smuggle out messages or sometimes even longer texts.

One cannot say, however, that these kinds of attitudes—support for Solidarity and the public expression of opposition to martial law—were universal among the Polish clergy. With only a few exceptions, the priests in villages and small towns did not share this attitude. In these contexts, expressions of any kind of protest or civil resistance were extremely rare. A large proportion of Poles lived in precisely these kinds of locations. According to SB estimates from December 1982, approximately 5–10 percent of priests sympathized with the opposition (in a way apparent to the authorities, of course).[29] Among those, probably not all would have been such good organizers and speakers, or simply as courageous, as Fathers Popiełuszko, Jancarz, and Jankowski. At least ten to twelve priests and monks were sentenced for "publicizing false information" and assisting the striking workers. A certain Benedictine monk from one of the most famous Polish monasteries, in Tyniec near Kraków, was sentenced to six and a half years in prison for distributing flyers.[30]

In the language of the SB, also used in the communist party, this was "church extremism"; the Episcopate representatives and bishop ordinaries were reminded of this at every opportunity. The authorities demanded that defiant priests be instructed, or even punished (by being transferred to smaller parish, for example).

The Church between Eternity and Solidarity 235

As one can see from the known sources, higher-ranking clergy generally limited themselves to lower-key ways of influencing the situation. In time, Primate Glemp was officially presented with a list of the names of sixty-nine "extremists" (including two bishops) who had ruined Church-state relations—which had, after all, been so good, as the government claimed.[31] Authorities also took other steps to pacify the clergy, such as organizing clubs of priests who were former soldiers—a group that numbered in the hundreds or even thousands, since seminarians had for many years been required to participate in military service. Although WRON launched this initiative in late April 1982, it is not clear, to what extent, if at all, it was actually carried out.

The communist regime was now resorting much more frequently to its traditional tool in the battle against the priests and Church: the security apparatus. During martial law, a special cell in Department IV of the Ministry of Internal Affairs, known as "Section VI" (earlier known as "Independent Group D"), became more active. While it had existed for almost a decade, it really gained momentum only after martial law was lifted. Section VI was involved in operations described quite enigmatically as "disintegrational." Actually, these activities were "aimed at limiting and liquidating the clergy's politically negative activities" by means of "special projects,"[32] which meant, for example, "provocations," the production of fake publications and brochures, assaults, beatings, destruction of vehicles, setting apartments on fire, and even murder. Section VI was an elite group numbering between ten and twenty individuals at the Warsaw headquarters, and somewhat fewer at the larger voivodship militia headquarters. Functionaries from this cell attempted to discredit the pope with the help of fabricated documents in February 1983. They also tried many times to discredit Father Adolf Chojnacki from the parish in Kraków's Bieżanów district. They made similar efforts in connection with Bishop Ignacy Tokarczuk, and in 1983 they launched a "disintegrational" operation against Father Popiełuszko.[33] Department IV grew from about 1,200 functionaries in 1980 to over 2,600 in 1981, and carried out numerous operations against the clergy, including generating fake underground publications directed at the clergy and Church circles, as well as producing anonymous letters and spreading rumors. A network of informers was particularly important in these kinds of activities. Their numbers grew very quickly, from about 6,400 individuals in 1980 to approximately 15,300 in 1983.[34] Of course, only some of these were members of the clergy, but it may be estimated that approximately 10 percent of priests and nuns (including those who were members of religious orders and those who were not) were collaborating with the secret police during that time. They provided the authorities with much valuable information, including some that facilitated the government's implementation of policies on the Church, or its influence on bishops and priests who held posts in the dioceses. It seems, however, that one of the main aims of such a large expansion of the network of agents was to use recruits as a means of "loyalizing the clergy," as it was called in the technical jargon. The point was not so much to subordinate the clergy so that they would inform on their confrères, but (or even mainly) so that they would be afraid of being demasked (i.e., discredited), and would feel they had been subordinated and incapacitated. In short, the aim was to get them not to speak out antagonistically against martial law, not to organize Solidarity Masses in their parishes, and to speak out negatively about those priests who did support the underground.

The secret police did not have to engage in "disintegrational" activities against most clergymen, or recruit them as secret collaborators. This was because priests were by nature loyal to the Church and its mission, which they profoundly believed was eternal. In contrast, they saw Solidarity as just a worldly, ephemeral phenomenon. They were thus serving eternity, and therefore did not feel obligated to serve an illegal trade union. Certain political and moral dilemmas facing Primate Glemp were alien to them. Although Glemp had to make political decisions, he did not actually intend to sacrifice any of the Church's vital interests for the sake of Solidarity.

Chapter Sixteen

Independent Society

Some, like Jacek Kuroń, had predicted that either a huge wave of spontaneous and uncontrolled anger would erupt on a mass scale, or that a general strike would be organized, which would absorb workers' social energy and provide it with direction. The real course of events proved these predictions wrong. Others, like Eugeniusz Szumiejko, believed that if Solidarity lost its influence in the large enterprises it would live on only as a myth or legend, and thus would not be able to initiate or influence current events. Their predictions also turned out to be off the mark. Reality took another path, one which was closer to the one anticipated by Szumiejko than the one Kuroń wrote about. In 1982, a Solidarity myth was already emerging, based on a very fresh memory of the sixteen months of the "carnival of freedom" that had preceded martial law, the sense of martyrdom immediately after December 13, and the romantic nature of the underground, which in its mythologized version was embodied by loyalty, suffering, and courage. Solidarity became implicitly linked with the series of brutally suppressed workers' revolts in 1956, 1970, and 1976, and, above all, the tradition of national uprisings dating back to 1830, 1863, and 1944, which had all ended in defeat. All this was the source of great myth-making power. The myth was especially attractive for young people, who were eager to run into the streets and join any incipient demonstration.

Solidarity was not, however, an uprising that could end in defeat. Rather, it was a social movement that could be subdued, but would be difficult to annihilate. This was because the real Solidarity also existed alongside the emerging myth, and was associated with Wałęsa, underground heroes, the TKK, the news sheets that were proliferating, and with the Masses for the Fatherland. Although the underground activists' appeals did not fill the streets with millions of vehement demonstrators who were ready for anything, they served as a positive example, even for most of those who preferred to stay at home. The difficulties of daily life, and particularly the fear of force and brutality, required that they remain passive. When people were sure that there would be no repercussions, that ZOMO would not charge the demonstrators, and that no tear gas or water cannons would be used, then people were suddenly revitalized. Certainly not everyone who went to see John Paul II did so because it provided them with the opportunity to manifest their (negative) attitude toward WRON and General Jaruzelski. Most were perhaps motivated purely by the desire for a spiritual experience and to show respect for the pope. In reality, however, these events became part of the phenomenon of "martial law religiosity," since John Paul II appealed to those present not only to pray, but also to think about their country. For those who were determined to act, the emotional intensity and mass nature of those meetings perhaps made them feel as if the millions who were standing before the Polish pope would stand behind them as well, if need be.

On January 22, 1983, TKK announced a platform document titled "Solidarity Today."[1] Perhaps few at the time paid attention to a particular change that TKK had introduced since their program announcement the previous July, but it seems significant in retrospect. While the July announcement had been titled "Underground Society," Solidarity leaders stated six months later that "the concept of an 'Independent Society' had crystallized" during various discussions among different groups. Although this difference is clearly not fundamental, "underground" is nevertheless not the same as "independent." The first necessarily imposes a certain eliteness and sets more difficult, or at least riskier, tasks for its members. The second is more open and primarily relates to activities that take place "above ground." In a certain sense, this change reflected the fact that a great variety of ways of expressing opposition to martial law took shape and grew stronger over the course of 1982. Often, these methods harked back to national traditions, whether in their newer or older forms. They ranged from planting bombs to organizing theatrical performances in people's homes, and were more complementary than competing. Taken together, they forged an amalgam whose core was Solidarity, which existed both as a myth in the making as well as a real organization. "Solidarity Today" was addressed "to all of society," which was an exaggeration to some extent, since it implied that the governing elite and their lackeys—whether civilian or in uniform—were excluded from society, as was everyone who supported the government or simply declared their obedience to it. In a certain sense, "all of society" probably did not even include those who were completely disinterested in public affairs and simply comprised the "silent masses"—those who answered "I don't know" or "I don't have an opinion" in public opinion polls. As some of the sociological studies from 1982–83 show, this kind of dichotomous image of societal reality, with a sharp division into "us" and "them," was prevalent among those who declared themselves opponents of martial law. It is thus not surprising that this kind of opposition emerges from the text, which, after all, was not a scholarly analysis but a call to action. If someone is convinced that most of society is following the same path that he is, this conviction undoubtedly reinforces that person's sense of correctness in choosing that path rather than another. Nevertheless, it is difficult not to feel that this kind of simplification bordered on wishful thinking, since the distribution of attitudes toward martial law at that time differed little from that which had been recorded in mid-1982 (see chapter 11), and antagonism or even animosity toward Solidarity was not at all a marginal phenomenon.

The union still had the workers' support, however, and this was most important, after all. The government, however, was not gaining support among the workers as fast as it wanted to. A unique and even somewhat odd example attests to this fact. In May 1983, the government Public Opinion Research Center (Centrum Badania Opinii Społecznej, CBOS) conducted a sociological experiment in which workers from a smaller enterprise in a small town were shown a television program titled "The Brothers' Conversation," based on footage that had been prepared during a meeting between Lech and Stanisław Wałęsa. Researchers waited to show the program to workers close to the time that the Nobel Peace Prize winner was to be announced, because it was expected that, once again, as in 1982, Wałęsa would be among the candidates. The researchers wanted to test viewers' reactions. In the report, 108 randomly chosen factory workers were in the projection room. A couple of minutes after the film started, close to one-third of the viewers left the room, followed by more, until finally only 25 people remained. After the projection concluded, the most tenacious viewers, who were "mostly representatives of the administration and party *aktiv*,"[2] asked questions like "Does Wałęsa know about the program?" "Who made the recording?" "Why was a private conversation . . . recorded?" and why were conversations of private people "being shown publicly?" The authors of the report refrained from making any "generalizing conclusions" because of the small sample size of the audience.[3] I also believe that one cannot generalize based on this example, but it probably does say something about the mood at a time when Solidarity's ability to be active in the workplace was, after all, already very limited.

In "Solidarity Today," TKK outlined three areas in which action should be taken: the "refusal front" (the boycott of pro-government organizations and state-controlled media), the "economic war," and the fight for an "independent social conscience." It also sketched out the prospects for a general strike, which was regarded as "inevitable," although it set no dates. The "international political situation" was considered, quite unexpectedly, to be one of the factors that would determine whether such a strike would start, or succeed.

The TKK members probably had not forgotten that they had written about a plan to call a strike not long before, in the spring of 1983, but the fact that they did not set even a vague date this time—and also taking into consideration the fact that Solidarity could not have any real influence (due to the international situation)—may indicate that they had distanced themselves to a certain extent from such an undertaking. The question of whether there should be a general strike prompted the most controversy in TKK and its intellectual circle, which is probably the reason why they eventually approved a compromise. It was obvious that they needed to write a strike into their program as a tool in the social conflict. In the framework of the "economic war," it was the "strongest and most effective" form of collective protest. It is one thing to hold an emergency strike in defense of the specific economic interests of a particular crew, and quite another thing to proclaim a nationwide general strike, which is clearly a political act, however. The authors of the program resolution were very cognizant of that fact, yet at the same time they could not renounce a concept that had already become semi-mythical.

According to TKK's plan, the strike was not supposed to be the prelude to or the first phase of a revolution that would overthrow the communist system. Its aim was still to "force [the government] to seek a compromise with society" and allow the "process of reforms" to begin, which the "current dictatorship" was not capable of undertaking. TKK even assumed that the strike preparations should include "formulating and agreeing upon a minimum social program" which would assure that the changes (reforms) would start and "would take into consideration the limitations stemming from the internal and international political realities." I do not believe that this reduction of the strike's aims resulted from a desire to camouflage TKK's real views out of fear that repercussions would worsen and its authors would be accused of inciting people to overthrow the regime. Most likely, these were their real beliefs—not only of Solidarity's underground leaders, but also of a significant number of their supporters. Radical moods are not always tantamount to revolutionary ones. But those were present, too.

"Fighting Solidarity" (Solidarność Walcząca) still continued to be in conflict with TKK's moderate leaders and most of the regional organizations. It was gradually garnering support outside of Lower Silesia. There were also other groups advocating very staunch resistance, and since this could not be shown through the means of fighting (such as terrorism or sabotage), it manifested itself in a radicalization of aims. One aim was thus not to achieve reforms by forcing the government to negotiate, as TKK's leaders wanted to do, but simply to overthrow communism and end the "Yalta servitude." Unusual ideas still did crop up, such as the idea of an alliance between the Church, Solidarity, and the army, which was treated as a self-reliant entity on the political scene, independent of the communist party. One of KOR's founders, Antoni Macierewicz, and the group associated with him at the journal *Głos* (Voice) presented this concept.[4] In a way, this was a variation on the concept behind TKK, and also an idea which alluded to some of the analyses from the first period of martial law whose authors had treated the events of December 13 as a military coup, somewhat like those for which Latin America was famous, and perhaps even similar to Józef Piłsudski's coup d'état of May 1926.

While the ideas of Kornel Morawiecki and members of MRKS had a certain resonance within independent society, the ruling camp did not take them seriously. They were also not known outside of Poland, and the West remained unaware of those who proposed them. In the West, only a few of TKK's members counted, other than Wałęsa and a few (such as Bronisław Geremek) who had been present in the foreign media even before martial law, some of whom had been known since the 1960s, such as Adam Michnik and Jacek Kuroń. Solidarity's moderate leaders had to reckon with radical members of the underground, and perhaps it was thanks to these groups that the union's underground platform document even included the goal of a general strike—albeit in the future. "Solidarity Today" mentioned the general strike proposal last, probably due to a lesser extent to the reservations expressed by some of TKK's members, and more to the fact that this form of protest was treated as the crowning achievement of independent society. Nonetheless, it was considered to be something that would take place at some distant point in the future.

TKK saw the "refusal front" as the main area of confrontation. Above all, this was a reaction to the government's plan—which had begun to be implemented—to create new, pro-government trade unions. The boycott principle encompassed not only the organizations that were "the substitutes for those that had been delegalized," but also those that "imitate social and political life" (like PRON) or "show support for the current dictatorial system." People were urged to refuse to participate in the "farcical elections" and "in mass rallies, official demonstrations, and celebrations organized by the government." The boycott was to be applied selectively, and it was possible to be active in institutions that strove to "meet the authentic needs of society," if that activity "does not serve to make lies credible and support the dictatorship." At enterprises, the boycott was to have a more limited scope, to include, for example, orders "restricting workers' rights." It is difficult to determine just how many people actually refused to participate in government-sponsored organizations and events. It was certainly noticeable in intellectual and artistic circles (see chapter 12).

It was just as irksome (and perhaps even more so) for the government at the enterprises, where the boycott affected the trade unions that had been created under the aegis of the Polish communist party. On the basis of fragmentary data collected by the party apparatus and the Ministry of Internal Affairs, one can conclude that the boycott was most widespread in large enterprises. Even party members were in no hurry to join the organizations, whose names almost invariably began with the words "independent" or "self-governing," which of course had clearly been stolen from Solidarity's own name. In the spring of 1983, over half of the 200 most important enterprises that the party's Central Committee directly controlled did not have cells of these "neo-unions," as they were called in the underground press. Where they did exist, their members consisted primarily of supervisors and people in the administration (and pensioners).

The appeals for a boycott were also quite effective as far as party-sponsored rallies were concerned, and also, to some extent, official government manifestations. The May Day celebrations were the most visible example. Because of fears that attendance would be low, these took place according to a new plan that was much more modest than usual. Calls to boycott the press did not garner much response (people were called on not to buy press publications on Wednesdays). To a certain extent, this situation recalled the one during the German occupation, when the Polish Underground State announced a boycott of the Polish-language German press (the *gadzinowa* press), which was not universally observed, just like the boycott on cinema-going.

In terms of the "economic war" that TKK was proposing, the aims were to oppose everything that would cause a "further decline in the standard of living"; to try to ensure that regulations defending workers' rights be observed (such as suitable working conditions); to indicate erroneous decisions made by the management or supervisors; and to use the workers' self-government to achieve these ends. It is difficult to say anything specific about the activities of the illegal union within enterprises in the social or production spheres. No one has undertaken any systematic research on this question yet, perhaps because it has been clear to researchers from the start that this work would be arduous and not terribly exciting. In the underground press, one can find a great deal of information about these types of activities, but for obvious reasons, people tried to avoid mentioning names or even specific Solidarity branches.

The authorities, however, did not take the matter lightly and went about reactivating workers' self-government very cautiously, precisely because the "former union" did exist. There was a fear that Solidarity would use workers' self-government for its own ends—a fear that was justified by knowledge of such cases. Oddly, TKK's program mentioned the secret enterprise commissions only very superficially. It only said that the program "also imposes obligations on them," though they did exist in many of the enterprises. Often, these commissions were involved not just in helping those who had suffered under martial law or in the field of symbolism and propaganda (such as publishing of illegal news sheets and flyers). The program also mentioned "regional structures" only in cursory terms, and did not outline their tasks and roles at all. Reading this document, one might come away with the impression that Solidarity still needed to be created. As a result, there is much evidence to suggest that TKK was appealing directly to society—going above the heads of those in the union's secret structures.

As a third area of its activities, "Solidarity Today" said that one of its aims was to counteract the "dangers that totalitarian government poses to the areas of consciousness . . . education and national culture, social morality and civic attitudes." This area was without doubt the most extensive and varied, and was also extremely important. It was in this arena that a significant portion of the battle was fought to delegitimize not only General Jaruzelski's group and martial law, but also the communist system as a whole, and to break the Polish communist party's monopoly in the sphere Marxists called the "superstructure." Solidarity was present in that sphere as an organization relatively infrequently (but not rarely)—more often as a point of reference or even a myth.

The borders between the union's structures and the initiatives that arose outside of them were exceptionally fluid in this area. Solidarity's leadership centers, in contrast, had just begun building institutions to mediate between the union and opponents of the regime in the field of social consciousness, to coordinate their activities to the best of their ability, and to determine channels of financial and organizational assistance. During the course of 1983, however, underground organizations such as the Committee of Independent Culture, Independent Education, and the Social Committee of Sciences were founded. The last of these was involved not only in providing assistance to academicians from universities and institutes who had lost their jobs, but also in financing research that official institutions did not want to subsidize (for example, studies on the destruction of the environment) and publishing scholarly books that censorship would have banned.

The activity with the widest impact was publishing. (On its beginnings during martial law, see chapter 11.) Both in the first few months after December 13 and during the next period, until the lifting of martial law, Solidarity publications clearly dominated among periodicals—i.e., underground news sheets. These Solidarity publications were issued on the factory, inter-factory, and regional levels, and in university towns by the Independent Students' Association. Nevertheless, initiatives not linked directly with the union's branches or student organizations gradually became increasingly important. This was most apparent among political and cultural periodicals, because the union organizations published almost exclusively informational news sheets. In the second half of 1982, but especially the following year, various political formations began to emerge (groups or parties), and with them came their publications. According to Władysław Chojnacki's estimates, the total number of news sheets showed a decline and signs of stagnation over the course of 1983: in 1982, as mentioned above, approximately 770 titles were published; in 1983, there were approximately 620, of which almost half were newly established publications.[5] While there was stagnation, there was also stabilization: in 1983 and the years that followed, there were no fewer than 350–80 titles that had been published for more than a year. With time, the circulations of underground news sheets and periodicals grew, which was not the result of increased demand, however, but because publishers' output increased as their ability to print materials improved.

Solidarity radio stations also should be included in the underground media. Beginning in mid-1982, these stations experienced a real boom.[6] In addition to those already mentioned in chapter 13, programs had begun broadcasting in Gliwice, Wrocław, Bielsko-Biała, Legnica, Głogów, Jelenia Góra, Kędzierzyn, Legionowo, Węgorzewo, Kłodzko, Bydgoszcz, Świdnica, Toruń, and Bielawa since late August; in February 1983, the Warsaw radio resumed broadcasting after its transmissions had been disrupted when its members were arrested; in April 1983, a Solidarity radio station in Świdnik began broadcasting, as well as in several other towns in the Lublin region. In the second half of 1982, the Fighting Solidarity Radio in Wrocław broadcast twenty-eight programs, and Poznań's Radio Solidarity broadcast forty-two. On August 31, 1982, Fighting Solidarity Radio managed to broadcast a short live transmission from a street demonstration in Wrocław, and in Toruń the radio's organizers came up with the idea of sending a transmitter up in a balloon that could float for many hours. The broadcasting equipment was not complicated, although their construction did require parts that were difficult to come by in Poland. Nevertheless, there were plenty of specialists who were willing to get to work. Broadcasting was a risky activity for the group that was engaged in it, but in some places this problem was overcome by remotely activating the transmitter. In 1982, the SB "acquired" eleven transmitters, which nevertheless did not interrupt broadcasting, except in Warsaw. The popularity of underground radio is perhaps best illustrated by the fact that even the SB used it for purposes of disinformation. In late April 1983, for example, it broadcast a program in Warsaw pretending to be Radio Solidarity, during which it was announced that the independent May Day parade had been cancelled.[7] Despite the increased number of broadcasts and varied programming, Solidarity's radio stations were more significant psychologically than as a source of information.

Beginning in late 1982, the number of books being published increased markedly. Of these, more were still booklets of modest length rather than bona fide books. In all of 1983, approximately 860 books and booklets were published, which was 40 percent more than in the previous year.[8] The print runs grew gradually, but they basically did not exceed a thousand or two thousand copies, rarely reaching several thousand. Little libraries run by secret factory commissions appeared immediately, reactivated after a hiatus because of the confusion following the imposition of martial law. Some of the union's cells were involved in distributing not only news sheets, which was the norm, but also books. Increasingly often (which is not to say often), underground publishing houses availed themselves of corrupt printers in state institutions that had printing shops, so publications were sometimes printed right in state printing shops.

The range of materials being published expanded, and essays, monographs, and memoirs gradually replaced occasional literature, which had been a direct answer to the imposition of martial law. One of the bestsellers in 1983 was a book by Jerzy Holzer titled *Solidarność 1980–1981: Geneza i historia* (Solidarity 1980–1981: Genesis and History) (published by Krąg Publishers), which even today is the most important monograph about the union during its legal existence. Many of the publications were reprints from émigré publishing houses; translations from Russian, English, and French were also common. Book publishing houses, at least the most ambitious ones, also published magazines. Although several galling disasters have been recorded, one can conclude on the basis of documents that have been studied up to now that the SB's knowledge about underground publishing was quite limited, despite the activities of its numerous informers. In any case, the SB did not succeed in paralyzing it. Nevertheless, the fact that there were several SB informers (like Lesław Maleszka and Henryk Karkosza) who were thoroughly initiated in the illegal publishers' various secrets seems to suggest that the SB consciously did not make use of all the information it had at its disposal, nor its destructive powers.

Paweł Sowiński, a leading expert on the subject, has written that, for many people, "independent books were a symbol that the union had survived, [and] buying them was treated like a donation to Solidarity."[9] If this really was the case, which seems highly likely, then the situation became ambiguous, at least as far as books were concerned, since publishing houses were becoming both more professional and commercial. Admittedly, there were numerous cases in which various union structures gave grants (these also began arriving from abroad), whether to publish a specific book or to start a publishing house. There is no evidence, however, to suggest that a financially successful publisher would share any of his profit with a Solidarity cell. So, if purchasing a book was treated like a "donation," then that money was destined more for independent society in a general sense than for the union itself. News sheets, periodicals, pamphlets, books, radio, and cassette tapes with not only songs but also feature-length articles or poetry—in short, the entire publishing scene—became just as much a synonym for popular resistance as the street clashes and patriotic masses.

Underground books and independent information were not the only kind of activities aimed at detoxifying society after decades-long indoctrination by government propaganda, when the government had a monopoly on media, education, and culture. They also encompassed various kinds of art. One of these phenomena was "art at churches" (sztuka przykościelna), as it was called. In April 1982, a boycott was announced that was to include galleries, exhibitions, museums, and competitions. The artists who wanted to protest against the imposition of martial law in this way thus condemned themselves to painting "for the drawer" or for "suitcase shows," which were organized in private apartments and studios, and meant they had deprived themselves of contact with the public. Some of them did nevertheless manage to find public places, while at the same time remaining outside state control—in the churches. The Weeks of Christian Culture that took place in Warsaw under the patronage of Primate Wyszyński encouraged this trend on a larger scale in 1975. As head of the Ministry of Artistic Circles, Father Wiesław Niewęgłowski wrote that the Church and its priests were concerned that "the voice of intellectuals and artists be able to herald truth, freedom, and hope."[10]

In March 1982, Janusz Bogucki, an art theorist and critic, began organizing artists' meetings at the Retreat House at Laski, near Warsaw, where there was a convent and home for blind children. In November 1982, a group show by several dozen artists took place in Warsaw's Holy Cross church. Beginning in the summer of 1983, exhibitions were underway almost without interruption at

Divine Mercy in Warsaw, too. Soon, similar events were being organized in other churches around Poland. In time, galleries were even created in the space that had been allotted to them in the actual churches, or in nearby buildings. The art at those shows and galleries included works that were purely religious in nature, as well as others that could be categorized as patriotic, or as patriotic and political. Most showed the subject's suffering through motifs from the Passion or by alluding to Polish national martyrological traditions, and the clichés of martial law: prison bars, barbed wire, batons, and blood. There were also many portraits, mainly of John Paul II. This tendency lasted all the way through the 1980s. In a play on the Stalinist-era term "socreaIism" (socialist realism), this current was ironically called "sacr-realism" or "liturgical socrealism."

It is difficult to say what the impact of these works was, and whether they were received as their authors had intended. Nevertheless, this "art at churches" constituted an important element of the independent social landscape, and it exposed many people to art who had never had any contact with it, other than sacral art or reproductions in school textbooks. Based on these activities, it should not be surprising that the Association of Polish Artists and Designers (Związek Polskich Artystów Plastyków, ZPAP)—just like ZASP and ZLP—was deemed an enemy of the government. On June 20, 1983, during John Paul II's visit to Poland, it was definitively dissolved. Solidarity's leadership appreciated the artists' strong engagement in independent society. In 1983, the first Solidarity Cultural Awards were presented; they became an annual event.

One other group of artists found a place for itself in churches during martial law, and also in private homes: these were theater people, particularly actors. The authors of a documentary work[11] list the titles of almost one hundred productions in 1982 and the first half of 1983, but it was in the following years that "church theater" peaked. To a large extent, these shows were poetry programs with religious and national or patriotic themes, often with musical accompaniment, or with vocalists. Sometimes they were literary and musical shows, or recitals. A large group of leading Polish actors from various generations took part in these performances, including the following artists, who were very well known at that time: Zbigniew Zapasiewicz, Hanna Skarżanka, Aleksandra Śląska, Katarzyna Łaniewska, Danuta Michałowska, Jan Englert, Teresa Budzisz-Krzyżanowska, Halina Winiarska, Anna Polony, Marian Opania, and Andrzej Szczepkowski. Most of those performing, however, were lesser-known artists, or those who were just starting their careers. The programs featured a great deal of nineteenth-century Romantic poetry, but it was the poetry of contemporary Polish poets that dominated, particularly that of Czesław Miłosz and Karol Wojtyła (later known as John Paul II), whose works were performed especially often.

Some of the productions were performed many times, and in different cities: the Katowice Underground Theater of Martial Law Poetry staged almost sixty performances (primarily in private apartments in Silesia), which were seen by over fifteen hundred people. The Andrzej Jawień Theater, founded at Poznań's church of the Dominican Fathers, had several dozen performances.[12] The Pilgrimage Theater in Łódź had about sixty performances of a program titled "Our Christmas Carol" in less than two months. The program "Songs of the January Uprising" inaugurated the Romuald Traugutt Philharmonic[13] in January 1983, which had dozens of literary and musical concerts in more than a dozen cities. The Home Theater, which began its activities in November 1982 with the show "Bringing Things to Order," started in the apartment of actress Ewa Dałkowska, and had over a hundred performances. Some of the shows took place during the Weeks of Christian Culture that was organized in many cities. Relatively few regular theater performances took place, such as T. S. Eliot's *Murder in the Cathedral* (see also chapter 12) or *Clang*, based on Beckett's prose (at the Closed Theater in Kraków); Kazimierz Brandys's *Both Very Old*; *Resurrection Through Love*, based on Dostoyevsky; and Pedro Calderón's *El principe constante*, in a free translation by Juliusz Słowacki. Traditional plays clearly could not be staged in apartments, and even church interiors did not have suitable equipment for the staging of large-scale productions, with costumes, full sets, and lights.

In many of the productions, "martial law religiosity" was present, whether through the texts, type of music, or performance venue. These aspects influenced the reception of these works: with only a few exceptions, these were churches (including cathedrals), cloisters, church grounds, parish halls, and other rooms. Artists' performances were very often incorporated into services or church celebrations. There is not even any way of estimating how many people watched these shows or how many came to church mainly to experience this type of art. Without a doubt, however, especially if one includes the presence of sculptures, paintings, and installations on church grounds, one can venture to say that an important part of independent art—an integral part of independent society—would have been impossible without the Church's support and the engagement of many priests at various levels. It is difficult to determine anything conclusively, but this was unquestionably an exceptional phenomenon—not only in Poland's history, but also on a more general global scale.

As I already mentioned in chapter 15, the delegalized ZASP suspended its boycott, which actors' circles regarded with some reservations, in late 1982. This did not mean that the presence of theater people in the churches had ended. Religious and patriotic performances continued to be held until 1989—partially because of momentum, in part at the clergy's urging, but probably mainly because there was a need. Underground leaders appreciated the role of art in the functioning of independent society, and in keeping alive—or even stirring up—patriotic sentiments, which were an important element in society's opposition to the government. This is why stage directors and theater troupes were among the winners of Solidarity's Cultural Award, and also why January 1–8, 1983, was proclaimed Polish Theater Week. That week, the theater-going public thanked actors with ovations and flowers for having persisted in their boycott for one year.

In 1982–83, underground culture existed in other cultural and intellectual fields, too. Various scholarly debates were waged, some more important than others, and some sociologists, historians, or philosophers published exclusively, or at least more frequently, in underground, émigré, or foreign publications, and published their books with underground publishers. Groups emerged that conducted "underground polling research," as Piotr Kwiatkowski calls it.[14] Their results were published in news sheets and periodicals; for example, in the autumn of 1982, the weekly *Kos* carried out a survey with approximately fourteen hundred respondents.[15] Various kinds of lecture series took place, often associated with the workers' universities that had existed before December 13, which Solidarity's regional boards had sponsored. As part of these programs, scholars from various disciplines would give lectures in churches and parish halls. Leading intellectuals (such as the sociologist and essayist Jan Strzelecki) and researchers (for example, the historian Krystyna Kersten) would go to small towns for these semi-underground events, where audiences were unaccustomed to these kinds of speakers. It was undoubtedly a new experience for them, too. People from literary circles, for whom publications were the most natural form of expression, were also very involved in such activities. Those who had been fired from the state media were also actively involved in these kinds of projects, and many of them manned the underground news sheets and periodicals.

One can thus say that, in the "battle for Poland's consciousness," independent society showed a high level of activity in various fields. The audience and also participants in these activities, however, were above all urban dwellers, not those of villages or small towns. The audiences were also comprised more of the urban intelligentsia than workers, although many sources do testify to workers' presence during various cultural events, as well as their quite wide readership of underground news sheets, and above all their participation on a mass scale in expressions of "martial law religiosity."

While all generalizations are risky, one should nevertheless conclude that all this activity did serve more to strengthen an already existing state of awareness, providing stimuli for individuals and groups who had an already-defined attitude toward the system and the rulers of martial law, rather than attracting those who belonged to the "silent masses," much less changing attitudes of the supporters of WRON or real socialism. Although many forms of this type of activity occurred in places that were readily accessible, such as the Masses for the Fatherland or other events in churches, it does not seem that people who did not feel, for whatever reason, that they were part of independent society attended these events. There were no signs anywhere that said "no entrance to strangers," and those who distributed flyers or news sheets were prepared to foist them on just about anybody. "Strangers," however, or even just those who were indifferent—which included many of Solidarity's former members—did not attend these events in any great numbers. The pope's visit was actually the only event at which independent society came into contact with the "bystanders."

TKK's January statement, which linked the ideological and action programs in a natural way, made no mention of street demonstrations, even though they had proven to be the most effective form of protest since the spring of 1982. Because enterprises were being strictly monitored, demonstrations had replaced strikes as the main instrument of resistance. The general atmosphere of fear and loss of confidence meant that factory halls and grounds could not become a place for preliminary mobilization. The various disciplinary and precautionary measures that the authorities had implemented also played a large role. These included strengthening the industrial guards and putting ORMO patrols in front of the larger factories, "warning" talks and preventative arrests by the SB, and constant video surveillance of hot spots, such as the areas in front of administration buildings or gates. The law "on the particular legal regulation during the period of the lifting of martial law," passed by the Sejm on December 18, 1982,[16] tightened the regulations meant to counteract mass demonstrations, including the introduction into the criminal code of a new article stating that "whoever undertakes activities with the aim of inciting public unrest or disturbances will be subject to a three-year prison term."

People were thus cautious in initiating protests in public places. I am not convinced that these arguments were sufficient to explain why TKK neglected to mention demonstrations in its document. Perhaps more significant was the sense of defeat in November, which meant that street demonstrations became a rarity. Even in December there were only a few, and even these were limited in scope, like those organized on the monthly "anniversaries" (the largest demonstrations took place in Gdańsk in March 1983). The demonstrations on the fifteenth anniversary of the events of March 1968 were limited to just several universities. Some groups gave up. For example, the Białystok regional Solidarity commission announced on January 15, 1983, that it would no longer take part in street protest demonstrations. On February 7 it released underground activists from the requirement that they stay in hiding, and on February 13 its chairman also revealed himself.[17]

Lech Wałęsa, who was carefully monitored by the SB, did not engage in extensive public activities. Wałęsa's return to work in the shipyard was the subject of deliberations at the highest levels of power. He worked repairing electric industrial vehicles, and was under tight SB surveillance, so he could not easily speak with colleagues outside the section in which he had been employed. He did give numerous interviews to foreign journalists, however, and met many people, including activists and advisors recently released from internment centers, either at home or in one of the Gdańsk churches (most often St. Brygida's). Wałęsa also traveled a little around the country. Sometimes he would only appear in public places, such as in March 1983, in Warsaw's Dramatic Theater at Sławomir Mrożek's play *Pieszo* (*On Foot*), where the audience gave him a warm welcome.[18] Thus, when Solidarity's chairman met with TKK members who were in hiding, which was announced in a special communiqué, it caused a sensation.[19] The three-day meeting (April 9–11) was above all informational in nature, according to participants' accounts.[20] Its aim was not to make group decisions, but rather to announce them.

The two paths that arose after Wałęsa's release were convenient for Solidarity from a tactical point of view, but did lead to misunderstandings. The activists from TKK noticed that Wałęsa was not only distancing himself from them to a certain extent, but was also showing a degree of contempt. The chairman disagreed with Jan Olszewski, who in 1982 warned of the danger that the underground would degenerate and the possibility of SB provocation. Wałęsa considered underground structures to be useful, but believed that they did not have enough power to influence the course of events in any fundamental way. He felt predestined for this role himself. Leaving behind the TKK "scheming," he admitted that he would limit himself to activities "above ground" that suited his vision and concepts, which were even more moderate than TKK's program. The meeting, although it was undoubtedly fruitful and necessary in view of his current and future activities, also had an important psychological impact. It demonstrated that the stubborn popular image of the omniscient SB had its limits, since people who had been under such tight surveillance or followed for as long as Wałęsa could still leave the SB high and dry.

The November 1982 strike ended in a fiasco, and the government released hundreds of prisoners from internment camps and repealed many onerous aspects of martial law, including militarization of most of the factories. After such a show of magnanimity, it might have seemed that independent society would be reduced to producing and reading news sheets and attending Masses for the Fatherland. Yet on March 20, 1983, Rakowski noted in his diary, "Our political influence is still negligible."[21] Was this pessimism on his part, or realism? Several days after Wałęsa's meeting with TKK in Gdańsk, General Kiszczak said that "the opposition has gone on the attack."[22] This was primarily because, on April 14, Solidarity's underground leadership appealed for a boycott of the official May Day parades, and for independent demonstrations to be organized. They used strong language: let May 1 be a "day of uncertainty and fear" for the government, they wrote, let it "find itself once again surrounded by lackeys, careerists, and the terror apparatus."[23] They appealed for parades and rallies, and for a large-scale flyer campaign. For the Third of May Constitution Day, however, people were advised about how they could express their opinions in individualized, "subdued" ways, such as dressing up in one's Sunday best, donning ribbons in national colors, and observing a minute of silence at noon.

Government and party propaganda, even the speeches of the highest echelon of government officials, treated Underground Solidarity as non-existent or depicted it as a group of troublemakers who had no support. A sense of unease is clearly apparent, however, in internal party documents and trustworthy personal accounts. In the second half of April, there was a nervous atmosphere among the ruling elite. "The political temperature is rising," noted Rakowski on April 21; a day later, he wrote, "It's getting hotter." According to the deputy prime minister, Jaruzelski was "uneasy" (April 21) and "upset" (April 28). During one of the Politburo's meetings, Kiszczak said that, on May 1, the threat would be "significant."[24] Thus, all routine steps were taken: on April 23, a communiqué was issued about the arrest of the TKK's Lower Silesian representative, Józef Pinior. Surveillance was heightened, more arrests took place, and printing shops were targeted. A suitably large number of law enforcement units were put on alert. As General Kiszczak reported, these were to be comprised of ninety-seven thousand militiamen from various formations, nineteen thousand ORMO men, and thirty-five thousand soldiers.[25] Hundreds of trucks were mobilized from factories. The military prepared convoys of vehicles, planes, and helicopters for the Ministry of Internal Affairs.

After a year and a half of experience, the Poles had undoubtedly one of the best-prepared formations in Europe for crowd control. Since the end of World War II, the Polish Army had appeared almost exclusively in the role of policemen on Polish (and Czech) streets, except for participating in parades and training exercises, or providing occasional assistance to the national economy (such as in the famous "Coal Corps," to which recruits with "bad" social backgrounds were sent during the years 1949–57). During the first postwar years, the army also played this role in the forests, when it assisted the security apparatus and militia in their fight against anti-communist partisans.

On May 4, before a session of the Politburo was set to start, its members watched a film of a counter-demonstration that had taken place on May 1: "It doesn't look so good," said Rakowski.[26] It was not only the Ministry of Internal Affairs that was ready for action; Solidarity had also prepared for the occasion. In the days before, an exceptionally large number of flyers was distributed, and local news sheets and mini-posters were hung in hundreds of locations, announcing the dates and places of the gatherings. In several cities Solidarity radio stations broadcast special programs. The Ministry of Internal Affairs reported that "incidents" had taken place in twenty cities across thirteen voivodships, and that the number of participants was estimated at fifty thousand. This time, the militia had no qualms and acted ruthlessly, despite the fact that it was International Workers' Day. They did run into problems, like in Wrocław, where some of the participants in the counter-parade, carrying Solidarity flags and banners, moved onto the official parade route and made it all the way to the honorary tribune. It was only there that ZOMO troops caught up with them, using tear gas. As a result, the legal demonstrators also found themselves coughing, and the dignitaries standing on the tribune had to flee.[27]

Similar situations—except without the tear gas—took place in Szczecin, where a large group of demonstrators marched in front of the tribune, as well as in Poznań. In Wrocław, several independent marches took place, and began from different locations, which hampered their pacification. The militia arrested over four hundred people. In Gdańsk, the marches and inevitable unrest that ensued began at noon and continued for many hours. The largest concentrations of demonstrators (numbering over ten thousand people) occurred in the vicinity of St. Brygida's, later at the former Solidarity headquarters, and finally during attempts to reach Wałęsa's apartment, which was heavily surrounded by ZOMO. The chairman himself did not even attempt to come out of his building, so it is not known whether he would have been allowed to do so. In Warsaw, a crowd of 10,000–20,000 was dispersed quite quickly with the aid of a mounted militia unit, used for the first time. The clashes in Gdynia and Kraków lasted for several hours. There were smaller counter-marches in Łódź, Lublin, Częstochowa, Katowice, Bochnia, and Siedlce. Some of the most serious clashes took place in Nowa Huta, where two marches merged on the Central Square. One had been coming from the church in Bieńczyce and another from the steelworks. The militia once again fought Homeric battles, defending the Lenin statue ("like independence"), and once again succeeded in carrying out its task. The clashes, however, lasted until the evening—several barricades were built and armored vehicles were called into action. A twenty-nine-year-old worker who had been shot in the throat with a tear gas grenade died on the spot near one of the barricades. In Kraków, one person died of a heart attack while fleeing the ZOMO as they charged. In Warsaw, one of the Third of May demonstrators who had been beaten by the militia died in the hospital.

Although fewer people took place in these demonstrations than on August 31 the previous year, it all made quite an impression, and in the context of the upcoming visit of John Paul II, one can say it really "did not look so good." Nowhere, however, was the army brought onto the streets, and no firearms were used. Bloodshed even on the scale of that in Lubin would throw the pope's visit into question. It would also mean another setback for General Jaruzelski's government and WRON, in the eyes of Poles as well as foreign observers. The Holy Father did not cancel his trip, despite the fact that there were at least two events in May that showed the authorities in a very bad light. First, on May 3, a storming party of plainclothes SB functionaries raided the headquarters of the Primatial Aid Committee, which was in the St. Martin's church complex in Warsaw's Old Town. Several people were beaten, and four men were kidnapped and taken outside the city, where they were abandoned. Ten days later, also in Old Town, a nineteen-year-old high school senior, Grzegorz Przemyk, was arrested and taken to the nearby militia headquarters. He was the son of the well-known poet Barbara Sadowska, who had been one of those beaten at St. Martin's. Przemyk was beaten horrifically by the militiamen on duty, and died two days later. His funeral took place May 19 at the Powązki Cemetery, after a Mass celebrated by Father Popiełuszko. More than ten thousand young people attended, primarily high school students. Although the funeral took place without incident, Przemyk's connection (via his mother) to the Metropolitan Curia and the chronological proximity of his death to the events of May 3 could have been interpreted as the evidence that there was consent for the use of violence against those associated with the Church, and perhaps even against the clergy. These events could also be seen as a sign of possible changes in the government's policies toward the Church.

The May Day demonstrations in 1983 were not a great success for Solidarity, but they showed that its ability to influence the behavior of the masses was still a force to be reckoned with, and that stabilization was still a long way off. The government, whether or not it wanted to, had to take the underground and TKK into account because of their influence, and also because the West was interested in events in Poland, partially as a result of Solidarity's increased activities abroad. Like every society, nation, or state that finds itself in oppressive conditions, "independent society" also had its émigré community, which had formed even before the union's interned or arrested activists left Poland. The core of this émigré group was comprised of people who had been active either in the pre-August opposition or in Solidarity, often in both, and who happened—for various reasons—to be abroad the moment that martial law was imposed. Those who had left Poland in the wake of the anti-Semitic campaign in 1968 aided them, having already assisted the democratic opposition (primarily KOR). Thus, many people from various waves and groups of Polish émigrés—including those who had fought in the Second World War—either assisted the new émigrés or (more often) undertook similar activities within existing émigré organizations, such as the Polish Ex-Combatants Association and the Polish American Congress. The latter played a role in the United States as the "Polish lobby," and somehow automatically became the "Solidarity lobby" as well. Radio Free Europe's Polish Section also became a strong base of support for independent society.

When martial law was imposed, several hundred activists and union members happened to be in the West, including more than a dozen who were there on official Solidarity business. Some of them decided that they should not limit themselves to participating in shows of support organized by Western trade unions, but that they themselves should instead begin to coordinate and organize. The first meeting of the most active individuals from several European countries took place in Zürich just four days after the imposition of martial law. Shortly afterward, the following organizations began their formal cooperation: the Solidarity

Coordination Committee in Paris, the Solidarity Action Committee in Brussels, the Solidarity with Solidarity Committee in Rome, and the Solidarity Office in Stockholm. Representatives of about fifty committees, including some from Canada and the United States, attended the congress that took place in mid-July 1982 in Oslo.

The main aims they set for themselves were: to initiate and help organize protests, to arrange the sending of packages and aid to Poland, and to collect information from Poland and convey it to media abroad, as well as to foreign political elites. These activities were facilitated by the fact that good contacts had existed between Solidarity and various trade unions in the West since August 1980. They sent printing equipment to Poland, and a charity drive was launched in autumn 1981, in response to Wałęsa's appeal. Most of the committees formed after December 13 were affiliated with their national union headquarters, which meant they were allotted space and funds for their day-to-day activities. Some Solidarity émigrés had good contacts with determined (albeit small) left-wing groups, mainly Trotskyite ones, who were accustomed to illegal activities. Their members were willing to undertake risky operations (such as those involving couriers) in support of the Polish working class. They seemed unbothered by the fact that Polish workers preferred John Paul II to Karl Marx.

It was not clear whether an executive center could be created for activities in the West, but TKK recognized, during its initial meeting in April 1982, that efforts in the West needed to be centralized, and Bogdan Lis was the person made responsible for doing so.[28] Jerzy Milewski was appointed director of Solidarity's Foreign Office. He was a physicist who had been a member of the Gdańsk strike committee in August 1980. When martial law was imposed, he was at an academic conference in the United States. It was decided that the office's headquarters would be in Brussels, because the International Confederation of Free Trade Unions and the World Confederation of Labor—the two largest headquarters of non-communist trade unions—were both located there. The leaders of these organizations enthusiastically agreed to accredit Solidarity's offices, which were given office space and funding for their day-to-day activities.

Solidarity's Foreign Office was formally created on July 1, 1982, but the tasks that TKK assigned to it were quite enigmatic: "to coordinate the activities of Solidarity members who are active outside Poland" and "to represent the interests of Solidarity to other trade unions."[29] In reality, the office had many more tasks than this, and some of them—such as sending equipment and money to Poland—could not be mentioned publicly. The Office was not involved in the organization of those "underground" matters, and because discretion was required, these activities were conducted by specific individuals or small groups. The Office's first spectacular operation was to send balloons with flyers from Denmark, but its principal and permanent activity was supplying printing equipment to Poland. The main people sending this equipment were Mirosław Chojecki, who lived in Paris, and Marian Kaleta from Malmö, who personally organized shipments by truck (the first left for Poland in June 1982). It took SB and intelligence a couple of years before they managed to get to the bottom of this vexatious problem: although it was clear who was doing the smuggling, and for whom ("the agents of imperialistic intelligence services"), they still did not know how increasingly new offsets and copiers were getting into the country.

For underground Solidarity, the public—not just clandestine—activities of the Office, committees, and even individuals were of considerable importance. Martial law's authorities treated these public activities as anti-state and even anti-Polish. Thanks to the bulletins that were published in English or French, and other forms of transmitting information, foreign media (including stations broadcasting in Polish), trade unions, and governments received extensive news and commentary from Poland, including TKK's announcements and appeals, and those of other Solidarity branches. Brochures with translations of Solidarity documents were published, as well as those with articles from the underground press. Contact was made with the main institutions involved in the defense of human rights—Amnesty International, the International Red Cross, and the Office of the UN High Commissioner for Refugees. With time, this became particularly important because of the new wave of émigrés from Poland: many people who had traveled abroad for "tourism" wound up asking for permission to stay, or for political asylum.

In November 1982, the Office arranged a meeting of representatives from the most important international trade union headquarters, at which it was decided that aid for Solidarity would continue indefinitely, and that relations with those unions not recognizing it would be suspended. The Office represented Solidarity in the International Labor Organization, which was important in that both trade unions and governments were represented there. Despite strong protests from Prime Minister Jaruzelski, Solidarity representatives participated in that organization's work. Efforts to obtain funds for the underground's activities were also quite effective, although more substantial sums would come only in later years. Nevertheless, the Office's financial situation in 1983 was stable, and its yearly budget totaled approximately $450,000. It was typical that in the first phase attempts were made only rarely to make direct contact with the top leadership in governments. The time for this would come later, after 1985, when Poland was becoming less isolated, the confidence of its government was waning, and increasing numbers of Western diplomats and politicians were visiting Warsaw. At that time, Warsaw became the center of gravity for "big politics," and a period of "underground diplomacy" began. In addition to the Office, many other contacts existed as well, some of which were informal, while others were professional—for example, scholars or journalists, who were mainly concerned with assisting people who had been imprisoned or fired. Fighting Solidarity also established its own foreign office.

After martial law was suspended on December 31, 1982, the atmosphere in Poland changed in ways that were beneficial to those in power. Although, from their perspective, things had improved, Poles who comprised "independent society" were of a different opinion. Despite the numerous announcements, reprisals persisted, except that people could no longer be interned on the basis of a militia commanding officer's decision on the voivodship level. Nevertheless, it was still possible, for example, to detain people for twelve hours or even a day or two, and the relevant services were perfectly willing to do so. They would summon people to the station under any pretext, or even with none whatsoever, and interrogate them repeatedly—something Lech Wałęsa also experienced. On May 6, 1983, for example, more than a dozen people were arrested from various now-illegal trade unions. They had met to sign an appeal to the Sejm demanding the release of prisoners and the reinstatement of those who had lost their jobs as a result of their union activities. After the May Day demonstration, about a thousand people were arrested in various cities, and many of their cases were sent to misdemeanor courts. In Poznań, on June 28, 1983, about two weeks before martial law was lifted, a crowd of many thousands of people was brutally dispersed. They had gathered on the anniversary of the 1956 strike and clashes. ZOMO used gas, and those detained were beaten at militia stations. People were arrested not only because they had taken part in the demonstration, or for illegal Solidarity-related activities, but also for crimes such as giving interviews to foreign magazines (for which Bronisław Geremek was arrested) or organizing a commemoration of the fiftieth anniversary of the Warsaw Ghetto Uprising (for which Janusz Onyszkiewicz was arrested). From the beginning of the year until mid-May, hundreds of criminal cases related to "anti-state crimes" were initiated.

The suspension of martial law did not change the scope of the SB's work; its operational activities intensified, and the ranks of informers continued to grow. According to statistics compiled by Tadeusz Ruzikowski, there were 10,000 more informers in 1983 than in the previous year (about 14,300 were recruited, and 5,000 were eliminated). The largest growth was seen in the sections dealing with Solidarity and the underground: from approximately 18,200 to 23,700.[30] We can assume that the information that the SB had at its disposal about illegal structures was significant and growing, but the actions taken against them were generally more like harassment—a printing shop, or a storeroom with magazines or books, would be raided, and elsewhere a couple of activists would be rounded up from secret enterprise commissions or regional offices. Some investigations, even prestigious ones related to leading members of the underground, were interminable. The search for Władysław Hardek began in February 1982 and lasted for a year and half—he was finally caught in August 1983. Kornel Morawiecki still eluded capture, as did leading activists from Warsaw and Gdańsk.

In the first half of 1983, no large-scale raids took place. The most spectacular was the arrest of Józef Pinior (mentioned above), and the largest propaganda operation was directly related to the lifting of martial law: in late July, the MKO was "unmasked." It was actually a provocation launched and run by the SB (see chapter 13), which was intended to encourage others to surrender officially. "Unmasking" MKO was a matter so serious that Jaruzelski and Rakowski were involved in making the decision to carry it out.[31] Hundreds of people were in prison who were either already sentenced or under investigation. Of these, eleven were leading Solidarity and KOR activists who had serious charges against them.

Political trials were still taking place: in February, there was one against Warsaw's Radio Solidarity, and in March one took place against the already-legendary crane operator Anna Walentynowicz, whose firing had served as the spark that set off the August 1980 strike. In May, the trial of the original leaders of the MRKS was held, as was the trial in absentia of Zdzisław Najder, director of the Polish Section of Radio Free Europe, which ended in a death sentence. In June, there was the trial of Edmund Bałuka, one of the leaders of the Szczecin strike in December 1970 who later escaped and returned illegally to Poland in 1980. Martial law had not actually been suspended at all for independent society—for those who the regime considered to be openly antagonistic to the government and system.

Chapter Seventeen

The Party Returns to the Ring

Shortly after martial law was imposed, Stefan Olszowski said at a Politburo meeting that the party needed to be "half a step behind the army" in the current situation.[1] Whether it was exactly half a step or not is open to debate, but in general this statement certainly corresponded to reality. While the communist party had always wielded power thanks to the support of the completely subordinate ministries of defense and the interior, they were increasingly crucial in guaranteeing the party's "leading role in the state" after the foundation of Solidarity. In fact, this "leading role" had actually been constitutionally guaranteed just recently, in 1976. Since February 1981, the higher and highest levels of power were in a sense militarized, as was the party itself, which stemmed from the need to prepare and administer martial law. Despite the increased presence of military men in party and state positions, from the perspective of an outside observer (i.e., all of society) it seemed like the army (and security apparatus) was "half a step behind the party," until that fateful night of December 12–13.

In discussing party-army relations, however, one should recall that the vast majority of officers (practically all those of the rank of colonel or above) belonged to the communist party (as was also the case among functionaries at the Ministry of Internal Affairs). Nothing can be said for sure about whether loyalty to the party or army was more important to them, except that both institutions required discipline and complete subordination. Perhaps Olszowski's statement should thus be modified: it was not the army that went out ahead of the party, but rather the communists in uniform who simply moved half a step ahead, in front of the civilian party members.

If the communist party's role as a political decision-making institution was weakened after the imposition of martial law—at all levels, including the party organizations at enterprises, too—this happened not because those who controlled the army had appropriated power, but because of a conscious decision by party leadership to transfer some of its power. In a formal sense, this transfer happened on December 5, 1981, when the Politburo authorized General Jaruzelski to order the imposition of martial law. Earlier decisions had nevertheless already pointed in this direction—for example, the appointment of General Jaruzelski to the post of prime minister in February 1981 and his appointment as first secretary in October.

The military was a fundamental tool in stabilizing the situation in Poland in part because of the militarization within the Polish communist party itself. This was the case not only in terms of higher-level positions, since "uniformed comrades" also took over some of the party offices (at the Central Committee and voivodship committees). It was also related to the fact that the party was now to be directed according to the decisions of a single individual in areas where executive power usually rested with collective bodies (such as voivodship executive committees). There were also more opportunities to co-opt and dismiss (i.e., remove) members at various levels. Finally, although Central Committee plenipotentiaries were appointed at the voivodship committees, whose role was vague—real chances for action depended to a significant extent on the political power of the local secretary. The iron principles of democratic centralism, the backbone of the totalitarian party, had of course been in force "forever," and the decision-making power of the first secretary (from the Central Committee down to the smallest party cell) was incomparably greater than that of the rest of the members of any given branch. Therefore, the instruction "On Party Leadership Under Martial Law Conditions"[2] does not appear to contain any radically new ideas. Implementing it, however, demonstrated that the top leadership did not have faith in the party's lower ranks. And with good reason—as was evidenced by the need to eliminate about ninety basal Polish United Workers' Party organizations (and even one municipal committee), as well as the dismissal (or resignation) of thousands of party activists and employees.

The local party organizations' ability to act was limited by the fact that the military commissioners and the security apparatus (formally the voivodship militia headquarters) assumed control in matters of personnel, at least as far as local state administration and enterprise management were concerned. Efforts were made not to infringe on the rules governing the party *nomenklatura*, according to which personnel decisions had to be approved by the relevant party body. Nevertheless the opinions of the military commissioners and SB, and information they provided, played a fundamental role in removing people from leadership positions. The Ministry of Internal Affairs even attempted to create personnel policies itself. This, however, was to a large extent the result of wishful thinking on the part of the ministry's leadership, at least as far as selecting and appointing new individuals was concerned. It was easier to identify those who should be removed because they could not manage under martial law conditions, or because they had some financial misdeeds or nepotism on their conscience, than to identify candidates to replace them and secure their appointment.

While the Ministry of Internal Affairs formally did not make any claims as far as influencing the party was concerned, WRON's internal documents foresaw strictly political activities for military commissioners as well as tasks related to the administration of martial law itself. These were actually even internal party matters, such as "completely rebuilding the connection between the party and government, and the working class and society . . . and reviving the party's mandate regarding its leading role."[3] It is not really known how these recommendations were to be implemented, but entrusting these kinds of tasks to military men meant that the party apparatus and *aktiv* were seen as inferior and less effectual; it was also evidence that the capabilities of the military were being overestimated. Perhaps the authors of these directives were more interested in words than in actual action.

As the sense of an immediate danger posed by Solidarity passed, there began to be signs of worry in the party apparatus and *aktiv* that the army was still not stepping down from its position "a half step ahead." In a questionnaire distributed on February 7, 1982, to participants at a meeting of military commissioners at the communal and municipal levels, twenty-nine of the ninety-seven commissioners who filled out the form said that party secretaries "do not aid them" in their work,[4] and twenty-five believed that the local administrative and party authorities "do not want the commissioners to remain active."[5] It is not known whether the Central Committee organized similar research in the party apparatus, too, but one can in any case conclude that—at least on the voivodship and local levels—conflicts did often arise in the system of martial law administration. At the communal and municipal levels, many commissioners also had misunderstandings with the local party bosses. They had known them since the autumn of 1981, when they were active as part of the military operational field groups and hence may have already formed negative opinions about them. The existing tensions lessened over time, but it was only after martial law was suspended that they diminished more markedly. At that time, 640 commissioners remained: 40 at the voivodship level (in the other nine, the voivods were military men), about 180 in the larger enterprises; the rest were in ministries, central offices, and the voivodship offices of school superintendents. Leaving commissioners in the school superintendents' offices, instead of turning these institutions over to the control of the appropriate party organizations, clearly attested to the fact that the leadership was gravely worried about the situation in education, especially among the youth. Because of young people's role in demonstrations and other forms of opposition, they became a subject of special concern.

Signs that people were discontented with the current state of affairs appeared in the central apparatus, too. Wojciech Wiśniewski, a Central Committee employee, recalled that the party's new position—not only behind the military, but even, as he believed, behind the state administration—"prompted a sense of degradation and marginalization." There was also a conviction that the party apparatus "had been pushed into the role of lecturers and propagandists who were supposed to persuade people of decisions being made by military and government organs."[6] Very often, however, the military was called in more readily for such tasks than were civilians, particularly when throngs of non-party workers or high school students had to be confronted.

In contrast, Kazimierz Barcikowski, who was in the top echelon of the party apparatus, noticed that the "attempt to bring military staff methods of operation to the party context led to a deepening of the apparatus's bureaucratic habits."[7] Moreover, he indicated that, as preparations were being made for martial law, the focus had been on the army and security apparatus, while political elements were being neglected. Although many propaganda activities were planned, assuming there would be quite an extensive symbiosis of the army, SB, and party, Barcikowski was correct in saying that propaganda and politics were not one and the same. While propaganda is supposed to serve politics, it is not supposed to be a substitute. Meanwhile, after the announcement of martial law, the political program was limited to include: maintaining relations with the Church that were as proper as possible, a vague plan (treated as secret) to take control of Solidarity from the inside, and sketchy slogans about reviving party activity.

On December 13, one of the key prerogatives of the various party organizations, including the Politburo, was seriously violated: no one was presented with a list of WRON's members for approval, or a list of the commissioners sent to ministries, central administration, and voivodships. At the time, this did not prompt anyone's reservations, at least in written form. These lists were drawn up by the Committee of National Defense and by military circles—the closest associates of General Jaruzelski, who were actually his subordinates. Similarly, voivodship party committees' rights were denied, since they were not asked to approve the commissioners who were being dispatched to the territories under their control. Somehow, no one objected, and all simply accepted Jaruzelski's authority.

By introducing new, additional conflicts—or perhaps only misunderstandings—to various elements in the government apparatus, martial law did not eliminate earlier conflicts, but perhaps even aggravated them. Most important of these was the conflict between the "hardliners," who advocated a return to the Stalinist model with only slight modifications, and the "moderates," also called the "reformers" or "liberals." It is not clear whether the existence of these groups can be seen as factions, since they were not very formalized. Nevertheless, it is clear from both internal party documents and especially accounts and memoirs that, during most of the debates, the individuals voting "for" or "against" were always the same, regardless of the subject under dispute. Thus, these clashes took place not as the result of different views on specific problems, but from different approaches in general. Stefan Olszowski, Stanisław Kociołek, Mirosław Milewski, Albin Siwak, and Tadeusz Porębski, for example, belonged to hardliners in the party leadership. Their support lay in a large portion of the middle echelon of the party apparatus, and especially in its *aktiv*. Hieronim Kubiak, Kazimierz Barcikowski, Mieczysław Rakowski, and Tadeusz Fiszbach belonged to the second "faction."

General Jaruzelski was fond of stressing that he was above all a military man who had actually found himself in politics by chance. After the imposition of martial law, however, he proved to be an expert in the techniques of party infighting, even if the Polish communist party's extraordinary situation undoubtedly facilitated their use. One of the most well-known tactics in purging the party's leading circles was referred to as "trimming the wings"—i.e., removing representatives of both "factions" (wings) from center stage, more or less at the same time. This kind of purge guaranteed that the party organization would be easier to control, and also opened the possibility of filling the newly emptied positions with individuals dependent on the main decision-maker (even if just by virtue of their advancement).

General Jaruzelski began "trimming the wings" very quickly: already in January 1982, the "liberal" Tadeusz Fiszbach (in Gdańsk) and the "hardliner" Andrzej Żabiński (in Katowice) were dismissed from their positions as first secretaries of their voivodship committees. As Barcikowski recalls, his party boss employed psychological manipulation to accomplish this task: he sent Olszowski, the informal leader of the hardliners, from Warsaw to carry out the change in Silesia, and dispatched Barcikowski (i.e., a liberal) to Gdańsk with that same mission. While Barcikowski admitted that "there was too much political calculation in that,"[8] he did nevertheless carry out the task. In May, Kociołek was dismissed from the post of first secretary of the party's Warsaw branch. He was then appointed ambassador in Moscow, which afforded him certain opportunities but deprived him of direct influence on events in Poland. At approximately the same time, the "liberal" Edward Skrzypczak was dismissed from the post of first secretary at the Voivodship Committee in Poznań. In July, the "liberal" Kubiak and the "hardliner" Olszowski were dismissed from their posts as Central Committee secretaries. Olszowski saw his appointment as minister of foreign affairs as a shift away from center stage, since that post—particularly in light of Poland's international isolation—was of secondary importance. Both men, however, remained members of the Politburo. Jan Łabęcki, an employee of the Gdańsk Shipyard, left its party cell at that time. Łabęcki believed that a compromise with Solidarity should be reached. In autumn, more maneuvering took place: Tadeusz Grabski, a leader of the hardliners, was officially reprimanded by the party, and his group's organization, the Reality Association (Stowarzyszenie Rzeczywistość) was pilloried. At that time, the same Politburo committee that was dealing with Grabski carried out a "purge" among the liberal intellectuals of Kraków who were linked with the Klub Kuźnica and the periodical *Zdanie*. Kubiak, who was associated with this group, was entrusted with the task of informing them that the club had been dissolved.

Finally, the Politburo passed a resolution on December 16, 1982, stating that continued existence was unwarranted for "those organizations, associations, and clubs whose activities in the current conditions cause the party to dissipate and do not further the consolidation of its ideological, political, and organizational unity, in accordance with its statutory requirements."[9] Thus, this resolution eliminated the remnants of any organizational pluralism within the party that had appeared during the post-August maelstrom, and had been a consequence of Solidarity's existence. Since pushing Solidarity out of public life had destroyed societal pluralism, there was no reason for any pluralism in the party itself. It is not clear how much time Jaruzelski spent arranging the dismissals of his party comrades. It was necessary, however, not only to maintain unity within the party, but also to affirm Jaruzelski's leadership, even though it was not seriously threatened. Incidentally, it was typical that those in one "faction" would attack those in the other, but no one dared to question Jaruzelski's position directly.

Before the imposition of martial law, the party leadership had been under intense pressure from Big Brother. The success of martial law—in defeating Solidarity, introducing harsh regulations governing how the state functioned, and gaining the upper hand inside the party—changed that situation significantly, however. The Soviet leaders could admonish their Polish counterparts to correct various things in Poland, or better conform to the general principles of socialism—by weakening private agriculture, curbing the Church, taking intellectuals and people from the cultural sphere down a peg or two, and dealing with the Solidarity underground more harshly, for example—but they no longer had much room to maneuver. One might even risk suggesting that, paradoxically, after December 13, Moscow was more dependent on the martial law team than the Polish generals (and secretaries) were on Moscow. Of course, the tools to exert political pressure still existed—it was possible to utilize Jaruzelski's opponents or competition within the party elite, of whom there were plenty. Nevertheless, no one approached his status in terms of authority within the party, or the loyalty the military showed him. For Moscow, the general, as the administrator of martial law, was the only guarantor of stability on the Vistula. And what could have been better? After all, the Soviet leaders had mounting problems of their own—new ones, compounded not only by their own advancing age, but above all by the fact that the Soviet economy was falling into an abyss, and by the ever costlier war in Afghanistan.

In November 1982, upon Jaruzelski's return from Brezhnev's funeral in Moscow, he told Rakowski that "the Soviets are slightly worried by Wałęsa's release, but their conclusion was: you know better what is expedient for you and what isn't."[10] A couple months later, Jaruzelski shared Józef Czyrek's account of his conversations with Soviet dignitaries, including Konstantin Chernenko, who was about to replace Iurii Andropov: "This is something completely new. No criticism, no signs of discontent . . . complete acceptance of our policies, complete understanding for the specific character of our situation and how difficult it is."[11] Moscow's reactions must have been a rude awakening for Jaruzelski's hapless competitors, since Soviet support was their only chance to play some kind of role. By imposing martial law, Jaruzelski's team not only decimated Solidarity, but also secured his group's control of the situation within the party itself, as well as the cool, calculated, neutral benevolence of the leaders in Moscow, if not their actual goodwill.

Despite this success, it was nevertheless clear that martial law could not last forever. The party would have to "build bridges" to the rest of society, and the ministries of defense and the interior could not be its only support in the long run. Having cleared the field of civic organizations, with varying degrees of subtlety, the Polish communist party then replaced the dissolved organizations with similar ones that were subordinate to the party. The Polish Journalists' Association was one of the organizations to meet this fate: it was replaced by the Association of Journalists of the Polish People's Republic (Stowarzyszenie Dziennikarzy PRL), whose board included no one from its previous leadership. The Union of Polish Stage Artists and the Association of Polish Artists had to introduce new boards. Other organizations had to limit their reach: for example, only a few of the fifty-five Clubs of the Catholic Intelligentsia that existed in December 1981 were granted permission to resume their activities.

"Building bridges" was accomplished primarily in two ways: by forging "a national agreement" and by organizing a trade union movement that would be subordinate to the communist party. These activities were launched relatively soon, as mentioned earlier, and had their origins in the Civic Committees for National Rebirth, which had already been founded by late December 1981, and the future trade unions' "initiative groups" that were established under SB control. The concept of a "national understanding" was embodied institutionally by PRON, which the Polish communist party and the "coalition powers" (the United Peasant Party, the Democratic Party, and approved Catholic groups) announced on July 20, 1982. (One of the Catholic groups, the PAX Association, had to be pacified beforehand with the introduction of a new leader, who replaced Ryszard Reiff. The night of December 13, Reiff was the only member of the Council of State not to demonstrate the required loyalty, voting against the decrees on martial law.)

Perhaps some individuals participating in the first phase of PRON's organization had hopes that the institution would have some autonomy, albeit limited. This quickly turned out to be a delusion. PRON simply became a dummy organization directed by the party, promoted heavily by General Jaruzelski's team. On November 19, 1982, the general paid a personal visit to PRON's headquarters, and the Initiating Commission took part in a meeting of the Government Presidium three days later. Soon afterward, it issued an appeal for the end of martial law, and its voivodship branches then called for the release of internees who came from their jurisdictions. This all was meant to convince public opinion that the PRON initiative was responsible for the Council of State's resolution to suspend martial law, since surely the highest state organ could not remain deaf to such a noble appeal. At a special meeting on December 17, the PRON Provisional National

Council was constituted, headed by seventy-two-year-old Jan Dobraczyński, a well-known Catholic writer associated with PAX who was not politically involved.

The new organization, which was officially established only at the congress in early May 1983, often acted as the voice of those in society who "passed the test of patriotic responsibility and realism." On July 9, it appealed to the Sejm, the Council of State, and the government to repeal martial law. As was to be expected, the appeal was heeded especially willingly because WRON had bombastically supported it. On July 20, the Sejm made changes to the constitution, to which PRON was added as a "plane on which society can be unified in the interest of the Polish People's Republic."[12] Predictably, what was created was a traditional, façade-like communist institution. Its directors were a "house blend," a colorful collection of lesser-known political activists, actors, intellectuals, athletes, and others. Although PRON's leader was a non-party writer, its general secretary was Marian Orzechowski, a party activist and Central Committee secretary, who was soon to be promoted to the Politburo. It is difficult to say whether anyone in General Jaruzelski's group believed this was really a "new bridge" to society. Rather, it seems they treated PRON purely instrumentally, since martial law was a means of returning to their tried and true methods of managing society.

PRON, the embodiment of the "national agreement," was organized relatively quickly, but trade unions necessarily had to be created more slowly. The courts registered a large number of enterprise-level union organizations—in mid-May 1983, about 13,500 of these had about 2.7 million members[13]—but many of them were small cells, and most of them were founded in smaller industrial plants, schools, offices, or institutions. Even the Trade Union of Party Employees was created during this wave. This organization was an oddity on a global scale; it was strange that its name skipped the two adjectives most often used in the names of new trade unions, "independent" and "self-governing." The "Independent, Self-Governing Trade Union of the Polish United Workers' Party" would have sounded nice! One should remember, however, that the communist party employed approximately twenty thousand people at that time, from Central Committee secretaries to cleaning ladies and custodians at village-level committees.

In April 1983, the Council of State made it possible to create national trade organizations. On June 11, the first of these was founded: the Federation of Metallurgical Trade Unions. Although many new trade unions were founded, their opportunities for growth were limited. The boycott of these organizations became quite widespread, having been supported by Solidarity, but the imposition of martial law itself had effectively convinced many people that they should not be members of anything at all. They were afraid to belong to underground Solidarity, or did not want to belong, but they also did not want to become members of the new pro-government unions. The creation of the new unions did more to embitter the atmosphere in the workplace than to calm it, both in terms of relations among workers, as well as between the new unions and the managers. While it is true that they were on the same side of the political barricade, the unions—whose national leader became Alfred Miodowicz, an annealer from the Lenin Steelworks—quickly began speaking out on salary-related and social issues, and on labor safety, so as not to lose their new position and compete effectively with Solidarity. In mid-1983, the Solidarity organizations in many workplaces had strong competition in the shape of these new pro-government unions, whose presence and activities reduced Solidarity's own influence. And this of course was exactly what those behind martial law had wanted.

During the first months of 1982, both the future movement for national rebirth and trade unions were getting underway, under the control of the military commissars and SB functionaries. Later, it was communist party branches and cells, above all, that were most active in filling the political space. Party apparatus functionaries and activists found themselves in positions that, until then, had often been occupied by military men. Since many of the most important factories and institutions had abandoned militarization and there had been a radical reduction in the numbers of military commissioners, the doors were once again open for local cells and party activists to act. There is no reliable information on the subject of the party's condition as a whole that would define the degree to which the party's lower and lowest levels had been revived, such as the communal or municipal district committees. Numerous reports from the field noted stagnation, low attendance at meetings, and unwillingness to participate in party events, but in Poland there had always been complaints about the indifference of rank-and-file members, as well as their lack of interest in party matters. Sometimes, in the 1950s for example, subscriptions to party publications were made mandatory. The communist party in Poland essentially never functioned the way that the leadership or party ideologues would have wanted it to, or as the party's statute envisioned.

It would be hard to expect that things would be different in the very exceptional circumstances that existed after December 13. It seems that the communist party was able to begin carrying out most of its functions as the party of power relatively quickly—surely by the autumn of 1982. This was particularly true in terms of its adherence to the principles of *nomenklatura*—i.e., in policies related to appointments. Clearly, it was not even able to mobilize its own members, whose fighting spirit left much to be desired. Neither is much known about power structure within the party as a whole. One can assume that among those who quit the party—a number amounting to over one million people (one-third of the membership) since the summer of 1980—most were those who supported the liberals rather than the hardliners. The purge that was launched during the autumn of 1981, which intensified after December 13, expelled many reformers of various ilks as well as supporters of an authentic (albeit probably impossible to achieve) social agreement. One may conclude that, as a result of martial law, a large part of the party's membership drifted toward the orthodox Left (the hardliners), which was hostile to any changes in the system. Martial law became an important factor in the polarization of views not only in society but also within the party itself, and somehow forced a unanimous, public declaration of belonging to one side or the other. Nevertheless, it was still a mass party, with a membership of over two million, representing over 5 percent of all Poles (of all ages, including infants). Most, however, undoubtedly kept their membership more out of conformity than for ideological reasons. Those party members who were conformists might have had a tendency not to make declarations in support of either side in internal party conflicts, and Jaruzelski's center position made it easier for them to maintain their typical neutrality.

For the pragmatists in General Jaruzelski's team—and for him—the most important instrument in terms of achieving a lasting stabilization and normalization was not PRON or the submissive trade unions, but rather success with the economy, which had been in crisis for years. The imposition and maintenance of martial law had also meant an additional burden on the budget—or at least one unforeseen in any five-year plan. Although Marx's thesis that "being shapes consciousness" is a serious oversimplification of social reality, it seems clear that living conditions and how they are perceived have a fundamental influence on people's attitudes in the political sphere. Looking at this from a longer perspective, one can say that those administering martial law were in a good situation: it could not be worse than late 1981 and 1982, so it could only get "better and better." The government survived the drastic price hikes that it had implemented on February 1, 1982, with a devastating impact on family budgets. According to some estimates, the real salaries in industry fell to just 57 percent of what they had been in 1980, and the gross national product fell by over 5 percent.[14]

During all of 1982, the situation in terms of consumer goods was extremely difficult: about 80 percent of the consumer goods market was in what was called the "unbalanced" sphere.[15] In other words, only one-fifth of consumer goods were more or less constantly available in the shops, with the other four-fifths either subject to rationing (on cards), or the object of time-consuming "hunting," which was conducive to corruption. Although the crisis in foodstuffs was worst in 1980–81, in 1982 the non-food market also collapsed. Inflation reached 100 percent. In the first six months of 1982, US sanctions had a negative impact—less so for individual consumers, and more for enterprises. Together with the severe shortage of hard currency, these sanctions caused even greater shortages of some raw materials, components, and spare parts. Despite the crisis, there was a push for more spending on the military and arms industry: the combined expenditures in that field reached 13 percent of the gross national product.

Martial law truly succeeded in blocking the economic reforms (albeit only partial and incohesive) that the 1980 summer strikes and the birth of Solidarity had sparked. Commissioners appeared in the enterprises, and in many cases they managed to check embezzlement and restore labor discipline, to some extent, and to limit minor, everyday thievery. Overall, however, they had a negative influence on enterprises' functioning, since they too often represented a "corporal's" way of seeing economic reality. This kind of lack of coordination is illustrative of the organizational changes: in order to increase enterprises' independence, 106 industry federations (zjednoczenia) were abolished, and 103 associations were formed in their place, encompassing basically all of the same enterprises—which was essentially pointless.

The traditional way of feigning action was to appoint advisory bodies, whose creation would be announced in the media. First, on March 26, 1982, the Sejm Presidium established the Social and Economic Council, which included representatives from various professions, such as workers, farmers, tradesmen, and artists—making it a rather inexpert body. The council's opinions, prepared by specialists, were not taken into consideration anyway. The Consultative Economic Council was established on April 1, and its significance was similar—it was more important in terms of propaganda than for reasons of substance. This was a relatively small group (twenty-nine people) of leading older economists, led by the well-respected Professor Czesław Bobrowski, who had played an important role in the Polish economy during the years 1945–48 and briefly again after 1956. In its work, the Council relied on the cooperation of research institutions, but its reports were met with no response.

For the duration of martial law, economic reforms were suspended, but projected plans did not include any fundamental changes. One can say that, for Polish reformers, the changes already underway for years in Hungary represented the maximum in terms of ideological, professional, and political possibilities. In any case, the height of the crisis had been overcome: production was no longer falling so dramatically, and the monetary overhang had been resolved to a large extent by the drastic increase in prices on consumer goods. This was not owed to commissioners or reforms, however, but rather to the fact that the situation in the enterprises had been resolved, the public mood calmed, and relations among the enterprises improved.

People managed in various ways, and "self-supplying" perhaps reached proportions close to those during the German occupation. For example, alongside the traditional methods of "working for oneself," such as selling bootleg alcohol or unlicensed trading in meat, garden plots—or better put, vegetable patches—became popular, and even appeared on the lawns in front of apartment buildings or in empty city lots. In cities, though not actually downtown, there were goats grazing or rabbits in cages—paupers' almost-forgotten friends. According to the Institute of the Domestic Market and Prices, fruits and vegetables were canned in 98 percent of households in 1983, one in three families repaired their washing machines themselves, and one in five fixed their own refrigerators. A year later, income from urban garden plots—of which there were approximately 850,000—comprised the equivalent of over 5 percent of spending on foodstuffs, and 16 percent of non-farm families raised small farm animals.[16] During the first half of 1983, rationing gradually began to end. This was due to a wide array of factors, including the desire to make a good impression and uphold propaganda's thesis that life had returned to normal. Thus, rationing cards on soap and laundry detergent were cancelled in February, on cigarettes in March (but then their price increased), on candy in April, and on shoes, cooking fats, butter, and milk in June.

These changes did not mean, however, that the shops filled with goods and lines disappeared. They were always an intrinsic part of communist Poland's landscape, where shopping for basic items on average took two hours a day—twice as long as fifteen years earlier. In 1983, the imbalance in consumer goods fell only several points, which in practice was barely perceptible on a daily basis. It was not surprising that, in some voivodships, temporary limits on purchases were even instituted on a local level, or local vouchers were distributed for goods that were not subject to official rationing. The "gray zone" grew: in 1983, it was the source for 10–12 percent of private income. This situation prompted authorities to launch a war against speculation and abuses, which became one of the main topics of propaganda. "Workers' brigades" were created, comprised of over sixteen thousand volunteers.[17]

Despite the oft-repeated slogans, the imposition of martial law did not have a positive influence on the economy. It remained the regime's Achilles' heel, regardless of which institution was "half a step ahead"—the army or the communist party.

Chapter Eighteen

The End of Martial Law

The Polish government not only planned carefully before imposing martial law, it also prepared assiduously for its end. There the similarities end, however, since those operations were diametrically opposed in terms of not only their formal aims, but also the basic principles by which they were introduced: martial law was planned as an operation to be carried out by surprise, and by the simultaneous use of all forces. It was, however, to be abolished in stages, which would be announced ahead of time. Some members of the ruling clique and their intellectual backers believed that serious changes could be carried out in the economy and state structures behind the façade of martial law, but these intentions were never clearly outlined. In reality, for a long time the only substantial activity in the economic sphere was the drastic price increases on February 1, 1982, which were supposed to rid the market of the enormous monetary overhang. It was clear that these price hikes could not be carried out without a heavy militia and army presence in the streets.

The document "Uwagi i propozycje dotyczące wyjścia z kryzysu politycznego i stanu wojennego" (Comments and propositions on how to overcome the political crisis and martial law),[1] prepared by the party's Central Committee apparatus in July 1982, mentioned the idea of creating a post of president of the Polish People's Republic, as well as controlled changes in the system of satellite parties, by which was undoubtedly understood permission for the foundation of a Christian Democratic party, with the support of the Episcopate. These projects were not part of the planned preparations for martial law, however, and there is also no sign that any of them were the subject of any serious discussion in decision-making circles over the course of the next year.

Preparing a plan for the repeal of martial law and the necessary actions afterward were once again primarily in the hands of military men, like everything related to its imposition. More specifically, they were within the purview of the Secretary of the Committee of National Defense and the Ministry of National Defense. This is illustrated by the fact that the person reporting on the legislative bills about the revocation of martial law at the Politburo session on November 18, 1982 (discussed in chapter 14), was the minister of national defense, General Siwicki, and not the justice minister or a representative of the Central Committee apparatus. It is thus not surprising that the basic document on the definitive end of martial law was drafted at KOK headquarters in early May 1983.

In "A Note on the Plan for the Repeal of Martial Law,"[2] it was not assumed that the conditions already existed to make this kind of decision. It was an interesting text, despite its complicated legal language. Those in power thought that before such a decision could be made, there should be a "thorough analysis of the country's social, political, and economic situation and its conditions and prospects for development." One would expect that this sort of document would have concluded with a clear statement about whether or not "the conditions making it possible to lift martial law exist." The "Note" was written before John Paul II traveled to Poland, and thus perhaps in response to a papal request that martial law be lifted before his visit, although the authors made no mention of it. General Jaruzelski steadfastly rejected the Vatican's request, assuming that how the visit went would be of fundamental importance in making the final decision about whether to continue or revoke martial law. Any link between the lifting of martial law and the pope's visit to Poland would have clearly been seen as a victory for John Paul II (and thus also for the Church). Such a move would have undoubtedly sparked an emotional, anti-government reaction by the crowds gathered to see the pope.

The authors of this "Note" assumed that the decision to call off martial law would nevertheless be made. They pointed out that, before it happened, "the existing threats [would need to be] neutralized and liquidated," including the "conspiratorial activities of the political opposition," "attempts to create a legal opposition," "the undesirable involvement of priests," "a mood of discontent stemming from a lack of market stability, the wage situation, and problems with supplies," and "the worsening speculation and corruption." These demands were practically impossible to fulfill quickly. If one were to take them seriously, martial law would have to become a permanent element of the system. The authors of the "Note" simply brushed off concerns about how realistic these requirements really were, because their main concern was what might happen after martial law was lifted. Thus, they stressed operations that would be essential "in the spheres of prevention, repressive measures, [ideological] education, and propaganda." Among the problems to be solved were "preparing a model for the continued existence and functioning of the Military Council of National Salvation" and "consideration of the relevance and the capacity" in which the military commissioners would be maintained. It is difficult to tell how this was seen, since keeping either WRON or the commissioners would clearly have cast doubt on the sense of lifting martial law in general, and would have meant that Poland had been transformed into a military dictatorship.

The "Note" proposed that, before the lifting of martial law, work be finished on an entire packet of regulations that would be accorded the same power as legislation. These included a law about the state of emergency, amendments to the criminal and labor codes, and approval of legislation useful in situations in which state security was threatened, but which "did not require any suitable special state." If these propositions were realized, Poland would be moving in the direction of becoming a country that was living in a permanent state of emergency. KOK's only constructive proposals were related to strengthening the legal framework that had facilitated the maintenance of a non-democratic, repressive system. There was no mention of changes that would have brought increased pluralism, of civic freedoms, or even of changes in the running of the economy and system of ownership. For the authors of this document—and probably also for the vast majority of the establishment and the ruling clique itself—the main aim was to maintain the existing system without any significant changes.

External factors undoubtedly played an important role in the decision to abolish martial law. Both the West and the Soviet bloc had already grown somewhat used to the army having the upper hand in Poland, rather than the party. For communist countries, however, even those who distanced themselves from Moscow, such as Romania, ideological factors rendered it an awkward situation. Moreover, it was not a good example for their own marshals and generals, either. For the West, martial law was a convenient weapon in the political and propaganda war, which the United States employed especially energetically and systematically. It is difficult to say whose opinion was more important for General Jaruzelski's group—that of the Kremlin, which was demanding that the party's importance be restored, or Washington, which was using martial law to justify painful economic sanctions. At every opportunity, the West would demand the release of prisoners and the legalization of Solidarity, which was embarrassing for communist Poland's representatives and reinforced their isolation. The following is a minor, but perhaps significant, example: in 1983, at a reception for Bastille Day organized by the French Embassy in Warsaw, no one from the government was invited.[3] The abolition of martial law would serve as an important step in reducing tensions between Poland and the West.

Despite the outward optimism regarding the degree of stabilization already attained, the party leadership feared that lifting martial law might cause serious problems. For this reason, the Polish government did not acquiesce to pressure from the Polish Church and the Vatican, whose expectation had been that Poland would no longer have repressive laws or political prisoners by the time John Paul II arrived. When preparations for martial law were underway, the SB's activities and the legal regulations designed to shield them were more important than any plans for efforts in the political sphere, or systemic reforms. At the aforementioned Politburo meeting on November 18, 1982, Jaruzelski called these regulations *bezpieczniki* ("safety catches"). Because of current fears, the situation repeated itself.

In the field of politics in the strict sense, however, it seems the ruling group's ability to act was simply limited, unless a presidential system were instituted as part of more fundamental changes to the system. It would have meant abandoning the "communized state"—i.e., a state completely in the control of the communist party. Instead, there would be a "nationalization of communism," which is to say a situation in which the party is an instrument in the hands of the state, as is the case in many authoritarian countries. If no decisions of this kind were made, what remained was to continue using PRON, parties and satellite groups, and subordinate civic groups (including trade unions), and persist in playing the game with the Church. This kind of "nationalized communism" would only be another type of dictatorship, since it would not lose its undemocratic nature. Considering the Polish and Soviet leaders' frames of mind, and those of their supporters, it is very doubtful that any true political liberalization would have been possible within the framework of "real socialism" (realny socjalizm), which would require that the opposition and Solidarity be allowed to operate above ground. For General Jaruzelski, even a simple step, like having the secret police stop infiltrating the Church, proved impossible—because it would have meant that the process of abandoning control over public life had begun.

It is not surprising, therefore, that only the question of the "safety catches" was raised during debates at this time, such as during a July 5, 1983, session of the Politburo, attended by invited members of the Sejm presidium and the Presidium of the Council of Ministers. These "safety catches" were the legal instruments protecting the system. The main one was to be the legislation titled "On the Special Legal Regulation for the Period of Emerging from the Crisis." This was to remain in force until the end of 1985—two and a half years. There was no agreement on details among the various party bodies: some believed that the regulations were too restrictive, and others believed the opposite—that the screws needed to be tightened still further. Rakowski mentioned a joke that conveys quite well the formal character of the legal measures: the legislation on overcoming the crisis should be comprised of two clauses, "clause 1—the Government is always right; clause 2—when in doubt, see clause 1."[4]

Debates also took place about the scope of the amnesty (considered inevitable) and its aims. There were no plans, however, to make it a general amnesty. In the opinion of the party leadership, its main aim was to create an incentive for people to come out from underground. TKK, however, in its announcement of July 3, diminished hopes that this strategy would be effective, saying that "the formal lifting of martial law and an amnesty do not make us inclined to discontinue our activities."[5] In an interview with *Tygodnik Mazowsze*, Zbigniew Bujak stated that society was "ready for compromise," and even to "forgive the injustices that were committed during martial law." Nevertheless, he remained skeptical as to the government's intentions and activities. He announced that after martial law was lifted, "there would be [only] a formal change in labeling."[6]

The skeptics were right. Of course, those who had publicly said for a long time that the "reds" were not to be trusted were also right: betting on an agreement with the government was politically naïve. Listening to the speech that General Jaruzelski gave at the Sejm on July 21, 1983, sufficed:[7] "Before the Earth bears its fruit," he began bombastically, "it will first be torn asunder by the plough. The birth of a new life is always accompanied by shouts and pain." The speech, albeit rhetorically impeccable, did not actually mark any real change. It was nevertheless saturated with lofty words, had populist accents ("a speculator who is growing fat at the cost of others"), and appealed for people to "take each other by the hand, to live in harmony, and to see the good of the socialist Fatherland as our common good, the only one, the highest one." The general used very well known platitudes about "socialist renewal," "democratic social life," "strengthening the position of the working class," "the development of class-based, independent and self-governing trade unions," "the practice of advising and consulting," and "profound economic reform." He thanked the militia and SB functionaries who had "proven their loyalty to the people's government," and announced that some of the officers would "continue to serve the country in civilian posts." He made strong declarations, such as "Anarchy will not return to Poland!" and all "attempts to undertake anti-state activities would be suppressed no less decisively than during martial law." "The organizers of the counterrevolution should have no illusions about this," he said emphatically.

"Point de rêveries, messieurs!" (No dreams, gentlemen!) was Tsar Alexander II's answer to the Polish notables who were paying him homage on May 23, 1856. They expressed their hope that he would deign to restore Poland's autonomy, which it had enjoyed under the Romanovs during the years 1815–30. General Jaruzelski did not cite the reformist tsar, of course, but he used those same words. Although in all likelihood he did not do so consciously, certain parallels nevertheless existed. There should be no illusions: the post-martial law state was to be a continuation of what the general had announced to Poland and the world early the morning of December 13, 1981.

The legislation about the amnesty, passed July 21,[8] was quite broad in scope, with approximately 500 individuals released as a result (more than 1,100 offenses were also "consigned to oblivion"). The sentences of approximately 100 people were reduced, and the proceedings against almost 800 others were discontinued.[9] As a result, 553 were released from prison and custody and, according to official figures, just 83 remained in confinement, including, however—which was significant—the entire group of eleven people from the National Commission and KOR, whose trials no one had even dared to begin yet. The possibility of expelling them from Poland began to be considered. The amnesty also included all those who reported to the appropriate office of the Ministry of Internal Affairs (or Polish diplomatic post abroad) by October 31 (this date was later extended to December 31), and declared in writing that they would cease their "criminal activities" and "reveal the type of deed and location where it was committed." Those who did so would either not have criminal proceedings launched against them, or would have any ongoing proceedings discontinued. According to an official communiqué,[10] about 1,100 people (twenty-five of whom were abroad) availed themselves of this offer. Many of them had not been involved in conspiratorial activities after December 13, and were thus confessing to the Ministry of Internal Affairs offenses that they had committed before that date.

The fact that the amnesty also included "offenses committed during the counteracting of strikes and protests" was of key importance, because this clause guaranteed impunity for militia and SB functionaries. Never before or after (until 1990) were any formal charges pressed against any functionary, even in connection with the Wujek mine massacre, or other cases in which firearms were used (such as in Lubin on August 31, 1982). There were cases (like the death of Grzegorz Przemyk) in which investigations were obstructed on orders from the highest circles of power. From December 13, 1981, to July 22, 1983, as the strikes were being broken and demonstrations dispersed, thirty individuals were killed or later died as a result of their injuries. About twenty were killed or later died as the result of beatings by the militia on the street, in prison, or under arrest. In addition, several people linked to Solidarity who were engaged in various types of underground activities were found dead, and it is suspected that the militia or SB murdered them. The case of Grzegorz Przemyk, who was fatally beaten, became symbolic, but at least three other young people his age who were connected to the underground in various ways also died after being beaten by functionaries.

Ending martial law involved a wide variety of activities, including those that fell into the categories of propaganda and even psychological manipulation. Such was the nature of the resolution passed on July 12 by the Sejm's Commission of Constitutional Responsibility regarding the former prime minister, Piotr Jaroszewicz, and a former deputy prime minister in his government, Tadeusz Wrzaszczyk, who were to be put before the State Tribunal. At the same time, the Commission put forth a motion to discontinue proceedings against two other high-ranking officials interned on December 13, 1981; in the case of First Secretary Edward Gierek and former Prime Minister Edward Babiuch, it declared that there was no legal basis for bringing them to justice.[11] Another propaganda move was the Sejm's passing of a resolution expressing the "highest admiration" for Jaruzelski.

Finally, it was announced that martial law was being lifted, on the strength of a Council of State resolution.[12] This document, comprised of just a few sentences, stated that the aims in implementing martial law "had been achieved," and that there was "political and social stabilization, and improved internal security and public order"—a declaration that did not reflect the actual state of affairs in the country. The resolution was passed on July 20 after a motion by WRON presented to the Council of State by General Tuczapski, who was already known to the members of this body because they had spent several hours together the night of December 12–13, 1981. The meeting's protocol indicates that WRON's motion was dated July 21, a day later than the meeting of the Council of State, but apparently no one attached much importance to these kinds of details.

An important element in the packet of "safety catches" was legislation passed on July 14 titled "On the Office of the Minister of Internal Affairs and the Fields in Which the Organs Subordinate to It Are Active."[13] It broadened some of the government's repressive powers; for example, the possibility of 48-hour administrative detention, and the authority to conduct searches. Most important in this legislation, however, was giving the SB a formal, legal status—the first time ever that this was done in communist Poland—and allowing SB functionaries to carry out "operational and reconnaissance activities" (article 6, paragraph 1), which would be extralegal (i.e., not based on the decision of a public prosecutor). Thus, this legislation sanctioned operational activities of all kinds, including those employing the services of informers, telephone and apartment tapping, and the monitoring of correspondence. Up until now, these types of activities had been illegal, meaning that information and materials gained in this way could not be used in court. This legislation "strengthened the legality of the activities carried out by that ministry's organs,"[14] in the words of General Tadeusz Walichnowski, who at the time was the rector of the ministry's Academy of Internal Affairs. It was high time, since it would soon be forty years since those methods had been employed based solely on decisions made by security apparatus functionaries.

Several changes to the constitution were also introduced in order to ensure that the government had a safe exit from martial law, and that the state would subsequently be able to function, both politically and in terms of the ministries of defense and the interior. One of these changes was that PRON would replace the existing Front of National Unity and become a "space for society to unite for the good of the Polish People's Republic."[15] This was essentially just a formality, like the introduction of a statement in the constitution to the effect that the Polish People's Republic "is realizing the national aspirations of the working class, drawing on its accomplishments and activity, and is increasing workers' participation in carrying out the affairs of the state."[16]

In light of what was done after December 13, 1981, with a trade union that encompassed most of the "working class," the only way to describe this wording is "cynical." As far as the state's actual functioning went, more important than these changes was an authorization in that same amendment for the Council of State to impose martial law "for [reasons of] defense or external threats," and that a state of emergency could be ordered "in all or part [of Poland] . . . if the internal security of the state was in danger, or in the event of a natural disaster." In addition, the state of emergency could take place "in matters of great urgency," announced personally by the chairman of the Council of State.[17] A separate piece of legislation on the state of emergency was passed half a year later (on December 5, 1983) as part of a set of additional legal "security catches" for the regime.

One of the "security catches" dating to July 1983 was the legislation mentioned above, "On the Special Legal Regulation during the Overcoming of the Social and Economic Crisis and the Modification of Some Other Laws."[18] It contained many restrictive regulations taken from various acts related to the implementation of martial law. For example, it foresaw the possibility of extending the workday, dissolving or suspending workers' self-government and the boards of associations, transferring teachers (on the basis of decisions made by voivods), suspending collegial bodies of post-secondary schools (senates and departmental councils), dismissing deans, and expelling students. It also postponed the possibility of having two trade unions active in one work place.

Changes to the criminal code were another "safety catch"[19] and included, for example, the introduction of a sentence of up to three years in prison for participating in a trade union that "had been dissolved or whose legalization had been denied"—in other words, for membership in underground Solidarity—and for "organizing or directing a protest action." The attributes of the military courts were also expanded so that their competence remained almost as broad as it had been under martial law. One more legal safeguard was the amendment of legislation on the monitoring of publications and of theatrical and other productions,[20] which among other things expanded the authority of the censorship offices, rescinded the freedom to reprint publications that had been published previously after having passed censorship, and also stipulated the monitoring of artistic and photographic exhibitions. By introducing phrases such as "threatening state security" and "contents that in an obvious way constitute a crime," the amendments created the "possibility of interpreting the regulations at will."[21]

All of these legal acts, passed between July 14 and 28, did constitute a substantial "safety catch" and consolidated the regime's repressive character, scrupulously concealed behind a screen of "democratic socialism" and "the people's law and order" (*ludowa praworządność*). Solidarity's underground leadership stated in a declaration on July 28 that the legal changes associated with the end of martial law meant that "the incapacitation of society had been recognized as a permanent element of the state's domestic policy,"[22] and that the lifting of martial law itself was a "propaganda gesture, an attempt to fool Polish society and international public opinion." In another statement issued on that same date, leaders of independent society announced that "the government has not broken the spirit of resistance . . . we exist and [continue to] fight."[23] They also declared that society was entering the next phase of the struggle, "having an incomparably better awareness" than before August 1980, and that the activists had been "hardened by the reprisals of martial law."

Sometimes underground Solidarity used the term "positional battle" to describe the current situation.[24] For the union, this involved launching activities in workplaces, organizing self-help (also through the churches), engaging in underground publishing activities, preparing union and self-government personnel in the secret workers' universities, and facilitating self-organization among teachers, academicians, and artists. Head-on clashes with the government were to be avoided, since the opposition's chances were not good. To a certain extent, these tactics recalled the "organic work" proposed by many Polish political circles during the Partitions, especially in the late nineteenth and early twentieth centuries. For those involved in that era's "organic work," the next national uprising—after three unsuccessful ones—still lay very far in the future, and they believed that all that remained was to build social consciousness, uphold national identity, and organize the life of society against the will of the three empires who had partitioned Poland in 1795. For Solidarity, general strikes were to assume the role of a national uprising, and "independent society" was to be the equivalent of "organic work."

At least in the common understanding, the term "positional battle" (or war) meant that those involved were focused on maintaining their territory. Staying with military terminology, it would seem that what was happening in Poland at this time was something other than a positional battle. For Solidarity, it was more of a defensive war, or even a war of survival—like that waged by the defenders of a fortress under constant siege from the enemy. Because of the disproportionate numbers and Solidarity's methods, the situation in Poland was also reminiscent of partisan warfare: the secret organization of street demonstrations by Solidarity or other associated groups (such as Fighting Solidarity) were the equivalent of assaulting the enemy in partisan warfare. Every once in a while, detachments of varying sizes would emerge from that "human forest" that General Jaruzelski spoke of in June 1982, and then go out into the squares and streets, after which they would retreat under pressure from the enemy's preponderance of forces. They would then hide among those who had not actively participated in the fighting.

What we call this situation or this type of warfare is not important, however, since in this case the concept of "positional battle" should refer to the political sphere and not the military one. It meant that neither side could definitively defeat the other, either because it was too weak, or because circumstances did not allow it to make use of all the forces at its disposal. Solidarity was not strong enough—i.e., it did not have enough active support from society in order to force the government to compromise, to say nothing of forcing it to an unconditional surrender. At the same time, the communist government was not capable of completely marginalizing or destroying its enemy, or of securing social peace, which it wanted to do by bringing Poland out of the crisis and guaranteeing the kind of standard of living to which most of society aspired. In this situation, the announcement that martial law was ending was more an act of propaganda than an acknowledgment of the actual state of affairs and the real balance of power. Normalization—returning to the status quo ante—began on December 13, 1981. After a year and a half, this process had not advanced far enough to say that the situation was already under control—and the economy still showed signs of collapse.

Solidarity's activities remained for the most part unchanged over the next few years. Adopted semi-spontaneously between May and September 1982, these actions included what came to be known as "independent society," with activities related to underground publications and also "martial law religiosity." There were also the regular sallies into enemy territory (demonstrations on various anniversaries). With time, new groups joined them, such as the pacifists, ecologists, and anarchists. Although new political projects emerged, too, the types of warfare (i.e., civil resistance) did not change much. The situation was similar in the enemy trenches. Since the army retreated from its positions in front of factories and in the streets, the standards of behavior and the measures the government took against the enemy had not fundamentally changed: these still included brutal propaganda attacks on Solidarity and its leaders, ZOMO charges against demonstrators, arrests (and then amnesties), SB maneuvers (called "operational games" in ministerial jargon, these operations were supposed to break the underground down from within), and attempts to neutralize the Church. So, after the lifting of martial law on July 22, 1983, there was no return to the old order, in which the communist state completely dominated society. Instead, what followed was simply a continuation of the events that had begun in August 1980.

Part 5

Endgame

Chapter Nineteen

Solidarity's Revolution

The Finale, 1988–89

"The worst is already behind us," General Jaruzelski announced in parliament on July 21, 1983, as he justified the lifting of martial law.[1] He was actually referring to the economic situation, but his words can also be interpreted more generally. For the governing clique and its numerous supporters, the entire period after August 1980 was "bad," and certainly "worse" than what had preceded it. In its very existence, Solidarity was undermining the status quo and posing a threat to the position of entire social groups: the party functionaries and a large portion of the state administration, members of the security apparatus and militia, and those in the professional army. They had a growing sense of being personally under threat. The rigors of martial law could not immediately alleviate all these fears. For many months, Solidarity had been trying to force the government to make concessions and negotiate. Street clashes, calls for strikes, distribution of flyers, anti-government graffiti, a selective boycott of state institutions, and conspicuous displays of religious participation accompanied these efforts. Solidarity's opponents and those who were indifferent to the union perceived the fact that the government did not yield under this pressure as a positive thing, while the lifting of martial law demonstrated that stability and order were beginning to return to Poland.

In his speech, First Secretary Jaruzelski did not clearly outline any tasks for the future. He did say, however, that a matter of "primary" importance was "to meet the material and cultural needs of society."[2] He believed that this could be achieved by "perfecting" the existing system through "more complete utilization of production assets" and "better management of labor resources."[3] These limitations stemmed from a phenomenon aptly described by sociologist Mirosława Marody: "people who support reform are against the government, and those who support the government are against reform."[4] To some extent, the signs of improvement over the course of 1983 did play a role; it seemed that, since the crisis had begun to abate, there was no longer any need to introduce changes. Although the country's economic situation played a fundamental role in legitimizing the system, the government's legal validity did not depend solely on how much meat was on the table.

Sociological research carried out in 1984 and 1985 identified four different stances: 1) affirming the existing political order; 2) contesting this order; 3) a middle (undecided) stance; and 4) a passive stance. In the spring of 1984—less than a year after martial law was lifted—the affirmative stance characterized 26 percent of those polled, with 23 percent opposing the existing order, 30 percent taking a middle position, and 21 percent having a passive attitude,[5] which indicated a relatively balanced range of attitudes. A year and a half later, in the autumn of 1985, 28 percent of those polled expressed an affirmative stance, 16 percent opposed the existing order, 23 percent had a middle stance, and 33 percent had a passive one. This data shows a clear fall in the number of those expressing opposition, and those who were undecided, as well as a small increase in the percentage of those who supported the system and a significant increase in the number of those expressing a passive stance. The sociologists' report stated unequivocally that there had been an "erosion of the camp of those contesting the ruling order and a consolidation of the camp supporting it."[6]

The conclusions, however, were cautious: "this does not mean a growing acceptance of the political order," since it was "more about the adoption of attitudes reflecting discouragement, and waiting" to see what would happen.[7] In this research, the large variation in attitudes is striking: the number of those opposing the current system was much higher (30 percent or more) among young people, professionals, skilled laborers, and urban dwellers than among older people, unskilled laborers, farmers, and rural dwellers (10 percent). With such a large fall in the number of Solidarity supporters, those contesting the status quo still remained significant—though not dominant—in the social groups that had a substantial influence on what went on in the public sphere.

The profound collapse of Solidarity's influence was clearly a success for the government team. For them, it was initially more important to weaken the opponent than to find new supporters. Prolonging a situation in which such a large portion of society harbored reservations toward or was indifferent to the government, meant, however, that the situation could become treacherous at virtually any moment. This might happen, for example, as the result of an economic collapse, or an event with a major impact on the triangle of government-society-opposition, to the detriment of those in power. One such dramatic event was undoubtedly the death of Father Jerzy Popiełuszko, one of the most popular Solidarity priests, who was brutally murdered by Security Service functionaries on October 19, 1984. Over two hundred thousand people attended his funeral. Mieczysław Rakowski, deputy prime minister, wrote in his diary that the day was "an ordeal for us" (*dzień próby dla nas*).[8] The funeral took place in a grave and sorrowful atmosphere, but without any mass protests. This shocking crime did not have the large impact on social attitudes that Rakowski had feared: the number of Solidarity's supporters did not increase, although Popiełuszko's death did reinforce the opinions of those who had already expressed a negative attitude toward the government. No event during the years 1983–85 that could have spurred a reorientation among the "silent majority" actually managed to have that effect.

There were many reasons for this: psychological exhaustion, lingering fear among many after the imposition of martial law, the lack of faith in the possibility of success, the desire for peace, and the need to concentrate on day-to-day hardships. Moreover, Jaruzelski's team pursued quite a clever "carrot and stick" policy, which was apparent in the treatment of political prisoners. In May 1984, there were over seven hundred. Although only a few dozen remained after the amnesty announced on July 21, 1984, there were once again about four hundred a year later.[9] They used a similar tactic toward the Church, taking advantage of the fact that some people within it were not favorably inclined toward Solidarity. In addition, maintaining proper relations with the authorities was important to many bishops and parish priests. The ruling group would give a "carrot," for example, by quickly granting permission for the construction of church buildings, which were being erected throughout Poland during that period.[10] Simultaneously, however, the government wielded its "stick," on occasion: "wars over crosses" broke out in schools, and propaganda ruthlessly attacked priests who sympathized with Solidarity. There were cases of beatings, cars set on fire, and other provocations.

The government saw to it that the trade unions under its control grew: in 1984, they already had 4.5 million members, many of whom were former Solidarity members. In artistic and intellectual circles, the situation was similar. After their organizations were disbanded in 1982–83, new ones were created with the help of the party and security apparatus, and most artists joined these groups. General Jaruzelski's team attempted to revive the communist party and managed to prevent a major exodus of members. There were no new applications for party membership, and most existing members in this ostensibly "workers'" party were bureaucrats and retirees. Nevertheless, the party still had over 2 million members, which meant that one in twelve Poles of working age were in the party. Most were card-carrying members out of conformism more than ideological engagement, but the degree of loyalty toward party leadership was quite high.

Populist means were employed to try to garner support among the "silent majority." The Workers' and Peasants' Inspection was formed, and set the task of prosecuting both real and imaginary speculators, who were blamed for consumer goods shortages. Hunting down speculators, however, could not be an antidote for the shortages, just as it could not prevent the price hikes—still the main tool for regulating the market. In 1985 alone, the official prices for meat and other foodstuffs increased, as well as for electricity, gas, and coal. Nevertheless, stores and warehouses were constantly besieged, and there was no guarantee that even the rationing cards in circulation could be fully honored. People felt threatened by inflation, which did not fall below 15 percent.[11] Military spending, increasing at a rate of 12 percent a year, as required by Moscow, was a burden on the state budget, as was the rapidly growing foreign debt: in 1985, it reached $33 billion, and in 1987 it was close to $38 billion. Because those in power proved unable to devise any solutions other than price manipulation, day-to-day problems were generally perceived as having "lost the status of being temporary sacrifices, and instead began to be seen as an intrinsic feature of social reality."[12] Though this did not necessarily mean they were ready to revolt, it did raise doubts as to how long stability would last.

In late 1985, one of the leaders of underground Solidarity, Zbigniew Bujak, estimated that 50,000–70,000 people were actively engaged in underground activities, and approximately 200,000 worked for the underground on a more irregular basis.[13] According to estimates of the Ministry of Internal Affairs, these numbers were 34,000 and approximately 100,000 people, respectively.[14] Even these figures testify to the large numbers of the opposition: more than 100,000 people constitute quite a sizeable army. In late 1985, a single print run of illegally published bulletins numbered about 200,000 copies,[15] and several hundred books and brochures were published every year. On national holidays and anniversaries of workers' revolts, invariably special Masses were said in dozens of churches, and rallies or demonstrations in some cities would also always take place afterward, which ZOMO would eventually disperse. They were rarely as large as during martial law, but up to ten thousand people would participate.

During the years 1983–85, many small but active political groups were founded. Along with those that already existed, these groups comprised the varied mosaic of a pluralistic political scene. Some of these groups declared radical aims (such as independence), and thus were opposed to Solidarity, which was inclined to conciliation. Solidarity, however, still set the tone, particularly its mainstream, which was centered on Wałęsa and the underground Temporary Coordinating Commission (TKK). Meanwhile, Wałęsa, winner of the 1983 Nobel Peace Prize, believed that "from the national point of view there is no other choice but to come to an agreement."[16] He did stipulate that "we are not going on our knees to [reach] an agreement," but he considered a compromise to be the only realistic path to change.

Neither side had any new political project even several years after martial law had ended: General Jaruzelski's team had strengthened its position but avoided real change like the plague, and rejected the possibility of concluding a new social contract. Solidarity repeated familiar demands, and was unable to fight using methods that it had employed up to that time (such as strikes). It was also not strong enough to force those in power to negotiate. Thus, there was a stalemate—and it seemed it could last for a long time. Meanwhile, in the second half of 1986, the ruling group took steps, which might be described as "the tactics of cooptation," that partially eased the situation. These measures were supposed to bring people associated with the opposition, or considered to be independent, into institutions controlled by the communist party. Analysts from the Ministry of Internal Affairs wrote frankly about "feigning dialogue"[17]—i.e., they considered it to be a political hoax.

These tactics were adopted for many reasons. Poland's situation in the international arena was undoubtedly the most important. Indeed, the first meetings with representatives from the West had already taken place at quite a high level (including foreign ministers), and some of the economic sanctions had already been lifted, but relations were still very cool. In the meantime, the Polish economy needed new loans, making proper relations with creditor nations extremely important. Renewing membership in the International Monetary Fund was also significant, because doing so would allow Poland access to its credit supplies. They also counted on the ability of official visits to influence Polish public opinion and legitimize General Jaruzelski.

The atmosphere in East-West relations after Mikhail Gorbachev came to power in the Soviet Union in March 1985 strongly influenced Polish leaders' decision to take liberalizing steps. Gorbachev undertook reforms ever more energetically. For these reforms, a reduction in military spending was necessary, which in turn meant an easing of international tension. President Reagan and other Western leaders supported this tendency, and saw the implementation of *perestroika* in Poland as a positive thing. The Soviet leader was encouraging new solutions. As early as 1985, he indicated clearly that the communist leadership in each of the "fraternal states" would be accountable to its own citizens, and that Moscow did not intend to interfere in their affairs. Gorbachev was satisfied with Jaruzelski's positive attitude toward reform.[18] Meanwhile, Jaruzelski was consolidating his own position—in November 1985, for example, he resigned his post as prime minister, which was the office directly responsible for economic matters (he was replaced by Zbigniew Messner, a professor of economics), and although he kept the position of first secretary, he assumed the post of chairman of the Council of State, which was in effect the post of president.

Jaruzelski also strove to become Gorbachev's closest collaborator of the communist bloc leaders. In November 1986, he told Gorbachev outright that the other communist leaders "will simply not be able to [reform]: they are old and have fallen behind. Let the two of us pull the load together."[19] Until now, Moscow and Washington had been pulling Poland in opposite directions—the Soviets pressed for a stricter regime, and the Americans expected Poland's leaders to liberalize. This time, however, the two superpowers began to form a common front. While it is true that they were doing so for different reasons, they were interested in sending Poland down the path of change. Gorbachev, on the one hand, believed that reforms introduced simultaneously throughout the bloc would save communism.

Reagan, on the other hand, believed that changes in Poland would weaken the system not only there, but also in the Soviet Union itself.

The ruling clique's own sense of having the situation under control was an important factor that encouraged the adoption of new tactics, as exemplified by the parliamentary elections in the autumn of 1985. After being postponed several times, and boycotted by Solidarity, the elections ended in a very moderate success for the opposition.[20] In late June and early July 1986, a communist party congress took place after a one-year delay—a fact that shows Jaruzelski's control of the situation in the party itself. Gorbachev honored the congress with his presence. Confident that both the party and society were under sufficient control, and that Moscow was encouraging innovations, Jaruzelski's team began trying to find new allies within Poland and improve its image in the West.

A fundamental prerequisite, however, was Poland's freeing of its political prisoners. This point had been one of the United States and NATO's demands after December 1981, and was something that most of the Polish public also hoped for. Under direct pressure from Washington,[21] on September 11, 1986, it was announced that the next amnesty would include all political prisoners, with the exception of those who had been sentenced for "spying" or "terrorist acts." From then on, opposition and Solidarity activists were no longer to appear before the courts. Although Poland could now officially be called a country "without any political prisoners," regulations were nevertheless tightened, making it possible to impose serious financial penalties and confiscate the "tools" used to commit the offenses (such as the cars with which the illegal publications were distributed).

The policy of "openness" was rickety, since it was really about changes that were only feigned, and not, for example, about recognizing Solidarity as a partner. Actually, the only thing that was done was to establish the Consultative Council of the Chairman of the Council of State, i.e., General Jaruzelski. Only a couple of this council's members were connected with the opposition, albeit loosely, and none had delegated powers. The public remained uninterested in the council's meetings, which had no decision-making powers. The opposition treated it as yet another sham. Nevertheless, the tension did ease, and, most importantly, people's fear of reprisals diminished. Solidarity and the opposition took advantage of the new situation: Wałęsa and a group of intellectuals wrote an open letter to President Reagan, appealing for the last remaining sanctions against Poland to be lifted, and Reagan took appropriate steps. They also made public the activities of the secret regional organizations. An above-ground national Temporary Council of Solidarity (Tymczasowa Rada "Solidarności") was created, as well as several oppositional political clubs, whose meetings, announced publicly, often had several hundred people in attendance.

This renewed political activity sparked other initiatives, including an anarchist performance group called the "Orange Alternative," which organized political "happenings." Probably the most important of these initiatives were those of the Working Group of National Commission (Grupa Robocza Komisji Krajowej), which was created in March 1987 by those who opposed Wałęsa in the union's former elite (including Andrzej Gwiazda and Anna Walentynowicz). They demanded that Solidarity's statutory authorities be reinstated and that a decidedly negative stance be taken toward General Jaruzelski. Wałęsa kept up the momentum and, in May 1987, in connection with the upcoming visit of John Paul II, gathered a group of intellectuals, who spoke openly in a published statement about Poles' right to independence and democracy.

The pope's visit itself clearly mobilized the regime's opponents. It took place on June 8–14, 1987, and this time he also visited Gdańsk, the "cradle of Solidarity." Millions of people went to see the pope, as during his previous visit, but there were significantly more Solidarity slogans and banners than in 1983. Many of the pope's statements—for example, about the inalienable rights "to truth," "to freedom," and "to association"[22]—played well with his audience's expectations. Just as during the pope's previous visits, the enormous crowds who came to see him demonstrated discipline and calm, despite the emotional tension, indicating that although Poles did expect changes, they did not show revolutionary tendencies. International contacts revived, but now it was not only Western diplomats who came to Poland. Now there were also politicians—like Vice President George Bush—and also experts seen by the government as anti-Soviet, such as Professor Zbigniew Brzeziński. The pope, before he came to Poland, received Jaruzelski at the Vatican. General Jaruzelski, already as the chairman of the Council of State, held talks, for example, with the president of France, François Mitterand.

Nevertheless, all this was accompanied by a deterioration in the popular mood: while only 38 percent of those surveyed believed that the economic situation was "bad" in December 1985, this number grew to 58 percent a year later, and by the spring of 1987—just before the pope's visit—it was already 69 percent.[23] This trend was permanent: in January 1988, only 13 percent of those surveyed were optimistic about the situation.[24] This result was worse than in July 1980, when the great wave of strikes was beginning. Inflation was over 25 percent and growing fast, and the shelves in the shops were still empty. Although the state and party leadership was aware of these problems, there was still no adequate reaction.

General Jaruzelski disregarded the warnings, just as he disregarded the propositions contained in the memoranda addressed to him in the autumn of 1987 by Rakowski and Wojciech Garstka, head of a group of analysts at the Ministry of Internal Affairs. Rakowski wrote, for example, that the current model of socialism "had exhausted its creative possibilities," and mentioned the need to legalize a moderate opposition, and Garstka demanded a "radical, bold, profound, and immediate reform" as a condition *sine qua non* for "saving socialism and the prospects for communism in Poland."[25] The experts in the wings were full of all different kinds of ideas and warnings. Nevertheless, on February 1, 1988, Messner's government introduced a price hike of 60 percent, the biggest in six years. It affected the prices of food, alcohol, cigarettes, gasoline, rent, and transportation, and was to be an introduction to the "Second Stage of the Economic Reform," as it was bombastically called.

Society's reaction was weaker than the opposition had expected, but there was nevertheless a reaction. In late April and early May, strikes took place at the "bastions of Solidarity," in Nowa Huta and the Gdańsk Shipyard, and elsewhere. These ended with militia intervention, but no one died. Although this was a clear warning, apparently it was not strong enough. In any case, General Jaruzelski was not favorably inclined toward any of the numerous propositions he had received from his advisors, who believed it was necessary to preempt the wave of strikes anticipated in the autumn. These predictions soon turned out to be correct. Strikes began at more than a dozen coal mines as early as August 15, and on August 17 the port in Szczecin went on strike, followed by the Gdańsk Shipyard on August 20, and Nowa Huta on August 22.

The situation appeared to be dangerous—and everywhere the fundamental demand was that Solidarity be legalized. It was also notable that young workers played an important role in the strikes: these were the "children of Solidarity," raised on clashes with ZOMO and romantic notions of the "underground." Recognizing that a new martial law would be more difficult to carry out than in 1981, Jaruzelski conceded, and on August 31 (not coincidentally, on the anniversary of the 1980 agreements) Wałęsa and General Kiszczak met for three hours. Bishop Jerzy Dąbrowski took part as well, which meant that the Church had assumed the role of moderator and the guarantor of the participants' credibility. A brief communiqué announced that talks would take place "at a round table," at which the situation in the country and possible resolutions to the crisis would be discussed. From that moment on, the expression "round table" entered the global political vocabulary and became a synonym for regime change achieved through compromise. In agreeing to the talks, the government had met the last of President Reagan's December 1981 demands—as it turned out, just a couple of months before his presidency came to an end.

The road to negotiations, however, was neither simple nor short. The ruling clique and its political backers did not want to bid farewell to a system that had guaranteed them complete power and privileges. A scenario involving negotiations was not, after all, the only possibility: in communist China, the reform launched in 1979 had reaped its first fruits, and the party had maintained its monopoly of power while reforming the country. In the Soviet Union, too, the changes initiated by Gorbachev had been dictated by the communist party, and if anything blocked them, it was intraparty intrigues. Paradoxically, Mieczysław Rakowski, considered to be a critic of the "real socialism," undertook the task of carrying out profound changes in the economy without undermining the political system. "You are my last hope," Jaruzelski told him when he offered him the position of prime minister.[26]

Rakowski assumed the post on September 27, 1988, and relatively quickly undertook a number of steps that society received positively. As a result, as many as 72 percent of those surveyed expressed trust in his government in November.[27] He enjoyed strong support despite the fact that he had made a controversial decision—to put the Gdańsk Shipyard in a state of liquidation, as an unremunerative enterprise. Society received this news calmly, but after Wałęsa's protest, preparations for the Round Table talks were at an impasse. That was, after all, what it was about: the government treated the talks as a trick to halt the wave of strikes and improve its reputation in the West. At a secret meeting with the secretaries of the voivodship party committees, Jaruzelski said outright that the Round Table was just a "move we had to make."[28]

As sometimes happens, an unexpected event resolved the impasse. Alfred Miodowicz, head of the pro-government trade unions, and also a member of the Politburo, came up with the idea that he and Lech Wałęsa should have a televised debate. Miodowicz believed that he towered over the Nobel laureate intellectually—although he himself was a worker. He assumed that he would beat his rival, and in doing so discredit Solidarity. The debate, broadcast live, took place the evening of November 30, and, according to 64 percent of those surveyed, Wałęsa won; 34 percent deemed it was a tie, and only 1 percent thought that Miodowicz won.[29] Moreover, 73 percent were in favor of legalizing Solidarity, and only 12 percent did not believe Solidarity should return to the public sphere. Not only did most Poles believe Wałęsa had won, but General Jaruzelski did, too: he admitted that opposing Solidarity's legalization any longer and delaying negotiations would mean a renewed danger of strikes and general destabilization. As he explained to his colleagues, "The gasoline has been spilled," and anyone could toss a match on it.[30]

Finally, on January 18, 1989, Jaruzelski broke the resistance of the party apparatus at a meeting of the Central Committee. The fact that about 30 percent of that body abstained or voted against the legalization of Solidarity as proposed by the first secretary testifies to the strength of that resistance.[31] This was a symptom of the crisis in the party itself, which admittedly did not threaten Jaruzelski's leadership, but did bode badly in the face of the upcoming negotiations and anticipated parliamentary elections. Nonetheless, there was a realization that the "Chinese road" (i.e., limiting reforms solely to the economy) could not work in Poland primarily because a well-organized opposition existed, with a large base of support in both Polish society itself and also the West.

Solidarity mobilized quickly. On December 18, 1988, without waiting for a final decision on the date of the Round Table talks, a one hundred-person

Civic Committee (Komitet Obywatelski, or KO) was founded, headed by Lech Wałęsa. Fifteen working groups were formed to prepare for the negotiations, and their members quickly got to work. Although Solidarity was still formally illegal, the process of creating openly operating cells at enterprises intensified. According to the Ministry of Internal Affairs, between ten and twenty of these cells were being formed daily.[32] More regional structures also came out of hiding, and underground news sheets were circulating openly in factories and at universities. Opposition groups that were against talks with the "reds" had no chance of influencing the course of events, although there were many of these, and they were active. The protesters played a role that was a little similar to that of the hardliners in the party, who believed that any efforts to find a compromise were tantamount to treason.

Both sides set what might be called "minimalist" goals for themselves. For Solidarity, most important was the ability to exist legally (including unions for farmers and students), and also having a check on the government, i.e., parliamentary representation. It was thought that these means of applying pressure would allow them to force the ruling camp to institute reforms in the sphere of civil freedoms: the freedoms of association and speech, access to mass media for the opposition, and changes in the court system and local self-government. For the party, the most important thing was to incline Solidarity to assume co-responsibility for the economic reforms that the Rakowski government had already implemented, at a high social cost. This was to take place through a joint election platform and the presence of candidates from the Civic Committee on a joint election list, where they were to be guaranteed approximately one-third of the seats. There was also talk of giving Solidarity several ministerial positions after the election.

While Solidarity's representation was homogenous, the opposite camp was not; it was comprised instead of several segments. In addition to representatives from the communist party leadership, there were also members of satellite parties who for some time had been showing signs that they were moving toward autonomy, as well pro-government trade unions. Their leader, Alfred Miodowicz, had his own political ambitions—and issues with Wałęsa. Jaruzelski and Rakowski did not take part in the talks, which demonstrated their reservations toward the Round Table, and also allowed them to disavow the entire operation if it failed to go according to plan. As a result, General Kiszczak became the single most important person—in short, policeman Number One. Of course, Jaruzelski did not entirely lose his influence on the negotiations, but his absence did complicate matters to the extent that Kiszczak had to consult with him quite frequently by phone about specific problems that arose during the discussion. Other than General Kiszczak, the government camp's most important participants were Politburo members Józef Czyrek, Stanisław Ciosek, Professor Janusz Reykowski, and the young politician Aleksander Kwaśniewski. In addition to Wałęsa, who attended only the most important meetings, Solidarity's main negotiators were Bronisław Geremek and Tadeusz Mazowiecki, along with experienced opposition leaders Adam Michnik and Jacek Kuroń. Solidarity was also represented by several young strike leaders from 1988 and heroes of the underground, whose role was more decorative. Especially significant for both sides was the presence of Church representatives at the Round Table, something that was very important for both sides, as well as for Polish society.

Moscow and Washington watched what was happening in Poland carefully, and with goodwill, but they were cautious in their comments. President George Bush, whose presidency was just beginning at that time, spoke out publicly about the Polish situation only on April 17, 1989, after the Round Table talks had concluded—as if he were attempting to avoid accusations that the United States was trying to exert pressure on the Poles. This restraint stemmed from the fact that, for Bush, the main "aim was becoming the stabilization of the Gorbachev government,"[33] which could be damaged by uncontrolled events in Poland. Thus, Americans avoided anything that could lead to Solidarity's radicalization. They did not, however, conceal their support for Wałęsa and his stance of compromise, a sentiment ambassador John Davies expressed on numerous occasions.[34]

The Soviets, in contrast, had been sending signals as early as the summer of 1988 that they were not excluding the possibility of Poland's acquiring a status similar to that of Finland—i.e., a neighboring state that had freedom in internal matters but respected Moscow's position in the military and international spheres.[35] Gorbachev believed that his Polish comrades would manage to overcome the crisis. The Polish ambassador in Moscow reported to Warsaw that in Gorbachev's circle the opinion prevailed that the existence of an opposition should be recognized as "an actual fact," that dialogue with it was "rational," and even that "Polish experiences might turn out to be useful in the future."[36] Extensive analyses of the situation in East Central Europe that had been prepared for Gorbachev in February were basically unanimous in their recognition of the fact that "the process of rejecting existing political institutions and ideological values . . . is already underway" in Poland and Hungary.[37] It was believed that this process might well have a negative impact on the Soviets' position in this part of Europe, but the possibility of military intervention was ruled out. Poles thus had essentially both American support and Soviet permission for their political experiment—i.e., they had a free hand. If anything was hampering them, it was their own views.

The talks began on February 5, 1989, in a seventeenth-century palace in downtown Warsaw. Nearly sixty participants sat around a table built especially for this occasion by a leading furniture manufacturer. The inauguration of the talks was broadcast live on television, but the actual negotiations, in which a total of about 450 participants took part, began a day later in various halls and rooms in the palace. Because they lasted so long, all the way until April 5, they became a real marathon, and—like all marathons—a media event. Separate working groups and subgroups, which had equal participants from both sides, met frequently—some of them a dozen or more times. Press conferences were held daily, at which accounts of the disputes were presented. Occasionally, however, the groups' members would prove unable to overcome their differences of opinion. In these situations, confidential meetings between the main negotiators were organized, but without the spotlights and journalists. Some of these meetings took place in Magdalenka, near Warsaw, which guaranteed a higher degree of discretion but also prompted suspicions that secret agreements were being made there, even though a representative of the Episcopate always attended the meetings.

The talks covered a huge array of problems: from local ones, such as the elimination of the four-shift system at the mines, to those affecting everyone, such as linking wage hikes to inflation, and questions related to the political system itself. Changes to state structures were one of the key topics of discussion: the creation of a second house of parliament and office of president, and also an election law. Jon Elster is correct in comparing the functions of Poland's Round Table (and others that took place later in other countries emerging from communism) to the German "pre-parliament" (*Vorparlament*) during the Spring of Nations in 1848, which prepared the principles by which the Constitutional Assembly would be called.[38]

As Solidarity's point of departure, it rejected a joint election platform and coalition after the election. The opposition's negotiators did not even try to propose holding a completely democratic election, since it was obvious that the ruling camp would not agree to it. Thus, they agreed that only communist party candidates (or those of its satellite parties) would run for 65 percent of the seats in the Sejm. For the other 35 percent of the seats, anyone could run. This way, the opposition got a chance—but not a guarantee—that a significant number of its candidates would be able to make it into parliament, while the ruling camp still secured a majority for itself. Jaruzelski's group decided that this provision was insufficient, which is why the government camp proposed establishing an office of president, with broad powers.

Fearing the results of a popular vote, they decided against a presidential system along the lines of the American model, or even the French one. Instead, the president was to be elected by the parliament, in which the communists had a guaranteed majority. The president's powers included dissolving parliament if legislation was passed that "threaten[ed] the President's constitutional prerogatives,"[39] which meant firm control over the power to pass legislation. He was also given the right to impose martial law and states of emergency, and would be the commander in chief of the armed services, and "stand guard over the state's sovereignty and security . . . [and] respect political and military alliances";[40] thus he also controlled executive power. No one said it outright, but it was clear to everyone that Jaruzelski was the only candidate for this position, especially since he did not hide his ambitions to wield personal power.

Equipping the office of president with such powerful tools dismayed Solidarity negotiators. This sentiment was compounded by suspicions that the architect and administrator of martial law would assume this post. As a result, in order to get Solidarity to agree, the government proposed that the 65:35 proportion of seats would not apply to the Senate election, which would be completely democratic. The opposition accepted this condition—for it, the principle of democratic elections itself was most important, even if the Senate was not very powerful.

The "political contract" was agreed upon after arduous—and at times even stormy—negotiations. This was indisputably the Round Table's most important achievement. It was all the more significant because none of the other discussions had resulted in decisions that would have had a far-reaching impact. For example, no plan for a territorial self-government reform was developed, nor was anything changed in the field of justice, and the communist party continued to wield its influence on the economy and nominations in the administration (what was known as the *nomenklatura* system). The party's monopoly in the state mass media was not undermined, nor was censorship lifted. The government camp did not agree to a general rehabilitation of those who were persecuted after the imposition of martial law. The question of the security apparatus was not addressed, despite the fact that in January "unknown perpetrators" had murdered two priests who had been cooperating with Solidarity. Military-related issues were not dealt with at all. Nothing was decided regarding privatization and the role of the state sector in the economy, nor was reprivatization mentioned.

The communist party could thus feel satisfied: while the Round Table did propose a profound reform of the system, it did not advocate changing the system entirely. Thus, both sides emerged from the talks without a sense of defeat. On the contrary, within Solidarity there was a belief that, thanks to the political reforms and newly guaranteed freedom of association, the opposition had now gained real instruments that would put checks on the government and create a bridgehead leading to a completely democratic system. For both the government camp and the opposition, and for Poles as a nation, the Kremlin's stance was of crucial importance. Gorbachev, in a conversation with Jaruzelski on April 28, was still favorably inclined to the "Polish experiment," and even said that "hampering the changes is not an option we are even considering."[41] Thus, nothing stood in the way of carrying out the "contract elections," as they were called.

The public turned out to be less interested in the talks than expected—both because they lasted so long, and because of the broad range of topics under negotiation. Thousands of people gathered in front of the Namiestnikowski Palace on the day the talks began, but only "a small group of curious onlookers" was there when the final meeting took place.[42] No rallies, manifestations, or other mass events accompanied the talks, like the strikes that had been held in support of Solidarity's demands. If one does not count several events organized by radical youth groups, one could even say that the negotiations took place in absolute societal silence. Although there was a general sense that the actual talks were indeed important, it was apparent that there was also skepticism about their outcome: in surveys, as many as 64 percent of respondents were not sure whether the agreement concluded would solve the country's most important problems, and a similar proportion believed that average citizens would not have any influence on what happened in Poland anyway.[43] Almost 60 percent believed that the opposition had stronger support in society than the government; just 2.5 percent of those surveyed claimed the opposite. It was thus becoming clear that the elections would be a crucial test—both of the agreement concluded at the Round Table, and of society's true mood.

Amendments to the constitution that reflected the compromise that had been reached were passed with lightning speed, and the election was set for June 4, with a second round to be held on June 18. There was not much time, which suited the government camp just fine: after all, it had at its disposal all the mass media (television, radio, dailies with large print runs), office space all over the country, tens of thousands of paid party functionaries, the state administration on regional and national levels, and the military and security apparatus. Meanwhile, the Civic Committee, which took upon itself the burden of the campaign, was just getting underway: its regional organizations were just being formed; it didn't have rooms, phones, or photocopiers; and its media presence was limited to the half-hour slots on television and radio, and to its allotment of paper—enough to print one daily newspaper (*Gazeta Wyborcza*), which began publication only on May 8, and one weekly, whose first issue came out on the eve of the election.

Keeping in mind the main actors' material potential, it seemed that the Solidarity camp would be doomed to defeat. In history, however, as we know, the "spirit" also plays a role—emotions, determination, and the sense of a mission. And the "spirit" in this case was on the side of Solidarity: the mobilization leading up to the election was reminiscent of the atmosphere during the first weeks of the union's existence in 1980. Thousands of volunteers of all ages and social groups reported to the committees, and from one day to the next election offices sprang up, flyers and posters were printed (often shoddily), signatures for candidate lists were collected on the streets and in front of churches, and hundreds of meetings and rallies took place. From their pulpits, many priests encouraged people to support Solidarity. While it is true that some non-Solidarity opposition groups submitted their candidates (as did the anti-Wałęsa Working Group), none of these activities had a Poland-wide character and they disappeared in the mass support for the civic committees. Each committee candidate received as his "dowry" a poster on which he was shown with the Nobel Prize laureate, although Wałęsa himself was not standing in the election (just like Jaruzelski and Rakowski). This is how "Wałęsa's team" was created. To avoid internal rivalries, only one person ran for each seat.

The election took on the character of a plebiscite: on one side, Solidarity; on the other, the "reds." Jaruzelski's team realized quite late that danger was looming, but proved unable to control its own ranks, where chaos was beginning to set in. For example, for each seat there were several candidates, even as many as a dozen or more, who were more often competing with each other than with the Solidarity candidates. Despite the cautionary survey results, the communist party leadership believed that the ruling coalition would manage to win a large proportion of the sizeable undecided electorate (approximately 30 percent of the voters), and that Solidarity would, in the best-case scenario, receive half the seats for which its candidates were running.

The first round of the election took place without any excesses, although some of the radical opposition groups had called for a boycott. During May, several violent clashes had taken place between youth groups and the militia, which heated things up. The results surprised—and even shocked—people: out of the 161 seats in the Sejm, which was open to all candidates, the Civic Committee won 160, as well as 92 of the 100 Senate seats. In the second round of the election, these "shortcomings" were compensated for—another seat was won in the Sejm and another seven in the Senate. A measure of the government camp's defeat was the fact that only three candidates from its list to the Sejm obtained at least 50 percent of the votes in the first round, and the rest (261 people) had to stand in the second round as well. In addition, only two people made it from the national list, which had 35 leading candidates from the ruling camp.[44]

The voters' verdict suggested that "further perfecting" of socialism was not so much an option as was changing to another system—the form of which, however, had not been discussed at all at the Round Table. *Vox populi, vox dei* ("The voice of the people is the voice of God")—but neither the "people" nor "God" knew what their goal should be, except that Poland should be democratic, independent, and rich. Society was essentially disoriented. After the elections, over 75 percent of those surveyed believed that a coalition government including Solidarity should be formed. Just under 9 percent supported the creation of a government by the opposition alone, and even fewer (3 percent) believed those who had been in power up to then should remain.[45] The low voter turnout was striking (just 62 percent of those entitled to vote participated), as was the significant number of people who answered "no opinion" or "difficult to say" in various surveys.

There was a clear belief that the country was entering a transition period and that, while the decisions made at the Round Table may have represented a point of departure, Poles, like the negotiating elite, did not have a clear picture of what the goal was actually supposed to be. Many probably felt confused because the utopian ideological project sketched out in 1981 during the emotional period following the August strikes collapsed when confronted with the brutality of martial law. That utopia, which is sometimes described as the "ethos of Solidarity," was based on values such as the dignity of a person as an individual and producer (dignity of work), communitarian coauthorship (including workers' self-government), egalitarianism, consensus, mutual aid, national tradition (the Romantic version), and Christianity as an important force for social cohesion. In 1989, this vision collided with the banality of political calculations that prevailed during the Round Table negotiations. As a result of these two opposing events—martial law and the Round Table—not much was left of the Solidarity revolution, which was to have been a moral and existential revolution, one that would have rested on the "power of the powerless," to use Václav Havel's famous expression.

It should thus not be surprising that, despite Solidarity's spectacular triumph, there were no displays of mass enthusiasm, no parades or mass rallies with thousands of people. Wałęsa and most of the Civic Committee activists instead strove to calm popular emotions rather than to stir them up, although the rapidly growing inflation could have fueled an attack on the ruling camp. In keeping with the logic of the Round Table, the main instrument was not direct social pressure, but a political game.

One of the first moves was an article by Adam Michnik with the unequivocal title "Your President, Our Prime Minister," published on July 3 in *Gazeta Wyborcza*. Gorbachev's advisor commented on it publicly, saying, "We will maintain relations with any government that will be elected in Poland."[46] The second move was a decision to enable the election of Jaruzelski as president, which was not guaranteed by the joint composition of the two houses of parliament, in which the opposition had 48 percent of the seats. During the voting, which took place on July 19, Jaruzelski was elected, thanks to the fact that several Solidarity MPs abstained. The results were humiliating for him: he got 270 votes, which was just one over the required minimum. Jaruzelski nevertheless put a good face on it, and after stepping down from his post as first secretary, a position which Rakowski assumed, he entrusted General Kiszczak with the task of forming a new government. This gesture bordered on provocation. After the recent period of martial law, having two generals in the country's highest posts was too much even for the most moderate oppositionists.

Wałęsa thus stepped into action. On August 7, he announced that the only solution would be a coalition of Solidarity and parties that had, until then, been satellites of the communist party. This time, Jaruzelski capitulated, although he managed to convince Wałęsa to agree to a coalition government with communist participation. Rakowski, as the new formal head of the Polish communist party, tried to protest, but was ignored by Jaruzelski and also by Gorbachev, who refused to meet with him personally and spoke with him only by telephone. The Romanian dictator Ceaușescu demanded that the Warsaw Pact intervene in Poland, but Moscow silently ignored his idea. As a result, on August 19, Jaruzelski entrusted one of the Round Table's main architects, Tadeusz Mazowiecki, with the task of forming a government.

Although the delicate negotiations on the government's composition still lay ahead, the weight of the government, and also responsibility for the country, had already shifted to Solidarity. In Mazowiecki's government, which the Sejm approved on September 12 with no opposing votes, Solidarity had twelve ministers in addition to the post of prime minister, the communist party had four, the other coalition members seven, and one was independent. Despite the fact that they held the post of president and the Ministries of Internal Affairs and National Defense, the communists found themselves very much on the defense, and did not realistically have much chance now to interrupt the process of change and regain their monopoly of power. In this way, Solidarity gained the primary tools needed to implement change, and soon, without deviating from the path of evolution and gradual change, it demonstrated that it was interested simply in getting rid of real socialism, not "repairing" it. To what extent the implementation of an increasingly mythical Solidarity "utopia" actually gave rise to Poland's political transformation is, however, another subject. Soon, it became apparent that real changes were moving Poland in the direction of the free market and privatization—far from the vision of a Self-Governing Republic that had reigned in the autumn of 1981.

Chapter Twenty

Escape from the Soviet Bloc
and the Fall of the Empire

While Poland may have indeed been the "weakest link" among communist states, this does not mean that the others were necessarily strong and intact. During the 1970s, the states founded on Marxist ideology were actually entering a deep economic crisis, which in turn prompted social and political crises. This also affected the Soviet Union itself, where the standard of living left much to be desired. Despite several decades of a nearly unblemished record of success, discontent was mounting there, too. The accomplishments of the engineers who designed the long-range missiles, nuclear weapons, and space vehicles contrasted sharply with the quality and quantity of consumer goods in Soviet homes. The Soviet Union's client states, comprised of poor Central American, African, and Asian countries, ranging from Fidel Castro's Cuba to Angola, Ethiopia, Mozambique, Laos, and Vietnam, increased the USSR's prestige, guaranteeing it several military bases as well as votes in the United Nations. This all helped the Soviet Union to maintain its status as a superpower. The costs of this expansion, however, seriously burdened its budget. In late 1979, Moscow involved itself militarily in Afghanistan, which prompted the United States to impose harsh economic sanctions. These affected, for example, the grain imports on which the Soviet economy was very dependent.[1] From the start, that war had high costs and was for many years a serious additional strain on the increasingly wobbly economy.

President Reagan did not limit himself, however, to his inspired anti-Soviet rhetoric, symbolized by his famous expression "the Evil Empire." In March 1983, he announced that work would begin on "Star Wars"—i.e., the Strategic Defense Initiative (SDI). This was to some extent a bluff, but the Pentagon's budget did double in several years,[2] which meant that a new phase was beginning in the arms race, one for which the Soviet economy was unprepared. In addition, the prices of crude oil had begun to fall on the world market, and this was the main source of hard currency required for Soviet industry, as well as for supplying the cities with bread. If this weren't enough, in 1982–85, Moscow experienced a "geriatric crisis": three of the party's general secretaries died while in office (Leonid Brezhnev, Iurii Andropov, and Konstantin Chernenko), as well as two other extremely important Politburo members (Mikhail Suslov and Dmitrii Ustinov). Uncertainty and rivalry plagued the highest echelons of power, which undoubtedly impeded the ruling of a superpower that was experiencing serious problems.

"Everything is rotten. Changes are necessary"—these were Eduard Shevardnadze's words in December 1984, when he was first secretary of the Georgian Communist Party and a member of the Soviet party's Politburo.[3] He was talking with Mikhail Gorbachev, who had joined that Soviet "super-government" along with Shevardnadze in 1978. Several months after their conversation, in March 1985, Gorbachev was elected general secretary, thanks to his organizational experience, his reputation as someone who was pro-reform, and also his age. He was just 54 years old, and alongside the "old men" who were dying off en masse, he seemed like a young, dynamic politician, who at the same time had already held high positions. Gorbachev rejuvenated the highest echelons of power, and made Shevardnadze one of his closest associates, entrusting him with the post of minister of foreign affairs, key to the general secretary's policies. He saw the relaxation of tensions between the Soviet Union and the United States as crucial to being able to resolve the situation, which was critical. The political project that Gorbachev was proposing, however, did not stem from a well-thought-out plan for revamping the communist economy, which was under the nearly complete control of the state, extremely bureaucratized and suffering from a lack of innovation. It was essentially based on intensifying investments in the machine industry (in effect the arms industry), and was somewhat reminiscent of the famous Stalinist-era "accelerated industrialization" campaign, or the Khrushchev-era "overtaking of America." Even the slogans were the same: "acceleration" (*uskorenie*) and "reconstruction" (*perestroika*). As a result, this maneuver was not a "cold, calculated plan, but rather a desperate leap into the unknown."[4]

A fundamental element of reform was that enterprises were granted their independence, which meant they could then begin acting in their own interest. This, however, "shattered the possibility of making a structural move on behalf of machine industry"[5]—i.e, attaining the main goal. Out of concern for the health of the population and work discipline, restrictions in the sale of alcohol were introduced; considering the size of the market for "intoxicating beverages," this meant a drastic fall in the income to state coffers. As a result, there was a shortage of funds for planned investments. Over the course of one year, the budget deficit increased three-fold. Western debt grew. In other words, the economy was beginning to break down rather than speed up. As a result, inflation grew, as did the "gray zone" and "black market," the disparity in salaries, speculation, and corruption. The mechanisms that had been controlling the economy up until that time had ceased to function, but no new ones took their place.

At a time when the economy was becoming destabilized and having a negative impact on the social mood, Gorbachev and his circle addressed a new challenge: liberalizing and democratizing the political system. The dissident movement had existed in the Soviet Union for a long time, with world-famous leaders such as Andrei Sakharov, Vladimir Bukovskii, and Aleksandr Solzhenitsyn. Unlike the Polish situation, however, the Soviet leadership was not being pressured by an organized opposition—it was not very large, and strictly monitored by the secret police. The political reforms were thus a "top-down" initiative, the work of a leader who relied on his closest associates and intellectuals from academic institutions. These changes are known as *glasnost'* (openness).

The disaster at the Chernobyl nuclear power station in Ukraine the night of April 25–26, 1986, provided *glasnost'* with momentum. At first, the government blocked information about the accident, but because of its magnitude (approximately a hundred thousand people were evacuated) concealing the facts proved impossible. Three weeks after the catastrophe, on May 14, Gorbachev made a statement on television in which he made society aware of the scope of this tragedy. To be sure, this was "directed openness," in Rudolf Pikhoia's words,[6] but its effects were spreading and the principles of *glasnost'* were being applied in new areas. On the surface, the phenomenon of "revisiting the past"—more specifically, Stalinist-era crimes—did not harm Gorbachev to any great extent. At first, there were novels (the most famous of these was Anatolii Rybakov's *Children of the Arbat*), stories, excerpts from memoirs, interviews, historical writings, and films. Then documents were published and historians took the floor. Newspapers and magazines were filled with hundreds of texts about the Great Purge of 1936–38, camps, deportations, and collectivization. The party, in short, had lost its control over the past. The problem was also how to keep a grip on current events: on May 28, 1987, a young German amateur pilot, unbothered by the anti-aircraft defenses, landed a small plane a few hundred meters from the Kremlin. The minister of defense was dismissed, as were over one hundred officers. The party leadership ordered the democratization of the party's internal procedures, as well as the rules governing local elections, which caused a real revolution in terms of who was involved, and also prompted innumerable conflicts that weakened the party and state administration.

Throughout Russia, various organizations were founded by ecologists, people protecting historical sites, or those calling for the rehabilitation and commemoration of Stalinist-era victims. Some organized demonstrations without obtaining the necessary permission. Every couple of days, there were marches through Moscow streets. Discussion clubs were set up, where everything was fair play—from the civil war of 1918–21, to shortages in the shops—but most discussions addressed the question of communism and what it is. In bazaars and improvised markets, one could buy not only meat, which was unavailable in stores, but also illegally reproduced cassettes with rebellious and ideologically "improper" songs. Discotheques were springing up that played "bourgeois music" (i.e., rock in its various forms), not Russian folk songs. Although censorship tried to stop the flood of anti-Stalinist publications, the security apparatus doggedly kept dissidents under surveillance. Both of these institutions were also subject to a particular kind of entropy, arising from the divisions and conflicts at the highest levels of power.

Despite having numerous opponents within the party elite, Gorbachev and his team strove steadfastly to implement further changes in the system, but did not intend to employ Western models. It was their own idea, for example, to create a Congress of People's Representatives via popular vote, based on a complicated electoral law. Over twenty-two hundred delegates were to take part. Its powers were vague: in part, it was to be an assembly of electors, in part a legislative body. Most importantly, however, the elections, which ultimately took place in March 1989, became a chance for various independent political, regional, professional, and ethnic groups to organize themselves outside communist party structures. The election campaign, which lasted many months, was very lively and brought new elements into public life. For people unaccustomed to freedom of speech, open differences of opinion regarding ideology or politics, and the public expression of conflicts of interest, the new situation might well have seemed like chaos and anarchy. So this important step toward civic freedoms and democracy at the same time created a sense of increasing destabilization at all levels of government. Most of the millions of communist party members were undoubtedly just as disoriented as the rest of society.

Gorbachev's specialty was foreign policy, the main principles of which he laid out in his 1987 book *Perestroika: New Thinking for Our Country and for the Entire World*. As Vlad Zubok wrote somewhat maliciously, Gorbachev presented a "foggy, messianic formula for the unification of the world, drawing on the ideals of a democratized communism."[7] Gorbachev had both an idealistic conviction about the need to abandon the use of force in international relations, as well as a vision of the convergence of a reformed Soviet communism and West European socialism, and the building of a "common European home." In the Soviet context, this really was "new thinking," since it broke with the Stalinist dogma about the inseparability of ideological interests (world revolution) and those of the state (imperial). Gorbachev no longer dreamed of global victory for the proletariat, or of further expansion for the Soviet Union. This did not mean abandoning the role of superpower, but there was an assumption that rivalry would cease, accompanied by disarmament and cooperation.

The Soviet Union's main claim to its international position was to be its initiation, thanks to *perestroika*, of the construction of a new, peaceful world order. It was clear that political practice diverged from these idealistic aims, and Gorbachev drove a hard bargain with Reagan. Nevertheless, it was important for Moscow that there be an end to the arms race and debt, so it made concessions. Most important of these were its withdrawal from Afghanistan, which eventually took place in February 1989, and the declaration presented in December 1988 at a session of the United Nations to the effect that the Soviet Union would cease putting military pressure on the satellite states and limit the number of Soviet troops stationed in them. For Soviet citizens, most important was, of course, to end the war in Afghanistan, in which about fifteen thousand Soviet soldiers had died and tens of thousands more had been injured, and which had caused the moral devastation of much of the generation that had been subject to the draft. These "Afghans" became a serious social problem for many years afterward, much as America's Vietnam veterans. When the last armored units returned to the Soviet Union, it meant that the war had been lost—something that had not happened in Soviet history since 1920, when the Red Army was expelled from Poland. For most, this brought a shocking sense of defeat.

From this great cauldron of *perestroika* and *glasnost'*, of hope engendered by the new freedoms, and of fear of growing chaos, a danger emerged that only very few Sovietologists had predicted. In May 1986, after Russian thugs attacked local students in Yakutsk, a demonstration took place featuring the slogan "Yakutia for the Yakuts":[8] the national liberation movements that Moscow had supported so willingly and persistently in Africa and Asia had made it all the way to Siberia—but not only there. In December 1986, serious ethnic unrest took place in Alma Ata, the capital of Kazakhstan, in which several people died. In the summer of 1987, the Crimean Tatars organized protests, and conflicts began between Armenia and Azerbaijan, which resulted in a pogrom of Armenians in Sumgait. In February 1988, thirty-two people died there. Over the course of 1988, "national fronts" began to emerge in the Baltic republics—Estonia, Latvia, and Lithuania—and there was loud talk of the "Soviet occupation." This was prompted to a large extent by the regional elections and preparations for the election of delegates to the Congress of People's Representatives. In April 1989, a demonstration in Tbilisi was brutally suppressed by special militia units; nineteen people were killed. On August 23, 1989, on the fiftieth anniversary of the signing of the Ribbentrop-Molotov treaty, in which the Third Reich agreed to the Soviet annexation of the Baltic states, several million people created a "living chain" between the Lithuanian and Estonian capitals, Vilnius and Tallinn. The multiethnic Moloch would crumble along ethnic lines. In short, even for the average observer, the Soviet superpower appeared to be a seriously destabilized state.

Perestroika and *glasnost'*—everything that was happening in the Soviet Union—affected the situation not only in Poland, but also in other East Central European countries. Each of them had their own internal problems, which were mainly, but not only, economic and social: Hungary felt the burden of Western debts, Romania had a poor population, Czechoslovakia and the GDR suffered a fall in production, Bulgaria and Romania were troubled by ethnic conflicts. Almost all had a "geriatric problem," since some of their leaders had been at the helm permanently since 1956 (Bulgaria, Hungary), 1964 (Romania), or 1969

(Czechoslovakia). With the exception of Hungary and Poland, where there were communist reformers, the other countries were dominated by orthodox Marxist-Leninists, reluctance to change, and a fear that they might potentially destabilize the situation. During the *perestroika* period, however, various opposition initiatives nevertheless existed everywhere.

In Bulgaria, a conflict with the Turkish minority had been smoldering since 1984. In December 1986, a group of determined individuals directed a letter to the Commission on Security and Cooperation in Europe about civil freedoms, and a year later the author of that letter, Ilia Minev, founded the Independent Association for the Defense of Human Rights. From the summer of 1987, ecologists organized demonstrations, and in the autumn of 1988 the "Salvation" Christian Union was created, as well as the Perestroika Club, whose founder was Zelio Zelev. In February 1989, when the Round Table talks were getting underway in Warsaw, a trade union called "Support" (Podkrepa) was established in Sofia; its name was a reference to Solidarity. A couple of weeks later, the very active association *Ekoglasnost'* emerged; its name, like that of Zelev's club, was not coincidentally alluding to what was happening in the Soviet Union.

In Czechoslovakia, where the organized opposition (Charter 77) was under strong pressure from the security apparatus, Catholic circles became more active. In late 1987 and early 1988, tens of thousands of people signed a petition demanding freedom for the Church. In March 1988, in Bratislava, several thousand people took part in a street demonstration in support of this petition. Similar scenes took place in downtown Prague on August 21 (on the twentieth anniversary of the Warsaw Pact invasion) and on October 28 (on the sixtieth anniversary of the founding of the First Republic), and in January 1989, when people demonstrated for several days in a row at the spot where the student Jan Palach had set himself alight in protest against the regime twenty years earlier. Many participants in this demonstration (including Václav Havel) were sentenced to prison. In June 1989, Charter 77 issued an appeal titled "Several Sentences," in which it demanded that political prisoners be released and that civil freedoms be granted.

In the GDR, there were scattered, but very numerous, initiatives critical of the regime, despite the fact that society was under very strict control there. These initiatives were primarily associated with local Lutheran churches, and many pastors were directly involved. They were of a pacifist or environmentalist nature, of which the best known was the Initiative for Peace and Human Rights, founded in 1986. In May 1989, a number of demonstrations of several thousand people took place in connection with the falsification of local elections. The East German situation was distinguished by a general desire to escape to the Federal Republic of Germany. In a travesty of Alberto O. Hirschman's well-known thesis, one can say that with the choice of "protest" (voice) or "escape" (exit),[9] East Germans chose the latter, while Poles generally chose the former. It was probably simply because the Poles were surrounded by "fraternal" countries (GDR, Czechoslovakia, and the Soviet Union) and the Baltic Sea, rendering escape virtually impossible. During the summer of 1989, tension grew in the GDR. It was influenced, among other things, by Poland's example, well known thanks to Western television and radio. In early September, some loose opposition groups began to transform themselves into parties (New Forum, Democracy Now), and in Leipzig several thousand people would participate in "prayers for peace" every Monday in front of the Church of St. Nicholas.

In Romania, where Ceaușescu's regime was exceptionally ruthless, there was essentially no organized opposition, although of course the system had no shortage of secret opponents. In November 1987, a workers' strike in Brașov, related to purely economic matters, was swiftly and brutally suppressed. The few activities that small groups or individuals undertook did not have an impact on Romanian public opinion. It was only in March 1989 that the first quasi-opposition initiative appeared, started by Silviu Brucan. It was known as the "Letter of Six" and was publicized widely because it originated with people from the communist elite who had fallen out of favor with the "Conducător," as the Romanian dictator called himself.

Thus, until late in the summer of 1989, the communist parties in these four countries did not show any reformist tendencies. At the same time, however, there were mass expressions of discontent and opposition, to varying degrees, influenced by what was happening both in the Soviet Union and in Poland.

The situation in Hungary was different. There, General Secretary János Kádár had for a long time been implementing piecemeal economic reforms, albeit not very consistently. Although these measures were not very effective, they did create a convenient situation for those within the party who were in favor of far-reaching reforms (even political ones), including Imre Pozsgay and Rezső Nyers, who became Politburo members in May 1988. Kádár, already ill, was sent into retirement as the party's "honorary chairman," thereby clearing the way for reformers to try to come to an understanding with the opposition, which was taking advantage of the broader scope of freedom that existed in Hungary compared to other communist countries (besides Poland). The Hungarian opposition was now moving from intellectual dissent to a more organizational stage. In September 1987, the Hungarian Democratic Forum was founded, followed by the Union of Young Democrats in March 1988, and the Union of Free Democrats later that autumn. In effect, these groups were already political parties, although they were cautious not to use this term. The defense of Hungarians in Romania was an important motivating factor for the Hungarian opposition. In March 1988, at a demonstration marking the 140th anniversary of the Hungarian Insurrection during Spring of Nations, nearly 10,000 people came to downtown Budapest. In June, however, tens of thousands attended a demonstration organized by the Democratic Forum in support of the Hungarians in Transylvania. Some estimates have even suggested this figure was over 150,000.

Unlike Mieczysław Rakowski, who believed that the best medicine for the Polish crisis was economic reforms, the Hungarian proponents of change were more focused on political ones. In January 1989, Pozsgay undermined the regime's legitimacy by publicly stating that it was not a "reactionary counterrevolution" that had taken place in 1956, but rather a national uprising. On February 11, the Central Committee passed a resolution stating that the foundation of democracy is a multiparty system.[10] A couple of weeks later, censorship was lifted, learning Russian in schools was made no longer compulsory, and the office monitoring churches and religious organizations was liquidated. In March, over 100,000 people attended a demonstration on the occasion of the 1848 insurection. In June, over 250,000 attended the reinterment of Imre Nagy, who had been hanged in 1958 and then secretly buried (face down) by the cemetery wall. Representatives of the Polish opposition attended the funeral as well, some of whom were newly elected MPs. On June 13, after preparations by the parties and opposition that had been underway since March, talks with the government began—after news that the Polish communists had suffered an overwhelming electoral defeat. Budapest's Round Table talks were concentrated on the question of parliamentary elections, because it was believed that only a democratically elected legislature would legitimately be able to decide what shape the state should take. The negotiations dragged on for a long time, and a compromise was reached only on September 18, by which time Tadeusz Mazowiecki's government had already been formed. The Hungarian parliament, which was still the same one chosen in government-controlled elections, gave way under the pressure of the mood in society, and by October had already reinstated Hungary's old official state name and symbols. The communist party reshaped itself into a social democratic one, which to a large extent was associated with an acceptance of democratic principles.

It is difficult to point to one main cause of the phenomenon that has been called 1989's Autumn of Nations, in an allusion to the famous Spring of Nations in 1848. This "Autumn" referred to the collapse of the East Central European communist regimes, one after another. To be sure, there were internal sources of social discontent in each of these states, including outrage at the shortages in consumer goods and a sense that development was stagnating. Also significant was the news from Poland about negotiations between the government and the opposition, the results of the June elections, and the formation of the Mazowiecki government. News about the changes in Hungary, albeit less spectacular, but nonetheless unequivocal, was similarly received. The examples of Poland and Hungary proved that the Soviet Union was abandoning the use of force and its role as Big Brother. Thus, it was ceasing to be both a potential aggressor and the powerful backer of the local communist elites, and now Gorbachev even urged them to reform. Increasingly, there was a general realization that, despite its efforts to modernize, the Soviet Union—fatherland of the World Proletariat—was in deep waters, and experiencing a profound crisis.

In Poland and Hungary, everything went peacefully, despite the fact that emotions were running high. In late summer 1989, *perestroika* and the changes launched in those two countries were able to serve as a catalyst for other countries in the region. The spark was probably the opening of the border between Hungary and Austria on September 11. Many Germans from the GDR were prepared for this, because in August several hundred East German citizens had crossed to Austria during a picnic organized by Hungarian oppositionists, with the slogan "We're knocking down the Iron Curtain." Over 150,000 Germans were still in Hungary, and when the border was opened, one and all set off for Austria. Thousands of others who were in Czechoslovakia or Poland stormed the West German embassies and consulates, and then were taken to the Federal Republic of Germany in special, closed trains that West German diplomats had managed to secure. As one of these trains went through Dresden, over 5,000 people stormed the train station, trying to make it into the train, which was filled to the brim with the lucky ones. The train station sustained serious damages, police dispersed the perpetrators (1,300 people were arrested), and the government closed the border with Czechoslovakia.

On Monday, October 2, over ten thousand people gathered in front of a Leipzig church, and similar demonstrations began to be organized in other cities as well. At a celebration for the fortieth anniversary of the founding of the GDR on October 7, a crowd of many thousands of people formed in Berlin and began to shout, "Gorbi, hilf uns!" (Gorby, help us!), not far from the official parade that Gorbachev was watching together with representatives from the other "fraternal parties." East Germany was transformed into a field of permanent street demonstrations, which the police left alone, while the party leadership feverishly searched for a solution. Instead of calming the situation, the East German leader Erich Honecker's dismissal from his posts prompted further demonstrations. On November 4, about half a million people gathered on East Berlin's Alexanderplatz. Two days later, the government stepped down. At 11:30 p.m. on November 9, the commandant of one of the border posts in Berlin misinterpreted a statement by the party spokesman that had been broadcast live on television and radio, and decided that border checks should cease. Crowds began to gather and a human flood rushed into West Berlin. Chancellor Helmut Kohl interrupted his "friendly visit" to Poland for two days and went to Berlin.

The Berlin Wall ceased to exist and the vision of a united Germany, whose division had been one of the cornerstones of the Cold War, began to come true. The communist system crumbled without tanks and rockets, much less nuclear weapons. For years, Poles have been arguing for the recognition of their leading role in the fall of communism, but the fall of the Wall is still seen as the most important symbol. (This is a bit like in soccer or basketball: although players who are good at passing might be valued by the experts, the public's hero is the one who shoots a goal or makes a basket.) It was not the fact that the Poles were first, however, that was really important, but that they had set off the dominoes, which then fell one after another.

In Sofia, from October 16 to November 3, Ekoforum took place, organized by opposition members. It attracted hundreds of participants, and over five thousand people came to its closing session. At the same time, the first changes were occurring among the ruling elite, and the minister of foreign affairs publicly criticized the party leadership. That day, as Berliners were beginning to flow through the Wall, Todor Zhivkov resigned, under pressure from the other members of the Politburo. He was at that time the longest ruling communist leader. Only Fidel Castro would beat that record. The political temperature in the country was heating up. A demonstration organized on November 18 in support of the rejuvenated party leadership got out of control, and the approximately a hundred thousand people who gathered demanded genuine liberalization and democracy. Some of the parties liquidated in 1947–48 were reconstituted, and on December 7, the Union of Democratic Forces was founded, which organized numerous rallies. The party gradually retreated, for example by agreeing to strike from the constitution the passage mentioning the party's leading role in the state. On January 3, 1990, the Round Table talks began and a date was set for democratic elections.

In Czechoslovakia, the Autumn of Nations began a week after the fall of the Berlin Wall, on November 16, with a student demonstration in Bratislava. The tempo quickened a week later, when about twenty-five thousand people gathered in downtown Prague in response to an appeal by student groups. The demonstration was brutally dispersed, but this made the organizers and participants more determined than scared. The students launched a boycott of classes and called on workers to hold a general strike. On November 19 in Prague, the oppositionists from Charter 77 announced the creation of a party called Civic Forum. In Bratislava, an organization called Public Against Violence was organized simultaneously. In large cities, demonstrations took place daily. Tens of thousands of people, even as many as a hundred thousand, would take part. The general strike that took place on November 27 was very successful. The strikers' main demand was that democratic parliamentary elections be held.

Just as in other cases, the communist party leadership attempted to save itself with a personnel tactic, by changing the general secretary, but it was already too late for half-measures. The "old" parliament, which was still in office, obeyed the public mood and removed the passage in the constitution about the leading role of the party, and on November 26—ten days after the first demonstrations—talks with the opposition began. On December 10, these talks resulted in the formation of a coalition government, with a communist prime minister and the participation of both opposition parties, and the election (December 29) of Václav Havel to the office of President of the Republic. The process of transforming the political system had begun.

The last domino to fall was Romania. There, events took a different course, albeit in the same direction. The first attempt to join the revolutionary changes sweeping the Soviet bloc was made in the provincial city of Iași, on the border with Soviet Moldavia, where *perestroika* was in full swing and people were demanding full sovereignty for the republic. In late November 1989, the Romanian Popular Front was created in Iași; it had about a dozen or so members, but soon they were all in prison. The chain of events that led to the toppling of the dictatorship began on December 15 in Timișoara, on the other side of the country. The protest was supposed to be only local, since it was in defense of a pastor who was to be moved elsewhere because of his contacts with the Hungarian opposition. Early in the morning on December 15, a picket stood in front of his apartment; by the afternoon, it had turned into an illegal demonstration, in which several hundred Hungarians and Romanians took part. The next day the situation repeated itself, and when the police attempted to remove the increasingly numerous crowds that had gathered, unrest spread through the city. As a result, the army intervened, using weapons, on December 17. The clashes continued, however, and there were fatalities. On December 20, there was a local general strike and the Romanian Democratic Front was created. It demanded that Ceaușescu step down and free elections be held. The army retreated and the demonstrators took control of the city.

What happened the next day in Bucharest was key, however: Ceaușescu called for a "rally of support," which got completely out of control and turned into a demonstration against the dictator instead. The army and special police units attacked the crowd; unrest ensued, followed by the first casualties. Despite the army's brutal intervention, tens of thousands of people appeared on the square in front of the Central Committee building on December 22. Even though shots were fired, the crowd began to storm the building, and Ceaușescu lost his nerve: he escaped with his wife by a helicopter that had landed on the roof, and took refuge in an army barracks in the countryside. For many hours, Romania's main focal point became Studio Number 4 of state television, which broadcast live speeches by various speakers with a broad range of views. In Bucharest and several other cities, clashes took place between military units and special police units loyal to the dictator. The fighting subsided only on December 25, after a summary trial that ended in the shooting of the Ceaușescus. A total of about twelve hundred people were killed, including almost a thousand after Ceaușescu had already fled. Provisional institutions assumed power in the country, such as the Council of the National Salvation Front, in which members of the opposition participated, but it was the communists who determined their tone, having quickly changed their colors. Nonetheless, political pluralism and complete freedom of speech were introduced, parties that had been liquidated in 1947–48 began to reemerge, and new parties were founded. Romania set off on the road to democracy, albeit under the aegis of the post-communists.

Regardless of whether or not the political changes began as the result of negotiations carefully prepared by the ruling communists and democratic opposition, like in Poland and Hungary, or negotiations that were undertaken ad hoc, under the pressure of mass street demonstrations, the government camp made concessions everywhere—except in Romania. Governments gave in to society's mood, while at the same time striving to guarantee for themselves a direct influence on the state as it was transforming. In this earliest phase of the transformation, which lasted roughly until the first free parliamentary elections, coalition governments were by and large headed by prime ministers who had their origins in the communist party, except in Poland and Romania.

The most active agents for change in Bulgaria and Romania were people from the establishment and opposition who were invoking *perestroika*. Jaruzelski and Pozsgay also invoked Gorbachev, and it was "Gorby" whom the Berliners asked to help them. When change got underway, however, Gorbachev and *perestroika* ceased to be of use. Admittedly, formal international structures (such as the Warsaw Pact and the Council for Mutual Economic Assistance) still existed, which up until now had helped Moscow shepherd the "fraternal parties." Now, however, they had become just empty phrases. One country after another "escaped" from the Soviet bloc, which had been bombastically called the "Camp of Peace and Socialism." The old saying that, in that camp, "Poland was the jolliest barracks, and Hungary was the one with the best grub" paradoxically lost its currency: the residents of all barracks, virtually en masse, or at least in quick succession, simply escaped, taking advantage of the fact that the guards were occupied with their own affairs.

During the talks in Malta in early December, President Bush assured Gorbachev that he was "stunned by the tempo of the changes taking place in Eastern Europe," and that Washington would try not "to do [anything] that could weaken [Moscow's] position."[11] Americans did not really have any influence on the course of events, however, and they would not have been in a position to preserve the camp's unity even if they had wanted to—which, of course, they didn't. Communists remained in the ruling cliques in those "former barracks," but they were trying more to adapt to the new situation than to halt the train that was speeding off toward the station called "sovereignty and democracy."

While *perestroika*'s influence on what was happening in the camp is clear and indisputable, it is nevertheless difficult to say anything objective about the impact that the events in East Central Europe had on the Soviet Union itself, and on

Gorbachev's policies. Although Gorbachev's own statements provide no evidence, we can assume that the imposition of martial law in Poland made an impression on him, since it testified to the ideological and political helplessness of the communist party when faced with a serious crisis and a society whose aspirations had been aroused. Gorbachev had undoubtedly watched the attempts at reform in Hungary and Poland since he took office, or perhaps even earlier. While implementing *perestroika*, Soviet specialists held consultations in Budapest about the reforms there in the field of enterprise management, and in Poland about Church-state relations and the functioning of private agriculture. Gorbachev's popularity was growing in the West, where there were even signs of real "Gorbymania." Admittedly, for Gorbachev, this much was more psychologically and politically important than applause in Warsaw or Budapest—though he did not underestimate this either. It is difficult to say, however, to what extent his good relations with Kádár and Jaruzelski helped him in his own clashes with internal enemies at the Kremlin.

In early 1989, the Soviet leadership had essentially reconciled itself to the fact that in the camp there would be further changes toward democratization, liberalization, the free market, and even "Finlandization." Nevertheless, if Moscow did undertake some discreet activities in any of those states, these would have aimed at encouraging changes, not hampering them. The Soviets engaged in these kinds of activities in the GDR, Bulgaria, and Romania only after Mazowiecki was already prime minister in Poland and Hungary's communist party had collapsed. As a result, one should presume that Gorbachev's group had accepted the speed and direction of these changes. They did not appreciate, however, that the most important part of the Soviets' External Empire—acquired as the result of the Second World War—would thus be lost. Even if "friendly and neighborly" relations were maintained, without ideological unity these could not possibly be as close as they had been up to this time.

Of these losses, the most important was the fate of the GDR, since for Moscow it had been either a key staging post to the West, or the furthermost line of defense, depending on its needs. Meanwhile, Chancellor Helmut Kohl announced on November 28 the "Ten-Point Program to Overcome the Division of Germany and Europe." The question of Germany was to become the top item on the agenda of superpower relations for nearly a year. German unification in October 1990 meant that Gorbachev had lost, which had a serious negative effect on his position in the Soviet Union. The loss of the bloc inevitably influenced the mood in Soviet society, and the examples from East Central Europe had an impact on the political and national demands of the Baltic states, Ukraine, and Moldavia. Although the Soviet Union still formally existed, its disintegration began in 1989, and in 1990 one Soviet republic after another—starting with Georgia and Lithuania—announced their independence. In June, the Highest Council of the Russian

Republic also approved such a declaration. This meant it was necessary to find some completely new political solution, which in the end failed. In December 1991, the state Lenin had founded ceased to exist.

The fact that a "weak link" (i.e., Poland) existed within the system of communist states undoubtedly had a role in this course of events, although what it was precisely is difficult to define. After this link began to crack in 1980, welding it (i.e., with martial law) did not help. After 1985, when Gorbachev and Jaruzelski's reforms overlapped, the system's mechanisms relaxed. This was especially true of the communist parties themselves, which were the backbone of both regimes. It is very likely that without Solidarity's revolution, the communist system would not have imploded, or its collapse would have taken a different course—perhaps a much bloodier one.

Conclusion

The Decade of Struggle and Its Legacy

In early December 1989, one of the banners in downtown Prague read: "Poland—10 years, Hungary—10 months, GDR—10 weeks, Czechoslovakia—10 days."[1] The author of the sign probably wanted to express his satisfaction that the Czechs (and Slovaks) turned out to be quicker (and thus better) at overthrowing communism than their neighbors, whom they hadn't much liked in general anyway. Regardless of the author's intentions, these words conveyed well the chronology of events. Above all, they implicitly underlined the Poles' long-running efforts to change the status quo. In essence, it was the Poles who were the most steadfast in undermining communism, which nevertheless does not mean that others elsewhere in the bloc had consented passively to its existence. The heroic efforts undertaken by the Czechs and Slovaks in 1968, the Hungarians in 1956, and the East Germans in 1953 nevertheless turned out to be isolated events. The oppositional activities in those countries never took place on a mass scale, and did not extend beyond intellectual opposition, articulated by just a few. While potentially irritating, this kind of opposition was not actually threatening to those in power.

Poles were not only steadfast, they also proved to be the most innovative in creating the tools that could help change—or even overturn—the communist system. The widespread wave of strikes during the summer of 1980 evolved into Solidarity, a mass social movement of unprecedented dimensions. This union was a Polish "invention" in the fight against an indigenous dictatorship and the outside forces supporting it. Solidarity's creation does not seem to attest to the Polish opposition's intellectual superiority, or exceptional predispositions. Perhaps it was above all the special cultural basis that existed in Poland—one that was both Romantic and insurrectionary—and the Poles' fresh memory of its traumatic twentieth-century experiences (mentioned in chapter 1), including the dramatic war with Bolshevik Russia in 1920 and the Soviet invasion of September 1939. All this encouraged an unusually large number of people to actively question a regime that had extensive means of repression at its disposal, as well as the support of a superpower. Often, this resistance was seen as an act of patriotism. Authentic leaders emerged who were able to set difficult tasks—both for themselves and for others. Some of these charismatic individuals had institutional support, such as the head of the Catholic Church, Primate Stefan Wyszyński; some were "ordinary citizens" in the opposition, such as Jacek Kuroń and Lech Wałęsa. Without these and other leading figures, the course of events might well have been very different.

Regardless of how long it took for communism to fall in specific countries, and whether we count it in years, months, or only days, and regardless of whether it was decided by votes cast (as in Poland in 1989), mass street demonstrations (as in East Germany and Czechoslovakia), or even bloodshed (as in Romania), the thrust of the regime change was generally the same: "democratic states of law," as they were called, emerged everywhere, based on Western European models, and respecting basic civil rights. Free elections to parliament were organized, and the rights to assembly and free speech were guaranteed. In addition, their economies were transformed (at varying tempos) from centrally and state-planned ones into economies based on the free market, open to the world. In July 1991, the formal structures of the Soviet bloc (i.e., the Warsaw Pact and the Council for Mutual Economic Assistance) definitively collapsed. All post-communist states, from the Baltic to the Black Sea, swiftly reoriented their foreign policy and announced that they would like to join European and Euro-Atlantic structures. The GDR, of course, was simply incorporated into the Federal Republic of Germany. These desires were not satisfied immediately. In the end, the first of these were accepted to NATO in 1999—ten years after the fall of communism. Joining the European Union in 2004 concluded a key phase in their political transformation.[2]

The lightning-fast fall of communism, which lasted no more than two years, first in East-Central European countries and then in the Soviet Union itself, inspired the catchphrase "the end of history," coined by the American political scientist Francis Fukuyama.[3] It soon became apparent that it was actually "only" the end of the Cold War; it was a breakthrough made possible when Soviet bloc attempts to achieve the Marxist utopia had been discredited, not because the entire world was now entering an era of universal happiness and democracy.[4] In any case, from the point of view of most Europeans from the former Eastern Bloc, it was undoubtedly the end of a "bad story," and thus the start of a new one—which of course would be "good," and definitely "better."

In these countries, the general direction of change was the same, and reforms posed similar, or even identical, difficulties (particularly in the economic sphere). There were also significant differences among them, and these still exist today. Some stemmed from history of the *longue durée*, from specific traditions reaching back sometimes hundreds of years, or from more recent experiences, such as the Second World War, during which the fates of the region's countries varied greatly.

Some, like Poland and Czechoslovakia, were victims of an invasion and members of the anti-German coalition, and others, like Romania, Slovakia, and Hungary, were allies of the Third Reich. Certain differences arose owing to the fact that, in more than forty years under Moscow, some countries were of key significance to the Kremlin (such as Poland), and others occupied a more secondary place (like Bulgaria). Some were less affected by the deteriorating economic situation (such as Czechoslovakia and the GDR), while others (like Poland and Romania) found themselves on the brink of disaster. Certain variations were rooted in the fact that, after 1989, they expressed their national or state interests in different ways, in which the varying compositions of the local political elites played their roles, as well as the personal traits of their leaders (it suffices to compare presidents Wałęsa and Havel). Differences in the methods of overthrowing communism itself were also a cause. One could thus say that the experiences accumulated over a long period—like during the "Polish decade"—were more effective over the long term in shaping society's behavior and political habits than those that were concentrated in time, such as the "ten Czech days."

In any case, many manifestations of public life in Poland after 1989 were the direct result of the period leading up to the fall of communism, and therefore naturally differ from those in other post-communist countries. Solidarity was undoubtedly the most important single ingredient that emerged from the many years of struggling to change the political system. After 1989, it functioned on at least two, only partially intersecting planes: the organizational one, as a trade union that continued to exist, and a mental one, since Solidarity represented a particular idea about how the collective and nation should be organized. In this context, it was about "solidarity"—without the capital "S."

After 1989, Solidarity did not regain the impressive dimensions that it had before the imposition of martial law. The entire organizational network was re-created on the central level (National Commission) and the local one (regional commissions), and cells in workplaces (factory commissions) were reestablished. Nevertheless, only about 20–25 percent of those who had been members before December 13, 1981, reconfirmed their membership. One can see that many people's decision not to join the reestablished union was to a certain extent a rational one. When Solidarity was being created, it was treated as a force whose aim was not only to defend workers' urgent needs, but also to initiate reform and changes in the political system. Since these changes were launched as the result of the Round Table compromise and the June 1989 election, Solidarity's functions as a force for reform were at least limited, if not entirely lost. Perhaps even more numerous were those who declined to renew their union membership because they felt guilty that they had "betrayed" the union after December 13 when they left it, or by hiding as passive observers, or even joining the "pro-regime" unions, which to some extent did meet the workers' basic need for trade unions.

Conclusion 317

Thousands of underground activists quit participating in Solidarity and were instead engaged in the creation of democratic institutions after 1989, such as political parties, new state structures, territorial self-government, and the free press. Many leading activists and advisors gradually left the union, primarily as a result of sharp internal conflicts that were already becoming fully apparent by the spring of 1990. These included the "legends of the underground"—Zbigniew Bujak, Władysław Frasyniuk, Adam Michnik, and Jacek Kuroń—and even Lech Wałęsa quit after being elected as president of Poland in December 1990. There were still many who believed that Solidarity should remain an organization that combined the role of a trade union and social movement with political aims. As a result, after 1991, the union had its own candidates in the parliamentary elections. While its success was only modest, it did manage to send its own representatives to the Sejm.[5] The union's political ambitions peaked in the September 1997 parliamentary elections. It was then that Solidarity Electoral Action (Akcja Wyborcza Solidarność, AWS) was created under its aegis, uniting most of the center-right parties. It received over one-third of the votes, which allowed it to form a government.

This victory was used to implement several important reforms (territorial self-government, pension, healthcare, and education). As far as the rebuilding of the state was concerned, however, one could say that this was the swan song of a power that for many years had been pushing Poland toward independence and freedom, as well as modernity. After a four-year term, AWS's societal support completely disintegrated. This was in part the result of the confusion that arose during the simultaneous implementation of the four reforms, affecting issues that concerned millions of people every day. The collapse of support was primarily brought about by the bickering and party particularism within Solidarity's support base. As a result, in the next elections (in 2001), AWS received just 5 percent of the vote, below the 8 percent threshold for coalitions to enter parliament.

From that time, Solidarity, in keeping with the tradition of European trade union movements dating back to the late nineteenth and early twentieth centuries, simply began supporting one of the political parties, abandoning its own attempts to enter parliament. Nevertheless, while British and French trade unionists most often supported left-wing parties, Solidarity supported the right, such as the Kaczyński brothers' Law and Justice party (Prawo i Sprawiedliwość). The brothers were in fact former union activists, and Lech Kaczyński had briefly served as a union chairman. Twenty-one years after its birth, Solidarity transformed itself from a political entity into a normal trade union. Its symbolic power was still significant, stemming from its history during the strikes of 1980 and resistance after martial law was imposed. People who had left the union and joined the world of party politics began to utilize this symbolic power for the realization of their own "aims and values."[6] Solidarity's symbolic character was emphasized through the celebration of August 31—the anniversary of the signing of the Gdańsk Agreement in 1980—as a state holiday. Paradoxically, in 2005, President Aleksander Kwaśniewski took part in the twenty-fifth anniversary celebrations. Kwaśniewski, a post-communist, had been a rising star in Jaruzelski's team in 1988–89. Or perhaps this was not a paradox, but rather a sign of democratic normality?

The fate of Solidarity's 1980–81 philosophy and program was more complicated than the history of the union itself. As I wrote in chapter 19, these began undergoing a metamorphosis after the introduction of martial law, and after 1989 their proponents had to confront the realities of a state that was democratic, but founded on the free market. The project of the Self-Governing Republic, which was approved at the union's First National Congress two months before the imposition of martial law, was based on what was to a large extent the utopian idea of a deliberative democracy. In this form of democracy, not only could everyone take part in debates, but everyone would also really participate. Another component of this ideology, which was called the "ethos of Solidarity," was that of "community spirit" (*wspólnotowość*), and the word "solidarity" itself was actually treated as a synonym for concepts such as "brotherhood" and "equality." The meaning of "community spirit" was also confirmed by the popularity of the idea—which was in effect a leftist one—that the workers would exercise self-government of the factories. They were the proper stewards of the factories, which were after all "ours"—common property, belonging to society, and not to the state.

The implementation of martial law entailed both a physical attack on the trade union, and aggression in the sphere of social consciousness. The previous status quo was restored, dominated by the Machiavellian principle (or that of Carl Schmitt) that politics is power and deceit, and not public debate concluding in a compromise. The experience of martial law, which many saw as being merely a cynical swindle on the part of the government, must have inclined millions of Poles to distance themselves from politics. This can be seen as one of the main explanations for why voter turnout has been so low: about half of citizens do not vote (even in the watershed elections of June 1989 only just over 60 percent took part). In Europe, including post-communist Europe, this is virtually unheard of. Martial law shattered the space that Solidarity had created for dialogue and polemics, and this space was never restored in the form that had existed before December 13. Since economic reforms were launched, both Solidarity and the workplace ceased to serve as the main points of reference for former union members in terms of engagement in the public sphere. The projects to move Poland toward a "third way" between capitalism and communism, or for the assumption of control over the factories by the workers ("workers' privatization"), either completely failed or were marginalized. Deliberative democracy and collective life based on "a solidary community" ceased to be a factor shaping people's beliefs and activities, as did the idea that individual freedom and justice for the collective were equal in importance, and politics understood as a civic duty. They became only an echo of a wonderful and not so distant past.

If some elements of the "solidarity" ethos do persist in public life, they are more an instrument of political battle or just a rhetorical ornament than any real profession of faith, or social project. That is the case, for example, with affirmations of the idea of a "community spirit," since this term usually only refers to the national community (an ethnically based one), and the demand for justice, which is sometimes understood simply as the equitable division of resources (by the state). In this sphere, however, there is a strong sense of an antagonism between the "community" ("we") and those in "power" ("they"). Of course, this is in a sense contrary to the idealistic vision of a pluralistic community, but the antagonism had already emerged in 1980–81, and was later greatly reinforced in the wake of martial law. This feeling was undoubtedly one of the reasons that the strikes during the summer of 1980 took on such a mass character. Later, the distinction between "us" and "them" was highlighted not only in situations involving direct conflicts, but also through the day-to-day rhetoric of the battle with the party-state apparatus.

This mood persisted after the watershed year of 1989 and quickly revived in conditions of democracy, freedom, and independence. To a significant extent, it became an expression of distrust, and often outright hatred, caused by the extremely high costs of the economic reforms ("shock therapy"), requiring many groups in society to make great sacrifices in the name of the free market. In this context, among others, various conspiracy theories were circulating, from traditional ("Jewish conspiracy" and even a "Masonic" one) to modern ones. These new conspiracy theories arose from people's perception that corruption and nepotism were key in Poland's transition from communism. The fact that the end of communism in Poland had emerged from negotiations and the signing of agreements (at the Round Table) was supposed to be proof that there had been a betrayal, resulting in an agreement between "them" (the communists and that dubious conduit, the opposition), swindling "us" (the people/nation). As a result—the proponents of these theories claim—the new, independent Poland has been governed not through democratically elected representatives and intellectual elites, but rather by people with well-concealed "connections" (*układy*), led by former security and intelligence apparatus functionaries, who still make use of their former secret agents. From time to time this antagonistic division between the governing (openly and covertly) and the governed continues to be apparent, sometimes in a violent fashion.

Although various political and social groups—especially populists and xenophobes—refer to this antagonism, it is part of Solidarity's propaganda arsenal as well. The union, although it now has only about 500,000–600,000 members, still has at its disposal (within Poland) a potential for mobilization, and skillfully uses well-known icons, and most of all its own logo—that magical masterpiece of typography. Some of the techniques of mass actions have simply been carried over from 1980–81. Among these is the use of armbands and banners in national colors (white and red) during strikes and demonstrations, which is not a part of trade union traditions anywhere else. When Solidarity was being created, however, it was simultaneously both a national and union movement, and many of its supporters thought of it more as a form of uprising against the partitioning powers or occupier than as a fight for pay hikes. In this context, the national colors were completely appropriate. In countries like Poland that went from communism to a free market democracy, and in democracies in general, protesting against government actions through demonstrations, strikes, or rallies is completely natural and quite frequent. Sociological research has found, however, that these types of events are more frequent in Poland than in other post-communist countries.[7] It seems certain that this stems from the tradition of Solidarity, for which strikes and street demonstrations were the main means of expression—with the national flag and the union's name as their main symbols.

This idealized image of Solidarity proved suggestive—and in many circles durable—as a force that was both faithful to its convictions, and also able to negotiate and successfully reach a compromise, which it demonstrated definitively in 1989. It is not surprising that during the Ukrainian "Orange Revolution" in 2004, which for geographical, cultural, and political reasons was close to Poland's heart, many Polish union activists and politicians traveled to Kyiv to support the fight for democracy there. In 2013, some charismatic former Solidarity leaders also traveled to Tunis and Cairo during the "Arab Spring" to teach the local revolutionaries how to conduct a peaceful revolution, to paltry effect. All this was taking place in countries far from Poland, where Warsaw had never had any political interest. Although one might see these kinds of activities as bordering on vanity, they nevertheless were supported by the image of Solidarity that had been (and continues to be) publicized in dozens of countries around the globe. The internationally recognized figure of Lech Wałęsa also contributes to this continued awareness of Solidarity outside of Poland.

This Nobel Prize winner and former Solidarity leader, as well as former president and worker, strives, in his travels around the world, to strengthen awareness of this movement. He reminds people of its main message, while accenting the role of mutual aid and solidarity in the life of communities (including the international one). The "Polish model" has been attractive to many—from the Philippines to South Africa and Tunisia, Chile, and Brazil. There is something important (and, for some, downright fascinating) about the fact that in an authoritarian state, an atomized society succeeded in creating such a mass movement. This movement was authentically plebian and spontaneous, motivated above all by ethics, and much less by questions of social welfare and political views. Just a few months after its founding, it became the subject of drastic and long-lasting oppression at the hands of state authorities. Nevertheless, it continued to base itself on the principles of non-violence and the ethos of a solidary community. The union proved so enduring that, in the end, it had a significant impact on the fate of the world in the late twentieth century: without it, there would have been no "Annus Mirabilis 1989."[8]

Notes

Preface

1. James G. Hershberg, *James B. Conant: Harvard to Hiroshima and the Making of the Nuclear Age* (New York: Alfred A. Knopf, 1993), 484.

2. Timothy Garton Ash, *The Polish Revolution: Solidarity 1980–1981* (London: Jonathan Cape, 1983); Abraham Brumberg, ed., *Poland: Genesis of a Revolution* (New York: Random House, 1983).

3. In this book, the term "militia" refers to the police force. During communist Poland, the Polish word "militia" (civic militia) came from the Soviet Union, where a "workers' and peasants' militia" was introduced to avoid creating a "bourgeois" police; thus, the communist militia is the "bourgeois police."

4. Andrzej Paczkowski, *The Spring Will Be Ours: Poland and the Poles from Occupation to Freedom, 1939–1989*, transl. Jane Cave (University Park: Pennsylvania State University Press, 2003).

5. The stenogram was published in Polish in Nina Smolar, ed., *Wejdą nie wejdą: Polska 1980–1982: wewnętrzny kryzys, międzynarodowe uwarunkowania* (London and Warsaw: Aneks, 1999).

6. In some I appeared as a coauthor; e.g., in Andrzej Paczkowski and Malcolm Byrne, eds., *From Solidarity to Martial Law: The Polish Crisis of 1980–1981: A Documentary History* (Budapest and New York: CEU Press, 2007). This publication appeared in conjunction with the conference in Jachranka mentioned above.

7. Significant for me was the work by Helene Sjursen, *The United States, Western Europe, and the Polish Crisis: International Relations in the Second Cold War* (Houndmills: Palgrave Macmillan, 2003). The work by Douglas J. MacEachin, *U.S. Intelligence and the Confrontation in Poland, 1980–1981* (University Park: Pennsylvania State University Press, 2002), based on CIA documents, deals with the period before martial law was imposed.

8. Gregory F. Domber, *Empowering Revolution: America, Poland, and the End of the Cold War* (Chapel Hill: University of North Carolina Press, 2014). Domber's book is based on extensive research in both US and Polish archives.

9. An exception is Georges Mink, *La force ou la raison: Histoire sociale et politique de la Pologne, 1980–1989* (Paris: Éditions la Découverte, 1989).

10. Including Nicholas G. Andrews, *Poland 1980–1981: Solidarity versus the Party* (Washington, DC: National Defense University Press, 1985); J. B. de Weydenthal, et al., *The Polish Drama, 1980–1982* (Lexington, MA: Lexington Books, 1983); Martin Myant, *Poland: A Crisis for Socialism* (London: Lawrence and Wishart, 1982); Adam Bromke, *Poland: The Protracted Crisis* (Oakville: Mosaic Press, 1983); Alain Touraine, François Dubet, Michel Wieviorka, and Jan Strzelecki, *Solidarity: Analysis of a Social Movement: Poland, 1980–1981* (Cambridge: Cambridge University Press, 1983).

11. George Sanford, *Military Rule in Poland: The Rebuilding of Communist Power, 1981–1983* (New York: St. Martin's Press, 1986).

12. Some of the reports were published in English. See Andrzej Paczkowski and Andrzej Werblan, "On the Decision to Introduce Martial Law: Two Historians Report to the Commission on Constitutional Oversight of the Sejm of the Republic of Poland" (Washington, DC: Woodrow Wilson Center for International Scholars, 1997).

Chapter One

1. These were the CIA, Bureau of Intelligence and Research (INR) at the Department of State, and the Defense Intelligence Agency (DIA).

2. "Interagency Intelligence Memorandum. Prospects for Eastern Europe" (August 1995), in *The United States and the Polish Crisis, 1980–1982: Sample Documents* (Washington, DC: The National Security Archives, 1995), 1.

3. Ibid., 13.

4. Of these, six (Bulgaria, Czechoslovakia, the GDR, Poland, Romania, and Hungary) belonged to the Soviet bloc, and two (Albania, since 1968, and Yugoslavia, since 1948) were independent of Soviet control.

5. As the protests were being quelled, about 2,700 people were detained (including 360 students). Of these, 150 were charged by the public prosecutor, but fewer than 20 were sentenced (to punishments ranging from 1.5 to 3.5 years in prison). In addition, several hundred people were inducted into the army as a means of punishment, and a similar number was expelled from their post-secondary institutions. Several departments were also simply dissolved. Piotr Osęka, *Marzec '68* (Kraków: Znak, 2008), 287 and 290.

6. During the five days of clashes, two demonstrators were killed, over five hundred people were detained, and about twenty were given prison sentences of six months to three years: Antoni Dudek and Tomasz Marszałkowski, *Walki uliczne w PRL, 1956–1989* (Kraków: Wydawnictwo Geo, 1999), 79.

7. An attempt to describe this phenomenon synthetically: A. Paczkowski, *Strajki, bunty, manifestacje jako "polska droga" przez socjalizm* (Poznań: PTPN, 2003).

8. Andrzej Friszke and Marcin Zaremba, eds., *Wizyta Jana Pawła II w Polsce, 1979: Dokumenty KC PZPR i MSW* (Warsaw: Biblioteka Więzi i Instytut Studiów Politycznych PAN, 2005), 5.

9. *Trybuna Ludu*, October 18, 1978.

10. Friszke and Zaremba, *Wizyta Jana Pawła II*, 140.

11. Raport K10/160/79 (survey conducted on June 11 and 12, 1979), Ośrodek Badania Opinii Publicznej (Center for Public Opinion Research; hereafter OBOP), Warsaw.

12. About eighty thousand workers participated in the strikes that took place in more than a dozen cities on June 25, 1976, in response to the price increases on food. In several cases, the striking workers emerged from the factories and there were riots in the streets. The largest of these were in Radom, Ursus, and Płock. Although the demonstrations were subdued without the use of firearms, four people were nevertheless killed. Several thousand workers were fired, and several hundred detained. Over three hundred were subjected to punitive arrests of up to three months, and fifty were given sentences of from two to ten years in prison by the courts. For details, see Paweł Sasanka, *Czerwiec 1976: Geneza, przebieg, konsekwencje* (Warsaw: IPN, 2006), passim.

13. A detailed history of this organization may be found in an older book by Jan J. Lipski, which is still a good source of information: *KOR: A History of the Workers' Defense Committee in Poland, 1976–1981* (Berkeley: University of California Press, 1985). The newest study in Polish is the monograph by Jan Skórzyński, *Siła bezsilnych: Historia Komitetu Obrony Robotników* (Warsaw: Świat Książki, 2012).

14. "Notatka" of Department III of the Ministry of Internal Affairs (July 24, 1981), Archiwum Instytutu Pamięci Narodowej [Institute of National Remembrance Archives] (hereafter AIPN), 0296/57, vol. 2, p. 32.

15. François Fejtő, *La fin des démocraties populaires: les chemins du post-communisme* (Paris: Éditions du Seuil, 1992), 94.

16. The main force behind this innovation was Professor Zbigniew Brzeziński, who was born in Warsaw. He also became the US president's national security advisor. People joked that "Poles rule the world," since the pope, the most important advisor to the American president, as well as US Secretary of State Edmund S. Muskie and Israeli Prime Minister Menachem Begin (who had even been an officer in the Polish army) all had Polish ties.

17. Janusz Kaliński, *Gospodarka Polski w latach 1944–1989: Przemiany strukturalne* (Warsaw: PWE, 1995), 172 and 194.

18. "Referat gen. Adama Krzysztoporskiego" (September 1979), in Łukasz Kamiński and Paweł Piotrowski, eds., *Opozycja demokratyczna w Polsce w świetle akt KC PZPR (1976–1980)* (Wrocław: Wydawnictwo GAJT, 2002), 273.

19. "Referat gen. Bogusława Stachury" (January 1980), in Kamiński and Piotrowski, *Opozycja demokratyczna*, 283. Though the situation was undoubtedly easier for dissidents in Poland, Stachura's use of the word "tenderly" here was surely a bit facetious since, for example, in the course of just one week in December 1979, 187 individuals were "held for clarification," 15 were "temporarily arrested," 75 searches were carried out, about 23,000 copies of illegal publications were confiscated, as well as 6,000 flyers and an unspecified (but "significant") amount of printing equipment, including typewriters (285).

20. Among the best known are a 1964 protest letter against publishing policies and censorship, which 34 writers and scholars signed; a speech by the famous philosopher Leszek Kołakowski in which he was very critical of Gomułka's policies in 1966; protest letters in 1971 and 1972 against the decisions in political trials; and a letter from December 1974 in defense of the rights of Poles living in the Soviet Union.

21. This description was actually used in February 1988 during one of the sessions of the Soviet Politburo. See Mezhdunarodnyi Fond Sotsialno-ekonomicheskich i politicheskich Issledovanii—Gorbachev Fond, Archive, Fond no. 2, "Dnevnik Medvedeva," no pagination.

Chapter Two

1. OBOP, *Skutki ataku zimy w opinii społecznej* (Warsaw: OBOP, 1979), 14.
2. OBOP, *Komunikaty z badań, marzec 1980* (Warsaw: OBOP, 1980), 22.
3. According to research conducted by OBOP during the years 1977–79, approximately one-third of Poles listened to RFE, BBC, or the Voice of America. See Jolanta Hajdasz, *Szczekaczka czyli Rozgłośnia Polska Radia Wolna Europa* (Poznań: Media Rodzina, 2006), 256–57.
4. The opposition called for a boycott of these candidates and distributed several hundred thousand flyers (the best known was "Voter! Stay at home—Brezhnev is voting instead of you"). After the elections, it was announced that there had been major fraud, which was probably true, but no one managed to prove it. See Skórzyński, *Siła bezsilnych*, 427–29.
5. Andrzej Paczkowski, "Le centre du pouvoir pendant l'été 1980: les mechanismes de la prise de decision," *Communisme* 93/94 (2008): 85–86.
6. Skórzyński, *Siła bezsilnych*, 440–41.
7. M. Jabłonowski, W. Janowski, and W. Władyka, eds., *Narady i telekonferencje kierownictwa PZPR w latach 1980–1981* (Warsaw: Wydział Dziennikarstwa i Nauk Politycznych UW, 2004), 20 and 46.
8. Paczkowski, "Le centre du pouvoir," 93.
9. Only this last idea was partially implemented: on August 20, more than a dozen KOR activists were detained, along with two members of KPN's leadership.
10. Grzegorz Majchrzak, "Informacje sytuacyjne MSW z sierpnia 1980 roku," *Zeszyty Historyczne* 145 (2003): 143. These figures were probably low.
11. Zbigniew Włodek, ed., *PZPR a "Solidarność" 1980–1981: Dokumenty Biura Politycznego*, 2nd ed. (London: Aneks, 1992; Warsaw: IPN, 2013), 84. (Citations are to the 1992 edition.)
12. Ibid., 73.
13. Because of the special role played by the strike in Gdańsk and the MKS there, it was treated as the center of protest. The Gdańsk Agreement is generally acknowledged to be the most important, and August 31 has become the symbolic date.

14. According to some estimates, from September 1980 to December 13, 1981, approximately 1,500 news sheets and periodicals were published. See Adam Konderak, *Bibliografia prasy opozycyjnej w PRL do wprowadzenia stanu wojennego* (Lublin: UMCS, 1998), 10.

15. Krzysztof Brzechczyn, "Program i myśl polityczna NSZZ 'Solidarność,'" in *NSZZ "Solidarność," 1980–1989*, vol. 2, *Ruch społeczny*, ed. Ł. Kaminski and G. Waligóra (Warsaw: IPN, 2010), 24–25.

16. "Kierunki działania Związku w obecnej sytuacji kraju (tezy do dyskusji)," in *Sprawy gospodarcze w dokumentach pierwszej Solidarności*, vol. 1, *16 sierpnia 1980–30 czerwca 1981*, ed. Jacek Luszniewicz and Andrzej Zawistowski (Warsaw: IPN, 2008), 232–49.

17. This term was used during a discussion about the program outline of February 1981, presented above. It was popularized thanks to the book by Jadwiga Staniszkis, *Poland's Self-Limiting Revolution* (Princeton, NJ: Princeton University Press, 1984).

18. For details, see Jarosław Kuisz, *Charakter prawny porozumień sierpniowych 1980–1981* (Warsaw: Wydawnictwo Trio, 2009), 376–462.

19. *Statut. Uchwała programowa z Aneksem. Dokumenty Zjazdu* (Gdańsk: BIPS, 1981), 23–61.

20. Ibid., 25.

21. Ibid., 45.

22. Ibid., 26.

23. Ibid., 61.

24. Paweł Rojek, *Semiotyka Solidarności: Analiza dyskursów PZPR i NSZZ "Solidarność" w 1981 roku* (Kraków: Nomos, 2009), 211.

Chapter Three

1. "Report on topic for discussion with the Polish leadership," in Paczkowski and Byrne, *From Solidarity to Martial Law*, 83–86.

2. *Polacy '81: postrzeganie kryzysu i konfliktu*, ed. W. Adamski (Warsaw: IFiS PAN, 1996), 86, 92.

3. Ibid., 94.

4. A. Paczkowski, *Droga do mniejszego zła: strategia i taktyka obozu władzy, lipiec 1980–styczeń 1982* (Kraków: Wydawnictwo Literackie, 2002), 87.

5. Manfred Wilke et al., "Kierownictwo SED wobec polskiego ruchu opozycyjnego w latach 1980–1981," in *Studia i materiały* 75 (Warsaw: PISM, 1994), 47.

6. Lech Kowalski, *Komitet Obrony Kraju (MON-PZPR-MSW)* (Warsaw: Semper, 2011), 391.

7. Stanisław Kania, *Zatrzymać konfrontację* (Warsaw: BGW, 1991), 91. It is possible that the maneuvers were just a bluff to force the Poles to make a decision, but there is no decisive evidence regarding this.

8. Paczkowski, *Droga do mniejszego zła*, 145.

9. Ibid., 146.
10. Paczkowski and Byrne, *From Solidarity to Martial Law*, 187.
11. Kania, *Zatrzymać konfrontację*, 111.
12. AIPN, 1405/92, pp. 4–13.
13. *Statut*, 95.
14. Jerzy Holzer, *"Solidarność" 1980–1981: Geneza i historia* (Warsaw: Krąg, 1983), 180 (underground publication).
15. "Transcript of CPSU CC Politburo Meeting. September 10, 1981," in Paczkowski and Byrne, *From Solidarity to Martial Law*, 348.
16. Kania, *Zatrzymać konfrontację*, 222.
17. "Protocol No. 002/81 of Meeting of the Homeland Defense Committee. September 13, 1981," in Paczkowski and Byrne, *From Solidarity to Martial Law*, 354–55.
18. "Position taken by the Presidium of the National Commission and Leaders of the Regions. December 3, 1981," in Paczkowski and Byrne, *From Solidarity to Martial Law*, 418.
19. For a brief discussion of the bill, see Paczkowski and Byrne, *From Solidarity to Martial Law*, 405–6.
20. "Radom—3 grudnia 1981," *Krytyka* 21 (1986): 68.
21. Mieczysław F. Rakowski, *Dzienniki polityczne 1981–1983* (Warsaw, Iskry, 2004), 8:126.
22. Paczkowski and Byrne, *From Solidarity to Martial Law*, 443; see 425–45 for entire protocol.
23. Ibid., 444.

Chapter Four

1. The cryptonyms "G" and "W" are used in many Polish documents; Christopher Andrew uses the cryptonym "Operation 'X.'" See Christopher Andrew and Vasili Mitrokhin, *The Mitrokhin Archive: The KGB in Europe and the West* (Warsaw: Muza SA, 2001), 922ff.
2. Apple Film Production Archives, Warsaw, Viktor I. Anoshkin, "Zeszyt roboczy" (translated from Russian), notebook no. 5, p. 3. (General Anoshkin was the personal secretary of Marshal Kulikov, and took notes about meetings and activities of his boss for archival purposes. They are of an entirely informal nature, and contain numerous personal assessments and comments by their author.)
3. Andrzej Krawczyk et al., eds., *Dokumenty: Teczka Suszowa* (Warsaw: Interpress, 1993), 69.
4. Rakowski, *Dzienniki polityczne*, 8:132.
5. Anoshkin, "Zeszyt roboczy," notebook no. 5, p. 3.
6. Ibid., 10–23.
7. Wojciech Jaruzelski, *Stan wojenny: Dlaczego* . . . (Warsaw: BGW, 1992), 390–91.

8. That same day in another conversation, Jaruzelski was even supposed to have expressed the fear that Glemp could become a "second Khomeini" (Andrew and Mitrokhin, *Mitrokhin Archive*, 921).

9. Peter Raina, ed., *Jan Paweł II, Prymas i Episkopat Polski o stanie wojennym* (Paris and London: Oficyna Poetów i Malarzy, 1982), 38.

10. Ibid., 39.

11. Jaruzelski, *Stan wojenny*, 391.

12. Ibid., 394.

13. Andrew and Mitrokhin, *Mitrokhin Archive*, 922.

14. Paczkowski and Byrne, *From Solidarity to Martial Law*, 448. The entire protocol is in that same book, pp. 446–53.

15. Ibid., 455.

16. Ibid., 38.

17. AIPN, 1405/99, p. 190.

18. AIPN, 1405/96, p. 244.

19. AIPN, 1405/311, p. 1.

20. AIPN, 1405/96, p. 4.

21. AIPN, 1405/103, p. 39.

22. Andrzej Golimont, *Generałowie Bezpieki* (Warsaw: BGW, 1992), 12.

23. *Jajakobyły: Spowiedź życia Jerzego Urbana*, comp. Przemysław Ćwikliński and Piotr Gadzinowski (Warsaw: BGW, 1992), 78.

24. Ibid.

25. Gabriel Meretik, *Noc generała* (Warsaw: Alfa, 1989), 30–31.

26. Ibid., 31.

27. "Tezy informacji zastępcy szefa Sztabu Generalnego do spraw operacyjnych" (November 18, 1981), AIPN, 1405/108, p. 118. (Entire document on pp. 114–19.)

28. Janina Jankowska, *Rozmowy niedokończone: Rozmowy z twórcami "Solidarności" 1980–1981* (Warsaw: Biblioteka Więzi, 2003), 465.

29. Ibid., 253–54.

30. Ibid., 295.

31. NSZZ "Solidarność," *Komisja Krajowa NSZZ "Solidarność": Posiedzenie w dniach 11–12 grudnia 1981* (Warsaw: Archiwum Solidarności, 2003), 256.

32. Maciej Łopiński, Marcin Moskit [Zbigniew Gach], and Mariusz Wilk, *Konspira: Rzecz o podziemnej Solidarności* (Paris: Editions Spotkania, 1984), 17. (Later published as *Konspira: Solidarity Underground* [Berkeley: University of California Press, 1990].)

33. Dorn related the results of research that was carried out after December 3, i.e., very recent, during a meeting of the National Commission. See NSZZ "Solidarność," *Komisja Krajowa NSZZ*, 152–56.

34. Jerzy J. Wiatr, *Życie w ciekawych czasach* (Warsaw: Europejska Wyższa Szkoła Prawa i Administracji, 2008), 126.

35. Mieczysław Rakowski commented on the article when it appeared, saying that this variant "is not possible to carry out." "It will be necessary to wait," he added, "for the Brezhnev generation to die out." See Rakowski, *Dzienniki polityczne*, 8:131.

36. *Tygodnik Solidarność* 37, December 11, 1981.
37. Ibid.
38. Meretik, *Noc generała*, 6.
39. As quoted by Andrzej Friszke, "Porozumienie – mimo wszystko: Prymasowska Rada Społeczna w stanie wojennym," *Więź*, 11 (2004): 84.
40. NSZZ "Solidarność," *Komisja Krajowa NSZZ*, 205.
41. It was published only in 1984 in a collection of texts by Kuroń titled *Zło, które czynię* (Warsaw: Nowa, 1984), 133.
42. NSZZ "Solidarność," *Komisja Krajowa NSZZ*, 176.
43. Łopiński, Moskit [Gach], and Wilk, *Konspira*, 10.
44. Anoshkin, "Zeszyt roboczy," notebook no. 5, p. 37.
45. Witold Bereś and Jerzy Skoczylas, *Generał Kiszczak mówi—prawie wszystko* (Warsaw: BGW, 1991), 130.
46. Andrew and Mitrokhin, *Mitrokhin Archive*, 922.
47. Rakowski, *Dzienniki polityczne*, 8:133.
48. Jaruzelski, *Stan wojenny*, 402.
49. AIPN, 1405/92, p. 4.
50. Kowalski, *Komitet Obrony Kraju*, 438.
51. Rakowski, *Stan wojenny*, 127.
52. Anoshkin, "Zeszyt roboczy," notebook no. 5, p. 43.
53. Ibid., 46.
54. Ibid., 15.
55. For the entire speech, see Tadeusz Walichnowski, ed., *Stan wojenny w Polsce 13.12.1981—22.07.1983: Dokumenty i materiały archiwalne* (Warsaw: Commandor, 2001), 81–85.
56. AIPN, 1405/62, pp. 76–78.
57. Walichnowski, *Stan wojenny w Polsce: Dokumenty i materiały*, 82.
58. Anoshkin, "Zeszyt roboczy," notebook no. 5, p. 49.
59. "Protokół z posiedzenia," AIPN, 1405/62, pp. 197–203. The typewritten manuscript was prepared only on March 25, 1982.
60. Kowalski, *Komitet Obrony Kraju*, 438.
61. *Polityka* 10 (March 5, 2011).

Chapter Five

1. Meretik, *Noc Generała*, 7–8.
2. "Protokół z posiedzenia Sztabu MSW" (January 8, 1982), in Bogusław Kopka and Grzegorz Majchrzak, eds., *Stan wojenny w dokumentach władz PRL, 1980–1983* (Warsaw: IPN, 2001), 121.
3. *Użyto broni: Relacja górników kopalni "Wujek,"* comp. Jacek Cieszewski (Kraków: Biblioteka Obserwatora Wojennego, 1988), 81.

4. "Ocena wyników działań podjętych przez Resort Spraw Wewnętrznych" (December 24, 1981), AIPN, MSW II, 1121, p. 61.

5. Jacek Kuroń, *Gwiezdny czas* (London: Aneks, 1991), 252.

6. Antoni Dudek, ed., *Stan wojenny w Polsce, 1981–1983* (Warsaw: IPN, 2003), 88.

7. Łopieński, Moskit [Gach], and Wilk, *Konspira*, 23.

8. "Protokół z posiedzenia Sztabu MSW" (January 8, 1982), in Kopka and Majchrzak, *Stan wojenny w dokumentach władz PRL*, 122.

9. Archiwum Kancelarii Prezydenta RP (Presidential Chancellery Archives), Rada Państwa, Vol. 26 "Protokoły posiedzeń," Issue 22/81, passim.

10. Ryszard Reiff, *Czas "Solidarności"* (Warsaw: Spotkania, 1988), 329.

11. Kazimierz Barcikowski, *U szczytów władzy* (Warsaw: Wydawnictwo Projekt, 1998), 309.

12. Teresa Torańska, *Byli* (Warsaw: Świat Książki, 2006), 235–36.

13. Barcikowski, *U szczytów władzy*, 312.

14. "Dziennik działań bojowych oficerów kierunkowych Dowództwa Okręgu, Śląski Okrąg Wojskowy," AIPN, 1405/132, pp. 1–10.

15. "Działalność sił zbrojnych w zakresie działań specjalnych," AIPN, 1405/95, p. 132.

16. "Wystąpienie przewodniczącego Wojskowej Rady Ocalenia Narodowego z dnia 13 grudnia 1981 r.," in Walichnowski, *Stan wojenny w Polsce: Dokumenty i materiały*, 81.

17. All the basic legal acts related to martial law are in ibid., 24–75.

18. AIPN, 1405/99, p. 135.

19. Andrzej Friszke, "Powstanie Tymczasowej Komisji Koordynacyjnej NSZZ 'Solidarność' w 1982 r.," *Zeszyty Historyczne* 155 (2006): 53–54.

20. "Protokół nr 19 z posiedzenia Biura Politycznego KC PZPR w dniu 13 XII 1981 r.," in Włodek, *PZPR a "Solidarność,"* 801.

21. Jabłonowski, Janowski, and Władyka, *Narady i telekonferencje*, 1260.

22. Ibid., 1267.

23. The MSW reports from December 13–28, 1981, were published in Peter Raina and Marcin Brożek, eds., *Operacja "Lato-80": Preludium stanu wojennego. Dokumenty MSW 1980–1981* (Pelplin: Bernardinum, 2003), 255–386.

24. H. Gontarz, "Strajk w Świdniku," in *Świadectwa stanu wojennego*, ed. A. Dudek and K. Madej (Warsaw: IPN, 2001), 77.

25. Translator's note: the wash and change house, "chain bath" (*łaźnia łańcuszkowa*), where the miners hang their workclothes from the ceiling to dry and air them out.

26. *Użyto broni*, 81.

27. Jerzy Fajerant [Jacek Cieszewski], ed., *Co powiedzą nasze dzieci? Relacja o strajku w kopalni "Ziemowit" (15–24 grudnia 1981 r.)* (Warsaw: Wydawnictwo Most, 1986), 8.

28. Łopieński, Moskit [Gach], and Wilk, *Konspira*, 22.

29. Andrzej Grajewski and Artur Kasprzykowski, eds., *Czas próby: "Solidarność" na Podbeskidziu w latach 1980–2005* (Bielsko-Biała: Region Solidarność, 2006), 65.
30. Jan Olaszek, ed., *Dokumenty władz NSZZ "Solidarność," 1981–1989* (Warsaw: IPN, 2010), 47.
31. Raina and Brożek, *Operacja "Lato-80,"* 281.
32. Włodek, *PZPR a "Solidarność,"* 807.
33. Aleksandra Mierzwińska and Jan Żaryn, "Episkopat Polski wobec wprowadzenia stanu wojennego," *Arcana* 6 (2005): 148.
34. Raina and Brożek, *Operacja "Lato-80,"* 267.
35. Raina, *Jan Paweł II*, 46.
36. Ibid., 52–53.
37. Lech Wałęsa, *Droga nadziei* (Warsaw: Rytm, 1989), 2:95.
38. "Zeszyt roboczy gen. Wiktora Anoszkina," in Łukasz Kamiński, ed., *Przed i po 13 grudnia: Państwa bloku wschodniego wobec kryzysu w PRL, 1980–1982* (Warsaw: IPN, 2007), 2:409.

Chapter Six

1. Rakowski, *Dzienniki polityczne*, 8:136.
2. Barcikowski, *U szczytów władzy*, 320.
3. Raina and Brożek, *Operacja "Lato-80,"* 288.
4. Such were the instructions, for example, of the Silesian Region, which were announced on December 10. For the text, see Jarosław Neja, *Grudzień 1981 roku w województwie katowickim* (Katowice: IPN, 2011), 67.
5. Katarzyna Zuzanna [Barbara Tchórzewska], *Czterech z "Andaluzji"* (Warsaw: NOW-a, 1985), 35.
6. For the text, see Neja, *Grudzień 1981 roku*, 88.
7. Fajerant [Cieszewski], *Co powiedzą nasze dzieci*, 16.
8. Ibid., 9.
9. Dudek, *Stan wojenny w Polsce*, 361. The examples above come from that same book, which is a mine of detailed information collected from all over Poland.
10. "Dziennik działań bojowych Stanowiska Dowodzenia MON," AIPN, 1405/132, p. 19.
11. Marian Terlecki, "Cztery pierwsze dni," in *13 Grudzień. Wspomnienia* (Kraków: s.n., 1989), 59.
12. *Użyto broni*, 90.
13. Raina, *Jan Paweł II*, 55–56.
14. "Dziennik działań bojowych Grupy Operacyjnej Stanowiska Dowodzenia MON" (December 14), AIPN, 1405/132, p. 9.
15. Zbigniew Solak, et al., eds., *Stan wojenny w Małopolsce w oczach świadków* (Kraków: Księgarnia Akademicka, 2001), 83.
16. Gontarz, "Strajk w Świdniku," 78.

17. *Użyto broni*, 97.
18. Solak et al., *Stan wojenny w Małopolsce*, 84.
19. Ibid.
20. "Działalność Sił Zbrojnych PRL w zakresie realizacji działań specjalnych w warunkach stanu wojennego," AIPN, 1405/103, p. 89.
21. Translator's note: That is, they were made to run a gauntlet—in Polish this was called a "path of health" (*ścieżka zdrowia*).
22. M. Kobylańska, "Nieznany strajk w KWK Staszic," *Gazeta Polska* 3 (January 24, 2007): 14.
23. This mine was named after communist Poland's "founding document," the Polish Committee of National Liberation's manifesto that was broadcast by Radio Moscow on July 22, 1944.
24. Account by Cz. Kłoska, in *Zeszyty Historyczne Solidarności Śląsko-Dabrowskiej* 7 (2003): 81.
25. *Użyto broni*, 92.
26. "Zapis rozmów prowadzonych przez dowódców jednostek wojskowych szturmujących kopalnię 'Wujek,'" in Kopka and Majchrzak, *Stan wojenny w dokumentach*, 81.
27. Fajerant [Cieszewski], *Co powiedzą nasze dzieci*, 33.
28. *Uparci z "Piasta": Relacje i głosy strajkujących górników*, compiled by Jacek Cieszewski (Bieruń: "Solidarność" KWK "Piast," 2001), 31.
29. Ibid., 99.
30. Kopka and Majchrzak, *Stan wojenny w dokumentach*, 89.
31. Raina and Brożek, *Operacja "Lato-80,"* 368.
32. Kopka and Majchrzak, *Stan wojenny w dokumentach*, 63.
33. "Działalność Sił Zbrojnych PRL w zakresie realizacji działań specjalnych w warunkach stanu wojennego," AIPN, 1405/103, p. 140.
34. Raina and Brożek, *Operacja "Lato-80,"* 373.

Chapter Seven

1. Walichnowski, *Stan wojenny w Polsce: Dokumenty i materiały*, 86.
2. Kobylańska, "Nieznany strajk," 15.
3. Kopka and Majchrzak, *Stan wojenny w dokumentach*, 380.
4. Details in the following collection of accounts and primary sources: Bogusław Gołąb and Władysław Kałudziński, eds., *Kwidzyn: W niewoli brata mego; Wspomnienia, refleksje, oceny* (Olsztyn: Pro Patria, 2005), passim.
5. Details in the following collection of accounts and studies: W. Kałudziński, ed., *Internowani w Iławie (1981–1982)* (Olsztyn: Pro Patria, 2006), passim.
6. A summary of that research can be found in Dudek, *Stan wojenny w Polsce*, 538–40.
7. Details and statistical figures can be found in Dariusz Stola, *Kraj bez wyjścia? Migracje z Polski, 1949–1989* (Warsaw: IPN, ISP PAN, 2010), 315–22.

8. Janusz Rolicki, *Edward Gierek: przerwana dekada; Wywiad rzeka* (Warsaw: Wydawnictwo Fakt, 1990), 231.

9. Kopka and Majchrzak, *Stan wojenny w dokumentach*, 376–78.

10. AIPN, 1405/131, p. 30.

11. Rakowski, *Dzienniki polityczne*, 8:140 and 145.

12. This trial was interesting insofar as one of those sentenced was the first secretary of the communist party's Enterprise Committee there.

13. Dudek, *Stan wojenny w Polsce*, 451. Other examples come from that same work.

14. Maria Stanowska and Adam Strzembosz, *Sędziowie warszawscy w czasie próby, 1981–1988* (Warsaw: IPN, 2005), 80.

15. Ibid., 294.

16. Grajewski and Kasprzykowski, *Czas próby: "Solidarność,"* 69.

17. Zuzanna [Tchórzewska], *Czterech z "Andaluzji,"* 55.

18. Ibid., 55.

19. Dudek, *Stan wojenny w Polsce*, 397.

20. Kopka and Majchrzak, *Stan wojenny w dokumentach*, 379.

21. Henryk Głębocki, *Policja tajna przy robocie: Z dziejów państwa policyjnego w PRL* (Kraków: Arcana, 2005), 431.

22. Rakowski, *Dzienniki polityczne*, 8:330.

23. Ibid., 8:323.

24. Stanowska and Strzembosz, *Sędziowie warszawscy*, 60–61.

25. Dudek, *Stan wojenny w Polsce*, 449.

26. "Informacja o wynikach weryfikacji kadr dziennikarskich," in Kopka and Majchrzak, *Stan wojenny w dokumentach*, 272.

27. Ibid., 150.

28. Dudek, *Stan wojenny w Polsce*, 41.

29. AIPN, 1405/99, p. 167.

30. Dudek, *Stan wojenny w Polsce*, 503.

31. Kopka and Majchrzak, *Stan wojenny w dokumentach*, 185.

32. Dudek, *Stan wojenny w Polsce*, 40.

33. Kopka and Majchrzak, *Stan wojenny w dokumentach*, 298.

34. "Debata poselska," *Trybuna Ludu*, January 27, 1982, 3.

35. "Odprawa aktywu kierowniczego MSW w dniu 7 czerwca 1982 r.," AIPN, 1585, p. 73.

36. Grzegorz Majchrzak, ed., "Ocena funkcjonowania cenzury w okresie obowiązywania stanu wojennego w PRL," *Karta* 29 (1999): 147.

37. Jolanta Muszyńska, Aneta Osiak, and Dorota Wojtera, *Obraz codzienności w prasie stanu wojennego* (Warsaw: TRIO, 2006), 72–73.

38. Translator's note: In these sales, the purchase of one type of item was dependent for example on something else, such as the return of empty bottles.

39. Quoted by Anna Skoczek, *Poezja świadectwa i sprzeciwu* (Kraków: Wydawnictwo SMS, 2004), 42–43.

Chapter Eight

1. Meretik, *Noc Generała*, 99.
2. "Current situation of the Polish crisis," in *Poland: The Long Journey to Freedom* (Brussels: NATO Multimedia Library, 2011), n.p.
3. MacEachin, *U.S. Intelligence*, 230.
4. Three possible scenarios were foreseen in a report prepared at the office of the NATO Secretary General in March 1981 ("outright invasion, with or without invitation," "intervention under guise of large-scale military deployment or exercises," and "use of force against the population by the Polish authorities, with or without appeal for Warsaw Pact assistance"), but proposed reactions were prepared only in case of the "Worst-Case Scenario," i.e., an invasion. See "Poland" (March 13, 1981), in *Poland: The Long Journey to Freedom*, n.p.
5. Meretik, *Noc Generała*, 170.
6. Ibid., 213.
7. Dietmar Bingen, *Polityka Republiki Bońskiej wobec Polski* (Kraków: Wydawnictwo Kwadrat, 1997), 201.
8. Paczkowski and Byrne, *From Solidarity to Martial Law*, 38.
9. "Protocol No. 19 of Politburo Meeting" (December 13, 1981), in ibid., 465.
10. Idesbald Goddeeris, ed., *Solidarity with "Solidarity": Western European Trade Unions and the Polish Crisis, 1980–1982* (New York: Lexington Books, 2010), 3.
11. Already on December 15, in information prepared for the "directorate," Minister Czyrek expressed his belief that "the West is going for appeasement (in the sense that it will still provide economic aid)." See Rakowski, *Dzienniki polityczne*, 8:137.
12. "Pilna notatka" (December 15, 1981), AIPN, 1405/194, p. 144.
13. Paczkowski and Byrne, *From Solidarity to Martial Law*, 483.
14. Ibid., 478.
15. Paul Kengor, *The Crusader: Ronald Reagan and the Fall of Communism* (New York: HarperCollins, 2006), 126.
16. Sjursen, *United States, Western Europe, and the Polish Crisis*, 70.
17. Ibid., 71.
18. "Compendium of measures taken or contemplated by the Allies concerning: Poland and USSR" (February 1, 1982), a total of thirteen pages, in "Documents Related to Events in Poland (1980–1984)," DC-R disc, edited by NATO Archives, December 2011, n.p.
19. Gary C. Hufbauer, Jeffrey J. Schott, and Kimberly A. Elliott, *Economic Sanctions Reconsidered: History and Current Policy* (Washington, DC: Institute for International Economics, 1983), 200. Exports to Poland were a little better, but decreases were also noted.
20. Wilke, Gutsche, and Kubina, "Kierownictwo SED," 75.
21. In Poland, the state of heightened combat alert had been cancelled a few days earlier, on March 29.

22. "Extract from Protocol No. 40 of CPSU CC Politburo Meeting" (December 13, 1981), in Paczkowski and Byrne, *From Solidarity to Martial Law*, 473–74.

23. Kamiński, *Przed i po 13 grudnia*, 422.

24. "Stenogram z posiedzenia Politycznego Komitetu Wykonawczego KC RPK" (December 17, 1981), in ibid., 465.

25. "Protokół posiedzenia Sekretariatu KC WSPR" (December 14, 1981), in ibid., 446.

26. Paczkowski and Byrne, *From Solidarity to Martial Law*, 505.

27. "Notatka" (December 16, 1981), AIPN, 1405/194, p. 144.

28. Paczkowski and Byrne, *From Solidarity to Martial Law*, 505.

29. Kamiński, *Przed i po 13 grudnia*, 430.

30. Rakowski, *Dzienniki polityczne*, 8:169.

31. "Report for the Politburo" (December 30, 1981), in Paczkowski and Byrne, *From Solidarity to Martial Law*, 502.

32. "Notatka informacyjna Departamentu I MSZ" (June 7, 1982), in Kamiński, *Przed i po 13 grudnia*, 570.

Chapter Nine

1. Włodek, *PZPR a "Solidarność,"* 585.

2. "Główne zadania realizowane aktualnie przez siły zbrojne" (February 1982), AIPN, 1405/131, pp. 94–95.

3. "Podsumowanie działalności Departamentu Kadr" (October 25, 1983), AIPN, 1405/99, p. 244.

4. Ibid., 245.

5. "Działalność Zarządu VI Sztabu Generalnego WP w okresie obowiązywania stanu wojennego," AIPN, 1405/99, p. 12.

6. "Główne zadania realizowane aktualnie," 96.

7. "Sprawozdanie Głównego Zarządu Politycznego Wojska Polskiego," AIPN, 1405/99, p. 171.

8. "Protokół z posiedzenia Wojskowej Rady Ocalenia Narodowego" (March 11, 1982), AIPN, 1405/62, p. 228.

Chapter Ten

1. "Protokół nr 002/81 z posiedzenia Komitetu Obrony Kraju" (September 13, 1981), Centralne Archiwum Wojskowe [Central Military Archive] (hereafter CAW), 1806/92/85, p. 180.

2. Andrew and Mitrokhin, *Mitrokhin Archive*, 520.

3. Paczkowski, *Droga do mniejszego zła*, 263.

4. Dudek, *Stan wojenny w Polsce*, 422.

5. J. Pniewski, "Kartki z historii," *Newsletter Instytutu Historycznego Uniwersytetu Warszawskiego* 27 (2003): 10.

6. "Informacja operacyjna" (December 23, 1981), AIPN, 00200/1432, vol. 3, pp. 209–12.

7. "Informacja naczelnika Wydziału III" (February 22, 1982), AIPN, 0236/273, vol. 2, p. 84.

8. Walichnowski, *Stan wojenny w Polsce: Dokumenty i materiały*, 84.

9. "Protokół nr 16 z posiedzenia Sekretariatu KC PZPR" (December 19, 1981), AAN, KC PZPR, 2260, p. 404.

10. Włodek, *PZPR a "Solidarność,"* 586.

11. AIPN, 0365/109, vol. 2, pp. 230–31.

12. "Koncepcja taktyki działania w zakresie odradzania i odbudowy związków zawodowych w Polsce" (January 1, 1982), AIPN, Gd.003/176, vol. 3, pp. 16–21.

13. *Tajne dokumenty: Państwo-Kościół, 1980–1989* (Warsaw and London: Aneks, 1993), 165.

14. "Referat Ministra Spraw Wewnętrznych" (June 6, 1982), AIPN, MSW II, 258, p. 24.

15. J. Reykowski, *Logika walki: Szkice z psychologii konfliktu społecznego w Polsce* (Warsaw: Książka i Wiedza, 1984), 90.

16. "Protokół z posiedzenia Biura Politycznego" (June 16, 1982), AAN, KC PZPR, V/172, pp. 516–17.

17. Walichnowski, *Stan wojenny w Polsce: Dokumenty i materiały*, 194.

18. Ibid., 205.

19. "Wystąpienie I Sekretarza Komitetu Centralnego PZPR" (June 6, 1982), AIPN, MSW II, 258, p. 73.

20. Andrew and Mitrokhin, *Mitrokhin Archive*, 930.

21. Kopka and Majchrzak, *Stan wojenny w dokumentach*, 94.

22. Wałęsa, *Droga nadziei*, 2:100.

23. Marzena and Tadeusz Woźniak, "Wałęsa, portret w ruchu," in *Wałęsa* (Gdańsk: Wydawnictwo Morskie, 1981), 180.

24. Ibid., 182.

25. Edmund Szcześniak, "Dookoła życiorysu," in *Wałęsa*, 24.

26. Sławomir Cenckiewicz and Piotr Gontarczyk described the matter most extensively in their monograph *SB a Lech Wałęsa: Przyczynek do biografii* (Warsaw: IPN, 2008), 46–81. This volume, based on solid archival research, is not favorable to Wałęsa.

27. M. and T. Woźniak, "Wałęsa, portret w ruchu," 187.

28. Alojzy Orszulik, *Czas przełomu: Notatki z rozmów z władzami PRL w latach 1981–1989* (Warsaw: Apostolicum, 2006), 9.

29. Ibid., 51.

30. Wałęsa, *Droga nadziei*, 2:103.

31. Orszulik, *Czas przełomu*, 54.

32. Full text of the memorandum in ibid., 27–30.

33. Note dated January 18. See Rakowski, *Dzienniki polityczne*, 8:174–77.
34. Ibid., 8:177.
35. Andrew and Mitrokhin, *Mitrokhin Archive*, 928.
36. *Tajne dokumenty: Państwo-Kosciół*, 163.
37. Wałęsa, *Droga nadziei*, 2:102.
38. That same day, the full text was published in both *Trybuna Ludu*, a central organ of the PZPR, and *Rzeczpospolita*, a semi-official government organ.
39. *Trybuna Ludu*, February 22, 1982, 2.

Chapter Eleven

1. Dudek, *Stan wojenny w Polsce*, 420.
2. Ibid., 88.
3. Andrzej Friszke, ed., *"Solidarność" podziemna, 1981–1989* (Warsaw: ISP PAN, 2006), 134. It was only at the beginning of 1984 that aid began arriving on a larger scale from the American National Endowment for Democracy. By late 1989, it had totaled around $9 million. For the official account, see Gregory F. Domber, *Empowering Revolution: America, Poland, and the End of the Cold War* (Chapel Hill: University of North Carolina Press, 2014), 283–88.
4. This story even served as the basis for the screenplay of the film *Eighty Million* (2011), directed by Sławomir Krzystek.
5. Ewa Kondratowicz, *Szminka na sztandarze. Kobiety w "Solidarności"* (Warsaw: Wydawnictwo Sic!, 2001), 38–39.
6. Dudek, *Stan wojenny w Polsce*, 416.
7. S. Rudka, *Poza cenzurą: Wrocławska prasa bezdebitowa 1973–1989* (Warsaw: PWN, 2001), 188.
8. Józefa Kamińska [Władysław Chojnacki], *Bibliografia publikacji podziemnych w Polsce, 13 XII 1981—VI 1986* (Paris: Editions Spotkania, 1988), 21.
9. Łopieński, Moskit [Gach], and Wilk, *Konspira*, 150.
10. Zbigniew Bujak, *Prawda raz powiedziana* (Warsaw: Archiwum Solidarności, 1987), 227.
11. Kondratowicz, *Szminka na sztandarze*, 23.
12. Piotr T. Kwiatkowski, *Stan wojenny w badaniach opinii publicznej w latach 1982–2003* (Szczecin: Szczecińskie Towarzystwo Naukowe, 2005), 10–11. All figures in this section of the book come from Kwiatkowski's work (passim).
13. Kamińska [Chojnacki], *Bibliografia publikacji podziemnych*, 17.
14. "Odezwa," in Walichnowski, *Stan wojenny w Polsce: Dokumenty i materiały*, 110.
15. Dudek, *Stan wojenny w Polsce*, 717.
16. Friszke, *"Solidarność" podziemna*, 501.
17. These were described in detail in an excellent article by Andrzej Friszke, "Tymczasowa Komisja Koordynacyjna NSZZ 'Solidarność' (1982–1987)" (in ibid.,

Notes to pp. 168–185

17–182). I have relied heavily on Friszke's work in writing the section dealing with this problem.

18. For the entire text, see Olaszek, *Dokumenty wladz NSZZ "Solidarność,"* 58–61.

19. The Karta Archives 76/IV; for an extensive discussion of this topic, see Friszke, *"Solidarność" podziemna*, 414–15.

20. "To było jedno z naszych wielkich powstań narodowych," *Tygodnik Mazowsze* 2 (February 11, 1982). For a complete transcription of that interview, see Bujak, *Prawda raz powiedziana*, 124–45.

21. Jacek Kuroń, "Tezy o wyjściu z sytuacji bez wyjścia," *Tygodnik Mazowsze* 8 (January 31, 1982).

22. For a discussion of Romaszewski's texts, see Friszke, *"Solidarność" podziemna*, 422–24.

23. Full texts of all declarations and communiqués were published in *Tygodnik Mazowsze* 11 (April 28, 1982). Reprinted in Olaszek, *Dokumenty wladz NSZZ "Solidarność,"* 63–68.

Chapter Twelve

1. Skoczek, *Poezja świadectwa i sprzeciwu*, 198.
2. Ibid., 210.
3. Ibid., 43.
4. Piotr Spiski, *Od trzynastego do trzynastego* (London: Polonia Book Fund, 1983), 38–39.
5. Daniel Przastek, *Środowisko teatru w okresie stanu wojennego* (Warsaw: INP UW, 2005), 42.
6. Ibid., 48.
7. Małgorzata Szejnert, *Sława i infamia: Rozmowa z Bohdanem Korzeniowskim* (London: Aneks, 1988), 165.
8. Dudek, *Stan wojenny w Polsce*, 186ff.
9. Ibid., 440.
10. Ibid., 444.
11. Ibid., 317.
12. Ibid., 54.
13. Ibid., 659.
14. Ibid., 310.
15. Łopieński, Moskit [Gach], and Wilk, *Konspira*, 80.
16. Dudek, *Stan wojenny w Polsce*, 54–55.
17. Ibid., 54.
18. Antoni Dudek and Tomasz Marszałkowski, *Walki uliczne w PRL, 1956–1989* (Kraków: GEO, 1999), 282–83.
19. Łopieński, Moskit [Gach], and Wilk, *Konspira*, 70–72.

Chapter Thirteen

1. "CDN" no. 4, May 6, 1982. ("CDN" was an underground news sheet. The title means "To Be Continued.")

2. Jan Skórzyński, Paweł Sowiński, and Małgorzata Strasz, eds., *Opozycja w PRL. Słownik biograficzny 1956–1989* (Warsaw: Karta, 2002), 2:227.

3. Dudek, *Stan wojenny w Polsce*, 244.

4. As cited by Grzegorz Majchrzak and Tadeusz Ruzikowski in "Radio 'Solidarność' w eterze na przykładzie Warszawy," in *Warszawa miasto w opresji*, ed. Kazimierz Krajewski and Magdalena Merta (Warsaw: IPN, 2010), 600. For more details on the entire undertaking, see ibid., 597–640.

5. Hajdasz, *Szczekaczka czyli Rozgłośnia*, 257. According to research conducted by the East European Audience and Opinion Research, based in the United States, the numbers were significantly higher (in 1982–83 listenership was said to have even reached 71 percent—ibid., 272), but the empirical basis for the research was not very representative, since it was Poles abroad who were surveyed.

6. M. Ochocki, *Byłem człowiekiem Kiszczaka* (Łódź: Athos, 1992), 176.

7. Łopieński, Moskit [Gach], and Wilk, *Konspira*, 166.

8. Rakowski, *Dzienniki polityczne*, 8:271.

9. Dudek, *Stan wojenny w Polsce*, 525–26.

10. Two others died or were fatally injured in the area where the clashes were taking place, but it not clear to what extent these cases were connected with the militia's activities.

11. Rakowski, *Dzienniki polityczne*, 8:274.

12. Ibid., 8:273.

13. Łopieński, Moskit [Gach], and Wilk, *Konspira*, 161.

14. "Referat na naradę aktywu kierowniczego MSW," AIPN, Wr.053/2153, p. 142.

15. "Referat ministra," AIPN, 1585/258, p. 26.

16. Ibid., 83.

17. For details on this operation, see Sławomir Cenckiewicz and Piotr Gontarczyk, *SB a Lech Wałęsa*, 143–46.

18. Almost three hundred documents related to the surveillance of this organization were published in Ł. Kamiński, W. Sawicki, and G. Waligóra, eds., *Solidarność Walcząca w dokumentach* (Warsaw: IPN, 2007).

19. AIPN, 1585/258, passim.

20. Głębocki, *Policja tajna przy robocie*, 62. The entire document is also published there, pp. 52–64.

21. *Solidarność Walcząca* Issue 1, June 11, 1982.

22. *Tajne dokumenty: Państwo-Kościół*, 201.

23. Walichnowski, *Stan wojenny w Polsce: Dokumenty i materiały*, 286.

24. Olaszek, *Dokumenty władz NSZZ "Solidarność,"* 70.

25. Ibid., 76.

26. For the entire text, see ibid., 72–75.

27. Ibid., 78.
28. "Protokół z posiedzenia Sekretariatu KC PZPR w dn. 30 VIII 1982," AAN, KC PZPR, 2265, p. 89.
29. AAN, KC PZPR, VII/62, p. 101.
30. Peter Raina, ed., *Rozmowy z władzami PRL: Arcybiskup Dąbrowski w służbie Kościoła i Narodu*, vol. 2, 1982–89 (Warsaw: Wydawnictwo Książka Polska, 1995), 47.
31. Raina, *Jan Paweł II*, 293.
32. Orszulik, *Czas przełomu*, 79–80.
33. AIPN, 0582/261, p. 120.
34. Dudek and Marszałkowski, *Walki uliczne w PRL*, 308.
35. Cited as in ibid., 316.
36. AIPN, 1405/62, p. 271.

Chapter Fourteen

1. Citation as per Dudek and Marszałkowski, *Walki uliczne w PRL*, 324.
2. Rakowski, *Dzienniki polityczne*, 8:334.
3. Peter Raina, ed., *Stan wojenny w zapiskach arcybiskupa Dąbrowskiego* (Warsaw: Wydawnictwo von Borowiecky, 2006), 103.
4. He was released soon for health reasons.
5. Raina, *Jan Paweł II*, 309.
6. Kolbe was a Polish monk who sacrificed his life at Auschwitz in order to save a young man's life.
7. "Charakterystyka kontrwywiadowcza województwa wrocławskiego za okres 1–31 sierpnia 1981 r.," in Kamiński, Sawicki, and Waligóra, *Solidarność Walcząca w dokumentach*, 54.
8. Łopieński, Moskit [Gach], and Wilk, *Konspira*, 163.
9. Friszke, *"Solidarność" podziemna*, 38.
10. Olaszek, *Dokumenty władz NSZZ "Solidarność,"* 84.
11. Ibid., 85.
12. Ibid., 86.
13. Dudek and Marszałkowski, *Walki uliczne w PRL*, 327.
14. Olaszek, *Dokumenty władz NSZZ "Solidarność,"* 90.
15. Dudek, *Stan wojenny w Polsce*, 530.
16. Ibid., 654.
17. Olaszek, *Dokumenty władz NSZZ "Solidarność,"* 96–98.
18. Rakowski, *Dzienniki polityczne*, 8:396.
19. Ibid., 8:389.
20. "Szyfrogram," AIPN, 0236/263, vol. 1, p. 373.
21. Paweł Piotrowski, "Kompanie polowe w 'ludowym' Wojsku Polskim jako forma represji politycznych," *Zeszyty Historyczne WiN* 32–33 (2010): 440–44.

22. Friszke, *"Solidarność" podziemna*, 47.
23. Dudek and Marszałkowski, *Walki uliczne w PRL*, 336.
24. Olaszek, *Dokumenty władz NSZZ "Solidarność,"* 100.
25. Ibid., 101.
26. Wałęsa, *Droga nadziei*, 2:126. Wałęsa and Jaruzelski only met in June 1989.
27. As quoted by Antoni Dudek, *Reglamentowana rewolucja: Rozkład dyktatury komunistycznej w Polsce, 1988–1990*, 2nd ed. (Kraków: Arcana, 2004; Kraków: Znak, 2014), 57. Citations are to the 2004 edition.
28. Orszulik, *Czas przełomu*, 82.
29. Ibid., 85.
30. Wałęsa, *Droga nadziei*, 2:110.
31. Rakowski, *Dzienniki polityczne*, 8:401.
32. Ibid., 8:359.
33. Ibid., 8:403.
34. Ibid., 8:406.
35. It did not serve this function because it was deemed a fake.
36. For the stenogram of this talk, which lasted many hours, see Cenckiewicz and Gontarczyk, *SB a Lech Wałęsa*, 358–86.
37. Olaszek, *Dokumenty władz NSZZ "Solidarność,"* 99.
38. Wałęsa, *Droga nadziei*, 2:137.
39. Rakowski, *Dzienniki polityczne*, 8:429.
40. Orszulik, *Czas przełomu*, 88.
41. AIPN, MSW II, 1004, pp. 95–108.
42. Ibid., 105.
43. "Protokół z posiedzenia Biura Politycznego," AAN, KC PZPR, V/186; for the complete protocol, see pp. 217–52.
44. Walichnowski, *Stan wojenny w Polsce: Dokumenty i materiały*, 388–96.

Chapter Fifteen

1. *Tajne dokumenty: Państwo-Kościół*, 163.
2. Raina, *Jan Paweł II*, 50.
3. Ibid., 60.
4. Ibid., 61.
5. Ibid., 69.
6. Walichnowski, *Stan wojenny w Polsce: Dokumenty i materiały*, 145.
7. Raina, *Jan Paweł II*, 191.
8. Full text in ibid., 210–19.
9. Full text in ibid., 247–90.
10. Ibid., 232. Full text of Father Blachnicki in ibid., 224–35.
11. Ibid., 303.
12. Rakowski, *Dzienniki polityczne*, 8:549.

13. Antoni Dudek and Ryszard Gryz, *Komuniści i Kościół w Polsce (1945–1989)* (Kraków: Znak, 2003), 398.
14. Ibid., 557.
15. Ibid., 562.
16. *Tajne dokumenty: Państwo-Kościół*, 293. According to Ministry of Internal Affairs estimates, approximately 50–60 percent of the participants were young people (ibid., 288).
17. Ibid., 298–99.
18. Rakowski, *Dzienniki polityczne*, 8:563.
19. *Tajne dokumenty: Państwo-Kościół*, 294.
20. Wałęsa, *Droga nadziei*, 2:194–95.
21. George Weigel, *Witness to Hope: The Biography of Pope John Paul II* (New York: Cliff Street Books, 2001), 463.
22. *Tajne dokumenty: Państwo-Kościół*, 274.
23. Ibid., 275.
24. Władysław Rodowicz, *Komitet na Piwnej: Fakty-dokumenty-wspomnienia* (Warsaw: Więź, 1994), 88.
25. Ibid., 112. 430 million marks was around $200 million.
26. A. Riechers, *Hilfe für Solidarność* (Bonn: Friedrich-Ebert-Stiftung, 2006), 23.
27. Friszke, *"Solidarność" podziemna*, 68.
28. Zygmunt Zieliński, *Kościół w Polsce, 1944–2004* (Radom: Polskie Wydawnictwo Encyklopedyczne, 2003), 304.
29. Dudek and Gryz, *Komuniści i Kościół w Polsce*, 385.
30. Dudek, *Stan wojenny w Polsce*, 395.
31. Dudek and Gryz, *Komuniści i Kościół w Polsce*, 403.
32. Jan Rokita and Antoni Dudek, eds., *Raport Rokity: Sprawozdanie Sejmowej Komisji Nadzwyczajnej do Zbadania Działalności MSW* (Kraków: Arcana, 2005), 166.
33. Ibid., 168–71.
34. Tadeusz Ruzikowski, "Tajni współpracownicy pionów operacyjnych aparatu bezpieczeństwa, 1950–1984," *Pamięć i Sprawiedliwość* 1 (2003): 131, Table No. 9.

Chapter Sixteen

1. For complete text, see Olaszek, *Dokumenty władz NSZZ "Solidarność,"* 103–10.
2. For complete research report, see Barbara Badura et al., eds., *Społeczeństwo i władza lat osiemdziesiątych w badaniach CBOS* (Warsaw: CBOS, 1994), 37–40.
3. Based on a personal decision by Jaruzelski, that film (*Pieniądze*) was broadcast on September 27, 1983, i.e., ten days before the Nobel committee announced that Solidarity's leader had been awarded a Nobel Prize.
4. Teresa Bochwic, "Antoni Macierewicz," in *Opozycja w PRL: Słownik biograficzny 1956–1989* (Warsaw: Ośrodek Karta, 2000), 2:221.
5. Kamińska [Chojnacki], *Bibliografia publikacji podziemnych*, 17.

6. Grzegorz Majchrzak, "Radio 'Solidarność': Niezależna działalność radiowa pod szyldem 'Solidarności,' 1980–1989," in *NSZZ "Solidarność" 1980–1989*, vol. 2, ed. Łukasz Kamiński and Grzegorz Waligóra (Warsaw: IPN, 2010), 387–452.

7. Rakowski, *Dzienniki polityczne*, 8:520.

8. Paweł Sowiński, *Zakazana książka: Uczestnicy drugiego obiegu 1977–1989* (Warsaw: ISP PAN, 2011), 297.

9. Friszke, *"Solidarność" podziemna*, 651.

10. W. Niewęgłowski, ed., *Kościół i kultura w latach osiemdziesiątych XX wieku: Doświadczenia warszawskie* (Warsaw: IPN, 2011), 11.

11. Joanna Krakówska-Narożniak and Marek Waszkiel, eds., *Teatr drugiego obiegu: Materiały do kroniki teatru stanu wojennego, 13 XII 1981–15 XI 1989* (Warsaw: Errata, 2000).

12. Andrzej Jawień was the pseudonym of Karol Wojtyła as poet.

13. Romuald Traugutt was head of the January Insurrection in 1863–64, and a romantic hero.

14. Kwiatkowski, *Stan wojenny w badaniach opinii publicznej*, 21.

15. Ibid., 35–38.

16. *Dziennik Ustaw* 41 (1982), pozycja 273. Reprint in Walichnowski, *Stan wojenny w Polsce: Dokumenty i materiały*, 388–96.

17. Dudek, *Stan wojenny w Polsce*, 446–47.

18. Daniel Przastek, *Środowisko teatru w okresie stanu wojennego* (Warsaw: INP UW, 2005), 169.

19. Olaszek, *Dokumenty władz NSZZ "Solidarność,"* 121.

20. For Lis's account, see Łopieński, Moskit [Gach], and Wilk, *Konspira*, 162; for Wałęsa's account, see Wałęsa, *Droga nadziei*, 2:150–52.

21. Rakowski, *Dzienniki polityczne*, 8:500.

22. Ibid., 8:507.

23. Olaszek, *Dokumenty władz NSZZ "Solidarność,"* 122.

24. Rakowski, *Dzienniki polityczne*, 8:515–17.

25. Ibid., 524.

26. Ibid., 523.

27. Dudek and Marszałkowski, *Walki uliczne w PRL*, 347.

28. Friszke, *"Solidarność" podziemna*, 62.

29. Ibid., 62.

30. Ruzikowski, "Tajni współpracownicy," 130–31, tables 8 and 9.

31. Rakowski, *Dzienniki polityczne*, 8:583.

Chapter Seventeen

1. Włodek, *PZPR a "Solidarność,"* 578.

2. For full text, see AAN, KC PZPR, 4759, pp. 5–13.

3. "Protokół z posiedzenia WRON odbytego w dniu 11 marca 1982 r.," AIPN, 1405/62, p. 234.

4. "Ankieta uczestnika centralnej narady pełnomocników KOK," AIPN, 1405/77, p. 287.
5. Ibid., 289.
6. W. Wiśniewski, *Dlaczego upadł socjalizm?* (Warsaw: Wydawnictwo Sprawy Polityczne, 2006), 61.
7. Barcikowski, *U szczytów władzy*, 368.
8. Ibid., 330.
9. Artur Jóźwik, *Krakówska Kuźnica: Historia, ludzie, idee* (Kraków: Trans-Krak, 2005), 103.
10. Rakowski, *Dzienniki polityczne*, 8:408.
11. Ibid., 8:497.
12. Walichnowski, *Stan wojenny w Polsce: Dokumenty i materiały*, 442.
13. Karol B. Janowski, *Źródła i przebieg zmiany politycznej w Polsce (1980–1989)* (Toruń: Adam Marszałek, 2003), 129.
14. Kaliński, *Gospodarka Polski*, 207.
15. Ibid., 229.
16. Mirosława Marody, *Długi finał* (Warsaw: WSiP, 1995), 41–42.
17. Jerzy Kochanowski, *Tylnymi drzwiami: "Czarny rynek" w Polsce, 1944–1989* (Warsaw: Neriton, 2010), 109.

Chapter Eighteen

1. AIPN, MSW II, 1004, pp. 95–108.
2. AIPN, MSW II, 3622, pp. 122–29.
3. Rakowski, *Dzienniki polityczne*, 8:581.
4. Ibid., 8:578.
5. Olaszek, *Dokumenty władz NSZZ "Solidarność,"* 127.
6. The entire interview, titled "Przesłanie dla 'Solidarności,'" is in *Tygodnik Mazowsze* 57 (July 14, 1983); for reprint, see Bujak, *Prawda raz powiedziana*, 163–65.
7. For full text, see Walichnowski, *Stan wojenny w Polsce: Dokumenty i materiały*, 443–51.
8. For the text of this legislation, see ibid., 456–62.
9. "Dane dotyczące stosowania ustawodawstwa związanego z wprowadzeniem, zawieszeniem i zniesieniem stanu wojennego," prepared at the Administrative Department of the Central Committee of the Polish United Workers' Party, August 1983, in Kopka and Majchrzak, *Stan wojenny w dokumentach władz PRL*, 382.
10. As quoted by Janowski, *Źródła i przebieg zmiany politycznej*, 138.
11. Rakowski, *Dzienniki polityczne*, 8:581.
12. Walichnowski, *Stan wojenny w Polsce: Dokumenty i materiały*, 443.
13. *Dziennik Ustaw* 38 (1983), pozycja 172.
14. Tadeusz Walichnowski, ed., *Ochrona bezpieczeństwa państwa i porządku publicznego w Polsce, 1944–1948* (Warsaw: Akademia Spraw Wewnętrznych, 1989), 220.

Notes to pp. 276–287

15. Walichnowski, *Stan wojenny w Polsce: Dokumenty i materiały*, 442.
16. Ibid.
17. Ibid.
18. For the complete law, see *Dziennik Ustaw* 39 (1983), pozycja 176.
19. For the complete law, see *Dziennik Ustaw* 44 (1983), pozycja 203.
20. For the complete law, see ibid., poz. 204.
21. Zbigniew Romek, ed., *Cenzura w PRL: Relacje historyków* (Warsaw: Neriton, 2000), 34.
22. Olaszek, *Dokumenty władz NSZZ "Solidarność,"* 129.
23. Ibid., 131.
24. Zbigniew Bujak was the first to use this term, in the title of an article that was published in *Tygodnik Mazowsze* on March 31, 1982. See Bujak, *Prawda raz powiedziana*, 149.

Chapter Nineteen

1. Walichnowski, *Stan wojenny w Polsce: Dokumenty i materiały*, 447.
2. Ibid., 447.
3. Ibid., 448.
4. Marody, *Długi finał*, 40.
5. Krzysztof Jasiewicz, *Polacy '84 z półtorarocznej perspektywy: Raport wstępny z badań* (Warsaw: Uniwersytet Warszawski, 1986), 30, table 21. The research was conducted on a representative sample of approximately a thousand people. The numbers are rounded here.
6. Ibid., 80.
7. Ibid., 81.
8. Rakowski, *Dzienniki polityczne*, 9:156.
9. Andrzej L. Sowa, *Historia polityczna Polski, 1944–1991* (Kraków: Wydawnictwo Literackie, 2011), 567.
10. According to official data, the construction of approximately three thousand buildings was underway, including several hundred churches. See Dudek and Gryz, *Komuniści i Kościół w Polsce*, 425.
11. Kaliński, *Gospodarka w PRL*, 102.
12. Marody, *Długi finał*, 55.
13. Bujak, *Prawda raz powiedziana*, 227.
14. AIPN 0752/1, 2:103.
15. Antoni Dudek, ed., *Zmierzch dyktatury* (Warsaw: IPN, 2009), 1:39. (MSW figures.)
16. *Polska pięć lat po Sierpniu*: Raport (London: Aneks, 1985), 5.
17. "Analiza aktualnych inicjatyw przeciwnika politycznego" (October 20, 1986), in Dudek, *Zmierzch dyktatury*, 1:62.

Notes to pp. 287–296

18. Svetlana Savranskaya, "The Logic of 1989," in *Masterpieces of History: The Peaceful End of the Cold War in Europe, 1989*, ed. Svetlana Savranskaya, Thomas Blanton, and Vladislav Zubok (New York: CEU Press, 2010), 5.

19. "Transcript of CC CPSU Politburo Session" (November 13, 1986), in Savranskaya, Blanton, and Zubok, *Masterpieces of History*, 238.

20. According to the opposition, approximately two-thirds of those entitled to vote took part, and according to an official communiqué, this figure was close to 79 percent (Sowa, *Historia polityczna Polski*, 585). In communist states, voter turnout usually reached 98–99 percent.

21. A. Paczkowski, "Playground of Superpowers, Poland 1980–89," in *The Last Decade of the Cold War: From Conflict Escalation to Conflict Transformation*, ed. Olav Njølstad (New York: Frank Cass, 2004), 388–89.

22. Dudek and Gryz, *Komuniści i Kościół w Polsce*, 429–30.

23. Marody, *Długi finał*, 51.

24. A study titled "Prognoza rozwoju sytuacji społeczno-politycznej," in Dudek, *Zmierzch dyktatury*, 1:172.

25. As cited in Dudek, *Reglamentowana rewolucja*, 106.

26. M. F. Rakowski, *Jak to się stało* (Warsaw: BGW, 1991), 119.

27. Dudek, *Reglamentowana rewolucja*, 209.

28. "Stenogram dyskusji roboczej," AAN, KC PZPR, 2639, p. 118.

29. Badura et al., *Społeczeństwo i władza*, 384. The survey was carried out the next day, after the debate.

30. Dudek, *Reglamentowana rewolucja*, 230.

31. *Trybuna Ludu*, January 20, 1989, 1.

32. Dudek, *Reglamentowana rewolucja*, 233.

33. Paweł Kowal, *Koniec systemu władzy: Polityka ekipy gen. Wojciecha Jaruzelskiego w latach 1986–1989* (Warsaw: ISP PAN-Trio, 2012), 313.

34. American policy toward Poland during this period is illustrated well in the following volume of documents: Gregory F. Domber, ed., *Ku zwycięstwu "Solidarności": Korespondencja Ambasady USA w Warszawie z Departamentem Stanu, styczeń-wrzesień 1989* (Warsaw: ISP PAN, 2006).

35. Kowal, *Koniec systemu władzy*, 287–88.

36. Dudek, *Zmierzch dyktatury*, 1:390–91.

37. "Memorandum from CC CPSU International Department," in Savranskaya, Blanton, and Zubok, *Masterpieces of History*, 354–55.

38. J. Elster, ed., *The Roundtable Talks and the Breakdown of Communism* (Chicago: University of Chicago Press, 1996), 4.

39. Dudek, *Reglamentowana rewolucja*, 261.

40. *Dziennik Ustaw* 19 (1989), pozycja 101.

41. Dudek, *Reglamentowana rewolucja*, 271.

42. Konstanty Gebert, *Mebel* (London: Aneks, 1990), 3.

43. Badura et al., *Społeczeństwo i władza*, 408. The survey was carried out just after the talks had concluded.

44. Paulina Codogni, *Wybory czerwcowe 1989 roku: U progu przemiany ustrojowej* (Warsaw: IPN, 2012), passim.

45. Badura et al., *Społeczeństwo i władza*, 434.

46. "Gazeta Wyborcza," July 4, 1989, 1.

Chapter Twenty

1. In 1984 imports amounted to 42 percent of the national production of the grain; see Rudolf G. Pikhoia, *Sovetskii Soiuz: istoriia vlasti, 1945–1991* (Moscow: RAGS, 1998), 370.

2. John Lewis Gaddis, *Strategies of Containment: A Critical Appraisal of American National Security Policy During the Cold War* (New York: Oxford University Press, 2005), 261.

3. Eduard Shevardnadze, *Moi vybor: V zashchitu demokratsii i svobody* (Moscow: Novosti, 1991), 65.

4. Włodzimierz Marciniak, *Rozgrabione imperium: Upadek Związku Sowieckiego i powstanie Federacji Rosyjskiej* (Kraków: Arcana, 2001), 110.

5. Vladimir Mau, *Ekonomika i vlast': Politicheskaia istoriia ekonomicheskoi reformy v Rossii, 1985–1994* (Moscow: Delo, 1995), 19.

6. Pikhoia, *Sovetskii Soiuz*, 488.

7. Vladislav Zubok, *A Failed Empire: The Soviet Union in the Cold War from Stalin to Gorbachev* (Chapel Hill: University of North Carolina Press, 2007), 330.

8. Pikhoia, *Sovetskii Soiuz*, 520.

9. Albert O. Hirschman, *Exit, Voice, and Loyalty: Responses to Decline in Firms, Organizations, and States* (Cambridge, MA: Harvard University Press, 1970), passim.

10. For text of the resolution, see András Bozóki, ed., *The Roundtable Talks of 1989: The Genesis of Hungarian Democracy* (Budapest: Central European University Press, 2002), 44–45.

11. John Lewis Gaddis, *The Cold War: A New History* (New York: Penguin Press, 2005), 289.

Conclusion

1. Stephen Kotkin and Jan T. Gross, *Uncivil Society: 1989 and the Implosion of the Communist Establishment* (New York: Modern Library, 2009), 9.

2. These changes took place also in the three Baltic states (Lithuania, Latvia, and Estonia) that were founded as a result of the Soviet Union's collapse.

3. Francis Fukuyama, *The End of History, and the Last Man* (New York: Avon, 1992).

4. Among other things, this was shown by the ethnic conflict in Yugoslavia and the "Operation Desert Storm" in Kuwait and Iraq, and especially by the later violent and

bloody events that were set off on September 11, 2001, by the terrorist attack on the World Trade Center in New York.

5. In 1991, it won approximately 570,000 votes (which was 5 percent of the total); in 1993, it won approximately 680,000 (just under 5 percent of the votes).

6. Ireneusz Krzemiński, *Solidarność: Niespełniony projekt polskiej demokracji* (Gdańsk: Europejskie Centrum Solidarności, 2013), 568.

7. Grzegorz Ekiert and Jan Kubik, *Rebellious Civil Society: Popular Protest and Democratic Consolidation in Poland, 1989–1993* (Ann Arbor: University of Michigan Press, 1999), passim.

8. Ralf Dahrendorf, *Reflections on the Revolution in Europe* (New York: Random House, 1990), 8.

Selected Bibliography

This list includes the important published primary and secondary sources that I cite throughout the book. In addition, I include here some English-language books that I do not cite directly but are helpful for understanding what was happening in Poland and in the international community during 1980–89.

Adamski, Wiesław, ed. *Polacy '81: postrzeganie kryzysu i konfliktu*. Warsaw: IFiS PAN, 1996.
Andrew, Christopher, and Vasili Mitrokhin. *The Mitrokhin Archive: The KGB in Europe and the West*. Warsaw: Muza SA, 2001.
Andrews, Nicholas G. *Poland, 1980–1981: Solidarity versus the Party*. Washington, DC: National Defense University Press, 1985.
Arbel, David, and Ran Edilist. *Western Intelligence and the Collapse of the Soviet Union, 1980–1990*. London: Frank Cass, 2003.
Ascherson, Neal. *Polish August: The Self-Limiting Revolution*. New York: Penguin Books, 1981.
Badura, Barbara, et al., eds. *Społeczeństwo i władza lat osiemdziesiątych w badaniach CBOS*. Warsaw: CBOS, 1994.
Barcikowski, Kazimierz. *U szczytów władzy*. Warsaw: Wydawnictwo Projekt, 1998.
Bereś, Witold, and Jerzy Skoczylas. *Generał Kiszczak mówi—prawie wszystko*. Warsaw: BGW, 1991.
Bernhard, Michael H. *The Origins of Democratization in Poland: Workers, Intellectuals, and Oppositional Politics, 1976–1980*. New York: Columbia University Press, 1993.
Bernstein, Carl, and Marcus Politi. *His Holiness: John Paul II and the Hidden History of Our Time*. New York: Doubleday, 1996.
Bingen, Dietmar. *Polityka Republiki Bońskiej wobec Polski*. Kraków: Wydawnictwo Kwadrat, 1997.
Bouyeure, Cyril. *L'Invention du politique. Une biographie d'Adam Michnik*. Lausanne: Éditions Noir sur Blanc, 2007.
Boyes, Roger. *The Naked President: A Political Life of Lech Walesa*. London: Secker and Warburg, 1994.

Bozóki, András, ed. *The Roundtable Talks of 1989: The Genesis of Hungarian Democracy*. Budapest: Central European University Press, 2002.
Bromke, Adam. *Poland: The Protracted Crisis*. Oakville: Mosaic Press, 1983.
Brumberg, Abraham, ed. *Poland: Genesis of a Revolution*. New York: Random House, 1983.
Brzechczyn, Krzysztof. "Program i myśl polityczna NSZZ 'Solidarność.'" In *NSZZ "Solidarność," 1980–1989*. Vol. 2, *Ruch społeczny*, edited by Ł. Kaminski and G. Waligóra, 13–74. Warsaw: IPN, 2010.
Brzeziński, Zbigniew. *Power and Principle: Memoirs of the National Security Adviser, 1977–1981*. New York: Farrar, Strauss and Giroux, 1985.
———. *The Grand Failure: The Bird and Death of Communism in the Twentieth Century*. New York: Collier Books, 1990.
Bujak, Zbigniew. *Prawda raz powiedziana*. Warsaw: NOW-a and Archiwum Solidarności, 1987.
Burakowski, Adam, Aleksander Gubrynowicz, and Paweł Ukielski. *1989—Jesień Narodów*. Warsaw: Trio, 2009.
Castle, Marjorie. *Triggering Communism's Collapse: Perception and Power in Poland's Transition*. Lanham, MD: Rowman and Littlefield, 2003.
Cenckiewicz, Sławomir, and Piotr Gontarczyk. *SB a Lech Wałęsa: Przyczynek do biografii*. Warsaw: IPN, 2008.
Chernayev, Anatoli. *My Six Years with Gorbachev*. University Park: Pennsylvania State University Press, 2000.
Codogni, Paulina. *Wybory czerwcowe 1989 roku: U progu przemiany ustrojowej*. Warsaw: IPN, 2012.
Curry, Jane, and Lubja Fajfer, eds. *Poland's Permanent Revolution: People vs. Elites, 1956 to the Present*. Washington, DC: American University Press, 1996.
Davis, Helen C. *Amerykanka w Warszawie*. Kraków: Znak, 2001.
de Tinguy, Anne, ed. *The Fall of the Soviet Empire*. New York: Columbia University Press, 1997.
de Weydenthal, J. B., et al. *The Polish Drama, 1980–1982*. Lexington, MA: Lexington Books, 1983.
Domber, Gregory F., ed. *Ku zwycięstwu "Solidarności." Korespondencja Ambasady USA w Warszawie z Departamentem Stanu, styczeń-wrzesień 1989*. Warsaw: Instytut Studiów Politycznych, 2006.
Domber, Gregory F. *Empowering Revolution: America, Poland, and the End of the Cold War*. Chapel Hill: University of North Carolina Press, 2014.
Dubiński, Krzysztof, ed. *Magdalenka: transakcja epoki. Notatki z poufnych spotkań Kiszczak-Wałęsa*. Warsaw: Sylwa, 1990.
Dudek, Antoni. *Reglamentowana rewolucja: rozkład dyktatury komunistycznej w Polsce 1988–1990*. 2nd edition. Kraków: Znak, 2014. First published 2004 by Arcana.
———, ed. *Stan wojenny w Polsce, 1981–1983*. Warsaw: IPN, 2003.
———, ed. *Zmierzch dyktatury: Polska lat 1986–1989 w świetle dokumentów*. Vol. 1–2. Warsaw: IPN, 2010.

Dudek, Antoni, and K. Madej, eds. *Świadectwa stanu wojennego*. Warsaw: IPN, 2001.
Dudek, Antoni, and Ryszard Gryz. *Komuniści i Kościół w Polsce, 1945–1989*. Kraków: Znak, 2003.
Dudek, Antoni, and Tomasz Marszałkowski. *Walki uliczne w PRL, 1956–1989*. Kraków: Wydawnictwo GEO, 1999.
Ekiert, Grzegorz. *The State Against Society: Political Crises and Their Aftermath in East Central Europe*. Princeton, NJ: Princeton University Press.
Ekiert, Grzegorz, and Jan Kubik. *Rebelious Civil Society: Popular Protest and Democratic Consolidation in Poland, 1989–1993*. Ann Arbor: University of Michigan Press, 1999.
Elster, John, ed. *The Round Table Talks and Breakdown of Communism*. Chicago: University of Chicago Press, 1996.
English, Robert. *Russia and the Idea of the West: Gorbachev, Intellectuals, and the End of the Cold War*. New York: Columbia University Press, 2000.
Fajerant, Jerzy [Jacek Cieszewski], ed. *Co powiedzą nasze dzieci? Relacja o strajku w kopalni "Ziemowit" (15–24 grudnia 1981 r.)*. Warsaw: Wydawnictwo Most, 1986.
Falk, Barbara J. *The Dilemmas of Dissidence in East-Central Europe: Citizen Intellectuals and Philosopher Kings*. Budapest: Central European University, 2003.
Fejtő, François. *La fin des démocraties populaires: les chemins du post-communisme*. Paris: Éditions du Seuil, 1992.
Friszke, Andrzej, ed. *"Solidarność" podziemna, 1981–1989*. Warsaw: Instytut Studiów Politycznych, 2006.
Friszke, Andrzej, and Marcin Zaremba, eds. *Wizyta Jana Pawła II w Polsce, 1979: Dokumenty KC PZPR i MSW*. Warsaw: Biblioteka Więzi i Instytut Studiów Politycznych PAN, 2005.
Gaddis, John Lewis. *Strategies of Containment: A Critical Appraisal of American National Security Policy During the Cold War*. New York: Oxford University Press, 2005.
———. *The Cold War: A New History*, New York: Penguin Press, 2005.
Garlicki, Andrzej, and Włodzimierz Borodziej, eds. *Okrągły Stół. Dokumenty i materiały*. Vol. 1–5. Warsaw: Kancelaria Prezydenta RP, 2004.
Garton Ash, Timothy. *The Magic Lantern: The Revolution of '89 Witnessed in Warsaw, Budapest, Berlin, and Prague*. New York: Vintage Books, 1991.
———. *The Polish Revolution: Solidarity*. 2nd edition. New York: Scribner's, 1984. First published 1983 by Jonathan Cape.
Gati, Charles. *The Bloc That Failed: Soviet–East European Relations in Transition*. Bloomington: University of Indiana Press, 1990.
Gebert, Konstanty. *Mebel* London: Aneks, 1990.
Gedmin, Jeffrey. *The Hidden Hand: Gorbachev and the Collapse of East Germany*. Washington, DC: American Enterprise Institute, 1992.
Geremek odpowiada, Żakowski pyta: rok 1989. Warsaw: Plejada, 1990.
Gerrits, Andre W. M. *The Failure of Authoritarian Change: Reform, Opposition, and Geo-Politics in Poland in the 1980s*. Aldershot: Darmouth Publishing Co., 1990.

354 Selected Bibliography

Gerner, Kristian, and Stefan Hedlund. *The Baltic States and the End of the Soviet Empire*. London: Routledge, 1993.
Głębocki, Henryk. *Policja tajna przy robocie: Z dziejów państwa policyjnego w PRL*. Kraków: Arcana, 2005.
Goddeeris, Idesbald, ed. *Solidarity with "Solidarity": Western European Trade Unions and the Polish Crisis, 1980–1982*. New York: Lexington Books, 2010.
Gołąb, Bogusław, and Władysław Kałudziński, eds. *Kwidzyn: W niewoli brata mego; Wspomnienia, refleksje, oceny*. Olsztyn: Pro Patria, 2005.
Golimont, Andrzej. *Generałowie Bezpieki*. Warsaw: BGW, 1992.
Goodwyn, Lawrence. *Breaking the Barrier: The Rise of Solidarity in Poland*. New York: Oxford University Press, 1991.
Gorbachev, Mikhail S. *Memoires*. New York: Doubleday, 1996.
Grajewski, Andrzej, and Artur Kasprzykowski, eds. *Czas próby: "Solidarność" na Podbeskidziu w latach 1980–2005*. Bielsko-Biała: Region Solidarność, 2006.
Grala, Dariusz T. *Reformy gospodarcze w PRL (1982–1989): próba uratowania socjalizmu*, Warsaw: Trio, 2005.
Hajdasz, Jolanta. *Szczekaczka czyli Rozgłośnia Polska Radia Wolna Europa*. Poznań: Media Rodzina, 2006.
Herschberg, James G. *James B. Conant: Harvard to Hiroshima and the Making of the Nuclear Age*. New York: Alfred A. Knopf, 1993.
Hirschman, Albert O. *Exit, Voice, and Loyalty: Responses to Decline in Firms, Organizations, and States*. Cambridge, MA: Harvard University Press, 1970.
Holzer, Jerzy. *"Solidarność" 1980–1981: Geneza i historia*. Warsaw: Krąg, 1983.
Hufbauer, Gary C., Jeffrey J. Schott, and Kimberly A. Elliott. *Economic Sanctions Reconsidered: History and Current Policy*. Washington, DC: Institute for International Economics, 1983.
Jabłonowski, Marek, Włodzimierz Janowski, and Wiesław Władyka, eds. *Narady i telekonferencje kierownictwa PZPR w latach 1980–1981*. Warsaw: Wydział Dziennikarstwa i Nauk Politycznych UW, 2004.
Jajakobyły: Spowiedź życia Jerzego Urbana. Compiled by Przemysław Ćwiklinski and Piotr Gadzinowski. Warsaw: BGW, 1992.
Jankowska, Janina. *Rozmowy niedokończone: Rozmowy z twórcami "Solidarnosci" 1980–1981*. Warsaw: Biblioteka Więzi, 2003.
Janowski, Karol B. *Źródła i przebieg zmiany politycznej w Polsce (1980–1989)*. Toruń: Adam Marszałek, 2003.
Jaruzelski, Wojciech. *Stan wojenny. Dlaczego . . .* Warsaw: BGW, 1992.
———. *Les chaines et les refuges: memoires*. Paris: Jean-Claude Latte, 1992.
Jasiewicz, Krzysztof. *Polacy '84 z półtorarocznej perspektywy: Raport wstępny z badań*. Warsaw: Uniwersytet Warszawski, 1986.
Jaworski, Paweł, and Łukasz Kamiński, eds. *Świat wobec "Solidarności," 1980–1989*. Warsaw: IPN, 2013.
Jóźwik, Artur. *Krakówska Kuźnica: Historia, ludzie, idee*. Kraków: Trans-Krak, 2005.

Kaliński, Janusz. *Gospodarka Polski w latach 1944–1989: Przemiany strukturalne.* Warsaw: PWE, 1995.

Kałudziński, W., ed. *Internowani w Iławie (1981–1982).* Olsztyn: Pro Patria, 2006.

Kamińska, Józefa [Władysław Chojnacki]. *Bibliografia publikacji podziemnych w Polsce, 13 XII 1981—VI 1986.* Paris: Editions Spotkania, 1988.

Kaminski, Bartłomiej. *The Collapse of State Socialism: The Case of Poland.* Princeton, NJ: Princeton University Press, 1991.

Kamiński, Łukasz, ed. *Przed i po 13 grudnia: państwa Bloku Wschodniego wobec kryzysu w PRL, 1980–1982.* Vol. 1–2. Warsaw: IPN, 2006–7.

Kamiński, Łukasz, and Paweł Piotrowski, eds. *Opozycja demokratyczna w Polsce w świetle akt KC PZPR (1976–1980).* Wrocław: Wydawnictwo GAJT, 2002.

Kamiński, Ł., W. Sawicki, and G. Waligóra, eds., *Solidarność Walcząca w dokumentach.* Warsaw: IPN, 2007.

Kamiński, Ł., and G. Waligora, eds. *NSZZ "Solidarność," 1980–1989.* Vol. 2–7. Warsaw: IPN, 2010.

Kania, Stanisław. *Zatrzymać konfrontację.* Warsaw: BGW, 1991.

Kengor, Paul. *The Crusader: Ronald Reagan and the Fall of Communism.* New York: HarperCollins, 2006.

Kennedy, Michael D. *Professionals, Power, and Solidarity in Poland: A Critical Sociology of Soviet-Type Society.* Cambridge: Cambridge University Press, 1991.

Kenney, Padraic. *A Carnival of Revolution: Central Europe 1989.* Princeton, NJ: Princeton University Press, 2002.

Kochanowski, Jerzy. *Tylnymi drzwiami: "Czarny rynek" w Polsce, 1944–1989.* Warsaw: Neriton, 2010.

Konderak, Adam. *Bibliografia prasy opozycyjnej w PRL do wprowadzenia stanu wojennego.* Lublin: UMCS, 1998.

Kondratowicz, Ewa. *Szminka na sztandarze. Kobiety w "Solidarności."* Warsaw: Wydawnictwo Sic!, 2001.

Kopka, Bogusław, and Grzegorz Majchrzak, eds. *Stan wojenny w dokumentach władz PRL, 1980–1983.* Warsaw: IPN, 2001.

Kotkin, Stephen, and Jan T. Gross. *Uncivil Society: 1989 and the Implosion of the Communist Establishment.* New York: Modern Library, 2009.

Kowal, Paweł. *Koniec systemu władzy: Polityka ekipy gen; Wojciecha Jaruzelskiego w latach 1986–1989.* Warsaw: ISP PAN-Trio, 2012.

Kowalski, Lech. *Komitet Obrony Kraju (MON-PZPR-MSW).* Warsaw: Semper, 2011.

Krakówska-Narożniak, Joanna, and Marek Waszkiel, eds. *Teatr drugiego obiegu: Materiały do kroniki teatru stanu wojennego, 13 XII 1981–15 XI 1989.* Warsaw: Errata, 2000.

Kramer, Mark. *Soviet Deliberations during the Polish Crisis, 1980–1981.* Washington, DC: The Woodrow Wilson Center, 1999.

Krawczyk, Andrzej, et al., eds. *Dokumenty: teczka Susłowa.* Warsaw: Interpress, 1993.

Kubik, Jan. *The Power of Symbols against the Symbols of Power: The Rise of Solidarity and the Fall of State Communism in Poland.* University Park: Pennsylvania State University Press, 1994.

Kuisz, Jarosław. *Charakter prawny porozumień sierpniowych 1980–1981.* Warsaw: Wydawnictwo Trio, 2009.

Kuroń, Jacek. *Gwiezdny czas.* London: Aneks, 1991.

———. *Zło, które czynię.* Warsaw: Nowa, 1984.

Kwiatkowski, Piotr T. *Stan wojenny w badaniach opinii publicznej w latach 1982–2003.* Szczecin: Szczecińskie Towarzystwo Naukowe, 2005.

Laba, Roman. *The Roots of Solidarity: A Political Sociology of Poland's Working-Class Democratization.* Princeton, NJ: Princeton University Press, 1991.

Levesque, Jacques. *The Enigma of 1989: The USSR and the Liberation of Eastern Europe.* Berkeley: University of California Press, 1997.

Lewis, Paul G. *Political Authority and Party Secretaries in Poland, 1975–1986.* New York: Cambridge University Press, 1989.

Lipski, Jan J. *KOR: Komitet Obrony Robotników Komitet Samoobrony Społecznej.* London: Aneks, 1983. (Later published as *KOR: A History of the Workers' Defense Committee in Poland, 1976–1981.* Berkeley: University of California Press, 1985.)

Luszniewicz, Jacek, and Andrzej Zawistowski. *Sprawy gospodarcze w dokumentach pierwszej Solidarności.* Vol. 1, *16 sierpnia 1980–30 czerwca 1981.* Warsaw: IPN, 2008.

Łopieński, Maciej, Marcin Moskit [Zbigniew Gach], and Mariusz Wilk. *Konspira: Rzecz o podziemnej Solidarności.* Paris: Editions Spotkania, 1984. (Later published as *Konspira: Solidarity Underground.* Berkeley: University of California Press, 1990.)

MacEachin, Douglas J. *U.S. Intelligence and the Confrontation in Poland, 1980–1981.* University Park: Pennsylvania State University Press, 2002.

Maier, Charles S. *Dissolution: The Crisis of Communism and the End of East Germany.* Princeton, NJ: Princeton University Press, 1997.

Majchrzak, Grzegorz. "Informacje sytuacyjne MSW z sierpnia 1980 roku." *Zeszyty Historyczne* 145 (2003): 65–155.

Mann, James. *The Rebellion of Ronald Reagan: A History of the End of the Cold War.* New York: Penguin, 2009.

Marciniak, Włodzimierz. *Rozgrabione imperium: Upadek Związku Sowieckiego i powstanie Federacji Rosyjskiej.* Kraków: Arcana, 2001.

Marody, Mirosława. *Długi finał.* Warsaw: WSiP, 1995.

Matlock, Jack F. *Autopsy on an Empire: The American Ambassador's Account of the Collapse of the Soviet Union.* New York: Random House, 1995.

Mau, Vladimir. *Ekonomika i vlast': Politicheskaia istoriia ekonomicheskoi reformy v Rossii, 1985–1994.* Moscow: Delo, 1995.

Melone, Albert P. *Creating Parliamentary Government: The Transition to Democracy in Bulgaria.* Columbus, OH: Ohio State University Press, 1998.

Meretik, Gabriel. *Noc generała*. Warsaw: Alfa, 1989.
Michta, Andrew. *Red Eagle: The Army in Polish Politics, 1944–1988*. Stanford: Hoover Institution Press, 1990.
Medvedev, Vadim A. *Raspad. Kak on nazreval v "mirovoi sistemie socializma."* Moscow: Mezhdunarodnyie Otnosheninya, 1994.
Mink, Georges. *La force ou la raison: histoire sociale et politique de la Pologne, 1980–1989*. Paris: Éditions la *Découverte*, 1989.
Muszyńska, Jolanta, Aneta Osiak, and Dorota Wojtera. *Obraz codzienności w prasie stanu wojennego*. Warsaw: TRIO, 2006.
Myant, Martin. *Poland: A Crisis for Socialism*. London: Lawrence and Wishart, 1982.
Neja, Jarosław. *Grudzień 1981 roku w województwie katowickim*. Katowice: IPN, 2011.
Niewęgłowski, W., ed. *Kościół i kultura w latach osiemdziesiątych XX wieku: Doświadczenia warszawskie*. Warsaw: IPN, 2011.
Njelstad, Olav, ed. *The Last Decade of the Cold War: From Conflict Escalation to Conflict Transformation*. New York: Frank Cass, 2004.
NSZZ "Solidarność." *Komisja Krajowa NSZZ "Solidarność": Posiedzenie w dniach 11–12 grudnia 1981*. Warsaw: Archiwum Solidarności, 2003.
Ochocki, M. *Byłem człowiekiem Kiszczaka*. Łódź: Athos, 1992.
Olaszek, Jan, ed. *Dokumenty władz NSZZ "Solidarność," 1981–1989*. Warsaw: IPN, 2010.
Orszulik, Alojzy, ed. *Czas przełomu. Notatki z rozmów z władzami PRL w latach 1981–1989*. Warsaw: Apostolicum, 2006.
Osa, Maryjane. *Solidarity and Contention: Network of Polish Opposition*. Minneapolis: Univeristy of Minnesota Press, 2003.
Osęka, Piotr. *Marzec '68*. Kraków: Znak, 2008.
Ost, David. *The Politics of Anti-Politics: Opposition and Reform in Poland since 1968*. Philadelphia: Temple University Press, 1990.
Ouimet, Matthew J. *The Rise and the Fall of the Brezhnev Doctrine in Soviet Foreign Policy*. Chapel Hill: University of North Carolina Press, 2001.
Paczkowski, Andrzej. *The Spring Will Be Ours: Poland and the Poles from Occupation to Freedom, 1939–1989*. Translated by Jane Cave. University Park: Pennsylvania State University Press, 2003.
———. *Droga do mniejszego zła: strategia i taktyka obozu władzy, lipiec 1980–styczeń 1982*. Kraków: Wydawnictwo Literackie, 2002.
———. *Wojna polsko-jaruzelska. Stan wojenny w Polsce 13 XII 1981–22 VII 1983*. Warsaw: Wydawnictwo Prószyński, 2006.
———. *Strajki, bunty, manifestacje jako "polska droga" przez socjalizm*. Poznań: PTPN, 2003.
Paczkowski, Andrzej, and Malcolm Byrne, eds. *From Solidarity to Martial Law: The Polish Crisis of 1980–1981. A Documentary History*. Budapest: Central European University Press, 2006.
Paczkowski, Andrzej, and Andrzej Werblan. *On the Decision to Introduce Martial Law: Two Historians Report to the Commission on Constitutional Oversight of the SEJM*

of the Republic of Poland. Washington, DC: Woodrow Wilson Center for International Scholars, 1997.

Patoka, Witold. *Poland under Pressure, 1980–1981: Crisis Management in State-Society Conflict*. Umea: Umea University Printing Office, 2001.

Pavlov, Witali G. *Rukovoditeli Polshi glazami razvedchika: krizysnyie gody 1973–1984*. Moscow: Terra, 1998. Originally published as *Byłem rezydentem KGB w Polsce* (Warsaw: BGW, 1994).

Penn, Shana. *Solidarity's Secret: The Women Who Defeated Communism in Poland*. Ann Arbor: University of Michigan Press, 2005.

Peszkowski, Stanisław [Andrzej Paczkowski], ed. *Ostatni rok władzy 1988–1989. Dokumenty Biura Politycznego*. London: Aneks, 1994.

Pfaff, Steven. *Exit-Voice Dynamics and the Collapse of East Germany: The Crisis of Leninism and the Revolution of 1989*. Durham, NC: Duke University Press, 2006.

Pikhoia, Rudolf G. *Sovetskii Soiuz: istoriia vlasti, 1945–1991*. Moscow: RAGS, 1998.

Pipes, Richard. *Vixi: Memoirs of a Non-Belonger*. New Haven: Yale University Press, 2004.

Pleskot, Patryk. *Kłopotliwa panna "S." Postawy polityczne Zachodu wobec "Solidarności" na tle stosunków z PRL (1980–1989)*. Warsaw: IPN, 2013.

Podgórecki, Adam. *Polish Society*. Westport, CT: Praeger-Greenwood, 1994.

Poland: The Long Journey to Freedom. Brussels: NATO Multimedia Library, 2011.

Polish Helsinki Watch Committee. *Poland under Martial Law*. Washington, DC: US Helsinki Watch Committee, 1983.

Poznanski, Kazimierz. *Poland's Protracted Transition: Institutional Change and Economic Growth, 1970–1994*. Cambridge: Cambridge University Press, 1996.

Przastek, Daniel. *Środowisko teatru w okresie stanu wojennego*. Warsaw: INP UW, 2005.

Rachwald, Arthur R. *In Search of Poland: Superpower's Response to Solidarity, 1980–1989*. Stanford: Hoover Institution Press, 1990.

Raina, Peter, ed. *Rozmowy z władzami PRL: Arcybiskup Dąbrowski w służbie Kościoła i Narodu*. Vol. 2, 1982–89. Warsaw: Wydawnictwo Książka Polska, 1995.

———, ed. *Stan wojenny w zapiskach arcybiskupa Dąbrowskiego*. Warsaw: Wydawnictwo von Borowiecky, 2006.

———, ed. *Jan Paweł II, Prymas i Episkopat Polski o stanie wojennym*. Paris and London: Oficyna Poetów i Malarzy, 1982.

Raina, Peter, and Marcin Brożek, eds. *Operacja "Lato-80": Preludium stanu wojennego. Dokumenty MSW 1980–1981*. Pelplin: Bernardinum, 2003.

Rakowski, Mieczysław F. *Dzienniki polityczne*. Vol. 7–10. Warsaw: Iskry, 2004–5.

———. *Jak to się stało*. Warsaw: BGW, 1991.

Raport: pięć lat po Sierpniu. London: Aneks, 1985.

Reiff, Ryszard. *Czas "Solidarności."* Warsaw: Spotkania, 1988.

Reykowski, J. *Logika walki: Szkice z psychologii konfliktu społecznego w Polsce*. Warsaw: Książka i Wiedza, 1984.

Riechers, A. *Hilfe für Solidarność*. Bonn: Friedrich-Ebert-Stiftung, 2006.

Rodowicz, Władysław. *Komitet na Piwnej: Fakty-dokumenty-wspomnienia.* Warsaw: Więź, 1994.

Rojek, Paweł. *Semiotyka Solidarności: Analiza dyskursów PZPR i NSZZ "Solidarność" w 1981 roku.* Kraków: Nomos, 2009.

Rokita, Jan, and Antoni Dudek, eds. *Raport Rokity. Sprawozdanie Sejmowej Komisji Nadzwyczajnej do Zbadania Działalności MSW.* Kraków: Arcana, 2005.

Rolicki, Janusz. *Edward Gierek: przerwana dekada; Wywiad rzeka.* Warsaw: Wydawnictwo Fakt, 1990.

Romek, Zbigniew, ed. *Cenzura w PRL: Relacje historyków.* Warsaw: Neriton, 2000.

Rudka, Szczepan. *Poza cenzurą: Wrocławska prasa bezdebitowa 1973–1989.* Warsaw: PWN, 2001.

Ruzikowski, Tadeusz. "Tajni współpracownicy pionów operacyjnych aparatu bezpieczeństwa, 1950–1984." *Pamięć i Sprawiedliwość* 1 (2003): 109–31.

Sanford, George. *Military Rule in Poland: The Rebulding of Communist Power, 1981–1983.* New York: St. Martin's Press, 1986.

Sarotte, Mary E. *1989: The Struggle to Create Post-Cold War Europe.* Princeton, NJ: Princeton University Press, 2009.

Sasanka, Paweł. *Czerwiec 1976: Geneza, przebieg, konsekwencje.* Warsaw: IPN, 2006.

Savranskaya, Svetlana, Thomas Blanton, and Vladislav Zubok, eds. *Masterpieces of History: The Peaceful End of the Cold War in Europe, 1989.* New York: Central European University Press, 2010.

Schweitzer, Peter. *Victory: The Reagan Administration's Secret Strategy that Hastened the Collapse of the Soviet Union.* New York: Atlantic Monthly Press, 1994.

Sebestyen, Victor. *Revolution 1989: The Fall of the Soviet Empire.* New York: Pantheon, 2009.

Shevardnadze, Eduard. *Moi vybor. V zashchitu demokratsii i svobody.* Moscow: Novosti, 1991.

Siam-Davies, Peter. *The Roumanian Revolution of December 1989.* Ithaca, NY: Cornell University Press, 2005.

Sjursen, Helene. *The United States, Western Europe, and the Polish Crisis.* Houndmills: Palgrave Macmillan, 2003.

Skoczek, Anna. *Poezja świadectwa i sprzeciwu: Stan wojenny w twórczości wybranych polskich poetów.* Kraków: Wydawnictwo SMS, 2004.

Skórzyński, Jan. *Siła bezsilnych: Historia Komitetu Obrony Robotników.* Warsaw: Świat Książki, 2012.

Skórzyński, Jan, Paweł Sowiński, and Małgorzata Strasz, eds. *Opozycja w PRL. Słownik biograficzny 1956–1989.* Vol. 1–3. Warsaw: Karta, 2002.

Slay, Ben. *Polish Economy: Crisis, Reform, and Transformation.* Princeton, NJ: Princeton University Press, 1994.

Słodkowska, Inka. *Społeczeństwo obywatelskie na tle historycznego przełomu. Polska 1980–1989.* Warsaw: Instytut Studiów Politycznych, 2006.

Smolar, Nina, ed. *Wejdą nie wejdą: Polska 1980–1982: wewnętrzny kryzys, międzynarodowe uwarunkowania.* London: Aneks, 1999.

Snyder, Sarah B. *Human Rights Activism and the End of the Cold War*. Cambridge: Cambridge University Press, 2011.
Solak, Zbigniew, et al., eds. *Stan wojenny w Małopolsce w oczach świadków*. Kraków: Księgarnia Akademicka, 2001.
Sowa, Andrzej L. *Historia polityczna Polski, 1944–1991*. Kraków: Wydawnictwo Literackie, 2011.
Sowiński, Paweł. *Zakazana książka: Uczestnicy drugiego obiegu 1977–1989*. Warsaw: ISP PAN, 2011.
Spiski, Piotr. *Od trzynastego do trzynastego*. London: Polonia Book Fund, 1983.
Staniszkis, Jadwiga. *Poland's Self-Limiting Revolution*. Princeton, NJ: Princeton University Press, 1984.
———. *The Dynamics of Breakthrough in Eastern Europe: The Polish Experience*. Berkeley: California University Press, 1991.
Stanowska, Maria, and Adam Strzembosz. *Sędziowie warszawscy w czasie próby, 1981–1988*. Warsaw: IPN, 2005.
Statut. Uchwała programowa z Aneksem. Dokumenty Zjazdu. Gdańsk: BIPS, 1981.
Stokes, Gale. *The Walls Came Tumbling Down: Collapse and Rebirth in Eastern Europe*. New York: Oxford University Press, 2012.
Stola, Dariusz. *Kraj bez wyjścia? Migracje z Polski, 1949–1989*. Warsaw: IPN, ISP PAN, 2010.
Stoner, Kathryn, and Michael McPaul, eds. *Transition to Democracy: A Comparative Perspective*. Baltimore, MD: Johns Hopkins University Press, 2013.
Szejnert, Małgorzata. *Sława i infamia: Rozmowa z Bohdanem Korzeniowskim*. London: Aneks, 1988.
Szlajfer, Henryk, ed. *Ku wielkiej zmianie: Korespondencja między Ambasadą PRL w Waszyngtonie a MSZ, styczeń-październik 1989*. Warsaw: Instytut Studiów Politycznych, 2008.
Tajne dokumenty: Państwo-Kościół, 1980–1989. London and Warsaw: Aneks, 1993.
Thomas, Daniel. *The Helsinki Effect: International Norms, Human Rights, and the Demise of Communism*. Princeton, NJ: Princeton University Press, 2001.
Tismaneanu, Vladimir, ed. *The Revolution of 1989*. New York: Routledge, 1999.
Tokes, Rudolf L. *Hungary's Negotiated Revolution: Economic Reform, Social Change, and Political Succession, 1957–1990*. Cambridge: Cambridge University Press, 1996.
Torańska, Teresa. *Byli*. Warsaw: Świat Książki, 2006.
Touraine, Alain, Francois Dubet, Michel Wiewiorka, and Jan Strzelecki. *Solidarity: The Analysis of a Social Movement: Poland, 1980–1981*. Cambridge: Cambridge University Press, 1983.
Trembicka, Krystyna. *Okrągły Stół w Polsce: studium o porozumieniu politycznym*. Lublin: UMCS, 2003.
The United States and the Polish Crisis, 1980–1982: Sample Documents. Washington, DC: The National Security Archives, 1995.

Uparci z "Piasta": Relacje i głosy strajkujących górników. Compiled by Jacek Cieszewski. Bieruń: "Solidarność" KWK "Piast," 2001.
Użyto broni: Relacja górników kopalni "Wujek." Compiled by Jacek Cieszewski. Kraków: Biblioteka Obserwatora Wojennego, 1988.
Wałęsa. Gdańsk: Wydawnictwo Morskie, 1981.
Wałęsa, Lech. *A Way of Hope*. New York: H. Holt, 1987.
———. *Droga nadziei*. Vol. 1–2. Warsaw: Rytm, 1989.
———. *Struggle and the Triumph*. New York: Arcade Publishers, 1992.
Walichnowski, Tadeusz, ed., *Stan wojenny w Polsce 13.12.1981—22.07.1983: Dokumenty i materiały archiwalne*. Warsaw: Commandor, 2001.
———, ed. *Ochrona bezpieczeństwa państwa i porządku publicznego w Polsce, 1944–1948*. Warsaw: Akademia Spraw Wewnetrznych, 1989.
Wedel, Janine. *The Private Poland: An Anthropologist's Look on Everyday Life*. New York: Facts on File Publications, 1986.
Weigel, George. *Witness to Hope: The Biography of Pope John Paul II*. New York: Cliff Street Books, 2001.
Weiser, Benjamin. *A Secret Life: The Polish Officer, His Covert Mission, and the Price He Paid to Save his Country*. New York: Public Affairs, 2004.
Wiatr, Jerzy J. *Życie w ciekawych czasach*. Warsaw: Europejska Wyższa Szkoła Prawa i Administracji, 2008.
Wilke, Manfred, Michael Kubina, and Reinhard Gutsche. "Kierownictwo SED wobec polskiego ruchu opozycyjnego w latach 1980–1981." In *Studia i Materiały* no. 75, 43–88. Warsaw: Polski Instytut Spraw Miedzynarodowych, 1994.
Wiśniewski, W. *Dlaczego upadł socjalizm?* Warsaw: Wydawnictwo Sprawy Polityczne, 2006.
Włodek, Zbigniew, ed. *PZPR a "Solidarność" 1980–1981. Tajne dokumenty Biura Politycznego*. 2nd edition. Warsaw: IPN, 2013. First published 1992 by Aneks.
Zieliński, Zygmunt. *Kościół w Polsce, 1944–2004*. Radom: Polskie Wydawnictwo Encyklopedyczne, 2003.
Zubok, Vladislav. *A Failed Empire: The Soviet Union in the Cold War from Stalin to Gorbachev*. Chapel Hill: University of North Carolina Press, 2008.
Zuzanna, Katarzyna [Barbara Tchórzewska]. *Czterech z "Andaluzji."* Warsaw: NOW-a, 1985.

INDEX

An asterisk (*) indicates that this organization's full name (in Polish/English) appears as an entry in the Abbreviations.

AAN. *See* Archiwum Akt Nowych
actors' boycott of martial law, 178–80; and Glemp, 229
Afghanistan, Soviet Union invasion of, vii, 122, 263, 300, 303–4
Agence France-Presse (AFP), 121
AIPN.* *See* Instytutu Pamięci Narodowej (Archiwum)
AK.* *See* Home Army
Alexander II (Tsar), 274
Alma Ata (Kazakhstan), 304
"Ambassador," martial law operation by MSW/SB, 194, 239, 343n3
amnesty, 219–20, 288; (July 1983), 273–75; (July 1984), 285
Amnesty International, 118, 255
Andaluzja mine (in Piekary Śląskie), strike in, 77, 82–83; miners' trials, 107. *See also* strikes/protests
Andropov, Iurii (KGB chief), 263; death of, 300; and Jaruzelski, 27–28, 36, 212
Anna mine (in Wodzisław Śląski), strike in, 90. *See also* strikes/protests
anniversaries/commemorations/memories of: Battle of Vienna, 196; Gdańsk Agreement (Aug. 31, 1980), 197–202, 318; January Uprising (1863–1864), 177; John Paul II, assassination attempt on, 191; March 1968, 249; martial law imposition, 100, 174, 178, 182, 186, 189, 198, 205, 206, 207, 208, 249; massacre on the Baltic coast (Dec. 1970), 8, 13–14, 36, 86, 105, 174, 199, 208, 216, 233; May Day (1982), 195, 250, 251; November Uprising (1830), 229; Poland's independence (Nov. 11), 7, 205, 208, 210, 211, 233; Polish Constitution (May 1791), 7, 189, 195, 233, 250; Poznań's "Black Thursday" (1956), 197–98, 256; Solidarity's registration, 205, 211; strikes of 1980, 198; Warsaw Ghetto Uprising (1943), 256; at Warsaw's Victory Square, 174; Wujek mine massacre (Dec. 1981), 174, 208, 216, 233
Anoshkin, General Victor I., 328n2; on Jaruzelski, 37–38, 39, 41; on martial law, 52; on Solidarity leaders/Wałęsa, 49, 71. *See also* Kulikov, Victor
Archiwum Akt Nowych (in Warsaw) (Archives of Modern Records), xii
Aristov, Ambassador Boris, 37; Jaruzelski and, 35–36, 39, 148. *See also* Brezhnev, Leonid; Kulikov, Victor
Arłamów. *See* Wałęsa, Lech
Armenia, 304
army. *See* Polish Army

Artistic and Academic Associations' Consultative Committee (Komitet Porozumiewawczy Stowarzyszeń Twórczych i Naukowych), 18, 47
Association of Journalists of the PRL, 264
Association of Polish Artist and Designers (Związek Polskich Artystów Plastyków, ZPAP), 246
Atlas, Michał, 218
AWS.* *See* Solidarity Electoral Action
"Azalea" ("Azalia"), martial law operation by MSW/SB, 54–55, 62, 94, 97, 121
Azerbaijan, 304

Babiuch, Edward, 15, 103, 275
Baibakov, Nikolai, 39
Bajerowa, Irena, 114
Baker, James, 121
Bałuka, Edmund, 257
Barcikowski, Kazimierz, 14; on AK, 146; and Church, 61, 70, 150, 152, 199, 225; "directorate" and, 72–73; and martial law, 42, 59–60, 66, 92, 219; and party, 261, 262; on Solidarity, 22, 143–44. *See also* Dąbrowski, Archbishop Bronisław; Wałęsa, Lech
BBC. *See* radio stations (foreign)
Bednarz, Piotr, 84, 209
Bednorz, Bishop Henryk, 91
Berlin (East). *See* German Democratic Republic
Berlin Wall, 122, 308, 309
Bern, demonstrations against martial law, 125
Białołęka prison (near Warsaw), 100, 170, 234
Białystok, 78, 141, 155, 159, 181, 249; demonstrations in, 189; reprisals in, 111, 112; Solidarity/underground structures in, 166–67; trials in, 105; TV boycott in ("television walks"), 180–81. *See also* strikes/protests; Zamet factory

Bielawa, 200; Radio Solidarity broadcast in, 243
Bielecki, Czesław, 156
Bielsko-Biała, 107, 191; demonstrations in, 189, 200, 206; strike committee in, 80; Radio Solidarity broadcast in, 243; Solidarity/underground structure in, 166–67; TV boycott in ("television walks"), 180. *See also* strikes/protests
Bierut, Bolesław, 75
Big Brother. *See* Soviet Union
Biuletyn Informacyjny (Informational Bulletin) (underground publication), 168. *See also* publishing
Blachnicki, Father Franciszek, 228
Bobrowski, Czesław, 268
Bochnia, 200, 252; trials, 105
Bogacz, Zbigniew, 91, 99
Bogdanowicz, Father Stanisław, 190
Bogucki, Father Teofil, 182
Bogucki, Janusz, 245
Bolczyk, Father Henryk, 80, 81
BOR. *See* Government Protection Bureau
Boratyński, Henryk, 59
Border Defense Troops (Wojska Ochrony Pogranicza) (MSW military unit), 54, 86, 91, 210. *See also* MSW*
Borowski, Adam, 164, 166, 186, 194
Borusewicz, Bogdan, 16, 68, 84, 167, 169
Borynia mine. *See* Rybnik Coal Area
Boston, demonstrations against martial law, 125
Bratislava, 309
Brezhnev, Leonid Ilyich, vii, 326n4; death of, 212, 263, 300; and Gierek, 13, 15; and Jaruzelski, 36, 129, 130–1; and Kania, 25, 27, 28; and Kulikov, 37, 38, 39; martial law, 128–29; Reagan and, 126. *See also* Soviet Union

Brucan, Silviu, 306
Brumberg, Abraham, 323n2
Brunné, Marek, 142
Brześć, 70; Soviet-Polish meeting in (April 1981), 27–28
Brzeziński, Zbigniew, xii, 289, 325n16
Bucharest. *See* Romania
Budapest. *See* Hungary
Budzisz-Krzyżanowska, Teresa, 246
Bujak, Zbigniew, 16, 158, 178, 200, 317; in hiding, 68, 80, 155, 156, 192; interviews with (*Tygodnik Mazowsze*), 169, 273, 339n20, 346n24; on Solidarity meeting (Dec. 13, 1981), 49; on Solidarity underground, 161, 286; and TKK, 171, 205. *See also* Solidarity; TKK*
Bukovskii, Vladimir, 302
Bulgaria (Sofia), 324n4; martial law and, 129; *perestroika* and, 304, 305, 309, 311, 312, 316; pressure on Jaruzelski, 28
Bundestag (West Germany), resolution on martial law, 125
Bush, George H. W., 121, 289; and Gorbachev, 311; stance on Poland, 293. *See also* US-USSR relations
Bydgoszcz, 133, 200; Radio Solidarity broadcast in, 243
"Bydgoszcz incident" (March 1981), 27, 45, 69. *See also* Rulewski, Jan
Bytom, 77; strike committee in, 80; trials in, 105

Carrington, Lord Peter, 123
Carter, Jimmy, 9
Castro, Fidel, 101, 300, 309
Catholic Church (Roman) (in Poland), 6; and "art at churches," 245–47; Church-state relations, 4–5, 21, 37, 42, 223–25, 285, 290, 346n10; and martial law, 61, 70, 224–29; Masses for the Fatherland, 182–83, 233, 237, 248, 250; Ministry of Artistic Circles, 245; and opposition, 7–8, 139–40; priests and (underground) Solidarity, 155, 158, 233–34; and Round Table, 293; as security apparatus target, 209, 235–36; and Solidarity, 69, 37–38, 144, 147, 204, 232, 236; and Wałęsa, 150–53. *See also* Episcopate; Glemp, Cardinal Józef; independent society
CBOS.* *See* Public Opinion Research Center
"CDN" (*Ciąg Dalszy Nastąpi*) (underground publication), 160, 340n1; "Agreement," 164
CDN (underground publishing house), 160. *See also* publishing
Ceauşescu, Nicolae, 299, 306; on army vs. party, 131, 132; and martial law, 129–130; trial and death of, 310. *See also* Romania
Cegielski, H. factory (in Poznań), 191, 207–8. *See also* Poznań; strikes/protests
Cenckiewicz, Sławomir, 100, 102, 337n26
Center for Public Opinion Research (OBOP*), 161–62, 326n3
Central Committee. *See* Polish United Workers' Party
Centralne Archiwum Wojskowe (in Rembertów) (Central Military Archives), xii
Charter 77. *See* Czechoslovakia
"Charter of Workers' Rights" (1979), 8. *See also* KOR*; WZZ*
Cheka (Soviet secret police), 181
Chełchowski, August, 114
Chernenko, Konstantin, 263, 300
Chernobyl nuclear power disaster, 302. *See also glasnost*; Gorbachev, Mikhail
Cheysson, Claude, 123
Chojecki, Mirosław, 203, 255
Chojnacki, Father Adolf, 235

Chojnacki, Władysław, 161, 164, 243
Chrzanowski, Wiesław, 200
Chyliczki. *See* Wałęsa, Lech
CIA (Central Intelligence Agency), 42, 43, 324n1
Ciastoń, General Władysław, 203
Cieszewski, Jacek, 55
Ciosek, Stanisław, 42, 143, 292; and Wałęsa, 61, 71, 81, 148–49, 150, 151–52, 214
"citizens' committees of national salvation," 135–36
Citizens' Militia (MO*) (militia; MSW military units), 44, 323n3; functionaries (militiamen) and martial law, 56–58, 76, 87, 91–92, 201; impunity of, 275; and Jaruzelski, 97, 195, 274. *See also* MSW*; SB*; ZOMO*
Civic Committee (Komitet Obywatelski, KO), 291–92; and election (June 1989), 296–98
Clubs of the Catholic Intelligentsia (Kluby Inteligencji Katolickiej, KIK), 5, 7, 70, 264. *See also* Catholic Church; opposition
Cold War, ix, 122; end of, 308, 315; and Solidarity, xiii
Cologne, demonstrations against martial law, 124, 125
COMECON (Council of Mutual Economic Assistance), 311; collapse of, 315
Committee of Independent Culture, 243. *See also* independent society
Committee of National Defense (KOK*), 272; martial law and, 25, 29, 51, 60, 261, 270; resolutions of, 64–65. *See also* Jaruzelski, General Wojciech; martial law
communist party. *See* Polish United Workers' Party

communist system (Poland/Soviet Bloc), 146; fall of, xii-xiii, 308–9, 315–16; functioning of, 4, 103, 223; and Solidarity, 19–20, 240, 242, 313, 314
Conant, James Bryant, prediction on Soviet Union, vii
Confederation of Independent Poland (KPN*), 6–7
Conference of Post-Secondary Rectors, dissolution of, 114
Conference of the Polish Episcopate. *See* Episcopate; Glemp, Cardinal Józef
conference on martial law (in Jachranka, 1997), xi-xii, 323nn5–6
Conference on Security and Cooperation in Europe (CSCE) (Helsinki Accords, 1975), 9; and human rights in Poland, 9–10, 325n19
Congress of People's Representatives, 303, 304. *See also* Gorbachev, Mikhail
Congress of Polish Culture (Dec. 11–13, 1981), 47–48; and martial law, 61
Consultative Economic Council, 268
Copper Basin (*Zagłębie Miedziowe*) (Silesia), 87, 90, 181
Coppola, Francis, *Apocalypse Now. See* Warsaw
Council of Ministers (*Rada Ministrów*), 74; martial law orders, 63–64, 134, 153, 219, 273
Council of National Understanding (*Rada Porozumienia Narodowego*), 30
Council of State (*Rada Państwa*), 52, 58, 60, 112, 265; and lifting martial law (July 1983), 264, 275–77; (martial law) decrees of, 63–65, 115–16; meeting of (Dec. 13, 1981), 58–60, 121
Cywiński, Bohdan, 8
Czabański, Krzysztof, 46
Czechoslovakia (Prague), 9, 306, 314–16, 324n4; Charter 77, 305, 309; martial law and, 129, 130; *perestroika*

and, 304–5, 308, 309; pressure on Jaruzelski, 28, 37; reaction to Solidarity, 24; revolts in (1953), 3; Soviet invasion of (1968), 24, 43, 122
Czerny-Stefańska, Halina, 179
Częstochowa, 155; Black Madonna of, 14; demonstrations in, 200, 201, 211, 252. See also Jasna Góra
Czogała, Jan, 76
Czuma, Andrzej, 16
Czyrek, Józef, 72, 123–24, 126, 263, 292, 335n11

Dałkowska, Ewa, 247
Danilecki, Tomasz, 112
Darłówko (Darłówek) (internment center), 99
Davis, Ambassador John R., 121, 293
Dąbrowski, Archbishop Bronisław, 199, 203; and martial law, 70, 234; and Wałęsa, 150, 215, 290. See also Barcikowski, Kazimierz; Episcopate
Department of State (US), 121, 122, 324n1
DIA (Defense Intelligence Agency), 324n1
"directorate" (martial law secret powerhouse), 72–73, 76, 147, 151. See also Jaruzelski, General Wojciech; martial law
Dobraczyński, Jan, 265
Dodziuk, Anna, 161
Domber, Gregory, xii, 323n8, 347n34
Dorn, Ludwik, 46, 329n33
Drzewiecki, Father Mirosław, 233
Dubrow, Steve, 121
Dudek, Antoni, 206, 324n6, 332n9, 333n6
Dybowski, Arkadiusz, 77
Dziekan, General Tadeusz, 134
Dziennik Telewizyjny ("Television Journal") (state run TV news program), 116; boycott of, 180–81. See also propaganda (government)
Dziennik Ustaw (Journal of Laws), and martial law, 60, 63
Dzierżek, Father Stefan, 106
Dzierżoniów, 211
Dzierżyński (Dzerzhinsky), Feliks, 195; monument of (in Warsaw), 181

Eagleburger, Lawrence, 126
East Berlin. See German Democratic Republic
East Germany. See German Democratic Republic
economy (Polish), 285–86, 287, 289–90, 291; economic aid from Soviet bloc, 129–130; failure of Gierek's policies, 9, 11–12; martial law and, 95, 118–19, 267–69, 270, 272, 279; and sanctions, 125–27, 207, 288, 335n19
Elbląg, 79; demonstrations in, 189, 190, 198, 200, 207; TV boycott in ("television walks"), 180; Zamech factory in, 208
elections, parliamentary: (1985), 288, 347n20; (June 1989), 291–92, 294–99
Elster, Jon, 294
Englert, Jan, 246
Episcopate (Church hierarchy), Conference of the Polish, 204, 227–28; Main Council's reaction to imposition of martial law, 81, 225; Round Table and, 294; and Solidarity, 226–27; and Wałęsa, 150–51. See also Dąbrowski, Archbishop Bronisław; Glemp, Cardinal Józef
Estonia, 304, 348n2 (conclusion)
European Parliament, on martial law, 125

Fejtő, François, 9

Fighting Solidarity (underground organization) (Solidarność Walcząca), 194, 196, 240, 340n18; foreign office of, 256; radio (in Wrocław), 244

Findeisen, Władysław, 142

"Fir" (Jodła), martial law operation by MSW/SB, 55–58, 99, 159

Firefighting Officers' School (in Warsaw) (Dec. 2, 1983), attack on (by MSW), 30, 36, 40, 45

First National Solidarity Congress of Delegates (Sept. /Oct. 1981), 28, 197; platform of (The Self-Governing Republic, *Rzeczpospolita Samorządna*), 19–20, 318

Fiszbach, Tadeusz, 57, 61, 261, 262

France, reaction to martial law, 125–26

Frankfurt, demonstrations against martial law, 125

Frasyniuk, Władysław 16, 45, 49, 168, 183, 185, 194, 317; arrest of, 206; in hiding, 84; and martial law, 58, 67; and TKK, 171, 205; trial of, 212. *See also* Wrocław

Freedom and Independence (Zrzeszenie Wolność i Niezawisłość), 168–69. *See also* Second World War

Free Trade Unionist. *See* Wolny Związkowiec

Free Trade Unions (WZZ*), 8, 13, 16, 139, 150, 171. *See also* KOR*

French Revolution, 73

Friszke, Andrzej, 66, 205, 210, 338–39n17

Front of National Unity (Front Jedności Narodu), 135, 197, 276

FSO car factory (in Warsaw), informers in, 193; strike in, 85. *See also* strikes/protests

Fukuyama, Francis, 315

Fund for Aid to the Repressed, 191

"G" (hour) (one of martial law's cryptonyms), 35, 40, 41, 42, 49, 53, 61, 93, 328n1

Gandhi, Mahatma, 45

Garstka, Wojciech, 289

Garton Ash, Timothy, 323n2

Garwolin, 200

Gazeta Krakowska (daily), 46

Gazeta Wyborcza (daily), 296, 298

Gdańsk, 209, 250; martial law imposition and, 57, 80, 90, 98, 133; Pope's visit in (June 1987), 289; Port, strike in, 68, 86; protests during martial law in, 183–84, 189, 190, 191, 198, 200, 201, 207, 249, 252; Radio Solidarity broadcast in, 193; Refinery, strike in, 86; reprisals in, 107, 110, 113–14; restrictions in, 117, 118; Solidarity/underground structure in, 166–67; strikes in (1970), 3; WZZ* in, 8. *See also* Gdańsk Shipyard

Gdańsk Agreement (Aug. 1980), viii, 15, 18, 19, 21, 23, 48, 197, 326n13; as a state holiday, 318

Gdańsk Shipyard (Lenin Shipyard), 8, 291; martial law imposition and, 80, 84, 85–86; protests during martial law, 204, 207, 290; reprisals in, 110; Solidarity's National Commission meeting in (Dec. 12, 1981), 48–49, 53, 56; strikes in (summer 1980), ix, 13–15, (1988), 290. *See also* Solidarity; Gdańsk; strikes/protests; Wałęsa, Lech

GDR.* *See* German Democratic Republic

Gdynia, 199; demonstrations in, 252; reprisals in, 110, 113–14, 202; strikes in (1970, 1980), 3

General Staff (of the Polish Army), and martial law preparations, 24, 41–42, 43, 53; and martial

law implementation, 79. *See also* Kukliński, Colonel Ryszard
Genscher, Hans Dietrich, 123
Georgia, 312
Geremek, Bronisław, 151, 219, 240, 256, 293
German Democratic Republic (GDR*) (East Berlin), 314, 324n4; martial law and, 128–130; *perestroika* and, 304, 305–6, 308, 312, 315, 316; pressure on Jaruzelski, 28, 37, 129; reaction to Solidarity, 24; revolt in (1953), 3. *See also* Honecker, Erich
German unification (Oct. 1990), 308, 312, 315
Germany (West; Federal Republic of Germany), reactions to martial law, 125, 128, 232, 305, 308, 312, 315
Gestapo, 155, 175. *See also* Second World War
Gierek, Edward, 3, 4, 5–6, 21; failure of economic policies of, 9, 11–12; internment of, 103, 115, 275; and strikes of 1980 (and Brezhnev), viii, 12–15; and Wyszyński, 223–24
Gieysztor, Aleksander, 142
Gil, Mieczysław, 16, 84
glasnost' (openness), xii, 302, 304. *See also* Gorbachev, Mikhail; *perestroika*
Glemp, Cardinal Józef (Primate), 224; actors' boycott and, 229; homilies of, 70, 200; Jaruzelski and, 210; John Paul II and, 226; martial law and, 44, 61, 225–26, 234, 235; and Primatial Social Council, 48, 227; and Solidarity, 37–38, 69, 171, 204, 227, 236. *See also* Catholic Church; Episcopate
Gliwice, 165; Radio Solidarity broadcast in, 243
Głogów, Radio Solidarity broadcast in, 243
Głos (underground publishing house), 160. *See also* publishing

Głos (Voice) (underground publication), 240. *See also* publishing
Główczyk, Jan, 153
Gocłowski, Archbishop Tadeusz, 158
Gołdap (internment center), 99
Gomułka, Władysław, 4, 5, 75, 223–24
Gontarz, Henryk, 66, 83–84
Gorbachev, Mikhail, x, 298–99, 308; and Bush H. W., 293, 311; foreign policy of, 303–4; and Jaruzelski, 287–88, 295; reforms in the Soviet Union by, 301–3; and Solidarity, xii-xiii; stance on Poland, 293, 298. *See also glasnost'*; *perestroika*
Górnicki, Wiesław, 61, 97
Gorzelany, Father Józef, 67
Gorzów Wielkopolski, 90; demonstrations in, 200–201
Gottwald mine (in Katowice), 88. *See also* strikes/protests
Government Protection Bureau (BOR), 231
Grabski, Tadeusz, 22, 262
"Grand Hotel" (Sopot), arrests of Solidarity members in, (Dec. 13, 1981), 56. *See also* martial law
Gromyko, Andrei, 28, 36; on John Paul II, 6
Gruba, Colonel Jerzy, 41
Grudzień, Zdzisław, 103
Gryfia Repair Shipyard (in Szczecin), strike in and pacification of, 87. *See also* strikes/protests; Szczecin
Grzyb, Zofia, 153
Gucwa, Stanisław, 218
Gulbinowicz, Bishop Henryk, 228
Gwiazda, Andrzej, 16, 45, 219, 289

Hague, The, demonstrations against martial law, 125
Haig, Alexander, 121, 123
Hall, Aleksander, 167, 169
Handzlik, Stanisław, 84, 194

Hanuszkiewicz, Adam, 179
Hardek, Władysław, 84, 168, 171, 205, 256–57. See also TKK*
Havel, Václav, 298, 305, 310, 316
Helsinki Accords. See Conference on Security and Cooperation Europe (CSCE)
Hermaszewski, Lieutenant-Colonel Mirosław, 52
Hiolski, Andrzej, 179
Hirschman, Alberto O., 305
Hobsbawm, Eric, xi
Hoffmann, Heinz, 128
Holzer, Jerzy, 244
Home Army (AK*), 146, 156. See also resistance; Second World War
Home Theater (in Warsaw), 247. See also independent society
Honecker, Erich, 123, 308; and martial law, 128, 129; reaction to Solidarity, 24, 28. See also German Democratic Republic
Hrubieszów (prison in), 108
Hubner, Zygmunt, 179
Hungary (Budapest), 128, 314, 316, 324n4; martial law and, 129, 130; *perestroika* and, 293, 304–8, 311, 312; pressure on Jaruzelski, 28; revolt of 1956, 122. See also Kádár, János
Husák, Gustáv, 129. See also Czechoslovakia

Iława (prison in), 100
Independent Education, 243. See also independent society
Independent Self-Governing Trade Union "Solidarity" (NSZZ* "Solidarność") (before martial law), "carnival" of, 31; as challenge to Soviet system, viii–ix, 21; creation of, viii, 16; gullibility of, 43–46; and opposition, 16; program/platform of (Self-Governing Republic) (at First National Solidarity Congress, Sept/Oct. 1981), 19–20, 28, 318; Radom meeting (Dec. 3, 1981), 30–31, 48; reaction to in Soviet Union, viii, 22; reaction to in the West, viii–x; registration of (1980), 22–23; as "self-limiting revolution," 19, 148, 327n17; as social movement, 16–18, 237, 314; threat to Poland's power structure, 283. See also Solidarity (underground)
Independent Self-Governing Trade Union of Individual Farmers Solidarity (NSZZ IR), 17, 23, 27, 165, 204
independent society, 238, 279; and "battle for Poland's consciousness"/ underground culture, 243–48; and émigré community, 253–56; and martial law, 277; and. See also publishing; Solidarity; TKK*
Independent Song Festival (at Opera Leśna, Sopot), 176
Independent Students' Association, 243. See also independent society
Independent Students' Union (Niezależne Zrzeszenie Studentów, NZS), 17, 23, 65, 155, 165
Individual Craftsmen's Solidarity (NSZZ Indywidualnego Rzemiosła "Solidarność"), 17
informers (secret collaborators of MSW/SB), 24, 93–94, 100, 108, 110, 141, 163, 193, 194, 235, 245, 256. See also MSW*; SB*
INR (Bureau of Intelligence and Research), 324n1
Institute of Theoretical Physics (Silesian University), dissolution of, 114
Instytutu Pamięci Narodowej (Institute of National Remembrance), xii
inter-enterprise founding committees of Solidarity (MKZ*), 15–16

Index

Inter-Enterprise Strike Committee (MKS*) (strikes of 1980), 13–15, 48, 326n13
Inter-Enterprise Workers' Committee of Solidarity (MRKS*), 164, 186, 189, 192, 240, 257
International Confederation of Free Trade Unions (in Brussels), 254
International Graphics Biennale (Kraków, 1982), 180
International Labor Organization, 124, 125–26, 255
International Monetary Fund, Poland's membership in, 127, 287
International Poster Biennale (Warsaw, 1982), 180
International Red Cross, 255
Inter-Regional Defense Committee of Solidarity, 194, 257
IPN. *See* Instytutu Pamięci Narodowej
Isakowicz-Zaleski, Father Tadeusz, 233
"isolation centers." *See* prisons/"isolation centers"
Iwanczenko, Dariusz, 78
Iwaniec, Colonel Władysław, 152

Jabłoński, Henryk, 58–59, 218
Jachranka (near Warsaw). *See* conference on martial law
Jagielski, Mieczysław, 14
Janas, Zbigniew, 68, 178
Jancarz, Father Kazimierz, 233, 234
Janiszewski, General Michał, 134; "directorate" and, 72–73; martial law, 41, 50, 51, 114, 209, 218, 230
Jankowski, Father Henryk, 233, 234
January Uprising (1863–1864), 169, 177
Jarocki, Jerzy, 180
Jaroszewicz, Piotr, 103, 275
Jaruzelski, General Wojciech, xii; and Aristov, 35–36, 148; on army/MSW/SB's "brotherhood," 194–95; biography of, 74–75; Brezhnev/Kulikov and, 28, 36–38, 129, 130–1; consolidation of power by, 287; Council of State's Chairman, 287, 289; "directorate" and, 72–73; and economy, 267, 289; first secretary of the party, xi, 29, 41, 194–95, 287; Gorbachev and, 287–88, 295; John Paul II and, 151, 226, 230–31, 271; KOK's chairman, 29; and martial law, x-xi, 60–61, 69, 105, 133, 218, 220, 283; and martial law (secret) preparations, 26, 27, 29–31, 35–39, 47, 53; martial law speech (Dec. 13, 1981), 63; meeting with academia, 142; meeting with Andropov/Ustinov, 27–28; Ministry of National Defense (head of), 29, 41, 74; and MSW/SB, 97; party purges by, 261–63; president of Poland, 217, 298; prime minister, xi, 26, 29, 41, 130, 197; on revenge, 115–16; and Round Table, 292; Sejm speeches by, 147, 142, 197, 274; and Soviets, 50, 212, 263; stance on Solidarity, 22, 144–45, 147–48, 192, 203, 291; and strikes of summer 1980, 14–15; unique position of, 29, 75–76; and Wałęsa, 150, 215, 343n3; Western image of, 122–23; WRON's chairman, xi, 41, 52, 60, 61, 74, 115, 124, 195. *See also* martial law; MSW*; Polish Army; PZPR*; SB*
Jasna Góra monastery (in Częstochowa), arrest of Solidarity activists at, 155; and Glemp's homilies, 70, 200, 228; and pope's homily, 231
Jastrzębie. *See* Rybnik Coal Area
Jaworski, Seweryn, 219, 220
Jaworze (internment center), 99, 166
Jedynak, Tadeusz, 188
Jelenia Góra, 66; Radio Solidarity broadcast in, 243

Jewulski, Father Bolesław, 105
John Paul II (Polish Pope; pope), 5, 238; and Jaruzelski, 151, 226, 231; and martial law, 124, 225–26, 271; and Reagan, 125; visits to Poland, (1979), 6; (1983), 196, 210, 229–31, 232; (1987), 289; and Wałęsa, 151, 230, 231. *See also* Wojtyła, Cardinal Karol
Joint Commission of the Government and Episcopate (Komisja Wspólna Rządu i Episkopatu), 146, 152, 196, 225. *See also* Barcikowski, Kazimierz; Dąbrowski, Archbishop Bronisław
Jurczyk, Marian (Szczecin), 219

Kaczmarski, Jacek, 176–77
Kaczyński, Lech, 317
Kádár, János, 129, 131, 306, 312
Kaleta, Marian, 255
Kalisz, Solidarity Mass in, 182
Kałkus, Stanisław, 218
Kamienna Góra (Gross Rosen) (internment center), 100
Kamiński, Aleksander, 156
Kania, Stanisław, 21; and Brezhnev/Soviets, 25, 27–28, 50, 212, 327n7; and "Bydgoszcz incident" 27; "commission," 73; and martial law preparation, 29; stance on strikes of 1980/Solidarity, 13–15, 22, 26, 140
Kantorski, Father Leon, 233
Karasek, Krzysztof, 176
Karkosza, Henryk, 245. *See also* informers
Karta (Charter) (underground publication), 165. *See also* publishing
Kartuzy, 200
Katowice, martial law imposition and, 58, 69, 89, 133; protests/demonstrations in, 252; Solidarity/underground structure in, 166–67; trials in, 105; Underground Theater of Martial Law Poetry in, 246–47

Katowice Steelworks (in Katowice), martial law imposition and, 80, 82, 85, 88, 90, 133; trials and reprisals, 105, 107, 110. *See also* strikes/protests
Katyń massacre, 4
Kelus, Krzysztof, 177
Kędzierzyn, Radio Solidarity broadcast in, 243
Kersten, Krystyna, 248
Khrushchev, Nikita, xiii
Kielce, under martial law, 165, 201
KIK. *See* Clubs of the Catholic Intelligentsia
Kiszczak, General Czesław, 134, 298; on AK, 146; and Bujak, 192; "directorate" and, 72–73, 76; and informers, 193; and preparations for martial law, 28, 38, 41; and implementation of, 50, 51, 53, 66, 199, 218–19; and pope's visit, 230; and Round Table, 292; and Wałęsa/Solidarity, 71, 152, 203, 213, 214–15, 250, 251, 290. *See also* MSW*; SB*
KKP* (Solidarność). *See* National Coordinating Commission of Solidarity
Klekowski, Janusz, 187
Klincewicz, Teodor, 198
Kłodzko, 200; Radio Solidarity broadcast in, 243
Kłosek, Czesław, 88
Kłosiński, Janusz, 179
Klub Kuźnica (in Kraków), 262
KO. *See* Civic Committee
Kobylańska, Monika, 88
Kociołek, Stanisław, 22, 42, 261, 262
Kohl, Chancellor Helmut, 308, 312
KOK.* *See* Committee of National Defense
Kołakowski, Leszek, 326n20
Kolbe, Father Maksymilian, 204, 341n6
Kołobrzeg, 117; demonstrations in, 211

Kołodziejczak, Colonel Bogusław, 134
Kołodziejski, Jerzy, 57
Kołyszko, Ryszard, 187
Komender, Zenon, 218
Konarski, Andrzej, 68, 168, 169
Konin, 200–201; "Konin" Aluminum Works in, 78; trials, 105
KOR.* See Workers' Defense Committee
KOS.* See Solidarity Defense Circles
Kos (Blackbird) (underground publication), 165, 178, 248. See also publishing
KOS (underground publishing house), 160. See also publishing
Kosmowski, Patrycjusz, 68, 107
Koszalin, demonstrations in, 200
Kowalczyk, Edward, 218
Kowalska, Bogumiła, 158
Kozakiewicz, Władysław, viii
KPN.* See Confederation of Independent Poland
Krąg (underground publishing house), 160, 244. See also publishing
Kraków, 165, 262; demonstrations in, 190, 191, 200, 211, 252; and martial law imposition, 66, 67, 90, 117, 118; Radio Solidarity broadcast in, 193; Solidarity/underground structure in, 166–67. See also Nowa Huta
Kremlin, 302. See also Soviet Union
Kropiwnicki, Jerzy, 105
Krosno (Polmo factory in), 110; Solidarity/underground structure in, 166–67
Krupiński, Mirosław, 68
Kryuchkov, General Vladimir, 27, 39
Kubasiewicz, Ewa, 107
Kuberski, Jerzy, 61
Kubiak, Hieronim, 48, 153, 218, 261, 262
Kuca, Colonel Władysław, 56, 193, 215
Kukliński, Colonel Ryszard, 42–43, 122
Kulerski, Wiktor, 178; strategy of, 169

Kulikov, Marshal Victor, xii; and Anoshkin, 328n2; and Jaruzelski, 37–39, 51; and martial law, 27, 28, 95, 128. See also Brezhnev, Leonid
Kultura (weekly) (Warsaw), 113
Kuroń, Jacek, 7, 16, 49, 139, 237, 241, 293, 315, 317, 330n41; arrest of, 56–57, 203; on Jaruzelski, 44; strategy of, 170
Kwaśniewski, Aleksander, 292, 318
Kwiatkowski, Piotr, 248
Kwidzyń (internment center), 100

Łabęcki, Jan, 147, 153, 262
Labuda, Gerard, 142
Łaniewska, Katarzyna, 246
Łapicki, Andrzej, 179
Laski convent (near Warsaw), artists' meeting in, 245. See also independent society
Latvia, 304, 348n2 (conclusion)
Law and Justice (Prawo i Sprawiedliwość, PIS) (political party), 317
Lech, Mieczysław, 142
Legionowo, Radio Solidarity broadcast in, 243
Legnica (Lower Silesia), 52, 188; Radio Solidarity broadcast in, 243
Leipzig (GDR), 306, 308
Lenin, Vladimir, vii, ix, 10
Lenin Steelworks (in Nowa Huta), 186, 191, 208; strike committees in, 67, 80; strikes in and pacification of, 78, 83, 86; and trials, 107. See also Nowa Huta; strikes/protests
Leś, Colonel Roman, 52
Lesiak, Colonel Jan, 56
Leszno, 191
Lewkowicz, Father Wacław, 233
Liga Kobiet. See Women's League
Lipiński, General Kazimierz, 59
Lipski, Jan Józef, 203, 325n13

Lis, Bogdan, 68, 155, 167, 169, 171, 205, 254. *See also* TKK*
Lithuania, 74, 304, 312, 348n2 (conclusion)
Łódź, 16, 67, 133, 233; demonstrations/strikes in, 86, 189, 190, 198, 200, 206, 211, 252; Pilgrimage Theater in, 247; reprisals in, 113; Solidarity/underground structures in, 164–65, 166–67; strike committees in, 67, 80; strikes in (1957), 3; trials in, 105, 107, 109. *See also* Słowik, Andrzej; strikes/protests
Lubin (Lower Silesia), 181–82; demonstrations in, 201, 211, 275; trials in, 105
Lublin, 133; demonstrations in, 189, 190, 200, 252; Maria Curie-Skłodowska University in, 114; Solidarity/underground structures in, 166–67; strikes in (July 1980), 12, 14; trials in, 109
Lublin region, Radio Solidarity broadcast in, 244
Łuczywo, Helena, 167–68
Ludwiczak, Jan, arrest of, 55–56, 97. *See also* "Wujek" mine
Luns, Joseph (NATO Secretary General), 123

MacEachin, Douglas J., 122
Macierewicz, Antoni, 240
Magdalenka (near Warsaw), 294
Main Council of the Polish Episcopate (Rada Główna Episkopatu Polski), 225; communiqué of (Dec. 15, 1981), 81
Main Political Directorate. *See* Polish Army
Main School of Rural Economy (Szkoła Główna Gospodarstwa Wiejskiego) (in Warsaw), strike in, 85. *See also* strikes/protests

Malara, Stanisław, 86
Maleszka, Lesław, 245. *See also* informers
Malicki, Colonel Tadeusz, 59
Malinowski, Roman, 218, 219
Małkowski, Father Stanisław, 233
Malmö (Sweden), 233
"*Mały Konspirator*" ("Little conspirator") (underground brochure), 156. *See also* Second World War
Manifest Lipcowy (July Manifesto) mine, strike in, and pacification of, 84, 87, 88–89, 90, 98, 333n23. *See also* Rybnik Coal Area; strikes/protests
"Maple" (*Klon*), martial law operation by MSW/SB, 57, 93; and "warning talks"/loyalty oaths, 102–3, 109–10
Maria Curie-Skłodowska University. *See* Lublin
Maritime College (in Gdynia), strike and trials, 107
Marody, Mirosława, 283
Marszałkowski, Tomasz, 206
martial law (*stan wojenny*) (Dec. 13, 1981–July 22, 1983) (cryptonyms "G," "W," "X"), x, 35, 328n1; arrests/internments of opposition/Solidarity, 55–58, 69, 98; and association with Second World War, 120; conference on (in Jachranka), xi, 323n6; costs of implementation of, 94–95; "directorate" (secret powerhouse), 72–74, 76, 143, 147, 151, 192, 335n11; and economy, 267–69; end of (and legal ramifications), 270–77, 279; food shortage and "black market" under, 118–120; impact on Polish society, 318–19; and internment of communist party leaders, 103–4; internment vs. arrest under, 98–99, 108; Kukliński and, 42–43; legislation, 63–65; and MSW/SB/Polish Army, 53, 62–63,

76–77, 79, 91–94; preparations for, 24–31, 35–40, 50–52; pretext to impose, 31, 35; purges and reprisals, 104–114, 334n12; reactions in Poland to imposition of, 66–69, 76–90; restrictions of, 117–18; and role of propaganda, 29, 35; SB's role in, 93–94; secrecy of preparations, 40–42; Solidarity unpreparedness for, 44–46; and Soviet Union/Soviet Bloc, 24–25, 26–28, 35–39, 50, 95, 128–132, 272; suspension of (Dec. 1982), 217–20; US/West reactions to, 121–128, 272. *See also* Jaruzelski, General Wojciech; propaganda; WRON*

Marx, Karl, 5, 73, 254

massacre on the Baltic coast (Dec. 1970), memory of, 14, 15, 233; monument (in Gdańsk), 8, 13

"Masses for the Fatherland," 182–83, 233, 237, 248, 250. *See also* independent society

Matyjas, Eugeniusz, 141

Mauroy, Pierre, 47, 127

May Day (International Workers' Day) celebrations, boycotts of, 241, 250; demonstrations ("counter-parades"), 189, 195, 253, 256

May 3rd holiday (Constitution of 1791) commemorations, 7, 189, 195, 233, 250

Mazowiecki, Tadeusz, x, 16, 151, 293; government of, 214, 299, 307; as prime minister, 312

Mazur, Father Franciszek, 106

Memling, Hans, 190

Meretik, Gabriel, 47, 54

Messner, Zbigniew, 153, 287, 290

Micewski, Andrzej, 48

Michałowska, Danuta, 246

Michnik, Adam, 8, 16, 97, 203, 241, 293, 298, 317

Miecznikowski, Father Stefan, 233

Mielec, State Aviation Works (WSK PZL) in, and martial law, 78. *See also* strikes/protests

"Mieszko." *See* OKO*

Mikulski, Stanisław, 142, 179

Milewski, General Mirosław, 22, 39, 214, 261; "directorate" and, 72–73

Milewski, Jerzy, 254

military. *See* Polish Army

Military Council of National Salvation (WRON*), 74, 88, 117, 135, 136, 142, 174, 175, 218, 203, 235, 259, 261; creation of, and its legality, xi, 51–52; first meeting of (Dec. 13, 1981), 59–60; and martial law end, 275–76; and martial law repeal, 197, 211, 265. *See also* Jaruzelski, General Wojciech; Sejm

militia. *See* Citizens' Militia (MO)

Miłosz, Czesław, 246

Ministry of Artistic Circles, 245. *See also* independent society

Ministry of Internal Affairs (MSW*/ SB* Security Service), 53–58, 116, 118, 192, 199, 206, 209; activities to disintegrate Solidarity, 140–43, 145, 163; battle against priests/Church, 234–36; cooperation with army, 79; Departments of, 93, 235; emigration program (exile), 101–2; and end of martial law, 276; Firefighting Officers' School attacked by, 30, 36; functionaries' brutality and impunity, 55–56, 98, 275; internment centers and, 100–103; Jaruzelski and, 97, 194–95; and martial law preparations, 25–27, 29, 35, 37, 40, 41, 43, 93–94; and MKO*, 257; "Operation Summer-80," 14, 326n9; and pope's visit ("Dawn" *Zorza*), 230; and Popiełuszko's murder, 235, 284; reports by, 15, 66, 190, 204, 230, 331n23, 343n16; Research

Ministry of Internal Affairs—*(cont'd)*
Office and efforts to penetrate the underground by, 193–95; stance against opposition, 97–98; strike-breaking tactics by, 78, 83–85; on underground publishing, 160; and Wałęsa, 213, 215–16. *See also* "Ambassador"; "Azalea" ; "Fir"; informers; Kiszczak, General Czesław; "Maple"; "Renaissance"; ZOMO*
Ministry of Justice, martial law preparations and, 25, 41, 100
Ministry of National Defense (MON*), 29; and martial law preparations, 26, 41, 53, 62–63, 270; Military Council of and Jaruzelski, 38, 52. *See also* Polish Army
Miodowicz, Alfred, 266, 292; TV debate with Wałęsa, 291
Mitterand, President François, 127, 289
MKO.* *See* Inter-Regional Defense Committee of Solidarity
MKS.* *See* Inter-Enterprise Strike Committee
MKZ.* *See* inter-enterprise founding committees of Solidarity
MO.* *See* Citizens' Militia
Modzelewski, Karol, 31, 44, 49, 219
Moldavia, 310, 312
MON.* *See* Ministry of National Defense
Montreal, demonstrations against martial law, 125
Morawiecki, Kornel, 156, 168, 186, 194, 196, 240, 257
Moscow (city), 95, 122, 302. *See also* Soviet Union
Moszczenica mine. *See* Rybnik Coal Area
Motorized Detachments of the Citizens' Militia (ZOMO*) (MSW military units), 40; arrests by, 56–58; street demonstrations attacked by, 184, 190, 191, 198, 201, 210–11, 252, 256, 279; strike-breaking by, 78, 83–91, 98. *See also* martial law
Movement for the Defense of Human and Civil Rights (Ruch Obrony Praw Człowieka i Obywatela, ROPCiO), 6
MRKS.* *See* Inter-Enterprise Workers' Committee of Solidarity
Mróz, Leonard, 179
MSW.* *See* Ministry of Internal Affairs
Myrdal, Alva, 194

Nagy, Imre, 307
Najder, Zdzisław, 257
Nance, Rear Admiral James W., 121
Napoleon Bonaparte, 73
Narożniak, Jan, 25, 192–93
Naszkowski, Eligiusz, 56, 143. *See also* informers
National Economic and Social Council, 49
National Commission (of Solidarity) (Komisja Krajowa Solidarność, KK), 45, 316; and creation of the National Stike Committee, 68; under martial law, 102, 143, 274; meeting in Gdańsk Shipyard and arrests of its members (Dec. 12, 1981), 48–50, 56–58, 68–69; meeting in Radom (Dec. 3, 1981), 30–31; and Wałęsa, 71, 150–51, 192. *See also* martial law; National Strike Committee; Solidarity
National Coordinating Commission of Solidarity (KKP*) (later KK), 16. *See also* National Commission (of Solidarity)
National Endowment for Democracy, 338n3
National NSZZ Solidarity Resistance Committee (OKO*) (pseudonym "Mieszko"), 168–69, 171
National Security Council, vii, 121, 122, 126

National Strike Committee (Krajowy Komitet Strajkowy), 68, 76, 80, 81, 168
NATO, 315; and martial law, 122–23, 125, 127, 288, 335n4. *See also* United States; West
Nawrocki, Jerzy, 142
Niedenthal, Chris, 47
Niepodległość (Independence) (underground publication), 165. *See also* publishing
Niewęgłowski, Father Wiesław, 245
Noel, Roger, 212
NOW-a (Independent Publishing House), 160. *See also* publishing
Nowa Huta (near Kraków), demonstrations in, 186–87, 189, 191, 198, 200, 201, 204, 206, 208, 210–11, 252, 290; Pope's visit in, 230; protest strike (1960), 3–4; TKK meeting in, 205–6. *See also* Lenin Steelworks; strikes/protests
Novocherkassk (Soviet Union), riots in (1962), 3
Nowy Targ, 200
NSDAP, 175. *See also* Second World War
NSZZ IR. *See* Independent Self-Governing Trade Union of Individual Farmers Solidarity
NSZZ* Solidarność. *See* Independent Self-Governing Trade Union "Solidarity"
Nyers, Rezsö, 306
NZS. *See* Independent Students' Union

Obodowski, Janusz, 219; "directorate" and, 72–73
OBOP.* *See* Center for Public Opinion Research
Obserwator wojenny (War Observer) (underground publication, Kraków), 160. *See also* publishing

"occupation code of conduct" (Bujak, Janas, Kulerski), 178. *See also* resistance
Ochocki, Marek, 188
Odom, General William, xii
Office for Religious Affairs, 61
Office of the UN High Commissioner for Refugees, 255
OKO.* *See* National NSZZ Solidarity Resistance Committee
Okrutny, Lieutenant-Colonel, 88
Olszewski, Jan, 16, 71, 200, 250
Olszowski, Stefan, 22, 42, 258, 261, 262; "directorate" and, 72–73; and martial law, 116, 230; and Soviets, 50
Olsztyn, 191; Solidarity/underground structure in, 166–67
Olympic Games, in Los Angeles (1984), vii; in Moscow (1980), vii, 122
Onyszkiewicz, Janusz, 117, 219, 256
Opania, Marian, 246
"Operation Summer-80" (Operacja Lato-80) (MSW), 14, 326n9
Operational Military Groups, 30
Opornik (Resistor) (underground publication), 177. *See also* publishing
opposition (anti-regime), 6–10, 325n19, 326n20; after 1985, 286, 288, 291, 293, 294, 295; role in summer 1980 strikes, 13, 18
"Orange Alternative," 288–89
Organika-Boruta plant (in Zgierz), 78
ORMO.* *See* Volunteer Reserves of the Citizens' Militia
Orszulik, Father Alojzy, 70, 228; and Wałęsa, 150–51, 152, 153, 200, 213, 217. *See also* Episcopate
Orwell, George, 161
Orzechowski, Marian, 265
Ostrowiec Świętokrzyski, 79
Otwock. *See* Wałęsa, Lech

Pabianice. *See* Polam factory

Paczkowski, Andrzej, xi, 323n4
Palach, Jan, 305
Palka, Grzegorz, 219
Pałka, Julian, 142
Pałubicki, Janusz, 44
Papandreu, Andreas, 127
Paris, demonstrations against martial law, 125
Paris Club, and Poland, 127
parliament. *See* Sejm
Paszkowski, General Roman, 88
Patriotic Movement of National Rebirth (PRON*), 197, 199, 211–12, 214, 219, 264–65, 273, 276
Pavlov, General Vitalii (KGB), 28, 38–39, 50, 140, 152
PAX Association, 48, 59, 218, 228, 264
perestroika ("reconstruction"), x, 287, 301; and *glasnost'*, impact on Soviet-bloc countries, 304–11; Gorbachev and, 303; and Poland, xii; in Soviet Union, 311–12. *See also* Gorbachev, Mikhail
Piaseczno. *See* Unitra-Polkolor factory
Piast mine (near Tychy), strike in, 83, 90–91, 99, 133, 177. *See also* strikes/ protests
Pichoja, Rudolf G., 302
Pietrzak, Jan, 176
Piłsudski, Marshal Józef, 8, 178, 240
Pinior, Józef, 84, 251, 257
Pińkowski, Józef, 26
Pinochet, General Augusto, 118, 175
Piórkowski, Jerzy, 142
Piotrowski, General Czesław, 88
Pipes, Richard, xii, 121
PIS. *See* Law and Justice
Pisuliński, Jan, 78
Placówka (The Outpost) (underground publication), 8. *See also* publishing
Płatek, Stanisław, 89, 90
Płock, strikes in (June 1976), 325n12
Pniewski, Jerzy, 142

Po Prostu (weekly), 3, 324n6
Poggi, Archbishop Luigi, 151, 226
Poindexter, Admiral John, 121
Polam factory (in Pabianice), strike in, 78
Poland (Polish People's Republic, PRL*), 203, 324n4; academic publications on, ix–x, xii; Church's position in, 4–5, 223; democratic opposition in, 6–10, 325n19; East-West/US relations and, 287–88, 293; IMF membership of, 127, 287; martial law and international isolation of, 128, 272, 287, 289; power structure after imposition of martial law in, 72–74; protests in, vii–viii, 3–4, 11, 324nn5–7, 325n12; resistance/underground tradition in, 4, 146, 156, 170, 314–15; transformation after 1989 of, 293–99; and Soviet Union/Soviet Bloc, 313; US/Western sanctions against, 128, 267; Western countries' aid for, 232. *See also* economy
Polish Academy of Sciences, 134, 142
Polish American Congress (USA), 253
Polish Army, the (Wojsko Polskie) (military), 206, 251; army-party relations, 258–61; cooperation with MSW/SB, 54, 195; draft and martial law, 36; Main Political Directorate of, 104, 114, 116, 136; and martial law, 35, 40, 43, 53, 62–63, 94; and militarization of state administration, 28, 133–34; strike-breaking ("unblocking" factories) by, 83, 85–90, 94. *See also* General Staff
Polish Ex-Combatants' Association (Great Britain), 253
Polish Filmmakers' Union, 18
Polish Journalists' Association (SDP*), 18, 264
Polish Philosophical Association, 18
Polish pope. *See* John Paul II; Wojtyła, Cardinal Karol

Polish Radio (state run), 63, 78, 188. *See also* propaganda
Polish Socialist Party (Polska Partia Socjalistyczna), 8
Polish Sociological Association, 18
Polish Television (state run), 55, 116, 180, 188. *See also* propaganda
Polish United Workers' Party (PZPR*) (communist party), viii, 175, 265, 285; vs. army, 258–61; Congress (1986) of, 288; crisis of, 130–32, 134–36, 266–67; Jaruzelski's purges in, 262; reaction to Solidarity and tactics against, 21–24; and Round Table, 295; Solidarity's challenge to, 21; and Solidarity membership, 111
Polish United Workers' Party (PZPR*), Central Committee (secretariat), 29, 73, 111; and martial law, 30, 209, 217, 241, 270; meetings/resolutions of, 12, 112, 126, 131, 147, 199, 291; stance on Solidarity, 139–40, 143–44
Polish United Workers' Party, Politburo (PZPR*), 73, 74, 114, 261; and martial law preparations, 24, 29, 35, 42, 114, 217, 220; meetings/resolutions of, 31, 66, 69, 71, 123, 131, 133, 144, 203, 217–20, 251, 258, 262–63, 270, 272, 273; stance on Solidarity, 139–40, 143–44, 147, 153; strikes (summer 1980) and, 13, 14–15; on Wałęsa, 213, 214
Polish Writers' Union (ZLP*), 18, 246
Polish-Russian/Soviet relations, 4
Polish-Soviet Friendship Society (Towarzystwo Przyjaźni Polsko-Radzieckiej), 135
Politburo. *See* Polish United Workers' Party
political prisoners (in Poland), 9, 13, 105, 108, 257, 272, 285, 288. *See also* prisons/"isolation centers"
Polityka (weekly), 26

Polony, Anna, 246
Pope. *See* John Paul II; Wojtyła, Cardinal Karol
Popiełuszko, Father Jerzy, 182, 233, 234, 235, 253; murder of, 284
Porębski, Tadeusz, 261
Poznań, 133; Andrzej Jawień Theater in, 247, 344n12; demonstrations in, 184, 191, 197, 211, 252; Radio Solidarity broadcast in, 193, 244; Solidarity/underground structure in, 166–67; strike committee in, 80; strikes in (1956), 3; and anniversary of, 197–98, 256. *See also* Cegielski, H. factory; strikes/protests
Pozsgay, Imre, 306, 307, 311
Prague. *See* Czechoslovakia
Primate. *See* Glemp, Cardinal Józef; Wyszyński, Cardinal Stefan
Primatial Aid Committee (*Prymasowski Komitet Pomocy*) (in Warsaw), 232, 252
Primatial Social Council (*Prymasowska Rada Społeczna*), 48; "Theses" of, 171, 227–28. *See also* TKK*
prime minister, the. *See* Jaruzelski, General Wojciech
prisons/"isolation centers," 99–100, 108, 220; SB's activities at, 100–103
PRL* (Polish People's Republic), 115. *See also* Poland
PRON.* *See* Patriotic Movement of National Rebirth
propaganda (anti-government/Solidarity), 169, 174–76, 245
propaganda (government), 4, 103, 124, 127, 245, 261, 269; anti-Solidarity campaign (as martial law tool), ix, 26, 28, 29, 35, 36, 97, 104, 116–17, 139–140, 142, 195, 209, 251, 257, 279, 285. *See also* Polish Radio; Polish Television; Urban, Jerzy

protests/demonstrations, 3–4, 249; against imposition of martial law, 76–79, 95; during martial law, 186–87, 189–91, 197–201, 206–8, 210–11, 233, 324n5–7; youth participation in, 184, 204–5, 343n16. *See also individual cities*; strikes/protests

Pruszcz Gdański, 57

Pruszków, underground structure in, 165

Przedświt (underground publishing house), 160. *See also* publishing

Przemyk, Grzegorz, 253, 275. *See also* MSW*; SB*

Przemyśl, 108, 200

Przetrwanie (Survival) (underground publication), 165. *See also* publishing

Przygodziński, Aleksander, 68

Przymanowski, Colonel Janusz, 116

Public Opinion Research Center (CBOS*), 239

publishing (underground) ("second circulation"/media), 7–8, 18, 159–61, 164, 187, 192, 243, 278, 327n14; publishing houses, 160, 244–45; as symbol of resistance, 245. *See also* independent society; Radio Solidarity

Pyjas, Stanisław, 97

Pytko, Colonel Zygmunt, 89

PZPR.* *See* Polish United Workers' Party

Radio Solidarity (Radio Solidarność), 177, 187, 189, 193, 244; trials, 203, 257, 313. *See also* independent society; publishing; Romaszewski, Zbigniew

radio stations (foreign), 13, 76, 188, 326n3; BBC, 14, 47, 188; RFE,* 12, 14, 47, 151, 177, 178, 180, 188, 253, 340n5; RFI,* 188; Voice of America, 188

Radom, strikes in (June 1976), 3, 325n12; trials, 105

Radom Solidarity meeting (Dec. 3, 1981). *See* Solidarity

Radomska, Maria, 142

Rakowski, Mieczysław F., 31, 48, 257, 261, 289, 290–91, 292; "Bydgoszcz incident" and, 27; as deputy/prime minister/first secretary, 26, 291, 298; diary's entries by, 50, 72, 105, 192, 209, 250, 251, 284; "directorate" and, 72–73; and Jaruzelski, 37, 105, 230, 257, 263; and martial law, 42, 60–61, 110, 142, 180; meeting with academia, 142; and new trade union project, 144, 153, 197, 338n38; and propaganda, 31, 116; and Wałęsa, 57, 71, 151, 214–15, 217. *See also* Urban, Jerzy

Rasiński, Marek, 187

Reagan, Ronald, vii, 290; and arms race, 300, 303; and Brezhnev, 126–27; and John Paul II, 125; martial law and sanctions, 125–26; and *perestroika* in Poland, 287–78; and Solidarity delegalization, 207; and Spasowski (Romuald and Wanda), 126. *See also* US-USSR relations

Reality Association (Stowarzyszenie Rzeczywistość), 262

Red Army. *See* Soviet Army

"Red Rowan" ("Jarzębina Czerwona"), martial law operation by MSW/SB, 71

Regional Executive Committee (Regionalny Komitet Wykonawczy), 167

Reiff, Ryszard, 59–60, 264

"Renaissance" (Renesans), martial law operation by MSW/SB, 93, 143, 163; failure of, 154

Repair Shipyard (in Gdańsk), strike in, 86

Research Office. *See* Ministry of Internal Affairs

Reserve Detachments of the Citizens' Militia (ROMO*), 89, 92, 199. *See also* MO*; ORMO*; ZOMO*
resistance (civic/social), 173, 279; active vs. passive (Kulerski), 169; forms of, 173–83, 233; Polish tradition of, 4, 156, 314–15; publishing (underground) as symbol of, 245; and Solidarity, 161, 277, 317. *See also* independent society; Second World War
Reykowski, Janusz, 146, 292
RFE* (Radio Free Europe). *See* radio stations (foreign)
RFI* (Radio France Internationale). *See* radio stations (foreign)
Ribbentrop-Molotov treaty (Aug. 1939), 304
Riechers, Albrecht, 232
"Ring" (Pierścień), martial law operation by MSW/SB, 49
RKW. *See* Regional Executive Committee
RMP.* *See* Young Poland Movement
Robles, Antonio Garcia, 194
Robotnik (The Worker) (underground publication), 8. *See also* publishing
Romania (Bucharest), 272, 306, 316, 324n4; and martial law, 129–130; *perestroika* and, 304, 310–11, 312, 315. *See also* Ceauşescu, Nicolae
Romaszewska, Zofia, 187
Romaszewski, Zbigniew, 155, 170, 187; arrest of, 194, 195; and "Radio Solidarity Trial," 203. *See also* publishing; Radio Solidarity
Rome, demonstrations against martial law, 125
ROMO.* *See* Reserve Detachments of Citizens' Militia
Romuald Traugutt Philharmonic, 247, 344n13

Round Table talks (Feb.–Apr. 1989, Warsaw), 291–95, 297–98. *See also* elections (June 1989)
Rozpłochowski, Andrzej, 219
Rozwalak, Zdzisław, 141
RSW "Press-Book-Movement" (Prasa-Książka-Ruch) (party publishing concern), 113
Rubinstein, Artur, 127
Rudka, Szczepan, 159, 160
Rulewski, Jan, 16, 219. *See also* "Bydgoszcz incident"
Rural Mutual Aid Society (Samopomoc Chłopska), 114
Rusek, Franciszek, 219
Ruzikowski, Tadeusz, 183, 256
Ryba, General Marian, 61
Rybakov, Anatolii, 302
Rybnik Coal Area (Upper Silesia), Borynia/Jastrzębie/Moszczenica mines, strikes in, 88. *See also* Manifest Lipcowy; strikes/protests
Rzeszów, demonstrations/strikes in, 189, 190; Solidarity/underground structures in, 166–67

Sadłowski, Father Czesław, 233
Sadowska, Barbara, 253. *See also* Przemyk, Grzegorz
Sakharov, Andrei, 302
Samsonowicz, Henryk, 142
sanctions. *See* United States; West
Sanford, George, xii
Sasin, Józef, 145
SB.* *See* Ministry of Internal Affairs
Schmidt, Chancellor Helmut, 123
Schmitt, Carl, 318
SDP.* *See* Polish Journalists' Association
Second World War (WWII), 4, 20, 146, 224, 253, 312, 315; martial law association with, 120, 157, 168–69, 173, 175, 178

Sejm (Polish Parliament), 36, 268; and martial law, 44, 52, 60, 103, 203, 206, 220, 249, 265; and 1989 election, 294, 297, 299, 317; and TKK, 197. *See also* Jaruzelski, General Wojciech

"self-defense" groups (party/MSW), 92–93, 199

"Self-Governing Republic" (*Rzeczpospolita Samorządna*). *See* Solidarity

"self-limiting revolution" (Solidarity), 19–20, 148, 327n17

Shevardnadze, Eduard, 301

Siedlce, 252

Sienkiewicz, Jarosław, 142

Sieradz, 66; TV boycott in, 181

Sikorski, Father Jan, 234

Siła-Nowicki, Władysław, 71

Silvestrini, Archbishop Achilles, 229–30

Siwak, Albin, 261

Siwicki, General Florian (head of General Staff), 134; "directorate" and, 72–73; and martial law, 37, 41, 50, 51, 52, 53, 72, 218–19, 230, 270

Skalski, Ernest, 46

Skarżanka, Hanna, 246

Skoczek, Anna, 176

Skóra, Tadeusz, 59

Skrzypczak, Edward, 262

SKS. *See* Student Solidarity Committee

Skwira, Adam, 55, 66, 80, 84, 90, 97. *See also* Wujek mine

Śląska, Aleksandra, 246

Słowacki, Juliusz, 5

Słowik, Andrzej, 16, 67, 105

Słowo (underground publishing house), 160. *See also* publishing

Słupsk, militia's cadet school in, 49

Śnieżko, Stefan, 112

Sobieraj, Andrzej, 219

Social Committee of Sciences, 243. *See also* independent society

Social and Economic Council, 268

Sochaczew, TV boycott in ("television walks"), 180

Sofia. *See* Bulgaria

Solidarity. *See* Independent Self-Governing Trade Union "Solidarity"

Solidarity (after 1989), "ethos" of, 298; transformation of, 316–318

Solidarity (bulletin), 14

Solidarity (in-exile) Congress (1982, in Oslo), 254

Solidarity (Solidarność) (underground), x; activists in hiding (and AK tradition), 155–58; and Church circles' support for, 158; Cultural Awards of, 246, 248; delegalization of (Oct. 1982), 203–4, 206–7; foreign office of (in Brussels), 254; funding of, 157–58; generational "changing of the guard," 184; martial law's end and "positional battle" tactics by, 277; as MSW/SB's target, 193–95; as a myth, 146–47; participation in, 161, 286; society's attitude toward, 161–62; strategies of (and debates about), 169–70, 186, 278–79; and TKK's founding, 171–72; transformation into underground structures, 163–71; and Wałęsa/TKK, 286. *See also* independent society; OKO*; NSZZ*; TKK*

Solidarity Action Committee (Brussels), 254

Solidarity Coordination Committee (Paris), 253–54

Solidarity Defense Circles (KOS*), 165

Solidarity delegalization (Oct. 1982), 203–4, 206–7; and protests against, 207–8

Solidarity Electoral Action (AWS*), 317, 349n5

Solidarity of Film and Stage Artists, statement of, 179

Solidarity Office (in Stockholm), 254
Solidarity with Solidarity Committee (in Rome), 254
Solidarity's First National Congress (Sept. /Oct. 1981), "Message to the Working People" by, 28; program/platform of ("The Self-Governing Republic"), 19–20
Solidarity's Temporary Coordinating Commission (TKK* NSZZ) (underground main headquarters), 189, 196–97, 204, 208–9, 211, 273; founding of, 171–72; secret meeting of, 205–6; and "Solidarity Today" program, 238–42; and Solidarity's Foreign Office, 254–55; and "Theses of the Primatial Social Council," 171, 227–28; and "Underground Society" platform, 197; and Wałęsa, 216, 250. *See also* independent society; OKO*
Sołowiej, Jerzy, 88
Solzhenitsyn, Aleksandr I., 302
Sopot. *See* Tri-City
Soviet Army (Red Army), 4, 146, 304; and martial law, 39, 128; and "Soyuz-81" maneuvers of, 27. *See also* Kulikov, Victor
Soviet Bloc countries' transformations, 311, 315
Soviet Committee of Economic Planning, 36
Soviet Union (Big Brother/Kremlin/Moscow/USSR), 9, 212, 316; abandoning of Brezhnev doctrine by, 293, 303–4, 307–8; collapse/disintegration of, vii, 312–13; dissidents in, 6, 301–2; economy, 300, 348n1(ch. 20); and end of arms race, 303; "geriatric crisis" in, 300–301; and Gorbachev's reforms, 301–3, 311–12; and Jaruzelski, 28, 35–36, 38, 50, 263–64, 287–88; and martial law, 29, 37, 39, 95, 128, 130, 263–64, 272; stance on Polish communist leaders, 10; and Round Table, 295; and Solidarity, viii, 15, 22, 24, 25, 28, 140, 192; and Soviet bloc countries' transformations, 304–11; and "Soyuz-80" and "Soyuz-81"maneuvers, 25, 26; war in Afghanistan, 122, 263, 300, 303, 304. *See also* Brezhnev, Leonid; Gorbachev, Mikhail
Sowiński, Paweł, 245
"Soyuz-80" maneuvers (Dec. 1980), 25, 327n7. *See also* Warsaw Pact
"Soyuz-81" maneuvers, 26–27, 28, 129. *See also* Warsaw Pact
Spasowski, Romuald, 124; and Reagan, 126
SPD*, on martial law, 125
St. Brygida's church (Gdańsk), 250, 252
St. Martin's church (Warsaw), 252–53. *See also* Primatial Social Council
St. Stanisław Kostka's church (Warsaw), 182. *See also* Popiełuszko, Father Jerzy
Stachura, General Bogusław, 9–10, 145, 325n19
Stalin, Joseph, vii
Stalowa Wola, 182; Steelworks, and martial law, 78
Staniszkis, Jadwiga, 148, 327n17
Stanowska, Maria, 106
Stasi (East German secret police), 218
Staszic mine (in Giszowiec), strike in, 67; pacification of, 88, 98. *See also* strikes/protests
State Tribunal (Trybunał Stanu), 103, 275
Stelmachowski, Andrzej, 16
Stockholm, demonstrations against martial law, 125
Stomma, Stanisław, 48
Strękowski, Jan, 165
strikes/protests (before martial law), 3–4, 6, 11, 324nn5–7, 325n12; summer 1980, 12–15

strikes/protests (under martial law), 76–80, 90–91, 332n9; army/MSW/SB/ZOMO's tactics to break/pacify, 83–90, 98; and Catholic masses/priests, 80–81; strike committees' creations and, 66–68, 80; and workers' unpreparedness for martial law, 81–83. *See also individual enterprises*; protests/demonstrations

Strzebielinek prison (near Gdańsk), 57; and SB's activities in, 100–103

Strzelce Opolskie, prison in, 108

Strzelecki, Jan, 248

Student Solidarity Committee (Studencki Komitet Solidarności, SKS), 6

Student Committee for the Defense of Democracy, 165

Supreme Court, 22, 106

Suslov, Mikhail, 50; death of, 300

Świdnica, 200, 206; Radio Solidarity broadcast in, 243; strikes in (Aug. 1980), 14. *See also* strikes/protests

Świdnik, 132; helicopter factory, strikes in and pacification of, 66, 76, 84, 86; Radio Solidarity broadcast in, 243; reprisals in, 110, 191; strike committee in, 80; TV boycott in ("television walks"), 180. *See also* strikes/protests

Świerczewski factory (in Warsaw), strike in, 85. *See also* strikes/protests

Szaciło, General Tadeusz, 116

Szczecin, 90, 133; demonstrations/protests in, 189, 190, 198, 200, 206, 252; Solidarity/underground structures in, 166–67; strikes in: (1970), 3, 75; (Aug. 1980), 14–15; (1988), 290; strike committee in, 80; trials in, 257. *See also* Gryfia Repair Shipyard; strikes/protests; Warski Shipyard

Szczecin Agreement (August 1980), viii, 8. *See also* Gdańsk Agreement

Szczepański, Jan, 59–60

Szczepkowski, Andrzej, 246

Szczytno, militia's cadet school in, 49, 208, 210

Szewczyk, General Józef, 59

Szmidke, Zenon, 98

Szumiejko, Eugeniusz, 48; and martial law, 68, 84, 168, 170–71, 205, 207, 237; and Wałęsa, 169. *See also* OKO*; TKK*

"tactics of cooptation" (by Jaruzelski), 286–87

Tbilisi (Georgia), 304

Tejchma, Józef, 48, 61, 180

Temporary Council of Solidarity (Tymczasowa Rada "Solidarności,"), 288

Terlecki, Marian, 80

TKK.* *See* Solidarity's Temporary Coordinating Commission

Tokarczuk, Bishop Ignacy, 229, 235

Tokarczyk, Antoni, 219

Toronto, demonstrations against martial law, 125

Toruń, demonstrations in, 189, 190, 211; Radio Solidarity broadcast in, 243–44; Solidarity/underground structure in, 166–67

(trade) union. *See* Solidarity

Tri-City (Gdańsk, Gdynia, Sopot), 81, 199; arrests in, 57; reprisals in, 113–14

Trybuna Ludu (daily), 64

Tu i Teraz (weekly), 113

Tuczapski, General Tadeusz, 42, 52, 59–60, 66, 276

Turowicz, Jerzy, 48

Tygodnik Mazowsze (Mazovian Weekly) (underground publication), 158, 167–68, 169, 187, 200, 210, 273. *See also* publishing

Tygodnik Powszechny (Catholic weekly) (Kraków), 5

Tygodnik Solidarność (Solidarity Weekly) (official Solidarity newspaper), 23, 46
Tygodnik Wojenny (War Weekly) (underground publication, Warsaw), 160, 165, 200. *See also* publishing
Tyniec (near Kraków), 106, 234

Ukraine, 312; "Orange Revolution" (2004), 320
underground. *See* Solidarity
union (trade). *See* Solidarity
Union of Polish Stage Artists (ZASP*), 229, 246, 247, 264
Union of Socialist Polish Youth (Związek Socjalistycznej Młodzieży Polskiej, ZSMP), 135, 144
United Nations, and martial law, 124, 126; and Soviet Union, 300, 303
United States (Washington), 9, 288, 311; and martial law, 121, 272; policy toward Poland, 293, 347n34; predictions on Eastern Europe, 3, 324n1, 324n4; reaction to Warsaw Pact maneuvers, 25; sanctions against Poland, 126–27, 128, 207, 267; sanctions against Soviet Union, 122, 127, 300, 348n1 (ch. 20)
Unitra-Polkolor factory (in Piaseczno, near Warsaw), 78. *See also* strikes/protests
Urban, Jerzy, 28, 175; and martial law, 42, 60, 124, 128. *See also* propaganda
Ursus (near Warsaw), demonstrations in, 198; TV boycott in ("television walks"), 180
Ursus factory (near Warsaw), informers in, 193; strikes in: (June 1976), 325n12; (July 1980), 12; (Dec. 1981), 85. *See also* strikes/protests
US-USSR relations, vii, 122, 127, 300, 301, 311; and arms race, 300, 303; and Poland, x, 287–88, 293. *See also* Bush; Gorbachev; Reagan

USSR. *See* Soviet Union
Ustinov, Marshal Dmitrii, 26, 28, 39, 50; death of, 300

Vatican (authorities/pope), 5, 6, 215, 226, 230, 271, 272, 289; reaction to Warsaw Pact maneuvers, 25
Vaught, John, 121
Voice of America. *See* radio stations (foreign)
voivodship defense committees, 65, 106, 199
Volunteer Reserves of the Citizens' Militia (ORMO*), 89, 92, 174, 178, 183, 249, 251. *See also* MO*; ROMO*; ZOMO*

"W" (one of martial law's cryptonyms), 35, 43, 328n1
Walentynowicz, Anna, 16, 257, 289
Wałęsa, Danuta, 71, 151, 213
Wałęsa, Lech (Solidarity's chairman), ix, xi, 16, 31, 249, 286, 315, 320; Arłamów, internment in, 153, 213–214; arrest/internment of, 57, 152, 227; biography of, 149–150; "Bolek," 149, 152, 337n26; "Brothers' Conversation," 213–15, 239, 342n35, 343n3; "Bydgoszcz incident" and, 27; Chyliczki (near Warsaw) isolation in, 149, 152; and Ciosek, 71, 81, 148–49, 150, 151–52, 214; and Civic Committee and election (June 1989), 291–92, 296–98; and Congress of Polish Culture, 48; Jaruzelski and, 148, 212, 342n26; John Paul II and, 151, 226, 230, 231; Kiszczak and, 214, 290; and letter to Reagan, 288; and National Commission meeting (Dec. 12, 1981), 48–49; Nobel Peace Prize and operation "Ambassador," 194, 343n3; Orszulik and, 150–51, 152,

Wałęsa, Lech—*(cont'd)*
  153, 200, 213, 217; Otwock (near Warsaw) isolation in, 57, 152, 215; president of Poland, 317; pressures on to capitulate, 148–49, 150–53; release of, 212–16; speech after release, 216–17; and strike of 1980, 13; and TKK, 216, 250; TV debate with Miodowicz, 291; and WZZ, 8, 13, 16, 150; and Zaspa housing, 216. *See also* Gdańsk Shipyard
Wałęsa, Stanisław, 213, 239
Walichnowski, General Tadeusz, 276
Waliszewski, Leszek, 68
Warsaw, 58, 121, 133, 193; actors' boycott in, 178–80; "*Apocalypse Now*" at Moskwa cinema in, 47; art shows in churches in, 245–46; Congress of Polish Culture in, 47–48; Operation "Azalea" in, 54–55; protests/demonstrations in, 67, 86, 90, 189, 190, 191, 198, 200, 201, 211, 230, 252; publishing (underground) in, 160–61, 165, 187; Radio Solidarity broadcast in, 177, 187, 243; reprisals in, 113; strikes in and pacification of, 85; trials in, 105, 106; underground structures in, 164–65; Victory Square in, 174
Warsaw Artists' Solidarity appeal, 180
Warsaw Pact (armies) (*Pakt Warszawski*), 122, 123, 311, 335n4; collapse of, 315; and martial law, 25, 26, 36, 38, 40, 43. *See also* Kulikov, Victor; Soyuz-80; Soyuz-81
Warsaw Steelworks, informers in, 193; strike in, 85. *See also* strikes/protests
Warsaw University of Technology (Politechnika Warszawska), strike in, 85. *See also* strikes/protests
Warsaw Uprising (1944), 4, 146
Warski Shipyard (in Szczecin), strike in and pacification of, 86–87; trials/reprisals in, 105, 110. *See also* Szczecin; strikes/protests
Washington, DC. *See* United States
Waszkiewicz, Jan, 68
Week of Christian Culture, 229, 245, 247
Węgorzewo, Radio Solidarity broadcast in, 243
Weigel, George, 231
Weinberger, Caspar, 121
West (Western Europe), reactions: to martial law, 121–28; sanctions against Poland, 127, 287; to Solidarity, viii–x
Wiatr, Jerzy J., 46
Wielowieyski, Andrzej, 228
Wierzchów Pomorski (internment center), 100
Wilczyński, Lieutenant Mieczysław, 89
Winiarska, Halina, 246
Wiśniewski, Wojciech, 260
Włosik, Bogdan, 208
Wojtalik, Lieutenant-Colonel Czesław, 152
Wojtyła, Cardinal Karol (Archbishop of Kraków), 5, 223, 246, 344n12; and opposition, 7. *See also* John Paul II
Wola (underground publication) (Warsaw), 164. *See also* publishing
Wolny Związkowiec (*Free Trade Unionist*) (underground publication), 105, 107. *See also* publishing
Women's League (Liga Kobiet), 135, 144
Workers' Defense Committee (KOR*), 6–7, 8, 97, 139, 171, 253, 325n13; members' trial, 192, 203, 257, 274; and strikes of 1980, 13–14. *See also* WZZ*
Working Group of the National Commission of "Solidarity" (Grupa Robocza Komisji Krajowej, Solidarność), 289
World Confederation of Labor (in Brussels), 254

World War II (WWII). *See* Second World War

Wrocław, 133, 181, 182, 209, 233; protests during martial law in, 183, 190, 191, 198, 200, 201, 204, 206, 207, 210, 251–52; publishing (underground) in, 159–60, 164, 165; Radio Solidarity broadcast in, 243, 244; reactions to imposition of martial law in, 58, 66–67, 77, 79, 84, 86, 87, 90; reprisals in, 111, 114–15; Solidarity/underground structures in, 157, 163, 166–67; strike committees in, 67, 80. *See also* Frasyniuk, Władysław; Morawiecki, Kornel

WRON.* *See* Military Council of National Salvation

WRON's chairman. *See* Jaruzelski, General Wojciech

Wrzaszczyk, Tadeusz, 275

Wujec, Henryk, 16, 203

Wujek mine (near Katowice), strikes and pacification of (massacre), 80–81, 84, 89–90, 98, 124, 148, 150, 275; and anniversary of, 208, 216, 233; and Glemp, 226; miners' trials, 97, 105, 106–7. *See also* strikes/protests

Wyspiański, Stanisław, 179

Wyszyński, Cardinal Stefan (Primate), 5, 7, 15, 139, 200, 223, 315; "Bydgoszcz incident," 27; death of, 224; and Week of Christian Culture, 245

Wytrwałość (Perserverance) (underground publication), 165. *See also* publishing

WZZ.* *See* Free Trade Unions

"X" (one of martial law's cryptonyms), 35, 328n1

Yakutsk (Siberia), 304

Young Poland Movement (RMP*), 6, 8, 14, 156

Zapasiewicz, Zbigniew, 246

Zamet factory (in Białystok), 78. *See also* Białystok; strikes/protests

ZASP.* *See* Union of Polish Stage Artists

Zawada, Stanisław, 142

Zawadzki, Sylwester, 219

Zazula, Jan, 177

Zdanie (Kraków), 262

Zhivkov, Todor, 309

Zieja, Father Jan, 7

Zierke, Wojciech, 141

Ziemowit mine (near Tychy), 66, 77, 110; strike in, 83, 90–91, 133; trials, 107. *See also* strikes/protests

Ziętek, Jerzy, 59

ZLP.* *See* Polish Writers' Union

ZOMO.* *See* Motorized Detachments of the Citizens' Militia

ZSMP. *See* Union of Socialist Polish Youth

Zubok, Vladislav, 303

Zürich (Switzerland), Solidarity activists' meeting in (Dec. 1981), 253

Żabiński, Andrzej, 22, 262

Żukrowski, Wojciech, 142